From Ming to Ch'ing

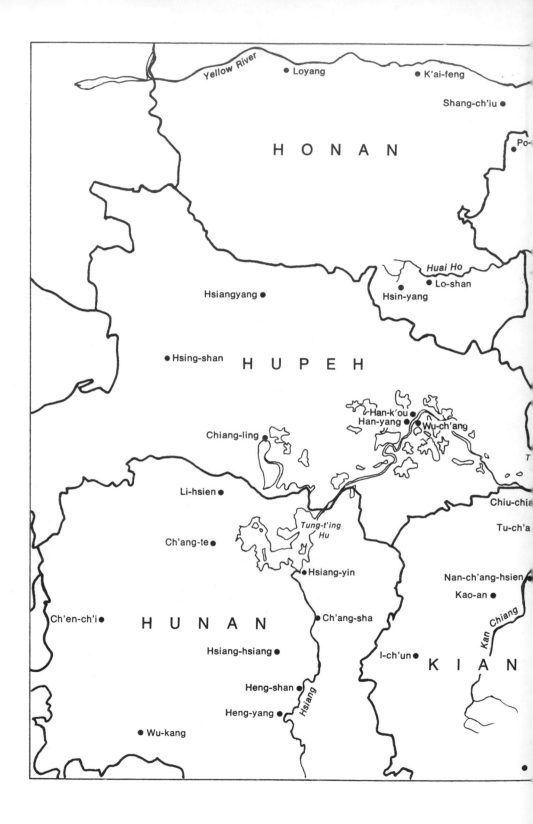

Yellow River   ● Loyang   ● K'ai-feng

                                  Shang-ch'iu ●

H O N A N   ● Po-

                                    Huai Ho
                                  ● Lo-shan
        ● Hsiangyang   Hsin-yang ●

    ● Hsing-shan   H U P E H

                              Han-k'ou ●
                              Han-yang ● ● Wu-ch'ang
    Chiang-ling ●   T

                                          Chiu-chia
    Li-hsien ●   Tu-ch'a

                    Tung-t'ing
                    Hu
    Ch'ang-te ●
                              Nan-ch'ang-hsien
                              Kao-an ●
                    Hsiang-yin ●
Ch'en-ch'i ●   H U N A N   ● Ch'ang-sha
                                        I-ch'un ●   K I A N
    Hsiang-hsiang ●

    Heng-shan ●
    Heng-yang ●   Hsiang

    ● Wu-kang

Central and Southeast China

CONTRIBUTORS

Hilary J. Beattie, Ph.D., Cambridge, has taught Chinese history at Yale University and is now working in the field of clinical psychology.

Jerry P. Dennerline, Ph.D., Yale, is Assistant Professor of History and Chinese at Pomona College and author of several studies of the Ch'ing conquest period in the lower Yangtze provinces.

Ian McMorran, Ph.D., Oxford, is Lecturer in Classical Chinese at Oxford and author of several studies of Wang Fu-chih.

Morris Rossabi, Ph.D., Columbia, is Associate Professor of History at Case Western Reserve University, and the author of *China and Inner Asia* and other studies of China and Islam.

Gertraude Roth, Ph.D., Harvard, is a specialist in early Manchu history.

Jonathan D. Spence, Ph.D., Yale, is George Burton Adams Professor of History at Yale. His most recent books are *Emperor of China: Self-Portrait of K'ang-hsi* and *The Death of Woman Wang.*

Lynn A. Struve, Ph.D., Michigan, is Assistant Professor of History at Indiana University. Her specialty is early Ch'ing intellectual history.

Frederic Wakeman, Jr., Ph.D., is Professor of History and Chairman of the Center for Chinese Studies at the University of California, Berkeley. His most recent book is *The Fall of Imperial China.*

John E. Wills, Jr., Ph.D., Harvard, is Associate Professor of History, University of Southern California. He is the author of *Pepper, Guns, and Parleys: The Dutch East India Company and China, 1662–1681.*

Tsing Yuan, Ph.D., Pennsylvania, is Associate Professor of History at Wright State University, Ohio. He is a specialist in late Ming economic history.

FROM MING TO CH'ING

Conquest, Region, and Continuity in
Seventeenth-Century China

Edited by
Jonathan D. Spence and John E. Wills, Jr.

New Haven and London   Yale University Press

Designed by John O. C. McCrillis
and set in IBM Press Roman type.
Printed in the United States of America by
The Vail-Ballou Press, Binghamton, New York.

Library of Congress Cataloging in Publication Data
Main entry under title:

From Ming to Ch'ing.

  Bibliography: p.
  Includes index.
  1. China–History–Ming dynasty, 1368-1644–
Addresses, essays, lectures. 2. China–History–
Ch'ing dynasty, 1644-1912–Addresses, essays,
lectures. I. Spence, Jonathan D. II. Wills, John
Elliot, 1936-
DS753.F74 1979   951   78-15560
ISBN 0-300-02218-2 (cloth); 0-300-02672-2 (paper)

11   10   9   8   7   6   5   4   3   2

This book is dedicated to

Chao-ying Fang
and
Lien-che Tu Fang

in admiration and gratitude for their many
contributions to Ming and Ch'ing studies

Contents

Preface

The year 1644—when the Ming dynasty fell, to be replaced by the last of China's dynasties, the Ch'ing—is rightly seen as a crucial moment in the history of late imperial China. Yet the very magnitude of the event has made it difficult to get any broad view across the seventeenth century as a whole, for the conventions of traditional Chinese historiography have placed pre-1644 events in the category of "Ming history" and those that came after as "Early Ch'ing," forming a conceptual barrier through which it has proved surprisingly difficult to pass. Also, the dominant categories within that same historiography tended to be those which dealt with institutional structures rather than with long-term trends; they concentrated on the pressing requirements and problems of the imperial bureaucracy, neglecting (or classing as deviant) behavior or organizations which ran counter to those requirements.

This book focuses around the dynastic transition from Ming to Ch'ing, but it is designed to show the ramifications of that event within the seventeenth-century historical context. At the present stage of our knowledge such a goal can only be achieved by a joint effort, for despite its apparent manageability, the topic demands familiarity with the military, institutional, economic, intellectual, and political history of two major dynasties, a detailed geographic knowledge that can range from southeast to northwest China, and a study of sources not only in Chinese but also in Manchu, Mongol, Russian, Dutch, and Portuguese. Accordingly, we made the decision to try to combine the expertise of a number of scholars who were working on various aspects of seventeenth-century China; and in November 1974, with the help of grants from the American Council of Learned Societies and the University of Southern California, sixteen scholars, many of whom had only recently finished their dissertations, assembled for a conference on the Ming-Ch'ing transition. The nine essays presented here are the revised versions of papers first presented at that conference.

From the beginning of our discussions we were interested in finding out what had changed from Ming to Ch'ing, and how. We knew that we would have to look at a longer span of time than just the twelve peak years of empire-wide turmoil from 1640 to 1652. At first some of us thought that we should focus our discussions within the span of a sixty-year process—1624 to 1683—of rebellion, militarization of politics, conquest, civil war, and consolidation of a new dynasty. That already is a substantial and important segment of the history of Ming–Ch'ing China; but as our discussions progressed, we realized that it was not sufficient for some analytic purposes. We became interested in defining the differences between the condition of state, society, and culture in "late Ming" and in "high Ch'ing," and found that neither could be seen clearly at the end-point of this sixty-year span; there were too many weaknesses of documentation, too many cross-currents of change, too many decadences or half-emergences of institutions. To get a clear vision of "late Ming" we had to go back to the middle of the Wan-li period, in the 1590s; while in order to focus clearly on the "high Ch'ing" we had to come down to the middle of the Yung-cheng period, ca. 1730. Moreover, we began to see this long period as having coherences of its own that spanned the dynastic transition: of an individuality and intensity of Confucian moral seeking, for example, that ran from the Tung-lin heroes through such great early Ch'ing scholars as Wang Fu-chih; or a continuity of half-controlled official exploitation of commerce that carried over from the eunuch mines commissioners of the 1590s to the "Emperor's Merchant" at Canton after 1700. The perception of the need to focus on this long time-span and the discovery of its internal coherence was a surprise to many of us, and was one of the more important results of our conference.

This volume begins with a chronological series of four close studies of events in the brief but complex military-political process for which the word *conquest* is an inadequate but convenient label. The final disintegration of the Ming and the initial establishment of Ch'ing rule over most of the vast area of the Chinese Empire took place in the amazingly brief span of twelve years, from 1640, when the rebel armies of Li Tzu-ch'eng and Chang Hsien-chung began to take and hold whole provinces, to 1652, when the last Ming restorationist emperor was fleeing into the southwestern mountains under the protection of the warlord Sun K'o-wang. Gertraude Roth's essay describes, largely from Manchu sources, some of the

crucial early stages of the development of the Manchu state, which
until now have been described primarily from much less comprehensive Chinese sources. We are forcefully reminded of one reason
for the swiftness of the Ch'ing consolidation after 1644, namely
that the Manchus invaded as a highly structured and disciplined
nation-in-arms, whose leaders already had shown remarkable capacity
for dealing with the complex problems of ruling and exploiting a
Chinese agricultural population and wooing a Chinese elite and integrating members of it into their own power structure.

In traditional historiography, the central drama of the conquest
begins with the fall of Peking to Li Tzu-ch'eng and ends with the
collapse of loyalist resistance in the Yangtze Valley just over a year
later, but though these events had apparently been studied in considerable detail, they reappear as new and strange in the studies of
Frederic Wakeman and Jerry Dennerline. Neither the Peking officials
who aligned themselves first to Li's Shun regime and then to the
Ch'ing, nor the Chiang-nan literati who struggled and argued among
themselves as the Ch'ing armies advanced, now seem to have been
blind fools; and if they sometimes seem to have been craven oppor-
tunists they were also far more than that. We can see that they were
protecting their own sources of public and private power in the complex and conflict-ridden structures of late Ming metropolitan bureaucracy and local administration. The Peking bureaucrats first sought
to accommodate themselves to the new reality of Li Tzu-ch'eng's
power, but then found Ch'ing rule preferable to Li's rampaging
troops. The Chiang-nan literati found some "loyalist" forces more
threatening to their own local power bases than the Ch'ing. In addition, we see these Chinese leaders playing out well-defined cultural
roles: for some, to use a phrase of Arthur Waley, this meant that
they "contrived to endow compromise with an emotional glamour";[1]
but for others this made suicidally futile resistance seem the only
moral option.

Finally, Ian McMorran's paper shows us somewhat less of the
institutional imperatives but far more of the bitter and futile personal
dimensions of Ming loyalism. Here we see how Wang Fu-chih, one of
the greatest philosophers of the age, who was soon to write of the
distinction and barrier between Chinese and barbarian as a fundamental moral principle,[2] could take part in organized resistance to a

barbarian dynasty only by joining in the sordid political wrangles of the court of the Yung-li emperor. When this sort of thing represented almost the only alternative to acceptance of Ch'ing rule, it is not hard to see why so many scholar-officials accepted the latter, or, like Wang, withdrew from active opposition to it, within just a few years.

The geographic settings of these "conquest" episodes were varied, but they were closely related to the central series of political-military events. The next two essays remind us that a comprehensive view of the conquest period must look beyond this central sequence at the many and varied regions of China which were somewhat more "peripherally" involved. The authors of these essays found that this requires substantial exposition of the histories of such areas over a long time-span, partly for the simple reason that this background is unfamiliar to most readers, but also because we must understand each area in terms of its own development rather than simply focus on the few episodes in which it became more or less tangentially related to the main process of the conquest. Morris Rossabi shows us that there was a Muslim element in the rebel armies of Li Tzu-ch'eng. At least as important, however, is his long-range picture of political disruption and economic decline on the northwest frontier and the central Asian trade routes leading out from it, and the associated turmoil in the Chinese Muslim communities, which so often have been slighted in general studies of pre-modern China. The southern maritime area studied by Wills is somewhat more familiar to Ming–Ch'ing scholars, and some episodes of the history of the Lung-wu emperor and the Cheng family are scarcely "peripheral" to the drama of the conquest; but Wills suggests that even these personalities and events can best be understood in the long perspective of the development of peculiar forms of leadership and economic and naval power in this area.

Although all six of these "conquest" and "region" essays show how patterns of power could be influenced by individual character and choice, all equally remind us of the ways in which individual action was shaped and constrained by long-range trends of social, economic, political, and cultural development. Even Wang Fu-chih's ideas and attitudes toward politics were shaped by family and regional tradition. The very fact that the merchant-mediator-admirals

described by Wills developed such a highly personal form of power
was, he suggests, a result of economic and geopolitical constraints.
These perceptions are very much in keeping with the focus on large-
scale trends and continuities in development that have dominated
European historiography and strongly influenced Chinese studies
in recent years, and the final group of three studies concentrates
more explicitly on such "continuities," in rural socioeconomic structure, in the urban communities and their relations with the state, and
in elite culture. But in each of these essays (except possibly Hilary
Beattie's on rural power in T'ung-ch'eng) a further point emerges,
and this common perception in the Yuan and Struve essays can be
seen as a second surprising and innovative product of our common
work: Even in these areas where continuity was strong, "Ch'ing"
was different from "Ming," and the differences were clearly related
to the events of the conquest and to the specific characteristics of
the new ruling elite.

The military and bureaucratic forces of the Ch'ing conquest were
totally inadequate to impose basic changes on China's immense
rural area and population, even if they had wanted to. Indeed,
Dennerline's and Beattie's essays suggest that traditional rural power
structures were of more benefit to the Ch'ing than vice versa; Dennerline's local elite refused to ally with "loyalist" groups that seemed
to threaten the traditional rural order, and Beattie shows that after
years of rebel occupation and incursion the T'ung-ch'eng elite
offered no loyalist resistance whatever. Ch'ing imposition of law and
order moved parallel to an astonishingly effective reassertion of
nonbureaucratic law and order, as landlords reoccupied without
opposition estates from which they had fled ten years before, and
imposed new discipline on their own clans. When we see the T'ung-
ch'eng lineage leaders focusing their attention on preparing young
clansmen for the examinations and on resisting a comprehensive
reregistration of land, we glimpse some of the sources of the solidity
of the traditional rural order that was reasserting itself in the early
Ch'ing in close alliance with, but far beyond the direct power capa-
bilities of, the new and vigorous Ch'ing bureaucracy.

Ch'ing state power, however, can be seen more effectively deployed
in the urban sectors described by Tsing Yuan; commercial wealth and
industrial enterprises were concentrated in relatively few locations

and were far more vulnerable to direct state action. Thus, though there is plenty of evidence that both in late Ming and in high Ch'ing trade was active, handicraft industries were thriving, merchants were making money, and officials sometimes were extorting it from them, we become aware from Yuan's essay that at the same time the merchant influence and the threat of mob violence that had intimidated late Ming officials did not have the same effect on those of the Ch'ing. In the long run, the Ch'ing were steadily to increase taxes on, and extortion from, the commercial economy, while the Ming had done so only sporadically and in the desperation of their last years.

The volume closes with Lynn Struve's essay, which deals with a different kind of continuity from Ming to Ch'ing and a different set of effects of the conquest. Struve shows how some late seventeenth-century scholars carried on the late Ming trends toward esteem for practicality and the active life and toward a more empirical and individual historiography. At the same time, they were working out their own complex responses to the utter failure of the literati to mount any "practical" resistance to the conquest, to the impressive practicality and vigor of the early Ch'ing elite, and to their own ambiguous status in an age of much private scholarship, occasional dazzling imperial and private patronage, but low mobility through the regular channels of examination and bureaucratic promotion. The subtle interplay of cultural continuities and effects of conquest, of nostalgia for the lost loyalist cause and fascination with the Manchus, the wide wanderings and geographic interests of some of these scholars, echo many earlier themes: continuity, "statecraft" interests in reform, the bitterness of futility and defeat, the organizational strengths of the Manchus, the diversity of regions.

The essays in this volume show an intricate network of interrelations between conquest and continuity, between event and trend. In concluding this preface, it may be useful to readers of these essays and to scholars hoping to contribute to our understanding of this period to outline one schematic way of classifying some of the most important of these varieties and interrelations, which other scholars may find worthy of elaboration or modification. We will move along a sort of spectrum from "continuity" to "conquest," drawing on a few points from other recent studies as well as on the essays in this volume.

First, we should note some very important secular trends that can be observed from mid-Ming through high Ch'ing, with only brief interruption by the conquest. These include commercial growth, urbanization, growing numbers of examination candidates, the wider dissemination of increasingly sophisticated classical scholarship and discussion of "statecraft." Second, from the early 1600s on there was a mounting current of elite reaction to late Ming "corruptions," especially the steady commercialization noted above, the concomitant increases in urban luxury and in the power of money in government, and the intellectual nonconformism associated with the T'ai-chou school of the followers of Wang Yang-ming. These reactions were in part the results of the growing numbers of examination candidates and the dissemination of classical and statecraft literature among them, which in turn were linked to the commercial expansion and urbanization, many of the effects of which the "reformers" deplored. These reactions affected very strongly the way early Ch'ing scholars viewed the late Ming, and many goals for reform survived and were even finally realized under the early Ch'ing.[3]

Third, we should notice a widespread "law and order" reaction—another important common perception from our conference discussions—to late Ming rebellions, Ch'ing massacres, the widespread turmoil and dislocation, and the frequent settling of private old scores which it made possible. This intensified the search for order and discipline that had been implicit in the late Ming reform programs, led to a tightening of clan discipline (as noted in Hilary Beattie's essay), and very much facilitated acceptance of any new ruling elite that could reimpose order, even if, as in the Ch'ing massacres, it sometimes began by contributing to the violence instead of suppressing it.

Fourth, we see a good deal of evidence for important shifts in elite political values as the vehement moralism, partisanship, and network politics of the late Ming were discredited by their limited success in achieving reform goals, maintaining law and order, or organizing resistance to the rebels and the Ch'ing, and especially as the continuation of late Ming partisan strife undermined the Nanking loyalist regime. Also, the rebellions and the Ch'ing conquest gave new and tragic scope to the ideal of the exemplar of moral purity, pursued with such intensity in the late Ming. In certain dramatically conspicuous areas of China, much of the flower of a generation sacrificed itself in futile resistance, often when there was a chance of withdrawing to fight another day, or refused to serve the rebels or the Ch'ing and went defiantly to execution. Lynn Struve has pointed out some of the ambivalences of the post-conquest generation toward the martyrs; an expression of unequivocal disillusionment is Yen Yuan's famous remark that "They could repay their prince only by committing suicide."[4] Perhaps these bitter examples and reactions help to account for a somewhat lowered intensity in pursuing the ideal of the moral exemplar in the early Ch'ing elite, as well as a relatively greater emphasis on administrative effectiveness and scholarly thoroughness.

Fifth, coming closer to the "conquest" end of our spectrum, it is useful to remember that some of the effects of the imposition of a new, vigorous ruling group had rather little to do with the fact that that group had an ethnically alien core. Any new dynasty, we suspect, would have brought an end to the dominance of the bureaucracy by the lower Yangtze elite and would have opened the way to the rise of many with military backgrounds, lower degree qualifications, and so on.[5] Any new dynasty would have decisively suppressed the academy agitation and network politics (already somewhat discredited, as we have seen) that had characterized the lower Yangtze domination of the late Ming. Any new dynasty would have been sufficiently security-conscious and sufficiently detached from local influences (in most areas) to impose the generally desired "law and order" with a heavy hand.

A sixth and last stage, then, is the question of the "Manchuness" of the Ch'ing conquest; in what ways *did* that alien core make a difference? First, conspicuous signs of alienness—customs, language, dress, diet—must have made a sharper psychological break from the old regime for the Chinese than probably would have been the case with a new Chinese regime. Resentment of the imposition of the queue was especially widespread. Ethnic anti-Manchuism never died out completely and was an important aspect of the growth of the secret societies, especially the Heaven and Earth Society. We also suspect that the conspicuous alienness must have heightened the Chinese elite's consciousness of its loss of autonomous modes of influence and increased dependence on the favor of those in high office. But there may have been a positive side to this psychological break. Manchus took over many of the functions of direct representation of the despot which under the Ming had been carried out by eunuchs, and Manchus, however alien, inspired nothing quite like the deeply rooted fear and loathing normal men felt for the eunuch. As Lynn Struve shows, the strenuous lives, military virtues, and strong military organization of the Manchus aroused a certain amount of ambivalent fascination and respect among early Ch'ing intellectuals.

Organizationally, the Manchuness of the Ch'ing conquest produced immediate and far-reaching changes in the military organization of the empire, with the imposition and elaboration of the Banner System. There were analogous changes in the structure of what might be called the extrabureaucratic elite, where Manchus from princes of the blood to bondservants performed efficiently, ruthlessly, and cohesively the functions of command, control, spying, and irregular exploitation that under the Ming had been divided among military officers, eunuchs and other imperial favorites, and occasionally imperial princes. The cohesiveness of the Manchus was reinforced by their awareness of widespread Chinese hostility, by the elaboration of the control mechanisms of the Imperial Household Department, and by strong kinship ties.[6] Indeed, down to the end of the K'ang-hsi period, the Manchus seem to have made much use of kinship in high-level Chinese politics as well, frequently relying on sons of their early Chinese allies in difficult political situations.

A final very important consequence of the Manchuness of the ruling house did not become fully apparent until the eighteenth century. Manchu orientation toward Inner Asia reinforced the concentration of Chinese foreign policy on that frontier. The Manchus combined their own organization and Inner Asian military and political skills with Chinese administration and economic power to establish a new level of control over China's inland frontier zones. This was a very basic change in the geopolitics of East Asia. The expenses and forced contributions of the Ch'ien-lung campaigns were an important factor in the political economy of that period. Foreign policy continued to be oriented toward the inland frontier and away from the coast, with immense consequences in the nineteenth century.

We are very aware that these essays are soundings in an oceanic subject. Almost everything remains to be done. Although the importance of institutional, economic, and other "continuities" approaches is well recognized in general, the peculiar problems and great potentialities of continuities across a conventional dynastic dividing line in this period remain to be exploited. Great "regional" topics also abound: Szechwan under Chang Hsien-chung and the Ch'ing, Yunnan from Mu T'ien-po to the fall of Wu San-kuei, Kwangtung from the loyalist courts through the Shang regime, and many more. We also believe that this regional approach to Chinese history deserves much wider application to other periods. But we are especially impressed by the drama and the interpretive importance of the "conquest" essays and by the immense variety of similar work that remains to be done, much of it starting from very easily obtained sources.[7] All our essays show, we believe, that conquest and continuity, event and long-run trend, affected *each other,* that sophisticated event-oriented history is essential to the understanding of many basic historical themes. All nine essays are also concerned with the personal dimensions of seventeenth-century lives, and sometimes we catch an insight into them as individuals, or read something that seems to come straight from the man, from Nurhaci's "I am now angry and spit in your faces" to Liu Hsien-t'ing's thoughts on mountain-climbing. Cumulatively, we gain an impression of this society in all its variety, and we have emphasized this point in the titles of the editors' introductions to each essay. It is our hope that by thinking of the essays as also dealing with such occupational, economic, or religious groups as seafarers, city dwellers, or Muslims, the reader will constantly have his horizons stretched beyond the dynastic transition itself. Some of these aspects, as well as the major thrust of each essay and its relation to the general theme of dynastic transition, are spelled out in our introductions; and it is hoped that this device will enable even the nonspecialist reader to read this volume as a book with its own continuities and its own coherence.

NOTES

1. Arthur Waley, trans., *The Analects of Confucius* (London, 1938; paperback, New York, n.d.), introduction, p. 37.

2. Wang Fu-chih, *Huang-shu*, p. 1, in Wang Fu-chih, *Huang-shu, O-Meng* (Peking, 1956).

3. Jerry Dennerline, "Fiscal Reform and Local Control: The Gentry-Bureaucratic Alliance Survives the Conquest," in Frederic Wakeman, Jr., and Carolyn Grant, eds., *Conflict and Control in Late Imperial China* (Berkeley and Los Angeles, 1975), pp. 86–120.

4. Tu Wei-ming, "Yen Yuan: From Inner Experience to Lived Concreteness," in W. T. de Bary, ed., *The Unfolding of Neo-Confucianism* (New York, 1975), pp. 511–41, at 522.

5. Lawrence D. Kessler, "Ethnic Composition of Provincial Leadership During the Ch'ing Dynasty," *Journal of Asian Studies* 28, no. 3 (May 1969): 489–511.

6. Chang Te-ch'ang, "The Economic Role of the Imperial Household (Nei-wu-fu) in the Ch'ing Dynasty," *Journal of Asian Studies* 31, no. 2 (February 1971):243–72. Preston Torbert, "The Ch'ing Imperial Household Department: A Study of its Organization and Principal Functions, 1662–1796," (Ph.D. diss. University of Chicago, 1973). For new perceptions of court politics, cf. two recent works: Robert Oxnam, *Ruling from Horseback, Manchu Politics in the Oboi Regency, 1661–1669* (Chicago, 1975) and Lawrence Kessler, *K'ang-hsi and the Consolidation of Ch'ing Rule, 1661–1684* (Chicago, 1976).

7. See, for example, the series *T'ai-wan wen-hsien ts'ung-k'an* (Taipei, 1958–), which contains inexpensive and generally well-edited editions of many of the most important sources on the conquest period, by no means limited to those related to the Cheng family and the history of Taiwan.

Acknowledgments

The discussions, plans, and meetings that led to this book began about seven years ago and have involved the efforts of many colleagues in addition to the contributors. Members of the Committee on Studies of Chinese Civilization of the American Council of Learned Societies and its Sub-Committee on Ming-Ch'ing Studies made valuable comments on several draft proposals. The committee funded a small exploratory preconference (attended by Jerry Dennerline, Joseph Fletcher, Philip Kuhn, Jonathan Spence, Frederic Wakeman, and John Wills), which helped immensely in focusing our approach to our many-sided topic and in identifying potential participants. The Committee on Studies of Chinese Civilization and the University of Southern California funded the full working conference in November 1974, and the University of Southern California also contributed efficient administrative support. In addition to the contributors to this volume, Joseph Fletcher, David Farquhar, Angela Hsi, Thomas Fisher, David Shore, and Richard Strassberg all participated in this conference and played important roles in its discussions. Susan Naquin served admirably as rapporteur. Florence Thomas has typed the entire draft and some pieces of it several times. Edward Tripp at Yale University Press was consistently patient and helpful, and Barbara Folsom proved a most alert manuscript editor. The maps were prepared for us by Karl Rueckert.

In the three and a half years since our conference was held, there have been some remarkable advances in the study of late imperial China that would have added much to our discussions and interpretations if we had had time to assimilate them fully. We think, for example, of the massive *Dictionary of Ming Biography,* edited by L. Carrington Goodrich and Chaoying Fang (Columbia University Press, 1976): though all the authors have checked the most obvious entries related to their topics, we all recognize that it will be years before we can digest the astonishing range of new ideas and research opportunities these volumes open up. They compound the debt of gratitude expressed in our Dedication. We are also very aware of the major advances in knowledge of urban China and in sophisticated thinking about its regional structure which are presented in G. William Skinner, ed., *The City in Late Imperial China* (Stanford University Press, 1977), as well as the complexity of argument in Thomas A. Metzger's analysis of Neo-Confucian political culture, *Escape from Predicament: Neo-Confucianism and China's Evolving Political Culture* (Columbia University Press, 1977). Here again, we regret that important findings could not be adequately taken into account.

In our conference we developed a strong sense of shared excitement about our subject and a commitment to the idea of cooperation in advancing knowledge of it, which we like to think is characteristic of the rapidly developing international community of Ming-Ch'ing scholars. This book attempts to contribute to that excitement and shared commitment, and to pay some part of our great debt to that community of scholars.

J. D. S.
J. W.

New Haven and Los Angeles
May 1978

1

The Manchu-Chinese Relationship, 1618–1636

by Gertraude Roth

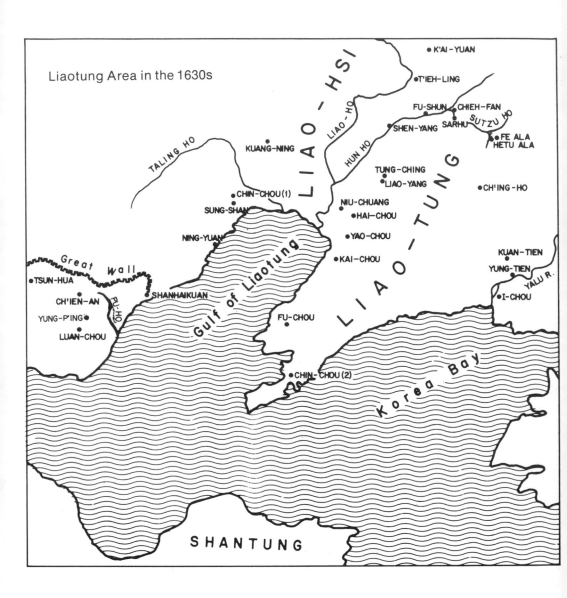

Liaotung Area in the 1630s

- K'AI-YUAN
- T'IEH-LING
LIAO-HSI
FU-SHUN • CHIEH-FAN
SHEN-YANG SARHU SUTZU HO
LIAO-HO
HUN HO
TALING HO
- KUANG-NING
- FE ALA
  HETU ALA
TUNG-CHING
- LIAO-YANG
- CH'ING-HO
- CHIN-CHOU(1)
SUNG-SHAN
- NIU-CHUANG
- HAI-CHOU
LIAO-TUNG
- NING-YUAN
- YAO-CHOU
Great Wall
- KUAN-TIEN
- YUNG-TIEN
- KAI-CHOU
- TSUN-HUA
Gulf of Liaotung
YALU R.
- CH'IEN-AN
FU-HO
SHANHAIKUAN
- I-CHOU
YUNG-P'ING
FU-CHOU
- LUAN-CHOU
- CHIN-CHOU(2)
Korea Bay

SHANTUNG

Manchus

To some contemporary observers, Chinese and European, and to many writers down to our own time, the Ch'ing conquest was a bloody and utterly alien "Tartar conquest," something like the Mongol devastation of Russia. From this perspective it is very hard to explain the ease of the conquest and the long success of Ch'ing rule, both of which stand in great contrast to the Mongol Yuan. Some of the reasons for these contrasts are to be found in the history of China in the late Ming and are pointed out in later essays in this volume. Others are the results of the development of the Manchu Ch'ing state before 1644. The Manchus did not come out of a steppe nomadic economy and society but out of a mixed hunting, farming, and pastoral economy. They were deeply involved in trade with China and were developing some small iron works and other handicraft industries, often employing skilled Korean slaves. They had had long and complex political relations with the Chinese tribute system and frontier military system. They had been influenced by Mongolian and Chinese political traditions as well as by the heritage of their ancestors who had ruled northern China as the Chin Dynasty (1127–1235).

Nurhaci and his followers rose out of a political environment of rapid rise and fall, marriage alliances, blood feuds, and boundless scope for ambition. The heritage of that world would continue to affect their political style as rulers of China at least down to the 1720s. In the late sixteenth century many chieftains tried to expand their power in the area we call Manchuria, including Wan, Khan of the Hada, Yangginu, chief of the Yehe, and Giocangga, Nurhaci's father. Nurhaci's success was more permanent than theirs in part because the Japanese invasions of Korea gave him more leverage in dealing with the Ming authorities and in part because the Ming authorities were losing the military power and the administrative coherence that had enabled them to control the frontier, either by halting the rise of an ambitious man or by forcing a compromise settlement on him.

We already know a good deal, primarily from the official account in Chinese called the K'ai-kuo fang-lueh, of the remarkable political-military-economic system Nurhaci and his successor worked out before 1644, drawing on Manchu, Mongolian, and Chinese patterns of

3

*organization. In Roth's account of the crucial period of this develop-
ment, based very largely on the contemporary records in Manchu
called* Man-chou chiu-tang, *we get a much more vivid sense than we
had from the Chinese sources of the false starts, the crises, the anxieties and angers amid which this system was evolved and by which it
was shaped. The striking talent for balancing relations among men,
land, and taxes, the evolving search for the right mix of segregation
and conciliation in dealing with the subjugated Chinese population,
the boldness with which political difficulties were met, the evolving
relations with the Chinese military commanders of Liaotung, all offer
important clues to the strengths of Ch'ing rule after 1644.*

*Knowledge of Manchu is rare among present-day students of the
early Ch'ing, and Roth's essay shows how profoundly our understanding of the conquest can be changed by exploring the original
records. And even if it is probable that no post-conquest sources in
Manchu exist that have the same freshness and interest as the ones
she has used here, we are now presented with enough evidence to
move beyond the hypotheses offered in Franz Michael's* The Origins
of Manchu Rule in China, *and to begin assessing the impact of these
earliest institutions and politics on the post-1644 Ch'ing state with a
new sophistication.*

INTRODUCTION

From the naming of the Dynasty in 1636 down past 1900, Ch'ing
politics involved, in shifting forms and combinations, preservation of
the cultural and organizational distinctiveness of the Manchu people,
selective cooptation of Chinese power-holders and appeals to Chinese
values, and watchful repression of Chinese anti-Manchu ideas and
actions. In this essay I will show how all these aspects of Ch'ing
politics already were highly developed by 1636. We also see in these
early years considerable Manchu interest in the devising of complex
systems of distribution of land and labor, systems that had their
roots in Inner Asian traditions as well as in Chinese. The years from
1636 to 1644 saw further important steps in the maturing of the
political attitudes and institutions that guided the conquest of China.
The Manchu archival sources used in this paper do not extend into

those later years, while the volume of Chinese sources and the problems of controlling their reliability increase enormously. Moreover,
preliminary research suggests that despite the defection of large
numbers of Ming officers and soldiers to the Ch'ing between 1636
and 1644, the basic structures of Manchu-Chinese social and economic relations did not change qualitatively in those years. Thus this
paper concentrates on the period between the Manchus' conquest of
Liaotung, between 1618 and 1621, which marks the beginning of
major contact between the Manchus and the Chinese, and the proclamation of the Ch'ing dynasty in Shen-yang (Mukden) in 1636. It
makes only a few general suggestions on developments after 1636.

The present study is based primarily on the *Man-chou chiu-tang*, a
collection of Manchu documents written before 1644. A copy of
these documents, which had been made during the Ch'ien-lung
period, was discovered in 1905 and has been romanized and translated into Japanese under the title *Mambun Rōtō*. These two
sources—for historical enquiries there seem to be only a few significant differences between the two—present a vast amount of new
data. They reveal political, economic, and social problems of the
early Manchu state which the official sources like the *Ch'ing-shih*, the
Shih-lu, or the *K'ai-kuo fang-lueh* do not mention at all, or only in
passing. Yet, as enlightening as the *Man-chou chiu-tang* is in many
ways, it still lacks a great deal of desirable information. The material
relating to the period before 1621 is scanty, leaving unanswered
many questions about the functioning of the government and the
early relationship between the Manchus and Chinese. The years between 1621 and 1636 are covered in more detail, but here too there
are gaps; and the source contains no records at all for the period after
1636.

A certain amount of contact between the Manchus and Chinese
had taken place throughout the Ming dynasty. During Ming times
some Manchus moved into territory inhabited primarily by Chinese
and some Chinese into areas with a Manchu population. Except for a
relatively small number of enslaved Chinese prisoners and occasional
conflicts between Manchus and certain Chinese officials, neither the
Chinese nor the Manchus exploited or oppressed the other generally
or systematically.[1]

When Nurhaci, the first Manchu khan, conquered several Jurchen

tribes around 1600 and organized them into companies (*niru*) and
banners (*gusa*), he treated his Jurchen and Chinese subjects equally.
Though the Chinese population was small, there seem to have been a
few Chinese companies as early as 1614[2] and Chinese could and did
obtain high office. The absence of evidence of friction in the Manchu
sources between the Manchus and the Chinese during the 1610s
cannot be taken as a purposeful omission by the writers of the documents, because Manchu oppression of the Chinese is freely acknowledged a few years later. It is much more likely that the relatively easy
relationship was the result of the fact that the free Chinese who lived
among the Manchus at this time were there out of their own will,
had not been subjected to Manchu rule by force or intimidation, and
in many ways were considered to have simply "become Manchu."
Perhaps the absence of major conflict in the past influenced Nurhaci's
thinking after the conquest of Liaotung and led him to believe that
Manchus and Chinese could easily live together.

If Nurhaci did in fact think so, he was mistaken. The Liaotung
Chinese were not pioneers who had ventured into Manchu territory.
They and their land belonged to the Manchu khan because of his military power. The local officials saw their best chance in submitting,
but the low degree holders (*sheng-yuan*) with the support of the
people mustered opposition to Manchu rule. Nurhaci's policy initially aimed at equality and it was only after the Manchus showed
their dissatisfaction and the Chinese their hostility that the early
policy of equality and integration turned into one of separation and
discrimination against the Chinese. The Manchu-Chinese relationship
was further strained by economic scarcities and the necessity to
temporarily house Manchus and Chinese together. A rebellion of the
Liaotung Chinese in 1623 led to the abandoning of Manchu-Chinese
equality on the official level, and another outbreak of Chinese discontent two years later to a reorganization of the Chinese in the
course of which they were distributed to Manchu officials with the
status resembling that of slaves.

The death of Nurhaci in 1626 marks a change in the Manchu-
Chinese relationship as well as in leadership. Nurhaci's successor,
Hung Taiji, again placed the Chinese under their own officials and
tried to achieve Chinese equality with the Manchus through separation. The reason for Hung Taiji's renewed emphasis on Chinese equality must be found in his need for Chinese political support. Hung

Taiji was not the heir-apparent under Nurhaci but usurped the throne. His title therefore should not be Huang Taiji, which is a later revision, but rather Hung Taiji, as it appears in the *Man-chou chiu-tang* and in at least two Korean sources. The title Hung Taiji almost certainly comes from the Mongolian though the meaning of the word *Hung* is not entirely clear. The origin of the name Abahai, commonly used in Western literature for Hung Taiji, has as yet not been established.[3]

In addition to a renewed effort to improve the status of the Chinese, another difference between the reigns of the two khans suggests a breaking point between Nurhaci's and Hung Taiji's reigns. While under Nurhaci most of the Chinese officials surrendering or submitting to the Manchus were of low rank, Hung Taiji appealed especially to the Chinese of high official rank. He did so with great success, partly because he was far more willing to make selective accommodations to Chinese culture and custom than his father had been.

FROM INTEGRATION TO SEGREGATION (1619-1626)

The period between 1619 and 1621 was one of conquest and rapid expansion. Already in 1618 Nurhaci had attacked the city of Fushun and induced its commander to surrender. In 1619 the Manchus fought a decisive victory over the Ming and their Korean allies at Sarhu, a victory followed by others at Shen-yang, Liao-yang, T'ieh-ling, and K'ai-yuan. The fall of Liao-yang in 1621 precipitated the surrender of most of the Liaotung peninsula. Nurhaci planned to head toward the strategic Shan-hai-kuan in 1623–24, but domestic problems demanded his attention and the presence of his troops in Liaotung.

At the time of the Liaotung conquest, Nurhaci already seems to have conceived of the possibility of expanding into China and setting up a Manchu dynasty in Peking, though on the basis of the present research it is impossible to determine how much of China he hoped or expected to win. Nurhaci's political ambition is apparent in his setting up the Latter Chin dynasty in 1616, reminding everyone of the parallel between the earlier Chin dynasty, which once controlled Northern China, and the latest developments in Manchuria. His ambition to become emperor also lies behind his interpretation of

natural phenomena, such as heavenly omens which proved that
Heaven supported him instead of the Ming, and in his propaganda in
general.

Strange lines of light in the sky were said to have appeared in 1612
and 1614. They supposedly occurred twice in 1615 as a proper
prelude to the establishment of the Latter Chin state in 1616.[4] But
the notion that the emperor is endowed by Heaven and receives
Heaven's approval or disapproval was adopted by the Manchus with
the greatest zeal at the beginning of the period of conquest. During
the year 1618 an overwhelming number of reports of such heavenly
signs aided the Manchus and the Chinese both to gradually become
used to the idea that a dynastic change was drawing near. Lines of
light in the sky appeared nearly every month, once staying for the
length of an entire month.[5] At other times, Nurhaci's scholarly aide
Erdeni interpreted good weather or a rainstorm as having been sent
by Heaven to facilitate Manchu victories.[6] Because the Manchus may
not have begun writing the documents now collected in the *Man-
chou chiu-tang* until 1618, the records for the earlier years seem to
have been written from recollection of the events. References to
heavenly omens before 1618 therefore may have been construed
later. The phenomena recorded for 1618, however, most likely
occurred in some form and were interpreted in the above way at
that time.

Propaganda through oral or written statements or through exemplary behavior was designed to win the support of the Chinese and
prepare them for Manchu rule. If Nurhaci had any hopes of setting
up a Chinese empire of whatever size, he had to work out a passable
relationship with the Chinese. By offering a better life to the common people through a redistribution of land and wealth, and by
promising to set up a just, capable, and corruption-free government
not based on hereditary privileges but on the selection of the truly
selfless, Nurhaci tried to convince the Chinese inside and outside the
Manchu borders that he possessed the traditional qualities to be the
founder of a new dynasty. Against the background of the conditions
in China, where the agricultural population was harassed by harsh
landlords, corrupt officials, and marauding troops and bandits,
Manchu propaganda could probably hope for some results, though it
is impossible to measure the degree of its success.

After the annexation of Liaotung, the Manchu government issued a

statement inviting the people of Liao-hsi, the area west of the
Liaotung River, to move to Liaotung and become free and equal
landowners: "Do not think that the land and houses will not be
yours, that they will belong to a master. All will equally be the
khan's subjects and will live and work the fields on an equal basis."[7]
The khan sent messengers to all villages to tell the people that "instead of letting the rich accumulate their grain and have it rot away,
or letting them pile up the goods for no use, one should nourish the
begging poor."[8] Especially during the period of 1618–21, but also
later, the Manchus were constantly aware of the effect their policies
toward the conquered and submitted people had on the population
beyond the temporary borders. After a tour of inspection, Nurhaci
instructed his supreme judges (*tu-t'ang*) never to maltreat the Chinese
newcomers, steal their clothing, or separate their families, and to
take extreme care to establish a good reputation by thoroughly investigating "the people who talk ill about us," because "if the people
of Kuang-ning hear it they will not submit."[9]

The Manchu troops had to observe strict discipline. For example,
after the surrender of the city of Hai-chou, the soldiers were forbidden to dismount from their horses in the villages through which
they passed, lest they rob or harm the population. Even the Manchu
princes (the *beiles*) who rode into the city in the company of a few
selected troops, dismounted only in front of the yamen, demonstrating a well-disciplined take-over. One or two soldiers who did
venture to steal something were caught and punished, and a few
among the soldiers who through carelessness finished their rations
of grain on the way, were not allowed to take anything from the
country but had to go hungry.[10]

Manchu military power undoubtedly played a major part in fright-
ening the people into submission, but the Manchus' efforts to attract
the people may also have elicited some positive response. No throngs
of people answered the invitation to come to the Manchu-occupied
territory. Even a voluntary surrender was degrading in that it required the people to submit with shaven heads to the town authorities and to kowtow to the khan, but when it was a question of
actually resisting the invading Manchus or quietly surrendering to
them, the latter choice was often taken. Thus the officials of Hai-
chou and Kuang-ning welcomed the Manchu liberators in the traditional way, with flutes and drums.[11] The *Man-chou chiu-tang* also

lists a great many Mongols who voluntarily joined the Manchus.

Having people submit was important to the spread of the idea that the Manchus were about to set up an empire, for along with the idea of a heavenly mandate goes the notion that a benevolent ruler attracts the people from afar. While history provided ample evidence that non-Chinese felt attracted to China and settled within its borders, the Manchus considered it a unique case that the direction of attraction was now reversed. "There is no precedent to Chinese people going over to another country but [because] they have heard that we take good care of our people, they have come to us to submit."[12] The well-being of the Chinese under the Manchus retained a high propaganda value even in times of economic crisis. In 1623, a year of economic hardship, the Manchu government took special care to provide the Chinese newcomers with grain.[13]

Another aspect of Manchu propaganda promised the appointment or promotion of capable officials regardless of social rank.[14] Propaganda and a proper treatment of the Chinese people and their officials formed a preparatory step to the establishment of a Manchu empire. The intention to pass through the Shan-hai-kuan and enter China appears as early as 1622, when Nurhaci warned the Chinese fleeing before his approaching Manchu troops in the Kuang-ning area: "Come out of hiding and down from the mountains, because even if you go inside Shan-hai-kuan . . . my great army will enter Shan-hai-kuan [in 1623–24]."[15]

There is no indication that expansion as a goal was ever abandoned at any time. In 1627, when the Manchu army was about to invade Korea, the Chinese memorialist Yueh Ch'i-luan advised the khan not to undertake the campaign to Korea, which would leave Liaotung under insufficient military protection, and urged him to return the Liaotung Chinese to China and make peace with the Ming government. Yueh Ch'i-luan predicted that otherwise the Manchu people would perish or be scattered. The khan's response left no doubt about his firm intention to continue a policy of expansion and about his view of peace negotiations with the Ming as a temporary, expedient measure only: "If the Chinese send someone to negotiate peace with us, let us obtain gold, silver, and silk and get our escapees back. It will be a peace in name only. Why should we return the Chinese, whom Heaven has given to us?"[16] The fact that Yueh Ch'i-luan was killed by enraged Chinese officials under the khan instead of by the

khan's order does not change the meaning of the event: peaceful coexistence with China was no longer a possibility under consideration.

After the conquest of Liaotung, the Chinese entered into all tiers
of society. There were slaves and servants, registered households, and
Chinese in high positions. Before the conquest the Chinese slaves
(*aha*) or bondservants (*booi niyalma*, lit.: "person of the household") were the private property of their master, who had complete
power over them. If the master chose to kill them, he was responsible
to no one. After the conquest of Liaotung, the social status of the
Chinese servant class became more differentiated, but there is little
information on the obligations or rights of the various bound people.
Some continued to be true slaves, while the bondservants seemed to
have been higher in status. The occurrence of the terms "household
slave" (*booi aha*), "bondservant" (*booi niyalma*), and "free person
of the household" (*sula booi niyalma*) suggests that the status of the
Chinese living in Manchu and perhaps in Chinese households ranged
from that of slaves to that of free people.[17]

The power of the master to punish and kill his slaves was also
limited after the conquest of Liaotung. Years earlier, when a company official killed a woman of his household and another woman
from his company on the ground that they were witches, nobody
accused him and he received no punishment. But in 1623, after he
maltreated and blinded still another woman, charges were brought
against him, and at the same time his former crimes also were dis-
closed. He lost his rank, was fined a sum of money, and had two
women taken away from him in compensation for the two he had
killed.[18] By 1623 the master could no longer punish his slaves on his
own authority but was required to report any crime committed by a
slave to the official in charge. A certain master who did punish a
Chinese woman of his household (*booi nikan hehe*) on his own
authority received thirty lashes.[19]

The khan decreed that the master-slave relationship should become
a more paternal one: the master should love the slave, and the slave
should love the master.[20] Although the decree described an idealized
picture of a paternal master and not reality, its importance lies in the
mere fact that a publicized legal guideline for the master-servant
relationship existed. Servants could also report their masters for illegal conduct. Depending on the severity of the offense, the servant
could be taken away and given to another master.[21] If the servant

knew of and reported traitorous activities on the part of his master,
he could even receive the reward of freedom. The slaves were originally people captured in battle and subsequently awarded (*shang*
or *tz'u*) to the military leaders and soldiers who had participated in a
particular campaign. But the misfortune of holding slave status was
not always a consequence of previous resistance on the battlefield.
On at least one occasion, households with a designated amount of
grain per person were made free, while those with less were enslaved.[22]

The origin of the people receiving the status of bondservant (*booi
niyalma*) in the 1620s and 1630s is not entirely clear. Quite likely
they were the people whom the khan gave (*buhe*) to imperial relatives,[23] to companies,[24] and to officials of all ranks to provide for
them in lieu of salary.[25] In those cases the master could draw a
fixed amount of revenue from a given number of people.[26] In referring to the Chinese so distributed, however, the Manchu source
usually does not use the term *booi niyalma,* but *aha,* and the Chinese sources use *chuang-ting* or *ting*—all terms which translate as
"free able-bodied man." The *K'ai-kuo fang-lueh* and the *Shih-lu,* in
recording an address which the khan made to the Chinese officials
in 1634 reproaching them for the excessively high number of Chinese belonging to them, refer to these Chinese as servants (*nu-p'u*)
in introducing the khan's speech, but in quoting the khan's words
use the term *ting.*[27] Unfortunately, there is no Manchu version of
the address, because quite possibly the ambivalence in the Chinese
text arose from the lack of a proper Chinese translation for *booi
niyalma,* whose status was one between *nu-p'u* and *ting.*

At some point—the date still needs to be established—the khan and
the beiles organized their bondservants into companies (*booi niru*)
and the Manchu word *booi* was transliterated into Chinese as *pao-i.*
The *Shih-lu* notes that a census held in 1630 also counted the number of people in the bondservant companies (*booi niru*), but this
may well have been a misconception dating from the later period
when the *Shih-lu* was written and the bondservants were formally
organized into companies. It does not necessarily mean that the
bondservants of 1630 also formed bondservant companies. The
ambivalent use of the terms *nu-p'u* and *ting* for the same group of
people, as well as the absence of the term *booi niru* in the *Man-*

chou chiu-tang, command caution about reading the existence and importance of bondservant companies of the postconquest time back into the period before 1636.

The large Chinese population of Liaotung, which had surrendered to the Manchus, were registered as households and administered by Chinese officials after the conquest. With the major exception of Li Yung-fang, the commander of Fu-shun, who surrendered in 1618, the officials under Nurhaci had not been high-ranking officials under the Ming. A list of officials taken over or appointed by the Manchus shows that the majority of the new officials were people who had held very low-level official positions or none at all. However, this may not be an accurate indication of the actual standing of these people in Ming Liaotung. The three names at the top of the list who received the highest ranks, T'ung Yang-hsing, Aita, and T'ung Yen, had no previous office listed. But Aita is not a Chinese name, and the other two were members of a famous Liaotung military family whose relations with the Manchus went back to 1616 or earlier. Higher-ranking Chinese officials, closer to the mainstream of the Ming bureaucracy, would not be attracted by the idea of service under rulers who were largely unfamiliar with the Chinese language, economically and politically below Chinese standards, and had very different customs, food, clothing, and so on. Also, Nurhaci believed that high officials taken over from the Ming were less likely to be loyal than those who were appointed or promoted by the Manchus, those owing their rise to the new rulers. Some Chinese officials apparently were attached to the Manchu banners, but those of high rank, like T'ung Yang-hsing and Aita, who were in command of large numbers of Chinese, were directly under the central government.

Although the surrender of the officials generally also meant the surrender of the population under their administration, opposition by the Chinese people to Manchu rule appeared almost immediately after the conquest. Some city dwellers burnt their possessions in preparation for their escape. They were sent to the countryside and ordered to till the fields. Others tried to poison their conquerors.[28] The circumstances of poisoning in Hai-chou show that the common people had a very different attitude from the Chinese officials and local gentry, for while the officials and members of the gentry

(*ba-i bayasa*) were greeting the arriving Manchus and entertaining
them in the yamen, the people poisoned the wells outside. There
are also frequent references to the Manchus being given poisoned
foods. Indeed, the Manchus were at a loss to discover the culprits,
and had to resort to taking a multiple number of precautions in
order to avoid being poisoned.[29] The extent and variety of poison-
ings showed that many Chinese participated in the opposition.
Judging from the later developments, the low-degree holders (*sheng-
yuan*) may have been behind the popular opposition, but at the
time of the conquest there is only one indication that this might have
been so: when the Manchu troops under the leadership of Aita
reached Chin-chou (2) in the south of the Liaotung peninsula, all
but two *sheng-yuan,* apparently of a large number, had fled to the
nearby islands.[30]

In order to secure Liaotung and prevent the Chinese from escaping, the Manchus settled and guarded the borders. They occupied
the houses of the Chinese residents along the borders and moved the
Chinese inward away from the border or to the north, which the
Manchus had left empty when they moved south.[31] Nurhaci also
planned to concentrate the Chinese into larger towns and cities
which could be easily defended against the enemy and where the
people could be kept from escaping.[32] When the officials made
preparations to distribute Chinese land and houses among the Manchus, the Chinese requested that they be allowed to stay where they
were and just share their houses, land, and food with the Manchus.
"We are all subjects of the same khan. Let us live together and eat
together. Why should we move?"[33] Their readiness to suffer a Manchu family to share their property may have been due to an official
statement—an unfounded statement as it turned out—that the concentration of the people in the towns was meant to last only for one
winter, for at the time the Manchu troops were on a campaign to
Liao-hsi and could not leave enough soldiers behind to guard all
places in the countryside.[34] Less than a month after the request,
cooccupant living began in several areas. Manchus and Chinese
lived, ate, and worked together.[35] The policy of cohabitancy was a
primarily economic measure. The Manchus had their food supply
secured without requiring transportation. The cooperative work
was also expected to be more economical, since more could be accomplished in less time.[36] In addition, cooccupant living could also

serve as a form of control over the individual Chinese household and give the Manchus, living with the more agriculturally skilled Chinese, a thorough training in agricultural work.

For the first winter 1621/22, just after the Manchus had moved into Liaotung and proceeded on to Liao-hsi, they had no grain reserves, and the Manchus received a monthly allowance of grain taken from the Chinese. According to the initial arrangement, only the Manchus were alloted four piculs (sin) of grain per month.[37] Many Chinese were probably left with less than that amount per capita for themselves. Therefore, only a month later a decree order that the Chinese be given equal rations.[38] To prevent either side from cheating the other in appropriating grain for themselves, both Manchus and Chinese were to be present when the stored grain was taken out.[39] In order to equalize the economic burden over the entire population—the cooccupant households were confined to the areas surrounding Liaotung—those Chinese not living together with Manchus had to compensate by giving more grain or making other contributions.[40]

The rationing of grain was an emergency measure only. The following year the Manchu government promised a redistribution of all land, giving each adult man five cimari (1 cimari equals 6 mu or about one acre).[41] There is no conclusive evidence that the promised redistribution of land did take place in 1623, but well into the 1630s it was a well-known law—though not always successfully implemented by the individual officials—that each adult man should have five cimari of land.[42]

Previously the tax system had been based on the banner organization, and each company had supplied ten men to cultivate public lands for government revenue. Now it was changed and made applicable to the Chinese outside the banner organization. Three men were to work one cimari of land jointly as alban (alban=public, corvée).[43] The grain tax was the same for Manchus and Chinese and remained the same after doubling a year later, bringing it to about 13 percent of the harvest.[44] The grain tax was not the only demand the government made on its subjects. The people had other corvée duties, but until this time there are no indications that according to the laws the Chinese received less land or paid higher taxes than the Manchus.

In 1622 free land that could be cultivated in the east, namely

Liaotung, was no longer plentiful. There was still free land around
Fu-shun, but the other parts of Liaotung were filled up: "The land
is extremely scarce. There are people who say that even if we till
there [around Fu-shun] there will not be enough because the land
is too small. Old or new people, if willing, should go to Shen-yang,
Pu-ho, I-lu, and Fan-ho [places along the Liaotung River north of
Shen-yang]. In Fu-shun the land is plentiful."[45] In addition to the
original Chinese population, Liaotung had already absorbed the Manchu population and many Chinese prisoners brought in from outside. After the campaign into Liao-hsi in the winter of 1621/22,
more Chinese, especially from the Kuang-ning area in Liao-hsi,
were moved to Liaotung. When they arrived in Liaotung many of
them could not be given land but had to be taken in by Liaotung
families and also live in units of two households. Thus, instead of
the cooccupant households being dissolved as had been promised,
more were formed. The basic economic difficulties resulting from the
sudden increase of population in Liaotung were aggravated by the
disruption caused by the moves. Grain shortages, already evident before the moves, became increasingly serious: during the summer of
1623 there was no salt, food was scarce, and famine occurred.[46]

In addition to the poor economic conditions, serious trouble
stemmed from the attitude of the Manchus toward the Chinese.
The policy of cooccupancy and Chinese equality was at variance
with the expectations of the Manchu military officials and soldiers
who saw themselves as conquerors and the Chinese as the conquered.
Instances of Manchus oppressing and robbing the Chinese were
numerous. In one case, the fishbuyers from the khan's own household slaughtered and ate Chinese livestock at will. They even killed
some Chinese and took their clothing and horses. To demonstrate
that standards of right and wrong applied to everyone, Nurhaci had
the leader of the fishbuyers executed and punished the other
participants.[47]

The Manchus living with the Chinese in cooccupant units frequently regarded their Chinese household not as equal partners but
as servants. They freely used the oxen of their Chinese family, had
the Chinese transport grain and grass on their carts for them, sent
them on errands, or even had the women do the household chores
for them.[48] Because of this attitude of the Manchu people it was nec-

essary to reduce the scope of cohabitation from a social and working
unit to a primarily social one: Manchu and Chinese households
should still live and eat together, but they should work separately,
working different parts of the land with separate animals.[49] Nurhaci
also set up a series of particular rules. Manchus were not to oppress
the Chinese, and not to steal anything from them. If a Manchu inflicted any harm on a Chinese, the Chinese had the right to file an
accusation, and two judges—the source does not specify whether one
of the judges was Chinese—were to decide the case; judgment had to
be unanimous. A further general order made it "illegal" to live in
discord with one's cooccupant partner.[50] Nevertheless, Manchu
oppression persisted and Chinese complaints did little to change the
situation. The various rules concerning the Manchu-Chinese relationship, trying to make cooccupant living a successful arrangement,
show that Nurhaci recognized that the Manchus were to blame for
most of the difficulties. Even though the Manchus had come as
conquerors, he tried to force them into line in order to protect
the Chinese.

Economic distress and Manchu oppression led to an open rebellion
of the Chinese throughout Liaotung in 1623. The first signs came in
the form of a series of simultaneous fires around Kuang-ning.[51] A
month later poisoning became prominent once more. Chinese invited
Manchus into their homes where they poisoned them with wine.
Other Chinese stole grain from grain collectors, killed Manchus, and
then went into hiding in the mountains.[52] In some cases, the Chinese
killed border guards and watchtower personnel and escaped across
the southern border.[53] In one case, as many as two hundred people
tried to escape, but the Manchu troops caught them and killed the
men.[54] In Yao-chou the Chinese killed Manchu women and children
as soon as the soldiers had left.[55] During this time of revolt many
officials received rewards for catching spies, which suggests that
Chinese unrest under the Manchus may have been connected with
Ming plans for a military offensive.[56]

The Manchus suppressed the rebellion easily, but the 1623 revolt
marks the turning point for the policy of Manchu-Chinese integration and equality. Just before the revolt there was another instance of
Manchus being punished for robbing Chinese.[57] It is the last entry
of its kind for several years. During the time of the revolts the policy

of integration began to be reversed: Manchu cavalry members and patrolmen were forbidden to visit Chinese homes and soldiers were warned that there was danger they might be beaten by the Chinese and therefore "should be on their guard day and night and not associate with the Chinese of the villages."[58]

The existing cooccupant living arrangements between Manchus and Chinese were not yet terminated, but from this time on no new ones were created. Certain returning troops received instructions "to go back where they had come from but not to live with the Chinese, but in different places."[59] In the moves of the households from the countryside into the towns, Manchus and Chinese for the first time were assigned separate quarters of the town. Later, Manchus were forbidden to enter the Chinese streets.[60] The clearest indication that Manchu-Chinese integration and equality were officially abandoned at this time were the new regulations concerning weapons.[61] It was illegal for the Chinese to possess weapons, while the Manchus were expected always to carry them, an unmistakable sign that one was master and the other subject.

The change from a policy of integration to one of segregation and discrimination also affected the high officialdom. There had been no discrimination against Chinese officials immediately after the conquest of Liaotung. Both Manchus and Chinese officials were in charge of Chinese subjects and received the same amounts when awards were given according to rank.[62] But as is seen from one case recorded in the *Man-chou chiu-tang* in great detail, the attitudes of the Manchu people impeded the performance of the Chinese officials just as they caused the failure of cohabitancy. After a Chinese subject sent in a complaint about being oppressed by his Manchu co-occupant household, the Chinese official in charge sent several messengers to the Manchu in question reminding him of the khan's edicts forbidding the maltreatment of Chinese. The Manchu thereupon refused to obey the Chinese high official, bound and beat the messengers, and destroyed the letter.[63] Although this case receives a somewhat lengthy treatment and therefore may have been special, still one suspects that there must have been many more cases of similar behavior which either escaped official notice or were not important enough to be included in the records.

With the outbreak of the 1623 revolts, Manchu-Chinese equality on the level of the officials was secretly abandoned. Because of its importance, Nurhaci's statement is quoted in full:

> Let us make all our beiles and officials live happily. If I [the khan] am now angry and spit into your faces, it is because your [the beiles' and Manchu high officials'] way of judging crimes is wrong. Why do you let the Chinese in high positions be equal to you? If a Manchu has committed some crime, look for his merits. Ask what he has accomplished. If there is any little reason, use it as a pretext to pardon him. If a Chinese committed some crime deserving capital punishment, if he did not make an all-out effort as he should, or stole things, why not kill him and all his descendants and relatives instead of letting him get away with a beating? Judge those Chinese who have been with us since Fe Ala [i.e. before 1619] on the same basis as the Jušens [i.e. Manchus]. Once a sentence has been decided upon, you cannot change it again. It is like a mule that does not know how to go backwards. You eight beiles read this letter in secret to the beiles and officials of the various banners. Do not let the people hear it. Do you not know that they [the Chinese] have killed and poisoned our women and children at Yao-chou after our troops left?[65]

Segregation on the psychological level took place simultaneously. It was remembered and written into the record that not only Chinese officials but also people without any rank had treated the Manchus in a haughty manner before the Manchus were in power. The Chinese were said to have freely entered the homes of Manchu nobles and behaved like masters. In comparison, since "we [the Manchus] obtained Liaotung, the Chinese haughtiness has been entirely dispelled."[66]

Separating the Chinese from the Manchu soldiers and keeping them apart in separate quarters of the towns probably eliminated some Manchu-Chinese friction among the people, but the new segregation, and the officially tolerated and secretly practiced discrimination against the Chinese, must have incited the opposition of the educated Chinese outside the Manchu officialdom. During the ninth lunar month of 1625 the most serious Chinese revolt of the pre-1644 period occurred. The Chinese killed Manchu soldiers, messengers, and people. They captured a Chinese official appointed by the Manchus and sent him to the Ming, but most of all they sought ways to escape themselves. They recruited soldiers or sent messengers to the Ming army asking them to come and safeguard their journey back to the Chinese side.[67] Since the Ming defeat at Sarhû in 1618, the Chinese had been making efforts to recover lost territory. However, since the uprising of the Chinese under the Manchus was again easily suppressed even with simultaneous Ming advances, one must assume that without outside activity there was no chance for a successful Chinese uprising under the Manchus.

In dealing with the 1625 uprising the Manchus distinguished between two main groups of people: one group consisted of people who had been low officials under the Ming but held no office under the Manchus, or low-degree holders, who were blamed for having incited the people to revolt; the other group, the common people in general, were considered to have been innocent, not to have harbored spies, and not to have made plans to escape. But even if this latter group had not been evil in themselves, neither had they shown themselves to be reliable. To cleanse the state of all rebellious elements, a nationwide purge took place in the eleventh lunar month of 1625. All Chinese people and officials, even in the areas where no open revolts had occurred, were investigated thoroughly. Many people and a large number of intellectuals (*saisa*) and low-degree holders were killed.[68]

Along with the purge came a new form of organization for the Chinese, the *tokso*. The term *tokso,* referring to imperial grants of cultivated land and people, had been in existence for some time. Before 1625 the number of men per *tokso* was not fixed,[69] but the creation of *tokso* on a large scale after the 1625 revolts brought standardization. The new *tokso* consisted of thirteen Chinese households under a Chinese headman (*jangturi*); they were administered by Manchu banner officials and thus belonged to one of the eight Manchu banners.[70] Each *tokso* owned seven oxen and worked one hundred *cimari* of land, eighty for their own sustenance and twenty as *alban,* which meant a tax increase from 13 percent of the harvest in 1623 to 20 percent in 1625. Nothing is known about a comparable tax increase for the Manchus; the 1625 increase seems to have been a vindictive measure against the Chinese after their revolt.

The organization into *tokso* existed for the remaining one and a half years of Nurhaci's reign. After Nurhaci's death in September 1626, Hung Taiji stated that the Chinese of the *tokso* had previously been given to the Manchu officials as slaves. "Because the khan [Hung Taiji] feared that the Chinese would be maltreated if they remained under Manchu officials for long, he abolished the *tokso* which had previously registered the submitted and surrendered people into units of thirteen men and which had distributed them as slaves to the Manchu high officials."[71] Hung Taiji's statement has often been cited to show that the Chinese under Nurhaci were slaves. However, as has been shown above, at least until the 1625 revolt most of the Chinese were not slaves. Even after 1625 they were not slaves, although they may have been *treated* as such by the Manchu officials. It is possible that Hung Taiji exaggerated the low position of the Chinese under Nurhaci in order to style himself their liberator.

SEPARATION: AN APPROACH TO EQUALITY? (1626-1636)

Hung Taiji (often later referred to as "Abahai"), the eighth son of Nurhaci, was not the recognized heir-apparent under Nurhaci, and although the exact circumstances under which he usurped power are not clear, he did not win the throne by the common consent of his brothers.[72] During his reign he encountered political opposition from his cousin Amin and his brothers Manggultai and Daišan, the three beiles (princes) who, together with Hung Taiji, had been the four most powerful men under Nurhaci and were called the Four Senior Beiles. In the struggle for power, the Chinese supported the khan and urged him to bolster his position against the beiles through political and economic measures. They advised the khan that booty from campaigns should no longer be divided equally among the leadership of the eight banners, the Eight Houses, which consisted of the banner beiles and groups of relatives. More booty should go to the central government under the khan than to the beiles, because "even if the beiles thus receive a little less, it is also for their own convenience, and although it may be somewhat troublesome for the khan, it has the benefit that he [the khan] alone is in command of things and receives human hearts."[73] On another occasion a Chinese memorialist warned "if ten sheep have nine shepherds . . . I feel that within a few years there will definitely be disorder and disunity and one cannot rule."[74] One Chinese official asked that the khan appoint "speaking officials" in order to get more objective information because "they [the speaking officials] will not embellish the mistakes of the beiles."[75]

In a collection of memorials to the khan written by Chinese officials between 1632 and 1635, the Chinese officials frequently urged the khan to take advantage of China's temporary weakness and embark on a major campaign against the Ming. By suggesting specific strategies on how to proceed with the conquest,[76] they showed the firm support of the Chinese officials for the khan's plan to conquer China. Although there are no memorials extant for the later years, quite likely more of a similar nature were written. In 1642 Tsu K'o-fa and Chang Ts'un-jen, two high-ranking Chinese under the Manchus, urged the khan to exploit the Manchu victory over Chin-chou (1) and extend the boundary of the Manchu state to the Yellow River,[77] and when the Manchus under the regent Dorgon entered Shan-hai-kuan in 1644, they did so on the advice of Grand Secretary Fan Wen-ch'eng, a Chinese who had been with the Manchus since 1618.[78]

Why did the Chinese officials so willingly support Hung Taiji? Their active participation suggests that their support was not merely the result of the collapse of the Ming defense in Manchuria, which took away the hopes for liberation of the Liaotung Chinese. Hung Taiji made a conscious effort to appeal to the Chinese official class. In doing so he even accused his father Nurhaci of having violated the basic principles of government by having killed so many Chinese after the 1625 revolt: "The killings of the people of Liaotung was the former khan's fault. I think it would compare to the killing of one body if we had two, or to destroying one head if we had two, at a time when the principles of government (doro jurgan) were not understood."[79]

Hung Taiji appealed to the Chinese official class by copying the form of the Ming government. He set up a chancellery (Shu-fang or Wen-kuan) that developed into a secretariat (Nei-ko), the Six Boards (Liu Pu) and a censorate (Tu-ch'a-yuan), and sinicized the process of official recruitment. Nurhaci had once used a kind of civil service examination,[80] but under Hung Taiji examinations took place on a more regular basis. Even though a frontier area like Manchuria did not produce a high number of degree candidates and the total number of officials recruited in this way was small, the examinations did offer a way to secure an official position.[81] A large group of high Chinese officials entered the Manchu bureaucracy after the siege and victory at Talingho in 1631. They subsequently urged the khan to look for more talent among the educated. The discussions on the matter of recruitment of officials after this time are couched entirely in Chinese terms.[82]

Hung Taiji's main concern was to attract the traditional upright scholar, but he did not bar people who made other kinds of contributions to the Manchu state from obtaining high official posts. He accepted the surrender of K'ung Yu-te, Keng Chung-ming, and Shang K'o-hsi. K'ung Yu-te and Keng Chung-ming had begun their military careers under Mao Wen-lung, the leader of Chinese resistance against the Manchus, who after the Manchu conquest of Liaotung first withdrew to Korea and then to P'i-tao, a small island located near the mouth of the Yalu River. Later, having been transferred to another superior after Mao Wen-lung's death, they staged their own revolt in Shantung; but when they were pressed by Ming forces they surrendered to the Manchus, bringing with them their military forces and a considerable amount of military equipment. They received the highest possible ranks, and on ceremonial occasions were seated on a level with Hung Taiji's brothers, the beiles Manggultai and Daišan. Shang K'o-hsi had also been stationed on P'i-tao, and after the surrender of K'ung Yu-te and Keng Chung-ming he stayed on for another year, but surrendered in 1634. Like K'ung and Keng, who continued to command their own troops under the Manchus, Shang K'o-hsi retained his army.

Opposition to appointing people who had questionable moral integrity in the Confucian sense was voiced by Hung Taiji's Chinese officials, who had entered the bureaucracy through the traditional channel of scholarship. Ning Wan-wo, one of the scholarly officials under Hung Taiji, strongly objected to promoting men like K'ung Yu-te and Keng Chung-ming, whom he called "boors without character,"[83] and in 1635 he again pointed to the hazards of recommendations by those without a proper education, particularly if there was no provision for making the sponsor responsible for his protégé.[84] Although K'ung, Keng, and Shang retained their eminent positions, Hung Taiji on the whole did heed the opinions of his

Chinese officials. On their advice, amenities traditionally attached
to the status of scholars and officials in China found their way into
the Manchu system, among them the exemption from corvée. In
1629 each successful candidate in the examinations was allowed
exemption from corvée for two adult men. After the later examinations the number of tax-exempt men varied, until in 1638 a regulation fixed the number for each rank.[85]

While Nurhaci had been extremely strict in dealing with the officials who tried to enrich themselves, for example, by hiding illegally
acquired animals or secretly keeping refugees, Hung Taiji seems to
have been very lax in this respect. No action was taken against
officials who were known to occupy more land than they were entitled to and to take the best land, leaving the poor land to the
people.[86] Conferring hereditary status or noble rank was another
way to reward and please Chinese officialdom. If an official had gone
over to the Manchus in time of peace the rank was given to his son
and made hereditary; the title was also hereditary if the official was
killed in battle for the Manchus or if he died from disease while in
office.[87]

Another area in which the Manchu leadership appealed to the Chinese people in general, and to the officials in particular, was in the
legal sphere. For several years after the conquest of Liaotung, officials could still receive corporal punishment.[88] Severing or piercing
the nose and ears was the most common form of punishment. Nurhaci, immediately after the Manchu entry into Liaotung, had ordered
the Chinese to write down the various customary laws of China.[89]
After 1631 punishment for killing an escapee, and quite likely also
for other crimes, depended on the status of the offender.[90] In 1632
Hung Taiji abolished the law that required the people to report the
misconduct of their family members, a law which stood in conflict
with the Chinese concept of family relationships. From then on, the
obligation of a son to report his father, the wife her husband, and so
on, was restricted to serious rebellious behavior; they were not required to report any other matter.[91] Thus, with the incorporation of
a sizable Chinese population, Manchu law was adjusted to the Chinese concepts of human relationships.

Because experience had shown that "togetherness" of Manchus and
Chinese resulted in Manchu oppression of the Chinese, Hung Taiji

tried to emancipate the Chinese through separation. Immediately upon his succession to the throne, he abolished the *tokso,* took the Chinese away from the Manchu officials, and again made them registered households administered by Chinese officials. The Manchu officials retained only a small number of Chinese as private servants.[92] Hung Taiji proclaimed that there should be no discrimination and that all corvée was to be equal.[93]

Chinese and Manchus were also separated in the courts. Chinese judges dealt with the crimes of Chinese, and Manchu judges with those of the Manchus, a policy in line with the desires of the Chinese officials. When Hung Taiji set up the Six Boards in 1631 and Chinese and Manchu legal cases were again handled together by the Board of Punishments, the Chinese approached the khan with the request for a renewed separation of Chinese and Manchu legal affairs to assure impartiality in justice.[94] Unfortunately the khan's response is not known.

The organizational separation of Chinese and Manchus was there to stay. The Chinese remained under their own Chinese officials and in separate quarters in the towns, and in 1630 formed their first independent banner.[95] In that year a census of all adult men took place,[96] and it was probably at this time that the Chinese quota for military service, which had been one out of twenty since the conquest of Liaotung,[97] was increased to one out of ten.[98] Those Chinese who had formerly been attached to the Manchu banners were included in the newly formed Chinese banner.[99] Already in the 1630s the Chinese soldiers had received instruction in the use of cannon.[100] After the Manchus built their own cannon for the first time in 1631, the Chinese banner soldiers continued to be in charge of the heavy artillery and came to be referred to as *ujen cooha* (lit. "heavy troops"). In 1637 the Chinese troops were divided into two and in 1639 into four banners.[101] Additional soldiers were recruited from among the Chinese who surrendered to the Manchus during this time, or even from among the slaves.[102] The last increase that completed the Chinese banner system by creating another four banners was again preceded by an increase in the quota for military service. In 1642 one out of three Chinese became a soldier, a quota which had existed for the Manchus for at least a decade.

As bannermen the Chinese were free people administered by Chi-

nese officials under Chinese commanders who were directly responsible to the central government. But even though Hung Taiji seems to
have intended to practice the equality he preached, Chinese equality
was limited. An authorized massacre of the Chinese civil population
at Yung-p'ing by his cousin Amin came as a major blow. There is
reason to believe that Amin, one of the eight beiles in charges of a
banner, had from the beginning opposed the incorporation of the
Chinese people on a level of equality with the Manchus, that he preferred to undertake campaigns for the sake of booty and to follow a
policy which did not aim at political control over the Chinese population.[103] According to the *Tung-hua-lu,* Amin attempted but failed
to win independence for himself and his banner after the death of
Nurhaci by proposing to move outside the borders of Nurhaci's
state.[104]

In 1629, the Manchus occupied four major cities inside the Shan-
hai-kuan: Ch'ien-an, Luan-chou, Yung-p'ing, and Tsun-hua. Because
Hung Taiji wanted to make these cities model areas of Manchu rule,
thus inducing other Chinese to surrender, he ordered that the Chinese of these cities should be treated with extreme care. But "Amin
after entering Yung-p'ing detested the Chinese residents and was
displeased with the khan's policy of caring for them."[105] He "did
not listen [to the other commanders and officials], killed all officials
and people of Yung-p'ing and Ch'ien-an, took goods, livestock and
women, and considering them [the booty] most important went
back."[106] In order to preserve his credibility, the khan made Amin
an enemy of the state, and through the mouth of the Beile Yoto,
who maintained that "the khan had nothing to do with the
crime,"[107] cleared himself for what had happened.

The Manchu-Chinese relationship was further adversely affected by
the steadily deteriorating economic conditions. The Manchus faced a
chronic lack of food which easily turned into a crisis. With a marginal
economy at home the Manchus could not afford to lose battles. "All
depends on sending out soldiers and horses and taking booty."[108]
Success in campaigns was not merely desirable, it was necessary.

In 1626 the Manchus suffered a major defeat at the hands of the
Ming army, a defeat which entailed high expenses without bringing
the needed supplementary income. In addition, the aftereffects of
the reorganization of the Chinese after the 1625 revolt and again

under Hung Taiji, as well as the arrival of a large number of Mongols coming to submit,[109] intensified the economic difficulties. Widespread famine that drove the people to cannibalism occurred in 1627-28[110] and economic hardship continued after the famine was over. While the troops may have relieved the economy somewhat by living temporarily off the enemy countryside and by bringing back booty, in the 1630s the campaigns increasingly added to the economic difficulties, because each time the army returned it brought with it a large number of captives and people who had surrendered. Since the Manchus made no comparative territorial gains—Talingho was taken but the Kuang-ning area remained insecure because of military activities, and Chin-chou (1) and Sung-shan were not conquered until 1642—the population increased out of proportion to the land under cultivation. In theory, the people who submitted were to receive a certain amount of grain for a period of adjustment and later five *cimari* of land per adult man. Reality was different; there was neither enough grain nor enough land for the newcomers. "Nowadays the land is small, but the people are many. . . . As for the incoming grain, there is not even enough to give out [to the newcomers]. The people who have to be fed have lately increased in number. The officials in charge say they have no grain. The granaries are empty."[111]

Many people were suffering because they had less than the official five *cimari* of land.[112] Natural disasters added to the suffering: ". . . the land of the people is small and there is not enough to care for all the people. Moreover, there has been a natural disaster this year (1632): the mulberry trees are all under water. In the villages nine houses out of ten are empty and the people do not have enough to live on."[113] In 1635 the Manchu state was heading into another period of crisis. The price of grain rose sharply and the people hoarded it.[114] In 1637 another famine occurred.[115]

Because there was no empty land to give to the large number of Chinese who entered the Manchu state in the 1630s, the beiles and the officials who had had some of their Chinese taken away when Hung Taiji dissolved the *tokso* after his succession and some when the first Chinese banner was formed, received again an increasing number of Chinese, including many officials. The prisoners and the people who surrendered in the 1630s were assigned not only on the basis of merit, as had earlier been the case, but also according to the ability of the master to care for them. The Eight Houses received the highest number, but other officials and even rich households without official rank had people assigned to them.[116] Chinese officials who had been with the Manchus for some time had to take in and care for newly surrendered officials.[117]

Except for a certain number of people who were given to the beiles personally, most of the people so distributed did not belong to their "masters," who only bore the responsibility for feeding these people but drew little or no benefit from them. Thus some of them neglected their duty. A memorial advising the khan to place the Chinese under the central government likens the Chinese officials under the Eight Houses to the khan's horses:

> Nowadays there are people called officials, which means that they are the people of the court and work for the court. They are like the horses of the khan which are distributed among the different Houses. . . . Since this [caring for the people] basically is of merit to the beiles, the beiles should nurture them and should be happy to do so. But if these people do not work for the beiles and the beiles care for them for nothing it is difficult for the beiles. . . . For this reason, if an official happens to be under a beile who understands the emperor's intention, who is happy to nurture the people, he will not have to worry about food and clothing, but if the official happens to be under a beile who does not understand the emperor's intention and who is not happy to care for his people, then he [the official] has to suffer from hunger and cold. . . . It is because the country's people do not belong to his House. The interest of a given House is not equal to the interest of the country.[118]

Though the economic conditions were such that both the Chinese and the Manchus suffered,[119] it seems likely that the burden was not shared equally and that the Manchus, on an individual basis, continued to oppress the Chinese and tried to shift the economic burden onto them. After the Yung-p'ing massacre, Hung Taiji repeatedly warned the Manchus not to rob and molest the Chinese and reminded the beiles and officials to treat their people well.[120] Not only was a massive killing not permissible, even individual cases of killing and robbing Chinese became capital crimes. Though it is impossible to estimate the extent of Manchu oppression at this time, the khan's admonitions and the new law indicate that the Manchus still tended to regard themselves as above the Chinese. Unfortunately there is no information on the amount of taxes levied during Hung Taiji's reign. We only know that labor services were different for the Chinese and Manchus. When the Chinese officials complained that their corvée was heavier than that of the Manchus, the khan grew very impatient and replied that the Manchus had a much larger variety of services to fulfill and that their corvée was even heavier than that of the Chinese.[121] This may have been true.

About 1636 Hung Taiji's attitude toward the Chinese underwent a change. The near-equality did not turn into discrimination as in 1623-25, but nevertheless Hung Taiji's focus of concern noticeably shifted from the Chinese to the Manchus. The main factor behind this development was an awareness of a weakening in Manchu fighting power.

Already in 1635 it was clear that the military fighting power suffered from the weaknesses of the economy. The government lacked adequate provisions for the army,[122] and some later campaigns may have been cover-up operations to procure food for the soldiers.[123] The poverty of the people also affected the quality of the individual soldiers: "If one pursues the enemy more than two thousand *li* the rich who have [good] horses can still proceed, but the horses of the poor are tired and fall behind."[124] The Chinese contingent of the Manchu army increased numerically from one banner in 1630 to eight banners in 1642, but the quality of the Chinese soldiers left something to be desired. When the Chinese banner soldiers were first used in 1630 to guard Yung-p'ing, each soldier had a sign with the words "new soldier" attached to his back, indicating that the Manchus felt they had to watch these recruits extra carefully.[125] After the Chinese had participated in battles more extensively, there was little doubt that their military performance was inferior to that of the Manchus. The khan rebuked them severely for looking on while the Manchu troops courageously faced death in battle.[126] The Chinese soldiers were also reprimanded for the evil practice of using inferior substitutes to do the fighting,[127] and on several occasions Hung Taiji accused the Chinese officials of harboring bipartisan feelings.[128] Although there is no question that the Chinese were

extremely important to the Manchu army because of their skill in
the use of cannon, it seems that the increase in the numerical strength
of the Chinese banner forces does not represent a proportional increase in the military strength of the Manchu army as a whole.

The awareness that the martial qualities of the Manchus themselves
suffered from exposure to Chinese civilization and from contact
with undisciplined Mongol troops weighed on the khan's mind, perhaps even more heavily than the military weakness that resulted from
lack of provisions and from the inferior quality of the Chinese
banners. Even the Manchus sent flunkies to go on duty in their stead.
"Before we had set up rules to prevent disorder. But now disorder is
abundant. When twenty soldiers go somewhere [on duty], twenty
flunkies (*uksin kutule*) are expected to go with them, when fifteen
soldiers go fifteen flunkies should go. But if one looks at the situation now, one discovers that the soldiers stay in camp and just let
the flunkies go."[129] In 1631 Hung Taiji still claimed that Amin had
committed his crime of killing the Chinese at Yung-p'ing because
"he did not study and did not know the principles,"[130] but in 1636
the very acquaintance with Chinese civilization was blamed for the
Manchus' weakness. Instead of being interested in going hunting as
the older generation had been when they were young, young people
preferred to "hang around the marketplaces and simply amuse themselves."[131] So far the military weakness of the Manchus had not yet
progressed to such a degree as to make hopeless any further attempt
to conquer China. But the realization of a gradual loss of strength
made an immediate conquest of China urgent. Time was not in the
Manchus' favor and Hung Taiji knew it.

While some Manchus easily submitted to the lure of Chinese civilization, others—Amin had been the most well-known and the most
powerful representative of this group—resisted Chinese influence and
resented Hung Taiji's efforts to appeal to the Chinese. They complained that "formerly T'ai-tsu (Nurhaci) executed the Chinese
and favored the Manchus. Now there are even some *wangs* and *tsung-
ping-kuan* (military generals) among the Chinese [in fact, there also
were Chinese *tsung-ping-kuan* under Nurhaci!—e.g. T'ung Yang-
hsing], and among the imperial relatives there are some officials and
some commoners. How could we fall this low?"[132] Because of the
crucial importance of the Manchu banners in a possible conquest of

China, Hung Taiji after 1636 paid more attention to the wishes and likes of the more traditionally minded and still more martial group among the Manchus and, in addressing the Manchus, emphasized the importance of the traditional Manchu qualities.[133] In 1631 he had ordered that all sons of Chinese and Manchu officials should study.[134] However, the Manchus considered such study as "something extremely bitter," and there is no indication that Hung Taiji ever tried to enforce a Chinese education on the Manchus. Most significantly, the large number of high counseling officials whom Hung Taiji appointed after 1636 were all Manchu.[135]

Hung Taiji could afford to stop actively courting Chinese officials because by 1636 he had eliminated his political opponents, the three Senior Beiles, and power rested securely in his hands. Amin was in prison where he died in 1640.[136] Manggultai, who had plotted against the khan in 1633, had died (or possibly was executed) in that year.[137] Daišan was intimidated by Hung Taiji, who accused him in 1635 of having committed a crime similar to that of Amin thereby indirectly threatening Daišan that he, like Amin, might be eliminated as a rival and put into prison.[138] In 1636 Hung Taiji had himself made emperor and assumed the name Ch'ing for his dynasty. Thus, as far as the domestic political scene was concerned, Hung Taiji sat firmly on the throne. Though China was still unconquered and the khan continued to welcome Chinese expertise and advice, the Chinese were no longer necessary as political support against Hung Taiji's internal rivals.

CONCLUSION

There is little information on the Manchu-Chinese relationship for the period between 1636 and 1644. Until further evidence becomes available, we can make some conjectures about these years on the basis of the official sources and of what is known about the situation around 1635 and 1636. The Chinese remained important to the Manchus for their technical skills, their knowledge of government affairs, and most of all for the building and servicing of the cannon. They were less important politically than before and as soldiers could not be entirely relied on to risk their lives. During the period when Hung Taiji actively appealed to the Chinese official class, he had promoted a fairly large number of Chinese to high posts. Almost all

of the great Chinese under the Manchus were people who submitted
to the Manchus or gained their prominence during Hung Taiji's reign
before 1636. Ma Kuang-yuan, the commander of the Chinese banner
after 1632, joined the Manchus in 1630; Liu T'ien-lu, Chang Ts'un-
jen, Tsu Tse-hung, and Tsu K'o-fa after Talingho in 1631; K'ung
Yu-te, Keng Chung-ming in 1633, and Shang K'o-hsi in 1634. Other
prominent names like Shih T'ing-chu, Ning Wan-wo, and Fan Wen-
ch'eng had submitted much earlier but remained relatively unim-
portant under Nurhaci. Only Hung Taiji promoted them to high
office: Shih T'ing-chu became the first commander of the Chinese
banner but died in 1632; Fan Wen-ch'eng had joined the Manchus
when Fu-shun fell in 1618 but came into the limelight only in 1629,
when he invented the story that the Ming commander Yuan Ch'ung-
huan was in league with the Manchus, a story which made the Ming
emperor suspicious and led to the execution of Yuan Ch'ung-huan.
Ning Wan-wo served for years under Sahaliyan, one of Nurhaci's
sons, before he was promoted to the Chancellery in 1629.

   None of the officials who surrendered after 1636 was of great importance. Shen Chih-hsiang seems to have been the one who was
given the greatest attention. It was not until 1642, the siege and
conquest of Chin-chou (1) and Sung-shan, that the Manchus achieved
the surrender of the two great Ming generals Hung Ch'eng-ch'ou and
Tsu Ta-shou. Tsu Ta-shou, in fact had surrendered once before, in
1631, but had then been allowed to return to Chin-chou (1) in order
to take the city for the Manchus. He remained in Chin-chou (1)
again fighting the Manchus. Hung Taiji did not make special over-
tures to the two Ming generals in 1642. The surrender of Tsu Ta-
shou and Hung Ch'eng-ch'ou was a great political success, but the
Manchus probably owed this success more to the desperate situation
of the Ming defense than to their own military strength. Even though
there is no equivalent to the *Man-chou chiu-tang* for these years to
reveal the weaknesses of the Manchus, the record of the official
sources is at least suspicious. Time and again the Manchus are said to
have won splendid victories, but instead of exploiting the situation
and making the final conquest of Peking, their army returned home.
It seems probable that the Manchus hoped with all their hearts to
make new territorial acquisitions but that their strength was insufficient. The fall of Chin-chou (1) and Sung-shan was a victory that was
long overdue.

The Manchus had been fighting over Chin-chou (1) for more than ten years. They had been repulsed many times. The recent reappraisal of Wu San-kuei's surrender by Angela Hsi[139] fits into the interpretation of a weakening Manchu military force. Wu San-kuei did not surrender to the Manchus. According to Hsi, he first singlehandedly defeated an army sent against him by the rebel Li Tzu-ch'eng and then abandoned the strategic Shan-hai-kuan in pursuit of Li Tzu-ch'eng. Thus, the Manchus who were outside the pass could easily enter. Subsequently, being caught between Li Tzu-ch'eng and the Manchus, Wu San-kuei had to negotiate with one of the two. He chose the Manchus. At the time Wu San-kuei decided to join the Manchus he was in command of a good and well-disciplined army. This was exactly what the Manchus needed. Previously when they had fought Wu San-kuei he had repelled them. Unable to defeat Wu alone, the Manchus could never have hoped to defeat a combination of Wu San-kuei and Li Tzu-ch'eng. Only with Wu San-kuei's army could they break the deadlock.

NOTES TO CHAPTER 1

Abbreviations

CT	*Man-chou chiu-tang* (cited by volume and page)
CTPC	[*Ch'in-ting*] *pa-ch'i t'ung-chih*
KKFL	[*Huang-Ch'ing*] *k'ai-kuo fang-lüeh*
MR	*Mambun Roto* (cited by volume and page)
THL	*Tung-hua-lu*
Tsou-i	*T'ien-tsung ch'ao ch'en kung tsou-i*

1. For a general discussion of the Jurchens prior to the rise of Nurhaci, see Morris Rossabi: "The Jurchen in the Yüan and the Ming," manuscript for the Chin Dynastic Project, edited by Herbert Franke, to be published by the University of Washington Press.

2. *Ta-Ch'ing Hui-tien* (Ch'ien-lung reign) and the *CTPC*, p. 3030 record a total of 400 companies for 1614. Thinking of a company as a unit of 300 households, some scholars question the reliability of the *Hui-tien* and the *CTPC* and believe that the passage refers to a later date (Fang Chao-ying: "A Technique for Estimating the Numerical Strength of the Early Manchu Military Forces," *HJAS*, 13:195; cf. also Chao Ch'i-na: "Ch'ing-ch'u pa-ch'i Han-chün yen-chiu," *Ku-kung wen-hsien*, 4.2:55–65. However, it is quite likely that the 400 companies of 1614 were not companies of 300 households but were of a much smaller size, and later were combined to form fewer but larger companies. Nurhaci had created four banners in 1601; in 1615 he completed the banner system by

adding another four banners, each consisting of twenty-five companies. He also set the size of a company at 300 households at this time. If in 1615 an average of two small companies were combined to form companies of 300 households, then the total number of 400 companies would be cut in half, accounting for the number needed to make up eight banners. It is probably the fact that these Chinese were, for all practical purposes, considered Manchus; the small number of their companies would explain the infrequent mention of Chinese companies before the establishment of a Chinese banner in 1630. The Chinese companies are mentioned only once (*CT* 5:2172; 2171; *MR* 3:1105–06) in an entry which is undated. According to Li Hsueh-chih's analysis, based on the handwriting and on the paper used, the year was 1623.

3. Li Hsueh-chih and Kuang Lu, "Lao Man-wen yuan-tang," *Annual Bulletin of the China Council for East Asian Studies,* no. 4 (1965), pp. 46–48.

4. *Shih-lu* (T'ai-tsu) 2:5, 7, 8.

5. *CT* 1:165, 343, 374–77, 383, 387; *MR* 1:81, 103–04, 109, 111–12.

6. *CT* 1:375–76; *MR* 1:103,106–07.

7. *CT* 2:1086; *MR* 2:579.

8. *CT* 2:725–26; *MR* 1:355–57.

9. *CT* 1:189, 191; *MR* 1:89. *CT* 2:682–83, *MR* 1:334.

10. *CT* 2:633–35; *MR* 1:298–99.

11. Ibid.

12. *CT* 1:553–54; *MR* 1:164–65.

13. *CT* 4:1627; *MR* 2:805.

14. *CT* 2:695–96; *MR* 1:341.

15. *CT* 2:1089; *MR* 2:581–82.

16. *CT* 6:2580–81; *MR* 4:15; and *Shih-lu* (T'ai-tsung) 2:7b.

17. *CT* 2:1561; *MR* 2:745.

18. *CT* 3:1380–81; *MR* 2:673.

19. *CT* 3:1330; *MR* 2:643.

20. *CT* 2:586–87; *MR* 1:267.

21. *CT* 3:1386, 1485; *MR* 2:677, 753.

22. In 1624, officials were instructed to "send those Chinese households with five to seven Manchu *sin* (1 Manchu *sin* corresponds to 1 Chinese *tou* 8 *sheng,* about 11.9 kg) of grain per capita. One will give them land and houses. . . . Put together those without grain and inform the khan of their number." (*CT* 4:1790–91; *MR* 2:887–88). Only a few pages further on, the *CT* states that those with less than the standard amount of grain were turned into slaves (*CT* 4:1828; *MR* 2:906).

23. *CT* 4:1829–30, 5:2060; *MR* 2:885, 908–09.

24. *CT* 2:614–15; *MR* 2:795.

25. *CT* 3:1367; *MR* 2:666.

26. *CT* 3:1354–56; *MR* 2:658–59.

27. *Shih-lu* (T'ai-tsung) 17:14b–15; *KKFL* (Hauer transl.), p. 334.

28. *CT* 2:631; *MR* 1:297–98. *CT* 2:680–81, 684–85, 1094; *MR* 1:333, 335, 2:584.

29. *CT* 2:693-94; *MR* 1:340.
30. *CT* 2:702-03; *MR* 1:344-45.
31. *CT* 3:1412; *MR* 2:697.
32. *CT* 2:805; *MR* 1:407.
33. *CT* 2:806; *MR* 1:407-08.
34. *CT* 2:824; *MR* 1:419.
35. *CT* 2:830-31; *MR* 1:422.
36. *CT* 2:1065; *MR* 2:564.
37. *CT* 2:856; *MR* 1:435.
38. *CT* 2:909; *MR* 2:465-66.
39. *CT* 2:832; *MR* 1:423.
40. *CT* 3:1412; *MR* 2:697. *CT* 2:857, 909; *MR* 1:435, 2:465.
41. *CT* 2:725-26; *MR* 1:356.
42. *CT* 3:1358-59; *MR* 2:660-61.
43. *Tsou-i,* pt. 1, p. 7.
44. Before 1623, three Manchus worked one *cimari* of land jointly as alban (*CT* 2:726; *MR* 1:356). Since one *cimari* of land seems to have produced about one *hule* of grain—the Western or Chinese equivalent to one *hule* still needs to be established—every adult man paid one-third of a *hule.* If he in fact had five *cimari* and could grow five *hule,* the tax before 1623 amounted to 6.7 percent of the harvest. Beginning in 1623, a Manchu company consisting of 300 men paid 200 *hule,* while the Chinese administered by Manchu officials paid two *hule* per three men.
45. *CT* 2:1065; *MR* 2:565.
46. *CT* 2:597; 5:2164; *MR* 2:778, 3:1103.
47. *CT* 2:678; *MR* 1:331-32.
48. *CT* 3:1242-45; *MR* 2:609-10.
49. *CT* 2:1081, *MR* 2:575.
50. *CT* 2:830-32; *MR* 1:422-23.
51. *CT* 3:1375-76, 1455, 1474, 5:2040; *MR* 2:671, 728, 742, 759, 772, etc.
52. *CT* 3:1424-25; *MR* 2:706-07.
53. *CT* 3:1451; *MR* 2:726.
54. *CT* 3:1439; *MR* 2:712.
55. *CT* 3:1504; *MR* 2:771-72.
56. *CT* 3:1416-19, 1435; *MR* 2:701-03, 713.
57. *CT* 3:1386; *MR* 2:677.
58. *CT* 3:1451; *MR* 2:726; *CT* 4:1786; *MR* 2:886.
59. *CT* 4:1795; *MR* 2:889.
60. *CT* 4:1647; *MR* 2:819. *CT* 7:3235-36, 3154; *MR* 3:1094, 4:354.
61. *CT* 3:1433-34, 1443-45, 1484-85; *MR* 2:712, 720-22, 752-53.
62. *CT* 2:629-31; *MR* 1:296-97.
63. *CT* 3:1242-45; *MR* 2:609-10.
64. Fe Ala was Nurhaci's capital before 1603. In that year he moved to the nearby Hetu Ala, where he stayed until 1619. Since the *CT* after the conquest of Liaotung frequently refers to the time of Fe Ala but never to Hetu Ala, it seems

likely that after 1621 Fe Ala as a time reference includes the period from 1603 to 1619.

65. *CT* 3:1585–87; *MR* 2:771–72.

66. *CT* 4:1846; *MR* 3:954.

67. *CT* 4:1935–38; *MR* 3:991–92.

68. *CT* 4:1938–40; *MR* 3:992–94.

69. *CT* 4:1829–30; *MR* 2:908–09.

70. *CT* 4:1939–40; *MR* 3:993–94.

71. *CTPC* 12:4865. *Shih-lu* (T'ai-tsung) 1:2.

72. According to the *KKFL*, the transition of leadership was smooth and simple. The three Senior Beiles under Daišan's initiative offered the khanship to Hung Taiji, who refused several times before accepting. Franz Michael, accepting the *KKFL* story, writes: "They [the beiles] elected with little delay or difficulty Nurhaci's eighth son, Abahai, as successor" (*The Origin of Manchu Rule in China*, p. 87). According to a *THL* entry for 1626, it was also Daišan who offered the khanship to Hung Taiji, but a later *THL* reference (3:14) records that Amin in 1626 took the initiative in offering Hung Taiji the title of khan in return for a promise to let him (Amin) depart with his banner and be his own master somewhere else. Two Korean sources written about that time have still another version of what happened. The Korean Veritable Records state that Nurhaci, shortly before his death, appointed Daišan to succeed him, but Daišan renounced the throne in favor of Hung Taiji. The other Korean account reports that before his death Nurhaci appointed Daišan to be the regent for a younger brother, Nurhaci's ninth son Abatai, but that Daišan let Hung Taiji take his place (both Korean sources are quoted by Kuang Lu and Li Hsueh-chih, p. 48). In all of the accounts of events in 1626, Daišan was involved, but in view of a conflict between Hung Taiji and Daišan in 1635, it is not impossible that Daišan was pressured into renouncing his claim instead of voluntarily offering the khanship to Hung Taiji.

73. *Tsou-i*, pt. 1, 11a–b.

74. Ibid., p. 42.

75. Ibid., pt. 2, 3b.

76. Ibid., pt 1, 3–4, 18–19, 17b; pt. 2, 15, 20–22, 34, 37b–39; pt. 3, 9, 13–14, 21b–22.

77. *Ch'ing-shih*, 3:30a.

78. *Ch'ing-shih*, p. 232.

79. *CT* 7:3579; *MR* 5:583.

80. *CT* 4:1940; *MR* 3:994.

81. Periodic examinations were more widespread as a means of evaluation. After 1632 the Chinese officials in local administration or in the Six Boards had to undergo an examination after every three years of government service (*Pa-ch'i t'ung-chih*, 1739 ed., 9:2976, 2980).

82. E.g. *CT* 9:4165–66. *Chiu Man-chou tang*, trans. Kanda Nobuo (Tokyo, 1972), pp. 75–76.

83. *Tsou-i*, pt. 2, 23.
84. *CT* 9:4159. *Chiu Man-chou tang*, pp. 70–71.
85. *CTPC* 14:5687.
86. *Tsou-i*, pt. 1, 45.
87. *Pa-ch'i t'ung-chih*, 1739 ed., 7:2458.
88. *CT* 3:1286–87; *MR* 2:617.
89. *CT* 2:644; *MR* 1:305–06.
90. *CT* 7:3431; *MR* 5:514–15.
91. *CT* 8:3737; *MR* 5:726.
92. *THL* (T'ien-ts'ung), 1:2a.
93. *CTPC* 12:4865.
94. *Tsou-i*, pt. 1, 2b.
95. Chao Ch'i-na, pp. 57–58.
96. *Shih-lu* (T'ai-tsung), 7:27b–29.
97. *CT* 2:851, 925–28; *MR* 1:432; 2:474–75.
98. *Tsou-i*, pt. 2, 4b.
99. *KKFL* (Hauer transl.), p. 319.
100. *CT* 2:1073–74; *MR* 2:571.
101. *CTPC* 7:2479–82.
102. *Shih-lu* (T'ai-tsung), 14:32; *CT* 8:3660; *MR* 5:633.
103. Already under Nurhaci, Amin had moved on his own authority from the area assigned to his banner, thus endangering the border defense (*CT* 3:1254–57; *MR* 2:554). In 1627 the Manchus, with Amin as their supreme commander, invaded Korea. After the Korean king had already accepted the Manchus' demands, Amin, against the advice of the other officers in the field, insisted on proceeding to the Korean capital, which undoubtedly would have yielded a rich booty. It was only because those under his command refused to join him that he gave up his plan (*CT* 7:3309–13; *MR* 4:404). He turned back, but not without getting a minimum of booty by pillaging Korean towns for three days.
104. *THL* (T'ien-ts'ung), 3:14.
105. *CT* 7:3335, 3338; *MR* 4:411–12.
106. *CT* 7:3343–46; *MR* 4:414–15.
107. *CT* 7:3579–80; *MR* 5:583.
108. *Tsou-i*, pt. 1, 11.
109. *CT* 6:2717; *MR* 4:111.
110. *CT* 6:2685; *MR* 4:87.
111. *Tsou-i*, pt. 1, 8b–9.
112. *Tsou-i*, pt. 1, 7.
113. *Tsou-i*, pt. 1, 22a–b.
114. *CT* 10:5196–97; *MR* 7:1362.
115. *CTPC* 14:5591–95.
116. *THL* (T'ien-ts'ung), 1:37.
117. *Tsou-i*, pt. 2, 27.
118. Ibid., pt. 1, 36b–37.

119. Ibid., p. 33b.

120. T'ao Hsi-sheng, "Man-tsu wei ju-kuan ch'ien ti fu-lu yü hsiang-jen," *Shih-huo*, 2.12:34–36.

121. *Shih-lu* (T'ai-tsung), 17:10b–12. *KKFL* (Hauer transl.), pp. 332–34.

122. *CT* 9:4151. *Chiu Man-chou tang*, p. 64.

123. Hsiao I-shan, *Ch'ing-tai t'ung-shih* (Shanghai, 1927–32), p. 206ff.

124. *Tsou-i*, pt. 1, 16.

125. *Shih-lu*, (T'ai-tsung), 6:7.

126. *Tsou-i*, pt. 2, 40.

127. *Shih-lu*, (T'ai-tsung), 53:24b. *KKFL* (Hauer transl.), p. 514.

128. Chao Ch'i-na, pp. 60–61.

129. *CT* 7:3565–67; *MR* 5:575.

130. *Man-chou lao-tang pi-lu*, Chin-liang, ed. and trans. (Taipei, 1929), ts'e 2, 34b–35.

131. *CT* 10:4992; *MR* 6:1211.

132. *Shih-lu*, (T'ai-tsung), 64:8. *THL* (Ch'ung-te), 3:37b.

133. *CT* 10:4992–93; *MR* 6:1211–12. *KKFL* (Hauer transl.), p. 419.

134. *Tsou-i*, pt. 1, 12b–13.

135. *Ch'ing-shih*, 3:23b, 26b, 27.

136. Ibid., p. 216.

137. Ibid., p. 218.

138. *THL* (T'ien-ts'ung), 2:32–33b.

139. Angela Hsi, "Wu San-kuei in 1644: a Reappraisal," *Journal of Asian Studies* 34.2:443–453.

2

The Shun Interregnum of 1644

by Frederic Wakeman, Jr.

Peking Officials

In the space of six weeks in the late spring of 1644, Peking fell to two conquering armies in succession: the rebel troops of Li Tzu-ch'eng on April 25, and the Manchu troops on June 5. Despite the extent and variety of the politicomilitary history of the Ming–Ch'ing transition from 1621 to 1683, these two events in Peking were of immense importance. The city itself had been of symbolic influence at least since the days when Yueh Fei had dreamed of the recovery of the "city of the Yellow Dragon" in the eleventh century.* For over two hundred years since the 1420s, the red walls and yellow tile roofs of the Imperial City, the audiences for metropolitan examination graduates and newly appointed officials, had figured in the hopes and dreams of every member of the Ming elite. Ming despotism, barring from politics the imperial princes enfeoffed in the provinces and undercutting most regional concentrations of bureaucratic power as well, had increased the political importance of the capital and reduced the possibility that the Ming could save itself, as the T'ang had in the 750s and 760s, by falling back on well-established provincial power bases.

The events in Peking during these weeks, from the suicide of the last Ming emperor on Coal Hill down to the flight from the city of Li Tzu-ch'eng, have received little attention in the official histories, since they were merely an interregnum between two dynasties. Instead, the exciting and often lurid stages of this drama were recorded by several contemporaries in the form of yeh-shih, *unofficial or "wild" histories, and it is on these that today's historian must draw if he seeks to understand the details of the transition of power within the capital itself. The* yeh-shih *are hard to use and hard to evaluate: their contents seem to range from precise documentation to wild invention or mythic distortion. Nevertheless, by comparing all of the accounts of the Shun interregnum, it is possible to reconstruct a reasonably accurate narrative of the rebel regime and of the actions of those who served it.*

This is especially so because, along with the yeh-shih *and later compilations like Chi Liu-ch'i's* Ming-chi pei-lüeh *(written sometime in the early Ch'ing) or Wen Jui-lin's* Nan-chiang i-shih *(published*

---

*Hellmut Wilhelm, "From Myth to Myth: The Case of Yueh Fei's Biography," in Arthur F. Wright and Denis Twitchett, eds., *Confucian Personalities* (Stanford, 1962), p. 151.

41

in 1830), there also survive contemporary accounts with an unmistakable ring of veracity. Ch'ien Hsing's Chia-shen ch'uan hsin lu, *for instance, makes a special point of indicating when only parts of conversations were overheard at court by attendant ministers, or when his account is based upon unreliable hearsay. The same insistence upon accuracy is voiced by Chao Shih-chin, the bureau director from the Ministry of Works who was held prisoner in Liu Tsung-min's encampment during the Shun reign. His* Chia-shen chi-shih *also gives the source of secondhand evidence, usually by name, as does Liu Shang-yu's journal, the* Ting-ssu hsiao-chi. *Accounts such as these, therefore, provide a yardstick against which to check other, more extravagant chronicles of the period.*

The task of deciding which of the yeh-shih *of the Ming–Ch'ing transition are to be trusted still remains to be done, but for this set of events, at least, the historian can usually decide for himself which are the likeliest versions. In the long run, there is probably no way to deal with this material short of a careful study of the filiations of all texts; factual assertions on which clearly independent texts agree; factual assertions that can be anchored in non-*yeh-shih *documentation, collating the dates and editions of works and the lives and prejudices of their authors; and so on. Perhaps as we do more of this kind of work we shall want to study and adapt to our own needs the canons of critical verification developed by fact-oriented nineteenth-century European historians from Ranke down to the classic handbook of Langlois and Seignobos.**

The kind of narrative political history for which these canons of verification were relevant has been in decline among European political historians for some decades, in part because so much already has been done so well, in part because of the increasing sense that narrative political history was "superficial," that social, economic, cultural, institutional history went "deeper," closer to the real springs of change and development in complex societies. But in Chinese history there has been very little really thorough narrative political history, and some of us are beginning to suspect that it may be less "superficial" than sometimes has been thought. In the episode described here, for example, the substance of the great changes in

---

*Ch. V. Langlois and Ch. Seignobos, *Introduction to the Study of History,* trans. G. G. Berry (New York, 1913).

institutions, political economy, and the power of classes and regions that took place in the Ming–Ch'ing transition cannot be separated from the sequence of Shun and Ch'ing conquests of Peking and the death of the Ch'ung-chen emperor on Coal Hill. The Ch'ing appeal to the Peking bureaucracy and elements of the rest of the Chinese elite surely would have been far less successful if the Ch'ung-chen emperor had escaped to form a new government elsewhere or if Li Tzu-ch'eng's Shun regime had not deteriorated into pillage and terror. And that appeal was an essential part of the great changes in institutions, political economy, and the power of classes and regions that marked the Ming–Ch'ing transition.

Sequence here becomes a vital part of substance, and the reader with some knowledge of Chinese history will notice one remarkable aspect of the cumulative record. The six-week period of Li Tzu-ch'eng's rule in Peking runs the whole gamut of gestures, stereotypes, and actions that we have been trained to observe in the maturation of a dynastic cycle: from populist rebel leader bringing hope of re-generation and relief, through administrative centralizer and emer-gent tyrant, down to the ravaged fugitive, his downfall spurred by the cruelties and excesses of a "bad last minister," in this case the general Liu Tsung-min. The cycle is a logical as well as dramatic one. And in the account here presented from many different sources it carries the ring of accuracy. Li Tzu-ch'eng was faced with similar problems to those which the last Ming rulers had had; he too needed money urgently and was threatened by Manchu armies, an evasive bureaucracy, and unreliable Chinese regulars. The members of the bureaucracy wavered, dared to hope, and were terrorized; with one wish-fulfillment denied them, they turned to another. And even if, as Wakeman shows, many had thought at first that the relieving armies on June 5, 1644, were Ming restorers rather than Manchu conquerors, they could still sigh with relief, "It was just like old times."

The lunar new year's day of 1644 was dismally celebrated in Peking. The ministers who assembled before dawn to wish the Ch'ung-chen emperor well, discovered the palace gate mysteriously

jammed shut, and when they finally did gain entry, found the
emperor in tears over the Ming dynasty's financial plight. Returning
to their official residences in the early morning light, the courtiers
were forced to struggle through a particularly harsh dust storm that
cast a blood-red pall over the city's inhabitants, many of whom were
suffering from the pustulent epidemic that afflicted north China
during those years. None of them knew, of course, that on that same
day, February 8, the rebel leader Li Tzu-ch'eng was inaugurating the
Shun dynasty (but not yet proclaiming himself emperor) 500 miles
to the southwest in Sian.[1]

The emperor's grief was understandable. The official who audited
the Ministry of Finance accounts that year reported that both the
old and new treasuries, filled to brimming twenty-five years earlier,
now contained only a few registers, some materials for the imperial
son-in-law's tomb, and a scant 4,200 ounces of gold and silver.[2] As
that same man, Chao Shih-chin, also explained in his diary:

> This morning [April 22, 1644] I met face to face with the Min-
> ister of Finance, Ni Yuan-lu. By then Ni had already resigned.
> Because our relationship had been that of teacher and student
> when I was at the National University, I asked him about our
> monetary reserves. Ni said, "It takes 400,000 [taels] a month
> to meet the cost of military provisions for defending our fron-
> tiers. In the first lunar month there were [still] receipts coming
> in from outside. We have just finished calculating [the min-
> istry's accounts] for the second month. In the second month
> there were no receipts coming in [at all]."[3]

Holding off the Manchus to the northeast, and attacked by powerful rebel armies to the southwest, the Ming government could not
afford to pay its own soldiers. For that reason alone it was bound to
fall. But the sense of doom that oppressed these bureaucrats was
inspired by more than certain knowledge of the besieged dynasty's
bankruptcy. The mood of apathetic hopelessness now settling over
Peking reflected their suspicion that the Ming house had lost its
legitimate right to rule. Although few dared mention this conviction
publicly, and although officials doggedly maintained the dull routine
of daily administration, many felt that the approaching rebels were
an expression of the populace's rightful discontent with the injustices

of the ruling regime. Tseng Ying-lin, a supervising secretary in the
Ministry of War, told the Ch'ung-chen emperor on February 24 that
the empire was in jeopardy because the people flocked willingly to
the rebels' side, fleeing social oppression.

> The gentry and the wealthy presently clothe themselves with
> rent and feed themselves with taxes, sitting at their leisure while
> they suck the bone marrow of the population. In peaceful times
> they manipulate trade so as to subordinate the people and mo-
> nopolize vast profits. When there is trouble, ought we expect
> [the people] to share the vicissitudes of the gentry and the
> wealthy, putting forth efforts [on their behalf]? Indeed, the
> rich grow richer, invariably fleecing the people; and the poor
> grow poorer, until they are unable to survive at all.[4]

The rebels' claim to social legitimacy was reinforced by reports that
filtered in of the Shun armies' inexorable march across Northern
China. On March 16 the capital of Shansi fell to Li Tzu-ch'eng's
men; and the bureaucrats of Peking learned that throughout the
entire province "the civil and military officials had all lost their confidence in each other," surrendering town after town to the enemy.[5]
    The reports also spoke of Li Tzu-ch'eng's efforts to keep his troops
from looting, and of his insistence that the markets of captured
towns be kept open so that the inhabitants could be fed.[6] Like some
hero out of the pages of the popular, though officially proscribed
novel, *Water Margin*, Li promised justice wherever his armies went.[7]
The people were told—and many Ming bureaucrats believed—that Li,
the "dashing prince" (*ch'uang-wang*), would live up to the promises
of the ditties sung in areas his soldiers soon would cross:

> You'll feed your mates,
> You'll dress your mates,
> You'll open wide your city gates.
> When Prince Ch'uang arrives there'll be no more rates.[8]

Ministry officials and clerks also learned of the broadsheets which
Li Tzu-ch'eng's excellent espionage corps had posted in advance of
his coming.

> The nobles all eat meat and dress in white silk breeches because
> [the government] relies on their support alone. The eunuchs all

nibble grain and wolf down suckling pigs because [the emperor] uses them as his spies. Convicts are strung together like beads on a string. The gentry has no sense of decency. Taxes grow heavier each day. The people are collectively filled with moral hatred.[9]

Fearing such moral hatred and troubled by rumors that myriads of the poor and outcast had swelled the Shun armies, the literati of Peking looked increasingly to their own interests. Tacitly acknowledging the legitimacy of the rebellion, they dreaded their own fate should the capital fall and thus guarded their private coffers all the more tightly.

The rebels' collective indictment of personal gain seemed confirmed by the *sauve-qui-peut* atmosphere of the capital during the dynasty's last days. This was why so many chroniclers emphasized the bureaucrats' "selfish" (*ssu*) refusal to respond to the emperor's appeals in mid-March for public donations to provide military rations (*hsiang*) for the capital garrison. "The civil and military officials [contributed] no more than several hundred or several tens [of taels] and that was all"; and even when a quota was assessed on each yamen, "the officials clamorously asked to be excused."[10] On April 12, the emperor went so far as to pardon seven prominent political prisoners after they agreed to contribute funds for the city's defense, and six days later sent the eunuch chief of his secret police to press his own father-in-law, Chou K'uei, for money. Ch'ung-chen also asked his two grand secretaries, Wei Ts'ao-te and Ch'en Yen, for donations; but even though both were wealthy men, the former contributed only 500 taels, and the latter nothing at all. It was obvious that those with "ample capital" were reluctant to volunteer any more than token sums.[11]

One reason for their reluctance was the commonly held belief that the Ch'ung-chen emperor had millions of taels of his own which he was selfishly refusing to release for military purposes. Estimates of these reserves ran as high as 30,000,000 ounces of silver and 1,500,000 ounces of gold.[12] The emperor himself repeatedly insisted that the palace treasury was virtually empty—a claim partly borne out by his inability to finance a southern expedition.[13] Yet even though the most reliable estimate was that the privy purse contained about 200,000 taels, contemporaries fancied that his coffers were filled to the brim.[14] Remembering how stingy the emperor had been with his own funds years earlier when the "bandits were only a few gangs of starving people," they blamed his miserliness for the downfall of the dynasty. As one court official put it, "Early on if he had spent one piece of cash, it would have covered costs equivalent to two pieces later. When the times grew critical, giving the people ten thousand cash wasn't even worth what that one piece [would have paid for earlier]."[15] The emperor's presumed avarice was thus used to justify his bureaucrats' unwillingness to part with their spoils of office.

The only seemingly selfless act during this dismal time was the offer made by Grand Secretary Li Chien-t'ai to contribute one million taels of his own to outfit an army for the relief of Shansi province.[16] Li's hastily recruited force of marketplace hangers-on and unemployed laborers had little chance of standing up to the rebels' well drilled cavalry units, but the very fact that it existed at all momentarily inspired the emperor's confidence.[17] Ch'ung-chen's hopes were short-lived. Less than four days after Li Chien-t'ai marched out of Peking on February 23, couriers brought news that the Shun rebels were spreading across Shansi. P'ing-yang and all the perfectures bordering the Yellow River were already in the rebels' hands.[18] On April 9 a despatch finally arrived from Li Chien-t'ai himself, describing the hopeless state of his army and urging the emperor to abandon Peking and flee south.[19]

This was not the first time Ch'ung-chen had been advised to seek refuge in the southern capital of Nanking. Thrice before—on February 10, March 6, and April 3—a group of southern officials had suggested that the emperor leave Peking in the hands of the crown prince and establish a second line of defense along the Yangtze, with Chiu-chiang as the pivot point of a southern economic and military stronghold. The three most prominent advocates were Li Pang-hua, former Minister of War in Nanking; Ni Yuan-lu, former Minister of Finance; and Li Ming-jui, lecturer in the Hanlin Academy.[20] The plan, which was modeled on the history of the Southern Sung, was first brought to the emperor's attention by Li Ming-jui, who insisted that Ch'ung-chen could save the dynasty's mandate if he acted promptly.[21] The emperor responded positively but cautiously, fearing the opposition of some of his other ministers.[22] In a series of secret meetings with Li, he even worked out the route of his escape, but hesitated to raise the matter publicly until a rash of memorials from the Hanlin Academy provoked a court discussion.[23] Opposition quickly developed among those who feared leaving the administration of the capital in the hands of the fifteen-year-old prince, and who stressed the importance of preserving the imperial altars and tombs of the Ming in the North.[24]

The southerners therefore proposed a compromise. In a secret memorial, Li Pang-hua requested that the crown prince be sent south to consolidate Ming defenses in Chiang-nan while the emperor stayed behind to protect the northern capital and preserve the altars of the grain and soil.[25] On April 3, Ch'ung-chen convened most of his high officials in court audience to discuss this new suggestion. As minister after minister indicated his support of the scheme, Ch'ung-chen grew visibly enraged. It seemed as though the proposal would be approved until Kuang Shih-heng, supervising secretary of the Ministry of War, angrily intervened. Li Ming-jui—Kuang loudly insisted—was the secret architect of the plan, and he and his clique were fostering "heretical" ideas behind the scene.[26]

Kuang Shih-heng's outburst was directed against those who would sacrifice the emperor's life and the nominal unity of the empire in order to strengthen the defense of the South. The crown prince could be used to rally support for a southern Ming regime because hereditary legitimacy was attached to his person. The more abstract legitimacy of the dynasty, however, was represented by the royal altars. If the heir was to go south, then the custodian of those altars—the emperor himself—would have to stay behind and preserve them to the end.[27] Because Li Pang-hua's compromise virtually ruled out the possibility of Ch'ung-chen's escape, the emperor quickly supported Kuang Shih-heng's opposition to the plan. Yet because the compromise proposal had publicly emphasized the necessity of maintaining the ancestral rites, Ch'ung-chen now had to acknowledge his duty to remain in the capital. His response was therefore both grieved and grandiose—"It is proper for a kingdom's ruler to die for the altars of the soil and the grain, and I will die happily!"—and again the matter was momentarily dropped.[28]

Li Chien-t'ai's April 9 despatch thus raised for the last time an extremely sensitive issue. Encouraged by this independent suggestion that the capital be abandoned, Li Ming-jui and his supporters pro-

posed once more that the crown prince be placed in nominal charge
of military affairs in Chiang-nan. But once again Kuang Shih-heng
halted all debate by interrupting angrily with a bitter accusation.
"What do all of you intend by having the heir ordered south? Do you
intend to repeat the history of Emperor Su-tsung at Ling-wu?"[29]

Kuang's allusion was strikingly familiar to all. In A.D. 756 the
T'ang emperor Hsuan-tsung had abandoned Ch'ang-an to An Lu-
shan's rebel army. After his praetorians killed his favorite concubine,
Yang Kuei-fei, enroute, Hsuan-tsung fled to Shu (Szechwan), leaving
the crown prince behind in western Shansi to placate army officers
who wished to retake Ch'ang-an. The young prince yearned to rejoin
his father, but his officers pointed out to him that it would be a
greater act of filial piety to rally the army at Ling-wu and recover the
capital. After five requests, the prince agreed to "accord himself with
their collective wishes and plan for the altars of the soil and the
grain."[30] Consequently he named his father emperor-abdicate
(shang-huang t'ien-ti), adopted the imperial name Su-tsung, and
established a temporary court at Ling-wu from which he eventually
reconquered Ch'ang-an.[31]

Kuang Shih-heng was suggesting, then, that if the Ming crown
prince were sent to Chiang-nan, he would surely become emperor in
his own right. Ch'ung-chen would be judged well by history for
guarding the altars of the dynasty, but that act would also doom him
either to forced abdication or imprisonment and death. Stunned into
silence by this pointed simile, the court officials "dared not say a
word." Ch'ung-chen himself still could have approved the proposal.
But he had already begun to adopt a new role for himself, self-
pitying, self-righteous, apparently little concerned with practical
measures to give the dynasty a chance to survive his own death.
During the April 3d debate he had complained: "There is not a single
loyal minister or righteous scholar to share the dynasty's troubles.
Instead they plot. Well, the monarch is going to die for the altars of
his ancestors like the morally upright of all time. My will is resolved."[32] Now, he laid all the blame upon his officials and angrily
absolved himself of guilt for the loss of the mandate. "It is not I, the
ruler, who has lost his realm. It is all of you, my ministers, who appear to be trying so hard to lose the realm!"[33] This motif of an aban-

doned and betrayed ruler colored all of Ch'ung-chen's remaining days —days that were to be capped by the emperor's self-ordained sacrifice.

However dignified his public resolve to "die for the altars of his ancestors," Ch'ung-chen's private behavior when that moment arrived was far from majestic.[34] On the evening of April 24, just as Li Tzu-ch'eng's soldiers were occupying Peking's suburbs, the emperor commanded the crown prince and his two brothers to hide in the homes of relatives. Ch'ung-chen then drank himself into a stupor and proceeded to try to kill his consorts. Empress Chou committed suicide, but it was the emperor's own sword that murdered Princess K'un-i, wounded another consort, and severed the right arm of the crown princess.[35] After this rampage Ch'ung-chen disguised himself as a eunuch, and near midnight tried to escape from the palace.[36] Fired on by his own palace guards, who failed to recognize him, he was turned back at the Cheng-yang gate and all possibility of escape was removed. As Ch'ien Hsing reconstructed the event:

> Filled with dread his majesty returned to the palace where he changed his robes and walked with [his chief eunuch, Wang] Ch'eng-en to Wan-shou hill. When he reached the [red pavilion on Mei-shan (coal mountain) which housed the] Imperial Hat and Girdle Department, he hanged himself. Shortly before one a.m. on the nineteenth day of the third month of *chia-shen*, in the seventeenth year of Ch'ung-chen (April 25, 1644), the emperor of the Great Ming ascended to heaven on a dragon.[37]

To the very end the emperor continued to blame his ministers for the fall of the dynasty. Many contemporary accounts stressed his sense of abandonment. On the morning of the 25th, when no officials appeared at the predawn audience, Ch'ung-chen is supposed to have said, "My ministers have failed me. As ruler of the country I [must] die for the altars of the soil and the grain. An empire that [has lasted] 277 years: lost in one day. It's all because of the mistakes of treacherous ministers that it has come to this. Alas!"[38] And later when he reached Coal Mountain, moments before strangling himself with his sash, he is said to have sighed again, "I await my literati but there are none assembled here. To come to this now! Why is there not a single one among all those ministers to accompany me?"[39]

Fact and fabrication are intertwined in accounts like these. Some chroniclers maintain, for instance, that Ch'ung-chen left a suicide note which read:

> Seventeen years ago I ascended the throne, and now I meet with heaven's punishment above, sinking ignominiously below while the rebels seize my capital because my ministers have deceived me. I die unable to face my ancestors in the underworld, dejected and ashamed. May the bandits dismember my corpse and slaughter my officials, but let them not despoil the imperial tombs nor harm a single one of our people.[40]

Yet an unusually reliable contemporary diarist reports that when the body of the emperor was eventually discovered three days later lying under a pine tree on Coal Hill, there was no such note. A palace servant who had seen the body told the diarist, Chao Shih-chin, that the emperor wore a blue silk robe and red trousers. His hair was disheveled in death, and the only written remains were the two characters *T'ien-tzu* (Son of Heaven) written with his left hand.[41]

There was also, both then and later, some skepticism about the emperor's effort to shift the blame for his fall upon his ministers. The nineteenth-century bibliophile and poet, Wu Ch'ien, commented: "Those who read history say that at the fall of the Ming, there was a ruler but no ministers. [This is] in order to deny that Ssu-ling [which was the posthumous name of Ch'ung-chen] was the ruler who lost his realm."[42] And a writer of Ch'ung-chen's own time remarked: "When a ruler is of a certain sort, then so are his ministers. Can posterity believe him when he said, 'I am not a ruler who lost his realm?'"[43] Yet despite these doubts, and despite the widespread accounts of the emperor's ignoble last night, most contemporaries were persuaded by Ch'ung-chen's efforts to blame his ministers for the debacle and portray himself as an aggrieved and abandoned martyr. In fact, many of the ministers so accused unquestionably shared a strong sense of guilt and accepted personal responsibility for the fall of the dynasty.

The most deeply affected were the thirteen or more who committed suicide on April 25, the day Li Tzu-ch'eng entered Peking. These men were not mourning Ch'ung-chen, for none of them knew that the emperor was dead. His body was to remain undiscovered for

three more days, and it was widely assumed at the time that he had
left the capital to establish a *hsing-tsai* (temporary court) elsewhere.[44] Ni Yuan-lu's contrition was typical of most. Before taking
his life, Ni faced north, symbolically regarding his ruler, and said,
"Your minister was a high official. His fault was that he was a minister who could not save the realm."[45] Others, like Shih Pang-yueh,
vice censor-in-chief, expressed similar feelings of guilt for the fall of
the dynasty. Before he hanged himself, Shih wrote a couplet which
read:

> I am ashamed to lack even half a plan to relieve the present distress,
> But I do have this body to offer in return for my ruler's grace.[42]

It would seem, then, that such loyalists died believing, like many contemporaries who survived them, that "the demise of the Ming [was
owing to] the way in which all of the gentry and officials turned
their back on the commonweal and pursued selfish goals."[47]

   This same accusation—that the Ming had been betrayed by selfish
ministers and factional cliques—was repeated on specially prepared
banners and placards carried by Li's soldiers and officials when they
formally entered the city that afternoon.[48] Li himself was met outside the palace gates by three hundred attendants, supervised by
Ch'ung-chen's chief eunuch Wang Te-hua, who led the "dashing
prince" through Ch'ang-an gate to the Great Within. Peking was now
his.[49]

   Li did not know that the emperor was dead, and one of his first
announcements was that he would reward the informer who brought
him news of Ch'ung-chen's whereabouts with 10,000 taels of gold
and a noble rank.[50] He certainly did not intend to punish the emperor, for he too blamed the emperor's officials for the downfall of
the dynasty. "His ministers only looked after their own selfish interests. They formed cliques and there were very few public spirited
and loyal ones at all."[51] Indeed, Li Tzu-ch'eng was apparently
shocked when his men finally did find Ch'ung-chen's body on Coal
Hill. Taken to view the remains, Li deplored the emperor's death.
"I came to enjoy [the profits of ruling] the rivers and mountains
together with you," he told the corpse. "How could you have committed suicide?"[52]

   Li Tzu-ch'eng was aware of the horrible onus attached to regicide

in Chinese political judgments, and he may also have realized that
usurpers seldom held the throne for long, usually being succeeded
by one free of blame for overthrowing the previous royal house.
This, at least, is one way of understanding why, just before the city
surrendered so readily to him, Li sent the eunuch Tu Hsun (who had
surrendered to him at Chü-yung pass) into the palace to offer Ch'ung-
chen a negotiated settlement. If the Ming emperor would ennoble Li,
give him one million taels, and acknowledge his control of the
Shensi-Shansi area, then Li in turn would destroy the other rebel
groups in China and defend Liaotung against the Manchus. Ch'ung-
chen failed to agree to these terms for fear of being labeled "expedient" (*pien*) by later generations, and the negotiations were never
concluded.[53] But the fact that Li did make this last-minute offer at
all indicates his desire, temporarily at least, to defer dethroning
Ch'ung-chen. Now, with the capital in his hands, he too had good
reason to blame selfish ministers, rather than his own military
attack, as the cause of the Ming's demise.[54]

Li Tzu-ch'eng's conviction that Ch'ung-chen's ministers were responsible for his fall was strengthened by the revulsion he felt for
collaborators—the "twice-serving ministers" who now offered to aid
him as they had aided Ch'ung-chen. Li already had a shadow government of his own, composed of gentrymen and officials who had surrendered to him before he captured Peking. Thus, he did not ride
into the capital at the head of a rebel army alone; he was also accompanied by a fairly large retinue of civil officials. These men had
surrendered at various times in the past. Perhaps the first official of
note to serve Li was a Shansi gentryman named Sung Ch'i-chiao who
had joined the rebel cause under duress in 1634 in Shensi.[55] Li had
gained many more gentry adherents when he occupied Honan in
1641–42. The two most important members of this latter group were
Li Yen and Niu Chin-hsing.

Li Yen was a former *chü-jen* whose father, Li Ching-po, had been
governor of Shantung under the T'ien-ch'i emperor. Li Yen's personal history—his public charity work, his disputes with more avaricious members of the Honanese gentry around Kaifeng, and his
moral decision to join the rebels—has already been told elsewhere.[56]
What has not been sufficiently stressed, however, is that Li Yen's
father had been publicly disgraced for his anti-Tung-lin activities and

his support of the eunuch Wei Chung-hsien.[57] Nor has it been widely known that Li Yen's classmate (*t'ung-nien*), Niu Chin-hsing, persuaded Li Tzu-ch'eng that many of the upper gentry of Honan, Shensi, and Shansi would be willing to serve him because they had been denied Ming office for similar factional reasons.[58] It was men like these who had supplemented Li Tzu-ch'eng's self-acquired knowledge of the Confucian classics with lectures on ethics and history.[59] And it was also they who had urged Li to establish a base in Shensi from which to attack Peking.[60] They were given ministerial rank in the Shensi regime and thus stood ready when Li's army moved through Shansi toward the capital to receive new gentry adherents like Chang Lin-jan, who was to become vice-minister of finance in the Peking government of the Shun.[61]

The key positions in the new Shun government were therefore occupied by men of gentry or official background who had surrendered to Li Tzu-ch'eng before he had taken power in Peking (see table). Most were northerners like Li himself: twelve from Shensi, Shansi, Honan, Shantung, and Northern Chihli; and only three from Hukuang, Szechwan, and Chekiang. The two most powerful men in this group—powerful in the sense of dictating appointments within the Shun bureaucracy—were Sung Ch'i-chiao and Niu Chin-hsing, neither of whom had been a Ming official at the time he joined Li. Although intimates of the Prince of Shun, they had never been military lieutenants with control over their own forces like Li Yen, the shaman Sung Hsien-ts'e, or Li Tzu-ch'eng's "sworn brothers," Liu Tsung-min and Li Kuo (his nephew). The absence of these latter military commanders from the official Peking roster of the Shun regime suggests the civil-military, public-private bifurcation of Li's government. The new regime, in other words, did not bureaucratically incorporate the Shun's "tent government," which remained outside regular government and above civil control.

Nor did this relatively small group of Shun officials have the manpower to control the existing bureaucracy without the collaboration of existing officeholders. The rebels had assumed from the moment they entered Peking that the clerks and attendants of the capital yamens would serve them, and in this presumption they were not wrong.[62] They also hoped to recruit a new cadre of regular civil servants unblemished by Ming service. Sung Ch'i-chiao had advised Li

Key Figures in the Shun Government[63]

Hanlin Academy				
Niu Chin-hsing	Honan	cj–1634	Grand secretary	Joined Li Tzu-ch'eng in Honan in 1641
Ho Jui-cheng	Honan	cs–1628	Grand secretary	Recommended by Niu Chin-hsing
Li Chih-sheng	Hukuang	cs–1634	Grand secretary	Joined Li in Shansi; in charge of exams
Personnel				
Sung Ch'i-chiao	Shensi	cs–1628	Minister	Joined Li in Shensi in 1634
Finance				
Yang Yü-lin	N. Chihli	cj–1630	Vice-minister	Joined Li at T'ung-kuan, where he had been attached to the Military Defense Circuit
Chang Lin-jan	—	—	Vice-minister	Formerly prefect of P'ing-yang (Shansi); surrendered to Li there
Yang Chien-lieh	Shansi	cs–1640	Bureau director	Joined Li when he took P'ing-yang
Chang Lu	Unknown	cs–1640	Bureau director	Formerly magistrate of P'ing-yang, who surrendered to Li
Chieh Sung-nien	Shensi	cs–1631	Bureau secretary	Surrendered to Li at Pao-ting
Rites				
Kung Yü	Shensi	cs–1631	Vice-minister	Surrendered to Li in Honan
War				
Po Ching-hsing	Honan	cs–1637	Bureau director	Surrendered to Li in Honan; a former Ming censor
Yü Chung-hua	Shantung	—	Bureau director	Formerly a bureau vice-director, he had been detached for duty in Shansi where he surrendered to Li
Lü Pi-chou	Shantung	cs–1628	Bureau vice-director	Joined Li in Honan; logistics expert
Justice				
Sheng Chih-ch'i	Chekiang	cs–1595	Vice-minister	Formerly an administration commissioner in Shensi, who joined Li while in that same province
Works				
Li Chen-sheng	Shensi	cs–1634	Minister	Regional inspector of Hukuang, who surrendered to Li in 1642
Censorate				
Liu Yin-tung	Szechwan	cs–1631	Censor-in-chief	Formerly regional inspector of Shun-t'ien, he had surrendered to Li at T'ung-chou

Tzu-ch'eng that, "Your minister feels that since these [officials] were unable to sacrifice themselves with complete loyalty and filial piety for their dynasty, then they are just as incapable of serving their new ruler with a pure and undivided heart."[64] Li was most sympathetic to Sung's feeling. Nurtured on *Water Margin* ideals of loyalty and justice, imbued with a primitive sense of Confucian righteousness, he could not forgive Ch'ung-chen's former ministers for their apparent betrayal of their ruler. His own retinue consisted of many officials who had served the Ming in the provinces, but the fact that they had joined him before the occupation of Peking placed them in a different category than the bureaucrats whom Li now blamed for the fall of the Ming. The latter had personally served Ch'ung-chen, and—in Li's eyes—were responsible for the dynasty's demise. Both of these attributes, personal proximity and individual responsibility, meant that they should have committed suicide like the loyalists who took their own lives on April 25; men such as those deserved respect. In fact, Li personally mourned Ni Yuan-lu's death, and had the words *chung-ch'en* (loyal minister) inscribed over the gates of the loyalists' residences, ordering his men not to enter them.[65] But metropolitan officials who had not sacrificed themselves incurred his opprobrium and distaste. Sung Ch'i-chiao's advice thus fell on receptive ears.

The difficulty was, however, that the new government could not be efficiently administered without relying upon those culpable former officials until a new cadre could be recruited. Li Tzu-ch'eng had taken immediate steps to appoint a few of the many northwestern *chü-jen,* and even *sheng-yuan,* who had come to Peking with the Shun armies in hope of bureaucratic spoils.[66] He had also encouraged Sung Ch'i-chiao to hold examinations for the *hsiu-ts'ai* degree in Shun-t'ien and Ta-t'ung prefectures, and for the degree of *chü-jen* in the capital. But the formation of a new civil service would take time, and provisions had to be made during the interim for staffing the middle and middle-upper rungs of the existing bureaucracy. At least some of the metropolitan literati would have to be kept in office despite Sung and Li's suspicions of the "twice-serving." To this end, Li ordered his grand secretary, Niu Chin-hsing, to announce that former Ming officials were to register with the new authorities on April 26 and must prepare to present themselves at court the morning of the 27th. At that time they would be given the option of serving the Shun regime or of returning to their native places "at their own convenience."[68]

The response of the literati to this announcement was ambivalent. Their initial reaction to the fall of Peking had been one of quite natural confusion. Early on the morning of the 25th, attendants had begun fleeing the palace, alerting pedestrians outside the Forbidden City that the emperor was no longer on the throne.[69] Many believed that Wu San-kuei's army had arrived from Ningyuan the previous night to save them from the rebels, but this hope was soon dispelled. By 9:00 A.M., as smoke and ashes filled the sky, panic began to infect the crowds that jostled through the streets and alleys. Ming soldiers retreating into the inner city alerted the Pekingese to the rebels' entry. The worst was expected until, moments later, residents rushing back from the walls shouted that there would be no massacre: "It's fine, it's fine, they're not killing people." Householders immediately began writing *Shun-min* (which means both "people who submit," and "subjects of Shun") upon their residence gates, or on yellow pieces of paper which they pasted on their foreheads or stuck on their hats.[70]

The Shun soldiers, wearing white hats and green clothing, moved steadily through the city. At first most people stayed indoors, and pedestrians hugged the sides of the streets as the columns of horsemen moved by, silent save for the clatter of hooves and the creaking of armor.[71] As rebels began spreading through the *hu-t'ung* (alleys) marking off billets, it became clear to the residents that this was, for the moment at least, a highly disciplined force. Looters were executed on the spot and nailed, hands and feet, to the wooden street posts west of Ch'ien-men.[72] By noon, when Li Tzu-ch'eng formally entered the city, the reassured inhabitants lined the streets, respectfully holding incense in their hands, or holding up placards with Shun's reign name, Yung-ch'ang, written out. And by that afternoon, as fears continued to subside, people could be seen strolling leisurely about as though nothing had happened.

The Ming officials reacted in different ways. About three hundred literati, led by Grand Secretary Wei Ts'ao-te and Minister of War Chang Chin-yen, obsequiously welcomed Li at the gates.[73] Others shed their official robes and burned their court regalia, buying used clothing (the price of which doubled in the capital's flea markets), or shaving their heads to pose as Buddhist monks.[74] Still others hid in the homes of their office clerks (*ch'ang-pan*), or with relatives. Almost all were greatly relieved when they heard of Niu Chin-hsing's

announcement, reported to them by the very clerks whose dwellings
they inhabited. However, their relief was tinged with some apprehen-
sion because they also learned that Niu had ordered the clerks to
report any officials who were concealing themselves.[75] Some bureaucrats did resolve to stay in hiding.

> Those who were determined not to serve tried to hide. Once
> all the literati came across the phrase [in Niu's announcement],
> "at their own convenience," in contrast to the coercion applied
> to the clerks, the professional hangers-on [in their midst] stirred
> excitedly. The moment this personnel entered [the court] they
> were attached to the bandits' [personnel rosters]. If [an official]
> was [morally] good, however, he hid from the bandits, who were
> unable to interrogate him.[76]

Later when systematic plundering began, these "good" officials were
quickly discovered.[77]

The officials that registered on the 26th presented themselves at
four different places: General Liu Tsung-min's billet, Li Kuo's billet,
Li Yen's temporary residence, and the headquarters of General
Kuo Chih-wei. Their fate was sealed from that moment on, because
after they had registered, these gentlemen were detained under guard
in each general's encampment (ying).[78] The only ones released were
officials who had known the major Shun leaders earlier in life. For
instance, at Liu Tsung-min's encampment where the registration was
being conducted by Sung Hsien-ts'e, the Ming officials waiting
uneasily to be questioned were startled when a messenger was sent
out to ask for Wu Tzu-ch'ang, a bureau secretary in the Ministry of
Personnel, by name. A little later, Wu was escorted out of the encampment with great politeness by the dwarfed shaman, Sung
Hsien-ts'e; and only then did the assembled officials realize that Wu
was a t'ung-hsiang (fellow townsman) of Sung from Honan.[79]

While these officials were presenting themselves for registration
and what amounted to temporary imprisonment, others were still at
large, pondering suicide, hesitating between flight or service, or even
actively seeking office under the new dynasty. There were inevitably
those who viewed the establishment of the Shun dynasty as a great
personal opportunity. The most notorious examples were "professional hangers-on" like Yang Chin-ch'i, a 1631 chin-shih who had
never before been given office. After sending a present to the Shun

minister of personnel, Sung Ch'i-chiao, Yang told family and friends
that "tomorrow at this time I'll no longer be a nobody (fan-jen)"—
a phrase that was soon lampooned around the capital to characterize
this kind of opportunism.[80] Sung also was the contact sought out by
a group of four prominent officials from Wu-hsi (Chiang-nan) who
had been among the officials welcoming Li Tzu-ch'eng as he entered
the city gates. Led by Ch'in Hsien, a bureau secretary in the Ministry
of War, the group also included his uncle, Chao Yü-sen, a graduate of
the Hanlin; Wang Sun-hui, a former magistrate who had contem-
plated suicide then lost his nerve; and Chang Ch'i, a bureau secretary
in the Ministry of Rites. On the 25th, as the Prince of Shun's retinue
approached the four men, they had bowed and announced their
willingness to serve the new ruler. But even though their physical
deference was visible, their words of submission were inaudible over
the sound of the horses.[81]

However, they soon learned of Niu Chin-hsing's order to register.
Chao Yü-sen, who had only received his *chin-shih* degree four years
earlier, rushed immediately to Wang Sun-hui's house. After a few
moments of polite discussion, he abruptly announced what was on
his mind.

> I have received the gracious bounty of Ch'ung-chen. Neverthe-
> less, the dynasty fell in retribution for its own acts. There is no
> rational necessity for me to give up my own life by dying [for
> the dynasty]. And [at the same time] I cannot bear to flee and
> abandon my wealth and station in order to requite [the em-
> peror's bounty]. What about you?[82]

Wang replied just as frankly. "This very moment is the beginning of a
new dynasty. Our group must strive to appear first [for office]."[83]
Because Chao had known Sung Ch'i-chiao years earlier, he was thus
able to lead Wang and Ch'in Hsien (who joined them later) to call
upon Sung at his residence. As they were being shown in, Wang Sun-
hui pulled a piece of paper out of his pocket and stuck it on his fore-
head. The characters on the paper read: "Announcing the entry of
Minister Wang Sun-hui." Since the word "entry" obviously indicated
Wang's desire to join the new government, Sung Ch'i-chiao smiled
and remarked, "Excellent words."[84]

For many officials, therefore, the Shun regime seemed to mark the
beginning of a new dynasty, holding the mandate and providing an

opportunity to participate in the founding reign. There were precedents for such a choice in the recognition that imperial legitimacy as
such was, in part, a matter of political power—power that Li Tzu-
ch'eng surely wielded. The Sung philosopher Ou-yang Hsiu, for
instance, had divided legitimacy (*cheng-t'ung*) into its binomial
elements, *cheng* being the moral right to succession, and *t'ung* the
fact of political unity. In this formulation imperial unification was
sometimes the prerequisite for imperial virtue, and ends could be
used to justify means.[85] For men who believed that the mandate had
passed on, service to Li Tzu-ch'eng represented their Confucian obligation to educate the rebel leader to appreciate imperial virtue and
righteousness.[86]

Chou Chung, a Hanlin bachelor of the class of '43 and one of the
most promising scholars of the realm, was one such person. A Fu-she
adherent, Chou Chung clearly believed that Li Tzu-ch'eng was in
Peking to stay. Chou acknowledged Li's brutality, but to him this
was simply evidence that the Shun dynasty was blessed with a dynamic monarch. "When [Ming] T'ai-tsu first arose," he told friends,
"it was just like this." And with Chou's help, political unity would
become even more of a fact. "Chiang-nan," he was fond of saying,
"is not hard to pacify." So it was that he called on the Shun grand
secretary, Niu Chin-hsing, before the court audience of April 27 and
announced his intention to serve the new ruler and help him unify
the empire.[87]

The audience that was supposed to be held on the 27th never in
fact took place. It simply provided an occasion for Li Tzu-ch'eng to
humble the bureaucracy. The night of April 26 saw a great flurry of
activity in officialdom as the literati tried to assemble clothing for
the next day's dawn audience. Because many of them had burned
their official clothing the day before, the attire required for a court
appearance was at an absolute premium. Tailors stayed up into the
late hours of the night in order to clothe their customers with official robes and hats at three or four times the going rate.[88] However,
few literati could reequip themselves in time, and it was a gray and
shabby group which assembled at the Tung-hua gate just before dawn
the next morning.[89] The officials who gathered did not include those
who had registered at the generals' encampments and were still being
held prisoner.

As the poorly attired literati entered the Forbidden City by the

Ch'ang-an gate, each man ceremonially handed over his calling card to the rebel guards. The cards were just as promptly tossed into a large pile and burned, leveling the crowd of officials into a single mob of undifferentiated office seekers. As they moved on into the palace, apprehensive and nervous, they found the Ch'eng-t'ien gate firmly closed. There they sat down to wait—a wait that lasted until noon. At that time, the eunuch palace director Wang Te-hua came out of the Great Within followed by several soldiers. Here for the first time the former Ming officials realized that all was not to be forgiven, that Ch'ung-chen's allocation of blame had been accepted by at least some members of the Shun regime. Wang spotted the former minister of war, Chang Chin-yen, in the crowd and singled him out for reproof. "It was all your crowd that ruined the Ming dynasty," he shouted, and when Chang tried to argue back, the eunuch had his attendants slap the minister across the face. After this incident the literati settled down once more to wait for their monarch. By sunset he had not appeared, and they finally left the antecourt, verbally abused and ridiculed by the soldiers around them.[90]

The same kind of treatment was meted out when the officials were told to present themselves for audience on the 29th, this time accompanied by the registered officials brought over from the generals' encampments under guard. Grand Secretary Wei Ts'ao-te and Duke Ch'eng Kuo tried to preserve regular order, but the bureaucrats were crushed together at the palace entrance and soon began pushing each other out of the way in order to get through the gateway first. The lictors on duty at the gate began to use their batons on the mob, and then finally had to call for help from some of Li Tzu-ch'eng's troopers, who kicked and cursed the officials into line. Cowed, their heads lowered in fearful respect, the literati let themselves be herded into the palace grounds. Once inside, they were forced to sit or kneel on the ground while the abuse continued. Gradually the soldiers tired of their sport and left the officials to themselves. There was no sign of their new ruler; for Li Tzu-ch'eng remained in the Wen-hua palace, dressed in breeches and undershirt, while the crowd outside awaited his whim. The hours slowly dragged by. The literati grew hungry, but there was no one to send for food; they grew tired, but there was nowhere to recline except upon the steps to the throne.[91]

At dusk, their wills completely broken, the scholars were aroused by a fanfare. Li Tzu-ch'eng was coming out of the inner palace.

Accompanied by his most trusted officers, the Prince of Shun slowly seated himself on the throne. His loathing was audible. "How could the empire not be in a state of disorder with such a bunch of immoral [officials] as these?"[92] Yet, no doubt advised by Niu Chinhsing and Sung Ch'i-chiao, he also realized that some among them had to be chosen to staff the bureaucracy. The Honan gentryman Ku Chün-en slowly began to call the roll from the ministry rosters. As each official responded to his name, there was a pause—time long enough for Grand Secretary Niu Chin-hsing to recite the misdeeds of that officeholder in full detail.[93] Then the roll call reached Chou Chung, the prestigious Hanlin bachelor who had already privately told Niu that he was willing to become a loyal servant of *ch'uang-wang,* the "dashing prince."

> Ku put down the list and said, "If your majesty is eager to acquire a worthy [official], then we ought to break our pattern and select some for employ." Then he said to Niu, "This is a famous scholar," and [suggested they] appoint Chou. Niu Chinhsing looked at *ch'uang* [*wang*] and praised [Chou] a great deal, saying, "He truly is a famous scholar." *Ch'uang* said, "In what way a famous scholar?" Niu answered, "He writes well." Then *ch'uang* said, "Could he not write upon the theme, '[The scholar trained in public duty] seeing threatening danger, is prepared to sacrifice his life?'"[94]

Having displayed his Confucian erudition with an ironically appropriate phrase from the *Analects,* Li Tzu-ch'eng magnanimously approved Chou Chung's appointment as a Shun official.

Chou's selection marked a change in the proceedings. As more names were called out, Niu Chin-hsing's "steady gaze" decisively evaluated each successive bureaucrat's capacity for office. "Those he deemed suitable were chosen [to serve], and those he deemed unsuitable were dismissed."[95] Sometimes, as in the case of Chou Chung himself, this meant choosing office-seekers who had already contacted him or Sung Ch'i-chiao.[96] In other cases, it was a matter of choosing friends or old acquaintances who were intended to become "Niu's men" in the new bureaucracy. For example, one of the prestigious Hanlin bachelors of 1643 was both Honanese and a member of the provincial *chü-jen* class of 1615—traits shared with Niu who

appointed him a censor.[97] Another man, Ho Jui-cheng, had been a
junior supervisor of instruction in the Ming government and was
appointed to the Hanlin Academy because he came from Niu's
hometown.[98] Yet a third example was Wei Hsueh-lien, whose friend
and fellow Catholic, Han Lin, was a former crony of Niu Chin-
hsing.[99] In all, 92 were chosen to be escorted back out the Tung-hua
gate to the Ministry of Personnel for appointment.[100] The several
thousand remaining were herded in the opposite direction to the
Hsi-hua gate, where they were forced into five columns and marched
off at swordpoint to General Liu Tsung-min and Li Kuo's encampments outside the city walls.[101]

The cohort selected for office was not, in general, a high-ranking
group. In principle, the officials were chosen from the fourth rank
and below. This clearly suited both parties' interests. Li Tzu-ch'eng
was concerned with recruiting a bureaucracy neither tainted by
ministerial betrayal of the personal relationship with Ch'ung-chen,
nor too senior to compete with his own retinue. The officials who
agreed to serve, on the other hand, were men whose bureaucratic
careers were just beginning (e.g. the Hanlin class of '43) or who had
not yet risen to the apex.[102] Of those who joined the Shun government, 90 percent had received their *chin-shih* since 1628, and one-
quarter belonged to the classes of 1640 and 1643.[103] Most of these
stayed in the same posts they had occupied before the fall of the
city. Three bureau directors in the Ministry of Personnel; two bureau
secretaries in the Ministry of Finance; one bureau secretary, two
bureau vice-directors, and one bureau director in the Ministry of
Rites; along with seven censors and the entire roster of chief clerks in
the Hanlin Academy all retained their previous positions. And, in
spite of being shifted from one ministerial responsibility to another,
all of the supervising secretaries of the Offices of Scrutiny were kept
in office. At an intermediate level, then, the bureaucracy remained
largely intact.[104]

As we have seen, the decision to serve was both a matter of selecting office over imprisonment and of believing that this was an
opportunity to "Confucianize" a newly established dynast. Li Tzu-
ch'eng certainly recognized the latter expectation and tried at times
to live up to the image of a humanized ruler, as when he appointed
the famous *li-hsueh* scholar, Yang Kuan-kuang, as palace lecturer

and minister of rites.[105] At the same time, a stubborn insistence
upon ministerial integrity tended to drive the Prince of Shun into a
rage, and those who wanted the opportunity to serve had to accept
the new leader on his own dictatorial terms. When the Hanlin bachelor Chang Chia-yü insisted upon Li's reciprocity after offering the
"dashing prince" his loyalty, Li simply had Chang tied in front of
the palace for three days, and then curtly threatened to kill his
parents unless he submitted and bowed in his new ruler's presence.[106] It was clearly much safer to follow the course of syco-
phancy. Liang Chao-yang, another Hanlin bachelor who had given
the Minister of Personnel Sung Ch'i-chiao five thousand ounces of
gold before the April 27th audience, was one of the few former Ming
officials actually promoted. This good fortune came to him after he
shamelessly compared Li Tzu-ch'eng to the sage rulers Yao, Shun,
Shang T'ang, and Chou Wu-wang.[107]

Li Tzu-ch'eng himself was confused by these imperial expectations, vacillating between his civil delight in Confucian forms of
flattery and his martial rage at effeminate ministers. Was he indeed a
potentially sage emperor? Or was he more fundamentally a knight-
errant who had captured the throne? As a rebel he certainly possessed the confidence of a dynastic aspirant. According to some
sources, he had begun talking about becoming emperor in 1638;
and when ridiculed by one of his followers for this aspiration, he had
compared himself to Liu Pang, founder of the Han.[108] His conviction about his historical mission had also been strong enough to carry
him through one of the nadirs of his military fortunes when, in the
fall of 1640, he was bottled up by Yang Ssu-ch'ang in the Yü-fu
mountains along the Shensi-Szechwan border. At that time, many
of his men, including even Liu Tsung-min, had wanted to surrender
to the Ming forces.

However, Li had insisted that he held the mandate (t'ien-ming) and
that it could be tested by divination. When the divination was held
at a nearby temple, three successive casts were all auspicious, persuading Liu to follow the "dashing prince" into Honan where, because of the famine conditions, Li Tzu-ch'eng recruited a vast new
army.[109] There, Li's belief in his mandate intensified even further.
In part this was simply because of his surname, since a common
prophecy in north China was that "eighteen sons" (shih-pa-tzu)

would combine into "Li" (made up of the characters for *shih-pa-tzu*) to conquer the empire.[110] Moreover, Li was both the name of the founder of the T'ang and, by earlier projection, the name of Lao-tzu himself. The T'ang association added a more conventional note of imperial legitimacy, which was exploited by Li at Niu Chin-hsing's suggestion. When the first Shun government was established at Hsiang-yang, T'ang government titles were adopted, and these were retained even after Peking was taken.[111] Li's own dynastic and reign titles also carried resonances of that earlier dynasty; for, there had been a Shun emperor (reigned 805), a Ta-Shun reign (890–891), and even a Yung-ch'ang era (689) during the T'ang period. Marching out of Shensi like Ch'in Shih Huang-ti, overcoming adversity like Han Kao-tsu, reincarnating ancient prophecies like T'ang T'ai-tsung, and forcefully establishing a government like Ming T'ai-tsu—Li Tzu-ch'eng certainly seemed to possess many of the historically legitimizing qualities of a dynastic founder. And these in turn were confirmed by the repeated requests that he cease being merely Prince Shun and actually enthrone himself as emperor.[112]

There were excellent political reasons for Li Tzu-ch'eng's assuming the title of emperor. As a rebel leader, even as a prince, he was only primus inter pares. Old comrades-in-arms, like Liu Tsung-min and Li Kuo, were treated as equals by him and with great deference by important civil ministers. Sung Ch'i-chiao, for example, always bowed obsequiously in Liu Tsung min's presence and addressed him as "Your excellency."[113] Obviously, there would be some difficulty in getting General Liu to recognize Li's ascendancy. When Niu Chin-hsing came to Liu's encampment on May 2 and invited him to come to court and request Li to ascend the throne, Liu Tsung-min answered:

> "He and I were highwaymen together. Why should I salute him? I absolutely refuse." Niu Chin-hsing urged him [to go], saying, "It isn't the same now as then. Just two visits of respect, and that's all." Then, an official from the Court of State Ceremonial delivered a memorial to Tsung-min which urged [Li Tzu-ch'eng] to enter [the Great Within and ascend the throne]. Tsung-min said, "What does it mean, 'to urge to enter'?" The official from the Court of State Ceremonial explained its meaning, and added, "I beg your excellency to carry out the [court] ceremonies."

> Tsung-min said, "What does it mean, 'to carry out the cere-
> monies'?" The official from the Court of State Ceremonial said,
> "Five salutes and three kowtows."[114]

Yet Liu Tsung-min had recognized Li's military mandate in the mountains of Szechwan, and confirmation of Li's civil mandate was now
forthcoming from officials like Chou Chung. If Li had held the enthronement ceremony, like all those other founding rulers whose
military mantle he wore, there is no doubt that Liu Tsung-min would
have attended, and that in the end Li's imperial charisma would have
elevated him above the status of comrade-in-arms to Liu. This new
legitimacy would have reinforced his authority, enabling Li to make
the final and necessary transition to civil rule. But time and again the
Prince of Shun hesitated. Enthronement was first scheduled for
May 11, and then postponed repeatedly—to May 13, May 17, May 20,
and finally May 22—by which time Li Tzu-ch'eng had left the capital
to fight Wu San-kuei.[115]

Why did Li Tzu-ch'eng hesitate until it was too late? One immediate reason for postponement may have been his desire to use the
Ming crown prince, now in his custody, as a bargaining pawn with
General Wu San-kuei, whose frontier defense forces were poised to
attack Peking. Yet, as Li Yen had pointed out to Li Tzu-ch'eng, his
enthronement would give him the imperial right to enfeoff Wu San-
kuei and thus stay his advance.[116] Therefore it made better political
sense to hold the ceremony as soon as possible. However, Li Tzu-
ch'eng continued to delay, almost as though he felt he did not
deserve the throne he had usurped. This kind of corrosive self-doubt
may have driven him to foist ever more blame upon the officials
which Ch'ung-chen had named scapegoats for the fall of the dynasty.
Frequent comments of Li Yen, Sung Hsien-ts'e, and Sung Ch'i-chiao
about the dubious loyalty of turncoats seemed to intensify Li
Tzu-ch'eng's outrage, which was vented upon corrupt survivors like
the imperial relative Li Kuo-chen, who was bitterly excoriated as a
"robber of his country" by the Prince of Shun for having embezzled
the capital's military funds.[117] Soon, Li Tzu-ch'eng was delivering
more than verbal lashings. At his command to "punish the disloyal,"
the Ministry of Justice brought charges against a number of bureaucrats, forty-six of whom were legally executed.[118]

Just as Li Tzu-ch'eng shared the former emperor's belief that official malfeasance had toppled the dynasty, so did he face the same kind of financial crisis as had Ch'ung-chen. The government simply did not control enough public funds to pay the Shun armies. Li Tzu-ch'eng was therefore quite receptive to Li Yen's advice that former Ming officials be forced to contribute to the public purse. These donations were even to be designated by the same term as the late Ming's supernumerary taxes: *hsiang* or "military rations." But whereas Ch'ung-chen's levied quotas and political ransoms had yielded relatively modest funds, Li Tzu-ch'eng was in a stronger position to enforce his demands. After all, at least eight hundred former Ming officials were already imprisoned in the generals' encampments. The Prince of Shun had only—so Li Yen suggested— to assess selective fines upon these men, who would be divided into three groups: the notoriously corrupt who should be tortured until they turned over their private fortunes; those who refused to serve the Shun who should have their property confiscated; and the relatively blameless who should be asked to "volunteer" contributions to the regime.[119]

Li Tzu-ch'eng approved this plan on May 1, and during the next day a schedule of quotas was drawn up. Former grand secretaries were expected to pay 100,000 taels, former ministers 70,000, and so on down to 1,000 for the lowest-ranking bureaucrats.[120] On May 3 the schedules were sent to each of the encampments.[121] There was a curiously bureaucratic quality to the arrangements for what was to become a grisly scene of bloodletting. The "military rations" quotas were not assigned to individuals but by official rank, and even in some cases to all the employees of a given ministry. And not only were the schedules formally observed and the sums regularly forwarded to Li Tzu-ch'eng's treasury, the differentiated quota system was also extended to areas outside of Peking under Shun occupation.[122]

The quota system was routinely observed by the Prince of Shun's generals, who had already established a system of "punishing" officials and gentry until they contributed to the rebel forces as they marched across Shansi.[123] Li Tzu-ch'eng's decision on May 1 was even anticipated by Liu Tsung-min, who had several days earlier ordered his men to construct special vises for crushing human bone.[124] These pincers were tried out on some of Liu's own clerks and then used sparingly to force several former Ming officials to "submit" and serve the Shun. Until May 3, however, the instruments were largely unused. Liu Tsung-min would certainly have abused his prisoners in any case, but it was Li Tzu-ch'eng's angry order to "kill the guilty, and punish the greedy and covetous" that unleashed the general altogether.[125]

As soon as the quotas were announced the officials' long ordeal began. A few high officials immediately paid Liu considerable sums to avoid "punishment" and were promptly released.[126] But most could not get the necessary cash from relatives and friends, and one by one they were hauled out into the courtyards of Liu's billet to be tortured. The same scene was enacted in the other encampments, and especially that of Li Kuo. But Liu Tsung-min's prisoners suffered the longest and harshest brutalities—beginning that morning, lasting on into the night, for ten days. In all, two hundred regular officials, several thousand functionaries and clerks, and numerous eunuchs were put to the vise. About one thousand died.[127]

At first the tortures seemed, both to the victims and to the torturers, to be retribution for the fall of the dynasty. The lingering sense of guilt for Ch'ung-chen's death led those who were being abused to speak of "being punished" (*shou-hsing*), as though they acknowledged Liu's right to apply to them the same instruments they had once used in routine judicial interrogations. And, at the same time, the rebels saw themselves as administering punishment to "selfish ministers" who had brought about the fall of the dynasty. Former Grand Secretary Wei Ts'ao-te, for example, was tortured for four days until he managed to find 10,000 taels to pay his captors. Yet Liu Tsung-min was still unappeased and berated Wei for "losing the realm." Wei painfully insisted that he was merely a bookish scholar who had had no real involvement in political affairs, while the person really responsible for the fall of the dynasty was Ch'ung-chen, who had "lacked the *Tao*." This remark infuriated Liu, who shouted back, "How could Ch'ung-chen have trusted you? And you defame him by saying that he had no *Tao*!" He then had Wei hit repeatedly across the face, and the "punishment" continued for one more day until the grand secretary died, his cheekbones split.[128]

Liu Tsung-min not only enjoyed his role as an instrument of Ch'ung-chen's vengeance; he also regarded himself as a righteous if crude judge of public morality. When a minor case of adultery among peasants in a village just outside Peking was brought to his attention, he indignantly sentenced two of the offenders to death and a third who had condoned the relationship to lingering death by slicing—a punishment far out of proportion to the crime.[129] In fact, his obsession with retribution, especially against high ministers, eventually overcame his desire to extract the necessary quotas. Wei Ts'ao-te's case is a perfect example of this. After Wei died, Liu Tsung-min had his son brought in. The younger Wei pointed out to Liu that there simply was no more money in the family coffers, but that he could have raised contributions from the grand secretary's former students and friends if Wei Ts'ao-te had been kept alive. Now it was too late, and Liu would get no more funds. The rebel general killed the young man for this belated advice.

Although Liu Tsung-min viewed himself as an instrument of moral retribution, he lacked the even-handedness of a Confucian judge. Punishments were excessive, and above all, arbitrary. As one survivor of the ordeal noted:

> Of all the ministers who were punished, a few [were tortured] beginning on May 2; and others beginning on May 3, or May 4, or May 5. There were many different reasons for their being punished. Some paid a lot of money and yet were tortured again. Some paid [only a] little and yet were not tortured again. Others paid all they had and were still tortured. Still others paid no money and in the end weren't punished at all. Those who knew [of this] supposed it was retribution for [the evil deeds of] previous generations. Of the regular officials who were flogged, some had not even paid money and yet were sent to the Ministry of Personnel and appointed officials. Some had already paid money, scheming obsequiously for office, and took [Liu] Tsung-min or Ta-liang's [i.e., Li Kuo's] calling-cards to present to the Ministry of Personnel. There were also those in the midst of being chosen [for office at court] who, when it was known that they had money, were sent to Liu or to Li to be tortured. There was no fixed standard.[130]

A lingering sense of guilt had made many officials feel, through their haze of pain and despite the fearful mutilation, that they may have deserved punishment. The quota system, so familiar to Ming bureaucrats who had served under Ch'ung-chen, seemed a reasonable form of monetary redemption. Accustomed to harsh judicial methods of their own, they were not even aghast at the brutality of the punishments. What terrorized them in the end was the unpredictability of their judges; and when they came to realize that there was no connection between crime and punishment, justice seemed like revenge, and guilt no more than their "retribution for previous generations."

As more and more trussed corpses were tossed into straw hampers and carried out of Liu Tsung-min's compound each morning, news reached Li Tzu-ch'eng of his general's excesses. On May 12, the Prince of Shun paid a call upon Liu Tsung-min's encampment, and was appalled by the sight of several hundred men being tortured in the courtyard. He turned to his old comrade and said, "The heavenly portents are not auspicious. General Sung [Hsien-ts'e] says that we should reduce the punishments. This group should be released."[131] Liu Tsung-min answered respectfully. And, indeed, the following morning an official order came for the release of the remaining prisoners. Liu obeyed.[132]

However, Liu's appetites had been too deeply whetted. His storerooms were already filled with gold and silver wine goblets, "mountains" of bolts of cloth, gold and silver coins and ingots, and his courtyards bulged with cartloads of clothing.[133] Yet he wanted more. Deprived of officials he turned to other victims, arresting almost a thousand merchants to torture for ransom.[134] Setting such an example for his troops, Liu Tsung-min found it increasingly difficult to maintain the discipline shown when his soldiers first entered Peking. How could he tell his soldiers not to plunder when his storerooms were so filled, or not to rape when he himself had abducted a daughter-in-law of the imperial household?[135]

At first the Shun troopers only plundered at night, when a curfew was imposed upon the city. "The soldiers forced open doors and entered, seizing gold and silver, violating wives and daughters. The people began to suffer. Every nightfall was the same."[136] Then they began abusing the homeowners with whom they were billeted.[137] In the streets, they casually rode down pedestrians or whipped laggards out of their way. First teahouse servants and singing girls, then the daughters of respectable households, were seized and sexually abused.[138] The citizens of Peking quickly coined a phrase for the looting that followed: *t'ao-wu,* "scouring things." Soldiers entered homes at random in small bands, each successive group "scouring" off whatever previous gangs had overlooked: money, jewels, then clothing, and finally food.[139]

As the disorder spread, Sung Hsien-ts'e was heard to ask Li Yen in despair, "Was not the prophecy of the eighteen sons to be fulfilled for the commonweal?"[140] Yet there was little that leaders like Liu Tsung-min could do to control their troups, who would probably have mutinied if denied their booty.[141] Consequently, when Li Tzu-ch'eng summoned his generals to a special audience and asked them, "Why can't you help me to be a good ruler?" their blunt response was: "The authority to rule was granted to you. But we have the power to plunder as well. There's no argument about that."[142] It would be hard to devise a more suitable epitaph for the Shun regime.

The populace of Peking suffered even more as Li's men took out their resentment over shifting military fortunes upon officials and commoners alike. When Li Tzu-ch'eng led part of his forces out of the capital on May 18 to attack Wu San-kuei, sixteen high Ming officials were beheaded together outside the Tung-hua gate.[143] And as some of the troops left behind under Niu Chin-hsing's command began to drift out of the city to return to Shensi, even more homes and shops were plundered.[144] Then, after Li was defeated near Shan-hai-kuan on May 27 by Dorgon and Wu San-kuei's armies, the returning rebels—mean with fatigue and drink—vented their rage upon the capital by sacking its yamens, looting more of its residences, and setting fires which destroyed entire sections of the city around the Chang-i gate.[145] Wu San-kuei's refusal to negotiate with the defeated rebel drove Li Tzu-ch'eng into a murderous rage. Thirty-eight members of the Wu household were murdered by Li's men, and the bloody head of Wu San-kuei's own father was hung over the city's wall. With no choice but flight or surrender, Li hastily enthroned himself on June 3 and prepared to abandon the capital. The next day the emperor of Shun set the Wu-ying palace ablaze and rode out of the city gates toward the West.[146] Behind him, "smoke and flames filled the sky" and fires burned in almost every district of the city.[147] The "dashing prince" had occupied Peking for forty-two days, only the last of which had been as emperor.

Li Tzu-ch'eng's last-minute effort to ceremonialize his imperial mandate came just as he was losing his rebel mandate as seeker of justice and defender of the people. The people of Peking had wept with relief when they heard that Li had lost his battles with Wu San-kuei.[148] Sung Hsien-ts'e was heard to sigh, "My master is only a horseback king,"[149] and in the marketplaces vendors gibed:

> Tzu-ch'eng hacked his way to power—
> But he's not the son of heaven.
> He mounted the throne on horseback—
> But not for very long.[150]

Now, as the main body of Li's army departed, laden with loot and reinforced with conscripted townsfolk, the inhabitants of Peking took revenge upon the stragglers. Mobs formed to seize stray Shun soldiers and throw them into burning buildings. Other rebels were decapitated in the streets, "and the people's hearts were gladdened."[151] Li's policies had lost him the hearts of the masses and the "subjects of Shun" were no longer his.

Li's misrule in Peking also hardened the Manchus' inclinations toward conquest into a firm decision to intervene in China.[152] Prior to Li Tzu-ch'eng's occupation of Peking, the Ch'ing rulers had hesitated between two different alternatives—alternatives that constituted the major motifs of Abahai and Dorgon's foreign policy. There was, on the one hand, the tribal tradition of military aristocratism, vested in the beile and expressed through raiding expeditions over the wall which earned them merit and wealth. The beile were less inclined toward occupation of North China, especially since that was bound to strengthen the hand of Prince Regent Dorgon. But there was, on the other hand, the Chin tradition of imperial rule, symbolized by the Shun-chih emperor and fulfilled in the Ch'ing dynasty's committment to realize Nurhaci's "great enterprise" (*hung-yeh*). This second motif had not previously entailed the occupation of China because the Ch'ing had been able to take pride in its dealings with the Ming, as though both were simply several among many *kuo* competing for paramountcy in northeastern Asia. What tilted the balance in favor of the imperial alternative when the Ming fell was yet a third factor, which was less a motif than a presence: the Chi-

nese bannermen and their leaders. It was to these men that Dorgon
turned when the news of Li Tzu-ch'eng's occupation of Peking
reached Mukden, four hundred miles northeast of the Chinese capital. Dorgon particularly confided in Fan Wen-ch'eng, who had surrendered to the Manchus in 1618, and whose opinion he now
sought.[153]

Fan Wen-ch'eng enthusiastically recommended intervention, and
the reasons he gave show how critical Li Tzu-ch'eng's loss of legitimacy was for the later history of China. Even though Li Tzu-ch'eng's
troops were said to number almost a million, Fan thought that they
could be defeated because Li had lost all political support. By initially overthrowing the Ch'ung-chen emperor he had incurred
heaven's displeasure. Then, by abusing the gentry and officials,
he had aroused the literati's opposition. Now, in looting the capital,
raping commoners' wives, and burning people's homes, Li's soldiers
had earned the masses' hatred. The soldiers of the Ch'ing, therefore,
would enter China as a "righteous" army. "We will make certain that
it is known we are punishing them for their crimes. Since we will be
motivated by righteousness, how can we fail?"[154] Dorgon agreed:
the justification for Ch'ing conquest was to be punishment of the
rebels who had brought about the Ming emperor's death.

It was also Fan Wen-ch'eng, supported by another Chinese collab-
orator, Hung Ch'eng-ch'ou, who emphasized the importance of a
change in military tactics after the Manchus did intervene. In Hung's
view, successful intervention would depend upon altering the Sino-
Manchu forces' conventional policy of raiding for loot, bounty,
slaves, and livestock.[155] So advised, Dorgon assembled his generals
and beile before they crossed the wall at Shan-hai-kuan, and pledged
a covenant (yueh) to "save the people" through imperial pacification
(cheng) by not plundering, burning, or killing needlessly.[156] And on
May 20, after the Ch'ing armies entered China proper, Fan Wen-
ch'eng began preparing special proclamations to the Chinese people
that were to be distributed well in advance of their westward march.

> The righteous army comes to avenge your ruler-father for you.
> It is not an enemy of the people. The only ones to be killed now
> are the ch'uang bandits. Officials who surrender can resume their
> former posts. People who surrender can resume their former
> occupations. We will by no means harm you.[157]

It was these reassurances that opened the gates of cities all along the route to Peking, and that brought Ming garrison commanders over to the side of the Ch'ing.[158]

In Peking itself there were rumors of a "great army" coming from the East. A few even mentioned the Ch'ing by name.[159] But most of the officials who marched outside the city on the morning of June 5 to welcome their rescuers assumed that they would be hailing Wu San-kuei and the Ming crown prince.[160] Instead, they found themselves greeting a large force of Manchus, foreheads and temples shaved in tribal fashion. Dumbfounded, they watched as one of the Manchu leaders climbed up on the imperial chariot which palace attendants had brought to seat the Ming heir.

> He spoke to the people, saying, "I am the prince regent. The Ming crown prince will reach all of you in due course. He has assented to my being your ruler." Everyone in the crowd was startled and stared [at him], unable to comprehend. Meanwhile he continued to speak to the crowd. Someone said that he was the descendant of [the Ming emperor] Ying-tsung [who had been abducted by the Mongols]. The people were too frightened to act and had no means [of opposing him]. Thereupon the regent proceeded to enter [the Forbidden City].[161]

Escorted by the silk brocade guard, Dorgon ascended the steps of the smoldering Wu-ying palace.[162] When he reached the top, he turned and addressed the assembled officials, asking them to bring forward the most noble (*kuei*) in their ranks. Li Ming-jui, who had survived Liu Tsung-min's encampment unharmed, was hesitantly led up to Dorgon, who graciously asked him to become vice-president of the Ch'ing Board of Rites. Li quickly demurred: he was old and ill, he—. But Dorgon interrupted him before he could continue:

> The emperor of your dynasty has not yet been [properly] buried. Tomorrow I intend to order all of the officials and people of the capital to observe public mourning. But how can there be [proper] public mourning if there exists no ancestral tablet? And how can there be an ancestral tablet if no posthumous name has been conferred [by the Board of Rites]?[163]

Moved to tears, Li Ming-jui bowed and accepted the appointment, promising to assume responsibility for the imperial sacrifices.

Li Ming-jui's tears were genuine manifestations of relief—a relief shared by all of the others present. Dorgon's words had reassured them that their physical ordeal was over and that they no longer faced imprisonment or torture. Instead, they were assured of prompt employment under the new regime. As Dorgon made clear in a proclamation later that day, "Scholars of resolve will reap upright administration, meritorious fame, and pursuit of their vocation."[164] In the days that followed, as registration proceeded normally, gesture after gesture was made in the direction of former Ming officials. Ming titles were restored, and Dorgon even went so far as to rescind his order that Manchu hairdos be adopted, which had offended the bureaucracy.[165]

Even though Dorgon did not hesitate to decry late Ming bureaucratic practices, he did not condemn their practitioners—the beleaguered officials who were now encouraged to reform themselves.[166] Whereas Li Tzu-ch'eng had been moralistically offended by collaborators, Dorgon seemed to hold a much more tolerant and expedient view of human foibles. Long accustomed to the notion of twice-serving ministers, yet sensitive to the sensibilities of Confucianists, Dorgon did not govern according to extremely formulaic notions of virtue. His public rhetoric, prepared for him by Chinese collaborators like Fan Wen-ch'eng, was laced with abstract Confucian sentiments, but his concrete perception of public service was quite flexible. Dorgon possessed, in other words, a forgiving sense of exigency (ch'üan) that contrasted sharply with the crude and overbearing righteousness that had betrayed Li Tzu-ch'eng's original intent.[167] During one impeachment hearing, for instance, a Ch'ing official accused a colleague of having served under the Prince of Shun. Dorgon, detached from the moral reproof of that riven generation of literati, merely laughed and said, "The only people who can reproach others are those who have already established their own loyalty and purity."[168] Tolerance thus made it possible for Dorgon to recruit intact virtually the entire Peking bureaucracy—or what had survived of it after the Shun regime—for his new dynasty. By June 14 as one diarist commented, "the [area] above Ch'ang-an marketplace [was filled] once again with officials high and low," and once more, "is was just like old times."[169]

On that first day of Ch'ing rule when Dorgon addressed Peking's officialdom from the Wu-ying steps, Li Ming-jui's tears of gratitude had expressed more than sheer physical relief. They had also been signs of moral relief—and that sentiment, too, was shared by all the Ming officials present. Dorgon's concern that Ch'ung-chen's demise be properly observed by the dead emperor's own ministers absolved them of guilt over the fall of the dynasty. There would be no more retribution for them now. Instead, punishment would be meted out to the rebel who had earlier so harshly condemned them all: Li Tzu-ch'eng himself. As Dorgon proclaimed a few hours later that same day:

> [The Ming dynasty] has been extinguished by roving bandits, and its service [to Heaven] belongs to the past. But we need say no more. The empire is not an individual's private empire. Whosoever possesses virtue, holds it. The army and the people are not an individual's private possessions. Whosoever possesses virtue commands them. We now hold it, and so take revenge upon the enemy of your ruler-father in place of your dynasty.[170]

Cheng and *t'ung*—morality and unity—were seemingly fused in a single claim upon the throne. The Ch'ing, avenger of regicide, ruled legitimately because it was pledged to exterminate the rebels who had destroyed its predecessor. In this way Ch'ing succeeded Ming, and the Shun reign passed into history as a mere rebel interregnum. In Peking, at least, the new cycle had at last begun.

NOTES TO CHAPTER 2

1. Liu Shang-yu, *Ting-ssu hsiao-chi* [A modest record to settle my thoughts], in Chao I-ch'en and Wang Ta-lung, eds., *Ting-ch'ou ts'ung-pien* [Selections compiled in 1937] (Wu-hsi, 1937), *ts'e* 2, p. 1; Li Ch'ing, *San-yuan pi-chi* [Historical notes covering the years 1637–45], in *Ku-hsueh hui-k'an* [Sinological compilations], ser. 1 (Shanghai: Kuo-ts'ui hsueh-pao, 1913), *fu chung,* 12; Ch'ien Hsing, *Chia-shen ch'uan-hsin lu* [A credible record of 1644], in Wang Ling-kao, *Chung-kuo nei-luan wai-huo li-shih ts'ung-shu* [Historical collectanea of China's inner turmoil and outer grief] (Shanghai: Shen-chou kuo-kuang she, 1940), 12:7.

2. Chao Shih-chin, *Chia-shen chi-shih* [Chronology of the year 1644], in *Chia-shen chi-shih teng ssu-chung* [*Chia-shen chi-shih* and four others] (Shanghai: Chung-hua shu-chü, 1959), p. 7.

3. Ibid.

4. Wan Yen, *Ch'ung-chen ch'ang-pien* [Annalistic record of the Ch'ung-chen period], in Wang Ling-kao, *Chung-kuo nei-luan,* ser. 10 (Shanghai: Shen-chou kuo-kuang she, 1947), pp. 77–78. T'an Ch'ien, the great early Ch'ing historian of

the Ming, has a slightly different version of this memorial, in which Tseng described the wealthy as "deluding" the people. "When trouble approaches, they want the impoverished people to put forth efforts for mutual protection. [This] is irrational." Tseng went on to report accounts of the bandits torturing local gentry for "military rewards" which were paid over to the rebels in order to secure the gentrymen's release—a practice that was carried on later during the occupation of Peking. Since "the gentry and the wealthy" had to pay ransoms anyway, argued Tseng, they might as well follow the "equal fields method" (*chün-t'ien chih fa*) and distribute money to the poor before it was too late and rebels reached their door. This would be "a policy both to rescue the people and to disperse rebellion." T'an Ch'ien, *Kuo-ch'üeh* [An evaluation of the events of our dynasty], collated by Chang Tsung-hsiang (Peking: Ku-chi ch'u-pan-she, 1958), p. 6013. I would like to thank Professor Frederick Mote for directing my attention to this passage, as well as to other sections in the *Kuo-ch'üeh* cited later in this article.

5. Liu Shang-yu, *Ting-ssu*, p. 1.

6. Ch'en Chi-sheng, *Tsai-sheng chi-lüeh* [A brief chronicle of rebirth], in Cheng Chen-to, ed., *Hsuan-lan t'ang ts'ung-shu* [Collectanea from Hsuan-lan hall] (Nanking: Nanking Central Library, 1947), p. 3. His armies marched according to slogans which ordered them to "kill no one, accept no money, rape no one, loot nothing, trade fairly." Cited in Hsieh Kuo-chen, *Nan-Ming shih-lüeh* [Outline history of the Southern Ming] (Shanghai: Jen-min ch'u-pan-she, 1957), p. 28. Ming intelligence was normally quite poor. See, for example, Hsiao I-shan, *Ch'ing-tai t'ung-shih* [General history of the Ch'ing dynasty] (Shanghai: Commercial Press, 1927), 1:249; and Ku Ying-t'ai, *Ming-shih chi-shih pen-mo* [A narrative of Ming history from beginning to end], Chi-fu ts'ung-shu ed. (1879), 79:1a; and Ch'ien Hsing, *Chia-shen*, p. 8. This point is also made in Angela Hsi, "Wu San-kuei in 1644· A Reappraisal," *Journal of Asian Studies*, vol. 34, no. 2, p. 445.

7. For the influence of *Shui-hu chuan* on the rebels, many of whom took their titles from the novel, see Li Wen-chih, *Wan-Ming min-pien* [Popular revolts of the late Ming] (Shanghai: Chung-hua shu-chü, 1948), p. 197.

8. Cited in Hsieh Kuo-chen, *Nan-Ming*, pp. 23–24.

9. This broadsheet was found by Li Chien-t'ai's officers when he led the military expedition out of the capital. Tsou I, *Ming-chi i-wen* [Hearsay from the Ming dynasty], preface dated 1657 (Taipei: Bank of Taiwan, 1961), pp. 20–21.

10. Chao Shih-chin, *Chia-shen*, p. 6. Mr. Ch'eng I-fan first alerted me to the historical symbolism of the "selfish" refusal to contribute.

11. Ch'ien Hsing, *Chia-shen*, pp. 11–12. Chou reluctantly handed over 10,000 taels of his enormous fortune and then secretly ordered his daughter, Empress Chou, to contribute another 5,000 from her savings in his name. Li Wen-chih, *Wan-Ming*, p. 141.

12. This is Chao Shih-chin's estimate based upon the year-dates he saw stamped upon some of the ingots shipped out of Peking to Sian by the Shun rebels. Chao Shih-chin, *Chia-shen*, pp. 17–18.

13. Ch'ien Hsing, *Chia-shen,* p. 7. There was plenty of jewelry when Li took the palace, but only 200,000 taels in cash according to Li Ch'ing, *San-yuan, fu chung,* p. 22a. There is also evidence for this in a conversation that reportedly took place on February 10, 1644, between Ch'ung-chen and one of his most trusted counsellors, Li Ming-jui. Li begged the emperor to cover military costs by contributing moneys from his privy purse. The emperor answered that, "The privy purse is cleaned out." However, Li was skeptical and incredulously asked how all of the wealth accumulated by three centuries of Ming rulers could have been entirely squandered. The emperor's answer, which I take to be a reasonably frank and forthright response, was that, "There really isn't any [money left]." Tsou I, *Ming-chi,* p. 20. Tsou I is a particularly reliable source for this conversation because he was Wu Wei-yeh's disciple, and Wu, in turn, was a close friend of Li Ming-jui who probably recounted this to him. I should add that the emperor did have enough money in the privy purse to pay several tens of thousands of taels to provision the military forces of the eunuch Tu Hsun. Ch'ien Hsing, *Chia-shen,* p. 11.

14. Li Ch'ing, *San-yuan, fu chung,* p. 22a.

15. Pao Yang-sheng, *Chia-shen ch'ao-shih hsiao-chi san pien* [Minor annals of the affairs of the dynasty in 1644, 3d compilation], in *T'ung-shih* [Painful history] (Shanghai: Commercial Press, 1912), no. 21, 4:15a.

16. Chi Liu-ch'i, *Ming-chi pei-lüeh* [An outline of the Northern Ming] (Taipei: Bank of Taiwan, 1969), p. 397. Although Li Chien-t'ai had almost no military experience, he had considerable interest in protecting his family and property in Shansi from Li Tzu-ch'eng. Li's speech to the emperor is given in slightly different versions in P'eng Sun-i, *P'ing-k'ou chih* [On the pacification of the bandits] (Peiping: National Peiping Library, 1931), 8:3; and in the so-called *Ch'ung-chen shih-lu* [Veritable records of the Ch'ung-chen reign], 17:1a. The *Ch'ung-chen shih-lu* is not an official compilation, and its author is unknown. It appears in the *Pao-ching-lou pen* copy of the *Ming Veritable Records,* published by Liang Hung-chih as: *Ming shih-lu* [Veritable records of the Ming], photolithographic reprint of the manuscript copy formerly kept in the Kiangsu Provincial Library (Academia Sinica, Institute of History and Philology, 1940).

17. *Ming shih-lu,* 17:2; Ch'ien Hsing, *Chia-shen,* p. 8; P'eng Sun-i, *P'ing-k'ou chih,* 8:6.

18. Wen Ping, *Lieh-huang hsiao-chih* [Minor reminiscences of Emperor Chuang Lieh], in Wang Ling-kao, *Chung-kuo nei-luan* (Shanghai: Shen-chou kuo-kuang she, 1947), p. 226; T'an Ch'ien, *Tsao-lin tsa-tsu* [Miscellaneous dishes from a forest of jujubes] (Taipei: Hsin-hsing shu-chü, 1960), *jen,* 1b.

19. Chi Liu-ch'i, *Ming-chi pei-lüeh,* p. 414. T'an Ch'ien mentions Li Chien-t'ai's dispatch under an April 10 entry. See T'an Ch'ien, *Kuo-ch'üeh,* p. 6034.

20. Ch'ien Hsing, *Chia-shen,* p. 63; Li Ch'ing, *San-yuan, fu chung,* p. 22a; Tsou I, *Ch'i Chen yeh-ch'eng* [Wild chronicles from the (T'ien-) ch'i and (Ch'ung-) chen periods], reprint of Palace Museum edition of 1936 (Taipei: Wen-hai ch'u-pan-she, n.d.), pp. 441–42 (12:1). For Ni Yuan-lu's ideas on this question, see Ray Huang, "Ni Yuan-lu: 'Realism' in a Neo-Confucian Scholar-

Statesman," in Wm. Theodore de Bary, ed., *Self and Society in Ming Thought* (New York and London: Columbia University Press, 1970), pp. 420–22.

21. The two most detailed accounts of this audience I have found are in Tsou I, *Ming-chi*, pp. 18–20, 24, and Chi Liu-ch'i, *Ming-chi pei-lüeh*, pp. 393–94. They tally closely, though the former is more detailed. Because Tsou I bore a special relationship to Li Ming-jui (see n. 13 above), this account presents Li in a most favorable light. However, there seems to be no question of Li Ming-jui's crucial role in the effort to get the Ch'ung-chen emperor to transfer his capital to Nanking. See, for example, the relatively disinterested account in Tai Li and Wu Shu, *Huai-ling liu-k'ou shih-chung lu* [The Huai-ling record of the wandering bandits from beginning to end], cited in Li Kuang-t'ao, *Ming-chi-liu-k'ou shih-mo* [The Ming period wandering bandits from beginning to end] (Taipei: Institute of History and Philology, Academia Sinica, 1965), p. 79.

22. Tsou I, *Ming-chi*, p. 18; Chi Liu-ch'i, *Ming-chi pei-lüeh*, p. 393.

23. Tsou I, *Ming-chi*, pp. 20, 22–23; Ch'ien Hsing, *Chia-shen*, p. 10; Li Ch'ing, *San-yuan, fu chung*, p. 22a; P'eng Sun-i, *P'ing-k'ou chih*, 10:6b.

24. These altars were the *she-chi*. The *she-chi* was a cult of ancient China that most scholars have understood as being sacrifices to the earth god (*she*) and the god of grain (*chi*). The connection of these altars with emperorhood was always very close. See Ling Shun-sheng, "Chung-kuo ku-tai she chih yuan-liu" [The origin of the *she* in ancient China], *Chung-yang yen-chiu-yuan: min-tsu hsueh yen-chiu so chi-k'an* [Academia Sinica: Bulletin of the Institute of Ethnology], 17:1–44. Recovery of the *she-chi* constituted one of the main Southern Ming appeals to retake the northern plain. See, for example, Ku Yen-wu, *Sheng-an pen-chi* [Basic annals of Sheng-an], Ching-t'o i-shih ed. (Taipei: Bank of Taiwan, 1964), p. 37.

25. The following account is based upon a comparative use of Tsou I, *Ming-chi*, pp. 22–24; Chi Liu-ch'i, *Ming-chi pei-lüeh*, pp. 394, 411, and 480–82; Ch'ien Hsing, *Chia-shen*, p. 10; Liu Shang-yu, *Ting-ssu*, 3a; Wen Ping, *Lieh-huang*, p. 228; Ku Ying-t'ai, *Ming-shih*, 79:5; Li Ch'ing, *San-yuan, fu chung*, 19a. All these sources agree upon essentials, save the date of the audience, and most seem to feel it occurred on April 3, 1644. T'an Ch'ien, however, dates the audience April 5. See *Kuo-ch'üeh*, p. 6031.

26. Liu Shang-yu, *Ting-ssu*, 3a. Although T'an Ch'ien refrains from mentioning Kuang Shih-heng's role in the court debate, he does mention later that Kuang had opposed the recommendations to move south. T'an Ch'ien, *Kuo-ch'üeh*, p. 6053. Some believed at the time that Kuang Shih-heng resisted these suggestions because he had already been in touch with Li Tzu-ch'eng and planned to surrender to the rebel. Tai Li and Wu Shu, *Huai-ling liu-k'ou*, cited in Li Kuang-t'ao, *Ming-chi liu-k'ou shih-mo*, p. 79.

27. Wen Ping, *Lieh-huang*, p. 228; Tsou I, *Ming-chi*, p. 24. The wherewithal for such a move may not even have existed by this time, since the main roads south were probably cut. Li Hsun-chih, *Ch'ung-chen ch'ao yeh-chi* [Unofficial annals of the Ch'ung-chen court] (Taipei: Bank of Taiwan, 1968), p. 184.

28. Wen Ping, *Lieh-huang*, p. 228.

29. Chi Liu-ch'i, *Ming-chi pei-lüeh*, p. 414.

30. Ssu-ma Kuang, *Tzu-chih t'ung-chien* [Comprehensive mirror to the aid of government], annotated by Hu San-sheng (Taipei: Hung-yeh shu-chü, 1974), 118:6982.

31. Ibid., 118:6973-82.

32. Chi Liu-ch'i, *Ming-chi pei-lüeh*, p. 411.

33. Ibid., p. 414. See also pp. 424-25; and Tai Li and Wu Shu, *Huai-ling liu-k'ou*, in Li Kuang-t'ao, *Ming-chi liu-k'ou shih-mo*, p. 77, for the emperor's penitential edict dated April 17.

34. Ch'ien Hsing, *Chia-shen*, p. 16. This appears to be the primary account from which most others are derived. It forms the basis of the narration given in E. Backhouse and J. O. P. Bland, *Annals and Memoirs of the Court of Peking*, reprint (Taipei: Ch'eng-Wen Publishing Company, 1970), pp. 101-03.

35. Chi Liu-ch'i, *Ming-chi pei-lüeh*, p. 433, presents a slightly more favorable version, showing the emperor in a less demented and more sober state. An account similar to this one is also given in Chang Tai, *Shih-kuei ts'ang shu* [Writings stored in a stone case] (Shanghai: Chung-hua shu-chü, 1959), p. 43. In T'an Ch'ien's version, the emperor's demise is quite dignified. His drinking is also minimized. After writing off a letter to the duke of Ch'eng-kuo, Ch'ung-chen "ordered wine to be brought in. He drank several cups in succession, and sighed, 'All over the city our people are suffering.'" T'an Ch'ien, *Kuo-ch'üeh*, p. 6043. This same impression of a tragic and noble death was shared by many contemporaries. See ibid., pp. 6052-53.

36. The K'ang-hsi emperor, who later interviewed some of the old eunuchs who had served in the palace during the Ch'ung-chen reign, also learned of the emperor's attempt to flee. Jonathan D. Spence, *Emperor of China: Self-Portrait of K'ang-hsi* (New York: Alfred Knopf, 1974), p. 87.

37. Ch'ien Hsing, *Chia-shen*, p. 16.

38. Pao Yang-sheng, *Chia-shen ch'ao-shih hsiao chi* [Minor annals of the affairs of the dynasty in 1644], in *T'ung-shih*, no. 21, 1:2a. Ch'ung-chen especially blamed Wei Chung-hsien. Five days before Peking fell, he secretly ordered that Wei's bones be gathered and burned, but the command was never carried out. Ch'en Chi-sheng, *Tsai-sheng*, 6a.

39. Chi Liu-ch'i, *Ming-chi pei-lüeh*, p. 434.

40. Hsiao I-shan, *Ch'ing-tai*, 1:65.

41. Chao Shih-chin, *Chia-shen*, p. 11.

42. Wu Ch'ien, *Tung-chiang i-shih* [Extant facts about the Yalu border], preface dated 1806 (edited by Lo Chen-yü and published in 1935), preface, p. 1.

43. Cited in Chao Tsung-fu, "Li Tzu-ch'eng p'an-luan shih-lüeh [The rebellion of Li Tzu-ch'eng], *Shih-hsueh nien-pao* [Historical annual], 2.4:147.

44. Chao Shih-chin, *Chia-shen*, p. 10. Grand Secretary Fan Ching-wen, the highest-ranking official to commit suicide that day, thought that the emperor had escaped south as originally planned. Tsou I, *Ch'i chen*, p. 420 (11:9b); *Ming-shih* [The Ming dynastic history] (Taipei: Kuo-fang yen-chiu yuan, 1962),

2993.3 (ch. 265); Hsü Tzu, *Hsiao-t'ien chi-nien fu-k'ao* [Annals of an era of
little prosperity, with appended notations], annotated by Wang Ch'ung-wu
(Shanghai: Chung-hua shu-chü, 1957), p. 34; *Erh-ch'en chuan* [Biographies of
ministers who served both the Ming and Ch'ing dynasties (Peking, ordered
compiled in 1776), 12:17. At least twenty-eight high officials took their lives
after the emperor's death, but not all on April 25. For a list of these men, see
T'an Ch'ien, *Kuo-ch'üeh*, p. 6048.

45. Tsou I, *Ch'i chen*, p. 424 (11:11b).

46. T'an Ch'ien, *Kuo-ch'üeh*, p. 6050. Slightly different wording is given in
Huang Tsung-hsi, *Nan-lei wen-ting* [Literary fixations from the Nan-lei studio],
Ssu-pu pei-yao ed. (Taipei: Chung-hua shu-chü, 1966), *ch'ien-chi*, 5:8b; Chi
Liu-ch'i, *Ming-chi pei-lüeh*, p. 483; and P'eng Sun-i, *P'ing-k'ou chih*, 9:10.

47. Wen Jui-lin, *Nan-chiang i-shih* [A continuous history of the southern
frontier] (Taipei: Bank of Taiwan, 1959), p. 237.

48. P'eng Sun-i, *P'ing-k'ou chih*, 10:1a. Many of these slogans were prepared
by Li Chih-sheng. Li, a *chin-shih* of 1634, was formerly a Shansi director of
studies. Li Tzu-ch'eng put him in charge of examinations within the Hanlin
Academy and made him a grand secretary. Ch'ien Hsing, *Chia-shen*, p. 116.

49. Ibid., p. 18.

50. Chao Shih-chin, *Chia-shen*, p. 9.

51. Hsiao I-shan, *Ch'ing-tai*, 1:255. This accusation was repeated in his conversation with the crown prince, who was assured by the rebel that he would
retain his wealth and noble status. Chao Shih-chin, *Chia-shen*, p. 9; Chang Tai,
Shih-kuei, p. 45; Ch'ien Pang-i, *Chia-shen chi-pien-lu* [An account of the transition of 1644] (Taipei: Bank of Taiwan, 1968), p. 13.

52. Chao Tsung-fu, "Li Tzu-ch'eng," p. 147.

53. Ch'ien Hsing, *Chia-shen*, p. 15.

54. Hsieh Kuo-chen, *Nan-Ming*, pp. 28–29; P'eng Sun-i, *P'ing-k'ou chih*,
10:1a.

55. Despite his prominent position in the Shun regime, little is said about
Sung Ch'i-chiao in the standard biographical sources. In fact, it is almost as
though his activities were expunged in shame, as he was among the collaborators
sentenced to death by dismemberment by the Prince of Fu's regime. A *chin-
shih* of 1628, he came from a prominent gentry family in Ch'ien-chou, Shansi,
serving as prefectural judge in Yangchow and vice-director of the Ministry of
Personnel before returning to his home district some time around 1634. In
1634–35, Ch'ien-chou was twice occupied by Li Tzu-ch'eng: once after he was
defeated by Hung Ch'eng-ch'ou at Hsiang-yang, and once again after a similar
defeat at Wu-kung. According to the local gazetteer, Li surrounded the walled
hsien capital and spread word that he especially valued Sung Ch'i-chiao. If Sung
were to surrender to him willingly, then he—Li—would spare the city. Tremendous public pressure was brought to bear upon Sung, and the street outside his
house filled with elders and townsmen pleading that he agree to serve the rebel.
He finally gave in and joined Li, even though his wife, the granddaughter of a
well-known official named Wen, committed suicide in protest. Chou Ming-ch'i,

comp., *Ch'ien-chou chih kao* [Draft gazetteer of Ch'ien-chou], 1884 ed. (Taipei: Ch'eng-wen Book Company, 1969), pp. 458, 496–97. See also Chi Liu-
ch'i, *Ming-chi pei-lüeh,* p. 621; *Ming-shih* (Kuo-fang ed.), 2977.9 (ch. 254),
3091.7 (ch. 275); Hsü Tzu, *Hsiao-t'ien fu-k'ao,* p. 27.

56. James B. Parsons, *Peasant Rebellions of the Late Ming Dynasty* (Tucson:
University of Arizona Press, 1970), pp. 91–92.

57. Chao Tsung-fu, "Li Tzu-ch'eng," p. 138.

58. Ibid., p. 147. Niu also cited the sixteenth-century philosopher, Li Chih,
as an example to Li Tzu-ch'eng of literati respecting great popular leaders.
Parsons says (p. 93) that Niu only held the *kung-sheng* degree, but other sources
place him in the *chü-jen* class of 1617 along with Li Yen. See, for example,
Ch'ien Hsing, *Chia-shen,* p. 74. According to Rossabi's essay in this volume, Niu
may have been a Muslim. Chao Shih-chin's jailer, Yao Ch'i-ying, told him that
Niu was from Pao-chi county in Honan and was a heavy drinker who developed
a foul temper when in his cups. He revealed this side of his nature to his son's
father-in-law, a prominent local *chin-shih,* who was also shocked when Niu
drunkenly beat up a district clerk. The father-in-law and magistrate had Niu
jailed on criminal charges and he was stripped of his *chü-jen* rank. Li Tzu-ch'eng
released Niu from jail. Chao Shih-chin, *Chia-shen,* p. 17. Other accounts suggest
that Niu was introduced to Li by a doctor named Shang Chiung and stress his
abilities as a military strategist and mathematician. Li Wen-chih, *Wan-Ming,*
p. 106. According to a 1647 memorial from the Ch'ing metropolitan censor,
Hang Ch'i-su, which appears in the *Ming-Ch'ing shih-liao* collection (*ping,* p.
618), Niu Chin-hsing later surrendered to the Ch'ing. See Li Kuang-t'ao, *Ming-
chi liu-k'ou shih-mo,* p. 86.

59. Li had studied the Confucian classics when he was holed up in the Shang-
lo mountains along the borders of Honan, Hupeh, and Shensi in the winter of
1638. Li Wen-chih, *Wan-Ming,* p. 100. According to Li Tung-fang, while Li
Tzu-ch'eng occupied Hsiang-yang, Niu lectured to him daily. Li Tung-fang,
Hsi-shuo Ming-ch'ao [Minutiae of Ming history] (Taipei: Wen-hsing shu-tien,
1964), p. 428. However, Li Tung-fang does not provide any reference for this
statement, for which I have been unable to find corroboration.

60. In the summer of 1643 Niu advised Li to march directly north from
Hsiang-yang to Peking. Another gentry adherent, Ku Chü-en, instead proposed
developing a base first in Shensi. Li Wen-chih, *Wan-Ming,* pp. 124–25.

61. Chao Shih-chin insisted that a regular government was left behind in Sian
when the rebels came to Peking and that the ministers appointed to the former
Ming yamens in the capital were all just vice-ministers of the Sian government.
Chao Shih-chin, *Chia-shen,* p. 12. This is not supported by other evidence. See,
for example, Li Wen-chih, *Wan-Ming,* p. 128. Chang Lin-jan surrendered P'ing-
yang to Li, who asked him and two other officials to write denunciations of the
Ming emperor. Because Chang wrote his in couplets, while the other two used
straight prose, Chang was singled out for recognition and made minister of works
in the rebel *hsing-tsai.* In Peking, Chang was put in charge of Li's personal
treasury and could come and go in the palace as he pleased. Chao Shih-chin,
Chia-shen, p. 10.

62. Chao Shih-chin, *Chia-shen*, p. 7.

63. This roster is basically derived from information given in Ch'ien Hsing, *Chia-shen*, pp. 74–88. There is a more inclusive list in Li Wen-chih, *Wan-Ming*, p. 138. It differs from mine in a few details, for example, in stating that Po Ching-hsing surrendered to Li in Shensi rather than in Honan.

64. Pao Yang-sheng, *Chia-shen hsiao chi*, 5:1b; Ch'ien Pang-i, *Chia-shen*, p. 15; Hsü Tzu, *Hsiao-t'ien fu-k'ao*, p. 126.

65. Li Wen-chih, *Wan-Ming*, p. 136; Chao Shih-chin, *Chia-shen*, p. 10.

66. There were so many office seekers of this sort that Sung Ch'i-chiao was heard to wonder aloud, "How are we going to employ such a mob?" Feng Meng-lung, *Chia-shen chi-wen* [Hearsay recorded from 1644], in Cheng Chen-to, *Hsuan-lan t'ang*, 11a.

67. Both examinations were arranged around the theme of the transfer of the Heavenly Mandate. P'eng Sun-i, *P'ing-k'ou chih*, 10:9b, 11a. Seventy sat for the latter examination and fifty were passed, going on in some cases to receive appointments as magistrates. Ch'ien Hsing, *Chia-shen*, pp. 95–100; Pao Yang-sheng, *Chia-shen hsiao chi*, 5:1b.

68. Feng Meng-lung, *Chia-shen*, 5b; P'eng Sun-i, *P'ing-k'ou chih*, 9:7; Ch'ien Hsing, *Chia-shen*, pp. 79, 91; Ch'en Chi-sheng, *Tsai-sheng*, 1:17b.

69. The following is mainly based upon Chao Shih-chin, *Chia-shen*, pp. 7–9.

70. Feng Meng-lung, *Chia-shen*, 5a; Hsü Ying-fen, *Yü-pien chi-lüeh* [A general record of experiencing dynastic change], Ching-t'o i-shih ed. (Tao-kuang period), 5b–6a.

71. Ch'ien Hsing, *Chia-shen*, p. 17; James Parsons, *Peasant Rebellions*, pp. 134–36. Before Li entered the city, Niu Chin-hsing had warned him that since he was now taking over the empire, he must not allow his men to slaughter indiscriminately. Liu Shang-yu, *Ting-ssu*, 2a. There were some shouted commands to the populace as the rebels entered: "If anybody has donkeys or horses, they must quickly contribute them. Any who dare conceal them will be beheaded." Chao Shih-chin, *Chia-shen*, p. 9.

72. Chao Shih-chin saw this himself. Chao Shih-chin, *Chia-shen*, p. 9.

73. *Erh-ch'en*, 12:17. Chang Chin-yen, who does not have a biography in the *Ming-shih*, was a native of Honan who had first served as a magistrate and then became a compiler in the Hanlin Academy. It was he who, while serving as a supervising secretary in the Ministry of War, impeached Yang Ssu-ch'ang and later became minister of war himself. *Ming-shih* (Kuo-fang ed.), 290.4; Hsü Tzu, *Hsiao-t'ien fu-k'ao*, p. 27.

74. Chao Tsung-fu, "Li Tzu-ch'eng," pp. 147–48. Parsons mistook their garb for convict's clothing, perhaps because of ambiguities in P'eng Sun-i, *P'ing-k'ou chih*, 9:12–14.

75. Feng Meng-lung, *Chia-shen*, 5b; Ch'en Chi-sheng, *Tsai-sheng*, 1:17b; Hsü Ying-fen, *Yü-pien*, p. 6; Chao Tsung-fu, "Li Tzu-ch'eng," p. 148; Ch'ien Hsing, *Chia-shen*, pp. 54–55; P'eng Sun-i, *P'ing-k'ou chih*, 9:12a.

76. Feng Meng-lung, *Chia-shen*, 5b.

77. Ch'ien Hsing, *Chia-shen*, pp. 33, 64.

78. Chao Shih-chin, *Chia-shen*, p. 10.

79. Ibid.

80. Ch'ien Hsing, *Chia-shen*, p. 76; P'eng Sun-i, *P'ing-k'ou chih*, 10:2; anon., *Kuo-pien nan-ch'en ch'ao* [Notes on suffering officials during the dynastic change], in *San-ch'ao yeh-chi* [Unofficial annals of the T'ai-ch'ang, T'ien-ch'i and Ch'ung-chen periods], Wang Ling-kao, *Chung-kuo nei-luan* (Shanghai: Shen-chou kuo-kuang she, 1947), p. 185.

81. Ch'ien Hsing, *Chia-shen*, pp. 92–94, 96–97; Hsü Tzu, *Hsiao-t'ien fu-k'ao*, pp. 117, 124.

82. Ch'ien Hsing, *Chia-shen*, p. 96.

83. Ibid., pp. 96–97; Chi Liu-ch'i, *Ming-chi pei-lüeh*, p. 584.

84. Where and how Chao and Sung became close friends is not mentioned. Chi Liu-ch'i, *Ming-chi pei-lüeh*, p. 584; Hsü Tzu, *Hsiao-t'ien fu-k'ao*, p. 117.

85. James T. C. Liu, *Ou-yang Hsiu: An Eleventh-Century Neo-Confucianist* (Stanford: Stanford University Press, 1967), p. 111.

86. *Ming-shih* (Kuo-fang ed.), 2779.8 (ch. 244); P'eng Sun-i, *P'ing-k'ou chih*, 11:3b–4a.

87. Ch'ien Hsing, *Chia-shen*, p. 76; Feng Meng-lung, *Chia-shen*, 8b. Chou Chung helped orchestrate the campaign to persuade Li Tzu-ch'eng to actually become emperor. Chao Tsung-fu, "Li Tzu-ch'eng," p. 149.

88. Chao Tsung-fu, "Li Tzu-ch'eng," p. 148.

89. Accounts of the audience differ with respect to dates. Because Chao Shih-chin's account seems so genuine, I am taking the 29th to be correct.

90. Chao Shih-chin, *Chia-shen*, p. 11.

91. Chao Tsung-fu, "Li Tzu-ch'eng," pp. 148–49.

92. Ch'ien Hsing, *Chia-shen*, p. 14.

93. Ibid., pp. 54–55.

94. Hsü Tzu, *Hsiao-t'ien chi-nien* [Annals of an era of little prosperity] (Nanking: 1887), pp. 115–16. The phrase is from the *Analects*, bk. 19, ch. i.

95. Ch'ien Hsing, *Chia-shen*, p. 73.

96. Such men were usually from Shensi.

97. Ch'ien Hsing, *Chia-shen*, p. 86.

98. Niu Chin-hsing had renamed the Hanlin Academy the *Hung-wen kuan*, but to avoid confusion I continue to use the Ming designation.

99. P'eng Sun-i, *P'ing-k'ou chih*, 9:16a.

100. Chao Shih-chin claimed that 96 were chosen and that he was among them. He refused to serve and was taken away with the other prisoners. Chao Shih-chin, *Chia-shen*, p. 11.

101. Ch'ien Hsing, *Chia-shen*, pp. 55, 73, 116.

102. Thus it was mainly older men of great repute who committed suicide, such as the censor-in-chief Li Pang-hua, of the class of 1604.

103. Ch'ien Hsing, *Chia-shen*, pp. 74–88.

104. Ibid.

105. Ibid., pp. 81–82; Chi Liu-ch'i, *Ming-chi pei lüeh*, pp. 578–79.

106. P'eng Sun-i, *P'ing-k'ou chih*, 10:2.

107. Ch'ien Hsing, *Chia-shen*, p. 83; Chi Liu-ch'i, *Ming-chi pei-lüeh*, p. 584; Hsu Tzu, *Hsiao-t'ien fu-k'ao*, p. 115.

108. Li Wen-chih, *Wan-Ming*, p. 102.

109. Ibid., p. 103. Parsons (p. 65) places this incident in 1638, when Li was defeated by Hung Ch'eng-ch'ou. I believe he may be mistaken.

110. James Parsons, *Peasant Rebellions*, p. 93; Susan Naquin, *Millenarian Rebellion in China: The Eight Trigrams Uprising of 1813*, (Yale University Press, 1976), p. 15.

111. Ch'ien Hsing, *Chia-shen*, p. 74; Hsü Ying-fen, *Yü-pien*, 9b.

112. Chao Tsung-fu, "Li Tzu-ch'eng," p. 149; James Parsons, *Peasant Rebellions*, p. 142. Chao Shih-chin steadfastly refused to believe Li ever really had the intention of becoming emperor, because his supply carts were constantly shipping treasure out of Peking to Sian. Chao Shih-chin, *Chia-shen*, p. 15.

113. Chao Shih-chin, *Chia-shen*, p. 16.

114. This conversation was overheard by Chao Shih-chin. Ibid., p. 12.

115. Ibid., p. 14.

116. Li Wen-chih, *Wan-Ming*, pp. 136–37.

117. Ch'ien Hsing, *Chia-shen*, pp. 57–58. He may even have ordered him beaten to death by Liu Tsung-min. One source claims that Li Kuo-chen hanged himself. Wu Wei-yeh, *Wu-shih chi-lan* [Collected readings of the poetry of Wu], Ssu-pu pei yao ed. (Taipei: Bank of Taiwan, 1966), 1 *shang*:14b.

118. Pao Yang-sheng, *Chia-shen hsiao chi*, 5:1b; P'eng Sun-i, *P'ing-k'ou chih*, 10:3.

119. Kuo Mo-jo, *Chia-shen san-pai nien chi* [The third centennial of 1644], revised edition (Peking: Jen-min ch'u-pan-she, 1972), p. 22. Kuo cites Chi Liu-ch'i, *Ming-chi pei-lüeh*. See also Huang Chih-chün, comp., *Chiang-nan t'ung-chih* [The provincial gazetteer of Kiangnan], 1737 ed. (Taipei: Ching-hua Book Company, 1967), p. 2585 (153:29a).

120. This schedule was harsher than Li Yen's original plan, which ordered officials of the first rank to redeem themselves by paying 10,000 taels, and those of lower ranks, 1,000. Li Yen's supposedly moderating influence may merely reflect traditional historiography. See James B. Parsons, "Attitudes toward the Late Ming Rebellions," *Oriens Extremus* 6:182.

121. Unless otherwise noted, the information on torture is from Chao Shih-chin, *Chia-shen*, pp. 12–14.

122. Li Wen-chih, *Wan-Ming*, p. 143.

123. Intelligence report appended to Chao Shih-chin, *Chia-shen*, p. 25.

124. These were modeled after regular judicial torture instruments, except that the nails were designed to protrude so that the flesh was torn as well. Thousands of these vises were manufactured and supplied to the other encampments as needed.

125. Ch'ien Hsing, *Chia-shen*, p. 56.

126. Former Grand Secretary Ch'en Yen, for instance, managed to secure 40,000 taels which he handed over to Liu in exchange for his freedom. Accord-

ing to T'an Ch'ien, Ch'en Yen was tortured by having his feet bound, perhaps in some kind of a press, until he turned over 360 ounces of gold and dug up another 10,000 ounces of silver. T'an Ch'ien, *Kuo-ch'üeh,* p. 6061.

127. Li Wen-chih, *Wan-Ming,* pp. 142–43; Chi Liu-ch'i, *Ming-chi pei-lüeh,* p. 447; T'an Ch'ien *Kuo-ch'üeh,* p. 6062. T'an Ch'ien, *Tsao-lin, jen*:2b, gives the figure of 1,600. Hsü Ying-fen, *Yü-pien,* p. 7a, a contemporary diary, reports 1,000 dead.

128. Chao Shih-chin, *Chia-shen,* p. 13; T'an Ch'ien, *Kuo-ch'üeh,* p. 6062. According to the latter, Wei Ts'ao-te paid 13,000 ounces of gold.

129. Chao Shih-chin, *Chia-shen,* p. 14.

130. Ibid., p. 13.

131. Ibid., p. 14.

132. Ibid., p. 15.

133. Ibid., p. 13.

134. Li Wen-chih, *Wan-Ming,* p. 142.

135. Chao Shih-chin, *Chia-shen,* p. 11.

136. Ibid., p. 9.

137. Hsü Ying-fen, *Yü-pien,* 7b–8a.

138. Ch'ien Hsing, *Chia-shen,* p. 55.

139. Ibid., pp. 30, 54; anon., *Pei-shih pu-i* [Supplementary remains of events in the North], in Cheng Chen-to, *Hsuan-lan t'ang,* 4a.

140. Hsiao I-shan, *Ch'ing-tai,* 1:251.

141. Hsieh Kuo-chen, *Nan-Ming,* p. 41; James Parsons, *Peasant Rebellions,* p. 134.

142. Ch'ien Hsing, *Chia-shen,* p. 56.

143. These included Ch'en Yen, Ch'iu Yü, and Chu Shun-ch'en.

144. Many people felt that Li would not return victorious. Hsü Ying-fen cast the changes that day and threw a *k'un,* which convinced him that a new ruler was on his way. Hsü Ying-fen, *Yü-pien,* 10b–12a.

145. Ibid., 12a.

146. Ibid., 14a; James Parsons, *Peasant Rebellions,* pp. 134–42.

147. Liu Shang-yu, *Ting-ssu,* 8a.

148. Ibid., p. 7a; Hsü Ying-fen, *Yü-pien,* p. 12.

149. Ch'en Chi-sheng, *Tsai-sheng,* p. 20a.

150. Ibid., p. 20b.

151. Liu Shang-yu, *Ting-ssu,* p. 8a. For the critical importance of Li's loss of support among the gentry and officials, see Li Wen-chih, *Wan-Ming min-pien,* pp. 165–66.

152. *Shih-lu (Shun-chih)* [The veritable records of the Shun-chih reign], photoreprint (Taipei: Hua-wen shu-chü, 1964), 4:42b, 44.

153. Fan had joined the Manchus when Fu-shun fell in 1618. Li Yuan-tu, *Kuo-ch'ao hsien-cheng shih-lüeh* [Biographical sketches of former worthies of the ruling dynasty] (P'ing-chiang, 1866), 1:1b. See also Fan Wen-ch'eng's biography by Fang Chao-ying, in Arthur O. Hummel, *Eminent Chinese of the Ch'ing Period* (Washington: Government Printing Office, 1944), pp. 231–32.

154. Hsiao I-shan, *Ch'ing-tai*, 1:258. Fan's role in promoting the Manchu conquest is also recognized in Li Yuan-tu, *Kuo-ch'ao hsien-cheng shih-lüeh*, 1:1b: "At the time when the Prince [Regent Dorgon's] army entered [Shan-hai-] kuan, [Fan] was the first to settle on the great plan, advising [Dorgon] to enter [with his] troops." This source also points out that all of Dorgon's decrees, edicts, announcements, and so forth, were written by Fan.

155. *Shih-lu (Shun-chih)*, 4:44.

156. Ibid., 4:45–48a; Hsiao I-shan, *Ch'ing-tai*, 1:261.

157. Hsiao I-shan, *Ch'ing-tai*, 1:261. The phrase *tai-pao chün-fu chih ch'ou* was repeated frequently. See Hsieh Kuo-chen, p. 55.

158. *Shih-lu (Shun-chih)*, 4:48.

159. Liu Shang-yu, *Ting-ssu*, 8b.

160. Chi Liu-ch'i, *Ming-chi pei-lüeh*, p. 33. The crown prince had disappeared after being held in custody by Li Tzu-ch'eng.

161. Liu Shang-yu, *Ting-ssu*, 8b.

162. *Erh-ch'en*, 12:4a–5b.

163. Chi Liu-ch'i, *Ming-chi pei-lüeh*, pp. 33–34.

164. Hsiao I-shan, *Ch'ing-tai*, 1:262.

165. Ibid., 1:265. Hsiao I-shan does not date this decree. It is given as the sixth lunar month, but with the days deleted, in T'an Ch'ien, *Pei-yu lu* [Record of travels in the North] (Hong Kong: Lung-men Book Company, 1969), p. 354.

166. Hsiao I-shan, *Ch'ing-tai*, 1:263, 380; Li Kuang-t'ao, comp., *Ming-Ch'ing tang-an ts'un-chen hsuan-chi* [Photographic reproductions of selected documents from the Ming and Ch'ing archives], 1st series (Taipei: Institute of History and Philology, Academia Sinica, 1959), pl. 5, p. 6.

167. Contrasting Yang Chu's egoism with Mo Ti's altruism, Mencius said: "Tzu-mo holds a medium [between these]. By holding that medium, he is nearer the right. But by holding it without leaving room for exigency (*ch'üan*), it becomes like their holding one point. The reason why I hate holding to one point is the injury it does to the Way. It takes up one point and disregards a hundred others." *Mencius* 7.1.27. This is a slightly altered version of the translation given in James Legge, *The Chinese Classics* (Oxford, 1894), 2:465.

168. Sun Chen-t'ao, *Ch'ing-shih shu-lun* [A detailed discussion of Ch'ing history] (Taipei: Ya-chou ch'u-pan-she, 1957), p. 37.

169. Hsü Ying-fen, *Yü-pien*, p. 18b.

170. Hsiao I-shan, *Ch'ing-tai*, 1:262.

3

Hsü Tu and the Lesson of Nanking
Political Integration and the Local Defense in Chiang-nan, 1634–1645

by Jerry Dennerline

Local Militia

In previous historical treatments, the Nanking regime of the Ming restorationist prince of Fu has been seen either as a dramatic case of court factionalism or as an example of the tensions among "loyalist" resistance, corrupt incompetence, and collaboration. We have received the picture of a Nanking court, dominated by Ma Shih-ying and Juan Ta-ch'eng, driving Shih K'o-fa and other loyalists into ineffective protest until those same loyalists launched a last desperate resistance to the Ch'ing that brought destruction on their heads, and upon their local communities. These were the "loyalist" heroes who stood in sharp contrast both to the Ch'ing collaborationists and the eunuch-ridden and helpless restoration courts, and they have been so presented in the histories of Tung-lin partisans, late nineteenth-century anti-Ch'ing writers, and twentieth-century Chinese nationalists.

By using the Hsü Tu affair as his focus, Jerry Dennerline radically changes these historical perspectives, for through Hsü Tu he shows that there was an intensely serious crisis of political organization and local control in the area around Nanking in 1643 and 1644. In this crisis we can see that there was not, at least in this area, any unified "gentry" that included both the local landowning elite and the holders of bureaucratic office, and could serve as an integrative force for purposes of national and local defense. If the restorationists (of whatever persuasion) were to succeed, they had to integrate the local society into the political structure, and in this task they failed.

This is local history, not just at the level of prefectural or hsien elites, but also below this, in the world of village organization, where one can find around 180 rural compacts in Chin Sheng's paramilitary organization in the one hsien of Hui-chou alone. This problem of paramilitary organization was perhaps the crucial one that separated out local activists linked to the "Tung-lin partisan" side of the bureaucratic elite from the local landowning powers: there was a real threat to local concepts of the status quo in either Chin Sheng's ideas for total participation of villagers of both sexes in a disciplined militia, or in Ch'i Piao-chia's expanded antibandit crop-watching corps, or in Ch'en Tzu-lung's land and riverine professionalized police force. Of Dennerline's four militia examples, only Hou T'ung-tseng

91

was for stricter "control" in the traditionally valid pao-chia *sense of that term.*

Hsü Tu dramatically threatened the local balancing act that restorationist leaders were trying to perform; as a committed and talented military commander, he could defend his local area from attack, but his defense forces cut across too many local elite prerogatives to permit the men he sought to protect to let him live. Since these local interests were needed by the restoration bureaucrats, since integration had not been achieved, they acquiesced in Hsü Tu's death. And it was this acquiescence, ironically, which could be turned against them when factional struggles in the prince of Fu's court grew more bitter in late 1644. Dennerline shows how such an analysis can be built up from a basis of late Ming Tung-lin sources by combining detailed reading in the local gazetteers with some unofficial chronicles and one rare diary of a key participant, Ch'i Piao-chia's Chia-i jih-li, *made available in Taiwan in 1969.*

THE HISTORIOGRAPHICAL CONTEXT

The fall of Peking in 1644 marked the end of the Ming dynasty. The Manchu conquest of China followed. Historians have aptly described these events in great detail, and their descriptions are full of lessons based on the behavior of the historical actors. Many of the figures involved in the struggle for political control have become legendary in modern times, and the tales of Manchu atrocities are legion.[1] Those figures which survive in popular historical narratives and fiction as national heroes were loyalists, men who chose to die for the Ming house rather than submit to the new Ch'ing overlords. Most were members of the bureaucratic elite—holders of Ming civil service degrees or sons and grandsons of Ming officials.[2] Recently, Chinese historians have added to the ranks of heroic figures the less prominent leaders of towns and village resistance movements, as well as shopkeepers, fishermen, peasants, menials, and other Ming subjects who fought against foreign domination. The popular view of the

This essay would not have been written without the help of a research grant from Pomona College during the summer of 1974.

period of conquest now involves elements of patriotism, nationalism, loyalism, and ethnic pride.[3]

But the modern historian who is concerned with the development of social and political forms rather than the transfer of dynastic power and its emotive symbols, finds most of his questions un-answered. Given the high rate of resistance throughout the Yangtze valley and the south, why was the native political structure unable to survive the Ch'ing challenge? If the resistance leaders were at once the representatives of Ming authority and the natural leaders of local society, why were they unable to retain control of their home districts when Ch'ing magistrates with no local reputation or connec-tions arrived to take office? With such an abundance of Ming princes and pretenders, provincial armies and powerful warlords, loyalist ministers and gentry stalwarts roaming the south until the 1680s, why did popular nativist sentiment not provide them with the strength to expel the invaders?

Traditional historians have explained the failure of China's defenses in terms of administrative ineptitude and factional conflict. In their view, Ming officialdom had become so corrupt that any attempt to marshal a force sufficient to defeat the disciplined Ch'ing army was doomed to failure. Moreover, the official elite was hopelessly divided by particularistic loyalties, revealing a callous disregard for common political goals. Unity was impossible and selfish interests prevented even the most able loyalists from organizing an opposition to the common enemy. Warlords switched sides; officials followed. Fac-tions fought factions and able men withdrew to hermitages. Private self-sacrifice and martyrdom replaced political leadership, and the resulting fragmentation left China easy prey to the efficient Manchu military machine.

In the People's Republic of China the traditional explanation still stands, enhanced by concepts of class conflict and a frustrated emer-gent bourgeoisie. Popular resistance threatened elite interests, and disloyal officials turned rapidly to the Ch'ing for protection against the forces which resistance had unleashed. Loyalists, too, frustrated the warlords in their attempts to expel the invaders; for, the war-lords' armies would upset the very political order which made civil officials the leaders of the loyalist cause. According to communist writers, the most progressive elements within the resistance were merchants, strong enough to help raise armies but helpless against the tide of rural reaction which turned to the Ch'ing for protection.

Both traditional and modern historiography stress a single theme in explaining the failure of resistance during the long period of conquest and consolidation—political fragmentation in the face of the efficient military regime. The arguments are persuasive but they continue to beg the question of local political structure. Every argument assumes that loyalists were the natural social leaders who represented the common interests of local communities, and that fragmentation was the result of private, isolated group interests. One is forced to conclude that local leadership was divided and that the reactionary elite took good advantage of the division to call on the Ch'ing protectors to preserve order in their own selfish interest. But, up to now, historians have presented the case so completely in the context of dynastic competition that they have never really examined the problem of local leadership itself. If we are to understand the meaning which the Ch'ing conquest and the fall of the Ming had for local society, it is time for a revision.

My purpose in this essay is to shift the focus of discussion from dynastic politics and factional intrigue to problems of political organization and local control. My subject thus relates one event which has attracted much attention in the annals of loyalism, the failure of the Ming restoration in the southern capital of Nanking in 1644, to another one which appears only as a footnote in scattered sources, the rebellion of Hsü Tu in the hills of central Chekiang some eighteen months earlier. The relationship is tenuous; but if overstated here, it should at least serve to stimulate further investigation into the unsolved maze of local politics which underlay the events historians have already described so voluminously.

The events of the restoration and their background are well known.[4] Shortly after the fall of Peking a group of ministers, officials, and noblemen in Nanking met to decide on a course of action for the south. After some deliberation, they decided to invite the Ming prince of Fu, grandson of the Wan-li emperor (reigned 1573–1620), to serve as head of a caretaker regime until the fate of the late Ch'ung-chen emperor's own sons could be known. The major bureaucratic faction in Nanking, under the leadership of Shih K'o-fa, the southern minister of war, accepted this decision with reservations. The prince was reputedly a ne'er-do-well and had the misfortune to be the scion of a branch which had caused one of the greatest dynastic crises in Ming history. His father had been the favorite of the Wan-li emperor during the early years of his reign, but some factions, traditionally assumed to be the progenitors of the one referred to as Tung-lin, argued that the favorite could not legitimately succeed the emperor and demanded that the rightful heir be formally designated. This argument eventually won out and the favorite was enfeoffed at Honanfu in 1601 with the title prince of Fu.[5]

This settled the succession dispute but the factional division at court only worsened. During the 1620s another faction had emerged by supporting the most powerful household eunuch, Wei Chung-hsien, and with paranoid consistency the eunuch-controlled regime purged the central bureaucracy of all who could be labeled Tung-lin, martyring six censors and solidifying the opposition of a significant portion of the southern bureaucratic elite. Tung-lin power rose again with the accession of the Ch'ung-chen emperor in 1628, and those who had associated themselves with the last regime fell into disrepute. The new emperor labeled the offending faction "seditious" (*ni tang*), listing its members and forbidding their participation in administrative affairs. Therefore in 1644, the appearance of the prince of Fu in Nanking threatened to revive the factional strife of the 1620s. Shih K'o-fa, who had taken the Tung-lin side himself in the 1620s, faced the problem of stilling the factional storm that threatened. The failure of the restoration was due, in part, to his inability to do so.

At first glance the distance from Shih K'o-fa to Hsü Tu seems great.[6] Hsü was dead before the fall of Peking, executed for open rebellion against the Ming magistrate in his native Tung-yang. Grandson of a Ming official, Hsü himself had not won elite status nor fought political battles at court but had withdrawn from competition in order to pursue the martial arts. He appears to have had a considerable following in the rural area around his home but traditional chroniclers have not provided much detail. His name appears in the annals of the restoration in a somewhat mysterious connection. In 1645, at the height of the factional struggle as the anti-Tung-lin forces began to turn the tide against Shih K'o-fa and his followers, the prince of Fu (emperor in his own right by then) conducted a personal investigation into the handling of the Hsü Tu affair. A fresh rebellion of Hsü's followers, apparently launched to avenge his death, occasioned the investigation, but the complications run extremely deep. It is my conclusion that this matter marked an important turning point in the factional struggle itself and that the reasons lead back to the very roots of political organization and local control.

As one shifts one's attention from court politics to local and regional defense, one expects to find some continuity—local powers or natural leaders turning for or against the dynasty in self-defense. The leaders should be the bureaucratic elite, and in some places this seems to have been the case. But, throughout much of the Yangtze delta and northern Chekiang there was conflict. The most prominent members of the bureaucratic elite were not always in control. I believe that restoration leaders in the Chiang-nan region were aware that the structure of local power was very delicately balanced in their favor, that the factor most essential to maintaining that balance was a well-coordinated central authority, but that a viable defense required the cautious integration of that authority with powerful local interests which could just as easily oppose the restoration attempt. This awareness led the local loyalists to oppose centralization on political and social grounds, in order to win local support, but it also prevented them from becoming the champions of local interests in the cause of self-defense. They were in the awkward position of supporting the Nanking regime while opposing its defense policies and courting local interests while opposing local power.

The Hsü Tu affair is one dramatic example of the ramifications of the loyalists' position. Its role in restoration politics is ironic, and it would be folly to conclude that it was the chief cause of the Tung-lin party's demise. But it does serve to point out the significance of local organizational problems and issues of local defense in the course of the resistance. The organizational problems were more complex than the issue of loyalty versus collaboration. Although these problems were clear long before the Ming collapse and the restoration in Nanking, the dynastic crisis demonstrated how far-reaching their effects could be. If there must be one, then, this is the lesson of Nanking.

THE NANKING RESTORATION AND REGIONAL POLITICS

Perhaps the most important point which traditional chroniclers of the resistance have failed to stress is that plans for a southern restoration preceded the fall of Peking. As the military situation in the north worsened in the winter of 1643–44, proposals to establish a regional line of defense circulated in eastern Kiangsu and northern Chekiang. These proposals clearly anticipated the ultimate failure of Ming defenses in the north and sought to assure the continuity of the ruling house should the central government be forced to relocate.[7] The restoration which southerners, especially Tung-lin sympathizers, would like to have directed, involved setting up the heir apparent in Nanking with a refurbished Nanking imperial guard under the control of the Nanking Ministry of War. At the end of 1643, Shih K'o-fa was the Nanking war minister, military governor of northern Kiangsu, and coordinator of "grain tribute," the tax which the south paid in kind to supply the armies of the north.

In December, Shih began to reorganize the Nanking capital brigade. First, he impeached those who held potentially key military posts as sinecures.[8] Then, he received permission to create a whole new command structure and to recruit and train a whole new regiment, including river patrols.[9] At about the same time, certain courtiers began to advance the proposal to move the heir apparent to Nanking.[10] At first the plan was only to facilitate the defense of Chiang-nan by making the imperial presence more clearly felt there. But when the proposal was finally aired in private audience on March 31, 1644, the capital was already imperiled. By that time a group represented in the bureaucracy by a young Tung-lin censor, Ch'en Tzu-lung, had already trained a naval force of 2,000 men and contracted for seagoing vessels to carry them.[11] Ch'en Tzu-lung, who was one of the founders of an activist literary society in Sung-chiang, proposed that this contingent be sent to Tientsin to receive the heir apparent and escort him to Nanking. If the southern restorationists had succeeded in that plan, the politics of the restoration, if not its outcome, would have been quite different. But, as Frederic Wakeman recounts in detail in his essay, the emperor refused to consider it. Within a month Peking fell to Li Tzu-ch'eng.

The restoration which these early planners did not direct was dominated by four northern warlords, their captive grand secretary, and his captive prince. I shall not recount the whole story; a brief outline will suffice. Shih K'o-fa and the Tung-lin faction, having lost track of the heir apparent after the fall of Peking, hoped to establish the Honan prince of Lu as guardian of the realm. This prince, although less closely related to the late emperor than the prince of Fu, had a reputation for refinement as well as an interest in the welfare of the Ming state. The case for the prince of Fu owed its strength primarily to the support of the governor of Feng-yang, Ma Shih-ying. Ma was a man from far-off Kweichow, lacking local connections among the Chiang-nan elite but having well-developed political connections in the southern capital itself. Unfortunately for him, as well as for Shih's party, these connections were related to the old "seditious" faction, out of power since the late emperor's succession in 1628. Perhaps the only factor which really mattered in the initial dispute between the parties was military strength. Ma Shih-ying had three generals and a half-million northern soldiers behind him.

Ma Shih-ying did not bring his military subordinates with him to Nanking. The south surely would have resisted such a move at the outset. He still needed to form some kind of coalition with the Tung-lin faction if there was to be any restoration at all. Shih K'o-fa agreed to move his command across the Yangtze to Yangchow, helping to balance the military power of the two factions on the perimeter of defense. Still, the Tung-lin faction maintained a strong hold on the Nanking bureaucracy, especially in the ministries of War and Personnel.[12] Thus the restoration government began with heavy Tung-lin participation. The key to the restoration story was Ma Shih-ying's successful recommendation of Juan Ta-ch'eng, a "seditious" party sympathizer, who rooted out the Tung-lin group and led the regime to ignominious defeat.

When describing the factional struggle in Nanking, it is difficult to depart from the standard interpretation. For years Juan Ta-ch'eng had sought to establish himself as an intellectual leader in Nanking. Tung-lin sympathizers had invoked the memory of the six martyred censors to expel him from the southern capital in 1639, and the bitterness between Juan and his antagonists was well known. Ma Shih-ying probably owed much of his own political strength in Nanking to Juan and his friends, and it was natural for Ma to doubt the intentions of Tung-lin protagonists, however logical their arguments for regional defense might be. Ma claimed that Tung-lin spokesmen sought to undermine not only his own position but that of the restoration emperor as well. In turning to Juan Ta-ch'eng he had two specific points to make.

First, he argued that Juan was an expert in military strategy.[13] Given the Tung-lin faction's own involvement in military planning at this point, it would be useful to have some examples of Juan's writings on the subject. Unfortunately, we have only the chroniclers' testimony that Juan would fortify the Yangtze, a strategy which appears less than brilliant but certainly deserves more detailed discussion. The Tung-lin strategists, as I shall explain below, stressed the importance of an integrated defense of the entire region, a plan which depended on the cooperation of the Kiangsu and Chekiang elite. That the Ma-Juan faction could not claim to guarantee such cooperation, as the Tung-lin faction could, is a fact worth bearing in mind.

Second, Ma intentionally used his recommendation of Juan to turn the charges of sedition around. The "seditious" party had originally charged Tung-lin with seditious behavior, after all, and Juan was prepared to renew that charge. The standard interpretation dwells upon Juan's careful purge of Tung-lin sympathizers from the bureaucracy. He founded his case on the involvement of two southern political figures in the regime of Li Tzu-ch'eng. The two Tung-lin proponents had surrendered to save their own lives and later returned to the south in hopes of receiving amnesty. Juan extended the case against them to include others, charging guilt by association, until he succeeded in having several offenders executed in April of 1645. Juan's charges of sedition tainted every Tung-lin proposal, from its initial support of the Honan prince of Lu to its recommendations for local defense, and the standard view blames Juan for the removal of the party's leaders from office during October of 1644.[14] This interpretation serves well enough to describe the hopelessness of the division in the capital city, but it fails to note the threat which Tung-lin and the southern bureaucratic elite did, in fact, present to the Nanking regime. It is now time to apply our new perspective to the logic of these events.

Although the case against Tung-lin sympathizers continued until the collapse of the restoration government, the decisive events of the factional struggle occurred between June and October of 1644. The Nanking government's first appointment as director of the Bureau of Investigation (censor-in-chief) was the Shao-hsing philosopher, Liu Tsung-chou (1578–1645). Liu was a respected elder statesman and straightforward spokesman for the Tung-lin faction.[15] Liu's appointment to this politically powerful post came on June 14, just as Ma Shih-ying reached Nanking. Liu did not hasten to assume his duties.[16] Before the fall of Peking he had already begun to agitate for broader militarization in Hangchow, Chekiang's provincial capital. When Peking fell, he advised the newly appointed Chekiang governor to send troops to Chen-chiang to help defend the Yangtze crossing that was the gateway to the south.

On June 24, when Shih K'o-fa left Nanking to establish his command at Yangchow, Liu and the governor were both in Chen-chiang. Before proceeding to Nanking, Liu presented a series of memorials defining the Tung-lin position. In the last of these he charged Ma Shih-ying with trying to set up a regime that was too highly centralized, depending on eunuchs and northern generals to the detriment of the state. He challenged Ma to prove his disinterest by assuming command of his generals in Feng-yang, as Shih K'o-fa had done by moving to Yangchow. He further demanded that new eunuch controllerships which Ma had recommended for the Nanking imperial armies be abolished and that new commands be established between Feng-yang and the south. He warned that historically eunuch interference in bureaucratic and military affairs had invariably led to warlord domination at the imperial court. It was thus essential that the prince of Fu's regime be demilitarized and that the one grand secretary who could easily be compromised by the warlords, Ma Shih-ying, return to the provinces.[17]

The annals of the restoration focus on Liu's challenges and his subsequent removal as one important element in the Tung-lin's faction's demise. The warlords memorialized in response that Liu was party to a plot to replace the prince of Fu, who already called himself emperor, with the Honan prince of Lu, whom Shih K'o-fa and other Tung-lin sympathizers had originally supported to lead the restoration. Men like Shih K'o-fa, Ch'i Piao-chia, Liu's old student who was the new governor at Soochow, and the Sung-chiang activ-

ist, Ch'en Tzu-lung, supported Liu's arguments and advised that this
was a civil affair in which the warlords themselves should have no
voice. Eventually Ma won out. Liu was removed and his supporters
followed. The last to go was Ch'i Piao-chia. Restoration annals make
his dismissal appear almost as an afterthought, but from our perspective Ch'i was the central figure. In order to show why, let us shift our
focus to the governorship at Soochow.

As governor of the four prefectures east of Nanking, Ch'i Piao-chia
provided the single most important link between the restoration
government and local defense organization in the south. In addition
to his own governor's brigade, the Su-sung guard, and a newly created Ching-k'ou brigade at Chen-chiang, Ch'i was in charge of five
thousand troops of the Chekiang governor's brigade that he had
brought with him.[18] He also traveled extensively, discussing problems of defense and local order with the region's leaders, and kept in
touch with his home province by messenger. Not only did he discuss
pao-chia organization with local leaders, but he also appealed successfully for financial and paramilitary help from private sources.[19]
By all appearances the newly appointed governor of Chekiang, who
had traveled to Kiangsu along with his troops, was taking advice from
Ch'i and Liu Tsung-chou. The latter, of course, were themselves
leaders of Chekiang's provincial elite. Finally, Ch'i was the man who
had to coordinate the defense of the Yangtze crossing between
Yangchow and Chen-chiang with Shih K'o-fa. In this capacity he
supported Ch'en Tzu-lung and recommended that the naval force
which the Sung-chiang group had trained earlier be commissioned
to patrol the Yangtze River itself.

The strategic importance of the Soochow governorship is evident.
With the support of two provincial brigades and the bureaucratic
elite of the region, Ch'i had the power to bring the Nanking regime
down if he had chosen. Neither Liu Tsung-chou nor Ch'en Tzu-lung
nor any other Tung-lin partisan had that kind of power. Ma Shih-
ying could not have failed to notice this fact. Moreover, the Honan
prince of Lu was then established at Hangchow and the Chekiang
provincial army was between him and Nanking. The prince had
stopped briefly in Chen-chiang on his way south, at which time he
met Ch'i and Liu Tsung-chou.[20] Liu's meetings with the Chekiang
governor at the time he demanded Ma Shih-ying's removal to Feng-

yang were cause enough for the warlords' alarm.[21] Ma surely needed
to break up this nexus to secure his position. But at the time of Liu's
famous memorial the new emperor had not yet succumbed to Ma's
partisan interests. Although Tung-lin's enemies began their attack as
early as June 24 and Ma had recommended Juan Ta-ch'eng by mid-
July, the Tung-lin partisans still held sway when Liu finally took up
his post in Nanking on August 19. Ch'en Tzu-lung in his capacity as
censor and others had persuaded the emperor to keep Ma at a safe
distance, and Tung-lin continued to control the Ministry of Personnel. The purge of Tung-lin partisans occurred between October 9 and
November 2. Even though Ch'i Piao-chia lingered in office until
December, the sequence of events that seems to have turned the
emperor against Tung-lin found Ch'i in the center.[22]

    The key event in Ch'i Piao-chia's demise was not his support of
Liu Tsung-chou, but a memorial he submitted on September 28 in
defense of the censor, Tso Kuang-hsien.[23] Tso was the brother of one
of the Tung-lin martyrs of 1626.[24] In July 1644, when Ma Shih-ying
first recommended Juan Ta-ch'eng for a position in the Ministry of
War, Tso had joined Ch'en Tzu-lung and others in condemning Ma
for the action, pointing out that the previous emperor had decided
which party was "seditious" and that Ma's contradiction of this
decision cast doubts on his own loyalty to the Ming house. Viewed as
part of the factional struggle, this was sufficient cause for the attacks
against Tso two months later. But the charges against Tso, to which
Ch'i Piao-chia responded, specifically involved an administrative
decision which he had made the previous winter. As acting governor
of Chekiang, Tso had ordered the execution of Hsü Tu, the rebellious
magnate from Tung-yang. When Hsü's followers rebelled once again
in early September the blame came to rest at Tso's feet. The investigation which the emperor had ordered pointed to nepotism, as Tso
was related by marriage to the magistrate against whom the original
rebellion was directed. The charges stated that Tso's in-law had
provoked the revolt and that Hsü's case had not received a fair
hearing.

    Ch'i Piao-chia argued, as Tso had done, that Hsü's rebellion was
treason nonetheless and that execution was entirely in order. Regardless of Hsü's intentions and abilities, unless he was executed his rebellion could only inspire the same kind of behavior among less

desirable elements.[25] The logic of Ch'i's defense mattered little. His support of Tso Kuang-hsien was damning. At that point Ch'i and, apparently, the entire Tung-lin faction lost the emperor's ear. Two days after Ch'i's memorial the emperor appointed Juan Ta-ch'eng to a high-level post in the Ministry of War with the job of policing the Yangtze River defenses.[26] That was a job which the Tung-lin partisans had surely intended for Ch'en Tzu-lung's navy.[27] In addition, the emperor prohibited official personnel recommendations for persons without proper degrees, limiting Ch'i's authority to grant commissions. From that time on the Tung-lin partisans had little influence in Nanking. Tso Kuang-hsien was not officially denounced until a month later. By that time there was no one in Nanking with enough influence to defend him. Ch'i Piao-chia learned that he himself was in trouble when Liu Tsung-chou and others were forced to retire between October 9 and October 16.[28] Their support of Chi's earlier policy arguments was instrumental in bringing them down. Finally, Ch'i's support of the discredited Tso Kuang-hsien officially forced his retirement on December 14.[29]

The effect of Ch'i Piao-chia's retirement on Chiang-nan's defenses was deleterious. He had won the respect of enough military men to stabilize the situation at Chen-chiang and he had widespread support among the bureaucratic elite. Once the climate changed in Nanking, the appearance of cohesion in eastern Kiangsu began to slip. Ma Shih-ying created a new censorial post as a wedge between the Soochow governor and Chen-chiang. Perhaps hoping to soften the blow, he appointed a man with Tung-lin connections to fill the post. This man, Yang Wen-ts'ung, was also from Kweichow and related to Ma by marriage. Ch'i refused to receive him.[30] Eventually the new censor became Ch'i's replacement. His chief contribution to the region's defense was to use the funds Ch'i had collected for militia building to fortify two small islands in the Yangtze.[31] Perhaps the hardest blow was to the attempted regional integration which Ch'i had symbolized. One of the last victims of the purge was an obscure *chü-jen* from Sung-chiang by the name of Ho Kang, whose case typified Nanking's reaction against paramilitary organization and the region's more creative leadership. Ho Kang was the military expert who trained and led the naval force for which Ch'en Tzu-lung had argued at court. He reached Nanking in October in time to receive a

favorable recommendation, but soon he was removed from the
Yangtze defense system to a distant prefectural post. Out of desperation Ho abandoned that post and returned to Yangchow to
fight at Shih K'o-fa's side. There he died in June of 1645, along
with his more famous commander, a victim of the war's best-known
atrocity.[32]

The role of the Hsü Tu affair in Tung-lin's demise is ironic. At first
glance it would seem that the Ma-Juan clique had chosen an event
otherwise unrelated to the Tung-lin cause in order to discredit a
troublesome censor, Tso Kuang-hsien. It would also appear that
Tung-lin sympathies alone served to implicate Ch'i Piao-chia and
others in the case. In fact, the Tung-lin group itself had had an
interest in Hsü Tu's survival in the winter of 1643–44; for he was
then part of the very same restoration plan which the attack on Tso
Kuang-hsien brought to an end. His rebellion was one of the early
signs of the movement's fatal flaw—the fact that integration of local
interests in plans for defense meant compromising Ming authority in
local control. The issues involved in the Hsü Tu affair thus run much
deeper than the factional dispute in Nanking. If Hsü Tu's execution
was a cause of Tung-lin's failure, his rebellion was perhaps a greater
cause. This is the proposition I shall consider in what follows, but before we return to Hsü Tu himself, let us examine the political and
social setting in which the restorationists developed their plans for
local defense.

THE SETTING FOR LOCAL DEFENSE

The problems which plagued restoration planners were already clear
to many in the decade preceding the fall of Peking. It was first in
1634 that rebel activities forced the government and the local elite
to deal with questions of regional defense and local military organization. There were many weak points in the Ming structure. The
administration of Nan-chihli, the area presently defined by the
boundaries of Anhwei and Kiangsu provinces, had been fragmented
intentionally by the Ming founder and remained so until the Ch'ing
reorganization of 1645.[33] Unlike the provinces, Nan-chihli had no
central treasury and no central surveillance office.[34] Military gov-
ernors had been established from time to time to coordinate the
affairs of given prefectures, but the only permanent governorship in

the 1630s was that for Ying-t'ien prefecture in Nanking. This governor was charged with coordinating the various regular military circuits north and south of the Yangtze from Chiu-chiang to Shanghai. Coordination of tax payments and tactical commands, however, was the responsibility of several regional officials spread throughout the area, each with his own line to the Ministry of War. During the last years of the Ming there was a rapid turnover of personnel in these posts, and the posts themselves proliferated dramatically, their jurisdictions randomly shifting with each new rebel threat.[35] In short, there was no effective administrative organization that could deal with the military problems of Nan-chihli at the end of the Ming.

If the region lacked political definition, it was not a well-defined unit in any natural sense either. The Yangtze River clearly provided some economic continuity through the region, but it also divided north and south strategically. This fact meant that the interests of An-ch'ing and Lu-chou in problems of defense would not always coincide with those of Nanking and Soochow. Moreover, the interests of the coastal prefectures of Soochow and Sung-chiang were demonstrably better integrated with those of northern Chekiang than with those of the middle Yangtze region.[36] As the coast united southeastern Kiangsu and northern Chekiang and the river split north from south, mountains separated Chekiang from Anhwei. Only Hui-chou was connected with Hangchow by river. The rest of southern Anhwei faced the central Yangtze valley. Because of this, the issue of defense cannot be seen simply in terms of provincial administration. In the present discussion the politics of southeastern Kiangsu and northern Chekiang merge. This area was the principal geographical locus of the Tung-lin faction. It was also here that the restoration had its strongest support. It is this connection that bears most directly on the issue of local political integration in the restoration movement.

Before the autumn of 1634, according to the historian Tai Ming-shih, no one in official circles was worried that the rebels from Shensi might descend into Nan-chihli. Suggestions that should the rebels decide to attack Feng-yang the south was also in danger were met with derision in Peking. The minister of war is reported to have said, "The bandits are men of Ch'in. They won't eat Chiang-nan rice, and their horses won't eat Chiang-nan grass. That the bandits won't harm Chiang-nan is clear."[37] When Chang Hsien-chung headed south after the rebel alliance had laid Feng-yang waste that winter, no one was laughing. Governor Chang Kuo-wei, who was later to play a role in the restoration movement, rushed to An-ch'ing and hastily organized a defense. Making do with the existing military organs of Nan-chihli's southwestern prefectures, he managed to oversee the rebels' passage out of the region and into Hu-kuang, but not without considerable damage to private property and Ming prestige.[38] From that time on there was a chorus of demands for more adequate defense measures in Chiang-nan. Political leaders from T'ung-ch'eng to Shanghai expressed anxiety about the fate of the south and offered strong opinions about how to save it. One obvious demand was for increased troop strength and more effective coordination. In June the government decided to create a new military circuit for Lu-chou and An-ch'ing separating it from the one south of the river. Shih K'o-fa, then a department chief in the war ministry in Peking, volunteered to take the new post.[39] Soon there was a new governor-general to coordinate the campaign east of Shensi. In 1637 the rebels came to An-ch'ing once more. This time they laid waste T'ung-ch'eng. Chang Kuo-wei demanded more troops, and a new governorship was established at An-ch'ing for Shih K'o-fa.[40]

While Shih was reorganizing the military administration of western Nan-chihli, the government in Peking was trying out a new policy. Yang Ssu-ch'ang, minister of war since the Ming debacle at Feng-yang, spurred the effort to beef up the Ming armies with heavy surtaxes. His strategy emphasized mobilization in order to eradicate the rebel strongholds in the northwest. Many southerners opposed this policy in the interest of stability within their own region. They would pay the heaviest taxes, but their own defenses would show no appreciable benefits.[41] Defense measures in Nan-chihli would have to depend on local efforts, and their expense would come on top of the tax surcharges due Peking. But Yang Ssu-ch'ang continued to dominate in Peking until his policies met with disaster in 1641. In March of that year, Chang Hsien-chung captured the imperial fief at Hsiang-yang. Soon thereafter Li Tzu-ch'eng took Honanfu and Yang committed suicide.

The failure and subsequent official repudiation of Yang Ssu-ch'ang's policies hardly improved the situation in the south. From 1641 to 1644 Nan-chihli was subject to marauding by rebel and Ming armies alike. Economic dislocation led to increased inflation. Peri-

odic drought led to rice riots and new military levies to open confrontation between administrators and populace. In 1642 the Ming
general Tso Liang-yü asserted his independence, refusing to fight and
allowing his own army to raid at will in Hu-kuang and western Nan-
chihli.[42] New rebel activity began in Chekiang and the people of
eastern Kiangsu failed to provide tax grain for armies in the north.[43]
Pirates resumed activities in the Yangtze estuary.[44] In the following
year the militia of Hui-chou attacked government troops as they
passed by on their way north.[45] Government transport troops nearly
killed a magistrate in northern Chekiang in a dispute over tax goods
and Hsü Tu launched his rebellion in mountainous Chin-hua prefecture to the south.[46] Within ten years of the first rebel incursions,
Ming control of Chiang-nan was in serious doubt.

During that decade local officials and local communities had to
develop their own plans to face the crises. Not only did the bureaucratic elite advance proposals for reorganization of Chiang-nan's
defenses as a whole, they also laid plans for local militia organization.
In some cases the planners were leaders of local militia forces themselves, conscripting and training men to defend their districts against
specific rebel threats. It is not surprising that many such local leaders
became key figures in the restoration movement. But the same crises
brought another sort of response at the local level: the proliferation
of private paramilitary organizations.[47] Families and individuals
raised their own police forces to protect their property or to sell
protection to others who were too small to protect themselves. Such
groups clearly did not have the same public obligations as the militia,
and one can easily imagine the sort of conflicts that arose. Some
bureaucratic leaders saw themselves as spokesmen for the public
interest and saw others as representatives of private wealth.[48] For
them, any extrabureaucratic organization was of questionable
loyalty. But the integration of these public and private interests was,
in the end, the problem which defense planners had to face. It was
also the key to a successful restoration.

THE PLANNERS AND THE PROBLEMS

It is clear that plans for local defense in southeastern Kiangsu and
northern Chekiang were developing prior to the restoration. It is also
clear, although the details are hazy, that some defense planners an-

ticipated and encouraged a restoration government in Nanking even
before the fall of the Ming capital. Perhaps as early as December
1643, a group of Tung-lin partisans was working on a plan to move
the heir apparent to Nanking and use him to coordinate Chiang-nan's
defenses.[49] It is impossible to say how the restorationists planned to
coordinate these defense efforts with local militia, but the political
connections among them and local leaders were quite extensive. That
there was some kind of nexus involving Tung-lin partisanship, local
militia organization, defense planning, and restoration sentiment is
obvious. What is perhaps most interesting is that the defense planners
who eventually became associated with the restoration, although
they shared Tung-lin sympathies, differed widely in their ideas concerning local defense.

The four planners I shall discuss here, two of whom I have introduced above, were active local leaders as well as successful bureaucratic officials. All were holders of the *chin-shih* degree. All were
intimately involved in Tung-lin politics. All held positions, at some
time during their careers, that involved them in military affairs. None
was eccentric. They were all men who felt the heavy burdens of
social and political obligation and chose actively to pursue reformist
goals. All were leaders in the restoration and resistance movements,
and all died for that cause. Their thoughts on local defense reveal
an ambivalence among men of like mind concerning the specific
problem of integrating public and private interests in local defense.

The first planner, Chin Sheng (1598–1645), was a man of daring.[50]
A native of Hui-chou, Chin Sheng received his *chin-shih* degree in
1628 and became a bachelor in the Han-lin Academy. This honor,
reserved for the most outstanding candidates in the metropolitan
examinations, gave him direct access to the Grand Secretariat, where
policy was most likely to be determined. In 1629 the Manchus raided
Chinese territory within the Great Wall. Through his connections
with the Tung-lin faction, whose influence then prevailed in imperial
councils, Chin won an extraordinary appointment to oversee the
organization of a new type of military unit based on Western military
technology. The experiment failed, apparently sabotaged by powerful opponents who demanded too much return for too little investment, and Chin retired in disgust to Hui-chou. By 1636, he was in
charge of his district's rural militia organization, and within a few

years he had produced the most effective local defense force in the region. In 1643 he led the militia in repelling a Ming army which had been summoned by Feng-yang governor Ma Shih-ying from his native Kweichow. The southwestern soldiers were much feared in Chiang-nan, and Chin reacted when their commanders allowed the troops to pillage in the vicinity of Hui-chou. Ma accused Chin of leading an insurrection, but with the help of Shih K'o-fa, Chin was exonerated and Ma reprimanded instead.[51] In 1644, Chin refused to serve the restoration regime because of Ma's role in it. When collaborationist armies descended on Hui-chou after the fall of Nanking, he led a guerrilla-like resistance in the area until he was captured and executed on December 5, 1645.

Chin Sheng's plan for local defense was relatively uncomplicated. In accordance with the Ming statutory regulations, he set about organizing a rural militia (hsiang-ping) system.[52] There was nothing new in this. Rural militia were a common feature of southern society at the end of the Ming. But they were often hastily recruited and poorly trained, and they were rarely based on conscription. The term militia seems to have stood for any kind of irregular or paramilitary outfit that turned up on the side of the government in a local fracas. To Chin Sheng, on the other hand, it meant what the term had traditionally entailed—an irregular fighting unit, well-trained, conscripted village by village, hierarchically ordered, and ready to respond at a moment's notice. Such an organization depended especially on the cooperation of village leaders and the commitment of the rural populace in general to the organization's goals. Chin Sheng's plan shows an awareness of these factors and a faith in their applicability to the local situation in Hui-chou. Significantly, in his description of the militia he avoided all reference to the formally structured and inflexible pao-chia system, which many planners insisted should be used for conscription. On the other hand, he made no concessions to local strongmen who might bid for preemptive leadership in pao-chia's absence. His was a genuine call to arms, in the interest of the local populace, appealing to all the native instincts of the small, earthbound peasant and the public-spirited rural dweller.[53]

Chin defined the rules for training and recruiting the militia in 1636.[54] In rough outline, the rules were as follows. The district was divided into "rural compacts" (hsiang-yüeh) in accordance with a

recent precedent for selecting headmen. There were probably about
180 such units, each with definite geographical boundaries.[55] To
facilitate conscription, Chin had the villages within the compacts
organize themselves into wards (*ch'ü*) for registration. A ward was
the size of an average village, but larger villages might form two
wards, and those too small to conscript a unit of their own would be
attached to a neighboring village. Then, depending on what was most
natural and convenient, the wards would subdivide themselves into
precincts (*lien*). A precinct might include twenty to fifty people. It
would select a headman and keep its own register, which was not
subject to alterations by higher authorities. The registers were to
include all able-bodied males, and to list their means of support.
Comings and goings would be meticulously recorded.

The precinct was the basic unit of a sophisticated alarm system.
Each was to man an alarm drum or bell, and to see that it sounded
if, and only if, there was due cause. Any bandit victim could au-
thorize an alarm, and the alarm would pass on from precinct to
precinct accordingly. Ultimately the precinct would also provide
militiamen for the rural compact leaders to train and organize.
But there seems to have been no quota system at all. Instead, Chin
consistently demanded total participation, apparently expecting
every able-bodied male to be armed and prepared to fight. He even
encouraged universal instruction in "street fighting," so even "the
women and girls are all capable of defending themselves and killing
the bandits." Moreover, the structure and the goals of the entire system were to become the common knowledge of women and children,
so that there would be no mistake as to how it should function. In
short, Chin's prescription for dealing with the crisis was the total
militarization of rural society.

Chin's course of action raises a question of great social significance.
If the population was to be so thoroughly militarized, who could
control it? The plan itself allowed for variations in unit size and a
degree of organizational autonomy at the local level. Chin's was not a
structure imposed on local society by the magistrate's yamen, but a
locally organized system cooperating with the yamen through the
intermediate rural compact. Did the compact itself, then, tend to
represent the interest of the state or of local groups? And how could
the yamen prevent local strongmen from dominating the structure

once the people were trained and armed? Chin Sheng did not address himself to these problems, and one assumes that if the leaders of 180 compacts shared his interests and ideals the problems did not exist. But that is hard to imagine. Chin himself remained a loyalist guerrilla after the surrender of Hui-chou in 1645, but lost control of the rural compacts, which probably soon were keeping order in the name of the Ch'ing.

Variations on the Hui-chou theme occurred elsewhere in Chiang-nan. Militia groups locally organized and coordinated by the bureaucratic elite were active in northern Chekiang in 1642 and in southeastern Kiangsu during the restoration.[56] Such groups could be distinguished from the street gangs and private forces that sometimes styled themselves "militia" for the sake of appearance. On the other hand, it must have been a fine line indeed which separated public and private interests in many rural compacts, and this was the issue coordinators had to face. Arming local leaders surely meant compromising the power of the state. That, in turn, meant lessening the local power which the elite itself derived from its privileges vis-à-vis the state. If men like Chin Sheng were willing to force this issue it must have dampened the loyalism of most; and even those who sympathized fundamentally with Chin's approach were presented with a serious dilemma.

The second planner of interest, the restoration governor Ch'i Piao-chia (1602–45), represents a more cautious approach.[57] Ch'i was a native of Shan-yin in Shao-hsing prefecture in northern Chekiang. Known also as a playwright, he was a disciple and friend of Liu Tsung-chou the philosopher, a descendant of several generations of bureaucrats, and an official of high rank. Receiving his *chin-shih* degree in 1622, he served briefly as provincial inspector (*hsün-an*) in Soochow in 1633 and retired to Shan-yin under the pressure of court politics. When drought reduced the rice crop of the lower Yangtze region in 1641, Ch'i and other members of the bureaucratic elite helped to organize relief measures and protect against bandit activity. Ch'i wrote several essays on village "crop watching" and defense at that time. Two years later he was among the regional coordinators of the militia which was preparing for trouble in the wake of Hsü Tu's uprising to the south. About the time Li Tzu-ch'eng was closing in on Peking, he was part of the movement to establish the heir apparent with an army in Nanking. Traveling north to assume a new post in Nanking, he first received news of the emperor's death and then the appointment of governor of southeastern Kiangsu at Soochow. The last of the Tung-lin party to be chased from office, he returned to Shan-yin and waited for the Nanking regime to fall. He committed suicide when Ch'ing forces took Shao-hsing.

Ch'i's discussions of "crop watching" are useful for pointing up the dilemma which a member of the bureaucratic elite faced in organizing militia.[58] He proposed that each village organize its own police force to guard against theft at harvest time. Ch'i thought that these local forces, which probably already existed in some places, should be separate from the *pao-chia* mutual surveillance system. One such unit Ch'i described was made up of local village residents hired by the village itself. The village landowners paid for their services, each contributing an amount consistent with his land holdings. The police were to raise the alarm in the event of theft and they were held responsible if theft was discovered when no alarm had occurred. They also received a bounty for catching thieves. But Ch'i did not believe that the "crop-watching corps," as it was called, should function independently of bureaucratic control; its leaders answered to the magistrate. He also proposed that the *pao-chia* system be implemented in the same villages. Should some local resident tamper with the crops after they were harvested, his neighbors might also be held responsible. Ch'i pointed out that this would pacify the indigent, subdue the treacherous, and repress the unlawful—in other words, one assumes, prevent local magnates from using the "crop-watching corps" to hoard rice and reap great profits against the orders of the magistrate and to the detriment of the public welfare. "Crop-watching corps" were thus organized in such a way as to guarantee both public and private interests, but Ch'i intended them to be neither a substitute for *pao-chia* nor a means of defense against major rebel incursions.

The dilemma arose when serious external threats challenged the ability of the state to defend the villages. As late as 1642 Ch'en Tzu-lung, then the Shao-hsing prefectural judge, led an elite company of the governor's brigade in successfully defending the region against bandits from the mountains to the south.[59] But by the

following year Ch'i Piao-chia and others were preparing the rural
militia locally for another defense.[60] We may never know whether
the militia was in fact an extension of the crop-watching corps under
the landowners' leadership. It is hard to imagine that men like Ch'i
would not take advantage of such a sophisticated local organization
for defense. But it is also clear from his discussions just two years
earlier that he recognized the danger to yamen control which such a
move entailed.

The third planner, the Sung-chiang activist Ch'en Tzu-lung (1608–
47), was perhaps the most adaptable and creative.[61] Remembered for
his literary talent, Ch'en was one of the founders of a literary society
called Chi-she (Incipient Awareness Society). At the age of nineteen
he shook the literary world with his contemptuous remarks about
the most prominent literateur of the dominant Kiangsi classical
school and joined with his Chi-she fellows in building an influential
intellectual-political movement of their own. As a part of the larger
Fu-she (Restoration Society) movement, a younger and farther-
reaching extension of the established Tung-lin faction, the group set
out to explore new approaches to classical and historical scholarship.
Ch'en helped to edit the impressive 500-chapter compendium of
Ming statecraft literature, *Ching-shih wen pien*—still a major source
for the study of administrative organization and theory—published in
1637. In the same year he received his *chin-shih* degree and, eventually, the Shao-hsing prefectural judgeship.

In Chekiang, Ch'en first won fame by successfully heading off rice
riots and managing local relief measues after the drought of 1640.
This he did by skillfully combining *pao-chia* with commercial subsidies and price controls.[62] In 1642 he devised the policies and led
the troops which rid the region of bandits.[63] Just before the Hsü Tu
uprising, he was raising supplies for Chiang-nan's defense and personally supervising their transportation to Nanking. After rushing
back to Chekiang and securing Hsü Tu's surrender in January of
1644, he resigned in protest against Tso Kuang-hsien's rejection of
amnesty in the case. From then on he was involved in the campaign
to move the heir apparent to Nanking, helped build the naval unit in
Sung-chiang, joined in the unsuccessful impeachment of Ma Shih-
ying and Juan Ta-ch'eng, and finally died resisting the Manchus in
1646.

Much less orthodox than either Chin or Ch'i in his approach to
Chiang-nan's defense, Ch'en Tzu-lung argued that neither rural
militia nor *pao-chia* conscription were workable there. In a series of
scholarly arguments relating to defense, he proposed an alternative
so radical that it could only be academic. Ch'en thought *pao-chia*
could work only if society were leveled. Poverty breeds sedition and
pao-chia encourages it, he argued, because *pao-chia* is manipulated by
those with political power. In the end, the privileged were no less
bandits than the underprivileged and neither could be controlled by
pao-chia.[64] As for the rural militia, it was an institution born of the
northern plains and completely inapplicable in Chiang-nan. The
people there were not suited for paramilitary activity, Ch'en thought.
What the region needed, he believed, was a new kind of police force,
controlled by military officials in the district cities and with officers
in every town and every village cluster. Full-time troopers should be
recruited and trained locally. The towns and villages would compete
in district-wide contests in the martial arts and each unit would be re-
warded or punished according to its performance in the event of
genuine disorders. Fishermen would be recruited for river and lake
patrols, since much of Chiang-nan's banditry originated among the
lake people and the fishermen were accustomed to fighting. This new
police force would be professional, paid by commuted conscription
levies and fishing taxes. It would be coordinated by military officials
of the province, and it would serve both as a defense against rebel incursions and as a means of local control. Moreover, it would function
independently of both the local elite and the yamen functionaries.[65]

Ch'en's proposal is further evidence of the restorationists' dilemma.
"This plan," he wrote, "does not disturb the people and does not
drain their resources. It embodies the old system in a new method;
its implementation has many merits. Once disorder was upon them,
the people would understand the hardship they must bear and each
would try to save himself. Only then could the people themselves
organize their rural militia. But if we hope to organize in advance, we
can only do so by letting the government administer the organization
and not by depending on the people."[66] This attitude was typical of
the noblesse oblige which statecraft proposals tended to display, and
it confirmed the loyalists' reluctance to depend on private local
leadership. But once the situation became critical, Ch'en, like Ch'i

Piao-chia, found himself trapped between the ineffectiveness of strictly bureaucratic measures and those private interests which were bound to develop alternative means to deal with the crisis. By 1644, he had already become enmeshed in a variety of privately organized military and logistic operations which increased his effectiveness as a leader but compromised his position as an agent of bureaucratic control. As the narrative will show, the Hsü Tu affair made this ambiguous position untenable and seriously weakened the chances of the Nanking restoration.

The last planner, Hou T'ung-tseng (1591–1645), of Chia-ting, Soochow prefecture, represented the hard-line opposition to Ch'en's position.[67] The son of a victim of the anti-Tung-lin purges, Hou received his *chin-shih* degree in 1625 and refused to take office under the eunuch faction's regime. While he was at home in Chia-ting, his family provided the focal point of the local intellectual-political activities that were a part of the larger Fu-she movement. His offspring married the offspring of other Tung-lin sympathizers to the south, and their ties with the Chi-she group were especially strong. Hou began his civil-service career in 1635, serving first in the Nanking Ministry of Personnel and then as education intendant in Kiangsi. As military intendant in northern Chekiang in 1643, he was credited with putting down a mutiny of grain transport troops and preparing Chekiang's defenses against incursions by Tso Liang-yü's rebellious troops. Hou stood with other provincial authorities in the Hsü Tu affair, advocating harsh punishments for the rebels, when Ch'en Tzu-lung proposed amnesty. Refusing to serve in Ma Shih-ying's government in 1644, he retired to Chia-ting, taking no extra-bureaucratic military action until the Ch'ing arrived in August of the following year. Then, together with family and friends, he led the attempt to restore Ming authority in Chia-ting itself. When restoration failed, they defended the city's walls and died in the resistance that made Chia-ting a landmark of loyalism.

Hou T'ung-tseng's arguments concerning local control and defense were the most conventional of the four. Reflecting Hou's experience with traditional statecraft theory, they emphasized the importance of social and economic stability and expounded the dangers of militarization. After Chang Hsien-chung's rebels fled An-ch'ing in 1635, Hou wrote to Governor Chang Kuo-wei and to the Nanking minister of war that mobilization was the worst course the south could take.[68] The best defense, he thought, was administrative efficiency and strict local control:

> When reports first arrived that T'ung-ch'eng was besieged, government banners all pointed in that direction and the bandits had to flee by night. One heard only that the rebels feared the government troops more than the government troops feared the rebels. It follows that wherever there are troops there surely will be no bandits. Now we fear that troops will appear where bandits do not.
>
> When troops are moved to fill a void, then it is not external but internal affairs that give us cause for anxiety. Moreover, those internal affairs do not involve big bandits but petty traitors. It is the petty traitor who summons the bandit. . . . If we have a worthy administrator to insure a military surplus and to proscribe the activities of treacherous elements, then rebellion from within will not occur and an end to anxiety over the external threat will follow accordingly.[69]

Hou also wrote to the newly appointed magistrate of Chia-ting, warning against the current proposals that local magnates be encouraged to organize militia privately. Hou believed that regardless of the crisis, any ad hoc organization was an invitation to chaos. The magistrate should beware of two types of "perfidious behavior." The first was that of local magnates and yamen functionaries, the second that of extortionists and common street gangs. Hou implied that in pleading for sanctions to organize private arms, the former had no more concern for the public interest than the latter. *Pao-chia* conscription, modified to fit local circumstances and adjusted to financial exigencies, was the only proper way to raise militia.[70] Hou and his friends in Chia-ting themselves had offered a plan for making *pao-chia* more efficient and more equitable. The details of the plan are lost, but extant references to it clearly indicate that they envisioned no resort to private aid or any extrabureaucratic local organization.[71]

The restorationists' dilemma is clear in Hou's case as it was in Ch'en Tzu-lung's. Throughout the critical period he consistently opposed government measures which increased the demand on Chia-ting's economy. He helped to win tax remissions for the district in 1637 and again in 1641. His argument was, quite simply, that a government which drains the people's resources to defend itself cannot retain their loyalty or respect. In 1641, in fact, a proposed tax increase had combined with shortages to cause rioting in Chia-ting. At that time, in an open letter to the imperial court advisors, Hou wrote:

> I have heard it said that there is nothing more to the way in which a loyal minister makes state policy than creating confidence. If a policy has the confidence of the ruler but not the confidence of the people, then it must not be recommended, even though it is profitable. If it has the confidence of the people but not the confidence of the ruler, then it should be implemented even though it is not profitable.[72]

He explained consistently that it was an official guarantee of tax remission and the clever use of *pao-chia* registration for managing relief efforts that had saved the district from popular rebellion. But the source of funds and the leadership for the relief effort remain obscure.[73] One can hardly imagine an increased confidence among the people at this point unless it was in the effectiveness of those who coordinated relief. And it seems likely that they were local magnates more interested in local control than in the Ming campaign against Manchus and rebels.

The previous discussion should demonstrate that the restorationists had no simple answer to the problem of how to guarantee local control while preparing for Chiang-nan's defense. Still, they were driven to action by the rapid course of events. If Chin Sheng's plan provided a model for military organization, the other three planners demonstrated the dilemma inherent in trying to realize it. To the restorationists and the loyalists, official coordination and control were essential to militarization. To what extent could they rely on private organization or popular action and remain loyal? The Hsü Tu affair of 1644 put the question perhaps more directly than any other single confrontation in the annals of resistance. The ambivalence in the restorationists' response revealed the flaw that was the movement's greatest weakness.

THE HSÜ TU AFFAIR

The Hsü Tu affair must be seen in the context of militarization and crisis. Bureaucrats were not the only ones with solutions for the defense problem. Many sons of the bureaucratic elite in the south turned to the martial arts to enhance their own careers or guarantee their status locally. Not all of them worried about coordinating their efforts with the magistrate's office. They often built small but sophisticated fighting units of their own and even held contests as a public display of power. One could hardly hope to describe these paramilitary leaders in terms of a single category. Some were protecting family wealth. Some may have practiced extortion; others may have fought it. Still others may have anticipated the dynasty's fall and hoped to win favor with the new, as yet unidentified rulers. But demonstrably there were those who shared the restorationists' sympathies and hoped to win commissions in the defense of Chiang-nan. One such man was Hsü Tu.

Hsü Tu was the grandson of an official from Tung-yang, Chin-hua prefecture, in northern Chekiang.[74] As a student in the prefectural school he took a special interest in military affairs. He established a reputation in the martial arts and attracted a group of young men as followers. Once he was well enough known he traveled north to Soochow in search of a patron. There he attached himself to Wu Ch'ang-shih, one of the original Fu-she founders. One evening in Hsü's presence a servant came to report that Wu's nephew had been robbed and wounded by members of a notorious band of brigands from the lake region. Seizing the opportunity to demonstrate his prowess, Hsü vowed on the spot to capture the bandit leaders themselves, a task to which local officials had long applied themselves without success. Within a few days, Hsü and twenty-odd men from his Chin-hua group had tracked the bandits down and routed them in ship-board combat, bringing the leaders back alive. With that his reputation spread throughout eastern Kiangsu.[75]

From Soochow, Hsü moved on to Sung-chiang, where he met Ho Kang (d. 1645). Ho was the descendent of an early Ming official from Shanghai.[76] He had passed the Nanking provincial examination in 1630 along with Ch'en Tzu-lung and joined the Chi-she movement in Sung-chiang. Ho decided not to compete further in the examinations and turned instead to the study of military strategy and organization. He joined Hsü Fu-yüan (1599–1665), another of the Chi-she founders, in planning strategies for the defense of the Yangtze.[77] Together with Ch'en Tzu-lung and others, they eventually began to build their own naval force to apply their strategies. The Chi-she group stressed the methods of the late Ming general, Ch'i Chi-kuang. They favored small, well-integrated fighting units with a command system strengthened by personal loyalties. They also advocated recruiting professional fighting men from areas that traditionally provided tough soldiers. Ch'en Tzu-lung's discussions of *pao-chia* and militia in the lake region show the influence of this persuasion.

Ho Kang and Hsü Fu-yüan must have welcomed the appearance of a bold personality like Hsü Tu on the scene. Not only had he proved his talent as a strategist, but he also was a native of the mountainous region of Chekiang, the birthplace of Ch'i Chi-kuang's own famous army. Ho Kang encouraged Hsü to return to his native Tung-yang and train a unit of fighting men that he felt capable of aiding in the defense of Chiang-nan. Ho felt certain that they would soon have their chance, that Hsü would easily win a commission and, perhaps, bureaucratic rank. Hsü Tu took Ho's advice. Together with a small group of men from Tung-yang and the surrounding districts he pieced together an army of considerable size.[78]

By the autumn of 1643, Hsü's followers were said to have numbered in the tens of thousands.[79] The figures are impossible to verify, but it is clear that many locally prominent men of less than bureaucratic elite status were involved, and that the organization extended throughout the prefecture. Such an organization, noted for its discipline and its association with prominent families, could hardly avoid dealing with the district magistrate. But Hsü Tu's relations with the magistrate were less than amicable. The Tung-yang magistrate was Yao Sun-fei, member of one of the most prominent families in T'ung-ch'eng, Anhwei.[80] Like all magistrates, Yao was under extreme pressure to meet tax quotas and surcharges in the midst of drought and political unrest.

Finally, in November, one of Hsü's subordinates attempted to raid the armory in a district south of Chin-hua. Hsü himself was implicated and all attempts to clear him failed. Unable to strike an agreement with the magistrate without agreeing to contribute a large portion of the tax quota, Hsü found himself in a very difficult position. Soon his enemies, with the help of Magistrate Yao, convinced provincial officials to move against him, warning that he was planning an insurrection. Because thousands of guests had assembled for the burial ceremony of Hsü's mother, provincial authorities accused him of plotting a rebellion and began to hunt down his lieutenants. With that Hsü had no choice but to rise.[81]

In no time the rebels controlled Tung-yang and two neighboring districts. The alarm sounded in Chin-hua, Shao-hsing, and Hangchow. Chekiang had a rebellion on its hands. The governorship was temporarily vacant. It fell to Tso Kuang-hsien, the provincial inspector (*hsün-an*), to meet the crisis. Tso was the younger brother of Tso Kuang-tou, the Tung-lin martyr, also from T'ung-ch'eng, and related to Magistrate Yao by marriage.[82] Obviously he would be subject to pressure from both sides. But irrespective of his sympathies in the Yao-Hsü dispute, he had to preserve order. First Tso dispatched the governor's brigade to Chin-hua prefecture. They proved to be no match for Hsü Tu's well-trained, well-disciplined, and popularly respected troops. The crisis deepened. Ch'en Tzu-lung, who had been in Sung-chiang laying plans for receiving the heir apparent in Nanking, rushed back to Shao-hsing in hopes of arranging a settlement. Meanwhile the governor's elite guard, which had been led by Ch'en Tzu-lung himself during the rebel incursions of 1642, succeeded in forcing Hsü Tu out of Tung-yang and into the hills nearby. Ch'en took it upon himself to mediate. First he obtained a tentative promise of amnesty from the authorities, at least until the case could be heard. Then he rode into the hills alone to discuss the matter with Hsü Tu.

Ch'en suggested to Hsü that surrender would be the best policy. At that very moment Ho Kang was submitting a recommendation, through channels cleared by Ch'en Tzu-lung and Shih K'o-fa, that Hsü Tu be offered a commission and brought to the defense of Nanking.[83] Ho's proposal linked Hsü with Liu Tsung-chou and others of the bureaucratic elite in northern Chekiang in a broad plan to experiment with advancement through local leadership. Hsü Tu had made the whole plan look absurd. Praised in Peking for his outstanding loyalty, he was leading an insurrection against the Ming magistrate in his hometown. Ch'en and his associates could save the situation only if they could make Yao Sun-fei appear to be the traitor and remove Hsü Tu expeditiously to points north. Ch'en Tzu-lung did not restrain his anger at Hsü and warned him that he would be lucky to escape with his life, but still, surrender was their only hope. After some heated argument with his lieutenants, Hsü convinced them of Ch'en's sincerity, ordered the rebels to disband, and led sixty of his men in surrendering to the governor's guard.

By the time Ho Kang's proposal reached the emperor, Hsü Tu was dead. Peking agreed to experiment with Ho's plan, offered Hsü and the others commissions, and appointed Ho himself as secretary of the Bureau of Operations in the Ministry of War. But opposition pressure in Chekiang had already taken its toll. As Ch'en Tzu-lung accompanied the captured rebels to Hangchow, leaders of the local elite blocked their way and demanded execution. Ch'en argued that the act of surrender at least warranted a fair trial, and managed to secure passage to Hangchow. The pressure continued to mount. By the time they reached the city's gates it was clear that a fair hearing would be impossible. At first Ch'en argued unsuccessfully that it boded ill to execute one who surrendered in good faith, sparing the government a battle. Then he pleaded that if blood must flow, it should be Hsü Tu's only. His followers had surrendered under orders and their lives, at least, should be spared. But Ch'en's arguments were all to no avail. All sixty of the rebels were executed without trial before the city's gate, by order of Tso Kuang-hsien.

From Ch'en Tzu-lung's perspective, Hsü Tu was the maligned hero of this episode and the traitor to the Ming cause was Yao Sun-fei.[84] But the true lesson of the whole affair, I believe, lies elsewhere. Ch'en's anguish was personal. He, more than any other, was responsible both for Hsü Tu's high expectations and his death. Hsü Fu-yüan had first recommended Hsü Tu to Ch'en, and it was through Ch'en that Hsü Tu could hope to achieve success. It was also Ch'en's unfounded promise of amnesty that led Hsü Tu to surrender. Still, it must have been clear to Ch'en that as long as the dispute between a magistrate like Yao Sun-fei and a local strongman like Hsü Tu could have such dramatic repercussions, the whole basis of the restoration was in doubt.

The planners we have considered above, including Ch'en Tzu-lung, did not abide the kind of independence that Hsü Tu exhibited.

Ch'i Piao-chia and Hou T'ung-tseng, both of whom were quite close
to the situation, praised Tso Kuang-hsien's action in the case. Had
Hsü Tu gone unpunished, they believed, Ming control of Chiang-nan
would have been lost.[85] No matter how sympathetic other restorationists may have been to Ch'en Tzu-lung's plan, they knew that
private military action and restoration were an explosive mix. But
what none, including Ch'en, was ready to admit was that without
building a restoration on an alliance of men like Hsü Tu—from the
bottom up—they could do little to determine the direction of Chiang-
nan's defenses regardless of its political color. Nearly two years
later Hsü Tu, the rebel, had his ironic revenge.

HSÜ TU AND THE RESTORATION

It remains for us to examine the full implication of the Hsü Tu affair
in the events of the autumn of 1644. Ma Shih-ying had failed in his
first attempt to win an appointment for Juan Ta-ch'eng in mid-
July. In August, Liu Tsung-chou assumed his post as director of the
Bureau of Investigation, guaranteeing Tung-lin control of the three
politically most important positions in the bureaucracy, while the
grand secretaries numbered three to two in Tung-lin's favor. On
September 15 news reached Soochow that followers of Hsü Tu who
had evaded capture the previous spring had launched a new rebellion
and taken control of Tung-yang once again. Ch'i Piao-chia immediately dispatched emissaries to learn the details.[86] In Nanking Ma
Shih-ying recommended sending the imperial guard to Chekiang.
Chang Kuo-wei, a Tung-lin partisan whose native place was threatened, said there was no need.[87] The emperor (the former prince of
Fu) then ordered Ch'i to send the Chekiang governor's brigade back
to Chekiang to put down the revolt. Ch'i did not really comply with
this order. He sent half the Chekiang troops back but kept those
units which, by his own admission, were the better trained. In addition, he reviewed Ho Kang's troops and found them as impressive as
he had hoped. He recommended that Ho be given an extraordinary
provincial appointment and sent to Chekiang also.[88] In appearance,
the Chekiang Tung-lin group was claiming the authority to control the local situation in Chekiang—a bold assertion of power
vis-à-vis the central authority in Nanking.

At this critical juncture the governor of Chekiang, who was under attack for not anticipating the revolt, blamed Tso Kuang-hsien for creating the restive situation by executing Hsü Tu without a trial. This accusation was a political windfall for Ma Shih-ying. Not only was Tso a vociferous critic of Ma, but he and the governor were also important links in the power structure on which the Tung-lin group depended. If they were allowed to discredit one another the repercussions could be quite dramatic. On September 23 the emperor ordered the military censors to report the views of all native Chekiang personnel in Nanking concerning Tso Kuang-hsien's handling of the Hsü Tu affair. Then Ch'en Tzu-lung, caught in the middle as he had been by Hsü Tu's original rebellion, told his version of the story, blaming the perfidy of the magistrate Yao Sun-fei for precipitating the crisis.[89] Ch'en himself could hardly have wished for Tso Kuang-hsien's dismissal; it was Yao not Tso, who was to blame. But the new governor had to depend on Ch'en's story to defend himself. Both lost in the end, and the whole regional power structure suffered as a consequence.

The new uprising itself was settled in Tung-yang by local magnates, but its repercussions continued to shake Nanking.[90] On September 28 Ch'i Piao-chia submitted his memorandum defending Tso Kuang-hsien, which led, as described earlier, directly to the emperor's turn to Juan Ta-ch'eng and away from the Tung-lin. Although the nature of Juan's policies is not entirely clear, all the evidence points toward a deterioration of locally integrated defense networks in favor of centrally controlled projects and imperial demands for funds.[91] The dissolution of Ho Kang's navy and the isolation of Shih K'o-fa at Hangchow cannot be overemphasized. Whether or not the regional integration for which the native Tung-lin leaders stood provided any greater hope for Nanking is a moot point, but that it could not succeed without imperial support is clear.

This was the ultimate significance of the Hsü Tu affair for the politics of the restoration movement. The rebellion revealed a hiatus in the structure of political power. Hsü Tu's interests were not dynastic. Loyalty appears not to have been a great matter for him, but that he wielded a great deal of local influence is obvious. To the restoration planners loyalty was a serious matter indeed. It is equally significant that Ch'i Piao-chia and Ch'en Tzu-lung did not bolt and join Shih K'o-fa in establishing a rival regime in Chiang-nan once Nanking was lost to the Ma–Juan clique. There is no better demonstration of their dilemma than Ch'en Tzu-lung's own argument. Ch'en had opposed Hsü's execution because he believed it was better to tolerate special interests and private power than to weaken the chances for Chiang-nan's defense, but the rebellion had already left him stranded between obligations of loyalty and a populace that was indifferent to the Ming cause.

The story of another Tung-lin leader, Yang T'ing-shu, also typifies the loyalists' dilemma. Asked to participate in guerrilla resistance in the Soochow lake region after the fall of Nanking, he questioned the movement's legitimacy. To its leaders, who were also Tung-lin partisans, he purportedly objected, "Your proclamation of loyalty (*i*) surely comes from your loyal (*chung*) hearts, but from where will you get your supplies?" They replied, "We will get them from the people; we are not afraid of lacking supplies." "If that is the case," he rejoined, "then you are bandits. What has that to do with loyalty (*i*)?" He preferred to die a solitary martyr for his cause.[92] Do we hear sardonic laughter from Hsü Tu's grave?

POLITICAL INTEGRATION AND THE MING–CH'ING TRANSITION— A HYPOTHESIS

In this essay I have stressed the impact of a single case of local political dysfunction on the factional politics of the Nanking restoration. My purpose has been to shift the focus of historical discussion from loyalism and the personalities of famous men to the problems of local leadership and political integration. It should be clear that the Tung-lin leaders in southeastern Kiangsu and northern Chekiang were more than just a faction struggling for political power at the feet of the emperor in Nanking. They represented a large elite nexus of bureaucrats with a special interest in securing order throughout the several prefectures which divided their native land. It should also be clear that any attempt to identify them as local leaders is dubious. The "gentry," or larger mass of local magnates, has yet to be identified with the political elite on this level. In fact, the Hsü Tu affair calls into question the integration of bureaucratic politics and local power which scholars so often assume to have developed by this

time. The lesson of Nanking, I must conclude, is that political fragmentation was related to a hiatus in the structure of local power.

The key to stability in a time of dynastic crisis was some kind of
integration of local society into the political structure of the empire.
The failure of the bureaucratic elite to organize a viable defense in
Chiang-nan at the end of the Ming confirms my suspicions that the
elite did not serve this function in the mid-seventeenth century. A
man like Ch'en Tzu-lung could see that conventional regular militia
organization would not suffice for the defense of Chiang-nan. Chin
Sheng's militia in Hui-chou probably served the Ch'ing better than
the loyalists. There were 180 rural compacts between Chin and his
militia. Chin ended his campaign not as a militia leader but as a
guerrilla; he had no control or command structure that would enable
him to control his militia in a military crisis.

On the other hand, Ch'i Piao-chia's more highly centralized approach was equally ineffective, for as governor it was not the coordinated "crop-watching corps" he led but a coalition of bureaucrats
with political interests. Insofar as that group would depend on local
organization for support it failed. Hou T'ung-tseng died in a futile
resistance effort, controlling the district city's gates but not the
countryside. Ch'i Piao-chia, who was perhaps more realistic about
the restoration's prospects, chose a less dramatic and less destructive
private suicide. Ch'en Tzu-lung continued his dream, hoping to
coordinate guerrillas, natural social units, and bureaucratic leaders in
support of one prince or another until treachery trapped him in
1647. The "Mandate of Heaven" had long since returned to the
Ch'ing. What, then, of the local leaders to whom the restoration
planners had turned?

The Hsü Tu affair leads to a hypothesis concerning this question.
Hsü Tu may well have been typical of the local leadership on which
the new Ch'ing regime came to depend in much of the south. To
the Manchus it mattered little if such men lacked the power and
status to influence court politics directly. Locally, the rural militia
and the *pao-chia* system—the fragmented forces of the bureaucratic
elite—paled in their shadow. In eastern Kiangsu at least, it was a
private paramilitary organization which guaranteed Ch'ing control in
T'ai-ts'ang, where the elite were remarkably swift in denouncing allegiance to the Ming house.[93] The same group could claim responsi-

bility for repressing further resistance in Chia-ting, where other obscure leaders seem to have competed for power with little regard for dynastic concerns.

It is the final irony of the Hsü Tu affair that men like Tso Kuang-hsien and Ch'i Piao-chia stood between Hsü and the political authority of the Ming state. The Ch'ing could turn to such men boldly. Not only did the new rulers have sufficient confidence to encourage such shows of local strength, but they also stood to benefit by changing the political complexion of magistracies long dominated by the special interests of the bureaucratic elite. Development of this hypothesis awaits further research and it may well prove to be mistaken. After all, most of the powerful families of the late Ming period survived well into the eighteenth century. The point I should like to stress is that the degree of political integration at the end of the Ming may by no means be taken for granted. The development of the late imperial polity may have owed something to the lesson of Nanking.

NOTES TO CHAPTER 3

1. For a comprehensive annotated bibliography of traditional sources, see Hsieh Kuo-chen, *Wan-ming shih chi k'ao* (Peiping, 1932; Taipei, 1968). The best modern analysis of the fall of the Ming is Li Wen-chih, *Wan-ming min-pien* (Hong Kong, 1948). For a summary of the military campaigns, see James Parsons, *The Peasant Rebellions of the Late Ming Dynasty* (Tucson, 1970). For recent work in English on the conquest and the Chinese resistance, see Frederic Wakeman, "Localism and Loyalism during the Ch'ing Conquest of Chiang-nan: The Siege of Chiang-yin," in Wakeman, ed., *Conflict and Control in Late Imperial China* (Berkeley, 1975), and Jerry P. Dennerline, "The Chia-ting Loyalists: A Study of Conflict in Seventeenth Century China" (MS of a forthcoming book, n.d.).

2. My definition of the political elite in local society includes specifically the holders of civil service degrees that made them eligible for appointment to public office. For this reason I refer to the "bureaucratic elite" rather than "gentry" or "local elite." For a detailed discussion, see Dennerline, "The Chia-ting Loyalists," chap. 3.

3. For some examples of popular historical narratives, see Chu Yü, *Chia-ting chih chan* (Peking, 1956), Hu Shan-yüan, *Chia-ting i-min pieh-chuan* (Shanghai, 1938), Li Tung-fang, *Hsi-shuo Ming-ch'ao* and *Hsi-shuo Ch'ing-ch'ao*. For examples of more sophisticated historical studies that combine traditional

and modern approaches with the popular view, see Hsieh Kuo-chen, *Nan-ming shih-lüeh* (Shanghai, 1957), Li Kuang-pi, *Ming-ch'ao shih-lüeh* (Wuhan, 1957), and Li T'ien-yu, *Ming-mo Chiang-yin Chia-ting jen-min ti k'ang-Ch'ing tou-cheng* (Shanghai, 1955).

4. For the Nanking restoration story, see Hsieh Kuo-chen, *Nan-ming shih-lüeh*. The most comprehensive traditional accounts are in Hsü Tzu, *Hsiao-t'ien chi-nien* (reprint, Taipei, 1962) and *Hsiao-t'ien chi-chuan* (reprint, Taipei, 1963), and Wen Jui-lin, *Nan-chiang i-shih* (reprint, Shanghai and Hong Kong, 1971). An earlier and equally comprehensive but somewhat less reliable account is Chi Liu-ch'i, *Ming-chi nan-lüeh* (reprint, Taipei, 1963). For the background of the factional struggle, see Hsieh Kuo-chen, *Ming-Ch'ing chih chi tang-she yün-tung k'ao* (Shanghai, 1934; reprint, Taipei, 1967); Charles Hucker, "The Tung-lin Movement of the Late Ming Period," in John K. Fairbank, ed., *Chinese Thought and Institutions* (Chicago, 1957); and Ulrich Mammitzsch, "Wei Chung-hsien (1568–1628): A Reappraisal of the Eunuch and the Factional Strife at the Late Ming Court" (Ph.D. diss., University of Hawaii, 1968).

5. See Hsieh Kuo-chen, *Ming-Ch'ing chih chi* (1967 reprint), pp. 17–22.

6. The Hsü Tu affair receives sparse attention in the chronicles of the restoration and the resistance. The most thorough account in this type of source is the biography of Ch'en Tzu-lung in Wen Jui-lin, *Nan-chiang i-shih* (1971 reprint), 14:99. For the details I have relied on other sources. See below.

7. Yang Te-en, *Shih K'o-fa nien-p'u* (Ch'ang-sha, 1940), pp. 30–31, and Ch'i Piao-chia, *Chia-i jih-li* (reprint, Taipei, 1969), p. 9. See Frederic Wakeman's account in this volume and note 49 below.

8. *Ch'ung-chen ch'ang-pien* (Taipei, 1969), p. 23.

9. Ibid., p. 43. Also see Yang Te-en, *Shih K'o-fa nien-p'u,* pp. 30ff.

10. Yang Te-en, *Shih K'o-fa nien-p'u.* See below, note 49.

11. Hsü Tzu, *Hsiao-t'ien chi-nien,* 6:266; Ch'en Tzu-lung, "Nien-p'u," in *Ch'en Chung-yü kung ch'üan-chi* (1803) 2:17. The "navy" was probably a fighting unit that used boats for patrolling the rivers and coastal region. For a discussion of Chinese "naval" forces, see Edward L. Dreyer, "The Poyang Campaign, 1363: Inland Naval Warfare in the Founding of the Ming Dynasty," in Frank Kierman and John Fairbank, eds., *Chinese Ways in Warfare* (Cambridge, Mass., 1974), p. 204.

12. Shih K'o-fa and Chiang Yüeh-kuang, who had memorialized as Nanking officials that the heir apparent should be sent there, were both grand secretaries under the new regime. Both had been Tung-lin partisans in political disputes since the 1620s. Shih was concurrently minister of war. Chang Kuo-wei, another partisan, was in charge of the Nanking brigade. Chang Shen-yen was the minister of personnel (see Li Yen, *Tung-lin tang-chi k'ao* [Peking, 1957], p. 48), who recommended the other partisans. Cheng San-chün (Li Yen, *Tung-lin tang,* p. 39), whom Shih and Chang were attacked for recommending, had probably tried to make Nanking a Tung-lin enclave in the early 1630s. See Dennerline, "The Chia-ting Loyalists," chap. 7. The politics of Nanking at the end of the Ming would be an excellent topic for research.

13. Chi Liu-ch'i, *Ming-chi nan-lüeh*, 4:85–88. Only one censor is reported to have argued specifically that Juan had no military expertise. On his strategies, see ibid., 2:32–33.

14. This view is presented in Hsieh Kuo-chen, *Ming-Ch'ing chih chi* (1967), pp. 99–116, without analysis of the sequence of events. For the date of the executions, see Wen Jui-lin, *Nan-chiang i-shih*, 2:27, and Chi Liu-ch'i, *Ming-chi nan-lüeh*, 2:41.

15. See Li Yen, *Tung-lin tang-chi k'ao*, p. 20; Yao Ming-ta, *Liu Tsung-chou nien-p'u* (Shanghai, 1934).

16. Yao Ming-ta, pp. 318–24.

17. See Hsü Tzu, *Hsiao-t'ien chi nien*, 7:289–91.

18. Ch'i Piao-chia, *Chia-i jih-li*, p. 47.

19. E.g., Ch'i Piao-chia, *Chia-i jih-li*, p. 69 (2/11 and 2/12), and passim; Hou T'ung-tseng, *Hou Chung-chieh kung ch'üan-chi* (1933), 8:17b. One local leader on whom there is some information was Ko Lin (1605–45; 1642 *chü-jen*). Ko had first addressed his plans for military organization to Shih K'o-fa by letter in 1643. His discussions of militia organization and strategy so impressed Ch'i that he made him coordinator of militia for Chen-chiang prefecture and liaison for the defense of Ching-k'ou. His plans included official positions for *t'uan-lien* leaders. See Ko Lin, *Ko Chung-han i chi* (1890), 2:8–12b; 3:1–4; Ch'i Piao-chia, *Chia-i jih-li*, pp. 62–63.

20. Ibid., pp. 37–38.

21. See Hsü Tzu, *Hsiao-t'ien chi-nien*, 7:291.

22. See Wen Jui-lin, *Nan-chiang i-shih*, ch. 1. The sequence of events does not include the debate over the Hsü Tu affair, leaving the impression that both Ch'i Piao-chia and Tso Kuang-hsien were relatively late victims of the purge. In fact, Tso's case arose before the purges began. See below.

23. For the date of this memorial, see Ch'i Piao-chia, *Chia-i jih-li*, p. 59.

24. On Tso Kuang-hsien, see *T'ung-ch'eng hsien-chih* (1673), 4:48. For his handling of the Hsü Tu affair, see below.

25. For the content of the memorial, see Chi Liu-ch'i, *Ming-chi nan-lüeh*, 5:146.

26. Wen Jui-lin, *Nan-chiang i-shih*, ch. 1. Perhaps the first sign of the emperor's disfavor was the appointment of Wang Ying-hsiung the day after Ch'en Tzu-lung's story (see below) was aired at court. The Tung-lin faction had engineered Wang's dismissal from office in 1635, blaming him for the rebels' first attacks on Chiang-nan. See *Ch'ung-chen shih lu* (reprint, Nan-kang, 1962–68), 8:12.

27. Ch'en Tzu-lung had been selected by Shih K'o-fa to present a strategy for defending the river. Ch'en, in turn, recommended that Ho Kang, the man who trained the Sung-chiang naval force, be put in charge of the Yangtze defense. See Ch'en Tzu-lung, "Nien-p'u," 2:18–19, and *Shang-hai hsien-chih* (Chia-ch'ing, ed.), 13:23b. Ho received a post subordinate to Juan Ta-ch'eng before the purge was completed, but eventually lost it. See below.

28. Ch'i Piao-chia, *Chia-i jih-li*, p. 63.

29. Ch'i himself noted that the case against Chiang Yüeh-kuang, the sympa-

thetic grand secretary, charged him with supporting Ch'i's subversive recommendations. See his *Chia-i jih-li*, p. 60. To my knowledge the only source which suggests that Liu Tsung-chou's case derived from the case against Ch'i is Ku Yen-wu, *Ming-chi san-ch'ao yeh-shih* (reprint Taipei, 1961), pp. 11–12; but Ku did not elaborate.

30. For Yang Wen-ts'ung, cf. Ch'i Piao-chia, *Chia-i jih-li*, p. 71. Ch'i did eventually see Yang, and Yang explained that Ma had originally harbored no prejudice against the Tung-lin faction but was cornered by Liu Tsung-chou's argument. (Yang appears as a central figure in K'ung Shang-jen's drama, *T'ao-hua shan*.)

31. Hsü Tzu, *Hsiao-t'ien chi nien*, 8:380.

32. *Shang-hai hsien-chih*, 13:23b, and below. A similar case was that of Shen T'ing-yang, who had hoped to divert "grain tribute" funds to train and supply a navy but eventually resigned because of conflicts with another of Ma's handpicked men. See *Ming shih* (Taipei, 1963), 276:3104; Hsü Tzu, *Hsiao-t'ien chi nien*, 6:225, *Hsiao-t'ien chi chuan*, 44:536.

33. The provincial administrations of Kiangsu and Anhwei developed between 1645 and 1667. See *Chiang-nan t'ung-chih* (1684), 2:4, 11:6; *An-hui t'ung-chih* (1830), 7:3–4.

34. For the Ming administrative institutions, see *Ming shih*, 40:434–42.

35. For a list of the appointments, see Wu T'ing-hsieh, *Ming tu-fu nien-piao* (no publication data, post-1911), 4:35–36.

36. Before the Yüan period, Sung-chiang had been attached to Chia-hsing prefecture in northern Chekiang. From the founding of the Ming until its fall, tax problems and problems of control often focused on the seven prefectures of eastern Kiangsu and northern Chekiang as a unit. See *Ming shih*, 78:824; Ku Yen-wu, *Jih-chih lu chi-shih* (Ssu-pu pei yao ed.), 10:7, 10:13. It is also clear that in the Fu-she political-intellectual movement, the social ties among members from southeastern Kiangsu and northern Chekiang were especially numerous. See Wu Shan-chia, *Fu-she hsing-shih chuan lüeh* (1832 ed.; Hangchow, 1961), passim.

37. Tai Ming-shih, *Chieh-i lu* (reprint, Taipei, 1969), pp. 3–4.

38. Ibid., pp. 2–5; Hou T'ung-tseng, *Hou Chung-chieh kung ch'üan-chi* 6:9; Li Wen-chih, *Wan-ming min-pien*, pp. 55–61.

39. Chang Ssu-shan, "Kung te chi," in Shih K'o-fa, *Shih Chung-cheng kung chi* (Shanghai, 1937), appendix, pp. 68 ff; Tai Ming-shih, *Chieh-i lu*, pp. 5–9.

40. On the personalized nature of this post and its administrative reorganization under Shih K'o-fa, see Chu Wen-chang, *Shih K'o-fa chuan* (Chungking, 1943), pp. 8–21; Chang Ssu-shan, "Kung te chi"; Sung Chih-cheng, "Liu-an-sheng tzu-chi," in Shih K'o-fa, *Shih Chung-cheng kung chi*, appendix, p. 70.

41. Hou T'ung-tseng argued this, see below, pp. 116–17; also see Chang Ts'ai, "Chün-ch'u shuo," *Chih-wei t'ang wen-ts'un* (1675), 11:18.

42. Tai Ming-shih, *Chieh-i lu*, pp. 27–28; Parsons, *Peasant Rebellions*, pp. 115–17.

43. Ch'en Tzu-lung, "Nien-p'u," 1:27–31. See Dennerline, "The Chia-ting Loyalists," chap. 6, and below.

44. *Chen-yang hsien-chih* (Ch'ien-lung edition), 12A:50b; *Pao-shan hsien-chih* (1882), 6:25.

45. See below, p. 109.

46. Hou Yüan-ching, "Nien-p'u," in Hou T'ung-tseng, *Hou Chung-chieh kung ch'üan-chi,* 3:2; *Hsiu-shui hsien chih* (1684), 5:8b.

47. Information on such groups organized before 1644 is sketchy. Most notable was Hsü Tu's. A similar group in T'ai-ts'ang was that of the P'u family; see *Chen-yang hsien chih,* 12A:48, and *Yen-t'ang chien-wen tsa-chi* (Shanghai, 1911), p. 3 and passim. For evidence of others in existence by 1644, see Wen Jui-lin, *Nan-chiang i-shih* (Taipei, 1962), 25:370—Lu of K'un-shan; *Pao-shan hsien-chih,* 8:36, 9:57—Hsü[a] of Chia-ting; *Yen-t'ang,* p. 3—Shih of Ch'ang-shu. Also see Dennerline, "The Chia-ting Loyalists," chaps. 9–10—Hsü[b] and Wang of Chia-ting; and note 20 above—Ko Lin of Chen-chiang.

48. Hou T'ung-tseng, *Hou Chung-chieh kung ch'üan-chi,* 7:4b.

49. Yang Te-en, *Shih K'o-fa nien-p'u* (Ch'ang-sha, 1940), pp. 30f., states that Shih and Chiang Yüeh-kuang memorialized the plan before the last month of 1643, citing Cha Chi-tso, *Tsui-wei lu. Tsui-wei lu* (Ssu-pu ts'ung-k'an ed.), 17:41, notes a secret memorial of Li Pang-hua before the ninth month urging that the emperor's other two sons be enfeoffed at T'ai-p'ing and Ning-kuo, south of the Yangtze. But *Tsui-wei lu hsüan-chi* (Taipei, 1963), p. 109, dates the memorial of Chiang and Shih to after the new year. Chang Tai, *Shih kuei shu hou-chi* (Taipei, 1960), 24:229, dates it before the new year. Ch'i Piao-chia discussed the plan with Ch'en Tzu-lung on March 22, 1644; see Ch'i Piao-chia, *Chia-i jih-li* (Taipei, 1969), p. 9. According to Li Ch'ing, *San-yüan pi-chi* (Wu-hsing, 1927), 3:12, the emperor called an audience with only the top bureaucratic officials in Peking to test rumors of such a plan on March 31, and Li Pang-hua then made the proposal directly to him.

50. *Ming shih,* 277:3110; Wen Jui-lin, *Nan-chiang i-shih* (1971), 14:96; *Hsiu-ning hsien-chih* (1693), 6:24b.

51. There is an interesting exchange of letters between Chin and Shih concerning this affair. See Chin Sheng, *Chin Chung-chieh kung wen-chi* (1888), 1:24–34, 4:53–58, 5:1–27; Shih K'o-fa, *Shih Chung-cheng kung chi* (1897), 2:11. Also see Ch'ien Ch'ien-i, *Mu-chai ch'üan-chi: Ch'u-hsüeh chi* (1910), 80:1–6.

52. *Hsiu-ning hsien-chih,* 6:24b. See Chin Sheng, *Chin Chung-chieh kung wen-chi,* 1:45–46b, 4:1–53, 8:40–48b.

53. One is struck by the similarities between this plan and the general spirit of the nineteenth-century *t'uan-lien* militia. That spirit was aptly described by Philip Kuhn, *Rebellion and Its Enemies in Late Imperial China* (Cambridge, Mass., 1970), p. 32, as "militarization that grew from the needs of the natural units of local organization." I would hypothesize that the only difference was a hiatus in leadership below the bureaucratic elite in Chin Sheng's time, meaning that the compacts themselves may not have shared Chin's loyalist sentiments.

54. Chin Sheng, *Chin Chung-chieh kung ch'üan-chi,* 8:41–48b.

55. *Hsiu-ning hsien-chih,* 2:17.

56. In Chekiang it was led by Ch'i Piao-chia and others. See Ch'i Piao-chia, *Chia-i jih-li*, pp. 1–10. During the restoration in Kiangsu, Ko Lin of Chen-chiang led a militia organization similar to Chin's. See above, note 19.

57. *Ming Shih*, 275:3094; Wen Jui-lin, *Nan-chiang i-shih* (1971), 11:81; Wang Ssu-jen, *Ch'i Chung-min kung nien-p'u*, in Ch'i Piao-chia, *Chia-i jih-li*, appendix.

58. See *Ch'i Piao-chia chi* (Shanghai, 1960), 6:122–26. Also see Kuhn, *Rebellion and its Enemies*, p. 33.

59. Ch'en Tzu-lung, "Nien-p'u," 2:1–4.

60. Ch'i Piao-chia, *Chia-i jih-li*, pp. 1–10.

61. *Ming shih*, 277:3113; Wen Jui-lin, *Nan-chiang i-shih* (1971), 14:99; Ch'en Tzu-lung, "Nien-p'u." Ch'en is the subject of a dissertation by William Atwell, Princeton University, 1975.

62. Ch'en Tzu-lung, "Nien-p'u," 1:27–31.

63. Ibid., 2:1–4.

64. Ch'en Tzu-lung, *Ch'en Chung-yü kung ch'üan-chi*, 22:17.

65. Ibid., 22:18b.

66. Ibid., 22:21b.

67. *Ming shih*, 277:3114; Wen Jui-lin, *Nan-chiang i-shih* (1971), 15:102; Hou Yüan-ching, "Nien-p'u." See Dennerline, "The Chia-ting Loyalists," chaps. 4 and 7.

68. Hou T'ung-tseng, *Hou Chung-chieh kung ch'üan-chi*, 6:9, 6:11.

69. Ibid., 6:9.

70. Ibid., 7:4b.

71. See Huang Ch'un-yüeh, *Huang T'ao-an chi* (1924), 2:4; *Chia-ting hsien-chih* (1673), 21:39.

72. Hou T'ung-tseng, *Hou Chung-chieh kung ch'üan-chi*, 8:4.

73. See Dennerline, "The Chia-ting Loyalists," chap. 6.

74. Wen Jui-lin, *Nan chiang i-shih* (1971), 14:99, says Hsü Tu was the son of a noted family. *Tung-yang hsien-chih* (Tao-kuang ed.), 6:23b, says he was the grandson of Hsü Ta-tao (1607 chin-shih; see *Tung-yang*, 17:10). "Tung-yang ping-pien," in *Ching-t'o i shih*, says he was the grandson of Hsü Hung-kang (1580 chin-shih; see *Tung-yang*, 13:12b).

75. *Tung-yang hsien-chih*, 12:7b.

76. *Ming shih*, 274:3080; Wen Jui-lin, *Nan-chiang i-shih* (1971), 11:80; *Shanghai hsien-chih* (Chia-ch'ing ed.), 13:23b. On his ancestor Ho Kuang, *Shang-hai*, 12:10.

77. See Wen Jui-lin, *Nan-chiang i-shih* (1971), 14:99; "Hsü An-kung hsien-sheng nien-p'u," in Hsü Fu-yüan, *Tiao-heng t'ang ts'un kao* (Chin-shan, 1926). See also Hsü Fu-yüan's "Defending Against the Rebels in Chiang-nan," *Tiao-heng*, appendix; and "Yangtze Defense," in Ku Yen-wu, *T'ien-hsia chün-kuo li-ping shu* (Shanghai, 1936), 8:25.

78. Hsü Fu-yüan took the blame for encouraging Hsü Tu; see *Hsü An-kung hsien-sheng nien-p'u*. According to Wen Jui-lin and others, it was Ho Kang's plan.

79. The account which follows is drawn from Wen Jui-lin, *Nan-chiang i-shih*

(1971), 14:99–101, Hsü Tzu, *Hsiao-t'ien chi nien* 3:102–04, *Tung-yang hsien-chih,* 6:23b, 12:7b–8b, and Ch'en Tzu-lung, "Nien-p'u," 2:8–15. The most convincing detail is in *Tung-yang hsien-chih,* which is favorable to neither Hsü Tu nor Yao Sun-fei.

80. On Yao Sun-fei, see *T'ung-ch'eng hsien-chih* (1673), 4:52b, where Yao is described as the hero of the affair, very unconvincingly. On the Yao family, see ibid., 4:40b, 4:39b, 5:5b, 5:6b, and chüan 3, passim.

81. According to *Tung-yang hsien-chih,* Hsü Tu's group had long been of questionable loyalty, and it is implied that Hsü Tu himself was plotting rebellion or collaboration with other rebels. The loyalist annals all treat Hsü Tu as a victim of powerful local enemies, with no hint of disloyal intentions prior to the arrest of his lieutenants. All accounts agree that Yao forced his hand and that Hsü's enemies were involved in Yao's decision to call in government police.

82. On Tso Kuang-hsien, see note 24 above. I have found no further evidence of the Tso-Yao marriage ties.

83. *Ch'ung-chen shih lu,* 17:1.

84. Ch'en wrote only that "perfidious functionaries" (*chien li*) were to blame. See his "Nien-p'u," 2:9.

85. Hou T'ung-tseng, *Hou Kung-chieh kung ch'üan chi,* 8:14, and Hou Yüan-ching, "Nien-p'u," 3:5–6. For Ch'i Piao-chia's position, see above.

86. Ch'i Piao-chia, *Chia-i jih-li,* pp. 55–56.

87. *Tung-yang hsien-chih,* 12:8b.

88. Ch'i Piao-chia, *Chia-i jih-li,* p. 57.

89. Chi Liu-ch'i, *Ming-chi nan-lüeh,* 5:144–46.

90. *Tung-yang hsien-chih,* 12:8b.

91. See Chi Liu-ch'i, *Ming-chi nan-lüeh,* 2:33, and Hsü Tzu, *Hsiao-t'ien chi-nien,* 8:380.

92. *P'ing-wu shih-lüeh* (Taipei, 1968), p. 47.

93. The collaborationist group was led by the P'u family of T'ai-ts'ang. See note 47 above.

4

The Patriot and the Partisans
Wang Fu-chih's Involvement in the Politics of the Yung-li Court

by Ian McMorran

Philosophers

One of the distinctive features of traditional Chinese civilization
was that most intellectuals played, or aspired to play, political roles
and, correspondingly, that many officials were actively interested in
the intellectual trends and conflicts of their time. Thus the historian
of China often has the opportunity to see political events through
eyes sharpened by the light of an intense, subtle, and highly trained
intelligence. This is true of many of those involved in the Ming resistance movements, and Wang Fu-chih offers a particularly fine
example because he combined philosophical brilliance with active
participation and recorded his observations with unusual sensitivity.

There is a tendency, as we scan the works of many of the leading
scholar officials of imperial China, to conclude that they were often
rather pedestrian in describing the events that they had lived through,
and that they often seemed to be saving their deepest moral and
political insights for their theoretical writings, or for historical
studies of earlier periods. But in this study of Wang Fu-chih's involvement with the Prince of Kuei during the so-called Yung-li reign
(1647–62), and of Wang's history of that period as written in his
Yung-li shih-lu, *Ian McMorran* shows us how to trace the philosopher's personal responses in a raw political situation where Confucian theory offered few—or confusing—guidelines.

During his actual service at the Yung-li court in Kwangsi during
1650, Wang Fu-chih was forced to participate in the murderous and
destructive politics that divided the Wu and Ch'u factions and to
analyze concepts of duty and loyalty in deadly earnest; the distinction between an emperor's function and the emperor's person
had extra poignance in this atmosphere where the fugitive Ming
forces were visibly weakening their own strength, just as had those
in the Nanking court of the prince of Fu, studied above by Jerry
Dennerline. Wang's responses were complex and McMorran helps us
to understand them. They included such elements as the nostalgic
adoption of a Ch'ü Yüan analogy to his own role, the continual
honing of a perfectionist and critical mentality in which Wang
showed himself more "blind to the good points of his enemies than
the bad ones of his friends," an unwavering concern for the moral
counsel offered by the I-ching, and a deep commitment to the on-

135

*ward and regenerative movement of the cycles of history. In this
last case the regeneration, far in the future, could still offer present
solace to the philosopher caught in a situation where politics seemed
too deeply out of phase with philosophy to offer hopes of meaningful personal action.*

In 1644 North China was the scene of two crippling blows to the
already crumbling Chinese polity. First the Ming emperor was
overthrown and Peking occupied by the peasant forces of Li Tzu-
ch'eng, and then the new masters of the capital were themselves
promptly ousted by the combined armies of the Manchu regent
Dorgon and the Ming general Wu San-kuei, whose defection to the
Ch'ing invaders thus helped to usher in a period of foreign domination which was to endure until the twentieth century. Yet while
the Ch'ing regime proceeded, with considerable collaboration on
the part of both the military and civil officials of the previous
dynasty, rapidly to consolidate its position in the north, in the
south resistance was sufficiently protracted for certain historians to
use the term "Southern Ming" to describe it—by analogy, of course,
with the Southern Sung. Such an analogy can scarcely be sustained in
terms of duration of rule or territory controlled, but for nearly two
decades after the fall of Peking various princes of the Ming imperial
house did provide focal points for resistance to the new dynasty.

These resistance-loyalist regimes were, however, plagued by political conflict both internally and, where the "reigns" of different
pretenders to the throne overlapped, amongst themselves. The establishment of the first of them in Nanking, for example, was the
occasion of a factional dispute over the rival claims of two princes[1]
similar to the struggle between the inner court and the "righteous
circles" which had erupted in Peking under the last Ming emperors.[2]
Later the supporters of two other claimants even went so far as to
meet in pitched battle in Kwangtung.[3] On the other hand, while the
new order in Peking constituted not only a change of dynasty but a
foreign occupation, the Ch'ing rulers had, even before 1644, created
a Manchu state sinicized enough to attract large numbers of Chinese
collaborators. Now they bolstered their claims to the legitimate

succession by representing themselves as righteous avengers punishing the unruly hordes that had destroyed the Ming and upholding the institutional order which the peasant insurrection had menaced. Indeed, they proceeded to adopt the Ming administrative apparatus as the basis of their government of the country. Consequently, the Chinese of this period were, in deciding where their loyalties lay, confronted with an exceedingly complex situation.

The complexity of this situation was reflected in the reactions of individual scholar-officials, and this essay is essentially a study of the response of one of them, the philosopher Wang Fu-chih, who was a *chü-jen* of twenty-five when Peking fell. Wang himself played only a minor part in the political events of his time, but he was throughout his life a passionately concerned witness of them, as is clear from his writings, and his *Veritable Records of the Yung-li Reign (Yung-li shih-lu)* is one of the basic sources for the history of the Yung-li period (1647–62).[4] However, although the focus in the following pages is principally on Wang and his efforts to reconcile the disparate and often contradictory demands of the situation in which he found himself as he understood it, a preliminary attempt is also made to identify and interpret some of the forces at work during the early part of the Yung-li period, in particular the various groups which constituted this center of loyalist resistance and the nature of their alliances and rivalries.

In 1658, when writing a *Brief Family History (Chia-shih chieh-lu)*,[5] Wang reflected ruefully that, if only he had heeded his father's warning not to compromise his ideals by becoming involved with contemporary political cliques, he might have avoided "the struggle with evil men" at the Yung-li court eight years previously. The consequences of this involvement, he went on to lament, were that he was forced to retire from the court and was thus prevented from either following the example of the Chin hero, Chi Shao,[6] and dying at his ruler's side or from finding "a single patch of uncontaminated soil whereon to die." Later, when composing his own epitaph, he described the undying chagrin he felt at having "nursed the solitary wrath of a Liu Yüeh-shih without finding any way of sacrificing my life."[7]

Such expressions of remorse were certainly genuine (though the salute to his late father's wisdom is probably colored by feelings of

filial duty) but Wang was generally inclined to depict himself less as
misguided than as maligned and misunderstood, a loyal servant of
the emperor frustrated by vicious intrigue. In his case, he felt, the
comparison with Ch'ü Yuan in which disappointed scholar-officials
were wont to indulge, was justified. In the preface to his commentary on the *Ch'u Tz'u,* he wrote:

> If one were to sum up Master Ch'ü in a word it would be "loyal."
> . . . His integrity filled the heavens and the earth, and it was
> because of this that he incurred the hatred of envious and resent-
> ful people. How vile it was! And it was all because he was as pure
> as snow. In appending (my own composition) the *Chiu-chao* as a
> sequel I do not wish to imply that I am as gifted or worthy as he,
> but there is a similarity in the circumstances of time and place
> and our solitary spirits do resemble one another.[8]

He took the comparison even further in the introduction to his own
Chiu-chao, declaring: "Wang Fu-chih of the Ming dynasty was born
in the homeland of Master Ch'ü, but encountered a greater sorrow
and nursed a greater ambition than Ch'ü."[9] A native of Heng-yang,
Wang was, of course, like Ch'ü a man of Ch'u, and the parallel between the story of Ch'ü Yuan and his own experiences at the Yung-li
court is implicit throughout this work. He also provides the reader
with a commentary to spell out the message when the poetry does
not make it clear. Thus, when he writes, "if only I had been able to
exterminate the evil men in time then Ch'u might still survive, so I do
not regret the fact that I brought disaster upon myself by struggling
against them,"[10] one understands that for "Ch'u" one may substitute "the Yung-li court." (The Yung-li emperor, the prince of Kuei,
was, moreover a prince of Ch'u insofar as the family estates were in
Heng-chou.)

Such quotations as those above epitomize that image of Wang's
loyalty and patriotism which, burning like some fierce beacon across
the years, was to earn for him a special place in the regard of both
nineteenth-century reformers and twentieth-century revolutionaries,
particularly among his fellow Hunanese, in whom his regional pride
as well as his nationalism kindled a responsive spark.[11] Thus Wang
himself eventually became a paradigm of the virtues of the scholar-
patriot and joined the lists of those conventional stereotypes which

he had once invoked as a regional and a national hero. The importance of such stereotypes is not to be minimized; for Confucian scholars imbued with historical lore, they provided vivid representations of continuing validity and immediate relevance to their own moral choices. Indeed, I am inclined to believe that such stereotypes provided more than mere pegs of reference or opportunities for vain literary posturing (though they did both), but actually influenced the conduct of men of the calibre of Wang Fu-chih, who treated them absolutely seriously—even to the point of acting out the roles appropriate to their adopted personae.[12] They were, moreover, closely bound up with the process of assessing and passing moral judgments on individuals which formed a central element in the traditional study of history—not least in the case of Wang's own historical writing, his concern with institutions and overall trends notwithstanding. In this respect, it is worth noting that there is a marked difference between the *Yung-li shih-lu* and Wang's major historical works, the *Sung lun* (*On the history of the Sung*) and *Tu T'ung-chien lun* (*On reading the "Comprehensive Mirror"*).[13] In both the *Sung lun* and the *Tu T'ung-chien lun,* the reader is presented with an interpretation of events and a critique of institutions and personalities according to a systematically intricate but coherent philosophy of history. Both works are couched in the form of discursive commentaries, which may be read as a series of essays in historical criticism, rather than records of events. A knowledge of the historical background on the part of the reader is largely, and justifiably, taken for granted.[14] The *Yung-li shih-lu* is almost their exact opposite in both form and content.

The *Yung-li shih-lu* consists of one *chüan* devoted to the basic annals of the reign, followed by over twenty *chüan* of biographies. The chronicle follows the bald annalistic style, but detailed accounts of events are given in the biographies of those who took part in them. The biographies themselves are often vividly descriptive and full of factual information, but evaluation is almost exclusively confined to passing moral judgments on individuals and groups. The grand historical perspective of Wang's other writing is strangely absent. The result is not, however, either as objective or as reliable as it might appear. Hsieh Kuo-chen, in his critical catalog of source materials for the late Ming period, the *Wan-Ming shih-chi k'ao,*

rightly draws attention to the partisan prejudice which occasionally
colors Wang's version of events and the factual errors and omissions
in his account of what happened after he had retired from court.[15]
For example, the *Yung-li shih-lu* biography of Wu Chen-yü, the
president of the Board of Revenue and a partisan of the faction
against which Wang struggled and lost, is a demonstrably unjust one,
and the so-called Disaster of the Pledge in Water (*Chou-shui chih
huo*) in 1661 does not appear in Wang's history.[16] Nevertheless,
Hsieh, who drew extensively on the *Yung-li shih-lu* in writing his own
history of the period,[17] notes that Wang's work is most detailed and
reliable for the time when he was personally participating in the
administration.

One might say as much of other contemporary accounts such as
So chih lu;[18] indeed, all interpretations of the Yung-li period tend to
fall into a limited series of patterns in which the stereotypes and
clichés vary according to the historian's standpoint. Hsieh is no more
innocent of the charge than Wang himself. Where the latter is undoubtedly inclined to present the activities of the Ch'u partisans,
whom he had supported, in a favorable light as those of public-
spirited and patriotic men, in contrast to the corruption and
self-seeking of the opposing Wu faction, Hsieh emphasizes the
bureaucratic and gentry decadence of which both factions were a
product and contrasts it with the realistic vigor and patriotic fervor
of Yung-li's peasant allies. For both Hsieh and Wang, however,
patriotism is a touchstone, and in this respect the Ch'u faction
emerges from their accounts with greater credit than the Wu. The
Ch'u faction is subjected to the severest criticism in sources used by
Chi Liu-ch'i for his *Ming-chi nan-lüeh*;[19] but even here, in a book
that was prohibited by the Ch'ing, one has to take into account the
tendency of Chinese historians to emphasize the decadence of the
last years of a dynasty, a tendency which Manchu inquisitorial
pressures could only encourage.

The very bias of the accounts of Wang and his contemporaries may,
however, prove to be as illuminating in some respects as it is confusing in others. Providing one can piece together the various versions,
one should at least obtain a wider perspective in which the stereotypes take on additional nuances and can be related to one another
in more meaningful terms than those of a manichaeistic morality—

be it Confucian or Marxist in inspiration. Not that it is merely a
question of comparing different sources and resolving their contra-
dictions. In order to understand Wang's position, one must supple-
ment his *Yung-li shih-lu* with whatever one can glean in the way of
relevant information and interpretation from elsewhere in his writings,
not only his other historical works but his philosophy, poetry,
miscellaneous essays, and family records. In the process one becomes
aware of the importance of setting the individual against the background of a particular family tradition as well as that of the prevailing trends in public scholarly debate.

Wang's dilemma was that of an orthodox Confucianist who believed, like his Sung master Chang Tsai, that philosophy and political
science, moral conduct and government service, were indivisibly
interconnected.[20] Such a position was, of course, characteristic of
the scholars of the Tung-lin movement and, as I have argued elsewhere,[21] Wang's attitude needs to be examined both in terms of the
Confucian philosophical tradition and in the context of such late
Ming politico-philosophical developments, because the immediate
pressures of contemporary events lent a particular perspective to
perennial problems. In fact, among the influences one may observe
at work on Wang during his formative years are an emphasis on
strict self-cultivation and the moral obligations of the individual,
inculcated in him by his father and elder brother, and the more
directly political and social focus of moral concern, encouraged in
him by those friends and teachers who were of a Tung-lin persuasion.
Such influences were not necessarily incompatible. Indeed, in this
period one increasingly sees them associated, as in the cases of the
Tung-lin leader Ku Hsien-ch'eng and Liu Tsung-chou, in a philosophical tendency to stress the congruence of certain key elements in
Ch'eng-Chu orthodoxy and the school of Wang Yang-ming.[22]

A significant trend in late Ming thought was a certain diminution
of the previous antagonism between the Ch'eng-Chu and Lu-Wang
traditions, furthered, paradoxically enough, by the extremist developments in the latter. A number of individual scholars, confronted
with what they considered to be the heretical and iconoclastic
developments in the T'ai-chou school and among the so-called
mad Ch'anists, found that the Ch'eng-Chu school and the moderate
Chiang-yu branch of the school of Wang Yang-ming, despite their

differences, shared important beliefs, particularly in their affirmation of the validity of moral values. Both, for example, were opposed to the T'ai-chou interpretation of "beyond good and evil,"[23] and both emphasized the actual social consequences of philosophical theory in its concrete application—what Professor Chan Wing-tsit has called "the actual demonstration of moral values."[24]

Out of all this something approaching a new synthetic orthodoxy, or at least a revision of the criteria of orthodoxy, often critical of both Sung and Ming predecessors, seems to have been emerging in the teachings of such leading thinkers as Ku Hsien-ch'eng, Liu Tsung-chou, and Huang Tsung-hsi. These frequently involved new conceptions of the proper equilibrium of, and relations between, externally validated orthodoxy and the personal authenticity of the individual. Ku Hsien-ch'eng, for example, was able to combine the moral introspection of his personal style of *chu-ching*[25] with an activism in the social and political realm which became the model for the *philosophes engagés* of the Tung-lin.

Wang Fu-chih's search for an analogous intellectual balance and reconciliation was complicated and intensified by his personal experiences of conflict between the demands of personal integrity and public service. He grew up in a family acutely aware of what it regarded as the moral and political decline of the country. His father withdrew permanently from public life in 1631 (when Fu-chih was twelve), disgusted and disillusioned by his firsthand experience of corruption in the capital, and thereafter devoted himself to the education of his sons and the study of the *Spring and Autumn Annals.*[26] Fu-chih's brother, who was thirteen years older than he, also retired temporarily in 1640 after a brief period of service in the Imperial Academy, for the same reasons as his father. In so doing they were reacting in a fashion sanctioned by Confucian precedents to the choice between engagement and withdrawal that perennially confronted the scholar. Engagement offered the opportunity to affirm authentic moral values and realize the true Way. On the other hand, by ill-judged intervention in unfavorable circumstances one risked perversion of one's personal moral integrity: withdrawal was the scholar's course when the Way could not prevail.[27] Fu-chih, however, while he respected his elders' motives and was himself eventually forced into withdrawal, was by his own account[28] tem-

peramentally something of a hothead even as a child, and he responded to the deteriorating situation by seeking actively to set it
to rights.

By the time he was twenty-one, in 1640, he had become an active
participant in the politico-literary societies then flourishing, and
against his father's wishes founded a local K'uang-she (Reform
Club) in Heng-yang. Wang's poem celebrating the founding of the
K'uang-she makes it clear that he regarded it as a club in the Tung-
lin tradition.[29] This identification undoubtedly was reinforced by
Kao Shih-t'ai, the nephew of Kao P'an-lung, a leading member of the
Tung-lin. Kao Shih-t'ai was assistant provincial director of studies in
Hu-kuang, and prepared Wang and others of the group for the provincial examinations of 1642.[30] The poems Wang was then writing
brim over with concern for the state of the country, as in these
lines presented to his brother when the latter was leaving to take up
his position in the Imperial Academy in Peking:

> While our parents have old kinsmen by,
> At court there are no upright officials . . .
> As you travel northwards across the wilds of Honan and
>   Chinan,
> You will see white bones lying in the confused heaps of
>   battle.
> Year after year the locusts swarm,
> And each spring produce fresh larvae.
> The whole court seethes with slander,
> Such remedies as are proposed only aggravating the
>   situation.
> Yet, if the emperor were made aware of the suffering
>   which exists,
> Surely the shame of it would bring some positive response![31]

His brother returned home almost immediately rather than compromise himself by remaining in the atmosphere of opportunism and
corruption which prevailed among his colleagues, while Fu-chih's
own official career from the outset was overwhelmed by the events
that brought the Ming dynasty to a close. In 1642, having succeeded
in the *chü-jen* examinations, his subsequent journey to Peking (in
the company of the same elder brother) for the *chin-shih* examina-

tions had to be abandoned on reaching Nan-ch'ang because the way north was blocked by rebels. Nor was it any consolation to him on his return home to Heng-chou that the peasant leader Chang Hsien-chung, after capturing the town, summoned him and his brother to take office in the rebel administration he was beginning to set up, holding their father hostage to secure their cooperation. Fu-chih's dramatic response was to show himself prepared to die rather than serve a rebel. He inflicted several wounds on himself, using drugs to produce a worse effect, and had himself carried into the rebels' head-quarters, pretending that his brother had actually committed suicide. He and his father subsequently escaped through the help of a literary associate of Fu-chih's who had gone over to the rebels.[32] Although Chang's forces withdrew from Heng-chou early in 1644, soon after-wards the news of the fall of Peking plunged Wang into despair, and he withdrew into the hills, building himself a hut in the Shuang-chi-feng area of Heng-shan, which he called, significantly, "The Refuge for Continuing Dreams."[33]

The story of Wang's life thereafter is one of alternate active par-ticipation in anti-Manchu resistance and chagrined retreat into a life of intense scholarship. By this time it was the Manchus who consti-tuted the real danger to those Chinese who were trying to salvage something from the ruins of the Ming dynasty. Of the rebels, Chang Hsien-chung settled in Chengtu, where he proclaimed himself "King of the West," while the remnants of Li Tzu-ch'eng's armies, still a considerable force (Wang estimated it at half a million),[34] joined the Ming troops in an uneasy alliance in Hu-kuang under the governor-general, Ho T'eng-chiao, and the governor of Hupeh, Tu Yin-hsi. This alliance succeeded in stemming the advance of Manchu power, in-flicting several defeats on the Ch'ing forces early in 1646, but to the east Chinese resistance was steadily overcome. The regime of one Ming pretender, the prince of Fu (Hung-kuang) had been destroyed with the fall of Nanking in 1645, and the reign of another, the prince of T'ang (Lung-wu), had only a few months to run when, in the summer of 1646, Wang set out from his refuge to visit the assis-tant censor-in-chief Chang K'uang in Hsiang-yin with plans for re-trieving the situation in Hu-kuang, where, he believed, the alliance was in danger of disintegrating.

Ho T'eng-chiao had, as Wang explains in the *Yung-li shih-lu,* experienced great difficulty both in controlling and feeding the enormous army under his command. Consequently, the troops continually plundered the region, to the distress of the populace who were already suffering from the effects of a severe drought. To make matters worse, Ho did not get on very well with his colleague Tu Yin-hsi, who was stationed in Ch'ang-te and commanded about half of the rebel troops who had restyled themselves the "Loyalist Brigade."[35] The personal animosity of the two leaders thus threatened to create a division in the Ming forces, which were at this time supporting the prince of T'ang. Wang pleaded with Chang to use his authority to mediate and effect a reconciliation between Ho and Tu. At the same time he set before Chang his own proposals for a solution to the problem of supplying the troops with provisions. Chang was a vigorous commander, and his personal courage was respected by the rebels whose support he had helped to secure. He was also the protégé of Ho T'eng-chiao, who had secured for him the post of military circuit intendant when he reorganized the Ming forces in Hu-kuang in 1645, just before the fall of the prince of Fu.[36] Wang thus had reason to believe that Chang had Ho's ear. Moreover, he himself had cause to expect a sympathetic hearing from Chang, because the latter had been one of his examiners in 1642 and they had subsequently found that they understood one another very well and shared the same anxiety about the current trend of events.[37] On this occasion, however, Chang rejected Wang's suggestions and declared that his fears were groundless.

For about a year Wang returned to his "Refuge for Continuing Dreams," where he worked on the *Book of Changes* and the *Spring and Autumn Annals*—two key books for a man whose chief purpose in studying history was "from the mistakes of the past, to draw lessons for the future," each book providing in its own way a universal code.[38] In devoting himself to the latter he was complying with the wishes of his aged father, who urged him to produce a commentary that would preserve the family interpretation of the history.[39] The *Book of Changes,* on the other hand, was to provide a basis for the philosophy of history which he first adumbrated when in 1655 he set forth the fruits of his studies in the *Chou-i wai-chuan.* Here for the first time one encounters Wang's monistic vision of a dynamic universe according to which all processes, both moral and material,

natural and human, are correlated, while the task of man at its center
is to decipher the patterns from the tangled web of circumstance
and conditions and thus control events.[40]

In 1653, looking back on this period in a composition entitled
Chang-ling fu, Wang recalled the suffering of such impotent withdrawal and how the very books he was then studying had strengthened
his determination to serve the Ming cause in an active capacity.[41]
Thus, in the summer of 1647, accompanied by a boyhood friend
Hsia Ju-pi, he set out in an attempt to reach Wu-kang (in southwest Hunan), where the Yung-li emperor, who had been enthroned
in Chao-ch'ing a few months before, had retreated. They planned
to make a northwesterly detour through the Hsiang-hsiang mountains and Tu Yin-hsi's camp in what is now Ch'en-ch'i county.
Tu had been prefect of Changsha in 1641 and subsequently circuit-
intendant there, and by the time he became governor of Hupeh in
1645 was appearing occasionally in the company of Wang and his
patriotic friends in Heng-yang.[42] In addition to Hsia Ju-pi, these
included Kuan Ssu-ch'iu and other members of the K'uang-she.

Heavy rains and hostile troops prevented Wang and Hsia from
making contact with Tu, and they were stranded for a month in the
Ch'e-chia-shan region. Then, receiving news that his father was
gravely ill, Wang returned home and remained in hiding with him in
Heng-shan until the old man died three months later expressing a
wish to be buried in the hills, not in the town, because the latter now
was enemy territory.[43]

The Yung-li regime whose establishment had prompted this journey
of Wang's was to remain throughout its existence an unstable one.
Not only was it constantly shifting its court and administrative
center, moving—frequently under pressure from the Ch'ing forces—
to various places in Kwangtung, Kwangsi, Hunan, Yunnan, and
eventually Burma; its constituent elements also changed, as generals
together with their troops defected to and from the Ch'ing forces or
were destroyed by them and officials came and went. Militarily the
Yung-li emperor could in theory count on an alliance of regular
Ming soldiers and remnants of the rebel armies, but both were in
practice split into various groups that regarded each other with a
mixture of hostility, rivalry, and suspicion. Military leaders might
change sides at any moment; according to Wang, the regular general

Ch'en Pang-fu, who eventually defected to the Manchus in 1651, had been on the point of doing so in 1648, but his "surrender" to Li Ch'eng-tung (a general then collaborating with the Manchus) was forestalled by the latter's return to Ming allegiance—for which Ch'en proceeded to claim the credit![44] This incident gives a fair indication of the prevailing climate, and it is worth noting that Ch'en and Li subsequently remained on opposite sides as leading elements in the Wu and Ch'u factions respectively.

The former rebel commanders proved thorny allies for the regular generals and were no less divided among themselves, the most obvious examples being Sun K'o-wang and Li Ting-kuo, two of the adopted sons of Chang Hsien-chung and rivals for the inheritance of the overall leadership of his forces, whose long struggle eventually led to a full-scale battle in 1657. As a result, military leaders were careful to retain a considerable degree of autonomy, and even one as devoted to the Ming cause as Tu Yin-hsi frequently disregarded official orders.[45] There was thus never one generally acknowledged center of authority, and real political power, internally as well as externally, depended almost entirely on the relative strength and prestige of such military leaders and their civil official allies. In their struggles for dominance, one fundamental strategy of each of these groups was to combine power and prestige by persuading the emperor to establish his court in its own power-base, where it could rely on the support of a strong military ally and legitimize the dominance of that group. Of the two dominant factions at court in these early years of the Yung-li period, the Wu party's military base was Wu-chou, where Ch'en Pang-fu was in command, while the centers of the Ch'u party's military support lay in Kuei-lin, with the metropolitan custodian Ch'ü Shih-ssu, and in Kwangtung, with Li Ch'eng-tung and his adopted son Li Yuan-yin.[46]

The Yung-li emperor was, moreover, quite lacking in the qualities which might have enabled him to act as an arbiter in this situation and impose his own authority on it. In fact, he was little more than a nominal ruler, less a king than a pawn helplessly dependent on the tutelage of his knights (as he would doubtless have been on his bishops had the Catholic missionary Michel Boym[47] had his way!). An indecisive, feeble, and perhaps cowardly person, his reign confirmed the judgment of his mother, who originally told those who

wished to enthrone him: "My son is a good and gentle person. He
certainly hasn't the ability to put down rebellions. I wish you would
choose someone else!"[48] Ironically enough, she herself, as empress
dowager,[49] proved a real force behind the throne, and Chin Pao, a
supervising secretary who became the chief spokesman for the Ch'u
faction, even went so far as to draw a parallel with the infamous
Wu Tse-t'ien of the T'ang dynasty.[50] Certainly she took a strikingly
important part in the imperial deliberations as recorded in such accounts as the *Ling-piao chi-nien* of Lu K'o-ts'ao.[51] Wang Fu-chih's
treatment of her in the *Yung-li shih-lu,* while recognizing her power,
is more restrained. He places greater emphasis on the roles of the
eunuch Hsia Kuo-hsiang, who enjoyed her confidence, and Ma
Chi-hsiang, the commander of the Embroidered-uniform Guard who,
working hand in glove with Hsia, influenced the emperor through
her.[52] In any case, it is hard to quarrel with Wang when he sees a
struggle between what were known as the "inner" and "outer" courts
as an essential feature of political life under Yung-li, as it had been
under the last emperors in Peking.[53]

In considering what the Wu and Ch'u parties represented one has
to remember that in the first place *tang* were not supposed to exist,
the term being generally applied pejoratively to any organized
pressure group within the imperial administrative structure. The
exact membership of such groups is hard to establish, particularly at
the fringes, and a completely satisfactory definition of such volatile
and unavowed political alliances is consequently difficult. However,
an important characteristic of the Wu party was, as Wang indicated,
its identification with the "inner court." The Wu party was led by
the commander of the Embroidered-uniform Guard, Ma Chi-hsiang
together with the grand secretaries Chu T'ien-lin and Wang Hua-
ch'eng, and the president of the Board of Revenue, Wu Chen-yü. It
also had important allies inside the palace in the eunuchs Hsia Kuo-
hsiang, Chiang Kuo-t'ai, and P'ang T'ien-shou.[54] The connection with
the palace was further strengthened by the fact that Wang Hua-
ch'eng exploited a close relationship with the elder brother of the
empress, Wang Wei-kung.[55] Other Wu supporters included the vice-
president of the Board of Rites, Kuo Chih-ch'i, the vice-president of
the Board of War, Wan Ao, and the supervising secretaries Chang
Hsiao-ch'i, Ch'eng Yuan, and Li Yung-chi. In addition to Ch'en

Pang-fu, military support came from Tu Yin-hsi, who had been made president of the Board of War by the Yung-li emperor.[56] The members of the Ch'u party, on the other hand, all held posts of a censorial nature in the "outer court." Chin Pao had, since his arrival in 1648, held the position of supervising secretary in the Office of Scrutiny for Rites; Ting Shih-k'uei and Meng Cheng-fa were also supervising secretaries in the Offices of Scrutiny for Personnel and Revenue respectively; Liu Hsiang-k'o was an assistant censor-in-chief; and Yuan P'eng-nien was censor-in-chief of the left.[57]

The outstanding figure among the Ch'u partisans was unquestionably Chin Pao, who made of his political career a veritable moral crusade. The Tung-lin style of political confrontation based on moral criteria was still current, and the image of Chin Pao which emerges from all the accounts, however unsympathetic, and his own memorials,[58] is of an "impetuous and uncompromising" (k'uang-chüan) scholar in the Tung-lin mold.[59] The Hsiao-t'ien chi-chuan records that when Chin was serving the Lung-wu emperor the latter was so delighted with his forthright memorial declaring that the court should be established in Hu-kuang because Ho T'eng-chiao was reliable whereas Cheng Chih-lung was not, that he (punningly) exclaimed that Chin Pao was a precious jewel.[60] His fellow officials, however, regarded him with as much trepidation as admiration. Chin was a fearless critic of anyone he considered wrong, regardless of power or position, and in fierce and occasionally indiscriminate memorials he impeached Ch'en Pang-fu, Ma Chi-hsiang, and even the upright grand secretary Yen Ch'i-heng.[61] The Yung-li shih-lu quotes a memorial attacking Ch'en Pang-fu and Ma Chi-hsiang, in which Chin diagnoses the political sickness of the Yung-li regime as follows:

> Nothing is more disastrous at the present time than the fact that the generals in the provinces take no heed of the court, while at court evil men hold the political power.[62]

In his memorials[63] Chin urged the emperor, whom he regarded as misled by the prevarication and slander of those who had access to him, to be a true ruler and assume the moral leadership of the government, taking responsibility for decisions himself instead of delegating power to the likes of Ma Chi-hsiang or temporizing when confronted with clear alternatives. Not that Chin was advocating any

form of imperial dictatorship; on the contrary, he pleaded in typical
Tung-lin fashion for a return to the partnership between emperor
and bureaucracy in which leading officials fulfilled the traditional
Confucian role of imperial counselors. The goal he held out to the
emperor was Restoration (*chung-hsing*), a goal that should be actively pursued by taking the offensive, with the emperor leading his
troops into battle in person.[64]

Yuan P'eng-nien was in several respects the odd man out among
the leading Ch'u partisans. The others all had pedigrees of honest
official service and loyal resistance to the Manchus. Chin, Ting, and
Liu all came to the Yung-li court as protégés of Ch'ü Shih-ssu, while
Meng Cheng-fa was recommended by Chang K'uang. Yuan, on the
other hand, joined the court along with generals Li Ch'eng-tung and
Li Yuan-yin, in 1648, after a period of collaboration with the Ch'ing.
Indeed, he was apparently largely responsible for persuading Li
Ch'eng-tung to defect. Yet although, as the *Yung-li shih-lu* points
out,[65] Yuan had previously opposed Ma Shih-ying's purge of Tung-
lin and Fu-she elements while serving in the Nanking administration,
Wang's biography throws some doubt on Yuan's place in these
"righteous circles." It describes how Chin Pao and Ting Shih-k'uei
were initially attracted to Yuan by his previous reputation, and adds
that Yuan was an "experienced administrator" who contrived to
find speedy solutions to problems. It also records that Chin was
already regretting his connection with Yuan by the time of their
impeachment in 1650, because the latter, despite talk about reinvigo-
rating the resistance movement, gave priority to his own interests and
those of the Li family. Wang further offers the opinion that it was a
sign of the times that of the five officials impeached Yuan alone was
pardoned on the grounds that he was a reformed traitor, while the
other four, who had been loyal throughout, were punished.[66]

In recounting the circumstances of Yuan's return to allegiance,
Wang suggests that as a native of Ch'u his decision was influenced by
the news that Ho T'eng-chiao and Tu Yin-hsi were recovering Hu-
kuang. Chin Pao and Ting Shih-k'uei's predisposition to favour Yuan
was also probably accentuated by their common regional background. Although neither faction referred to itself by the name Ch'u
or Wu, one should not ignore the significance of these names, which
do in fact reflect a regional element in the composition of the two

factions. Yuan, Meng, and Ting were all from Hu-kuang, while Chin Pao, who was from Chekiang, had resided in Hunan[67] and during the Lung-wu regime had advocated making it the center of that court's resistance. Liu Hsiang-k'o was (despite his name)[68] a native of Shensi. The Wu party, for its part, consisted almost entirely of men from Kiangsu (Chu T'ien-lin, Wu Chen-yü, Tu Yin-hsi, Chang Hsiao-ch'i), Kiangsi (Wang Hua-ch'eng and Wan Ao), and Chekiang (Ch'en Pang-fu). Wang Fu-chih, of course, as a Hunanese with a highly developed sense of regionalism,[69] would have been predisposed to regard men of Ch'u with some sympathy.

The rise of the Ch'u party coincided with the period (1648–50) when the Yung-li emperor was living in Chao-ch'ing; he had gone there at the invitation of Li Ch'eng-tung, who returned to allegiance in Kwangtung in 1648. With the metropolitan custodian Ch'ü Shih-ssu stoutly defending Kuei-lin, and Chin Sheng-huan and Wang Te-jen reverting to the Ming cause in Kiangsi, Ho T'eng-chiao and his ex-rebel ally Ma Chin-chung set about recovering the territory lost previously in Hunan and Hupeh.[70] Two months before Ho finally recaptured Heng-chou, Wang and his K'uang-she comrade, Kuan Ssu-ch'iu, raised troops in Heng-shan in an unsuccessful attempt to accelerate the recovery of Hunanese territory. Wang nowhere gives a complete account of this exploit, although he mentions that Kuan's brother was captured and imprisoned after they had been defeated.[71] Wang and Kuan Ssu-ch'iu then made their way via Kuei-lin (where Wang seems first to have made the acquaintance of Ch'ü Shih-ssu) to Chao-ch'ing, where the Yung-li emperor had now settled. This again involved a long and hazardous journey, but Wang, recalling his military ancestors who had fought both for the Ming founder and Yung-lo, declared:

> My ancestors rose to fame in following the emperor, so how could I relinquish such an undertaking or begrudge the long march south! Nevertheless, when I reached the Imperial Court in the winter of 1648 what I saw there caused me great sorrow, and after much hesitation I withdrew and returned home, though my heart was still bound to my ruler.[72]

Something of the nature of Wang's disillusion with the Yung-li court on this his first direct contact with it is spelled out in the

Yung-li shih-lu. [73] "In the three or four years since the court was established," he writes, "the scholar-official class had declined." Some officials, after the earlier setbacks, had "lost the will to resist"; others, separated from the court by great distances and cut off by enemy troops, were "unable to resist, and could only turn with a melancholy sigh towards the south and pour out their feelings in poetry" from hiding-places in the hills. Some "had sacrificed their lives in serving their country," while others "had become itinerant priests." Many of those who had gathered at the court were of an "inferior or mediocre quality," and "for the most part arrivistes," so that although Chin Pao and Yen Ch'i-heng tried to set high standards of probity and ability, they could find no candidates who corresponded to them and "numerous posts remained vacant." Moreover, "after the emperor had moved to Wu-kang . . . [in 1647, as the Ch'ing forces advanced into Hunan] . . . many officials had fled, and as nobody wished to serve in the regime," replacements had been recruited from the ranks of "village school-teachers, itinerant fortune-hunters and yamen-clerks."

During this visit Tu Yin-hsi recommended Wang for a position as a Hanlin bachelor, but he declined, asking to be excused on the grounds that he was in mourning for his father. [74] This was perhaps a doubly filial gesture. In addition to fulfilling his obligations to his late father (from which he could conceivably have been absolved), withdrawal from the cockpit of the Yung-li court was in line with his father's precept and example. Tu Yin-hsi had not as yet become closely associated with the Wu party, nor Wang Fu-chih with the Ch'u, so it is unlikely that partisan considerations entered into his decision. Wang's biography of Tu in the *Yung-li shih-lu* is a fairly generous one; he is full of admiration for Tu's patriotism and courage, and in the factional struggle portrays him as the dupe of the Wu leader Chu T'ien-lin, who played on his resentment over Chin Pao's attacks to secure his support. (Tu was, moreover, to die at the end of 1649, before the final crucial clash between the factions.) [75] In any case, Wang once again used mourning as justification when he declined a post for which he was recommended by the Ch'u faction leader Ch'ü Shih-ssu in 1649. [76]

In 1650, however, his period of mourning at an end, Wang returned to the Yung-li court, which had just moved to Wu-chou in Kwangsi, and took up a post as *hsing-jen,* declaring that this was no time for a man to be a recluse but one in which to share his ruler's fate in life and death.[77]

Wang's direct involvement in the politics of the Yung-li court was nasty, brutish, and short. The imperial move to Wu-chou was a turning point in the factional struggles at court, and indeed in the life of the regime, and Wang's arrival there coincided with the crisis that was to end in the destruction of the Ch'u party as a political force and assure the supremacy of the ex-rebel general Sun K'o-wang for the next five years or so. During the previous year the Ch'u party had achieved such a degree of dominance that two of their leading opponents in the Wu party, the grand secretaries Chu T'ien-lin and Wang Hua-ch'eng, temporarily withdrew from the court, but in the same year Li Ch'eng-tung died after suffering a severe defeat at the hands of the Ch'ing forces; and early in 1650, with the enemy troops gathering for an attack, the emperor was persuaded to seek refuge in Wu-chou.

The Wu party, with the emperor on its "home ground," lost no time in demonstrating that the boot was now on the other foot. Chu T'ien-lin and Wang Hua-ch'eng emerged from retirement, and the leaders of the Ch'u faction, who had become known as "the five tigers" (or, more correctly "the five-part tiger")[78] were impeached for having monopolized the administration of the state.[79] With the exception of Yuan, they were imprisoned in an old temple by the Embroidered-uniform Guard, and Chin Pao was tortured. Despite pleas from Ch'ü Shih-ssu for their release, the emperor took no action. Wang Fu-chih, who had taken up his official post just previously, then went with his friend Kuan Ssu-ch'iu (who had been made a drafter) to urge Yen Ch'i-heng to intercede on behalf of the imprisoned partisans. They argued that they were all loyal men who had sacrificed everything in order to serve the emperor, and emphasized the disastrous effect their punishment would have on the morale of other supporters of the emperor's cause.[80] Yen, although he had himself been impeached on one occasion by Chin Pao, went and prostrated himself in front of the emperor's boat (the so-called "Water Palace") to plead for his release, but the emperor refused to receive him, and the only result was that Yen in his turn became a target for Wu party attacks. He was impeached by a Wu party supporter, Lei Te-fu, and sought permission to resign in an effort to escape the vengeance of his enemies.

Wang and a colleague in the Messenger Office, Tung Yün-hsiang, then interceded on Yen's behalf, submitting a memorial defending his right to resign, and urging the emperor not "to precipitate a second fall into evil or bring further humiliation on the nation and despair to the people."[81] Tung resigned and departed without waiting to see what would result from their memorial, but Wang remained to brave the wrath of the Wu clique and proceeded to submit memorials denouncing Lei Te-fu, Wang Hua-ch'eng, and Ch'en Pang-fu. Their riposte was swift and dangerous. Wang Hua-ch'eng produced a "scurrilous poem" with a title similar to one Wang Fu-chih had just written, with a preface in his name, and used this as a pretext to have him imprisoned. Fu-chih's life was saved only by the strenuous efforts of the ex-rebel general Kao Pi-cheng,[82] who secured his release along with that of Yen Ch'i-heng and the four imprisoned tigers. Fu-chih was allowed to retire from the court and, after a brief stay in Kuei-lin, he made his way back to Hunan.

Wang portrays the campaign of the Ch'u partisans—he does not, of course, use the word *Ch'u* or *party* but refers to them as the "righteous circles" (*ch'ing-liu*)[83]—as another episode in the struggle for an administration composed of good Confucianists, and thus endorses their own conception of their role. Conversely, in typically Tung-lin terms, he depicts the members of the Wu clique as villains concerned only with achieving their own ends and unmoved by the disintegration of the territory still under Chinese control.[84] In so doing he was less than just, for however much opprobrium they might merit, they were by no means all unmitigated blackguards. Wu Chen-yü in particular receives harsh treatment in Wang's biography of him. An important point of contention between the rival factions concerned the negotiations between the court and the ex-rebel general Sun K'o-wang. In 1649 Sun made it known that he would be prepared to ally himself to the Yung-li emperor in exchange for the title "Prince of Ch'in." Ch'en Pang-fu, seeing the possibility of acquiring a strong ally against his political rivals, gave his support to Sun's claims, and even sent him a fraudulent document which purported to recognize him as an autonomous ruler.[85] The Ch'u partisans were among those who spoke out against the scheme and, along with Yen Ch'i-heng and others, succeeded in getting it watered down, so that Sun was temporarily given an innocuous title.

Eventually, however, in 1651, after the "five tigers" had been ousted from court, Sun had Yen and others who had opposed him put to death, and according to the *Yung-li shih-lu,* it was Wu Chen-yü who provided Sun with a list of their names.[86] This is almost certainly a slander on Wu; there is no evidence to corroborate it, and Wu is described in other sources as an opponent of the scheme from the very beginning. Both the *Ming-chi nan-lüeh* and the *Hsiao-t'ien chi-chuan* attribute Wu's survival at this stage to his being away on a mission when Sun's men struck.[87] The *Yung-li shih-lu* certainly slanders Wu by omission elsewhere, for although Wu was one of the "Eighteen Gentlemen" who in 1654 died defending the rights of the Yung-li emperor against Sun's imperial ambitions (Sun was no longer satisfied with the title Prince of Ch'in, which he had by then arrogated to himself), there is no mention of this in Wang's biography of him.[88] Yet Wang's bias tended to blind him more to the good points of his enemies than the bad ones of his friends. His support of the Ch'u group was by no means uncritical, and in his biography of Yuan P'eng-nien he does not conceal his distaste for his vaingloriousness and opportunism. Nevertheless, Wang was sufficiently convinced of the correctness of his own judgment to stake his career, and even risk his life, in support of Yuan and his colleagues.

While Wang's condemnations of Ch'en Pang-fu, Ma Chi-hsiang, and Hsia Kuo-hsiang are surely justified despite their occasional purple passages, he also dealt harshly with other members of the Wu faction who appear to have been men of some integrity. Chang Hsiao-ch'i had a reputation for being "pure and not consorting with the vulgar elements of the day." Like Wang Fu-chih (and as Wang records), he had raised troops soon after the fall of Peking, and attempted to commit suicide when defeated. He also (as Wang fails to record) died heroically after being captured by the Ch'ing forces.[89] Kuo Chih-ch'i, whom Wang depicts as habitually corrupt, was, according to the *Hsiao-t'ien chi-chuan,* a stickler for proper procedure who had offended the notorious Wen T'i-jen under Ch'ung-chen and Cheng Chih-lung under Lung-wu,[90] while the *Nan-chiang i-shih* records that he opposed Sun K'o-wang's ambitions and declared, "In life and death I shall follow my lord, and never leave him."[91]

The case of Chu T'ien-lin is perhaps the most revealing, however. Chu enjoyed the confidence of the emperor, and when Chu, forced to retire by the Ch'u partisans, took leave of his ruler, they were both reduced to tears, the emperor declaring, "If you depart I shall be even more alone!"[92] Chu seems to have tried at one stage to act as a mediator between the emperor and the Ch'u partisans, hoping to restrain the latter by remonstrating with Yuan P'eng-nien and urging him not to neglect the obligations of a minister toward his ruler.[93] He advocated granting Sun K'o-wang the title "Prince of Ch'in" on grounds of expediency, arguing that it would encourage the powerful Sun to remain loyal and protect the emperor, whose forces were dwindling, from the increasing menace of the Ch'ing troops.[94]

The loyalty of such men as Wu, Chu, Chang, and Kuo was probably as sincere as that of the Ch'u partisans. Perhaps, however, one may detect a spirit of genuine conservatism in their attitude and a different concept of loyalty from that of their opponents. The loyalty of a man like Chu appears to have been a loyalty to the emperor's person—a loyalty that did not distinguish between the emperor and his imperial function—and it would have been strengthened by the close and even intimate relationship which might develop naturally between the imperial family and those who were constantly in contact with it in the "inner court." In the eyes of men of a Tung-lin persuasion who, like Huang Tsung-hsi, insisted[95] on the distinction between the emperor and his office, this notion of loyalty was a concomitant of the imperial despotism and degradation of ministerial status which had come to be accepted as the norm under the Ming. Thus, Huang's attack (in the *Ming-i tai-fang lu*) on the currently established idea that loyalty to the emperor was analogous to the duty a son owed his father may throw some light on the attitudes of both Ch'u and Wu partisans. Though he brings a clarity to a problem which was perhaps only dimly perceived by most of his contemporaries, its existence is implicit in much of their argument and action.

Wang Fu-chih, for his part, explicitly distinguished between the emperor's functions and his person. His strongest statement of this distinction is in the *Huang-shu,* written in 1656, not long after the factional struggles described above. He affirms that the first duty of a ruler is to protect his people from foreign invasion:

Now even the ants have rulers who preside over the territory of
their nests and, when red ants or flying white ants penetrate
their gates, the ruler organises all his own kind into troops to
bite and kill the intruders, drive them far away from the ant-
hill, and prevent foreign interference. Thus he who rules the
swarm must have the means to protect it. If, however, a ruler
fails to make long-term plans, neglects the integrity of his territory, esteems his own person more than the empire, antagonizes
colleagues, creates divisions among his own kith and kin, is
driven by suspicion to exercise a repressive control, and weakens
the central region, then, while he clings desperately to his privileged status and enjoys the advantages of his position without
fulfilling its obligations, disaster strikes and he is incapable of
overcoming it. Confronted with an external menace, he is unable
to stand firm against it. He can neither keep the succession for
his own descendants nor protect his own kind. Such an extinction of the Way of the true king was what the *Spring and Autumn Annals* mourned.[96]

Wang would have refused to serve even another Chinese dynasty
once he had held office under the Ming, as his criticism of Feng Tao
makes clear.[97] But his nationalism and his desire to expel the foreign
invaders lent an added urgency to his efforts to restore Ming sovereignty over all China. He never ceased "to continue dreaming" of a
Chinese recovery. Nor were his dreams entirely idle. The Manchu
hold on south China remained precarious for most of his life, and on
two occasions he was invited to resume active participation in the
anti-Manchu resistance. In 1652, when Sun K'o-wang had the emperor in his tutelage in An-lung, Li Ting-kuo, who had moved from
Kwangtung to Heng-chou, summoned Wang to join him. It was only
after much hesitation that Wang decided against it, and in his hesitation one may perhaps discern a man torn between conflicting notions
of loyalty as well as between the desire to reestablish Ming (and
Chinese) sovereignty and the conviction that the real power was
now irretrievably in the wrong hands. His dilemma, as he explains in
the *Chang-ling fu,* was that while he wished to serve his ruler, he
could not bring himself to trust those who formed his entourage:

At the time the emperor was supposed to be under the protection of Sun K'o-wang, but was in reality his hostage, and Sun was thus flouting the bond between ruler and subject. The grand secretary Yen [Ch'i-heng] from Shan-yin, who had made a just stand in court against the enfeoffment of Sun as a prince, had been murdered by Sun's brigands. How could such a man, one responsible for seizing the emperor and slaying his minister, possibly be trusted? This was why I withdrew to dwell in obscurity by the source of the river Cheng. And yet when Sun K'o-wang's lieutenant, Li Ting-kuo, emerged in Kwangtung and Hunan he achieved several victories, and his military power was impressive. At the time I wished on the one hand to remain where I was, but could find no uncontaminated place to hide, and on the other hand I wished to go and join the emperor but could not bear to take orders from those who had unlawfully seized power in his court. So I hesitated, not knowing where my duty lay. . . . Now here am I, a solitary minister a thousand *li* away, while my ruler is in a situation between life and death. The path I took in the past is now cut off, while the road to take in the future is still unknown. If amid the darkness there were a sign, then I might hope that my integrity would prevail. . . . When I think of my ruler I am sad and troubled. When I seek after what is right then I am strengthened in my moral stand and feel no resentment.[98]

In his perplexity Wang consulted the *I-ching,* which confirmed him in his decision, the message of the "K'uei" hexagram (38) about "meeting one's lord in a byway" being nullified by the counsel of no action of the "Kuei-mei" hexagram (54).

A similar situation arose in 1678 when Wu San-kuei, who had been in rebellion against the Manchus since 1674, proclaimed a Chou dynasty in Heng-chou. But Wu had not only collaborated with the Manchus in the capture of Peking in 1644 but had also been responsible for the capture and execution of the Yung-li emperor in 1662. Wang refused to cooperate with him.[99]

To some extent Wang's retirement into the hills of Hunan was a form of symbolic suicide, but there was about it a provisional quality due to his refusal to abandon all hope, which leads one to think of him rather as having "gone underground." When he first built himself the "Refuge for Continuing Dreams" in Heng-shan after the death of the Ch'ung-chen emperor in 1644, his dreams were those of a Ming restoration. Later they became simply dreams of a revival of Chinese power. As he wrote in 1670, eight years after the Yung-li pretender was captured and executed:

> Now that the old dreams are no longer continued,
> One had better awake to new dreams.[100]

He believed that it was natural for dynasties to flourish and decay, but while he came tacitly to accept that the mandate of the Ming house had passed from it, he looked forward to the resurgence and renewal which should, in the nature of things, follow the decline.[101] The events of his lifetime were the long night that would eventually give way to a new dawn,[102] the long winter during which he longed for spring.[103] Such a belief in the alternation of growth and decay was, of course, inherent in his philosophy of evolution; growth and decay were universal processes to which all phenomena alike were subject, and dynasties were no exception. The Ming, like the Sung before it, had reached and passed the point beyond which there was no return except through the "great reversal" that accompanied the peak of disaster—the overthrow of the dynasty.[104] Thus, in the *Tu T'ung-chien lun,* he wrote:

> In a world in which disaster has reached its climax and one stands alone, trying to bring the country back to moral consciousness, one must not grieve over one's loneliness. In the future there will arise those who will carry on the task.[105]

Wang certainly felt that he was, if not entirely alone, then one of a very small minority, but in what he himself referred to as "these degenerate times"[106] to be in a minority was almost a touchstone of true Confucian orthodoxy. He may have had some such thought in mind when, anticipating criticism of the relevance and utility of his writing, he wrote:

> A critic may say ". . . You may be said to have bolted the stable door after the horse has gone". To which I should reply, "Confucius, in writing the *Spring and Autumn Annals,* made many subtle criticisms of the times during which Duke Ting and

Duke Ai ruled. At the time when one speaks no one understands.
In setting forth what I have mentioned I am also trying to advise
future generations."[107]

In addition to pursuing his research and writing, Wang also attracted a small group of followers during his retirement in Hunan,
among whom were the sons of Kuan Ssu-ch'iu, and Chang K'uang
and the Ch'u partisan, Meng Cheng-fa, who spent the rest of his life
in Heng-yang.[108] Wang's experiences at the Yung-li court certainly
left their mark on his writings—as Liu Yü-sung pointed out, certain
passages in the *Shang-shu yin-i* may be understood as veiled criticisms
of late Ming events[109]—but they were gradually integrated into a
comprehensive critique of Chinese history. Nevertheless, on the
occasions when, in his historical investigations, he saw a parallel with
his own political struggle, his writing assumes an added vehemence
and passion. Discussing the party strife of the Eastern Han period,
for example, he wrote:

> As regards the worthies involved in the prohibition of political
> parties, there are those who say of them "They were loyal to the
> point of sacrificing their lives. Theirs was a great moral integrity."
> Others say of them "Headstrong and perverse,[110] to the point of
> bringing disaster on themselves, theirs was an egregious activity."
> The latter adduce all sorts of plausible arguments in order to
> discredit the prestige of scholars.[111] The verdict "great moral
> integrity" is closer to the mark, but still not definitive. A min-
> ister devotes his life to serving his ruler, and, if it should be of
> benefit to the state, even death should not be shunned. Where
> the ruler is unenlightened, and does not employ (a worthy man),
> but slanderous ministers form cliques, to sacrifice one's life re-
> sisting them, even though it be of no benefit to the state, still
> has the merit of a suicide inspired by integrity. However, the best
> course is to correct the ruler's moral faults directly and assist
> him towards the right. The next best course is to regard the mis-
> appropriation of political power and treachery as the root of
> disaster, and treat them with mortal hatred, and in this way one
> is still performing the function of a loyal minister. But no sooner
> has one disposed of one manifestation of treachery than another
> springs up, and one cannot strike down all of them. As for the
> mean and inferior fellows who rely on the perversion of author-

ity in order to peddle their evil, one cannot execute them all, nor are they worth executing. If one can make the ruler change, then the perversion of authority will disappear . . . but the mean and inferior fellows can easily provoke worthy men to anger and drive them into committing injustices. . . . It was because he struck directly at Yen Sung that Yang Chi-sheng's death was righteous. It was because he picked-out the eunuch Wei for impeachment that Yang Lien's death was glorious.[112]

Like Huang Tsung-hsi, Wang looked forward, as he declares in the *Huang-shu,* to the appearance of an enlightened ruler, one who would make use of his counsel. There was no shred of ambiguity as to the nature of such a ruler in Wang's case, however. He would be one who would "restore sovereignty to the country, accomplish its mission, stabilize its frontiers, and thereby guard the central territory and drive off the barbarians forever!"[113] Eventually, he ceased to believe that he would live to see this happen, but he still hoped to be of service to future generations to whom he would pass on the torch.[114] In his *Tu T'ung-chien lun,* he reflected on his position and his contribution:

With my country ruined and my home destroyed, I set forth my opinion for posterity. Although I have not been able to retrieve the situation, I have not aggravated the disaster, and besides, there are times when a gentleman cannot remain silent.[115]

Elsewhere he was much more pessimistic about his achievements, and generally regarded himself as a failure—but perhaps only a relative failure, for as he consoled himself in a late—and prophetic—poem:

It is after the tortoise has rotted that men use it for divination,
Before the dream is completed there can be no interpretation.[116]

NOTES TO CHAPTER 4

Abbreviations

ECCP, Eminent Chinese of the Ch'ing Period, A. Hummel, ed. (reprint of 1943–44 edition, Taipei, 1964).

References prefaced by TPY are to the T'ai-p'ing yang edition of the *Ch'uan-shan i-shu* (Shanghai, 1933). The numbers immediately following TPY refer to the *ts'e* of this edition.

SPPY, Ssu-pu pei-yao.

1. The princes of Lu and Fu, the latter being established with the reign-title Hung-kuang. *EECP,* pp. 195–96.

2. The supporters of the two princes tended to divide along established partisan lines, those with Tung-lin and Fu-she associations supporting the prince of Lu and their old inner-court opponents, led by Ma Shih-ying, backing the prince of Fu, whose father's claims to the succession had been opposed by Ku Hsien-ch'eng fifty years earlier.

3. At the battle of San-shui in 1647, when the Yung-li emperor's forces were defeated by those of the Shao-wu emperor. *ECCP,* p. 193.

4. The *Yung-li shih-lu* is one of many contemporary accounts and private histories which bear on the Yung-li regime. Other basic sources include: Ch'ien Ch'eng-chih, *So-chih lu;* Lu K'o-ts'ao (probable author), *Ling-piao chi-nien;* Chi Liu-ch'i, *Ming-chi nan-lüeh;* Wen Jui-lin, *Nan-chiang i-shih;* Hua Fu-li, *Liang-Kuang chi-lüeh;* the anonymous *Nan-ming yeh-shih;* and Hsü Tzu's *Hsiao-t'ien chi-chuan* and *Hsiao-t'ien chi-nien fu-k'ao,* which though later are based on contemporary material often no longer extant. Despite the pioneer work undertaken by Hsieh Kuo-chen (in *Wan-Ming shih-chi k'ao*) and W. Franke (in *An Introduction to the Sources of Ming History*), no modern scholar has as yet produced a full-scale study of the Yung-li period. Brief accounts appear in Hsieh Kuo-chen, *Nan-Ming shih-lüeh* (Shanghai, 1957) and Chien Po-tsan, *Chung-kuo shih-lun chi* (Shanghai, 1948). David Shore of Princeton is, however, at present engaged in a study which promises to fill this gap (Ph.D. diss., Princeton University, 1976).

5. TPY 69 *Chiang-chai wen-chi,* 10:5b.

6. Chi, son of the philosopher Chi K'ang, died in battle in 304 defending the emperor against rebels; his blood actually spattered the emperor's clothes.

7. TPY 69 *Chiang-chai wen-chi pu-i,* 2:11a. Liu Kun was a loyal servant of the Chin dynasty against the barbarians who was unjustly slandered, imprisoned, and killed in 317.

8. TPY 67 *Ch'u-tz'u t'ung-shih, hsü-li,* 1b.

9. TPY 67 *Ch'u-tz'u t'ung-shih, chüan-mo,* 1a.

10. Ibid., 8a.

11. T'an Ssu-t'ung, the martyr of the 1898 Reform Movement, incorporated certain of Wang's ideas in his *Jen Hsüeh* (cf., for example *T'an Ssu-t'ung ch'üan-chi* [Peking, 1954], p. 56), while both Ho Shu-heng and Mao Tse-tung joined the Ch'uan-shan Academy, founded to promote the study of Wang Fu-chih in Ch'ang-sha in 1914 by Liu Jen-hsi. All were Hunanese.

12. Wang's models, all mentioned in contexts where emulation is either his explicit or implied goal, include Ch'ü Yuan, Liu Kun, Chi Shao, Wen T'ien-hsiang, Chang Tsai, and Ku Hsien-ch'eng. Wen died for refusing to serve the Mongol dynasty that replaced the Sung. Chang and Ku were both philosophers who, in Wang's view, aimed at restoring the Confucian Way to its true course.

13. The *Tu T'ung-chien lun* was, of course, based on Ssu-ma Kuang's history, *Tzu-chih t'ung-chien.*

14. Most scholars would have at least read Chu Hsi's abridged version of Ssu-ma Kuang's work, the *T'ung-chien kang-mu.*

15. Hsieh Kuo-chen, *Wan-Ming shih-chi k'ao* (Peking, 1933), *Tzu-hsü*, 3b and ibid., 11:10a–10b.

16. Ibid., 11:10a.

17. Hsieh Kuo-chen, *Nan-Ming shih-lüeh*, especially pp. 146–77.

18. Ch'ien Ch'eng-chih, the author of *So-chih lu*, was like Wang sympathetic to the Ch'u faction. He arrived in the Yung-li court in 1648 and remained there until the crisis of 1650. He was a friend of Liu Hsiang-k'o, the Ch'u partisan, and relies on Liu's diary for events preceding his arrival. If, as Hsieh Kuo-chen believes, Lu K'o-ts'ao was the author of the *Ling-piao chi-nien* (cf. Hsieh Kuo-chen, *Wan-Ming shih-chi k'ao*, 11:33b–34a) this account, which is hostile to the Ch'u faction, is also a firsthand one.

19. See, for example, Chi Liu-ch'i, *Ming-chi nan-lüeh* (Shanghai, 1958), pp. 306–07, 323–24, and 348.

20. Chu Hsi, *Chin ssu-lu chi-chu* (*SPPY* edition, Shanghai, 1934), 8:6a–6b.

21. See my paper "Wang Fu-chih and the Neo-Confucian Tradition," in de Bary, ed., *The Unfolding of Neo-Confucianism* (New York, 1975), pp. 413–67.

22. T'ang Chün-i, "Liu Tsung-chou's Doctrine of Moral Mind and Practice and His Critique of Wang Yang-ming" in de Bary, *Unfolding of Neo-Confucianism*, pp. 305–29, and H. Busch, "The Tung-lin Shu-yuan and its Political and Philosophical Significance," in *Monumenta Serica* 14:113–17.

23. de Bary, pp. 305–12 and 430–31.

24. Chan Wing-tsit, "The Ch'eng-Chu School of Early Ming," in de Bary, ed., *Self and Society in Ming Thought* (New York, 1970), p. 45.

25. Busch, "Tung-lin Shu-yuan," pp. 117–19, and Huang Tsung-hsi, *Ming-ju hsüeh-an* (1882 edition), 58:6a.

26. TPY 69 *Chiang-chai wen-chi*, 10:4b–5a.

27. *Lun-yü* 5:20, 8:13, 14:1, 15:6, etc.

28. TPY 69 *Chiang-chai wen-chi*, 10:7a.

29. TPY 72 *I-te*, 1b.

30. TPY 60 *Lien-feng chih*, 2:1b and 3:4a, and TPY 73: *Nan-ch'uang man-chi*, 2a.

31. TPY 72 *I-te*, 2a.

32. TPY 64 *Lung-yuan yeh-hua*, 3b.

33. TPY *I-te*, 7a.

34. TPY 59 *Yung-li shih-lu*, 7:2a.

35. Ibid., 7:2b–6a.

36. Ibid., 7:8a–10a, and *Ming-shih* (*SPPY* edition) 280:1b–2a.

37. TPY 1: *Chiang-chai kung hsing-shu*, 1b.

38. TPY 51: *Tu T'ung-chien lun*, 6:9a, TPY 28 *Ch'un-ch'iu chia-shuo*, 1:12a and 2:9a, and TPY 64 *Huang-shu*, 4b.

39. TPY 28: *Ch'un-ch'iu chia-shuo hsü*, 1a.

40. de Bary, *The Unfolding of Neo-Confucianism*, pp. 448–50.

41. Ibid., pp. 420–21.

42. TPY 60 *Lien-feng chih*, 2:1b.

43. TPY 69 *Chiang-chai wen-chi*, 10:8a.

44. TPY 59 *Yung-li shih-lu,* 26:4a.

45. Ibid., 7:5a.

46. Yuan P'eng-nien, who became leader of the Ch'u faction, had persuaded Li to support the Ming cause. See TPY 59 *Yung-li shih-lu,* 11:3b–5a.

47. Considering the success of the Catholic mission in converting several members of the imperial household (including the empress dowager and heir-apparent) and the fact that P'ang T'ien-shou, Ch'ü Shih-ssu, and Chiao Lien were all Catholics, there is surprisingly little mention of Catholicism in the *Yung-li shih-lu* or other contemporary Chinese records.

48. Chi Liu-ch'i, *Ming-chi nan-lüeh,* p. 273.

49. The empress dowager Wang was in fact the official wife of the Yung-li emperor's father. His natural mother was named Ma. Some confusion between them and over their titles exists in the contemporary accounts, but see Hsü Tzu, *Hsiao-t'ien chi-chuan* (Peking, 1958), pp. 97–98.

50. Ibid., p. 328, and Nan-sha san-yü shih, *Nan-Ming yeh-shih* (Shanghai, 1930), *hsia,* 38b.

51. See, for example, Lu K'o-ts'ao (?) *Ling-piao chi-nien* (Ko-feng ts'ao-t'ang manuscript edition), 4:12b–13b.

52. TPY 59 *Yung-li shih-lu,* 25:3b.

53. Ibid. 19:1b–3b and 25:2b and 3b. See also C. Hucker, "The Tung-lin Movement of the Late Ming period," in J. Fairbank, ed., *Chinese Thought and Institutions* (Chicago, 1957), pp. 136–38.

54. According to Wang's account, P'ang was less a villain than a faithful servant of the emperor, but one whose lack of literacy and poor grasp of procedure led him to become the dupe of Hsia Kuo-hsiang. The devious Hsia had originally been a profligate youth who had castrated himself in an unsuccessful attempt to gain entrance to the court of the Hung-kuang emperor in Nanking, and subsequently served under the Lung-wu emperor in Fukien before P'ang introduced him into the Yung-li court. Ibid., 25:3a–3b.

55. Ibid., 3:2a and 25:3b.

56. Hsü Tzu, *Hsiao-t'ien chi-chuan,* p. 297.

57. Ibid., pp. 324–26.

58. Chin Pao, *Ling-hai fen-yü* in *Shih-yuan ts'ung-shu* (1916 edition).

59. See, for example, ibid., *chung,* 28a, and de Bary, *Unfolding of Neo-Confucianism,* pp. 426–28.

60. Hsü Tzu, *Hsiao-t'ien chi-chuan,* p. 325.

61. Ibid., p. 326.

62. TPY 59 *Yung-li shih-lu,* 21:2a.

63. Chin Pao, *Ling-hai fen-yü, chung,* 1a–3a.

64. Ibid., *chung,* 5b–7a.

65. TPY 59 *Yung-li shih-lu,* 19:1a–1b.

66. Ibid., 19:2b–3a.

67. Ibid., 21:1b.

68. Literal meaning is "Hunan visitor."

69. See, for example, TPY 63 *Ssu-wen lu wai-p'ien,* 19b–20a.

70. TPY 69 *Yung-li shih-lu,* 1:4a, 7:4a–4b and Ch'ien Ch'eng-chih, *So-chih lu* (Taipei, 1960), *chung,* 34–37.

71. TPY 69 *Chiang-chai wen-chi,* 8:2a, and TPY 70 *Wu-shih tzu-ting kao,* 26b–27b.

72. TPY 69 *Chiang-chai wen-chi,* 8:2a.

73. TPY 59 *Yung-li shih-lu,* 20:2a, and ibid., 4:1a–1b.

74. TPY 64 *Lung-yuan yeh-hua,* 1a–1b.

75. TPY 59 *Yung-li shih-lu,* 7:5a–8a.

76. TPY 64 *Lung-yuan yeh-hua,* 1a–1b.

77. TPY 1 *Chiang-chai kung hsing-shu,* 2a.

78. Chi Liu-ch'i, *Ming-chi nan-lüeh* (Shanghai, 1958), pp. 323–24, and Lu K'o-ts'ao (?) *Ling-piao chi-nien,* 4:3a. The Ch'u partisans were identified with five parts of a tiger (which vary according to accounts).

79. Hsü Tzu, *Hsiao-t'ien chi-chuan,* p. 328.

80. TPY 59 *Yung-li shih-lu,* 1:7a, TPY 1 *Chiang-chai kung hsing-shu,* 2a, and Ni Tsai-t'ien, *Hsü Ming chi-shih pen-mo* (Taipei, 1962), p. 348.

81. TPY 59 *Yung-li shih-lu,* 2:7a, and Ni Tsai-t'ien, p. 350.

82. Ibid., TPY 72 *Ho Mei-hua pai-yün shih,* 1a, and Ch'ien Ch'eng-chih, *So-chih lu, hsia,* 56–57 and 62 et seq. Both Wang and Ch'ien portray Kao as a man of considerable moral scruples, interested in Confucianism.

83. TPY 59 *Yung-li shih-lu,* 20:3a.

84. Ibid., 13:4a and 20:3a.

85. TPY 59 *Yung-li shih-lu,* 1:6a and 26:5a, and Chi Liu-ch'i, *Ming-chi nan-lüeh,* p. 340.

86. TPY 59 *Yung-li shih-lu,* 20:3a.

87. Chi Liu-ch'i, *Ming-chi nan-lüeh,* p. 340, and Hsü Tzu, *Hsiao-t'ien chi-chuan,* p. 746.

88. But see Hsu Tzu, pp. 316–17.

89. Ibid., p. 338.

90. Ibid., p. 317. See also TPY 59 *Yung-li shih-lu,* 20:1a–2a.

91. Wen Jui-lin, *Nan-chiang i-shih* (Hongkong, 1971), p. 162.

92. Ibid., p. 156, and Hsü Tzu, p. 310.

93. Wen Jui-lin, p. 156.

94. Ibid., pp. 156–57.

95. Huang Tsung-hsi, *Ming-i tai-fang lu* (Peking, 1955), pp. 1–5.

96. TPY 64 *Huang-shu,* 2b. On Wang's nationalism, See also Wang Gung-wu, *Nation und Elite im Denken von Wang Fu-chih (1619–1692),* (Hamburg, 1968).

97. TPY 49 *Ssu-shu ta-ch'üan shuo,* 10:52b–53a. See also Wang Gung-wu, "Feng Tao: An Essay on Confucian Loyalty," in A. Wright and D. Twitchett, eds., *Confucian Personalities* (Stanford, 1962), pp. 123–45.

98. TPY 69 *Chiang-chai wen-chi,* 8:2b–4b.

99. TPY 1 *Ch'uan-shan hsien-sheng chuan,* 2b, and *Wang Ch'uan-shan hsüeh-shu t'ao-lun chi* (Peking, 1965), pp. 547–48.

100. TPY 70 *Liu-shih tzu-ting kao,* 5b.

101. See, for example, TPY 54 *Tu T'ung-chien lun,* 20:31a, and TPY 58 *Sung lun,* 8:7b–8a.

102. TPY 69 *Chiang-chai wen-chi* 8:2a, and TPY 70 *Liu-shih tzu-ting kao,* 13a.

103. TPY 69 *Chiang-chai wen-chi,* 8:1a.

104. TPY 58 *Sung lun,* 8:7b–8a.

105. TPY 56 *Tu T'ung-chien lun,* 28:13a.

106. TPY 63 *E-meng hsü,* 1a.

107. TPY 64 *Huang-shu, hou hsü,* 1b.

108. TPY 73 *Nan-ch'uang man-chi,* 5b, and TPY 71 *Chiang-chai shih fen-t'i kao,* 1:5b, and Meng Cheng-fa, *San-hsiang ts'ung-shih lu* (Shanghai, 1947), pp. 215–20.

109. Wang Fu-chih, *Shang-shu yin-i* (Peking, 1962), p. 174.

110. The very expression used to describe Wang himself in the imperial verdict on his memorial impeaching Lei Te-fu. TPY 64 *Lung-yuan yeh-hua,* 3a.

111. This passage bears a close resemblance to Wang's defense of the Tung-lin. TPY 17 *Li-chi chang-chü,* 3:23b–24a, and de Bary, *Unfolding of Neo-Confucianism,* pp. 424–25.

112. TPY 52 *Tu T'ung-chien lun,* 8:10b–11b.

113. TPY 64 *Huang-shu, hou-hsü,* 1b. Wang's nationalism, whose philosophical basis was a theory that universal order depended on maintaining the distinctions between natural categories and restricting each to its natural sphere of activity, precluded any thought of collaboration.

114. TPY 53 *Tu T'ung-chien lun,* 13:11b.

115. TPY 56 *Tu T'ung-chien lun,* 28:5b.

116. TPY 1 *Chiang-chai kung hsing-shu,* 3b.

5

Muslim and Central Asian Revolts

by Morris Rossabi

Muslims and Rebels

Thanks to the efforts of James B. Parsons, Li Wen-chih, and others, we know a good deal of the main narrative line of the great rebellions that brought down the Ming: the explosive spread of rebellion among peasants and military deserters in Shensi in the drought year of 1628; the long rebel cavalry raids across north China; the apparent near-success and then utter collapse of Ming suppression efforts in 1637–41; the days in 1644 when Li Tzu-ch'eng sat in the Imperial Palace in Peking and Chang Hsien-chung ruled Szechwan; the quick collapse of both forces before the Ch'ing advance in 1644–46. We know some of the contexts necessary for a full understanding: factionalism and bankruptcy in the Ming administration; the special burdens of poverty and heavy taxation in the unforgiving mountains of northern Shensi. But we know little of the many local disorders in other areas of China before and after the great outbursts of 1628: a White Lotus rebellion in Shantung, 1622–24; aboriginal revolts in Szechwan and Kweichow from 1621 to 1637; the south coast piracy described by Wills and the rebellions in the lower Yangtze mentioned by Beattie and Dennerline. We suspect that the proximity of the Mongols and the presence in the northwestern rebel forces of many deserters from the Great Wall garrisons may have stimulated the rebels' development of effective cavalry, but we know very little of the history of the Mongolian frontier after the pacification of Anda in 1570.

In this essay Morris Rossabi introduces us to the Muslim contexts of the great rebellions. Much of this will be new to most students of China, who view Islam in China as of marginal importance, not quite Chinese, and not worth the effort required to study it. Certainly it is not an easy subject, requiring substantial knowledge of the languages and cultures of both China and Islam. But Rossabi here shows how important the study of Islam within and beyond the northwestern frontier is to an understanding of the changes in the brittle commercial and political economy of the northwest, how Muslims were important participants in the great rebellions, and how they made their own separate contributions to the great variety of anti-Ch'ing rebellion and resistance in 1645–48. Out of these changes emerged in the 1670s a new pattern of relations between China and Muslim

169

Central Asia which eventually would draw the Ch'ing into the conquest of vast territories in Turkestan and would leave the Chinese Muslims uneasy subjects of the Ch'ing.

We tend to think of Chinese history as internally determined, being touched externally only in the sense that disorder brings invasion. But here, as in Manchuria, and in some ways on the coast and in the southwest, foreign relations were much more a permanent and normal part of the region's polity, economy, and society. To comprehend this, we have to adopt the long timespan of Ming relations with Central Asia, because the evidence is much thinner and more spotty than for most other Chinese frontier areas. We have to take note, also, of the thinness and fragility of the Central Asian commercial economy, its extreme vulnerability to changes in its relations with China. This essay is consciously introductory, and almost every part of the succeeding development of Ch'ing relations with Central Asia and of the troubled history of the Chinese Muslims (both in the northwest and in Yunnan) awaits the kind of full bicultural and multilingual study Rossabi has given us here.

In the spring of 1638, the rebel leader Li Tzu-ch'eng and his followers were crushed by the military forces of the Ming dynasty at Tzu-t'ung in the province of Szechwan. Li eluded the pursuing troops, and after riding for over six hundred *li* (approximately two hundred miles) on a donkey, reached the camp of another insurgent leader, Lao Hui-hui (literally, "Old Muslim"), where he received sanctuary. He remained with Lao Hui-hui for about six months while he recuperated from an injury sustained during the battle. On Li's departure, his host helped him to build the foundation for a new army by giving him a detachment of several hundred soldiers.[1] Chang Hsien-chung, the other renowned insurgent leader instrumental in causing the collapse of the Ming dynasty, also sought asylum with Lao Hui-hui. Seeking to regroup his forces after being routed by a Ming army in the winter of 1641, Chang turned to his Muslim counterpart for refuge. Like Li Tzu-ch'eng, Chang left within a short time with the nucleus of a new military force.[2]

These two examples indicate that the Muslims in northwest China, located primarily in the modern provinces of Shensi and Kansu, played a role in the events preceding and immediately following the fall of the Ming dynasty in 1644.[3] Not only did the Muslims within China affect the late Ming and early Ch'ing dynasties, but the Muslims in the nearby towns and oases of the Tarim river basin and in the more distant cities and regions of Transoxiana also exerted an influence on political and military developments in China during that time.[4] The Chinese Muslim role was not limited to the immediate period of the rebellions that led to the downfall of the Ming. Their participation in the revolts of the 1630s and 1640s was the culmination of a large number of Muslim border incursions and local uprisings, which were often provoked by economic factors rather than ethnic or religious issues, throughout the sixteenth century. And the establishment of the Ch'ing dynasty in 1644 did not bring peace to northwest China and to the neighboring border regions. The new government was forced to send several expeditionary forces to quell the Chinese Muslim disturbances. In many of these uprisings, the Chinese Muslims received the support and assistance of their co-religionists in Central Asia.

This essay seeks to trace and assess the significance of the uprisings of the Muslims of China and Central Asia in the rebellions of the late Ming and early Ch'ing. Two difficulties have limited study of the Muslim role in the fall of the Ming. One is that the Muslims who participated in the revolts often joined the Chinese rebels and rarely formed separate units, making it virtually impossible to identify them as Muslims. Some were Han Chinese and some were not Chinese, but the sources often do not distinguish between them. The extent of Muslim participation in the rebellions has thus been difficult to gauge and has perhaps been underestimated in earlier studies of the late Ming rebellions. Another problem is that the sources on the Chinese Muslims are few and fragmentary. Many of the traditional Chinese and Persian histories, which are the principal primary sources, scarcely refer to relations between the Chinese and Central Asian Muslims and China, and some simply offer no information about the people and conditions in the neighboring territory.[5] Yet even the limited evidence available, as we shall see, shows that the Muslims in China and in Central Asia played important roles in the Ming-Ch'ing transition.

THE DECLINE OF CENTRAL ASIA AND THE RISE OF THE KHOJAS

In the sixteenth and seventeenth centuries, the settled population of Muslim Central Asia was confronted with grave threats to its political and economic security. The Timurid empire, which had brought unity to much of Central Asia, collapsed in the first decade of the sixteenth century, leaving the principalities and towns in the area to fend for themselves. Taking advantage of the fall of the Timurids, such nomadic groups as the Kazakhs, the Kirghiz, and the Turkmen raided the towns and oases of Central Asia, attacked the caravans transporting goods across Eurasia, and forced the sedentary Muslims to launch costly military expeditions to prevent additional incursions. The commercial and political relations of the predominantly Sunnite Central Asian Muslims with Persia were disrupted as the population of the Iranian Safavid state converted to the Shi'ite order of Islam, curtailing Central Asian links with the Middle East. The extension of the Russian empire into North and Central Asia was still another threat to the Muslim states of the region.[6]

In addition to these difficulties, the Central Asian states were plagued by succession struggles. Kashgar and Yarkand, the two most powerful towns in the western fringes of the Tarim river basin, were politically unstable from the middle of the sixteenth century. The succession of a feeble ruler, 'Abd al-Karīm (or 'Abd al-Latīf), in 1565 ushered in a period of dynastic squabbles that weakened and eventually resulted in the collapse of the Chaghatay khanate which governed the two towns.[7] Despite this decline, Kashgar managed to expand toward China by annexing the town of Turfan, which was located in the eastern fringes of the Tarim basin. By the late sixteenth century, however, the political leaders of Kashgar·were no longer fully in control of their realm.

The heads of a Muslim religious brotherhood filled the vacuum created by the political ineffectiveness of the Chaghatay khans. This Sufi order, known as the Naqshbandiyya, was a religious group that emphasized direct experience with God through silent "remembrance" (*dhikr*) of the divine and through head-bobbing, body-shaking, and other evidences of ecstasy.[8] It sought to return to a pure form of Islam untainted by foreign ideas or customs, be they Buddhist, Shamanistic, or Christian. Its leaders, known as "khojas," claimed descent from the Prophet and moved from one oasis and town to another seeking converts.[9] They were extremely successful as a result of "the proselitizing [sic] zeal and activity of the Musulman merchant priests who traversed the country in all directions, and spread their doctrine more by example and persuasive devices than by force."[10]

Though the Naqshbandiyya and the other Sufi orders were basically conservative *religious* movements, it appears that they attracted much of their Central Asian (and eventually Chinese) support because of their political and economic, rather than religious, views. No doubt the khojas originally believed that some political involvement would help them attain their religious objectives, but within a short time political and economic power became an end in itself. Their political power grew as a result of the influence of the khojas on the khans and potentates in the oases and towns.[11] Gaining the trust of their patrons, they rapidly became decision-makers rather than mere advisers. By the end of the sixteenth century, they overshadowed the Chaghatay khans as the wielders of political power in Kashgar and Yarkand. They engaged in commerce through their hostelries (khānaqāh), which welcomed merchants and were located along important thoroughfares. They also received grants of land from Central Asian rulers and landlords, which offered them additional income and power.

It might appear that the rise of the khojas would have promoted a revival of political centralization and power in the region. Instead, in the late sixteenth century, disputes rose among two lines of khojas, which prevented the unification of Central Asia. The Aqtaghliq ("White Mountain") khoja reigned supreme in Kashgar while the Qarataghliq ("Black Mountain") khoja governed in Yarkand, and their rivalry no doubt weakened them both.[12]

Similarly, economic problems apparently bedeviled Kashgar, Yarkand, and the surrounding regions. Repeated and regular natural disasters caused great agrarian distress. Since both these towns were, in addition, commercial entrepots, some segments of the population relied on trade. The caravan trade, which entailed long travels from China through Central Asia to the Middle East and Europe, dealt primarily in luxury products (silk, ceramics, etc.), and was of less economic consequence than local trade between the towns and the nearby steppe nomads.[13] Yet the governments, which levied tariffs on the caravan commerce, and the merchants, camel herders, and others who participated in the trade must surely have been affected by the growth of maritime trade from Europe to Asia. An important recent study by Niels Steensgaard[14] has shown that it was not the opening of this route by the Portuguese in the early sixteenth century but its expansion by the English and the Dutch early in the seventeenth that ruined the caravan trade across Persia and the Near East to the Mediterranean. Ocean-going vessels carried bulkier goods and were free of the bandits, tariffs, and protection costs that plagued the caravans; but, according to Steensgaard, it was the northern Europeans, not their Portuguese precursors, who took advantage of this to lower their prices in Europe and drive overland goods off the market.

This decline in the western branches of the caravan network must have had some impact on its eastern branches, but it is very hard to measure. It may well be that some historians have overestimated the importance of the long-range trade and luxury goods for the Central Asian towns, and thus have exaggerated the impact of its decline, but it certainly signified a loss, though perhaps not a devastating one, in revenue for the governments and merchants of these towns.[15] By the early eighteenth century, however, a few Central Asian merchants were employed as middlemen in the growing trade between China and Russia. Thus some of the prosperity for those associated with the caravan trade was again noticeable.

It is more difficult to assess trends in the more consequential trade between these towns and the neighboring nomads during this time. The raids of the Kazakhs, Kirghiz, and Turkmen may have disrupted trade, but the lack of data stymies efforts to analyze commercial developments.

Data on Chinese–Central Asian economic relations, however, are available and reveal a decline in tribute embassies to China. The Central Asian towns (excluding the nearby oases of Hami and Turfan) had dispatched fifty-seven embassies to China from 1410 to 1430, and each embassy consisted of several hundred or, in some cases, several thousand men, many of whom were merchants.[16] The envoys and merchants no doubt traded with the peoples living in the oases enroute to China and then received as gifts, or bought, vast quantities of silk, ceramics, robes, tea, and other goods while in China. In the period from 1600 to 1630, only two embassies from Central Asia reached the Chinese capital. Some merchants undoubtedly arrived at the Chinese frontier and traded with Chinese merchants during this time, either under official supervision or illegally. By the early seventeenth century, however, the official border markets were, as we shall note, chaotic. And some of the goods that could earlier have been obtained in the interior or in Peking were unavailable on the frontier.

In sum, succession struggles, rivalries among the khojas, nomadic raids, and economic disruptions all diverted Central Asian attention from and limited direct relations with China. Yet political events and economic and religious currents in Kashgar and Yarkand had repercussions in China, for the town of Turfan acted as the transmitter of Central Asian influence on the Middle Kingdom.

TURFAN AND THE LATE MING DYNASTY

Turfan faced some of the same difficulties as the rest of Central Asia. Located just north of the Taklamakan desert, Turfan had developed a subsistence agriculture that was utterly dependent on the waters descending from the nearby T'ien Shan mountains. The town was particularly vulnerable to variations in weather, and a severe reduction in the water supply threatened the survival of the community. The Chinese accounts occasionally mention such natural disasters in the town, but the frequency with which they occur is not specified. Despite the lack of specific data, it is clear from the Chinese records that the precarious balance in Turfan's agriculture was from time to time upset, contributing to its political instability.[17]

This fragile subsistence economy was supported by trade with the nearby nomads and with China. A large group among the inhabitants of Turfan relied upon commerce for their livelihood, and these merchants, camel and horse grooms and attendants, and innkeepers sought a continuation and even an expansion of trade. They also acted as a powerful lobby in prompting Turfan's rulers to resist commercial restrictions imposed by other states, mainly China.

The Chinese of the early Ming, however, did not restrict trade or tribute. Instead, the Ming court initiated relations with Turfan and welcomed embassies dispatched by the rulers of the town. By the middle of the Yung-lo emperor's reign (1403–24), an average of one Turfanese embassy a year reached China, offered tribute to the emperor, and traded with Chinese merchants. This arrangement suited both sides, for they each received valuable goods, and China secured peace along its northwestern border. But by the middle of the fifteenth century, larger embassies from Turfan arrived in Peking, and the expense of feeding, entertaining, and lodging the envoys and merchants proved extremely burdensome to the Chinese court.[18]

The Ming was also faced with serious difficulties all along its northern borders. In 1449, the Oirat Mongols captured the Ming emperor when he campaigned against them; the Jurchen of Manchuria, on several occasions in the mid-fifteenth century, raided Chinese communities in the northeast frontier lands; and at the same time, the Eastern Mongols and the Chinese clashed repeatedly.[19] The tensions along the northern border persisted into the sixteenth century and prompted the Chinese court to limit relations with the "barbarians." In 1465, the emperor decreed that only one Turfanese embassy every three years be permitted entry into China and that only ten men from each mission be escorted to Peking. Such regulations were certainly not popular with the merchants and the government of Turfan.

As a result, disputes between the Ming court and Turfan's rulers flared up as early as the 1470s. Commercial and tributary arrangements were the main source of contention between them and the Ming emperors. The Chinese denounced the merchants and envoys of Turfan for evading the economic regulations devised by the Ming court, while the latter insisted that Chinese frontier and provincial officials exacted illegal customs duties and demanded bribes from foreign merchants. The Ming court accused its neighbors from Turfan of buying contraband goods, of offering defective products in trade, and of trading illegally with merchants and officials not specifically designated by the Chinese government. It complained that Turfan sent too many tribute embassies with too many men on each embassy and that the envoys, some of whom were accused of theft, drunken sprees, and even murder, stayed too long in China. The Ming chronicles also allege that the Chinese Muslims helped the Muslims of Turfan to defy the court's regulations. Some of these accusations are corroborated by contemporaneous Western travelers.

Several accounts written by European merchants and missionaries describe the efforts of merchants from Turfan and Central Asia to forge official credentials in order to gain entrance into China as government envoys[20]—a privilege which the Chinese court would have denied them had they applied as private citizens, and particularly as merchants.

On the other hand, Turfan was suffering severe economic reversals. Some Chinese officials were, in fact, victimizing merchants and chieftains from Turfan. These corrupt Ming officials demanded a percentage of the profits from the transactions of Turfanese merchants in China. The merchants also complained that they were offered defective and inferior goods in trade and as tribute. Such complaints, together with the pressures engendered by occasional natural disasters and the ensuing agricultural failures, prompted the rulers of Turfan to request ever more insistently that the Chinese government remove its limitations on trade and tribute and order Chinese merchants and officials to offer unadulterated and superior products to Turfanese envoys.[21] Though Turfanese merchants sometimes took matters into their own hands by trading illicitly with Chinese merchants, their rulers persisted in seeking an expansion of officially sanctioned trade.

The Ming court's rejection of many of their requests precipitated conflicts between China and Turfan and weakened both. Clashes between Ming troops and the forces of Turfan were common in the late fifteenth and early sixteenth centuries. They culminated in Turfan's conquest of Hami, an important town adjacent to China's northwestern border, in 1513 and in raids on Su-chou in 1517 and throughout the 1520s.[22] Despite these pressures, the Ming court maintained (without total success, to be sure) commercial and tributary restrictions. In the thirty-three-year period from 1594 to 1627, six missions, or an average of one every five and one-half years, from Turfan reached China, which was a sharp decline from the average of one a year recorded during the Yung-lo era. The official trade in tea, horses, silk, salt, and other commodities in the Chinese frontier markets also declined drastically during this period. A few Turfanese merchants no doubt dealt with Chinese smugglers, but the products that could now be obtained on the border were fewer and less varied than those earlier available in the

interior and in the capital. Thus the Chinese commercial and tributary restrictions, together with natural disasters, crop failures, and
other factors not presently perceived, exacerbated the domestic
political difficulties confronting Turfan.

Dynastic squabbles plagued Turfan starting in the middle of the
sixteenth century. Mansūr, the last unchallenged ruler of the region,
died in 1543/44, and the struggle for succession among his descendants wrought havoc in Turfan. The ensuing confusion permitted
the khans and the khojas of Kashgar and Yarkand to invade and
conquer Turfan in the late sixteenth century.[23] The religious and
political leaders of the more distant towns in the western Tarim basin
now had bases, Turfan and Hami, on China's northwestern border
from which their religious views could be disseminated and from
which they could influence developments in China.

Equally significant, they had potential sympathizers within the
Chinese border among Muslim refugees, consisting primarily of
Muslims from Hami and neighboring towns who fled their homes
during the early sixteenth-century battles between China and Turfan.
They sought and readily received sanctuary within China. The Ming
court resettled most of them in Su-chou, Kan-chou, Liang-chou,
and other towns in northwest China and invited a few to the capital.[24] It granted them grain, clothing, and building materials and
occasionally bestowed military titles and ranks on their leaders.[25]
Those refugees who went to Peking served in the Embroidered-
uniform Guard (*chin-i wei*), the College of Translators (*ssu-i kuan*),
and the College of Interpreters (*hui-t'ung kuan*).[26] The vast majority
of the migrants, however, were permitted to settle along the vulnerable northwestern frontier.

The court's policy of allowing a potential fifth column to reside
in a strategic border area is, at first glance, baffling. It pursued the
same policy with Mongols who migrated to China, and according
to the leading student of Ming-Mongol relations, "the Court itself
and the responsible ministers rarely seem to have become excited
and never thought that the situation involved any real danger and
called for extra measures."[27] To be sure, toward the end of the
sixteenth century, some Chinese officials complained that the
subsidies to the refugees were costly.[28] And at least one suggested
that the Muslim refugees be settled, as individuals, throughout the

empire rather than on the northwestern border where they could pose a threat to China's security.[29] The court apparently ignored these suggestions, for it did not attempt to disperse its new Muslim subjects throughout China. Perhaps it did not regard such a small group, which certainly amounted to no more than twenty to thirty thousand people, as very dangerous. Or the Chinese may have prized the skills offered by the Muslim migrants. The refugees served as horse traders and breeders, merchants, postal station attendants, and interpreters, and the Chinese needed people in all these occupations, especially in the northwest.

Though the Chinese motivation for the settlement policy is unknown, it is clear that some of the Muslims eventually proved disloyal. As the Ming dynasty declined in the late sixteenth and early seventeenth centuries, and as economic conditions in the northwest deteriorated, the refugees from Hami and the other Tarim basin oases became increasingly hostile to the court. Since many of them relied upon commerce for their livelihood, the disruption of the border markets and the caravan trade impoverished them. Along with poor harvests resulting from natural disasters, this calamity forced some of them to turn to banditry for self-preservation. Ultimately, they joined the late Ming rebels in the northwest, but it is uncertain whether their aim was to topple the dynasty or merely to profit from the unrest. Even before the full-scale rebellions of the 1630s or 1640s, they were accused by Ming officials of plotting with the agents of such Central Asian towns as Turfan and Yarkand and with the Chinese Muslims to attack Chinese border settlements, an indication, perhaps, that they were closer to banditry than to rebellion.[30]

CENTRAL ASIA, THE CHINESE MUSLIMS, AND THE MING

The Chinese Muslims were a large and influential group and presented additional problems for the Ming dynasty. It is beyond the scope of this essay to deal with the relations of the Chinese Muslims and the Chinese starting with the arrival of Arab and Persian traders in the T'ang (A.D. 618–906) dynasty, but a brief note on Chinese policy toward the Muslims in the later dynasties is essential. The Mongol Yuan dynasty (A.D. 1271–1368) was the first to bring Muslims into political and economic prominence in China. It used

Muslims, rather than its potentially "untrustworthy" Chinese subjects, as financial advisers, tax collectors, and merchants.[31] In these
capacities, the Muslims dealt frequently with the Chinese in generally
unpleasant circumstances, and Chinese bureaucrats and merchants
considered the Muslims agents of their oppressive Mongol rulers.
They began to characterize the Muslims as avaricious, aggressive, and
shrewd.

It should be noted that Chinese officials resented the Muslims from
purely economic and political motives; there is no evidence that the
Chinese were perturbed by the religious doctrines of Islam. They did
not, at least during the Yuan and Ming dynasties, discriminate against
the Muslims on religious grounds. These dynasties treated them as
foreigners, not as exponents of an alien religion, and did not attempt
to suppress the expression of Islamic beliefs by the Muslim communities. Certain Muslim practices (for example, the ban on the eating
of pork, fasting during Ramadān) offended the Chinese, but the
Ming dynasty, which ousted the Mongols in 1368 and reestablished
Chinese rule, did not impose restrictions on Islam.[32]

Ming policy toward the Muslims who lived in nonstrategic areas
was, in fact, fairly tolerant. The court employed them as astronomers
calendar-makers, and diviners in the Directorate of Astronomy
(*Ch'in-t'ien chien*)—all certainly critical occupations in an agricultural society. Muslims retained their preeminent positions in the
directorate until the Jesuits successfully challenged their influence
in the 1600s.[33] Starting in the Yung-lo reign (1403–24), the Ming
also used Muslims as envoys, translators, and interpreters and occasionally accorded them prominent positions and offered them
generous rewards.[34] Other Chinese of Muslim background were
renowned as explorer-ambassadors (Cheng Ho), philosophers (Li
Chih), and military men (Ch'ang Yü-ch'un).[35]

Two of the Ming emperors were attracted by Islam, and some
Chinese Muslim accounts, which are not very trustworthy, report
that they may have become Muslim converts. The Hung-wu emperor (1368–98), the first of these rulers, had two Muslim cousins;
it is alleged that his wife, surnamed Ma (the most common surname
among Chinese Muslims), was a Muslim; and three major mosques
were built, with imperial approval, during his reign. The Cheng-te
emperor (1506–21) was favorably disposed toward Muslims. He

surrounded himself with several Muslim eunuchs and advisers; he authorized the production of bronzes and porcelains which contained Arabic inscriptions and were sold to Muslim patrons in China and Central Asia; and he invited to his court and was solicitous to a Muslim chieftain from Hami who had collaborated with China's Turfanese enemies, while he demoted some of his own officials who had imprisoned the chieftain.[36] One source claims that he even prohibited the eating of pork for several months in 1519.[37]

It is unlikely that these two emperors actually considered conversion to Islam, but that such reports circulated throughout the dynasty indicates that the court did not foster a climate in which persecution of the Muslims was rampant. This is not to say that some Chinese in the northwest did not despise or discriminate against the Muslims. Nor does it imply that all the Ming emperors necessarily approved of and patronized Islam. It is merely that the official court policy was one of toleration toward the Muslims.

The Ming did not attempt to split up and disperse the large concentrations of Muslims living along the northwestern border, which is undoubtedly the most tangible proof of its policy of toleration. Starting as early as the Han dynasty (206 B.C.–A.D. 220), Chinese rulers had been concerned about raids and invasions across the northwestern frontier by the Hsiung-nü, the Turks, the Mongols, and other Inner Asian peoples. The Hung-wu emperor himself had on several occasions referred to this threat and urged his officials to concentrate on the defense of the north and northwest rather than on expansion along the southern borders or overseas.[38] Yet it was precisely in the northwest (modern Shensi, Ninghsia, and Kansu) that the largest and most closely knit Muslim communities resided. By allowing the Muslims to remain in this vulnerable strategic region, the Ming court showed either its faith in their loyalty and allegiance or its need of their expertise in trade, foreign languages, and horse breeding.

The Muslims, for their part, pursued a policy of peaceful coexistence in the early Ming. That is, they were not overly assertive in the practice or expression of their religious beliefs, though they attempted to live according to the fundamental injunctions of Islam. The Muslims in northwest China were organized into small communities centered around one or a few religious figures and did not, at least during the Ming, unite and offer their allegiance to a single leader.

They retained their cohesion partly by living in separate quarters in the Chinese towns and partly by following the dictates of their religion discreetly. The prohibitions on the eating of pork, the fasting during Ramadān, the alms-giving, and the ritual slaughter of animals were all important to them, and they apparently sought to fulfill these obligations without offending Chinese sensibilities. They also built mosques and trained a few of their number in Persian and Arabic so that they had access to the original works of Islam. A few Muslims even traveled westward to carry out the cardinal responsibility of a pilgrimage to Mecca.

Yet the Muslims made some accommodations to Chinese society. They adopted Chinese dress, erected tablets near their mosques proclaiming their allegiance to the Chinese emperor, and learned to speak Chinese. Starting in the Yung-lo period, most began to assume Chinese names, and some intermarried with the Chinese.[39] A few studied the Chinese classics and became so familiar with the rudiments of Confucian civilization that they passed the civil service examinations and were accepted into the Chinese bureaucracy. In this way, some were sinicized, but the remarkable fact is that so few Muslims were actually assimilated into Chinese civilization. Instead of decreasing as some of its members intermarried with the Chinese, the Muslim community in northwest China expanded and its devotion to Islam did not diminish. By the end of the Ming, the Muslims had retained their identity and were a sizeable minority within China. Most of the intermarriages were between Muslim males and Chinese females, and the offspring were generally reared as Muslims. The Islamic community also increased through adoption. Wealthy Muslims on occasion adopted young Chinese boys, raised them as Muslims, and thus had marital partners for their daughters.[40]

The success of the Muslims is in sharp contrast to the fate of the Chinese Jews during the same time. Though the Jews who settled in Kaifeng and other towns in eastern China in the twelfth century survived intact through the Sung and Yuan dynasties, there were unmistakeable signs of decline by late Ming and early Ch'ing times. Very few Jews could now read Hebrew, and many had only vague notions of the contents of the Old Testament.[41] According to an early Ch'ing inscription in their synagogue in Kaifeng, "in matters concerning capping, marriage, deaths, and funerals, the Chinese

(Hsia) rites are followed."[42] The Jews did not actively proselytize, and in fact they began to intermarry with the Chinese Muslims or with the Chinese and were assimilated into Islamic or Confucian society.

What explains the differences in the response of the Muslims and the Jews to Chinese society? It certainly cannot be explained by Jewish ignorance or lack of interest in identification with their heritage. The original Jews who landed in China in the twelfth century were no less tenacious in adherence to their faith than the Muslims were to theirs. Jews and Muslims both had the same opportunities for integration into Chinese society, for the Ming court accepted foreigners into the civil service as long as they adhered to Confucian doctrine. It is true that there were fewer Jews than Muslims in China. Their paltry number may have intensified the difficulties the Jews faced in retaining their identity, but size is not the sole explanation for the assimilation of this or any other minority. Their efforts to avoid total immersion in Chinese civilization were undermined by the lack of contact among the various Jewish communities within China and, most important, by the absence, from Ming times on, of relations with Jews in other lands. Cut off in this way from the support and nurture of their coreligionists, they began to lose their Jewish identity.

Unlike the Chinese Jews, the Muslims in Ming China were in touch with the world Muslim community through Central Asia. During the Yuan, Chinese Muslims could travel, with scant if any interference from the government in Peking, to the Middle East, though in the Ming they limited their voyages to Central Asia. There is certainly no doubt that the Muslims were well traveled. As one scholar has observed, "Muslim merchants had a thriving network of communications between their widely scattered centres, and all Muslims were ensured a friendly reception and if need be free board and lodging in the mosque communities which lay on their route—they were therefore great travellers."[43] The mosques and religious hostelries of Central Asia and northwest China welcomed Muslim merchants as well as other itinerant Muslims. The Ming sources confirm the close relations between the Muslims within China and the Muslims in adjacent lands. They frequently accuse the Chinese Muslims of meeting with the Muslims of the Western Regions (*Hsi-yü*) and either collaborating to evade the commercial regulations of the court or planning raids on unguarded Chinese border settlements.[44] In sum, it is undeniable that the Chinese Muslims of the Ming period were involved with the Muslims of Central Asia.

Their bonds were strengthened by the type of work performed by the Chinese Muslims. Since several of the trade routes to Central Asia and Mongolia traversed northwest China, many Chinese Muslims had the opportunity to take part in commerce. Thus the Muslims served as merchants, interpreters, postal station attendants, conveyors of goods, and held other commercial positions. By default, they tended to monopolize work that involved horses and camels.[45] The Chinese had few proficient camel and horse breeders and depended upon the Muslims and other foreigners to rear and train their animals. They relied, in part, upon the Muslims to purchase and make available a supply of superior horses and camels from Central Asia and Mongolia. As a result, Muslims played an important role in the *Yuan-ma ssu* (Pasturage Office) and in the tea and horse trade with Central Asia.[46] The livelihood of many of the Chinese Muslims was thus directly related to trade with fellow Muslims from Central Asia.

Consequently, the apparent decline of the caravan and frontier trade, particularly in the late sixteenth and early seventeenth centuries, was as disruptive to the economic welfare of the Chinese Muslims as to that of the Muslims of Turfan, Yarkand, and other Central Asian towns. The northwestern border trade in tea and horses, for example, had become, by the late sixteenth century, chaotic and undependable as a source of income.[47] As Ray Huang has noted, "The decline of the horse trade on the frontier undoubtedly contributed to the economic depression of Shensi in the early seventeenth century. The trade in its heyday was extremely complex, involving officials, merchants, tea growers, army officers, and soldiers, and its importance cannot be measured simply by the figures in the official records. In 1589, the surveillance commissioner of Shensi stressed that it was essential to the province's local economy."[48] Similarly, the trade in textiles, camels, and jade along the frontier was disrupted. The backwardness of northwest China where many Muslims lived, together with the severe natural disasters afflicting the region in the late sixteenth and early seventeenth centuries, exacerbated their economic problems.[49]

It is not surprising that the Chinese Muslims and the Muslims of Central Asia, who faced similar problems in agriculture and commerce, should cooperate, particularly in relations with Chinese officials. And, as we shall note, they did work together in the late Ming and early Ch'ing. What remains unclear is the extent of the Chinese Muslims' knowledge of the religious views of the Central Asian Muslims. The Chinese sources on this, as in so many other matters involving the Muslims in China, are silent, but given their frequent dealings with the Muslims of Central Asia, it seems likely that some Chinese Muslims were acquainted with the Naqshbandī teachings of the khojas. It is difficult to assess the influence of these fundamentalist doctrines, which emphasized a militant version of Islam uncorrupted by foreign ideas, on devout Chinese Muslims and on the Muslim rebellions in the late Ming, but the fact that the Muslims on several occasions were willing to cooperate with non-Muslim Chinese implies that a dogmatic, anti-Chinese ideology did not inspire the Muslim insurrections. The economic problems of the Chinese Muslims offer a more credible explanation for their rebellions, and the Muslim rebels in Ming China probably cooperated with the khojas because of similar political and economic interests rather than a shared devotion to a holy war against nonbelievers.

THE CHINESE MUSLIMS AND THE LATE MING REBELLIONS

The agrarian distress and the commercial restrictions confronting the Muslims inevitably resulted in clashes with the Ming government. According to late Ming sources, some Muslim merchants repeatedly and deliberately sought to circumvent Chinese commercial and tributary regulations,[50] thus challenging and alienating the Ming court. Starting early in the sixteenth century, tensions between the court and the Muslims precipitated several insurrections. Even earlier, in 1476, a Muslim named Yang Hu-li had raided Chinese northwestern border settlements and was subjugated, with great difficulty, by Ma Wen-sheng, who was later to become the minister of war. This seems, however, to have been an isolated instance and unrelated to Muslim grievances. But in 1514 a certain Li Ta-lu harassed the towns of Han-chung and Sian in Shensi and initiated a series of Muslim raids on towns in northwestern China. According to several Chinese accounts, the Muslims in these cases often posed as mer-

chants, offering horses or medicines in trade. Having gained the
confidence of the Chinese authorities in a particular town, they then
unleashed a surprise attack on the unprepared inhabitants. This is,
of course, the Chinese view. The Muslim merchants charged that
Chinese commercial restrictions and abuse prompted them to engage
in such raids. And even the Chinese accounts concede that some of
these outbreaks were precipitated by Chinese officials and eunuchs
(the latter, in particular, acquired great political power in the Cheng-
te period), who discriminated against or sought bribes from Muslim
traders.[51]

The incidents became more serious and more frequent as China's
border defenses deteriorated. In 1513, Turfan had exposed China's
weakness in the northwest by occupying the town of Hami. Encouraged by the success of Turfan, many Muslims within China, who
had grievances against the Ming government, rebelled against the
Chinese authorities or raided border settlements. The Chinese chronicles of the Wan-li reign (1573–1620), for example, record Muslim
uprisings or raids in 1573, 1575, 1582, 1595, 1599, 1603, and
1612.[52] The Chinese histories yield pitifully few details about these
incidents, and such accounts emphasize the military pacification of
the raiders and insurgents. It is clear from these descriptions, however, that the raids were by no means major rebellions and usually
involved several hundred or a few thousand disgruntled Muslims.
On occasion, the Muslims collaborated with Mongols located beyond
the northwestern border in attacks on Chinese garrisons or frontier
settlements. The Ming sources attribute these outbreaks to natural
disasters that resulted in food shortages and to commercial disputes.
Food shortages and actual famines in the relatively poor farmland
of northwest China repeatedly provoked Muslim raids during this
period. Also, Chinese denunciations of and attempts to prevent
illegal trade transactions by Muslim merchants incited the latter to
avenge themselves through attacks on neighboring Chinese villages.

Meanwhile, the Ming dynasty was heading toward the collapse
which has been described by several scholars and which requires only
brief recounting here.[53] Costly military expeditions against the
Japanese in Korea in the 1590s and against the Manchus in the early
seventeenth century, excessive court expenditures, corruption among
some court and local officials, and the activities of avaricious and

politically powerful eunuchs had created severe financial problems
for the government by the early seventeenth century.[54] To defray
the rising costs, the court imposed additional taxes, primarily on the
peasantry. Land taxes doubled between 1618 and 1636, and many
of the officials who collected taxes were bribed by local landlords,
who in this way escaped from the tax rolls.[55] Fewer of the bureaucrats assigned to such distant regions as northwestern China had obtained the highest academic degree (the *chin-shih*), probably indicating a decline in the quality of officials.

In northern Shensi, a remote and relatively unprosperous region,
these economic abuses were devastating. With its limited cultivable
acreage, its poor communications and transport, and its isolation
from the wealthier provinces in China, this area suffered more
seriously than most regions from the deteriorating economic conditions.[56] Any unexpected or unforeseen circumstances could prove
disastrous. In 1628, just such a disaster, a prolonged drought, did in
fact occur. This drought and the resulting famine provoked unrest,
initially consisting of raids by small armed groups but eventually
organized into actual revolts by Li Tzu-ch'eng and other rebel
leaders.

The military colonies on the border, which might have been
expected to subjugate the rebels, instead often instigated or led the
uprisings. Originally meant to be self-supporting, the frontier soldiers
had, within a short time after the founding of the Ming, proved
unable to supply themselves and had come to rely on the government
for provisions.[57] By the early seventeenth century, however, the
government was unable, either through its own resources or through
requisitions from merchants, to provide the needed supplies. Nor did
it have sufficient horses for its frontier forces, particularly after the
gradual elimination of the horse markets on the northern borders.[58]
Thus the ill-supplied, demoralized, and often hungry common
soldiers in the military colonies frequently deserted and joined the
insurgents. And some scholars assert that the early rebellions were
led by and composed of deserters, outlaws, and others on the fringes
of peasant society rather than the peasants themselves.[59]

The postal station attendants fit into this nonpeasant category,
and they too joined the rebels. In an effort to reduce expenses, the
government in 1629 had abolished about one-third of the postal sta-

tions in Shensi. The unemployed and disgruntled attendants then
turned to antigovernment activities, frequently allying themselves
with the insurgents. Many of the attendants were, as noted earlier,
Muslims. So too were some of the military colonists and army deserters.[60] These Muslims were important and highly visible because
they had their own horses and weapons. They were also proficient
at combat on horseback and at raising and breeding horses, all of
which made them valuable to the rebel forces.

Muslim prominence in the early phases of the rebellion is attested
to by one of the reliable primary sources on the revolts, which notes
that "among the rebels there are hungry people, frontier soldiers, and
Muslims."[61] A number of Muslims are mentioned en passant as
leaders of early raids and revolts, but the Chinese histories offer few
details about them. They come down to us merely as names with no
other distinguishing features. A certain Ma Lao-hu ("Tiger Ma")
appears repeatedly in the Chinese accounts as one of the more successful Muslim leaders, but the location of his base, the size of his
forces, and the social composition of his followers are all left to the
reader's imagination.[62] One conclusive and unmistakeable fact
emerging from the sources is that the Muslims cooperated with
the Chinese rebels, and it appears that the Muslims had Chinese
soldiers in their ranks and the Chinese rebels had contingents of
Muslims in their bands, which supports the view that economic
motives were more important than religious ones for the Muslim
rebels.

It is difficult to assess the precise role of the Muslims in the rebellions of the 1630s and 1640s. They certainly took part in the
revolts that contributed to the collapse of the Ming dynasty, but
they were probably too few in number to determine the course of
the rebellions. They offered indispensable military skills but relatively few recruits to the insurgents. One Japanese scholar has suggested that the leader of the rebellions in Shensi, Li Tzu-ch'eng
himself, was a Muslim, but the evidence he presents is not conclusive and is subject to varying interpretations. It appears that Li
was adopted at the age of ten by an old Muslim woman to help her
care for her horses. He received some instruction in Islamic practices during his stay with her but certainly did not convert. Later
he became a postal station attendant, a popular occupation with the

Muslims. He was one of those who were dismissed when the Ming eliminated some postal stations in Shensi in 1629. There is no evidence, however, that his early exposure to Islam really influenced Li's life prior to his involvement in the rebellions.[63]

With the start of the rebellions, his relationship with Islam and the Chinese Muslims can be more easily traced. One of his prominent and most esteemed advisers was a Han Muslim named Niu Chin-hsing. Li's closest Han Muslim ally was Ma Shou-ying, who is more commonly known as Lao Hui-hui and was one of the early leaders of the rebellions. At one time, Lao Hui-hui is reported to have had 200,000 men under his command.[64] As noted earlier, he offered sanctuary to the two most important rebel leaders, Li Tzu-ch'eng and Chang Hsien-chung, when they had suffered severe setbacks at the hands of the Ming forces. He participated in nearly all the major conferences of the rebel leaders during the early stages of the rebellions and played a role in the formulation of policy and strategy.[65]

Though the number of Muslims who joined Lao Hui-hui and Li as rebels is uncertain, it is clear that those who did were a diverse group. Some were postal station attendants whom the Ming court dismissed in 1629; a few were peasants who, like their Chinese counterparts, had suffered from the Shensi drought in 1628; others were soldiers in the military colonies who had not received supplies or even the basic necessities from the government; and a large number were merchants whose livelihood was threatened by the commercial and tributary restrictions on the border and in Peking imposed by the Ming. They received encouragement and perhaps some supplies from the Muslims of Central Asia, but there is no textual evidence that their fellow Muslims across the northwestern border took part in the late Ming rebellions. During the early Ch'ing, only a few years later, the towns of Central Asia were, however, directly involved in the uprisings of the Chinese Muslims.

CENTRAL ASIA AND THE EARLY CH'ING REBELLIONS

The establishment of the Ch'ing dynasty did not dissipate the discontent of the Muslims of Central Asia and the Chinese Muslims. It is clear that the economic problems of Central Asia had not been resolved. Central Asian border trade with China was disrupted as a result of the rebellions and the ensuing political instability; the Ch'ing court devised restrictive commercial and tributary regulations; and natural disasters, including hailstorms, still plagued the Muslim farmers in the northwest in the late 1640s. Many of the Muslims of Central Asia and China apparently assumed that the new dynasty would pursue the same policies in the northwest as its predecessor. The town dwellers among them, in addition, still feared the incursions of the nomadic Kazakh and Kirghiz peoples. By the middle of the seventeenth century, they also had to contend with the growing power of the Zunghar Mongols. Under the leadership of their rulers, Qaraqula and his son Batūr Qung Tayiji, the Zunghars had conquered the lands of the other Mongol peoples in Western Mongolia and were attempting to form a unified state through the promotion of Buddhism, the creation of a new Mongol script, and the development of agriculture.[66]

Confronted by Mongol neighbors who seemed bent on conquest, it is not surprising that the Central Asian towns sought political unity. They appear to have been at least partially successful, for by the early 1640s the members of one family ruled nine of the strategically located towns in the Tarim basin. The khojas, with their emphasis on Muslim solidarity, also contributed to political centralization. A-pu-tu-la ('Abd Allāh) of Yarkand was the supreme potentate, and he had dispatched his eight younger brothers to rule in the various oases that were presumably part of his domain.[67] Pa-pai Khān (Bābā) of Hami and Sultān Khān of Turfan were the two brothers who dealt most frequently with China.

At the outset of the Ch'ing dynasty, the non–Han Muslims of Central Asia found that they faced commercial restrictions in China. In 1646, Turfan sent an embassy which requested a resumption of the trade and tribute relations that had been disrupted during the disturbances of the late Ming.[68] The Ch'ing court responded favorably, but reimposed the old Ming regulations on trade and tribute. It limited Turfan to one embassy every five years, required the envoys to follow a prescribed route from the border to Peking, and permitted only thirty men from each mission to travel to the capital.[69] The envoys could trade, under official supervision, with specifically designated Chinese merchants and officials at Lan-chou and at Peking. These restrictions, along with other, more minor regulations, no doubt frustrated and antagonized merchants from Turfan and the rest of the Central Asian towns.

Another disruption for the Muslim merchants was the court's inability to revive the tea and horse trade. The early Ch'ing chronicles indicate that the court wished to reestablish this trade.[70] It founded six branches of the Horse Trading Office (*Ch'a-ma ssu*) in northwestern China and imposed regulations in an attempt to monopolize this commerce.[71] Despite these efforts, the tea and horse trade did not flourish. By the 1670s, much of the tea collected by the government was used to pay its soldiers (who, in turn, sold the tea to obtain supplies) on the northwest frontier rather than to purchase Central Asian horses.[72] Within fifty years, the Ch'ing had discovered new and more profitable outlets for its tea. It began to export more of its tea to Russia and western Europe, and the Muslims of Central Asia were thus excluded from the trade.[73]

Like their coreligionists in Central Asia, the Chinese Muslims were suffering from the agrarian and commercial distress and the general economic instability of late Ming and early Ch'ing times. The Ch'ing court apparently recognized their economic problems, for on several occasions in the 1640s, it waived or reduced the taxes on Muslim regions in the northwest. Those areas afflicted by such natural disasters as hailstorms received special dispensation and aid from the Ch'ing rulers.[74] But some Muslims in China and Central Asia were still not pacified.

Starting in 1646, a Muslim named Mi La-yin united fellow dissidents in Kan-chou and rebelled against the Ch'ing court. Within a few months, the troops of another Muslim, Ting Kuo-tung, augmented the rebel forces. According to Ch'ing sources, the rebel leaders commanded one hundred thousand men, and with this large force they quickly occupied Lan-chou, Min-chou, and other northwestern towns. They claimed that their main objective was to assist in the restoration of the Ming dynasty.[75] Their candidate was related to the Ming royal family, and they proclaimed him emperor in the occupied town of Kan-chou. Here again the Chinese Muslims cooperated with the Chinese, which is still another indication that they were not motivated solely by religious considerations and did not plan to establish a purely Muslim state.

Yet they received support from their fellow Muslims in Central

Asia. Turfan undoubtedly provided assistance in the form of supplies, and possibly manpower, to Mi La-yin and Ting Kuo-tung.[76]
Hami's support was ensured by a clever tactical maneuver. The
Muslim leaders offered to enthrone the son of Hami's ruler as prince
of the town of Su-chou.[77] With this assurance that his son T'u-lun-
t'ai (Turumtay) would have a prominent position, the ruler of
Hami, Pa-pai Khān, enthusiastically assisted the rebels. Pa-pai Khān
may also have helped them in order to manifest his displeasure with
the Ch'ing restrictions on commerce and tribute. Or perhaps he
viewed the Ch'ing leaders as rebels and sought to assist the "legitimate" Ming rulers regain the throne. But he chose unwisely for his
son.

The Ch'ing government acted quickly to crush the Muslim dissidents. It assigned Meng Ch'iao-fang, the governor-general of Shensi,
to pacify the rebels.[78] A discussion of the details of his military
campaigns is beyond the scope of this paper. Suffice it to say that
he took advantage of the divisions among the insurgents and fought
against one rebel force at a time.[79] By 1650, Meng had crushed the
Muslims, killing Mi La-yin in Kan-chou and capturing and executing
Ting Kuo-tung in Su-chou.[80] According to the Ch'ing records, the
casualties in these campaigns were enormous. Over ten thousand
Muslims were killed in one battle in 1648. Another eight thousand
Muslims were beheaded in Ting Kuo-tung's last campaign. One
Ch'ing source estimates that a total of one hundred thousand Mus-
lims, which seems to be a grossly inflated figure, died during the
rebellions.

Despite this victory, the pacification of the Muslims of China and
Central Asia was not entirely successful. The Chinese Muslims remained dissatisfied with their economic status, and from this time
on began to assert and preserve their own unique culture. A true
intellectual revival was fostered among the Muslims in the seventeenth and eighteenth centuries. They produced over thirty major
works about Islam during this period, and these texts helped to
preserve their heritage and to maintain their identity as a distinct
group.[82] Similarly, the Muslims of Central Asia remained hostile to
Ch'ing China. Tribute and trade missions between Turfan and Hami
and China were resumed in 1656, but commercial disputes continued. In 1678 the White Mountain khoja Ḥaẓrat-i Āfāq, with the

aid of the Zunghar Mongols, finally overcame the Black Mountain khoja and the last Chaghatay ruler, ending the long quarrel between the two khoja lines and beginning the intermittent involvement of the Muslim towns in the Zunghar challenge to Ch'ing China. This conflict ended only with the Ch'ing conquest of Zungharia and Chinese Turkestan in the 1750s. But even after the entire Tarim basin was incorporated in the Ch'ing empire, the relations of its towns with the Ch'ing authorities remained strained at best.[83]

These later conflicts between the Ch'ing court and the Muslims differed from those of the late Ming and the early Ch'ing. Economic problems receded for a time, as trade between some regions in Central Asia and China and Russia expanded and as the Ch'ing dynasty sought to promote the economic recovery of the Central Asian territories it conquered in the 1750s. Religious and ethnic issues gave rise to the majority of the Muslim uprisings of the late eighteenth and nineteenth centuries. Unlike the Ming rulers, the Ch'ing court enacted regulations (including restrictions on the construction of mosques) that circumscribed the practice of Islam. The Ch'ing officials dispatched to the Muslim areas in the northwest were generally more corrupt and less tolerant of Islam than their counterparts in the Ming. In turn, the Muslims became more truculent and embraced the Naqshbandī and other militant orders. When they rebelled, they did not collaborate with the Chinese. The uprisings were purely Muslim in origin and were prompted by discrimination against Muslims. One of the rebel groups even sought to establish an independent Muslim state. It is possible that the more repressive Ch'ing policy was due to the empire's expansion into Central Asia and the sudden incorporation of a large Muslim minority, which the government apparently viewed as disloyal. Further study of Ch'ing policy toward the Muslims is needed, however, before its motivation can be understood.

Central Asia greatly influenced late Ming and early Ch'ing China. Without the support of and direct relations with their coreligionists in Central Asia, the Muslims in China, like the Chinese Jews, might have failed to preserve their community there. The Muslims of Central Asia and China not only shared a common religion but also had common agrarian and commercial problems. The commercial restrictions imposed by the Chinese, along with the agrarian and

194 MORRIS ROSSABI

political deterioration of the late Ming in the northwest, provoked
the Muslim revolts of late Ming and early Ch'ing China. The Central
Asian Muslims played a role in the Chinese Muslim uprisings of the
sixteenth century and may have been involved in the northwestern
rebellions that led to the downfall of the Ming dynasty. There is no
doubt that Central Asian Muslims from Hami, Turfan, and other
Tarim river-basin towns joined with the Chinese Muslims in opposing
the newly founded Ch'ing dynasty in the late 1640s. And these revolts were prompted by economic distress rather than by religious
or ethnic discrimination.

NOTES TO CHAPTER 5

1. Ku Ying-t'ai, *Ming-shih chi-shih pen-mo* (Shanghai, 1934 reprint), ch. 78,
p. 58.
2. Tazaka Kōdō, *Chūgoku ni okeru Kaikyō no denrai to sono guzū* (Tokyo,
1964), 2:1210.
3. Some useful guides to the sources on the Chinese Muslims are available.
Claude L. Pickens, Jr., *Annotated Bibliography of Literature on Islam In China*
(Hankow, 1950), though badly dated and lacking any references to Japanese
sources, is still a handy and well-organized description of the sources. Hajji
Yusuf Chang's "A Bibliographical Study of the History of Islam in China"
(M.A. thesis, McGill University, 1960) supplements Pickens, but it too omits
the important Japanese secondary accounts. The Japanese works are compe-
tently described in "Japanese Materials on Islam in China: A Selected Bibliography" by Mark S. Pratt (M.A. thesis, Georgetown University, 1962) and in
Shinkyō kenkyū bunken mokuroku, Nihon-bun [Classified bibliography of
Japanese books and articles concerning Sinkiang, 1866–1962] (Tokyo, 1962)
by Yüan T'ung-li and Watanabe Hiroshi. Russian contributions to the study of
the Chinese Muslims are listed in two works by Rudolf Loewenthal: "Russian
Materials on Islam in China: A Preliminary Bibliography," *Monumenta Serica*
16 (1957):449–79, and "Russian Contributions to the History of Islam in
China," *Central Asiatic Journal* 3, no. 4 (1962):312–15, and in Petr Emel'ianovich Skachkov, *Bibliografiia Kitaia,* 2d ed. (Moscow, 1960). J. D. Pearson,
Index Islamicus, 1906–1955 (Cambridge, 1958) and its various supplements
list periodical articles on Chinese Muslims found in obscure journals.
4. Claude P. Dabry de Thiersant, *Le mahométisme en Chine et dans le Turkestan oriental* (Paris, 1878), 1:154, is wrong in asserting that "l'histoire de
l'islamisme dans la province de Chen-si, n'offre rien de remarquable sous les
dynasties des Song, des Yuen, et des Ming."
5. A typical example of such indifference is the history of Mirza Muhammad
Haidar. As Ney Elias, the editor of the English translation of Muhammad Haidar's
work, notes, "Haidar's history nowhere speaks of intercourse with China."

See N. Elias, ed., *A History of the Moghuls of Central Asia being the Tarikh-i-Rashidi of Mirza Muhammad Haidar, Dughlat,* trans. E. Denison Ross (London, 1895), p. 63.

6. For more on this, see B. Spuler, "Central Asia from the Sixteenth Century to the Russian Conquest," in P. M. Holt, Ann K. S. Lambton, and B. Lewis, eds., *The Cambridge History of Islam* (London, 1970), pp. 468–70.

7. See Gavin Hambly, ed., *Central Asia* (New York, 1969), pp. 135–36, and B. Spuler, ed., *Geschichte Mittelasiens* (in *Handbuch der Orientalistik* 5, no. 5) (Leiden, 1966), pp. 240–41, for more details about the Chaghatay.

8. See Joseph Fletcher's unpublished paper, "Central Asian Sufism and Ma Ming-hsin's New Teaching," which has been extremely useful in the preparation of this essay.

9. For more on its teachings, see J. Spencer Trimingham, *The Sufi Orders in Islam* (London, 1971), pp. 91–94, and B. G. Martin, "A Short History of the Khalwati Order of Dervishes," in Nikki R. Keddie, ed., *Scholars, Saints, and Sufis* (Berkeley, 1972), pp. 275–78.

10. H. W. Bellew, "History of Kashghar," in T. D. Forsyth, ed., *Report of a Mission to Yarkund in 1873* (Calcutta, 1875), p. 174.

11. "Shinsho no tai Kaikyō seisaku" [Government policy toward Islam in the early Ch'ing], *Kaikyō jijō* 2, no. 4 (1939):33–53; Ch'en Ch'ing-lung, "Lun pai-shan tang yü hei-shan tang" [On the Aktaghlik and Karataghlik], *Bulletin of the Institute of China Border Area Studies, National Chengchi University,* no. 2 (July 1971), pp. 209–31.

12. The White Mountain khoja Ḥazrat-i Āfāq, who finally overcame his rival in the late seventeenth century, was considered a saint, and until modern times many came to worship at his tomb. For him and his tomb, see W. Barthold, "Kāshghar," in *The Encyclopedia of Islam* (Leiden, 1927 ed), 2:788, and A. N. Kuropatkin, *Kashgaria: Eastern or Chinese Turkestan,* trans. Walter Gowan (Calcutta, 1882), pp. 103–05.

13. For more on the operation of this trade, see my "Trade Routes in Inner Asia," in Denis Sinor, ed., *Cambridge History of Inner Asia* (London, forthcoming).

14. Niels Steensgaard, *Carracks, Caravans, and Companies* (Copenhagen, 1973), p. 170.

15. See, for example, Spuler, "Central Asia," pp. 470–71, who writes of the Russian expansion into Asia: "This also had the effect that traffic between eastern Europe and eastern Asia moved over to Siberia in the next centuries and went through Russian territory; there was a considerable decline in the economic importance of Turkistan." Owen Lattimore, *Inner Asian Frontiers of China* (Boston, paperback ed., 1962), p. xix, also emphasizes the decline of the caravan trade as an explanation for the decline of Central Asia.

16. Based on my own studies of the *Ming Shih-lu.* The *Mindai seiiki shiryō* (Kyoto, 1973), a compilation of all the *Shih-lu* references to Central Asia, appeared too late for use in this essay but will prove invaluable for all future studies of Ming–Central Asian relations.

17. See my "Ming China and Turfan, 1406–1517," *Central Asiatic Journal* 16, no. 3 (1972):206–07, for more on the economy and geography of Turfan.

18. Mao Jui-cheng, *Huang Ming hsiang-hsü lu* (Shanghai, 1937 reprint), ch. 7, 5a, for some of the complaints by Ming officials about the excessive cost of these embassies.

19. On the Jurchen, see my "The Jurchen in the Yüan and the Ming" for the Chin Dynastic History Project directed by Herbert Franke.

20. C. Wessels, *Early Jesuit Travellers in Central Asia, 1603–1721* (The Hague, 1924), p. 26. Note also the remarks of the sixteenth-century Jesuit Matteo Ricci, who resided in China for almost three decades: "Even at present it is an annual occurrence for Persian merchants to make excursions into China, under the pretence of being official legations." Louis Gallagher, trans., *China in the Sixteenth Century: The Journals of Matthew Ricci, 1583–1610* (New York, 1953), p. 106.

21. Tazaka, (see n. 2 above), pp. 972–77.

22. T'an Ch'ien, *Kuo-ch'üeh* (Peking, 1958 reprint), p. 3181.

23. For the last years of Turfan, see B. Spuler, "Central Asia," pp. 473–74.

24. Ch'en Jen-hsi, *Huang Ming shih-fa lu* (Taipei, 1965 reprint), pp. 1965–66, 1971.

25. See Chung Fang, *Ha-mi chih* (Taipei, 1967 reprint), pp. 18–21, and Chang Hung-hsiang, "Ming hsi-pei kuei-hua-jen shih-hsi-piao" [Genealogical tables of the naturalized citizens from the northwest in the Ming], *Fu-jen hsüeh-chih* 8, no. 2 (1939):98–118, for examples of the treatment accorded such refugees.

26. Lü Wei-ch'i, *Ssu-i-kuan tse* (Kyoto, 1928 ed.), ch. 7, 4a–5a.

27. Henry Serruys, "The Mongols in China, 1400–1450," *Monumenta Serica* 27 (1968):244.

28. T'an Ch'ien, *Kuo-ch'üeh*, p. 5055.

29. Tazaka, p. 1105; *Ming shih-lu (Hsien-tsung)* (Taipei, 1962–68 ed.), ch. 141, 1b–2b.

30. Tazaka Kōdō, "Mindai koki no Kaikyōto ryūzoku" [The Muslim bandits in late Ming times] *Tōyō gakuhō* 37, no. 1 (June 1954):58–61.

31. John W. Dardess, *Conquerors and Confucians: Aspects of Political Change in Late Yüan China* (New York, 1973), pp. 21, 51. For more on the Muslims in the Yuan, see my "The Muslims in the Early Yuan Dynasty."

32. J. F. Ford, "Some Chinese Muslims in the Seventeenth and Eighteenth Centuries," *Asian Affairs: Journal of the Royal Central Asian Society* 61, pt. 2 (June 1974):144–47.

33. On their role in the directorate, see Ho Peng-yoke, "The Astronomical Bureau in Ming China," *Journal of Asian History* 3, no. 2 (1969):137–57.

34. Chang Hung-hsiang, (see n. 25 above), pp. 118–21.

35. In this connection, Timoteus Pokora notes in his "A Pioneer of New Trends of Thought in the End of the Ming Period," *Archiv Orientalni* 29 (1961): 471: "The manysided connections of Li Chih and his ancestors with foreign countries and foreigners are very important for the evolution of his thought." The foreigners to whom he refers are the Muslims.

36. "Mindai no Kaikyō ni tsuite" [Concerning Islam in Ming times], *Kaikyō*

jijō 2, no. 3 (1939):5; Kamer Aga-Oglu, "Blue-and-White Porcelain Plates Made for Moslem Patrons," *Far Eastern Ceramic Bulletin* 3, no. 3 (September 1951): 12–16; B. Laufer, "Chinese Muhammedan Bronzes," *Ars Islamica* 1, no. 2 (1934):133–46; on the Muslim chieftain, see Paul Pelliot, "Le Hōja et le Sayyid Husain de l'histoire des Ming," *T'oung Pao* 38 nos. 2–5 (1948):81–198.

37. "Mindai no Kaikyō ni tsuite," p. 8.

38. See Lo Jung-pang, "Policy Formulation and Decision-Making on Issues Respecting Peace and War," in Charles O. Hucker, ed., *Chinese Government in Ming Times: Seven Studies* (New York, 1969), p. 52. The concern over defense of the northwestern border even affected important decisions in the nineteenth century. See Immanuel C. Y. Hsü, "The Great Policy Debate in China, 1874: Maritime Defense vs. Frontier Defense," *Harvard Journal of Asiatic Studies* 25 (1964–65):212–28. In this connection, it is all the more surprising that Ming China made so few preparations to thwart the planned assaults of the great Central Asian ruler Temür. See my "Cheng Ho and Timur: Any Relation?" *Oriens Extremus* 20, no. 2 (December 1973):129–36.

39. Tazaka Kōdō, "Mindai ni okeru gairaikei isuramu kyōto no kaisei ni tsuite" [Concerning the changing of family names among the foreign Muslims in the Ming], *Shigaku zasshi* 65, no. 4 (1956):49–66.

40. Islamic law prohibited adoption, but the Chinese Muslims apparently ignored this regulation. See Fletcher, "Central Asian Sufism," p. 18.

41. See my "The Jews in China," in Herbert Franke, ed., *Handbuch der Orientalistik* (Leiden, forthcoming).

42. William C. White, *Chinese Jews* (Toronto, 1942), 2:61.

43. Ford, "Some Chinese Muslims," p. 148.

44. See Tazaka, *Chūgoku ni okeru Kaikyō* 2:1195, for examples.

45. Raphael Israeli, "Chinese Versus Muslims: A Study of Cultural Confrontation," (Ph.D. diss. University of California at Berkeley, 1974), p. 67.

46. See Tani Mitsutaka, "A Study on Horse Administration in the Ming Period," *Acta Asiatica* 21 (1971):73–97, and Tani's *Mindai basei no kenkyū* (Kyoto, 1972) for more on the importance of horses to the Ming. A brief survey of the role of the horse in Inner Asia is found in Denis Sinor, "Horse and pasture in Inner Asian history," *Oriens Extremus* 19, nos. 1–2 (December 1972):171–83.

47. See my "The Tea and Horse Trade with Inner Asia during the Ming," *Journal of Asian History* 4, no. 2 (1970):159–62.

48. Ray Huang, *Taxation and Governmental Finance in Sixteenth-Century Ming China* (Cambridge, 1974), p. 260.

49. Larisa V. Simonovskaia, *Antifeodal'naia bor'ba kitaiskikh krest'ian v XVII veke* (Moscow, 1966), p. 52, offers a graphic description of the poverty in northwest China.

50. T'an Ch'ien, *Kuo-ch'üeh*, p. 5055.

51. *Ming shih-lu (Shen-tsung)* (Taipei, 1962–68 ed.) ch. 446, 2b.

52. T'an Ch'ien, *Kuo-ch'üeh*, pp. 4229, 4261, 4426, 4752, 4826, 4907, and 5055.

53. The earlier cited work by Simonovskaia, as well as Li Wen-chih's *Wan-*

Ming min-pien (Hong Kong, 1966 ed.) and James B. Parsons's *The Peasant Rebellions of the Late Ming Dynasty* (Tucson, 1970) are the standard sources for the rebellions in the late Ming. For an interesting appraisal of these three works, see John W. Dardess, "The Late Ming Rebellions: Peasants and Problems of Interpretation," *Journal of Interdisciplinary History* 3 (1972):103–17.

54. Albert Chan, "The Decline and Fall of the Ming Dynasty: A Study of the Internal Factors" (Ph.D. diss., Harvard University, 1954), pp. 16–135, for more detail on these problems.

55. For the decline in local government in late Ming, see John R. Watt, *The District Magistrate in Late Imperial China* (New York, 1972), pp. 136–38.

56. Li Kuang-pi, ed., *Ming Ch'ing shih lun-ts'ung* (Wuhan, 1957), pp. 106–09; Shimizu Taiji, "Mindai no ryūmin to ryūzoku" [Drifters and rebels in Ming times] *Shigaku zasshi* 46, no. 2 (February 1935):200–06.

57. Ray Huang, "Military Expenditures in Sixteenth Century Ming China," *Oriens Extremus* 17, nos. 1–2 (December 1970):40–46; Philip Kuhn, *Rebellion and Its Enemies in Late Imperial China* (Cambridge, Mass., 1970), pp. 21–22.

58. T'an Ch'ien, *Kuo-ch'üeh*, p. 4449; Chan, "Decline and Fall," pp. 228–34.

59. See Dardess on "The Late Ming Rebellions," pp. 103–17, for a concise presentation of this viewpoint. There are some valuable studies of the distinction between peasant rebels and bandits. Two important ones are Euclides Da Cunha, *Rebellion in the Backlands,* trans. Samuel Putnam (Chicago, 1944), and E. J. Hobsbawm, *Social Bandits and Primitive Rebels* (Glencoe, Ill., 1959).

60. Chan, "Decline and Fall," pp. 218–23.

61. Wu Shu, et al., *Huai-ling liu-k'ou shih-chung lu* (Taipei, 1969 reprint), p. 60.

62. Fang Hung-hsiao, *Ming mo liu-k'ou chi-shih* (Taipei, 1960), p. 7.

63. Tazaka, *Kaikyō no denrai,* 2:1212–16. For the translation of one important source on Li, see E. Hauer, "Li Tze [*sic*]-ch'eng und Chang Hsien-chung: Ein Beitrag zum Ende der Ming Dynastie," *Asia Major,* o.s. 2 (1925):436–98; 3 (1926):268–87.

64. Li Kuang-pi, ed., *Ming Ch'ing shih lun-ts'ung,* pp. 109–10.

65. Simonovskaia (see n. 49 above), p. 148.

66. For a brief summary, see C. R. Bawden, *The Modern History of Mongolia* (New York, 1968), pp. 50–51.

67. Tseng Wen-wu, *Chung-kuo ching-ying Hsi-yü shih* (Shanghai, 1936), pp. 242–43; Haneda Akira, "Minmatsu Shinsho no higashi Torukistan" [Eastern Turkestan in the Late Ming and Early Ch'ing;] *Tōyōshi kenkyū,* vol. 7, no. 5 (September–October 1942).

68. Maurice Courant, *L'Asie centrale aux xviie et xviiie siècles, empire kalmouk ou empire mantchou?* (Paris, 1912), p. 51; *Shih-lu (Shun-chih)* (Taipei, 1973 reprint), p. 309.

69. *Ta Ch'ing hui-tien* (Yung-cheng ed., 1732), ch. 104, 37b–38a; *Shih-lu (Shun-chih),* p. 310.

70. *Shih-lu (Shun-chih),* pp. 232, 311, 354.

71. Li Ti, et al., *Kansu t'ung-chih* (1737 ed.), ch. 19, 1a–3a.

72. B. H. Whitbeck, "The Tea System of the Ch'ing Dynasty" (B.A. thesis, Harvard College, 1965), pp. 38–39.

73. Ibid., p. 12. Nonetheless, as late as 1753 a modified tea and horse trade was still in existence. See Wang Yeh-chien, *Land Taxation in Imperial China, 1750–1911* (Cambridge, Mass., 1973), p. 71.

74. *Shih-lu* (*Shun-chih*), pp. 230, 338, 353, 453.

75. Pai Shou-i, ed., *Hui-min ch'i-i* (Shanghai, 1952), 3:3–4.

76. Sung Po-lu, et al., *Hsin-chiang chien-chih chih* (Taipei, 1963 reprint), ch. 2, 2a.

77. See Chung Fang, *Ha-mi chih,* ch. 3, for a full account of this episode.

78. Hsieh Kuo-chen, *Ch'ing-ch'u nung-min ch'i-i tzu-liao chi-lu* (Shanghai, 1956), pp. 279–82.

79. M. Camille Imbault-Huart, "Deux insurrections des mahometans du Kan-sou (1648–1783)", *Journal asiatique,* ser. 14 (November-December 1889), pp. 499–501. See also Wei Yüan, *Sheng-wu-chi* (Taipei, 1967 reprint), ch. 7, 26a.

80. See Meng's biography by E. S. Larsen and Tomoo Numata, in Arthur W. Hummel, ed., *Eminent Chinese of the Ch'ing Period* (Washington, D.C., 1934–44), p. 572.

81. Pai Shou-i, *Hui-min ch'i-i,* pp. 4–5.

82. For lists of some of these works, see A. Vissière, *Études sino-mahomé-tanes* (Paris, 1911), pp. 102–35.

83. Hung Liang-chi, *Ch'ien-lung fu-t'ing-chou-hsien t'u-chih* (1803 ed.), ch. 49, 28a, for more on their later relations; cf. also Joseph Fletcher, "China and Central Asia, 1368–1884," in John K. Fairbank, ed., *The Chinese World Order,* pp. 206–24.

6

Maritime China from Wang Chih to Shih Lang
Themes in Peripheral History

by John E. Wills, Jr.

Seafarers

In this essay, John Wills makes a preliminary exploration of China's southern coast, and of the seafarers, merchants, militarists, and officials who managed or exploited its resources. We can see how, across the span of a century and half between the 1550s and the 1700s, the history of the coastal zone related to continental history rather than merely echoed it. And study of this area shows how important were the intermeshings of military leadership, overseas trade, and the playing of a mediating role between the conflicting forces of bureaucracy and various foreign powers.

The figures who dominated the region during this period provide many different permutations in this military-merchant-mediator triad: Wang Chih (from the development of his Hirado base to his surrender and execution) shows how the individual career could rise and fall at the interface of wide-scale pirate activity and bureaucratic factionalisms. Just as the breaking of Wang Chih also illustrates a regrowth of Ming prosperity in the south as a distracted government turned its attention to northern problems, so the rise of Li Tan and the Cheng family illustrates how bereft the Ming were of options by the 1620s—enabling the most vivid example of international merchant-mediator to flourish in the person of Cheng Chih-lung. The Cheng family then became—inevitably we can see now—one crucial component within the transition from Ming to Ch'ing, but one also that was doomed to weaken as the power of the Ch'ing center was asserted at the expense of the periphery, and the state could enforce new prerogatives over its coastal populations. Thus, the two men who end this survey—Shih Lang and Wu Hsing-tso—were both dependent on the center and used by it even as they still continued, occasionally and profitably, to exploit the periphery.

Wills sets these events within a broad but still definable world context; in this context not only are the emerging European powers (along with the Japanese) important factors in the mediators' equation, they are themselves the observers and recorders of the Chinese scene, revealing data otherwise omitted from the Chinese record. Furthermore, the inescapable imperatives of the seafarers' world enable us to venture certain comparisons and to highlight certain features of the Chinese coastal world. In particular, we can see how

203

ultimately frail were the possibilities in the Chinese case for a truly fruitful and long-term *interaction between coastal profit and military power; and how, because the Chinese periphery could never have long periods of independence from the continental center, it failed to develop lasting structures that might have legitimated such interactions.*

ON PERIPHERIES

Our central images of China include the rice-paddies of the center and south, the brown plains of the north, the Grand Canal, the Great Wall. We know of other Chinas—the oases of the northwest, the gorges, tribes, and mountain-top forts of the southwest, the pirates, fishing fleets, overseas merchants, and trade ports of the south coast—but we see them as "peripheral" to the main patterns of Chinese history. Nothing in the following pages will lead us to revise that judgment of the peripheral character of maritime China, but I do hope to suggest ways in which the histories of peripheries in general, and maritime China in particular, can enormously enrich our understanding of late imperial China. I also hope to suggest how the impact of maritime China on the course of late imperial history was limited not only because it was geographically peripheral but also because of two other sets of factors. The first set relates to particular geopolitical weaknesses of the area itself, best seen by comparing it to other maritime areas; the second set concerns the modes of mobilization of power within maritime China, which eventually reduced the openness of its power structure both to association with the power-holders of other areas and to the cooptation of their scholar-official elites.

Every phase of the Ming–Ch'ing transition had a maritime element. The complex of internal corruption and external threat in the 1550s involved Wang Chih and Hu Tsung-hsien as well as Altan-qaγan and Yen Sung. The Hideyoshi invasions and Ming counterexpeditions of the 1590s, in addition to reshaping Ming-Manchu-Korean relations, were a turning point in, and almost the end (until modern times) of the long history of Japanese commercial-military aggressiveness on the continent. The breakdown of the 1620s, most clearly visible in the northwestern rebellions and the rise of the Manchu state in the northeast, had a smaller but still important counterpart in the rise of piracy and the emergence of Cheng Chih-lung on the south China coast. In 1645–46, it seemed possible that Ming resistance might find its strongest bases in the regimes of the prince of Lu and the prince of T'ang, both of which ruled coastal areas and depended partly on maritime power and maritime trade. In 1659 Cheng Ch'eng-kung's Yangtze expedition gave the Ch'ing court its only real scare between 1648 (at the latest) and Wu San-kuei's rebellion in 1673. The conquest of Taiwan in 1683 was the last stage in the consolidation of Ch'ing rule over areas inhabited by Chinese. But that bare catalogue reminds us that the story of maritime China in this period is a story of failed efforts and dissipated power, that maritime China, although it never ceased to be a source of wealth and trouble for the Ch'ing regime, never after 1659 posed a real threat to the dominance of the political and economic system that linked the Yangtze Valley and the North China plain and focused its military efforts on Mongolia and Inner Asia.

But there are several reasons why a recognition of the dominance of this core system must not keep us from paying adequate attention to maritime China and other "peripheral" zones. First, the dominant system was shaped by its relations with such areas, which at various times absorbed excess population, offered opportunities for the exploitation of trade routes and mines, and kept government forces busy putting down various kinds of banditry and rebellions. If we do not yet see how core-periphery relations can have been as structurally central for early modern China as Wallerstein suggests they were for early modern Europe,[1] it is clear that we cannot ignore them. Second, a knowledge of the peripheral areas and comparison of them enlarges our sense of the varieties of institutions, political cultures, and political economies that could develop at roughly the same time out of a common Chinese political heritage. There was nothing inherently "un-Chinese" about polities that gave larger roles than did the core polity of Ming-Ch'ing China to, for example, ethnic differences and tribal territorial organization, military leadership, or expansion of trade as a source of government revenue. The areas in which these and other variant traits could take root were often on the peripheries of the empire, so that the

geographical extent of their influence was limited in periods of
political instability and they were more or less repressed, exploited,
and distorted by the dominant core system in times of stability. But
these limits of the influence of variant traits, and more particular
ones such as those discussed in this essay for the maritime region,
do not reduce the exemplary and comparative importance of peripheral regions.

A VIEW OF A REGION

This essay focuses on the history of the south China coast and the
adjacent ocean from the Yangtze delta to Hainan. North of the
Yangtze delta wide shallows and mud flats limited coastal settlement and activity, and north of them Shantung and Liaotung formed
a different complex only occasionally linked with the south coast.
This south Chinese maritime region included the offshore islands,
the Pescadores, and Taiwan. In certain contexts it also included the
ports of Kyushu, the Ryukyus, Luzon, and the major ports of
maritime Southeast Asia.

There are many potentially fruitful approaches to the history of
this region. We have admirable work on the technology of Chinese
seafaring.[2] Bodo Wiethoff has shown us what can be learned by
careful analysis of types of state political activity in the region over
a long time span.[3] The politics of center-periphery relations in the
campaigns of the 1550s are fairly well understood, thanks especially
to So Kwan-wai's recent study,[4] but for all later episodes thorough
work on center-periphery relations remains to be done. The same is
true for the politics of the coastal Ming loyalist courts, especially
well documented in "unofficial histories" (*yeh-shih*). Local gazetteers yield excellent information, so far little exploited, on local
economies of fishing and trade and on such important topics in
local political history as *pao-chia* and militia organization against
piracy and the tremendous dislocations and shifts in settlement patterns caused by the Ch'ing coastal evacuation policy.

These promising approaches are pursued only in passing in this essay.
Rather, it begins from the perception that this naval-commercial
world had some foci outside China, and that in this period foreigners,
especially Europeans, were frequent participants in it and observers

of it even on the China coast. This opens up some special opportunities both in documentation and in interpretation. Chinese bureaucratic sources and local gazetteers, which could be very detailed for coastal areas, rarely took cognizance of anything out of sight of land. Diaries of sea voyages are limited to some by ambassadors sent to confirm the succession of Ryukyu kings[5] and a few others.[6] European sources tell us much about settlement and traffic along the coast we could never learn from Chinese sources.[7] For Luzon, for Taiwan before 1661, and for the Chinese in Southeast Asia, we are almost completely dependent on European witnesses.

The special opportunities for interpretation are largely comparative, broadly analogous to the comparative potentialities of the study of peripheral regions described above. When Chinese and Europeans met, differences in the ways they dealt with "objectively" similar circumstances of maritime trade and warfare highlight some important points of comparison. For example, when we read Dutch merchants' complaints that early Ch'ing officials cornering trade for their own clients "act more like merchants than like princes," we are reminded that for all its overt anticommercialism and laws against officials engaging in trade, Chinese politics had no counterpart to the urban and other "rights" that protected some merchants from official interference in Europe, and that Chinese officials did have extensive private financial interests which very frequently led them to ignore anticommercial laws and ideologies.

Another kind of comparison cuts deeper and leads to some fundamental geographical points about maritime China. All human orders, of course, are shaped by their natural environments. But if we seek to compare these environments and their influences, we find our work immensely complicated by man's transformation of his environments and by the great difficulties of comparing land-holding, local social structure, and so on, across basic cultural differences. But man cannot transform the patterns of winds, waves, and ocean currents. Thus it is relatively easy to compare the geographical imperatives of various maritime zones of the world and the human technical and organizational responses to similar imperatives. Even in arrangements for commerce and for peaceful relations among people of different cultures and religions, large elements of objectivity and comparability can be seen.

Traders from across an ocean generally have presented themselves as nonmediated aliens, unlike the situation on a land frontier where they form part of a complex, mediated interaction of cultures and of migrating peoples. They must be controlled, but they must be treated with some regularity and fairness for the sake of a mutually beneficial trade. Their internal affairs, being based on totally alien cultures and laws but representing, as long as isolated, no real threat to the host culture and polity, frequently are best delegated to their own "headmen." Thus, for example, these objective imperatives produced, in a kind of convergent evolution, broadly similar institutions for control of foreign trade in situations otherwise as different as those of Canton and Ouidah, Dahomey, in the eighteenth century.[8] For our period, the comparison of maritime zones of the world is enormously facilitated by the presence in all of them of Europeans, recording similar information from similar points of view. Thus we are brought full-circle to the interest in European involvement and witnesses with which we began, and we see why it is that of all the peripheral zones of China the maritime zone is the one in which the potentialities and limits of the Chinese heritage are most fully illuminated not only by comparisons among the core and peripheries of China but also with other geographically comparable areas of the world.

When we compare maritime China to other maritime areas in which Europeans were involved, such as the Baltic, the Mediterranean, and the shallow seas joining the Malay Peninsula and the main Indonesian islands, some striking contrasts emerge. In the other areas mentioned, power centers facing narrow and relatively safe seas sought to profit from their relations with each other through trading, piracy, plunder, raiding to force better conditions of trade, and colonization. Naval power could be used to concentrate wealth in one center at the expense of another, and the wealth would pay for the fleets. Concentration of power facilitated control of trade routes and brought the increased profits of trade monopolies. Elements of this pattern can be seen in the behavior of the commercially active princes of maritime Southeast Asia,[9] but its locus classicus is the Mediterranean. Here the geographical tendency toward a positive and centripetal interaction of profit and power, sketched above, was reinforced by two political cultures, European and Muslim, which encouraged leaders and followers to unite in active efforts to enlarge the wealth, power, and territory of their people, city, or nation, frequently at the expense of a rival group. If we wished to push studies of mutual reinforcement further, we could show how these tendencies in European culture had been enhanced by its development in the competitive city states of ancient Greece and Rome and of Renaissance Italy, all of which had been shaped by their Mediterranean environment.

Maritime China, by contrast, offered only meager opportunities for such positive interactions between profit and power. The south China coast confronted an open ocean which the Dutch, who knew all the maritime areas mentioned above, considered exceptionally dangerous. The only destinations within five hundred miles were Vietnam, a minor center of maritime trade whose political entanglements were along her land frontiers with China and Cambodia; Luzon, and Taiwan, only marginally attractive as entrepots and sources of a few mineral and other natural products, very promising for rice- and sugar-farming colonization, but requiring a very substantial concentration of economic and military power to transport colonists and protect them from the natives; and southern Japan and its outpost in the Ryukyus, which were south China's only real potential partners in a profit-and-power interaction.

But the Ryukyus were very small. Kyushu was about five hundred miles across those dangerous seas; and the opportunities for plunder and commerce-raiding along the Chinese coast were far greater than off southern Japan. Although the daimyo and samurai of Kyushu invested and participated in trade and piracy along the China coast in order to enhance their own wealth and power, no political authority in the single Chinese empire could take a similar positive attitude toward Chinese raiding along the Chinese coast. Thus the geographical imperatives of this area also were reinforced by its political traditions, in this case by the Chinese pattern of political unity and bureaucratic administration, so different from the competitive, multicentered politics of the Mediterranean.

European sources make it possible for us to set our story of political change in maritime China in a matrix of commercial change and growth, in broad trends for the late sixteenth century, in highly specific statistics for parts of the seventeenth. Despite its impressive commercial growth, the area was so thinly provided with bases, so much subject to the changes and pressures of the Chinese continental system, that long-lasting political institutions with their own processes of legitimation did not emerge within it. Rather, we see episodes of emergence of maritime profit-and-power structures, frequently tied to one man's combining of naval leadership, commercial connections, talents for mediation with Chinese officials and with foreigners. The careers of five such leaders form important focal points of our story: Wang Chih, Li Tan, Cheng Chih-lung, Cheng Ch'eng-kung, Shih Lang.

THE WAKŌ CRISIS AND WANG CHIH

From 1549 to 1561, the rich delta rice-lands and thriving commercial cities of the lower Yangtze were repeatedly thrown into alarm by invasions of "Japanese pirates" (wo-k'ou, Jap. wakō), who were in fact mostly Chinese. In 1556, for example, one band camped unchallenged outside the north gate of Wu-hsi, fanning out every morning to pillage and returning to their camp for the night.[10] In the same year, another band of sixty or seventy came ashore between Hangchow and Ningpo and set out on a pillaging and burning expedition past Hangchow, up-country to She-hsien in Anhwei, and down to the Yangtze at Wu-hu.[11] By the time they reached the great walls of Nanking they probably had been joined by other bands of pirates and by bandits from the countryside, but it is not likely that they ever had more than a thousand men. The garrison of Nanking shut the gates and did not come out to attack them. Defeated near the T'ai-hu by Yü Ta-yu, one of the few competent Ming generals, they finally were surrounded near Ch'ang-shu and over six hundred were killed. Along the coast the situation was even worse, as larger and better-organized groups of pirates repeatedly took *hsien* cities and garrison fortresses. Nor were the common people much better off when the pirates went away and the government troops came—a wild assortment of southwestern aborigines, miners, salt-workers, local militia-men, mercenaries, and even some Shao-lin monks. Hard to manage at best, they were especially likely to riot when corrupt officials cheated them on their rations.[12]

But by the end of 1557 measures against the pirates were beginning to take effect. By the end of 1561 only remnants were left on the Chiang-nan and Chekiang coasts. Some pirate forces moved into Fukien, where they briefly occupied the prefectural city of Hsing-hua in 1562, but government forces were in control on the Fukien coast from 1564 and on the Kwangtung coast from 1566. In 1574 one Ming fleet pursued a pirate force all the way to Luzon.

How could such a prosperous, densely settled area as the Chiang-nan–northern Chekiang coast fall prey to such small bands of invaders? What changed the balance of forces so rapidly after 1557, and why was there no comparable revival of piracy in subsequent decades? Most obviously, the expansion of the attacks had begun in 1550, after Chu Wan broke up long-established and thriving centers and networks of illicit maritime trade, and did not revive after 1567, when Chinese maritime trade to all points except Japan was legalized. Almost equally well known are the achievements of recruiters and trainers of new and effective militia forces, including Yü Ta-yu and Ch'i Chi-kuang, that began to be effective in resistance to the pirates about 1557. Professor Kwan-wai So has added the very interesting suggestion that in this period many farmers were driven from their land and into piracy and associated disorders by the unbearable exactions connected with the labor-service system, and that this situation must have been alleviated by the spread of the single-whip system in this area in the 1560s.[13]

But there were substantial elements of political negotiation, as well as of military organization and government policy, in these events. An important part of the shift of the balance of forces on the Chiang-nan-Chekiang coast was the surrender of the important leader Wang Chih in 1558, followed by his execution in 1559. These changes were enormously facilitated by this individual's distinctive maritime background and relations with important Ming officials.

About 1540 a center of piracy and illegal trade had developed at Shuang-hsü on the south side of Chusan Island under Hsü Tung of She-hsien, Anhwei, and Li Kuang-t'ou of Fukien, both merchants who had escaped from Fukien prisons. Wang Chih, also a She-hsien merchant, began as a supervisor of storehouses (*kuan-k'u*) under Hsü Tung, which would seem to imply some measure of specialization in trade and finance and perhaps some measure of control over the wealth of his superior. He soon became a commander of patrol squadrons (*kuan-shao*) and a councillor on military affairs (*liao-li chün-shih*). Earlier in his career he had made trading voyages as far as Patani on the Malay Peninsula. He may have played some kind of intermediary role in one of the first Portuguese voyages to Japan in 1543 and in bringing Japanese traders to Shuang-hsü in 1545. He made at least one voyage to Japan for Hsü Tung, and was especially trusted by the Japanese.

Wang's foreign contacts and control of Hsü's wealth may have helped him to emerge as the new leader of the organization after Hsü Tung was killed in Chu Wan's attacks in 1548–49. These attacks broke up the relatively stable centers of illegal trade and the credit arrangements that had grown up with them, forcing many to turn from trade to piracy. The collapse of Ōuchi power in western Japan in 1551 made the fine harbors of that area available as bases for any and all pirate forces.[14] Thus Wang came to power in one group just as piracy in general was expanding explosively. No doubt there were many pirates who were never under his control, but many were defeated by him or accepted his suzerainty. His rise seems to have owed as much to guile and mediation as to military leadership. In one case, for example, he defeated a rival by capitalizing on a split in his forces forces, allying with family militia of illicit-trade-connected gentry, and even arranging for the passive cooperation of a nearby official garrison. He then sent the defeated leaders to the government and kept their goods and ships for himself. In Japan he called himself the "King of Hui-chou," was received by Lord Matsuura of Hirado, and had especially large and secure bases in the Goto Islands west of Hirado.

Wang seems to have remained more a merchant-mediator than a military leader. As far as we can tell, he always remained in the island bases or in Japan, and never led an attack on the mainland. As early as 1552 he petitioned the Ming government for permission to trade. Thus, when his fellow-townsman Hu Tsung-hsien was given a key role in the campaigns against him, the stage was set for an intricate process of intrigue and negotiation in which Hu gradually won some measure of trust from Wang while at the same time instigating Wang's commanders to attack each other, turn each other in to the government, or surrender on promises of favorable treatment. Finally Wang, pressed by the defections and by the growing power of the militia forces, secured promises of favorable treatment, including the partial legalization of maritime trade in Chekiang, and surrendered. Hu

Tsung-hsien and his associates seem to have supported a policy of relaxing restrictions on maritime trade and may also have intended to allow Wang Chih to "redeem himself" by attacking other pirate forces on behalf of the government. Hu's power, if not necessarily these controversial policies, was supported by his alliance with the powerful grand secretary Yen Sung. But Yen had many opponents in the high bureaucracy, and in 1559 they persuaded the emperor to reject Hu's policies and order Wang Chih's execution. Thus, personal connections both among bureaucrats and between a bureaucrat and a pirate seem to have supported a policy of cooptation of pirate forces and adjustment to maritime trading interests. This policy was frustrated by bureaucratic politics without disastrous consequences because the militia gave the government sufficient military strength, because the government did eventually legalize maritime trade, and because the accommodation policy had led, before its final rejection, to the dismemberment of Wang Chih's organization and his surrender.

COMMERCIAL GROWTH AND OFF-SHORE ALARMS, 1570–1620

The half-century from 1570 to 1620 was generally one of peace and prosperity on the south China coast. Portuguese ships carried Chinese silks and other goods to Japan and returned with Japanese silver, perhaps 400,000 taels per year in the 1580s, 1,000,000 or more in the early 1600s. The mines of Mexico and Peru and the Acapulco Galleons added another million taels or more a year to the peak flow of silver into China around 1600.[15] Portuguese carrying of a large part of Sino-Japanese trade reduced the opportunities for Sino-Japanese conflict or collusion; Chinese carrying of the trade to Manila eliminated the need for any arrangement with another set of Europeans in addition to the Portuguese. Trade to Taiwan, almost certainly for the purpose of trading with Japanese coming there, was legalized, and Chinese probably began to go to Japan under the cover of trade to Taiwan.[16] With the legalization and regulation of trade and its steady expansion, the heirs of the positions and interests of Li Kuang-t'ou and Wang Chih could follow the commercial pursuits their predecessors had been denied by official policy. Pirates did not disappear from the coast, but the strengthened Ming naval forces generally were adequate to deal with them, and they frequently found better hunting in Southeast Asian waters.

Strains in Ming culture and politics intensified in the 1590s, with the great expeditions against the Hideyoshi invasions of Korea, the eunuch searches for new sources of revenue in the provinces, the controversy over the imperial heir apparent, and the varied intellectual quests of Li Chih, Hsü Kuang-ch'i, Chiao Hung, Kao P'an-lung, and many others. There were some links between these strains and the coastal situation described above. The silver imports and the commercial growth to which they contributed were basic causes of the fiscal difficulties of the Ming state in this period. Eunuch efforts to find new sources of revenue led to two confrontations with foreigners. In 1603 eunuch envoys went to Manila in search of a "mountain of gold" somewhere in Luzon. After they left, Spanish fears of a Chinese invasion and Chinese fears of a massacre led to armed conflict, ending in the massacre of as many as 23,000 Chinese.[17] In 1604, Chinese merchants at Patani—one of Wang Chih's old haunts—told officers of the Dutch East India Company they could secure trade for them through the eunuch in charge of the Fukien maritime customs, and the Dutch sent ships to the Pescadores to begin negotiations, but a military official denounced the intrigue to the court.[18]

A more important source of offshore alarms, and a more basic reason why they stayed offshore, was the changing nature of Japanese expansion. The Hideyoshi invasions of Korea revived Chinese fears of Japanese piracy and stimulated a brief revival of the prohibition of maritime trade, but military action did not spread to the south coast, and many of the Japanese who might have been attracted to a resumption of piracy were killed or exhausted their fortunes in these campaigns.[19] "Japanese pirates" occupied harbors of Taiwan several times, and were driven out by a Ming expedition in 1603.[20] A Satsuma expedition in 1609 brought the Ryukyus into fuller subjection than before. In the same year, Ieyasu sent Arima Harunobu on an exploratory expedition to Taiwan, but he returned without having been able to get much information from the inhabitants. In 1616, Murayama Tōan, a powerful and wealthy official in charge of maritime trade at Nagasaki, outfitted a fleet of eleven (some accounts say thirteen) ships to invade Taiwan, but it was dispersed by a storm, only one ship reached Taiwan, and its crew committed suicide when attacked and surrounded by aborigines.[21]

Japanese were still firmly excluded from Chinese ports, and Chinese vigilance in keeping them out can be seen from their constant pressure on the Portuguese to keep them out of Macao.[22] The Japanese, although armed and dangerous, were looking for trade or small plunder, not major confrontations with Ming China, and so they found ample profit and adventure in Taiwan and Southeast Asia. In the late 1620s Japanese traders came to blows with the Dutch on Taiwan, but by 1634 Japanese maritime trade had been entirely cut off as the "closed country" policy emerged. Chinese, too, not only carried on their old lines of trade in Southeast Asia, but settled in increasing numbers in the ports of Kyushu and in rough-and-ready trade-and-piracy outposts on the coasts of Taiwan. Thus Chinese and Japanese trader-adventurers, who had ravaged the south China coast from bases in Kyushu and the Chekiang islands in the 1550s, now found far fewer allies in a Chinese population absorbed in a thriving legal trade and a new scope for their energies in Taiwan.

In this period of expansion of maritime trade, although the Ming government gained some revenue from the taxation of legal maritime trade the sums were fixed and small. There was no return to the government encouragement of maritime trade and dependence on it for revenue that had characterized the Southern Sung and to some extent the Yuan. To officials, the sea represented problems, not opportunities, and statecraft stopped, if not at the water's edge, certainly short of the high seas. *Pao-chia* and other registration and control techniques; forts, garrisons, and coastal control squadrons; and management of government shipyards, were among the foci of their interest. Chinese seafarers' solid knowledge of areas beyond the seas rarely found its way into discussions of statecraft and other official documents. Pirate fleets, and official fleets pursuing them, voyaged to Taiwan and Luzon, but the only proposal I know of for the systematic colonization of Taiwan was one by Cheng Chih-lung in 1628.[23] The positive interaction of profit and power was focused not at the state level, as it had been in many ways from Southern Sung to early Ming, but in the private activities of merchants and gentry.

MILITARIZATION: LI TAN AND THE RISE OF THE CHENG FAMILY

In the 1620s this coastal picture of prosperity and uneasy peace
was abruptly shattered, in the same years that saw the bitter eunuch–
Tung-lin controversies, the rise of the Manchu state, and the outbreak of rebellions in the northwest. There were some causal links
among these crises. Factionalism, corruption, incompetence, and
fiscal bankruptcy undermined Ming efforts to respond to military
challenges on the coast as well as in the northeast and northwest.
The Ming court threw large armies against the Manchus, further re-
ducing the forces that might have been available against other threats
In 1628 a drought facilitated recruitment by both Li Tzu-ch'eng
and Cheng Chih-lung. Other causes of the coastal turmoil were
specific to that area. Silver imports from Manila may have been on a
plateau, or even declining a little. Far more important was the
sudden intrusion of a new and dangerous power, the Dutch East
India Company, whose ships and troops attacked Macao and then
occupied the Pescadores in 1622, and attacked coastal settlements
and shipping from then until 1624. The Ming government tried to
starve the Dutch out of the Pescadores by a one-year ban on maritime trade, further disrupting trade, throwing people out of work,
and facilitating the recruitment of pirates and smugglers. Finally,
in 1624, it assembled a large fleet which occupied all the Pescadores
except the peninsula on which the Dutch had built their fort, and
the Dutch were forced to agree to withdraw to Taiwan, where Chinese traders would come to them. But the Dutch continued to cruise
for junks trading to Manila, and pirates were everywhere on the
south coast, under a variety of leaders.[24]

   This situation offered golden opportunities for men of the merchant-
intermediary-military leader type, which they were not slow to
seize. Negotiation for Dutch withdrawal from the Pescadores was
handled by one Li Tan, captain of the Chinese community at Hirado,
Wang Chih's old base. The famous diary of Richard Cocks, merchant
of the English East India Company at Hirado from 1615 to 1621,
gives us a fragmentary but fascinating picture of the activities of this
remarkable man.[25] Cocks recorded in 1616 that Li "was governor of
the Chinas at Manila in the Philippines and in the end the Spaniards
picked a quarrel on purpose to seize all he had, to the value of
above 40,000 taels and put him into the galleys, from whence he es-

caped some 9 years since and came to Firando [Hirado] where he
has lived ever since." If Li escaped from the galleys in 1607, he may
have been sent to them in the aftermath of the bloody conflict of
1603. But he had not completely broken his ties with Manila; in
1615 we find a Spanish merchant seeking him out in Hirado to try
to collect on a debt for which he had stood surety. Li's brother was
the headman of the Chinese community at Nagasaki, and he had
another brother in China with whom he kept in touch. He exchanged
presents, social visits, and banquets with the English, the Dutch, and
Lord Matsuura, the daimyo of Hirado, and various members of the
Matsuura family. He carried on long negotiations with the English,
and took money from them to make the necessary presents to
officials, in the hope of obtaining for them permission to trade on
the China coast. He did not succeed, and the English thought they
had been given a runaround, but he may actually have been frustrated by the corruption and instability of the end of the Wan-li
period and the court crises of 1620–21.

Li Tan apparently came down to the Pescadores to mediate between the Dutch and the Ming officials early in 1623, then returned
to Hirado that summer, probably leaving behind as his agent a capable
young man named Cheng Chih-lung. Li returned to the Pescadores or
to the Taiwan coast at the end of 1623, and stayed until early in
the summer of 1625, overseeing the delicate period when the Dutch
withdrew to Taiwan and there made their first contacts with traders
from the mainland—all of them agents or licensees of another branch
of the Li Tan network headed by one Hsu Hsin-su. Early in 1625,
Cheng Chih-lung took a more independent role, commanding three
junks and about a hundred armed men as part of a Dutch expedition
against Chinese trade to Manila. Back in Taiwan, the Dutch un-
covered evidence that he was levying tolls on Chinese maritime
trade and plundering those who would not pay; such "water payments" (*pao-shui*) had precedents at least as far back as Wang Chih's
time and were the backbone of Cheng's sytem for the next twenty
years.[26] A later letter to the Dutch from Li Tan's son asserts that
these collections were made without Li's knowledge.[27] In the summer of 1625, Cheng was off to the north on another privateering
expedition, apparently having some kind of agreement by which the
Dutch provided some of the capital for his expedition and would
receive half the returns.

Thus, when Li Tan died in August, Cheng was at or near Hirado with enough arms and money to take control of the Japan and Taiwan branches of the Li Tan network. Hsü Hsin-su took over the Fukien branch, but his wealth was more vulnerable to official exaction than Cheng's.[28] Also, he had no military forces of his own and had to depend on shaky alliances with pirates and with a corrupt and strikingly incompetent Ming admiral named Yü Tzu-kao, a son of the great Yü Ta-yu. Cheng defeated various rival pirate forces, and in December 1627 overcame Yü's fleet and advanced to occupy Amoy and nearby island bases. Negotiations for him to "surrender" and turn his forces against the other pirates were probably already underway. His forces did not all owe him unqualified personal allegiance, and he had neither the iron resolve nor the wariness of a good military leader. In the summer of 1628, one-third to a half of his subordinates rebelled rather than accept the tamer life of a Ming garrison. But he managed his developing relations with the officials superbly, and the magistrate directly in charge, Ts'ao Lü-t'ai, argued his case in reports to his superiors.[29] Not only was he finally given military rank; when he was hard-pressed militarily he was given rations, boats, and the cooperation of some very tough coastal militia.

In 1629, although still facing formidable challengers, Cheng was more firmly placed in charge of the defense of Amoy, and earlier official talk about the eventual dispersal of his forces was dropped. He had major rivals at sea as late as 1634—the last was the son of Li Tan—but his official position and the fundamentals of his system were sound. "Water payments" and profits of trade paid for some, perhaps all, of the fleets and garrisons he controlled, and he also remitted funds to the capital both publicly and as private payments to various officials.[30] A network of merchant and other agents facilitated his trade and kept him informed of affairs in various parts of the empire. He had strong personal and commercial connections with the Portuguese of Macao and the Chinese communities in Macao, Taiwan, and Japan. In 1636, after much animosity and one major naval engagement, he and the Dutch on Taiwan resumed peaceful trade relations, and in 1640–41 they discussed, but could not agree on, a pact by which Cheng would stay out of the Japan trade and would provide the Dutch with a large quantity of goods for it, receiving a share of their profits.[31] He owned large estates in Fukien, and in 1640 settled 150 families of weavers under his control at An-hai.[32] His position as an international merchant-mediator could be seen even in the trappings of his private life: the great castle at An-p'ing-chen with direct access by boat to the inner quarters, the private chapel with both Buddhist and Christian figures, the bodyguard of escaped African slaves from Macao.[33]

Cheng's bureaucratic position also remained secure. His wealth may have helped obtain military *chin-shih* degrees for his brother Hung-k'uei and "adopted brother" Ts'ai, and may have influenced the court's rejection of proposals in 1642 that his fleet be moved north to attack the Ch'ing along the coast of Liaotung.[34] At the end of 1643, as the crisis deepened, Cheng Hung-k'uei was placed in charge of three thousand Ming troops in southern Kiangsi, while Chih-lung's position on the coasts of Fukien and eastern Kwang-tung remained secure.[35]

A comparison of the rise and fall of Wang Chih and the rise of Cheng Chih-lung is fascinating. Wang and Cheng relied on broadly similar combinations of commerce; mediation among foreigners, Chinese officials, and Chinese merchants and pirates; and control of their own naval forces. Each secured the mediation of a bureau-crat to argue that he be allowed to redeem himself by attacking other pirates. But at this point the two stories diverge. Wang was executed after he surrendered; Cheng was confirmed as a military commander. In 1559, officials saw an alternative hope for defense against pirates in the new militia; in 1628 there was no adequate alternative. In 1559 the Ming state was solvent; in 1628 it was bank-rupt. The wakō crisis of the 1550s, like the contemporary crisis in Sino-Mongolian relations, was an episode of military activity that was managed and brought to an end within the framework of a bureaucracy dominated by civil officials. The crises of the 1620s—coastal, Manchu, and northwestern—could not be so controlled and began an open-ended process of militarization that ended in the domination of many areas at various times in the 1640s by rebels, semiautonomous forces opposing the rebels, Manchu and Liaotung Chinese components of the Ch'ing military, and loyalist courts supported and/or held in thrall by regional militarists. This mili-tarization eventually yielded to civilianization, but not until a single dominant military structure had been established, in ways discussed below and in the Introduction to this volume.

There is some evidence that the militarization of the late Ming period carried with it some measure of increasingly positive valuation of military men and military pursuits in general elite culture, especially in the emerging statecraft school,[36] and of interest in reform on the part of military men. We have seen a military man protesting collusion among a eunuch, merchants, and foreigners in 1604. Jerry Dennerline has described some exceptionally far-reaching reform proposals made by a military *chü-jen*.[37] Such a change in the climate of opinion would help to explain Cheng Chih-lung's unwillingness to defer to the literati at Foochow in 1646, and his son's dramatic gesture of renunciation of scholar-official status at the end of that year.

THE LOYALIST COURTS

If the Nanking court had been able to organize an effective defense against the advancing Ch'ing forces in 1644–45, it would have had to have an effective naval force on the Yangtze. Ch'en Tzu-lung's preparations of a small force of river boats, mentioned by Jerry Dennerline in his essay in this volume, showed no awareness of the special expertise required for war on the water; the man to be placed in charge, Ho Kang, seems to have had no special background in river warfare, and Ch'en was simply buying boats and planning to put soldiers and sailors on them, not utilizing an existing force. However, he did point out the need for many local plans and efforts if the Yangtze were to be defended.[38] But as Dennerline has shown, there was little centralized official military structure in this area. Nor was there any really large irregular structure that could provide an alternative focus for organization, as Cheng Chih-lung's did in coastal Fukien. Perhaps this was because the lower Yangtze was much more complex geographically and economically than coastal Fukien, and had not had the two decades of militarization in which the Cheng structure had risen and matured.

Chih-lung, Hung-k'uei, and Ts'ai were given noble ranks by the Nanking regime and played ambiguous roles in the resistance. Cheng Ts'ai's participation in the campaign against Tso Liang-yü's son was marred by a territorial dispute with a fellow defender of Nanking.[39]

After the fall of Yangchow, Ts'ai and Hung-k'uei were in command
of the defenses at Chen-chiang, where the Ch'ing got their first foot-
hold on the south bank of the Yangtze. They accomplished this,
according to a usually excellent source,[40] by a ruse so simple-minded
that the Cheng brothers must have been incompetent, not in full
control of their garrisons, negotiating with the Ch'ing, or possibly all
three. The Chengs then took their forces out to sea and soon arranged
to accompany the prince of T'ang to Foochow, where the Cheng
family would be much more in control of the situation.

After the fall of Nanking, the coast quickly became a major focus
for Ming resistance, as many forces and individuals escaped from the
advancing Ch'ing forces by putting out to sea. If coherent resistance
was possible anywhere, it should have been here, in an environment
completely alien and alarming to the Manchus and many of their
Chinese allies, with quick movement of forces and supplies, supplementary financing from maritime trade and taxation of it, and the
special incentives to unity provided by the centripetal relation between profit and power in the maritime world. Because China was
such a great continental mass, maritime power could not be a determining factor in its political destiny, but it could be a strong
support for a regime in one or more coastal and lower Yangtze
provinces. But by 1650 coastal resistance was largely confined to
islands and peninsulas and had no significant links to inland regimes.
Why?

The conflict between the court established by the prince of T'ang,
later known as the Lung-wu emperor, at Foochow, and that established by the prince of Lu as "administrator of the realm" in Chekiang, was a minor cause of this failure.[41] The Chekiang court did
not assert full imperial claims. Many of its scholar-officials were
ready to negotiate with the Foochow court. Some local power-
holders were sanctioned by both courts. In time, the whole Chekiang
Fukien area probably would have been united under the Foochow
court. But there was very little time, because of the conflicts between scholar-officials and the extrabureaucratic power of military
men, within each court. The Chekiang literati opposed Fang Kuo-an
because he sheltered the despised Ma Shih-ying and because he reserved the most reliable sources of food supply for troops under him
and his allies.

The Fukien scholar-officials, unlike their Chekiang colleagues, had no really effective alternative to reliance on the military and financial power of Cheng Chih-lung and his relatives; but "effectiveness" was all too easily stigmatized as "expedient" compromise and rejected in favor of total, sometimes suicidal, loyalty to prince and principles. The scholar-officials saw the Chengs as ministers who did not behave like ministers, who used their extrabureaucratic control of troops and finance to dictate to the emperor, who, although military men, demanded honors above all civil officials, and who mixed private and public finance in drawing on government funds and supporting troops and fleets with funds not under government control. Moreover, the literati, with their networks of contacts and relationships all over south China, their sense of the empire as a single unit and the court as its center, were not much interested in stable regional bases. They may have sensed that their skills in mediation and in management of an extensive bureaucracy would be less essential to such regional regimes than to a unified empire; this can be seen much more clearly in the following discussion of Cheng Ch'eng-kung's regime on Amoy. Fang and Cheng stood to gain the most by a system of stabilized regional powers within which they could dominate and exploit their provinces, and there is some evidence that they communicated with each other and supported each other when they could. Cheng Chih-lung, who could not afford to separate himself from his maritime bases of power, refused to support major expeditions inland and began to negotiate with the Ch'ing when his emperor set out inland in person.

If Cheng Chih-lung could have delivered his entire power structure to his new masters, he probably could have retained much of his structure of military command and commercial exploitation, at least as long as it was militarily useful to the Ch'ing. For a decade the Ch'ing had been accommodating the personal, hereditary, military power structures of the Liaotung generals within the framework of their own personal, hereditary, military Banner System. Ch'ing generals and high officials often manipulated military supplies for their own profit and monopolized trade, and they could have accepted a new Chinese ally who did the same. All this is somewhat speculative, however, since Chih-lung could not deliver his whole power structure. Hung-k'uei, Ts'ai, and Chih-lung's son Ch'eng-kung all hesitated to follow him. The Ch'ing then confirmed Cheng

suspicions and assured the success of their resistance by arresting
Chih-lung, depriving him of any opportunity to control his fleets,
the trading ships returning from Japan, or the family reserve funds
in Japan. Such defections from defections also occurred in land-
based systems, but rarely with any success. Ch'ing military and
financial resources were supreme on land, but could not reach the
Cheng fleets, their island bases, or the commercial sources of the
financial strength.

At the end of 1646, Cheng Ch'eng-kung, mourning his mother's
death in the fall of An-p'ing-chen and bitterly condemning his
father's betrayal of the prince of T'ang, proclaimed the continuation of loyalist resistance on the islands, dramatically consummated
the family bias toward *wu* over *wen* by burning his literati robes, and
seized the Japan trade junks as they came in.

THE FAILURE OF COASTAL RESISTANCE, 1650–1664

After 1646, the loyalist court structure that had provided at least
some hope of cooperation between gentry/civil official leaders and
regional militarists was gone from Fukien, never to return. Coastal
resistance survived on the islands and in harbors remote from major
population centers. Sometimes such remnants developed impressive
cohesion and strength, but they were unable to articulate a structure
that would also draw on the latent Loyalist strength on the mainland. The sources of internal strength and cohesion are examined
below by means of a contrast between Chusan and Amoy. The failure of ties to the mainland is an equally interesting and considerably more complex question, which comes into focus especially in
relation to the internal composition of Cheng Ch'eng-kung's regime
and the politics of his Nanking expedition in 1659.

Huang Pin-ch'ing, a Fukien native, had been a military commander
under the late Ming, and then, like Cheng Hung-k'uei and Cheng
Ts'ai, had been involved in the Yangtze campaigns of 1644 and 1645
and had put out to sea as resistance collapsed. The Foochow court
placed him in charge of Chusan, and he refused to accept office from
or give refuge to the nearby prince of Lu, preferring allegiance first
to the Foochow court and later to that of the Yung-li emperor,
establishing ties with resistance centers in the Yangtze estuary and

on the Shantung peninsula.[42] In 1649, Huang Pin-ch'ing finally gave refuge to the prince of Lu and a few troops loyal to him, but soon was killed by agents of the Lu commanders. The ensuing conflicts between commanders and troops loyal to the prince and those which had served under Huang paved the way for the Ch'ing conquest of Chusan in 1651. The Lu commanders held Chusan from time to time later in the 1650s, and some Chekiang naval commanders joined them, but the financing came from Cheng Ch'eng-kung, and Chusan never again was an independent or permanent center of maritime resistance.

At Amoy, by 1651 Cheng Ch'eng-kung had deprived Hung-k'uei and Ts'ai of power and brought under his control their forces and all the outposts along the Fukien coast. Ch'en Pa, at Nan-ao just across the Kwangtung border, was well entrenched and only loosely under Cheng's power, but other outposts and commanders were effectively controlled.[43] Cheng gave refuge to the prince of Lu but refused to give him any substantial authority, preferring, as Huang Pin-ch'ing had, to accept offices and honors from the more distant Yung-li court and thus remain virtually autonomous. No doubt the Cheng family began with far greater resources than Huang Pin-ch'ing, having the wealth, fleets, and reputation Cheng Chih-lung had built up from 1626 to 1646. Cheng Ch'eng-kung's brother controlled the family reserve funds in Japan, and Ch'eng-kung's connections with the Chinese community in Dutch Taiwan were strong. Ch'eng-kung was as adept as his father at negotiation, and another brother provided able assistance in commercial and logistical matters. But Cheng Ch'eng-kung went far beyond this commercial-mediator heritage, combining it in his own person with a carefully cultivated loyalist mystique and great attention to military discipline, training, and organization. He was the spiritual heir not only of his turncoat father but also of the loyalist martyrs, not only of Wang Chih but also of Ch'i Chi-kuang. It should not surprise us to find that such combinations in one person, although enormously effective, required an immense effort of will, led to a regime very tightly focused on one individual, and, combined with Ch'eng-kung's rejection of his father's summons to surrender, to severe psychological tensions in that one individual.

Cheng Ch'eng-kung's harsh discipline occasionally was counter-productive; it frightened a few of his commanders into defection to the Ch'ing. Huang Wu's surrender of Hai-ch'eng in 1656 was a severe blow, and his recommendations probably helped shape the increasingly harsh Ch'ing policies of the late 1650s. Another defector, Shih Lang, later was invaluable to the Ch'ing as a naval strategist and organizer, and provides in the next section our last great example of the man who is at once mediator, naval commander, and exploiter of commerce. For civil officials, life on Amoy and Quemoy may have been a little less dangerous, but it offered few opportunities for advancement or genuine power. The Cheng family and its private agents controlled trade and finance, military men the troops and fleets. A good many scholar-officials had taken refuge from the Ch'ing under Cheng Ch'eng-kung, but most were "civil officials at leisure" (wen-hsien-yuan) and the remainder were honored but apparently powerless advisers or strictly subordinated bureaucratic technicians.[44] The Cheng regime was not an imperial court, with all the forms, rituals, and offices such a court required. Its leader was not a Li Tzu-ch'eng or Dorgon who needed literati advisers to give him respectability in the eyes of the Chinese elite, to draft documents and advise on the management of bureaucratic institutions, but a well-educated member of that elite who had publicly burned his civil-official robes and developed a military-commercial form of political power.

In the early 1650s, Cheng Chih-lung was kept in comfortable captivity in Peking and allowed to communicate with Cheng Ch'eng-kung, in the hope that he could help persuade his son to surrender. The Cheng family was also allowed to maintain its commercial network within the empire, an accommodation that fitted well into the negotiation strategy and also into the partial reversion to late Ming corruption characteristic of this period. But after the negotiations broke down in 1655, large Ch'ing forces pushed Cheng Ch'eng-kung out of most of his conquests on the Fukien mainland, maritime trade was prohibited, and there were more prosecutions of individuals accused of trading with the Cheng regime.[45] These measures, and Cheng quarrels with Dutch Taiwan, aggravated the effects of the general disruption and reduction of trade by the wars of the Ch'ing conquest, the expulsion of the Portuguese from Japan, and the falling-off in the Manila trade, the latter linked to the declining production of the Mexican and Peruvian mines and thereby to the European depression of the mid-seventeenth century.[46] Pressed by Ch'ing military advances and this commercial contraction, Cheng Ch'eng-kung had to seek supplies in wider-ranging expeditions into Chekiang and Kwangtung, and these expeditions came to rely more and more on force to get what they needed.

In the summer of 1659, a great force of over 1,000 vessels and 50,000–100,000 men under Cheng Ch'eng-kung sailed into the Yangtze, defeated Ch'ing forces at Kua-chou and Chen-chiang, and besieged Nanking, symbol of hope and disaster for the Ming cause. This expedition was an extension of the great coastal raids of the previous years and perhaps a sign of Cheng's growing megalomania or desperation or both. The Ch'ing court in Peking was profoundly alarmed. Many local magistrates along the Yangtze went over to Cheng. If he had taken Nanking, or if the old gentry-loyalist forces had joined him, he might have gained sufficient momentum to encourage other militarists, some still associated with the Yung-li emperor in the southwest and others allied with the Ch'ing, to join in a general counterattack on the Ch'ing. Very much remains to be done in the study of these events through local gazetteers and biographical materials. But a first impression from Cheng-related sources is that not many gentry-loyalists raised their heads. Troops of one Chekiang loyalist leader, Chang Huang-yen, fought bravely and effectively at Kua-chou and Chen-chiang but then were sent off to Wu-hu, up-river from Nanking, to block Ch'ing reinforcements, threaten Nanking from that direction, and consolidate the surrenders of local magistrates. This sounds sensible, but Chang tried to excuse himself from going and later complained that thereafter he knew nothing of the plans of Cheng's headquarters.[47]

Cheng Ch'eng-kung may not have been consciously rejecting the active cooperation of a force that was not personally loyal to him, but certainly the tight discipline and personal loyalty that held his forces together would have posed many obstacles to full cooperation with gentry-loyalist forces. At least as important, the Cheng regime could offer the Chiang-nan elite liberation from the alien yoke, but in other respects it probably had less to offer them than the Ch'ing. The regime that controlled most of the empire offered far more opportunities to the bureaucratic careerist than a challenger; an important political corollary to the well-known theory of the changing Mandate of Heaven. And as we have seen above, even in its coastal base areas the Cheng regime offered scholar-officials even fewer opportunities for advancement than most regional militarist regimes.

Why did Cheng Ch'eng-kung allow his troops to rest and celebrate his birthday rather than press the siege of Nanking, thus giving the Ch'ing time to bring up reinforcements? Whatever combination of overconfidence, waiting for loyalist allies who never came, expecting the Ch'ing to negotiate, and other unknown motives led to his decision, the result was a final catastrophe for Ming loyalism, as his fleet fled down the Yangtze and on to its Fukien bases. Of course it had to get back to the ocean before the Ch'ing could cut it off, but as far as we can tell, no thought was given to trying to hold a major base on Chusan and again seeking allies in Chiang-nan. Perhaps Cheng now was convinced that Chiang-nan loyalism had no military potential; but certainly he must have regarded the preservation of his fleets and Fukien bases as his most important task.

Cheng managed to hold those bases against a Ch'ing attack in 1660. His next move, the invasion of Dutch Taiwan in 1661, made excellent sense in terms of maintaining his own power base and finding a new source of food for his armies, but it was a further move away from offering any support to actual and potential allies, as is clear from Chang Huang-yen's vehement protest.[48] The prospect of a move away from coastal trade connections to fever-ridden southern Taiwan also conflicted with the commercial opportunism and instinct of self-preservation of Cheng's commanders, who ignored his orders to join him early in 1662. At this point, discussion of "objective" considerations of the sources of power and internal cohesion of the Cheng regime become inseparable from a family melodrama of parricide, incest, madness, and disputed succession.

The execution of Cheng Chih-lung on November 24, 1661, was one of the first of the harsh measures against the Cheng regime taken by the regents for the K'ang-hsi emperor. Ch'eng-kung, of course, had gone far to seal his father's fate by refusing to surrender in the 1650s, and by invading Taiwan had made it clear that he intended to remain autonomous. But according to the novelistic *T'ai-wan-wai-chi*,[49] when he learned of his father's execution, even in his demonstrative grief he insisted that it would not have happened if

Chih-lung had listened to him! Then Ch'eng-kung learned that his
son Ching, on Amoy, had fathered a child on the wet nurse of his
youngest brother; the wet-nurse being one of the "eight mothers,"
this was incest. Ch'eng-kung sent orders for the execution of his
son, the wet-nurse, the infant, and his own principal wife, because
she had not kept order in her household. Refusing to execute the
wife and son, and still resisting Ch'eng-kung's demands that they
come to Taiwan, the Amoy and Quemoy commanders were near
open rebellion as Ch'eng-kung's insanity worsened and he died on
June 23.

SHIH LANG AND THE NEW BALANCE, 1662–1690

Chinese and foreign sources leave no doubt about the brutality and
callousness with which the great coastal evacuation campaigns of
the early 1660s were carried out.[50] But they accomplished their
goal; they made most of the coastal outposts untenable for the
Cheng regime. The conquest of Taiwan might have solved the grain
supply problem and made them tenable again, but it was followed
almost immediately by a political crisis in which personalized and
familized politics showed some crucial weaknesses.[51] Family politics intensify disputes in a way that bureaucratic politics do not.
A disputed succession is an either-or proposition, especially likely to
give new heat to old differences, and it can come at the most in-
convenient time. After Cheng Ch'eng-kung's death, the Taiwan
commanders recognized as his heir his younger brother Hsi, not
Cheng Ching. On Quemoy, Cheng T'ai, the powerful manager of the
family's finances, probably tried to keep on good terms with both
camps and also was negotiating with the Ch'ing. But even if he had
supported Ching unreservedly, Ching probably would have eliminated
him as a potentially dangerous rival. When Ching imprisoned T'ai,
who then was murdered or committed suicide, T'ai's relatives took
their troops and fleets and surrendered to the Ch'ing.

Other Cheng commanders surrendered in 1663 and early 1664
because of ties to Hsi or T'ai, distrust of Ching, or disinclination to
abandon their posts and go to Taiwan. The Ch'ing used the surrendered fleets, and even a Dutch squadron, in the conquest of
Amoy and Quemoy in November 1663. Thus a combination of family rivalry, Ch'ing military action, and geography reduced the Cheng

forces by one-fourth to one-half in two years, and forced their withdrawal from all their coastal posts. The process of negotiation, surrender, and use of surrendered forces against their former allies was reminiscent of 1628–30, but far less risky, because the Ch'ing court was in complete and detailed control and because it had great financial and military resources and in the long run could get along without the surrendered forces.

Some of the surrendered Cheng commanders were quickly absorbed into the Ch'ing provincial garrison system. Away from the coast, split up into relatively small units, they were effectively neutralized. Ironically, this process was facilitated by the high degree of discipline and order that had prevailed in Cheng Ch'eng-kung's forces; the surrendered forces were soldiers, not pirates. But these small garrisons could not provide the offensive power and unity of command that would be required for an attack on Cheng Taiwan. This power was provided, in 1664–65 and again in 1680–83, primarily by Shih Lang. In him, and less clearly in his patron, ally, and fellow defector from the Cheng forces, Huang Wu, we see a modest and ultimately controllable reemergence of the merchant-mediator-admiral pattern of Wang Chih and the Cheng family, in the service of the continental power.

The Ch'ing elite had neither experience in (nor taste for) maritime warfare, which helps to account for Shih's being placed in exclusive command of two expeditions against Taiwan in 1664–65. In the first of these, in December 1664, it is likely that Shih deliberately turned back, alleging bad weather, in order to keep his power intact for a few months more.[52] But then, in the summer of 1665, other officials refused to cooperate with him (or perhaps to give him control over their forces), no further expeditions were sent, and Shih was summoned to Peking and was inactive until 1681. Then he found new patrons, including Li Kuang-ti, obtained an imperial decision excluding the governor-general of Fukien from a share in his command, and conquered Taiwan in 1683. Was the K'ang-hsi emperor in the 1680s, unlike his regents in the 1660s, simply astute and secure enough to allow an overbearing general to succeed and *then* discard him? In any case, Shih quickly lost influence after 1683, and in the late 1680s could not even monopolize trade in his home base of Amoy.[53]

Turning from the admiral to the merchant and mediator sides of

Shih Lang, we see him trying to trade with the Dutch at Hai-ch'eng in 1665 but being frustrated by strict Ch'ing surveillance. Both he and Huang Wu, however, seem to have managed to send a few of their own ships abroad in these years despite the strict prohibitions of maritime trade. After he conquered Taiwan, he boasted to the English and the Dutch of his influence at court and the privileges he could obtain for them (shades of Li Tan and the English at Hirado!), but it soon became clear that his influence was waning.[54] He still had client-merchants on Amoy, but they were competing with others, not cornering the trade. I know of no evidence that he used his commercial wealth to pay for his fleets; it is more likely that he used his surplus profits to protect his position by filling purses in the bureaucracy. It was very hard to maintain the maritime positive interaction of profit and power under the shelter of a vigilant, rapacious, and highly competent continental regime. Moreover, Shih had many competitors inside the early Ch'ing elite in his efforts to corner and exploit trade and mediate with overseas foreigners: Manchus, Liaotung Chinese generals and officials, even an imperial bondservant.[55] Such people had little or none of the antimilitary and (probably) anticommercial prejudices that had plagued Cheng Chihlung's relations with the loyalist court at Foochow, but their own commercialism must have contributed to their unwillingness to allow Shih to have his own way in maritime trade as Cheng had.

Concentration of mercantile power in the hands of a few high officials and their clients also was very conspicuous in the Cheng regime that revived a little and reoccupied part of coastal Fukien during the Rebellion of the Three Feudatories,[56] and in the regimes of the feudatories themselves, both before and after their rebellion. But the Cheng regime was a shadow of its strength of 1661, and the Keng and Shang feudatory regimes do not seem to have devoted much attention to naval power. In any case, studies of coastal areas will remain marginal to our studies of the Rebellion of the Three Feudatories and its suppression. Here the central conflict was between the Ch'ing and the structure Wu San-kuei had built up in the southwest. But the changes in Kwangtung and Fukien do provide some interesting case studies of politics and political economy on both sides, especially when further information is available from the records of European traders.[57]

It is clear, for example, that the various challengers of the Ch'ing were hampered by mutual suspicion and lack of a single central authority. In Canton in the fall of 1676, Shang Chih-hsin was in control but wary of his father, the retired prince Shang K'o-hsi, and of a representative sent by Wu San-kuei to keep an eye on the Canton regime. None of the above had any control over, nor apparently any close cooperative relations with, the Cheng regime, whose authority reached down the coast from Fukien to Tung-kuan, northeast of the Bogue. As far as we can tell, none of these regimes was able to match the dynamic and disciplined commitment to a cause or the mutually reinforcing relation of commerce and military power we saw in the regime of Cheng Ch'eng-kung.

We also have a good picture of the situation at Foochow after it returned to Ch'ing jurisdiction. General supervision of the continuing campaign against the Cheng regime was entrusted to the emperor's uncle Giyešu, but there also were two high-level Manchu officials sent from the capital to keep an eye on the situation, as well as a younger brother of Keng Ching-chung, the former rebellious feudatory, and the regular provincial hierarchy. Here the ethnic ties of the Manchu people, the family ties of the Imperial Clan and of the Keng family, and the regular structures of the bureaucracy, reinforced one another in a political structure far stronger than anything the Three Feudatories could provide, and linked to the court and the capital in so many ways that regional concentration of power was very difficult. Taiwan was conquered in 1683 not only by Shih's naval talents but also by Ch'ing negotiations that led to splits within the Cheng regime,[58] a tactic also pursued by the central power in 1559 and 1661, as described above, and by the superior financial resources of the Ch'ing regime, which enabled it to take the Cheng soldiers into its service at full pay, while food was scarce and military pay in arrears on Taiwan.[59]

On the pacified south China coast after 1683, trade by foreign ships revived somewhat and the trade of Chinese ships going overseas grew very rapidly,[60] but there was no revival of the maritime positive interaction of profit and power. Rather, detailed and sophisticated arrangements for the resettlement and peacetime garrisoning of the coast and for the control and taxation of maritime trade went hand in hand with the evolution of practices for the private exploitation of the profits from maritime trade by Ch'ing bureaucrats.[61] The central figure here was Wu Hsing-tso, governor-general of Kwangtung and Kwangsi from 1681 to 1689, the only imperial bondservant ever to become a high provincial official. Wu was the son of a Chekiang man who somehow became the commander of the bodyguard of the enormously influential Manchu Prince Daišan He was an obscure provincial official with some administrative reform to his credit, including land registration and equalization of labor service at Wu-hsi, until Giyešu, Daišan's grandson, picked him out and recommended him for rapid promotion at Foochow in the late 1670s.[62] According to a rumor recorded by the Dutch,[63] both Wu and Yao Ch'i-sheng sought the post of Kwangtung-Kwangsi governor-general, and Wu won out by offering 10,000 taels more than Yao for it. This may have referred to a simple bribe, but more probably to some kind of contribution to funds for the war against Feudatory remnants in the southwest or the Cheng regime.

Here we see a hint of a transition from all the various kinds of irregular and extortionate plunder in the name of financing armies that had plagued China during the Ming–Ch'ing transition to the systematic squeezing of merchant and other fluid wealth, often in the name of contributions to the Inner Asian campaigns, that was so important in the eighteenth century. The anticipations become even more striking when we find Wu Hsing-tso presiding over the dismemberment of Shang Chih-hsin's commercial empire in Canton. The confiscated fortune of Shang's leading client-merchant, Shen Shang-ta, was officially reported to be over 400,000 taels, and far more must have gone into the private coffers of Ch'ing officials.[64] Dutch records for the rest of the 1680s show Wu overseeing an abortive attempt to form a general association of merchants and high officials engaged in trade, a sort of anticipation of the later Co-hong; standing behind the activities of various client-merchants; and even sending merchant envoys to Batavia to discuss a contract for Dutch delivery at a fixed price of Japanese copper for the Canton mint.[65] These negotiations, a last item in our record of negotiation and mediation with foreigners, were unsuccessful, and about a year later Wu was dismissed for corruption in the minting of copper cash.

THE CH'ING PEACE

We are a long way from having a general picture of the development of maritime China between 1690 and 1720. For coastal Fukien, important trends included expansion of trade with and emigration to both Taiwan and Java. A sharp break with this relatively open and expansive situation came in 1717, with the prohibition of all trade to the "Southern Ocean," motivated by mistrust of Chinese who sailed to foreign countries and fear that they might collaborate with foreigners. The Dutch at Batavia also were told that these restrictions were made "because of the advanced age of the Emperor . . . in order to give less occasion for turbulence to the detriment of the Empire."[66] Even at this distance and in this connection, the Yung-cheng succession crisis seems to have stood out as something of a turning point. A few junks got through to Manila every year, but none to Batavia until 1722.[67] Worries about the unruly Chinese population on Taiwan probably had contributed to the decision to restrict trade, but the restrictions in turn probably exacerbated the unrest that led to the Chu I-kuei rebellion there in 1720,[68] which in turn reinforced the Ch'ing tendency to see the maritime world as a center of subversion. The Yung-cheng and early Ch'ien-lung periods saw increasingly strict and elaborate measures to control Chinese overseas trade from Amoy and European trade in Canton. In both cases, a guild of merchants was given large administrative responsibilities, prospered, then declined because of official squeeze and administrative difficulties late in the century.

At the end of the eighteenth century, trade was expanding, though much of it outside legal channels, and piracy was on the rise again. Although most aspects of this period await detailed study, it seems clear that maritime China in the ages of Nelson and Palmerston did not, could not, equal the impact on the history of the empire it had had in the ages of Drake, Piet Heyn, and Cheng Ch'eng-kung. The vast tea trade was carried in European ships; there were large numbers of armed European ships in the South China Sea every year; the squeeze on the fortunes of Canton and Amoy merchants was unrelenting; the superiority of European seamanship and gunnery was overwhelming even before the first steamships appeared. In 1842, with British guns trained on those same walls of Nanking that Cheng Ch'eng-kung had besieged, China entered its modern age powerless even to defend its coasts, much less to join actively in the struggle among the competitive maritime-commercial powers.

As we have seen, two of the basic causes of this decline of the power and influence of maritime China were its position on the periphery of the empire and some of the special limitations and hazards of the marine environment. Maritime forces could affect mainstream Chinese politics only when continental structures were weak. The pirates in the lower Yangtze in the 1550s almost certainly were abetted by internal dislocation and banditry; Cheng involvement in 1644–45 was only one aspect of a chaotic multisided civil war; and Cheng Ch'eng-kung's position at Nanking in 1659 was a very hazardous and exposed one.

The strategies of comparison outlined at the beginning of this essay shed some more light on the strengths and weaknesses of maritime China and on its continuities and discontinuities with the mainstream of the Chinese tradition. The mainstream and many variants of that tradition had prominent roles for the three types we have seen in the maritime scene; the merchant, the mediator, and the military commander. But in the maritime variant the three were occasionally and very powerfully combined in one person; mediation with foreigners was an important part of the mediative function; and there was much less need than in the mainstream and most variants for the mediative and administrative skills of ordinary scholar-officials. The last point, as we have seen in relation to Cheng Ch'eng-kung, helps us to understand the limits of the appeal of a maritime regime to potential allies on the mainland. Moreover, the case of Cheng Ch'eng-kung also suggests that the maritime interaction of profit and power fully realized its political potential only in combination with strict military discipline and strong commitment to a political cause. In the events discussed here, this happened only in a narrow focus on an extraordinary individual, not in an often-repeated pattern of personal power and legitimation, still less in the involvement of a whole community in the pursuit of maritime profit and power. Cheng Ch'eng-kung was neither a Shih K'o-fa nor a K'ang-hsi; Amoy was not a Venice or an Amsterdam.

NOTES TO CHAPTER 6

1. Immanuel Wallerstein, *The Modern World-System: Capitalist Agriculture and the Origins of the European World-Economy in the Sixteenth Century* (New York, 1974).

2. For an excellent survey and full references to this literature, see Joseph Needham, *Science and Civilization in China* (Cambridge, 1954 et seq.), vol. 4, pt. 3, pp. 379–699.

3. Bodo Wiethoff, *Chinas Dritte Grenze: Der Traditionalle Chinesische Staat und der Küstennahe Seeraum* (Wiesbaden, 1969).

4. Kwan-wai So, *Japanese Piracy in Ming China During the 16th Century* (East Lansing, Mich., 1975).

5. Ta-tuan Ch'en, "Investiture of Liu-ch'iu Kings in the Ch'ing Period," in John K. Fairbank, ed., *The Chinese World Order* (Cambridge, Mass., 1968), pp. 135–64, 315–20.

6. See, for example, Laurence G. Thompson, "The Junk Passage Across the Taiwan Strait: Two Early Chinese Accounts," *Harvard Journal of Asiatic Studies* 28 (1968):170–94.

7. For more on European sources and their uses, see John E. Wills, Jr., "Early Sino-European Relations: Problems, Opportunities, and Archives," *Ch'ing-shih wen-t'i* 3, no. 2 (December 1974):50–76.

8. Karl Polanyi, *Dahomey and the Slave Trade* (Seattle, 1966).

9. M. A. P. Meilink-Roelofsz, *Asian Trade and European Influence in the Indonesian Archipelago between 1500 and about 1630* (The Hague, 1962), especially chaps. 5, 7.

10. Cheng Jo-tseng, *Chiang-nan ching-lueh* (Ssu-pu ts'ung-k'an chen-pen, 2d collection, vol. 179–81, Taipei, 1971), 5A:43. Some basic works on the "Japanese pirates" are Kwan-wai So *Japanese Piracy;* Ch'en Mao-heng, *Ming-tai wo-k'ou k'ao-lueh,* Yenching Journal of Chinese Studies Monograph Series, no. 6 (Peiping, 1934; reprinted Peking, 1957); Akiyama Kenzō, *Nisshi kōshōshi kenkyū* (Tokyo, 1939); Ishihara Michihiro, *Wakō* (Tokyo, 1964); Li Kuang-pi, *Ming-tai yü-Wo chan-cheng* (Shanghai, 1956). For further bibliography and an excellent example of the kind of detailed analysis that sometimes is possible in the study of these campaigns, see Charles O. Hucker, "Hu Tsung-hsien's Campaign Against Hsu Hai, 1556," in Frank A. Kierman, Jr., and John K. Fairbank, eds., *Chinese Ways in Warfare* (Cambridge, Mass., 1974), pp. 273–307. For more detail on Wang Chih, see Goto Shukudō, "Wakō-ō Ō Choku," *Rekishi Chiri,* vol. 50, nos. 1, 2, 4, pp. 32–40, 106–26, 289–309.

11. Li Kuang-pi, *Ming-tai yü-Wo,* 50–51.

12. Li Kuang-ming, *Chia-ching yü-Wo Chiang-Che chu-k'o-chün k'ao,* Yenching Journal of Chinese Studies Monograph Series, no. 4 (Peiping, 1933).

13. Kwan-wai So, *Japanese Piracy,* pp. 154–55. On legalized trade and control measures after 1567, see Charles W. MacSherry, "Impairment of the Ming Tribute System as Exhibited in Trade Through Fukien" (Ph.D. diss., University of California, Berkeley, 1956), chaps. 4,5; Bodo Wiethoff, *Die chinesische Seeverbotspolitik und der private Überseehandel von 1368 bis 1567* (Hamburg, 1963), pp. 114–25.

14. Yobuko Jōtarō, *Wakō shikō* (Tokyo, 1971), especially the excellent map of the Kyushu pirate bases on p. 444; George Sansom, *A History of Japan, 1334–1615* (Stanford, 1961), p. 266.

15. For the Macao trade these estimates are based on C. R. Boxer, *The Christian Century in Japan, 1549–1650* (Berkeley and Los Angeles, 1951), pp. 105–09, and idem, *The Great Ship from Amacon: Annals of Macao and the Old Japan Trade* (Lisbon, 1959), p. 183. For some very convincing figures from

1,500,000 to 2,000,000 taels for 1637, see Boxer, *Great Ship,* pp. 6, 153, 196. For the Manila trade, I use Chaunu's figures for customs duties on Chinese trade, divide them by the statutory rate of the duty, and double to allow for untaxed trade. Chaunu has suggested that the ratio of untaxed to taxed trade may have been even higher than I assume here. Pierre Chaunu, *Les Philippines et le Pacifique des Ibériques (XVIᵉ, XVIIᵉ, XVIIIᵉ Siècles): Introduction Méthodologique et Indices d'Activité* (Paris, 1960), pp. 34, 200–05, 268. William S. Atwell, "Notes on Silver, Foreign Trade, and the Late Ming Economy," *Ch'ing-shih wen-t'i* 3, no. 8 (December 1977): 1–33, adds much useful detail and discussion.

16. *Ming ching-shih wen-pien hsuan-lu, Tai-wan wen-hsien ts'ung-K'an* (Taipei, 1958–) no. 289, p. 179 (hereafter cited as *TW*); Liu Chien-shao, *Fu-chien t'ung-chih cheng-shih-lueh* (ms, n.d. Harvard-Yenching Library), 14:14a–b.

17. William L. Schurz, *The Manila Galleon* (New York, 1939; paperbound ed., 1959), pp. 85–89; Chang Wei-hua, *Ming-shih Fo-lang-chi, Lü-sung, Ho-lan, I-ta-li-ya ssu-chuan chu-shih,* Yenching Journal of Chinese Studies Monograph Series, no. 7 (Peiping, 1934), pp. 90–101.

18. W. P. Groeneveldt, *De Nederlanders in China, Eerste Deel: De eerste bemoeiingen om den handel in China en de vestiging in de Pescadores (1601–1624)* (The Hague, 1898), pp. 11–23; Chang Wei-hua, *Ming-shih,* pp. 116–23.

19. Ishihara Michihiro, *Bunroku-Keichō no eki* (Tokyo, 1963); Li Kuang-t'ao, *Ch'ao-hsien jen-ch'en Wo-huo shih-liao* 5 vols. (Taipei, 1970).

20. Shen Yu-jung, *Min-hai tseng-yen, TW,* no. 56.

21. Iwao Seiichi, "Shih-ch'i shih-chi Jih-pen-jen chih T'ai-wan chin-lueh hsing-tung," *T'ai-wan ching-chi shih pa-chi* (T'ai-wan yen-chiu ts'ung-k'an, no. 71, 1959), pp. 1–23.

22. Chang Wei-hua, *Ming-shih,* pp. 64–67; Chang T'ien-tse, *Sino-Portuguese Trade from 1514 to 1644* (reprint, Leiden, 1969), pp. 118–21.

23. *Ming ching-shih wen-pien hsüan-lu,* drawn primarily from the *Huang Ming ching-shih wen-pien* of Ch'en Tzu-lung et al., is an extremely important and convenient collection of material on these topics. On Cheng Chih-lung's proposal, see Fang Hao, "Ch'ung-chen ch'u Cheng Chih-lung i-min-ju-T'ai shih," *Taiwan wen-hsien,* vol. 12, no. 1, pp. 37–38.

24. W. P. Groeneveldt, *De Nederlanders in China,* passim; *Ming-chi Ho-lan-jen chin-chü P'eng-hu ts'an-tang, TW,* no. 154.

25. Richard Cocks, *The Diary of Richard Cocks, Cape-Merchant in the English Factory in Japan, 1615–1622,* 2 vols., Hakluyt Society, ser. 1, vol. 67 (London, 1888). Many of the important passages on Li Tan are cited in Iwao Seiichi's excellent study, "Li Tan, Chief of the Chinese Residents at Hirado, Japan, in the Last Days of the Ming Dynasty," *Memoirs of the Research Department of the Toyo Bunko* 17 (1958):27–83.

26. On Cheng's relations with the Dutch, see Iwao, "Li Tan," pp. 71–82, and archives of the Dutch East India Company, Algemeen Rijksarchief, The Hague, Koloniaal Archief (hereafter KA), 997: 228–33, 999: 317–84, 999: 394, 1002: 179. On *pao-shui* see Ts'ao Lü-t'ai, *Ching-hai chi-lueh, TW,* no. 33, 1:4; Chou K'ai, ed., *Hsia-men chih, TW,* no. 95, 16:666; Lin Shih-tui, *Ho-cha ts'ung-t'an, TW,* no. 153, 4:156.

27. Iwao, "Li Tan," p. 81.

28. Among the most important sources on Cheng Chih-lung in the late 1620s are Ts'ao Lü-t'ai, *Ching-hai;* Chiang Jih-sheng, *T'ai-wan wai-chi, TW,* no. 60, 1:3–39; P'eng Sun-i, *Ching-hai chih, TW,* no. 35, 1:1–4; *Cheng-shih shih-liao ch'u-pien, TW,* no. 157.

29. Ts'ao Lü-t'ai, *Ching-hai,* especially 2:28–42.

30. Yang Ying, *Ts'ung-cheng shih-lu, TW,* no. 32, p. 43; Chi Liu-ch'i, *Ming-chi nan-lüeh, TW,* no. 148, "fu-lu," p. 520.

31. C. R. Boxer, "The Rise and Fall of Nicholas Iquan," *T'ien-hsia Monthly,* 11 (1941):401–39, at 430–32; *Dagh-register Gehouden in 't Casteel Batavia, 1628–1682* (Batavia, 1887–1931), 6 December 1640, pp. 110–13; 31 December 1640, pp. 147–50; 29 January 1641, pp. 175–77; 13 December 1641, p. 59.

32. *Dagh-register,* 6 December 1640, p. 117

33. Lin Shih-tui, *Ho-cha,* 4:156; Boxer, "Rise and Fall," pp. 427–29, 437.

34. Lin Shih-tui, *Ho-cha,* 4:156; *Cheng-shih shih-liao ch'u-pien,* pp. 174–81.

35. P'eng Sun-i, *Ching-hai chih,* 1:7.

36. Examples would include Mao Yüan-i's famous *Wu-pei chih* (T'u-shu-chi-ch'eng ed.) and the very extensive military material in Hsü Kuang-ch'i, *Hsü Kuang-ch'i chi* (Shanghai, 1963). Topical indexing of the late Ming *ching-shih* collections would enormously facilitate their use in the kind of content analysis that is needed here as well as in research on particular topics.

37. Jerry Dennerline, "Fiscal Reform and Local Control: The Gentry-Bureaucratic Alliance Survives the Conquest," in Frederic Wakeman, Jr., and Carolyn Grant, eds., *Conflict and Control in Late Imperial China* (Berkeley and Los Angeles, 1975), pp. 86–120, at 101–02.

38. Hsü Tzu, *Hsiao-t'ien chi-nien, TW,* no. 134, 6:266–68.

39. P'eng Sun-i, *Ching-hai chih,* 1:7.

40. Hsü Tzu, *Hsiao-t'ien chi-nien,* 10:459.

41. These paragraphs are based on the most important Chinese sources on the Cheng family, most of which are listed in John E. Wills, Jr., *Pepper, Guns, and Parleys: The Dutch East India Company and China, 1662–1681* (Cambridge, Mass., 1974), p. 15, n. 33. Most of these sources are organized chronologically. On the Lu Court, see also Cha Chi-tso, *Lu ch'un-ch'iu, TW,* no. 118, and Huang Tsung-hsi, *Hai-wai t'ung-k'u chi, TW,* no. 135.

42. On Huang Pin-ch'ing see, in addition to the above, Hsü Tzu, *Hsiao-t'ien chi-chuan, TW,* no. 138, 64:917–20.

43. On Ch'en Pa, see P'eng Sun-i, *Ching-hai chih,* 3:60, and Hsü Tzu, *Hsiao-t'ien chi-chuan,* 20:961.

44. *Cheng-shih kuan-hsi wen-shu, TW,* no. 69, pp. 9–13; Hsü Tzu, *Hsiao-t'ien chi-chuan,* 57:787–58:832.

45. Many documents on cases of this kind, arranged roughly chronologically, are to be found in *Cheng-shih shih-liao hsü-pien, TW,* no. 168.

46. Chaunu, pp. 204–11; Louis Dermigny, *La Chine et l'Occident: Le Commerce a Canton au XVIIIe Siècle* (Paris, 1964), 1:124–36.

47. Chang Huang-yen, "Pei-cheng lu," in his *Chang Ts'ang-shui chi* (Shanghai, 1964), pp. 192–202, at 194.

48. Ibid., pp. 18–20

49. Chiang Jih-sheng, *T'ai-wan wai-chi,* 5:207.

50. Information on this policy is scattered through Wills, *Pepper;* see p. 17, n. 36, for some basic bibliography. A full study from all sources, especially local gazetteers, would be an important contribution to our understanding of this period.

51. Ibid., pp. 27–28, 41–43, 51–53, 81–82.

52. Ibid., pp. 98–100.

53. Sino-European relations in the 1680s are discussed in chapter 5 of the long draft of my *Pepper;* I am revising and extending this chapter for separate publication. Scholars are welcome to consult my copy of this draft or the one on deposit at the East Asian Research Center, Harvard University.

54. Algemeen Rijksarchief, KA, 1304:956–60v, 1327:736–42v; M. Paske-Smith, *Western Barbarians in Japan and Formosa in Tokugawa Days, 1603–1868,* 2d ed. (reprint, New York, 1968), pp. 112, 115.

55. Information on the commercial practices of early Ch'ing officials is scattered throughout my *Pepper,* including the above-mentioned chapter 5 of the long draft.

56. Ibid., pp. 154–57, and the sources cited there.

57. Ibid., chap. 4. For studies and sources on English trade with the Cheng regime, see p. 152, n. 9.

58. Chiang Jih-sheng, *T'ai-wan wai-chi,* 9:387–95; P'eng Sun-i, *Ching-hai chih,* 4:92–93.

59. Paske-Smith, pp. 116–17.

60. Chaunu, pp. 208–11; figures from Dutch and other sources are assembled in the appendixes of my long draft.

61. See, for example, Tu Chen, *Yüeh-Min hsün-shih chi-lüeh* (n.d.); copies in the Kuwabara Collection, Library of the History Department, Kyoto University, and in Ssu-k'u ch'üan-shu, Palace Museum, Taiwan. P'eng Tse-i, "Ch'ing-tai Kuang-tung yang-hang chih-tu ti ch'i-yuan," *Li-shih yen chiu* 1 (1957):1–25; Chou K'ai, *Hsia-men chih, TW,* no. 95, chap. 5.

62. *Ch'ing-shih-kao T'ai-wan tzu-liao chi-chi, TW,* no. 243, pp. 501–03.

63. Algemeen Rijksarchief, KA, 1275:693v–94.

64. Li Shih-chen, *Fu-Chiang fu-Yüeh cheng-lüeh* (n.d.), 7:37–38v. The Toyo Bunko has a copy of this very valuable collection by the Kwangtung governor in the 1680s.

65. Algemeen Rijksarchief, KA, 604:318–20, 325–27, 335–39, 606:18, 84, 93, 169–70, 249, 819:341–49, 1346:157v–60, 1351:38v–40.

66. J. de Hullu, "Over den Chinaschen Handel der Oost-Indische Compagnie in de Eerste Dertig Jaar van de 18ᵉ Eeuw," *Bijdragen tot de Taal-, Land- en Volkenkunde van Nederlandsch Indië* 73 (1917):32–151, at 42.

67. Ibid., p. 47; Chaunu, pp. 180–81.

68. A. W. Hummel, ed., *Eminent Chinese of the Ch'ing Period* (Washington, D.C., 1943), pp. 181–82.

7

The Alternative to Resistance
The Case of T'ung-ch'eng, Anhwei

by Hilary J. Beattie

Local Notables

*It is impossible to analyze developments in the Ch'ing countryside
without reference to the local elite or "gentry." The dominant trend
in defining this class or status group has been to think in terms of
official positions and degree-holding, and much valuable work has
been done along this line by Ho Ping-ti, Chang Chung-li, Ch'ü T'ung-
tsu, and others. Hilary Beattie, however, comes at the problem from
a different perspective, a perspective that in part emerges from the
sources she uses; for the lineage genealogies—which are particularly
rich for seventeenth-century T'ung-ch'eng—enable her to identify a
local elite "based on wealth, education, kinship and marriage ties, as
well as official titles."*

*The genealogies, in contrast to most official or semiofficial sources,
make degree holding and official position essentially irrelevant to the
data presented. Hence we learn about the powers of lineage organizations in the nonpolitical sphere and can study the patterns of survival in such lineages as those of the Chang, Yao, and Fang. Beattie's
evidence points to the existence of a late Ming social fabric in the
area of T'ung-ch'eng that was too strong to be torn apart by the midcentury rebellions or the Ch'ing conquest. (This contrasts in significant ways with Jerry Dennerline's findings for the area around
Nanking in the same period.) We are able to see how the T'ung-
ch'eng elite rode out the storm, and the variety of means they used
to do so: by using political influence to get provincial government
support for their localities, by sending some of their families off to
safety in other areas, by defusing local unrest with concessions or
gifts, by mobilizing local militia defense corps, and by taking tough
action against their own deviant members.*

*The essay also illuminates another method employed to bolster
elite lineage power, namely, the systematic lobbying effort mounted
to frustrate the government's attempt to resurvey and reclassify landholdings in the interests of fairer taxation. Just as the local elite had
managed to modify the Chang Chü-cheng 1581 surveys, so they
managed to nullify the 1663 survey attempts. From a long view
we can see that successful campaign as ultimately self-defeating,
since the roots of inequality in the countryside were thereby firmly
entrenched; but at the time the elite must have seen avoidance of re-*

241

*assessment as being as important in bolstering their power as the firm
establishment of lineage rules and organization—further proof, if
any were needed, that the Ch'ing conquest would not deleteriously
affect their privileged way of life.*

One of the most striking features of the Ch'ing conquest of central
and south China after 1644 is the great variety of local reactions and
responses that it engendered. Even within the Yangtze delta, the cultural and commercial heartland of the country, the Manchus and
their north Chinese allies were met with everything from willing surrender to furious defiance, defiance that was crushed with a thoroughness and ferocity probably unparalleled since the Mongol conquest
nearly four hundred years earlier. Understandably, it is the latter
type of response that has so far captured the Chinese, and Western,
historical imagination. The heroic loyalty, readiness for self-sacrifice,
and terrible sufferings of elite and townspeople in places like Yangchow, Chia-ting, and Chiang-yin, where thousands were butchered,
and many officials committed suicide rather than surrender to their
barbarian conquerors, had a particular appeal for many Chinese in
the late nineteenth century, when they could be invoked to arouse
anti-Manchu feeling.[1]

There is a serious danger, however, that the dramatic impact of
such events and the disproportionate amount of attention devoted to
them may create by default the impression that they were more
typical than in fact they were and thus distort our picture of the
conquest as a whole. The admittedly impressionistic evidence thus
far available suggests, in fact, that such extreme occurrences were the
exception rather than the rule. This essay will accordingly investigate
the events of the Ming-Ch'ing transition in a county outside the delta
region, T'ung-ch'eng in Anhwei, which, despite the fact that it was in
the central arena of revolts and warfare for ten years or so up to and
during the conquest, and was the home of numerous officials with
apparently strong loyalties to the Ming government, by no means
exhibited any marked desire to resist alien rule. On the contrary, its
"gentry" elite, the key social group in this as in any other locality,
seem to have made successful efforts to minimize the effects of this

traumatic period by cooperating with rather than defying the new regime.[2] If some of them did subsequently retire from government office, their actions, as will be seen, cannot necessarily always be interpreted as diehard loyalty to their former rulers.

How and why this remarkable social continuity and stability were maintained in the face of great odds, and what compromises of interest were required on both sides, will be discussed in what follows. It must be emphasized at this point, however, that many more such local studies, drawn from a broader area than merely the Yangtze delta, will be required if we are ever to have a balanced picture of the events of the Ming-Ch'ing transition. Ideally, it should thus eventually be possible to chart much more precisely the pattern of warfare and devastation caused by revolts or conquest, or both, in central and south China in the 1630s and 1640s, and to ascertain to what extent these determined a given locality's subsequent resistance or collaboration.

Source material for this type of local study is generally abundant. T'ung-ch'eng offers a particularly promising starting point in that, in addition to good gazetteers, it affords large numbers of genealogies compiled by the lineages that by the seventeenth century were becoming a highly important form of social organization in the area. Those genealogies that contain detailed biographies, dated prefaces and rules, and so on, can often give valuable clues to social conditions in the area over long periods. T'ung-ch'eng moreover, as a place with strong scholarly traditions and many officials, can boast very large numbers of private writings, some of which, such as those of the noted scholar Tai Ming-shih (1653–1713), deal directly with the events of this epoch. Though the elite who compiled all these works tended, out of concern for their reputation with posterity, to be somewhat evasive when it came to recording actions and events that might discredit them, it is still possible to reconstruct a convincing, albeit still incomplete, picture of their aims and activities in the transition period and its aftermath.[3]

T'ung-ch'eng is one of the six counties of An-ch'ing prefecture, in south-central Anhwei; it lies immediately to the north of the Yangtze, roughly 130 miles up-river from Nanking and slightly to the northeast of the provincial and prefectural capital of An-ch'ing (or Huai-ning). The northwest part of the country is hilly or mountainous, and was originally well-wooded, while the southeast is low-lying, fertile, and well-watered, but subject to frequent inundation; the marshes, sandbars, and reedlands lying along the Yangtze itself were destined in the Ming and Ch'ing to be largely reclaimed and turned into rich farmland. The county city is situated on a small plain amid the northern hills, well away from the dangers of flooding.[4]

The great turning point in the county's history came in the period of prolonged revolts and warfare that marked the Yuan-Ming transition, when T'ung-ch'eng and the surrounding area (which had escaped the worst of the damage) seem to have been flooded with refugees from devastated parts of north Kiangsi and Hui-chou prefecture in southern Anhwei.[5] This marked the beginning of much more intensive agriculture and increasing prosperity in the county, accompanied in the fifteenth century by the rise of numerous well-to-do landowning families. It was not, however, until the sixteenth century, when the economy of much of the Yangtze valley and of southeast China was becoming rapidly more commercialized and more prosperous, and some of the resulting wealth was frequently channeled into education, that T'ung-ch'eng gradually began to be transformed from a relatively minor agricultural backwater into a place renowned for its espousal of scholarship and production of great officials. Toward the end of the dynasty it could boast of men who were fairly eminent in the central government—among them Yeh Ts'an, president of the Board of Rites in the T'ien-ch'i reign (1621–27); Tso Kuang-tou, the censor who in 1625 became the martyred hero of the Tung-lin party; Ho Ju-ch'ung, grand secretary early in the Ch'ung-chen reign (1628–44); and numerous others in lesser positions.[6]

Most significant from the point of view of the social historian is the fact that this kind of academic and official achievement began to be concentrated to some extent in certain families, most of whom throughout their history show strong evidence of landowning traditions. The most notable were undoubtedly the Fang family, who produced their first *chü-jen* as early as 1399, and four others in the course of the fifteenth century (two subsequently became *chin-shih* and four held official posts—all were related in a direct line of descent). During the sixteenth and early seventeenth centuries, fourteen of their descendants became *chü-jen,* and nine *chin-shih.* Their closest challengers in the Ming were the Yao family, who produced their first *chin-shih* in 1451, and many more degree-holders and officials (including six *chin-shih*) in the course of the sixteenth and first half of the seventeenth century. Among the other local families who enjoyed a certain degree of academic and official success at this time were those of Tso, Tai (later to produce the unfortunate seventeenth-century scholar, Tai Ming-shih), Wu, and Ma. One other name of which special note should be taken is that of Chang. Four of this family became *chin-shih* and officials after the 1520s; they were destined for even greater heights 150 years later.[7]

Rising affluence and intensified competition for both scholarly attainment and local prestige seem to have been the spurs to another vitally important social development in T'ung-ch'eng in the sixteenth century, namely, the gradual formation of extended kinship or lineage organizations, both by families who had already achieved some success and those who aspired to it. Naturally these lineage organizations in the early stages were fairly rudimentary, entailing sometimes little more than the compilation of a handwritten genealogy (listing all known kinsmen traceable to a single common ancestor, and thus defining the membership of the group), attempts to celebrate collective sacrifices and festivals (sometimes in an ancestral hall built for the purpose), and, more important, the acquisition of a modest amount of land, the income from which would finance joint activities. Management was still somewhat haphazard and rules for the regulation of members' conduct usually absent.

The lineage nonetheless proved to be a reliable way of maximizing a family's influence and status in the locality, and also of building up some joint resources that could be used to finance aid to and education of members, and thus help to perpetuate social advantages already gained. Not surprisingly, the first efforts at lineage organization were made by members of the Fang and Yao families in the fifteenth century;[8] they were followed by many others in the sixteenth century, particularly toward its end. The social prestige of these groups was further enhanced by deliberate and enduring strategies of intermarriage, the most notable examples being first the Fangs with the Yaos, and later, from the early seventeenth century onward, the Yaos with the Changs.

Greater affluence and desire for a more sophisticated life style were also the inducement for some (though by no means all) members of prestigious families to move from their landholdings in the countryside to take up residence in the county city. This, from the mid-sixteenth century, was coming to be a place of wealth, cultivation, and some intellectual and literary distinction (though the gazetteer's boast that its reputation in these matters grew to be "the foremost north of the Yangtze" need not be taken absolutely literally).[9] The presence of increasing numbers of wealthy families in the city, and its strategic position on the main road leading north from the provincial capital, An-ch'ing, to Peking, were good reasons why its magistrate in 1576 was able to persuade the provincial governor and the resident elite to have it fortified with walls. Though the need for defenses was not apparent to everybody at the time, the city's residents were to have reason to be grateful for them sixty or so years later, when many less well-fortified towns in the region were overrun by rebels.[10]

On the specific nature of the intellectual developments taking place in T'ung-ch'eng in this period much research remains to be done. One trend that can already be perceived (significantly, in view of the direction taken by the so-called T'ung-ch'eng literary school in the eighteenth century and later) is toward a severely moralistic type of Confucian thinking, with strong emphasis on practical conduct. Its foremost exponent seems to have been Fang Hsüeh-chien, of the first branch of the Fang lineage, who had espoused some of the doctrines of the Wang Yang-ming school. He produced, in addition to more purely philosophical writings, two exceedingly didactic works in which biographies of outstanding local people are used to exemplify and illustrate the highest ideals of virtue in all spheres of human life.[11]

Fang Hsüeh-chien, though he never held any official post, was a well-known, respected, and highly influential teacher in the area in the late sixteenth century. If his kind of moralistic doctrines were at all prevalent in the county it could perhaps be among the reasons why several of its officials (among them his own grandson, Fang K'ung-chao, who held office in the Board of War) became Tung-lin partisans in the 1620s and suffered for the stand they took. Most seem to have been previously involved with each other through family or scholarly ties, or both; the most famous was the censor Tso Kuang-tou, who was imprisoned and tortured to death in 1625. A later biographer of the notable men of the county, Ma Ch'i-ch'ang, at one point states that in total no fewer than thirty-five persons from T'ung-ch'eng were involved in the "eunuch catastrophe."[12] Though it has proved impossible to trace all of them, there can be no doubt that the events were well known in the county, and that there must have been a strong climate of sympathy for the sufferers and, conceivably, for their moralistic ideals of government service.

It is therefore not surprising to find that at least twenty-four persons from T'ung-ch'eng (and probably nearer thirty or thirty-five), some of them directly related to those involved in the Tung-lin affair, subsequently joined its successor movement, the Fu-she. In fact, of the total membership for An-ch'ing prefecture, all but two appear to have come from T'ung-ch'eng. Among them were all of Tso Kuang-tou's four sons and some of Fang K'ung-chao's relatives, namely his eldest son, the famous scholar and later Buddhist monk, Fang I-chih, and two of his first cousins, the *sheng-yuan* and poet Fang Wen, and the *sheng-yuan* Fang K'ung-shih; also his son-in-law Sun Lin, who was a friend and companion of Fang I-chih.[13]

Though the kind of moral idealism evidenced in the political struggles of the 1620s was in many cases perfectly sincere, there are also indications that it was on occasion not free from the more purely partisan and self-seeking types of motivation of which the idealists were wont to accuse their opponents.[14] This being the case, one is less startled by the discovery that T'ung-ch'eng's elite, in their conduct in their home locality and in their relations with the local population, did not necessarily exhibit the same kind of idealism as some of them may have done in the sphere of national politics. By the 1620s severe social tensions were arising in the county, tensions that were invariably attributed to the extravagant and overbearing behavior of the affluent local elite families, most notably those residing in the county city. Unfortunately, it is not possible to provide specific instances of this kind of inconsistent behavior, for scholars were clearly not anxious to leave explicit accounts of their own or their families' misdeeds.

Gazetteer accounts of the social situation in this period, obviously anxious to avoid offending powerful local interests, are likewise deliberately vague as to the ways in which frictions arose. The seventeenth-century edition, compiled when events were still recent enough to be painful, merely states in its description of customs in the county city that "by the Ch'ung-chen period (1628–44) extravagance became excessive and distinctions were confused," and also intimates that in the prosperous central district affluence and extravagance resulted in chronic conflicts.[15] The 1827 edition, which in fact reprints, without acknowledgment but virtually unaltered, Tai Ming-shih's invaluable account of the revolts in T'ung-ch'eng, is rather more explicit. "Previously the scholar-officials and worthies of the county had all been noted for virtuous conduct in their localities, while the common people stood universally in awe of the authorities and respected the scholar officials. But by the T'ien-ch'i and Ch'ung-chen reigns many of the long-established families and powerful lineages had become accustomed to license and extravagance; their young men and serfs [nu-p'u, tenant farmers of low status, subject to more obligations than were free tenants] made depredations everywhere, which the common people resented."[16]

No details are given, but these descriptions accord with what is generally known of rural discontent elsewhere in the Yangtze valley and southeast China at this time. Though the causes and even precise nature and extent of this unrest are still subject to considerable controversy, it appears that in some areas growing commercialization and prosperity may have led to rising expectations among tenants and serfs, as well as to increasingly exploitative behavior by landlords. This in some places (notably parts of Fukien) began to engender rent resistance, riots, and even revolts.[17] The rural situation was worsened in the late Ming by the corruption and demoralization of local government, and by a series of seven extra levies on the land-tax. Wealthy families with local influence and power (especially those numbering prominent officials or degree-holders in their midst) found it fairly easy to evade these, in the same way as they evaded much regular taxation and labor service, and thus left most of the burden to be borne by the poorer section of the community. Many great families also became notorious for extravagance and for terrorization of the local population.[18]

The precise nature of the exploitation carried on by the elite families of T'ung-ch'eng is very hard to establish, in particular because there is almost no evidence on the nature of serfdom there and the relations of landowners with tenants and serfs. There are, however, definite suggestions from the sixteenth century onward of tax and service evasion and attempts at obstruction of accurate land registration by rising elite families. The Ming permitted generous rates of exemption from labor service and from service levy (assessed on the basis of the land-tax) to all officials and degree-holders, ranging from 30 *ting* (fiscal individuals) and 30 *shih* of grain for the highest central government officials, down to 2 *ting* and 2 *shih* for *sheng-yuan*.[19] There is no doubt that in T'ung-ch'eng there were persistent efforts, especially in the lower ranges, to extend these privileges illegally to other family members; a case in point is that of a non-degree-holding member of the Yao lineage in the mid-sixteenth century who expected the *sheng-yuan* among his relatives to afford him protection from labor services as a matter of course.[20] If kinship solidarity in the face of administrative demands was strong even before many local families could boast of members in important official positions, one might infer, especially taking into account the admissions of elite misbehavior referred to above, that there could have been considerably more abuse of privilege by the early seventeenth century.

Similarly, when in 1581 an attempt was made by the county magistrate to resurvey T'ung-ch'eng's cultivated acreage (as part of the national land survey ordered by Chang Chü-cheng), resulting in a new and more uniform scheme of converting actual to fiscal *mou*, strong protests arose, led presumably by the most powerful landowning interests. As a result, yet another survey was made, which returned to the pre-1581 scheme of *mou* conversion and to virtually the original early Ming acreage quota (though this can be shown to have been by now far less than the amount of land actually under cultivation in the county).[21] Though for this reason the tax burden in T'ung-ch'eng was never extremely high, it seems plausible that the local elite families with any degree-holding members at all would try to use their exemption privilege to the maximum in order to protect themselves from it. The fact that the elite's arrogance and exploitation are described as having worsened sharply in the 1620s could be connected with the imposition of the successive extra levies on the land-tax itself, which are likely to have been borne mainly by those lacking the influence to escape them.[22] Such behavior, coupled with increasing ill-treatment of their tenants and the rest of the local peasantry, may have been enough to set the elite families and their immediate relatives apart, and to create a gulf of dangerous antagonism between them and the rest of the society.

One direct piece of evidence that some of the local elite themselves recognized the dangers of the situation is afforded by the earliest dated set of lineage rules from T'ung-ch'eng, those of Tso Kuang-tou's own lineage, drawn up late in 1634 by one of his older brothers. These contain a section entitled "Forbidding what should not be done," which strongly warns members against cheating the government of taxes and swindling other people, counterfeiting currency, "intimidating officials and worming their way into authority," and many other illegal schemes that are but darkly alluded to. Another section castigates those who deliberately foment litigation between other parties with the aim of enriching themselves and buying landed estates with the proceeds, while another, entitled "Condemning love of litigation," laments the readiness with which people currently become embroiled in quarrels and lawsuits over very trifling matters, and the ease with which these lead to enmities and loss of property.[23]

The need for such rules surely betrays the prevalence at the time of the very behavior they condemn, and the anxieties this aroused among the more far-sighted of the elite. The anxieties were well founded, for it was in this very same year, 1634, at around the same time, that the popular discontent that had been simmering for some time suddenly erupted, as cogent leadership emerged.[24] According to one source (unfortunately unavailable in its entirety to Western scholars), the first move to organize a rising was made earlier in the year by a serf, Chang Ju, in response to rebel movements already afoot in Kiangsi and Hupei. His adherents grew steadily in numbers, and fairly soon leadership was taken over by two other local desperadoes, Wang Kuo-hua and Huang Wen-ting. Though their band remained hidden, rumors of their ferocity and huge numbers (popularly estimated at 10,000 or more) reached the city, whose inhabitants trembled in hourly expectation of an attack. "The great and important families were torn between doubt and confidence. Some wanted to defend the city walls, others the streets. They regarded all their family serfs as savage wolves, none of whom would protect them." Since nothing happened for some time, they

were lulled into a false sense of security and evidently relaxed precautions. Then one night the rebels launched a sudden raid on the
city, started a fire that burned down "hundreds" of houses belonging to rich families, and escaped before dawn, laden with their
valuables.[25]

This event inaugurated more than ten years of violence, bloodshed,
and devastation in the county. T'ung-ch'eng's situation was made
infinitely worse by the fact that, in addition to suffering from repeated local uprisings, it lay directly in the path of the great rebel
armies from the northwest, notably that of the dreaded Chang
Hsien-chung. It was thus in the main theater of internal warfare
throughout most of this time and witnessed the antirebel campaigns of several important late Ming generals, including Shih K'o-fa,
Tso Liang-yü, and Huang Te-kung. In these chaotic years, T'ung-
ch'eng experienced a demoralizing succession of sieges and battles,
famines and epidemics, and the local elite suffered the effects of
violent popular hostility. From the outset "almost all the great
gentry families had their property burned and plundered." One of
the very few exceptions is said to have been Tai Chün-ts'ai (a retired county magistrate of the Tai lineage, and thus a relative of the
early Ch'ing scholar, Tai Ming-shih), whose fields and houses were
not attacked because his conduct had won the good will of the local
population.[26] Another popular figure who escaped attack was Fang
K'ung-chao. He had been restored to office at the beginning of the
Ch'ung-chen reign but at this point was living at home to observe
mourning. He subsequently managed to inveigle a large number of
the rebels into coming to him and then had them all killed.[27]

Not all the local elite had the strong nerves of Fang K'ung-chao.
As early as 1636 many of the great families were said to have fled
south across the Yangtze, as did many of the people who lived
along its banks. By 1642 "over half" the gentry (shen-chin) were
said to have gone.[28] Some, like members of the Fang, Hu, and Chang
families, simply went down the river to the Nanking area and stayed
there for the duration of the troubles. Others took members of their
families to safety but then returned to look after their interests in
T'ung-ch'eng as best they could.[29] Those rash enough to stay on
their estates often did not survive long. An older member of the
Chang family who did this was murdered in 1637, after a gallant

defense against the rebels, along with his four sons who had come to his aid.[30] The same year saw the death of a member of the most prominent branch of the Yao lineage, the *sheng-yuan* Yao Sun-lin, who with his elder sister was waylaid in the mountains.[31] Ma Ch'i-ch'ang devotes a collective biography to several others who suffered the same fate, while attempting to defy the rebels; they are likewise commemorated in the gazetteer.[32]

Most of the elite who remained behind were thus forced to take refuge in the county city where from the beginning they played a leading role, along with two successive magistrates, in organizing its defense in the frequent sieges that ensued. Tai Ming-shih at a later date attributed the survival of the city (in contrast to the fate of so many others) to the effectiveness of this combined effort.[33] Several members of the leading families, including some Tung-lin and Fu-she sympathizers, appear to have been particularly active in these operations. Among them were Fang K'ung-chao (in intervals spent out of office), Tso Kuang-tou's sons, and members of both the Chang and Yao lineages, notably Yao Sun-lin's second cousin, Yao Sun-fei (whose name will recur below).[34] Also celebrated as outstanding defenders of the city were two *sheng-yuan,* Ch'iu Shan and Wang Wen-yao, who were held in special esteem by the local authorities for their ability to calm down outbursts of popular feeling "with a single word"; presumably they were persuasive orators.[35] The efforts of these men and others were effective, not only in saving the city, but perhaps also in winning back the support of the local population. They issued grain rations in time of famine; Chang Ping-i, father of the notable early Ch'ing official Chang Ying, made gruel from his own grain stocks for this purpose, and also canceled all the debts owed to him. In 1642 the "elders and gentry" gave out five hundred oxen captured from the rebels in order to assist the people of the surrounding countryside in ploughing during a temporary respite from attacks.[36]

The elite remaining in T'ung-ch'eng undoubtedly found that one of the most effective ways of assisting the defense effort was to utilize the influence of those of their number serving in official positions in order to obtain outside help. In 1635 messengers had been sent to Soochow to ask for extra troops from Governor Chang Kuo-wei, and the same request was made at court that year by Sun

Chin (an elder brother of Sun Lin, Fang K'ung-chao's son-in-law) who was then a supervising secretary in the Board of War.[37] (This latter was the famous occasion on which the board president Chang Feng-i replied that the rebels from the northwest posed no threat to Chiang-nan because they were not used to eating southern rice, nor could their horses eat southern fodder.) Tso Kuang-tou's youngest son, Tso Kuo-ts'ai, likewise asked general Shih K'o-fa for more supporting troops; his request was granted because of Shih's great respect for his father.[38] Similarly, in 1642 the elite of the county successfully petitioned one of the Yao lineage, Yao Sun-chü, then serving in provincial office in Hu-kuang, to have unruly Hu-kuang troops withdrawn from the area.[39]

On at least one or two occasions, though information is fragmentary, the elite appear to have organized more active military measures on their own initiative. An early effort at forming some kind of local defense corps was made under the leadership of Fang K'ung-chao's son-in-law, Sun Lin, the brother of Sun Chin; its effectiveness is unknown. Another band, formed by a local man named Wu Chin-chao, was defeated by the rebels; Wu was killed and four of his family committed suicide.[40] In general, however, as Frederic Wakeman has convincingly shown, the imperial authorities were anxious at this period to prevent military power from falling directly into local gentry hands. It was with great reluctance, and at the very last moment, in April 1644, that an edict was issued authorizing the formation of militia on a nationwide scale. It is therefore not surprising that the only other militia force known to have existed in T'ung-ch'eng (an ad hoc band recruited and led in the early 1640s by the *tien-shih* or jail warden, who was not himself a local man), was soon dispersed, not by the rebels but by imperial troops who accused its members of having killed some of their own men.[41]

By 1642, when Chang Hsien-chung subjected the city to a siege worse than any that had gone before it, the plight of T'ung-ch'eng was becoming desperate. Food was in short supply and pestilence spreading; the water in the city's wells was polluted and the people reduced to eating the flesh of corpses. Many who had elected to stay behind must by now have regretted it, for it was said that "those who had property worth tens of thousands of taels outside in the

county were now dying of starvation in the city." Toward the end
of the year, food was so short that the magistrate warned that the
gentry were prepared to kill themselves and their wives, and the
commoners and troops to flee, unless relief were sent immediately.
At this Huang Te-kung did come to the rescue with a force from
An-ch'ing, but this help afforded the city only a brief respite.[42]

The county's worst problem by this time was in fact not so much
continued attacks by the rebels as the burdens imposed on the area
by the imperial Ming troops that were supposed to be defending it.
One major difficulty was simply that of provisioning large numbers
of government troops from the county's depleted resources, as more
and more land went out of cultivation and was laid waste. In 1640
the efforts of the military authorities to obtain grain supplies from
T'ung-ch'eng (at a time when the population was said to be reduced
by half and already had difficulty in paying the regular taxes) led to
a riot outside the local military headquarters; the *sheng-yuan* of the
county were blamed for inciting it. From this year onward there
were repeated famines, and the people lived in constant fear of the
troops pillaging their scanty supplies. By 1643 70 to 80 percent of
the county's cultivated acreage was said to have been devastated, and
its payments of grain tribute were hopelessly in arrears; the major
burden of exactions now fell on the east district, which alone had
escaped extensive damage. A raid by general Tso Liang-yü's troops,
followed the same year by a plague of field-mice that ate the crops,
was, so to speak, the last straw. The people had already petitioned
one of their officials at court, the supervising secretary, Kuang Shih-
heng, to try and avert the renewed efforts of the provincial authorities to collect and increase the grain tribute; now the *sheng-
yuan* of the county pressed the new governor at An-ch'ing, Chang
Liang, to ask for a 70 percent tax remission on their behalf, but in
the chaos of the times it is likely that the request went unheeded.[43]

Plundering by imperial troops became even more troublesome as
time went on. The reason was largely the increasingly arrogant and
insubordinate attitude of the local military commander, Lo Chiu-wu,
aided and abetted by his fellow-officer, Sun Te-sheng. Chang Liang
evidently could do little to control either of them. When in 1644
there was another famine and Chang ordered them to make their
troops open up waste land as military colonies (*t'un-t'ien*), the

soldiers simply forced the local people to farm for them, stole their oxen, and roamed around looting. The behavior of Lo and Sun grew worse in mid-1644, after the fall of Peking, when they took advantage of the prevailing confusion to increase their raids.[44]

The new Ming government at Nanking fairly soon fell under the control of the notorious Ma Shih-ying, an old enemy of the Tung-lin party, who appointed as president of the Board of War none other than his friend and former classmate, Juan Ta-ch'eng. This must have been a blow to many of the T'ung-ch'eng elite, who detested Juan, both because of the ambivalent and opportunistic role which he had played in the Tung-lin affair, and also, very likely, because of his family's unsavory reputation in T'ung-ch'eng itself, where they had lived for a time.[45] When Juan, banished from office in 1629, had tried to form a literary society of his own in An-ch'ing as a rival to the Fu-she, it had soon withered, apparently owing to the hostility of Fu-she supporters in T'ung-ch'eng, led by Fang I-chih.[46] Some of these men had subsequently been among the signatories of the petition to have Juan driven from Nanking in 1639. It is therefore not surprising that when Juan, in September 1644, made a personal expedition to An-ch'ing to inspect the military situation, he put on a tremendous show of pomp and ceremony, no doubt to impress all his old enemies. Yet despite his magnificent entourage and the outwardly cooperative demeanor of Lo Chiu-wu and Sun Te-sheng, he was quite helpless, as Tai Ming-shih mockingly relates, to prevent further ravages by their troops over the whole area between An-ch'ing and T'ung-ch'eng.

One of the main concerns of Juan and Ma at this time was to fortify An-ch'ing against possible attack from their opponent, General Tso Liang-yü, who, they feared, was beginning to attract many of their enemies into his camp. When Tso Liang-yü's troops came east to attack An-ch'ing, however, Lo and Sun took advantage of the situation to loot the granaries of T'ung-ch'eng and humiliate the new magistrate, who had rashly tried to assert himself against them. The troops at An-ch'ing soon mutinied and surrendered the city to Tso's son, Tso Meng-keng, forcing its commander Yang Chen-tsung (recently installed there by Juan and Ma) to flee to T'ung-ch'eng for refuge. Here, however, he found Lo Chiu-wu beginning an uprising and could only look on helplessly at the sight

of his and Sun Te-sheng's troops burning, looting, and taking young
women and boys captive. No wonder that the people of T'ung-ch'eng
were described at this time as being "as if placed between flood and
fire, constantly uncertain of their fate."

Their plight was only relieved after Ch'ing troops, commanded by
Dodo, had taken over the lower Yangtze area, including Nanking.
Dodo sent a force to pacify the rest of the Yangtze valley, a detachment of which, led by two Chinese officers, came to T'ung-ch'eng
in the summer of 1645 to deal with Lo Chiu-wu and Sun Te-sheng.
These two were by now contemplating first sacking the city and
then allowing their troops to disperse with their loot, but were
somehow persuaded to desist by the influential *sheng-yuan* Wang
Wen-yao.[47] They and some of their henchmen were in due course
executed, mainly on the advice of the erstwhile military commander
at An-ch'ing, Yang Chen-tsung, who went over to the Ch'ing and was
reinstated in his former post. Thus, ironically, the submission of the
Ming troops to the invaders was brought about by a representative of
the local elite whom they were supposed to be protecting, and by a
Ming general.

This course of events is in striking contrast to the heroic resistance
put up by some towns in the Yangtze delta regions, such as Chiang-
yin and Chia-ting, but is not greatly to be wondered at. Both the
local peasantry and the families of the local elite must by this time
have been utterly weary of protracted warfare and devastation, especially when it was carried out not by the rebels but by the armies of
their own generals. They must have longed to return to a state of
peace and normality, so that the surviving population could begin
once more to cultivate the overgrown fields, repair the dikes and thus
gradually restore the prosperity of the area. It is understandable,
therefore, that the representatives of the Ch'ing were welcomed as
the forces of law and order; it is claimed that once the unruly Ming
commanders had been arrested and the population calmed and reassured, it was possible to disband the pro-Ch'ing troops without a
shot having been fired.[48] In this part of Anhwei, unlike southern
Kiangsu (which had not suffered such devastation from internal
rebellion) there was subsequently very little sign of overt loyalist
resistance to the new dynasty. One or two sporadic risings by troops
calling themselves "righteous forces" did occur, notably in 1648

and 1649, but were easily suppressed owing to absence of popular support.[49] The way was thus open for rehabilitation and recovery which, as will be seen, took place fairly rapidly.

Nevertheless, there were a few manifestations of loyalism and cultural trauma among Tung-ch'eng's elite, in particular those idealists who had been members of the Fu-she or those who held important government posts in the final years of the Ming. For example, it is related that in 1644, when the news of the fall of Peking to Li Tzu-ch'eng reached T'ung-ch'eng, the people "joined in lamentation, unable to sleep or eat." Two of the scholars of the county, one a relative by marriage of Tso Kuang-tou, the other a *kung-sheng*, subsequently starved themselves to death.[50] These acts were quite exceptional, however, and were not so much anti-Ch'ing in motivation as expressions of ritualized loyalty to the fallen dynasty. No such demonstrations are recorded as having taken place when T'ung-ch'eng surrendred to the Manchu forces, and there is no mention anywhere of local reaction to the notorious edict of July 1645 that the people of China should henceforward conform in outward appearance to their conquerors by shaving the fronts of their heads and growing the queue. It was the hair-cutting edict, more than any other act, that has been considered to have symbolized utter submission to the barbarian regime, and to have engendered the desperate acts of resistance that occurred in Chiang-nan. The fact that in T'ung-ch'eng it appears to have provoked no violent opposition probably also indicates an easy acceptance of the new order of things.[51]

Among the thirty or so individuals who had joined the Fu-she, and who might have been expected to share some of the values and principles of those who carried on resistance to the Ch'ing elsewhere, only four, so far as is known, transformed feelings of loyalty to the southern Ming cause into direct action. The most famous was Fang I-chih, who had become a *chin-shih* in 1640 and tutor to one of the emperor's sons. After the fall of Peking he eventually managed to flee south to join the Ming regime at Nanking. Although forced to flee again when Ma Shih-ying and Juan Ta-ch'eng initiated a wholesale purge of Fu-she members (something that, as will be seen, discouraged many from following the Ming any further), he persisted in his support of the Ming cause and eventually in 1646 joined the prince of Kuei in Kwangtung. The following year he was dismissed

from office as vice-president of the Board of Rites and grand secretary, survived a brief period of capture by the Ch'ing, and ended
his life as a Buddhist monk.[52]

His brother-in-law Sun Lin, who seems to have had considerable
experience in the military campaigns of the late Ming, was equally
repelled by Juan and Ma's conduct of the government at Nanking.
Instead he joined the staff of the Ming general Yang Wen-ts'ung and
with him fought for the prince of T'ang, whose regime at Foochow
was finally crushed in October 1646. Sun and Yang died together at
the hands of the Manchus at P'u-ch'eng in Fukien.[53] Ch'ien Ping-
teng, a native of T'ung-ch'eng who had earlier been much influenced
by Fang I-chih and was a determined opponent of Juan Ta-ch'eng,
served in turn the prince of T'ang in Fukien and then the prince of
Kuei at Chao-ch'ing. Rather than follow the Yung-li court to Kwangsi
in 1650, however, he returned home with the help of a local Ch'ing
official from T'ung-ch'eng. He subsequently wrote much on the
history of this period.[54] The only other overt loyalist from T'ung-
ch'eng seems to have been Wu Te-ts'ao, a gifted poet and writer from
an eminent local family. After the fall of the Ming he traveled around
northeast China for a time and then also entered service with the
prince of Kuei in the southwest, but he died fairly soon somewhere
in Kwangtung or Kwangsi.[55]

There were at least eight other cases in which Fu-she members or
officials from T'ung-ch'eng retired ostentatiously into private life,
but there is not usually enough evidence to show whether they acted
out of principled antagonism to the new dynasty or from a more
complex variety of motives.[56] Only one of them, Sun I (the elder
brother of Sun Chin and Sun Lin) is known for certain to have been
offered and to have refused a government post. Another of the six,
Chiang Ch'en, seems to epitomize what may have been a prevailing
mood of realism and resignation. Having served for a brief spell in
the Board of Revenue in Peking, he too fled south to Nanking.
Yet, when requested by Shih K'o-fa to take up a military post with
his army, he merely sighed and said, "How can five wolves be kept
at bay with one sheep?" He then presented a few suggestions for the
conduct of the Ming campaigns and returned home forthwith to
T'ung-ch'eng.[57] Two others among the eight, Sun Lin's brother
Sun Chin (the former vice-president of the Board of War) and Fang

I-chih's father Fang K'ung-chao (superintendent of military settlements in Shantung and Chihli at the time of the fall of Peking),
abandoned or were forced out of the Nanking government because of
professed hatred for Ma Shih-ying and Juan Ta-ch'eng. But they took
no further loyalist action as far as we know, and probably also hoped
to enhance their chances of surviving the Ch'ing conquest by cutting
short their public and active manifestations of loyalism.[58]

Another pressing motive for retirement, which may also have
affected Sun Chin and Fang K'ung-chao, was not so much hatred of
the Manchus as the fear of Chinese political opponents who, in the
aftermath of the bitter factionalism that had characterized the late
Ming, might still be anxious to pay off old scores. This certainly
seems a probable explanation in the case of Yao Sun-fei, noted
earlier as having played an important role in the defense of T'ung-
ch'eng. At the end of the Ming he was serving as magistrate of Tung-
yang county in Chekiang, where he took steps to crush what he
considered to be an attempted rebellion by Hsü Tu, the local elite
organizer of an independent militia force.* Hsü Tu later was persuaded to surrender and was summarily executed, along with many
of his supporters, by another T'ung-ch'eng man, Tso Kuang-tou's
brother Tso Kuang-hsien, in his capacity as regional inspector of
Chekiang. Tso, as one who was passionately identified with the
Tung-lin faction, subsequently opposed Ma Shih-ying's efforts to
promote Juan Ta-ch'eng to major office at the Nanking court; he was
then arrested by Juan on charges of sedition in connection with the
Hsü Tu incident, but managed to escape. An attempt was made to
bribe Yao Sun-fei to withdraw his support from Tso; when it failed
he too was imprisoned and was only freed when the Ch'ing took
Nanking. He then returned home to T'ung-ch'eng where he lived for
nearly twenty years as a respected and influential member of the
community, on good terms with the local magistrate and doing all he
could to promote his family's and lineage's interests.[59] To judge
from Jerry Dennerline's unraveling of the complex issues involved in
the Hsü Tu incident, Yao Sun-fei was widely held in Chiang-nan to
have acted dishonorably and treacherously in this affair, and may
well have been too afraid of reprisals to remain any longer in govern-

*Hsü Tu's militia is discussed in detail in Jerry Dennerline's essay (pp. 89–132 above)

ment, even under the Ch'ing. At all events, the episode gives a further hint of the labyrinthine intricacies of politics in this period and the historiographical biases which make it so difficult to attribute motives with confidence.

Overall, however, collaboration seems to have been more common in T'ung-ch'eng than retirement. Even among those associated with the Fu-she group, at least eleven (including one of Tso Kuang-tou's sons and one of Fang I-chih's) passed examinations or held office under the new dynasty.[60] The most striking case of this type occurred in the Chang family, which had earlier, in 1639, provided a noted martyr to the Ming cause, Chang Ping-i's brother Chang Ping-wen, who died defending the city of Chi-nan in Shantung against a Manchu raiding force led by Dorgon himself. This did not prevent their cousin Chang Ping-chen, governor of Chekiang at the end of the Ming, from going over to the Ch'ing in 1645 and rising ten years later to become president of the Board of War.[61] Chang Ping-i himself did all he could to promote the entry of his sons, especially Chang Ying, into official careers under the Ch'ing.

A glance at the county's lists of candidates successful in the *chü-jen* and *chin-shih* examinations in the early Ch'ing instantly confirms that among the important local elite families this attitude of cooperation prevailed.[62] The lists from the very beginning are thickly crowded with the names of all those who had been powerful and influential before the change of dynasty—notably Fang, Yao, Chang, Wu, Sun, Tso, Ma, Tai, and others. Some, particularly of the Changs and Yaos, and to a lesser extent, Fangs, were destined for great eminence in office. A man like Chang Ping-i's son Chang Ying (*chin-shih* 1667), who rose by the end of his career to become Hanlin chancellor, president of the Board of Rites, grand secretary, and trusted confidant of the K'ang-hsi emperor, might indeed be said to typify the "confident new men" of the K'ang-hsi era.[63] Clearly the elite families who had been prominent before the conquest were determined to remain so afterwards. Success in the higher examinations was one certain means of maintaining social position, and evidently few were willing to compromise their chances of continued local eminence for the dubious moral benefits of loyalty to a defunct dynasty. This general preference for expediency over strict moral principle among T'ung-ch'eng's elite may indeed be one reason why

the events of the actual transition to Ch'ing rule are very much
played down in all available local records.

To understand the real aims and interests of the elite in the aftermath of the transition, it is necessary to investigate their activities on
the local scene as opposed to the stance they took on issues of national politics. This reveals some of the ways in which they attempted
to entrench themselves in their previous position and maintain good
relations and influence with the local authorities, at the same time
moderating the behavior that had brought about such extreme social
antagonism and terrifying violence in the county in the late Ming.

First of all, it was evidently quite easy for the members of elite
families who had fled down the Yangtze or taken refuge in the
county city to recover their personal and lineage landholdings, the
foundation of their local wealth and power, once the area was finally
pacified; possibly they were even able to extend them to include the
property of deceased neighbors. Members of the Hu family, who had
spent the years of the revolts in Nanking, afford one example of this;
one of them was delighted to discover that his holdings had prac-
tically escaped the disasters.[64] This phenomenon may not be as
remarkable as it seems, given the basic, underlying attitude of deference to landlord rights and fear of landlord power that seems to
have persisted in many parts of rural China well into the twentieth
century.[65] Chang Ying himself, in a famous treatise on investment in
land, written at the end of the seventeenth century, emphasized that
it was the only type of property that would survive wars and rebellions, and summed up what had evidently been his own family's
experience: "Even if people should have to leave their homes because
of the ravages of war or rebellion, once things have quieted down
they will return. There may be nothing worth mentioning left of
their houses and stores, yet the plot of land that belonged to the
Chang family will still belong to the Changs . . . . When the wilder-
ness has been cut down and the land reopened to cultivation they
will still be as prosperous as before."[66]

The Changs, and probably many others like them, seem, moreover,
to have employed a strategy for survival characteristic of the Chinese
elite in emergencies—that of sending some members away to safety
while leaving others behind to safeguard the family interests as best
they could. Chang Ying's father, Chang Ping-i, in 1635 had taken his

children to the Nanking area, but returned the following year and remained in T'ung-ch'eng throughout the worst of the crisis. It is quite
certain that those of the Changs who had gone to Nanking did recover their property on their return. Though the land registers were
stated to be "in confusion," those relating to the Chang holdings
(which were mostly in the same district) were sorted out with help
from another member of Chang Ping-i's generation, Chang Ping-
ch'ien, who was evidently better versed than some of his kinsmen in
the complexities of land registration and taxation.[67] In general, the
references to the recovery of property in this way are so casual as to
suggest that it was taken for granted.

The surviving peasantry must have returned with equal alacrity to
their holdings, for economic recovery was remarkably rapid. It was
aided by fairly generous tax remissions; between 1645 and 1647
roughly one-third of the registered cultivated acreage in the county
was granted exemption. In the following fifteen years there were
successive reports that varying amounts of this had been returned to
cultivation, until in 1663 the total corresponded to the original Ming
figure for taxable acreage. The population was said to have been de-
creased (through death or flight) by as much as half in the course of
the revolts, something that may in itself have provided favorable
economic opportunities for the survivors, but by 1672 the official
population totals were also back to what they had been in the late
Ming.[68]

By the 1660s the county's former prosperity was definitely re-
viving. In 1659 a major irrigation system to the south of the county
city (which had probably been damaged during the fighting) was
extended on the orders of the magistrate, and a few years later was
further repaired and overhauled. Recovery was aided by favorable
weather conditions and good harvests; after 1647 there were no
major droughts until 1671–72 and grain supplies were abundant.[69]
Trade also revived quickly. The market-town of K'ung-ch'eng in the
northeast of the county had been so severely damaged by the revolts that commercial activity virtually ceased there, but some years
later it appears that "the brokers and peddlers there were becoming
prosperous; over five hundred trading households settled there, and
K'ung-ch'eng again became an important town."[70] In the 1670s
and 1680s, when a new edition of the gazetteer was compiled, its

descriptions attest that economic activity in the county was thriving and growing, almost as if the revolts had never happened.

The administrative measures of the new regime and the reactions of the local elite to them were too complex and too ramified to permit detailed discussion here, but a few examples will be given to try and test the hypothesis that the Ch'ing may have attempted in T'ung-ch'eng a rationalization and streamlining of local government that had been impossible in the Ming. The most important sphere of local administration was of course the fiscal one. In one respect at least, the Ch'ing were anxious to make no changes that would alienate local opinion, for, in T'ung-cheng as elsewhere, the land-taxes (once the exemptions had been ended) appear to have been imposed at the same rates as in the late Ming, before the surcharges of the seventeenth century. They were raised only once, but very slightly, in 1671. The Ming system of land classification and *mou* conversion was likewise adhered to, save for very minor adjustments, and once the total acreage in 1663 reached the late Ming figure of 410,061 *mou,* no further increases were registered. (But land registration did occasion some conflict, as will be explained below.) The county's total number of *ting* or fiscal individuals (here levied on acreage, at a rate of approximately one *ting* per 50 *mou*) was likewise never allowed to rise much higher than the late Ming figure.[71]

The Ch'ing government's willingness to placate the local elite by maintaining the fiscal status quo was, however, qualified in at least one respect. Though the tax quotas were in effect rather modest, it was essential to the survival of the new regime that the taxes actually be collected, in other words, that some way be found to check the elite's selfish and disruptive exploitation of excessive tax privileges and the resulting huge tax arrears that, between them, had drastically eroded the foundations of the Ming fiscal system and helped bring about social chaos at the end ot the dynasty, above all in Chiang-nan.[72] This was surely the reason for the abrupt change in the laws of tax exemption, an act which so far has not received the attention it deserves. In 1657 the former generous scale of exemptions allowed to officials and degree-holders was abolished. Henceforward they were to be permitted no exemptions whatsoever from the service levy assessed on land, and when it came to labor service they were to be granted a personal exemption of only one *ting* each, a privilege that was not to be extended to any family members. This limitation applied also in the case of exemption from *ting* assessed on land.[73]

It is still hard to gauge with certainty the effects of these reductions in the legal exemption rates, but it is surely no coincidence that soon afterward serious efforts were made to enforce the cooperation of the elite in the matter of tax payment. These culminated in the celebrated Chiang-nan tax clearance case of 1661, when over 13,000 degree-holders and officials and 240 yamen employees were investigated for tax default and subsequently punished by dismissal, deprivation of degrees and titles, confiscation, imprisonment, and flogging.[74] At least one similar case (albeit on a much lesser scale) has come to light in northern Anhwei, and there is some indication that similar methods may on occasion have been resorted to in T'ung-ch'eng itself.[75] Clearly, much more research needs to be done, particularly on the purely fiscal (as opposed to the political) implications of the Chiang-nan tax case itself, if we are ever to have a more accurate picture of early Ch'ing taxation policies and their consequences. One fact that does emerge from all the writings on this tangled subject is that although in many areas of China, even in the mid-Ch'ing, the "gentry" did in practice often pay somewhat lower rates of land-tax (and could still take advantage of their status to reduce or defer payments) the extent of this de facto privilege varied widely, depending on the district and the attitude of the local authorities.[76] From the data available for T'ung-ch'eng, it does appear that official fiscal privileges for the elite *were* effectively reduced, especially after 1728, when even the *ting* charge was merged with the regular land-tax.[77]

One may therefore hypothesize that this change in T'ung-ch'eng, following on the traumatic shock of the late Ming uprisings, may indeed have induced a somewhat chastened mood in the local elite, helped to reduce their blatant exploitation of excessive privilege and protection of relatives that had helped to bring about the revolts, and to convince them that a slightly greater degree of cooperation in the matter of tax payments was probably in their own long-term interest. It appears that the elite in the Ch'ing did not venture to set themselves apart so obviously and so arrogantly from the mass of the population;[78] other reasons for this will be suggested below, in connection with the further development of lineage organizations here in the early Ch'ing.

Although in the matter of ceding most of their earlier tax exemption privileges the elite may have been forced, or have seen reason, to compromise with the Ch'ing authorities, when it came to other proposed fiscal reforms they showed themselves far from powerless in defending their own interests. A case in point is the local reaction to the national land survey proposed by the Board of Revenue in 1663, out of the no doubt justified conviction that long-standing inaccuracies in the registration of land and *ting,* combined with deliberate perversion of the registers by gentry and clerks, were largely responsible for continuing tax arrears.[79] This would have meant drawing up new and accurate "fish-scale" registers, as had been done at the beginning of the Ming dynasty, a procedure that threatened to reveal much unregistered land and expose many malpractices.

To avert this alarming prospect, the T'ung-ch'eng elite resorted to the subtle tactic of having one of their currently most prestigious members, Yao Sun-fei's son, Yao Wen-jan (at home in temporary retirement from his post of junior metropolitan censor in Peking), make persuasive representations to the provincial authorities. He argued that the whole project should simply be abandoned on grounds of expense. The cost of surveying and making new registers for T'ung-ch'eng alone would come to over 2,000 taels, and would be vastly greater if the survey were carried out on a province-wide scale. He subsequently "discussed" the matter with the magistrate, and ensured that the Ming system of land classification and registration was adhered to unchanged; in fact, with one very minor exception, no increases in acreage were registered in the county thereafter, and no further attempts were made to revise the grading of land.[80] Yao's intervention may have had wider repercussions, for in 1665 the governor of Anhwei, Chang Ch'ao-chen, memorialized the throne with a request to abandon the survey entirely, arguing in terms too strikingly similar to Yao Wen-jan's to be coincidental.[81]

The new regime was thus effectively prevented, in T'ung-ch'eng as elsewhere, from starting out with a comprehensive and relatively accurate survey of taxable land as the Ming had done, and from thereby broadening its fiscal base at the outset. It therefore seems reasonable to view early Ch'ing administrative innovations, in T'ung-ch'eng at least, as not so much a comprehensive and streamlined program of local government reform as a series of pragmatic adjustments and compromises. These were designed to secure the minimal concessions regarded as indispensable to stable social order and sound governmental finances, at the same time avoiding any disastrous clashes with local opinion and interests, even if this meant abandoning reform plans on occasion.

Apparently the local elite in this part of China were by now so firmly entrenched that sweeping action in total disregard of their interests, such as had been undertaken by Ming T'ai-tsu in the late fourteenth century, was simply no longer possible. At the same time, it appears that in order to secure these interests they resorted less to factional allegiances, as in the late Ming period, and more to the direct exploitation of personal patronage and influence within the central and provincial governments. This conclusion accords with the impression of many scholars working on the transition period, that the "horizontal" politics of the local elite in the late Ming began, in the Ch'ing, to give way once more to the "vertical" politics of direct exercise of central power and patronage.[82]

If this is true, it helps also to explain the increasing assiduity with which T'ung-ch'eng's elite families continued to compete for examination success and office, the obvious means of direct access to, or at least contact with, power and patronage. Yet although many of the families that had risen to prominence in the second half of the Ming continued to be eminent or rose to even greater heights in the Ch'ing dynasty, it should not be imagined that they had survived the upheavals of the seventeenth century without damage. The revolts worsened the already disturbed situation in T'ung-ch'eng by disrupting social relationships there for over ten years and decimating the membership of many important families. As one later genealogy put it, entire households had been massacred or had died of disease, "so that the lineage was barely saved from extinction"; even thirty years later some of the survivors were unable to name their ancestors and degree of kinship to one another.[83] Moreover, the embryonic lineage organizations which some of them had begun to create in the late Ming were in most cases also shattered in the 1630s and 1640s. What little land they had went out of cultivation or was illicitly sold off, ancestral shrines were destroyed, and handwritten genealogies lost.

It was obviously imperative for the surviving members of elite families to find some means both of reasserting their threatened position in the locality and of alleviating the social hostility that had led

to the uprisings. Part of the solution seems to have been to rebuild
earlier lineage organizations on a firmer basis or to commence them
where they did not already exist; very many kinship groups can be
observed doing this in the aftermath of the revolts, sometimes as
early at the 1650s and 1660s. Though the ostensible reasons for this
may have been to renew proper kinship ties and make possible the
continued veneration of common ancestors, one may hypothesize
that the underlying motive was to enhance the proper hierarchical
relationships and tighten control over unruly members, as well as to
promote friendly feelings among kinsmen of very different social and
economic standing, and to help ensure better relationships between
different kinship groups.

Numerous positive measures were necessary if all these aims were
to be achieved.[84] One of the most basic was to trace the lineages'
scattered members and to recompile their genealogies; in addition,
many genealogies were for the first time printed, as an insurance
against loss. Both the Yaos and the Changs carried this out in the
early 1660s, at the instigation of Yao Sun-fei and Chang Ping-i
respectively (though most of the work on the Chang genealogy was
done by Chang Ying). In addition, land had to be recovered and put
under more systematic management; in the Chang lineage this was
done by Chang Ping-i who, it was noted earlier, had stayed in T'ung-
ch'eng through the revolts, presumably to try and safeguard the
family interests. Ancestral halls were repaired, rebuilt, or constructed
for the first time.[85]

It was at this time, too, that many lineages felt the need to compile
detailed rules, both for the management of property and the control
of members. The Yaos in 1657 instituted an exceptionally severe set
of regulations dealing with the proper care and maintenance of all
tomb areas, following the discovery that in 1642, during the chaos of
the revolts, one unworthy member had violated all rules of filial and
ancestral piety by secretly burying his father next to the hallowed
grave of an early lineage ancestor.[86] The Chous of Yao-shih were
greatly troubled in the post-rebellion period and possibly earlier by
the lax and disrespectful conduct of their younger members, and
feared that it would in time endanger and shame the whole group.
Accordingly, in 1661 their elders drew up a set of formal family
regulations (*chia-kuei*) and at the same time appointed branch heads
to enforce them. Recalcitrant members were to be reported to the

elders in the ancestral hall for punishment and, if that failed, to the local authorities.[87]

One of the remarkable features of T'ung-ch'eng's lineage rules is in fact their generally strict and comprehensive nature, especially with regard to matters like tax abuses and evasion, the avoidance of litigation, the need to control servants so as to prevent them from damaging a family's good name, the decent treatment of tenants, and the provision of aid to members in distress.[88] Such concerns must surely have been enhanced by memory of the conflicts in the county during and before the strife-torn period of the revolts. There can be little doubt that it was the social crisis of the transition era, as well as competition for local prestige and influence, that greatly stimulated and speeded up the formation of lineage organizations in the early Ch'ing. Their usefulness as instruments of social control must have been enhanced during the eighteenth and nineteenth centuries, when population increased out of all proportion to the resources of local administration. This fact was consciously recognized in neighboring Huai-ning county (An-ch'ing), whose gazetteer describes the ways in which the lineages there promoted good behavior and mutual welfare in the eighteenth century.[89]

The other most striking feature of the rules of T'ung-ch'eng lineages is their emphasis on the pursuit of socially respectable occupations, and in particular on the value of education, as the way, if not always to office, at least to elite status and social esteem. Many began to devote a substantial part of the income from their joint landholdings to educational purposes and, to judge from the county's outstanding number of successes in *chü-jen* and *chin-shih* examinations in the second half of the seventeenth and in the eighteenth century, the elite's competitive and aggressive energies, manifested in more overt ways in the late Ming, were now channeled more exclusively into competition for academic advancement.[90]

As was already mentioned, many of the same families who had first become prominent in the sixteenth century or earlier, experienced remarkable academic and official success in the first half of the Ch'ing. Most dazzling of all were the Changs. The career of Chang Ping-i's son, Chang Ying, has already been outlined. His own son, Chang T'ing-yü (1672–1755), did even better, becoming one of the first and most influential members of the Grand Council, and probably one of the most powerful Chinese ministers of the entire dynasty.[91] Their relatives by marriage, the Yaos, never attained such heights, but still produced some notable men, including a president of the Board of Punishments, Yao Wen-jan (1621–78), and the scholar and philosopher Yao Nai (1732–1815).[92] Though their tenure of high office could not last indefinitely, there is abundant evidence to show that they, and other families of lesser distinction, used their advantages (foremost among which was patronage) very well while they had them. They were often able by these means, and by continuing to build up their lineage organizations, to establish their position securely in their home locality right down to the end of the dynasty and well into the republic.[93]

There is little doubt that the foundations of these achievements were being consolidated throughout the seventeenth century, regardless of war and conquest. All the evidence indicates that the social fabric of the county was already so strongly woven by the end of the Ming dynasty that not even violent disturbances were able to tear it apart, nor to change the course of social development in any really fundamental way. This basic cohesion did facilitate rapid recovery after the revolts but by the same token seems to have made it virtually impossible to carry out any sweeping and immediate rationalization of local administration that might clash drastically with elite interests. The case of T'ung-ch'eng demonstrates vividly the extent to which the social order in the Ming and early Ch'ing was becoming stabilized and developing resilience against outside shocks and disturbances, a quality that was to be demonstrated even more strikingly in the nineteenth century.

With regard to the actual Ch'ing conquest, its impact seems to have been rather slight as compared to that of the revolts of the 1630s and 1640s. It was these, in fact, which probably facilitated acceptance of the Ch'ing government as the only alternative to prolonged chaos. Though some individuals did show signs of loyalty to the Ming cause, they were very few in number. Most of the elite, even those in office, undoubtedly put local, family interests and the maintenance of their position and prestige a long way above the abstract notion of loyalty to a fallen dynasty or to a few outward symbols of Chinese cultural identity. If the new regime was prepared to refrain from sweeping attempts to alter the local status quo, and to maintain through the

examination system the same channels of social advancement as
had the Ming, then it could be accepted without too much heart-
searching. The elite of T'ung-ch'eng, when it came to a political and
moral crisis, showed themselves in the main to be hard-headed men
of the world rather than passionate idealists.

NOTES TO CHAPTER 7

Abbreviations

FSHSCL	Wu Shan-chia, Fu-she hsing-shih chuan-lüeh
HC	-hsien-chih
MS	Ming Shih
STP	-shih tsung-p'u / -shih tsu-p'u
TCHC	T'ung-ch'eng hsien-chih

Numbers in parentheses after genealogies refer to listings in Taga Akigoro,
Sofū no kenkyū (Tokyo, 1960). Those beginning with T. are genealogies in
Japanese libraries, and are to be found on pp. 80–186. Numbers beginning with
C. refer to those in Columbia University East Asian Library, which are listed on
pp. 370–450.

1. The two most important Western studies on these acts of resistance to date
are Frederic Wakeman, Jr., "Localism and Loyalism during the Ch'ing conquest
of Chiang-nan: The Tragedy of Chiang-yin," in Frederic Wakeman, Jr., and
Carolyn Grant, eds., Conflict and Control in Late Imperial China (Berkeley,
1975); and Jerry Dennerline, "The Mandarins and the Massacre of Chia-ting: An
Analysis of the Local Heritage and the Resistance to the Manchu Invasion in
1645" (Ph.D. diss., Yale University, 1973). Detailed references to the Chinese
sources on the subject will be found therein. A translation of the famous account
of the massacre at Yang-chou by Lucien Mao is given in T'ien-hsia Monthly
(1937), pp. 515–37.

2. In general I prefer to avoid the term gentry, with its almost automatic
connotations of officials and degree-holders, and use instead local elite. My research on T'ung-ch'eng shows that the social elite there was a broader, less
distinctly defined group based on wealth, education, kinship and marriage ties,
as well as official titles. For detailed discussion, see my Land and Lineage in
China: A Study of T'ung-ch'eng county, Anhwei, in the Ming and Ch'ing Dynasties (Cambridge, forthcoming, especially chaps. 2, 4, and 5.

3. The greater part of the evidence for this paper has to be drawn from the
county gazetteer TCHC (of which there are three main editions, dated 1490, 1696,
and 1827; the last reprints Tai Ming-shih's account of the seventeenth-century
revolts); Ma Ch'i-ch'ang's T'ung-ch'eng ch'i-chiu chuan (1911; reprinted, Taipei,
1969); and some genealogies of local lineages, supplemented where possible with
the standard sources for the period.

4. The account of T'ung-ch'eng's social history which follows comes mainly from the local gazetteers and is discussed in far greater detail in chap. 2 of Beattie, *Land and Lineage in China.*

5. Almost all the lineages of T'ung-ch'eng record in their genealogies that their "first ancestor" moved to the area in the Yuan-Ming transition period.

6. It should be noted that despite commercialization there were apparently no great merchant families among the T'ung-ch'eng elite. Most local wealth was basically derived from landowning, sale of rent grain, and usury. For another sixteenth-century case of local wealth being translated into education, see E. S. Rawski, *Agricultural Change and the Peasant Economy of South China* (Cambridge, Mass., 1972), pp. 88–94.

7. See the lists of the county's examination results in *TCHC* (1827), chap. 7. The relationship of individuals with the same surname to each other can be corroborated from their genealogies or, in the case of the Fangs (for whom no genealogy is available), from the biographies given in Ma Ch'i-ch'ang's work. The concentration of Changs and Fangs among T'ung-ch'eng's officials in the Ming has been noted by James Parsons, "The Ming Dynasty Bureaucracy: Aspects of Background Forces," in C. O. Hucker, ed., *Chinese Government in Ming Times* (New York, 1969), pp. 212–13.

8. *Yao STP* (T.428), first preface; Ma Ch'i-ch'ang, 4.1a–2a. For more detail, see Beattie, *Land and Lineage in China,* chap. 4.

9. *TCHC* (1696), 2, *feng-su,* 3a.

10. Ibid., 1, *ch'eng-chih,* 2a–b; *TCHC* (1827), 9.6b–7a.

11. Ma Ch'i-ch'ang, 4.1a–2a. The works in question are *T'ung-i chi hsü* and *Erh-hsün* (both reprinted 1883).

12. Ma Ch'i-ch'ang, 4.20b. On Fang K'ung-chao, see ibid., 5.18a, and *MS* (reprinted, Taipei, 1962), 260.2953. On his relative, the censor Fang Ta-jen (a friend of Tso Kuang-tou who was also involved in the affair), and on Tso Kuang-tou himself, see Charles O. Hucker, *The Censorial System of Ming China* (Stanford, 1966), pp. 199, 281–85, and passim. Another local casualty, who seems to have been connected with these last two, was Wu Yung-hsien (a commander in the Liao-tung campaigns), on whom see Ma Ch'i-ch'ang, 4.18a–19a. Ma gives accounts of all these persons in chaps. 4 and 5.

13. Most of the T'ung-ch'eng participants in the Fu-she are listed, in some cases with brief biographical notes, in chap. 4 of Wu Shan-chia's *Fu-she hsing-shih chuan-lüeh* (1831; reprinted Hangchow, 1961). Other names have been culled from the K'ang-hsi edition of the *Fu-she hsing-shih* (Rare Books of the National Library of Peking, no. 562, microfilm), Lu Shih-i's *Fu-she chi-lüeh,* and the list of signatories to the 1639 petition to have Juan Ta-ch'eng driven from Nanking. The most important of these persons have entries in Ma Ch'i-ch'ang, chap. 6. For these references on the Fu-she, I am indebted to Jerry Dennerline. T'ung-ch'eng does not, however, with the possible exception of Fang I-chih, appear to have provided any of the most important leaders of the movement, on which see the detailed account by William S. Atwell, "From Education to Politics: the Fu-she," in de Bary, ed., *The Unfolding of Neo-Confucianism,* pp. 333–67.

14. This can be seen in the bitter factionalism that continued to the very end of the Ming and was carried over into the southern Ming courts long after the original issues were dead; see references, later in this essay, to the T'ung-ch'eng elite's continued hostility to Juan Ta-ch'eng, and also contributions elsewhere in this volume by Frederic Wakeman, Jerry Dennerline, and Ian McMorran.

15. *TCHC* (1696), 2, *feng-su,* 3a–b.

16. *TCHC* (1827), 23.11b. This account (apart from some deletions at the beginning and end) is virtually the same as Tai Ming-shih's *Chieh-i lu,* which forms ch. 14 of his collected works, *Nan-shan chi* (reprinted, Taipei, 1970). The term "serf" is not an ideal translation of *nu-p'u* (since the latter were certainly not equivalent to medieval European serfs), but it is hard to find a better term that still preserves the distinction between *nu-p'u* and free tenants.

17. The most useful accounts of agrarian unrest in the Ming and of the revolts in central and south China are still probably those given by Fu I-ling, especially in *Ming-tai Chiang-nan shih-min ching-chi shih-t'an* (Shanghai, 1957), and *Ming-Ch'ing nung-ts'un she-hui ching-chi* (Peking, 1961). A succinct but controversial version of the social implications of these events is given by Mark Elvin in *The Pattern of the Chinese Past* (Stanford, 1973), chaps. 6, 15. In this paper it is unfortunately impossible to investigate in detail the effects of commercialization and rebellion on the status of serfs and tenants, and on their relations with landlords, as there is simply very little evidence for T'ung-ch'eng. All that can be said is that agricultural serfdom does appear to have died out in T'ung-ch'eng, as in other parts of Chiang-nan, by the eighteenth century.

18. Chao I, *Nien-erh shih cha-chi* (*SPPY* ed.), 34.13a–14b. The gazetteer of neighboring Huai-ning county makes it clear that similar extravagance and competition between great families were arising there at the very end of the Ming; see Huai-ning *HC* (1915), 10.1b.

19. *Ta-Ming hui-tien* (1587), 20.19b. *Ting* originally, in theory, signified an adult male liable for the performance of labor service, but as Ho Ping-ti has shown (*Studies on the Population of China, 1368–1953* [Cambridge, Mass., 1959], chap. 2), came increasingly to be used as an abstract unit of taxation levied on households on the basis of property ownership. In T'ung-ch'eng after the Single Whip reform in the 1560s, one *ting* was assessed as 50 *mou* of land.

20. *Yao STP* (T.428), 1.8a–9a; ibid., *hsien-te chuan,* 1.3a–b.

21. *TCHC* (1696), 2, *t'ien-fu,* 36a–42b. A detailed account of this whole episode is given in Beattie, *Land and Lineage in China,* chap. 3. On Ming methods of converting actual to fiscal *mou* for tax purposes, see Ho Ping-ti, *Studies on the Population of China,* chap. 6.

22. On the surcharges, see Ray Huang, "Fiscal Administration during the Ming Dynasty," in Hucker, ed., *Chinese Government in Ming Times,* p. 118.

23. *Tso STP,* (T.126), 2, *chia-hsün,* 11b–13a.

24. *TCHC* (1827), 23.11b, states, following Tai Ming-shih, that the first uprising occurred in the eighth month of that year (Ch'ung-chen 7), whereas the Tso rules are dated in the ninth month, though they could have been in preparation earlier.

25. This version of events comes from a work entitled *T'ung-pien jih-lu,* "A diary of the revolts in T'ung-ch'eng," by the local scholar and Fu-she member Chiang Ch'en, one of whose works was proscribed in the Ch'ing. (A list of T'ung-ch'eng writers who suffered this fate, several of them Tung-lin or Fu-she sympathizers, is given by Yao Ying in his *Shih-hsiao-lu,* 5.25a–26a, in his collected works, *Chung-fu t'ang ch'üan-chi,* 1867.) His account, which appears to be more detailed in some respects than the others available, has not yet been located in any Japanese or Western library but is quoted by Fu I-ling, *Ming-Ch'ing nung-ts'un she-hui ching-chi,* p. 98

26. *Tai STP* (T.1136), 22.33b; Ma Ch'i-ch'ang, 5.21a.

27. *TCHC* (1827), 23.11b.

28. Ibid, 23.13b; 9.9a.

29. Ma Ch'i-ch'ang, 3.17a; 8.26a; *Chang STP* (T.656), 27.6a.

30. *Chang STP* (T.656), 26.14b–15a.

31. *TCHC* (1696), 5, *chung-chieh,* 6b.

32. Ibid., 5, *chung-chieh, wu-pei;* Ma Ch'i-ch'ang, 6.9b–11b.

33. Tai Ming-shih, "Chieh-i-lu tzu-hsü," in *Nan-shan-chi,* 2.35a–b.

34. Ma Ch'i-ch'ang, 5.18a; 6.13b; *Chang STP* (T.656), 26.13a–14a, 28a–b; *Yao STP* (T.428), *hsien-te chuan,* 2.19a, 8a ff.

35. Ma Ch'i-ch'ang, 6.19a–b. The names of one or two other defenders are also mentioned here, though nothing more is known of them.

36. *Chang STP* (T.656), 26.23b; *TCHC* (1827), 23.20b.

37. On Chang Kuo-wei and his concern for T'ung-ch'eng's defense, see *MS* 276.3099–3100; also Arthur W. Hummel, ed., *Eminent Chinese of the Ch'ing Period* (Washington, D.C., 1943–44), p. 180. For Sun Chin's request and the response to it, see *TCHC* (1827), 23.12a–b; Ma Ch'i-ch'ang, 5.24b–26b.

38. Ma Ch'i-ch'ang, 6.13b.

39. *TCHC* (1827), 23.18b.

40. Ma Ch'i-ch'ang, 6.5a, 11a.

41. *TCHC* (1827), 23.18a. On imperial resistance to the formation of local militia, see Frederic Wakeman, Jr., "Localism and Loyalism," pp. 49–53. He also notes that in Chiang-yin local defense efforts were kept firmly in the hands of the *tien-shih* precisely because he did not have local ties. When in 1644 a memorial was sent to the emperor urging him to allow the formation of gentry militia, T'ung-ch'eng was cited as one of the places where this was being done, by the *sheng-yuan* Chou Ch'i, but I have found no direct confirmation of his role in such efforts.

42. *TCHC* (1827), 23.18b–19b; *TCHC* (1696), 1, *hsiang-i,* 11a.

43. *TCHC* (1827), 23.17a, 21a–b. The request to Kuang Shih-heng is described by Ma Ch'i-ch'ang, 5.27b. Ma, incidentally, is anxious to defend Kuang from the charge of collaboration with Li Tzu-ch'eng after the fall of Peking; see Wakeman, chapter 2 of this volume.

44. Most of the details in the account of the fall of T'ung-ch'eng given in this section are drawn from Tai Ming-shih's *Chieh-i-lu,* pp. 21b–23b.

45. Hummel, *Eminent Chinese,* pp. 558, 398–99. For a detailed account of Juan

Ta-ch'eng's career, see Robert B. Crawford, "The Biography of Juan Ta-ch'eng," *Chinese Culture* 6, no. 2 (March 1965): 28–105.

46. Hsieh Kuo-chen, *Ming-Ch'ing chih-chi tang-she yun-tung k'ao* (Taipei, 1967), pp. 172–73. A Fu-she member from T'ung-ch'eng, Ch'ien Ping-teng (Ch'eng-chih), had been tempted to join Juan's new society but was dissuaded by Fang I-chih; this move apparently crystallized local opinion against it. Ch'ien continued to be an active opponent of Juan and, as will be seen, was one of the very few Fu-she members from T'ung-ch'eng who later served any of the southern Ming courts.

47. Ma Ch'i-ch'ang, 6.19a–b.

48. *TCHC* (1696), 5, *wu-pei*, 5a.

49. Ibid., and Tai Ming-shih, *Chieh-i-lu*, p. 23b.

50. Tai Ming-shih, *Chieh-i-lu*, p. 21b; Ma Ch'i-ch'ang, 6.9b.

51. Cf. Wakeman, "Localism and Loyalism," pp. 58–60.

52. Hummel, *Eminent Chinese*, pp. 232–33; Ma Ch'i-ch'ang, 6.15b–17b. On Fang I-chih's later years, see Yü Ying-shih, *Fang I-chih wan-chieh k'ao* (Hong Kong, 1972).

53. *FSHSCL*, 4.16b–17a; Ma Ch'i-ch'ang, 6.5a–7a; *MS*, 277.3115.

54. See note 46 above, and also Lynn Struve, "Uses of History in Traditional Chinese Society: The Southern Ming in Traditional Chinese Historiography" (Ph.D. diss., University of Michigan, 1974), p. 73;

55. *FSHSCL*, 4.16b; Ma Ch'i-ch'ang, 6.17b–18a.

56. *FSHSCL*, ch. 4, lists most of these.

57. Ibid., 4.14b–15a; Ma Ch'i-ch'ang, 6.20a–22b, 5.26a.

58. Ma Ch'i-ch'ang, 5.24b–26b; 19a; *MS* 260.2954.

59. Ma Ch'i-ch'ang, 5.22a–b; 6.13b–15b. Yao Sun-fei's collected works were among those proscribed in the eighteenth century (see n.25 above); his son Yao Wen-jan, however, rose to become a president of the Board of Punishments under the Ch'ing. See *Ch'ing-shih* (reprinted, Taipei, 1961), 264.3896–97, and note 80 below.

60. Tso Kuang-tou's third son, Tso Kuo-lin, became a *chü-jen* in 1645 and eventually a subprefect in Honan; Ma Ch'i-ch'ang, 6.12b–13a. Fang I-chih's second son, Fang Chung-t'ung, became a subprefect; ibid., 7.29b–31b.

61. *TCHC* (1696), 5, *chung-chieh*, 4a–b; ibid., 4, *shih-hsü*, 57b–58a; *Chang STP* (T.656), 26.28a–b.

62. *TCHC* (1827), ch. 7. I have checked that in the majority of cases persons with the same names were related to each other.

63. A very brief outline of his remarkable career is given in Hummel, *Eminent Chinese*, pp. 64–65. See also Jonathan D. Spence, *Ts'ao Yin and the K'ang-hsi Emperor* (New Haven, Conn., 1966), pp. 141–44.

64. Ma Ch'i-ch'ang, 3.17a.

65. For twentieth-century examples, see: Fei Hsiao-t'ung, *Peasant Life in China* (London, 1939), p. 189; Mark Selden, *The Yenan Way in Revolutionary China* (Cambridge, Mass., 1971), pp. 48, 59–60; and William Hinton, *Fanshen* (New York, 1966), pp. 112–16 and passim.

66. Chang Ying, *Heng-ch'an so-yen* [Notes on real estate], *Ts'ung-shu chi-ch'eng* ed., p. 3. A complete, annotated translation is given in Appendix C of Beattie, *Land and Lineage in China.*

67. *Chang STP* (T.656), 27.6a; 26.33a–b.

68. *TCHC* (1827), 2.1aff.; *TCHC* (1696), 2.2a–3a.

69. *TCHC* (1696), 1, *shui-li,* 17b; ibid., 1, *hsiang-i,* 11a–13a.

70. Ma Ch'i-ch'ang, 6.19a.

71. *TCHC* (1696), 2, *t'ien-fu,* 5a–8b; 20b–21b; 36aff.

72. For an analysis of late Ming fiscal problems, showing in particular the government's inability to expand its fiscal base so as to keep pace with rising population and productivity, and to check tax evasion and arrears, see Ray Huang, "Fiscal Administration during the Ming Dynasty," especially pp. 112–28, and *Taxation and Governmental Finance in Sixteenth Century Ming China* (Cambridge, 1974), passim. Wang Yeh-chien, in *Land Taxation in Imperial China, 1750–1911* (Cambridge, Mass., 1973), pp. 9ff., also shows that the Ch'ing were unable to make radical changes in the basic fiscal structure they inherited from the Ming.

73. The changes are summarized by Li Wen-chih, "Lun Ch'ing-tai ch'ien-ch'i ti t'u-ti chan-yu kuan-hsi," *Li-shih yen-chiu* 5 (1963):75–108, on p. 81; he considers them to be a major stage in the reduction of the gentry's fiscal privileges. Hsiao Kung-ch'üan, in *Rural China: Imperial Control in the Nineteenth Century* (Seattle, 1960), p. 125, merely notes the cut in exemption rates without really considering its implications.

74. Hsiao Kung-ch'üan, *Rural China,* p. 127, notes that the campaign against gentry malpractices in fact began in earnest in 1658, the year after the change in the exemption laws. For a detailed account of the events of the Chiang-nan tax-case, see Hsiao I-shan, *Ch'ing-tai t'ung-shih* (Shanghai, 1927), 1:425–28. For its political background, see Lawrence Kessler, "Chinese Scholars and the Early Manchu State," *HJAS* 31 (1971):179–200, and Robert Oxnam, "Policies and Institutions of the Oboi Regency, 1661–1669," *JAS* 32, no. 2 (February 1973): 265–86.

75. The Anhwei case occurred in Feng-yang prefecture; see *Pei-chuan-chi,* 93.9b–11b. More detail on all this is given in Beattie, *Land and Lineage in China,* chap. 3.

76. Wang Yeh-chien, *Land Taxation in Imperial China,* pp. 38–39; Hsiao Kung-ch'üan, *Rural China,* p. 131; Ch'ü T'ung-tsu, *Local Government in China under the Ch'ing* (Cambridge, Mass., 1962), pp. 185–86.

77. *TCHC* (1827), 2.21b–22a.

78. Ibid., 3.14b–15a, gives an account of the polite and scholarly behavior prevalent in the county city in the eighteenth century which, however idealized, still contrasts significantly with gazetteer descriptions of the same place in the late Ming.

79. *Shih-lu* (K'ang-hsi) 8.4a–b.

80. *Ch'ing-ch'ao hsü-wen-hsien t'ung-k'ao,* 1.7501; *Yao STP* (T.428), *hsien-te chuan,* 2.16a; *TCHC* (1827), 2.22a. See also note 59 above.

81. *Shih-lu* (K'ang-hsi) 15.6b–7a; cf. Huang, "Fiscal Administration during the Ming Dynasty," p. 122.

82. This point of view is perhaps best summed up by Frederic Wakeman, Jr., on pp. 15–17 of his essay "High Ch'ing, 1683–1839," in James B. Crowley, ed., *Modern East Asia: Essays in Interpretation* (New York, 1970), See also the essay by John E. Wills, Jr., in this volume (chap. 6). Chang Ying's son, Chang T'ing-yü, proved to be a superlative master in the exercise of patronage, even if he did go a little too far for his own good; see Hummel, *Eminent Chinese*, p. 55.

83. *P'an STP* (C.818), *chiu-p'u fan-li*, 2b–3b.

84. A much more detailed discussion will be found in chap. 4 of Beattie, *Land and Lineage in China*. The genealogies of almost seventy T'ung-ch'eng lineages are still extant, most of them in Japan (they are listed on pp. 212–13 of Taga Akigoro's *Sofū no kenkyū*). Several other lineages are known to have survived, even though their genealogies are not available.

85. *Yao STP* (T.428), second preface (1661); *Chang STP* (T.656), third and fourth prefaces (1666); ibid., 26.23a. See also note 67 above.

86. *Yao STP* (T.428), second preface (1661), p. 3b; ibid., *chin-yueh*, 1a–b.

87. *Chou-shih Shang-i-t'ang chih-p'u* (C.291), *ch'ung-ch'ih chia-kuei hsu* (1661), 1b–2a.

88. Almost all the T'ung-ch'eng genealogies contain, not only *chia-hsün*, "family instructions" (fairly general injunctions on correct moral behavior), but also *chia-kuei*, "family regulations" (which are much stricter and more specific, and constitute one definite indication of a lineage's organizational strength). Cf. Hui-chen Wang Liu, *The Traditional Chinese Clan Rules* (New York, 1959), p. 30. Careful selection and treatment of tenants is also a major theme of Chang Ying's *Heng-ch'an so-yen*.

89. *Huai-ning HC* (1915), 10.8b.

90. *TCHC* (1827), chap. 7; Beattie, *Land and Lineage in China*, end of chap. 2.

91. Ho Ping-ti, *The Ladder of Success in Imperial China* (New York, 1962), pp. 137–38.

92. Hummel, *Eminent Chinese*, pp. 900–01.

93. The Changs and the Yaos became notorious for their exploitation of patronage; see note 83 above. Several T'ung-ch'eng lineages were still able to compile large and elaborate editions of their genealogies as late as the 1920s and 1930s.

8

Urban Riots and Disturbances

by Tsing Yuan

City Dwellers

We can see from Tsing Yuan's essay that, contrary to much accepted wisdom on the subject, the cities in late Ming and early Ch'ing had a distinctive ethos; far from being merely administrative centers, they were powerful economic units that required special handling by the state. Drawing on local histories and collections of urban inscriptions, as well as on the wide range of recent Chinese and Japanese studies on urban history, Yuan surveys urban riots across a span of a hundred and fifty years, presenting yet another example of the importance of the Ming-Ch'ing transition for the longer process of socioeconomic change. His findings suggest that strengthened state power was reflected in the loss of a sense of autonomy shown by urban workers. Late Ming workers had been goaded by comparatively light increases in taxation to take the law into their own hands; partly because the tax increases were associated with eunuch malfeasance, but also because the workers were strong members of the community, with their own powerful leaders. This was in marked contrast to the Ch'ing situation.

Different dimensions of workers' power can be seen in the Soochow weavers' riots of 1601, led by the popular hero Ko Ch'eng; in the Ching-te-chen potters' riots of 1601 and 1604; and in the series of Soochow riots in 1626. In the last of these, the city workers and the urban gentry clearly combined in pursuit of common goals; but even in the other Ming riots, when there was no clearly shared interest, members of the elite seem to have given a sympathetic hearing to rioting workers. Yuan suggests, persuasively, a certain connection between these elite attitudes and the type of political moralism being taught in the Tung-lin and other late Ming reform associations.

The early Ch'ing period, by contrast, was much less receptive to urban protest; the elite were generally aloof, unless directly involved in their role as examination students, and officials were harsh and suspicious. Yuan discusses this new harshness partly in terms of the idea of "conspiracy," partly in terms of the complex demands that K'ang-hsi, and especially Yung-cheng, placed on their officials. The potential of urban workers' power was still present, as can vividly be seen in the cotton calenderers' riots of 1723 and 1729, but the state's response seems to have been savage and efficient. If one facet

279

of Yung-cheng's reign was the reemergence of a fundamentalist statecraft frugality and discipline, as scholars have suggested, then we can see from Yuan that its effects must have been felt as much by the city workers as by bureaucrats or merchants. Here we have some suggestive evidence for the repression of trends which, in comparable situations in Europe, had led to the emergence of forces we can identify as bourgeois.

INTRODUCTION

Urban riots in traditional China have not been much studied. Part of the explanation is to be found in the view that traditional Chinese cities were the seats of government and symbols of central authority, not the locales for social unrest.[1] It has often been assumed that popular riots and disturbances tended to begin in the countryside before they could reach the cities. As an administrative center, the traditional Chinese city lacked the dynamism and heterogeneity of her counterpart in the early modern West. Until recently, there has been very little empirical study to test these assumptions regarding urban order and stability in traditional China. The evidence of the riots should make us view the traditional Chinese city with much greater ambivalence: it was not only a place of officialdom and high culture, but also of some instability, where control required constant official vigilance. This essay seeks to examine the phenomena of urban riots in their various forms during the late Ming and early Ch'ing periods in order to elucidate the social tensions and problems within the traditional urban scene.

Indeed, the Chinese cities of the seventeenth and eighteenth centuries were far from the quiet and stable centers of administration we have generally believed they were. Between 1590 and 1626, at least twenty-five instances of urban riot occurred; between 1660 and 1729, there were at least fourteen abortive as well as actual urban disturbances. Although most of the riots happened in one given city at a time, during certain periods, particularly the years 1601–03, 1626, and 1729, the disorders broke out in a number of different cities at about the same time. Occurring as many of these riots did in the richest and most cultured region of the empire, the

Lower Yangtze or Chiang-nan area, they for a time threatened to disrupt the commercial lifeblood of the empire and challenged the authority of the central government in some of its important administrative centers. Although the total number of the riots may not seem large, they were concentrated in very important cities at critical times and had repercussions in the politics of the empire. Still other examples of urban unrest might yet turn up in sources that have not been thoroughly studied, but the recent interest of Chinese and Japanese historians in "capitalist" development and social change in this period has led to a relatively thorough search for sources.[2] These newly published materials give hints of new forms of labor organization and leadership in these cities. These sources also point to the serious concern of the authorities, whether Ming or Ch'ing, with these challenges to their control over the urban areas.

These urban riots ultimately proved abortive and had little effect on the shape of politics and society in the mid-eighteenth century. But why? Before we can begin to answer this complex question, we need to discuss some more concrete ones. What were the locations of these riots and what relationship did they bear to the various trades? Who were the leaders of these riots? What were some of the issues that touched off these riots? How widespread was the participation and how long the duration?[3] In examining the following cases, we can discern certain continuities as well as significant changes from the late Ming to the early Ch'ing in terms of the class relations of these disorders and the officials' handling of them.

GEOGRAPHIC, ECONOMIC, AND SOCIAL FACTORS

Most of the urban riots occurred in the most economically advanced region of the empire, the Chiang-nan area. Of the many cities there, Soochow, the commercial and handicraft capital of the empire, stood foremost in the number of its riots: 1601, 1602, 1603, 1636, 1661, 1723, and 1729 were some sample years for Soochow riots. But during the period from the 1560s to 1720s, some twenty-five other cities also experienced at least one riot. Most of these cities, such as Chiang-yin, Nanking, Sung-chiang, and Ch'ang-shu, were also located in the Chiang-nan area. But there were riots at Lin-ch'ing toward the northern end of the Grand Canal, the Wuhan cities in the Middle Yangtze, Ching-te-chen in Kiangsi, the pottery capital of China, as

Distribution of Urban Riots in China
1560s — 1740s

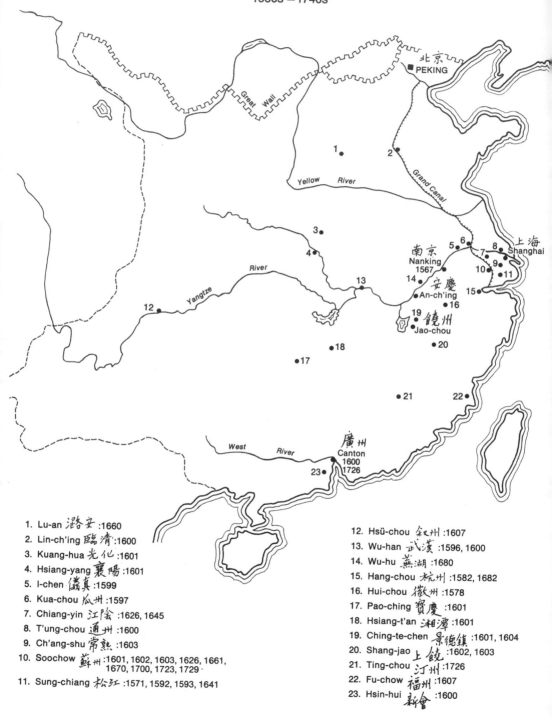

1. Lu-an 潞安 :1660
2. Lin-ch'ing 臨清 :1600
3. Kuang-hua 光化 :1601
4. Hsiang-yang 襄陽 :1601
5. I-chen 儀真 :1599
6. Kua-chou 瓜州 :1597
7. Chiang-yin 江陰 :1626, 1645
8. T'ung-chou 通州 :1600
9. Ch'ang-shu 常熟 :1603
10. Soochow 蘇州 :1601, 1602, 1603, 1626, 1661, 1670, 1700, 1723, 1729
11. Sung-chiang 松江 :1571, 1592, 1593, 1641

12. Hsü-chou 叙州 :1607
13. Wu-han 武漢 :1596, 1600
14. Wu-hu 蕪湖 :1680
15. Hang-chou 杭州 :1582, 1682
16. Hui-chou 徽州 :1578
17. Pao-ching 寶慶 :1601
18. Hsiang-t'an 湘潭 :1601
19. Ching-te-chen 景德鎮 :1601, 1604
20. Shang-jao 上饒 :1602, 1603
21. Ting-chou 汀州 :1726
22. Fu-chow 福州 :1607
23. Hsin-hui 新會 :1600

well as at Foochow and Canton along the southern coast.[4] Since
most of these cities were centers of commerce and handicrafts, their
riots had the participation of artisans, weavers, dyers, potters, the
unskilled calenderers and laborers, and the unemployed, as well as
students and members of the gentry.

There was probably some correlation between the size and population of the cities and their susceptibility to riots. The existence
within the population of a large free labor force, for example, in
Soochow and Ching-te-chen, might be a key explanation for the high
incidence of trouble in certain cities, probably because a certain
"critical mass" of poor people was necessary to get mob action
started.[5] There are, unfortunately, few reliable population statistics
for the late Ming and early Ch'ing cities from which to draw firm
conclusions. The population of Soochow was been variously estimated from about the half-million mark in the sixteenth century
to approximately two million at the beginning of the seventeenth
century.[6] Soochow was not only a populous city, but it was also the
heaviest contributor of land-tax to the state since the early Ming
period, paying as much as 3,000,000 piculs of rice per year.[7] The
population of Ching-te-chen, on the other hand, was much smaller,
about 100,000 by the end of the Ming period.[8] But as the porcelain
capital of China, it had many seasonal potters and laborers, whose
livelihood was insecure at best. Both in 1601 and in 1604, there were
serious riots at Ching-te-chen, which, had they continued, could have
brought about a sharp curtailment of chinaware for the imperial
court as well as the overseas market. In the case of Ching-te-chen,
the incidence of riots was due not so much to the sheer size of its
population as to the peculiar composition of its labor force.

Since many of the riots occurred in large commercial and handicraft centers, the organizational framework of the artisans and
workers needs to be considered. The gradual emancipation of the
artisan class during the Ming period fostered the growth of autonomous workshops and corporations, which flourished increasingly
during the Ch'ing period. As more and more artisans were freed from
their compulsory statutory obligations to the state through commu-
tation by payment in silver, there emerged by the late Ming period a
class of skilled workers: weavers, dyers, smiths, potters, and printers,
whose services could be hired.[9] As the handicrafts such as silk

weaving, cotton weaving, and porcelain manufacturing advanced in sophistication in the late Ming and early Ch'ing, the various trade corporations (*hang*) and workshop owners (*chi-hu*) played an increasing role in determining wages and working conditions. But there was a higher proportion of skilled workers among the rioters in the late Ming than in the early Ch'ing. It can be shown that the corporations and workshops played a greater regulatory role in the early Ch'ing in supervising their members' activities.[10]

The existence of a large number of urban poor, especially when they lacked stable employment, lent momentum to many urban riots. Soochow, for example, had a large population of poor and unemployed who easily swelled the ranks of the malcontents. As the official report of the Soochow riot of 1601 noted:

> The people without families who wander around in search of a living cannot make plans in the morning for the evening of the same day. If they find employment, they live. If they lose employment, they perish. When the dyeing shops closed [during the strike], I saw several thousand dyers scattered.[11]

By early Ch'ing times, a particular group of cotton laborers, the calenderers, constituted a significant element of the lower social stratum of Soochow. Relatively unskilled laborers whose duties consisted of applying the stone rollers to the cotton cloth to produce glossiness, the calenderers were men of robust physique with few ties or obligations to the city in which they worked. In his confidential report to the Yung-cheng emperor in 1730, the governor of Kiangsu, Li Wei (1687?–1738), referred to the calenderers as "single men who assemble like crows and do not attend to their proper functions, but relying upon their numbers, collude to victimize the good people."[12] No doubt, the presence in Soochow of an estimated 10,900 calenderers, who had no families of their own and few skills, did present a threat to public order. Since these workers were casually employed and frequently dismissed, it is not difficult to understand their discontent and unruly behavior.

To be sure, there were other elements in the composition of the urban "rabble" in the eyes of the government. Beggars, vagabonds, secret society members, and local toughs were equally suspect. By early Ch'ing times, the fear of underworld elements had merged with dynastic concerns with anti-Manchu forces, real or imagined. There is, in fact, a remarkable similarity between the outlook of Ch'ing authorities such as Li Wei and that of Gustav LeBon. In his classic study *The Crowd: A Study of the Popular Mind,* first published in France in 1895, LeBon allowed his ideological hostility to the French Revolution and modern "mass society" to prejudice his feelings toward the crowd, whose characteristics he described as "impulsiveness, irritability, incapacity to reason, the absence of judgment and of the critical spirit."[13] Indeed, the French sociologist noted that the crowd was dominated by a criminal mentality and that "thieves, beggars, indifferent workers without employment" constituted the bulk of these potential social subversives.[14] On the other hand, recent studies from the People's Republic of China of commercial growth and "sprouts of capitalism" in this period tended to emphasize and praise what they regarded as the "proletarian" origins of the urban uprisings. The wary historian has to try to avoid this conceptual Scylla and Charybdis by focusing on individual case studies. By investigating the specific circumstances in which these riots took place, first for the late Ming, then for the early Ch'ing, we may be able to generalize with greater authority about their nature and scope.

THE LATE MING URBAN RIOTS

Ming disturbances were concentrated in the late sixteenth century and culminated in 1601–03. Although many of the riots were localized and of short duration, the riots of 1601–03 were not only widespread but also witnessed the alliance of *sheng-yuan,* the lowest degree holders, with "the mob." At first glance this seems surprising; while the mob had little to lose, a member of the elite might lose his rank and his property in the event of government reprisal.

If one examines the social composition of the urban rioters, the *sheng-yuan* stood near the top of the social pyramid. Immediately below them were the students who were candidates for the *sheng-yuan* degree or academy students. The holders of the two higher degrees, *chü-jen* or *chin-shih,* rarely participated. The *sheng-yuan* were far more numerous than the higher degree holders, and had less to lose in a confrontation with the authorities. Imbued with a Confucian sense of morality, many of the *sheng-yuan* and student rioters had a sense of noblesse oblige toward their fellow townsmen and their grievances. They also had their own grievances, involving the fairness and probity of the examinations on which their chances of upward mobility depended.[15] Yet the very nature of such student protests against examination abuses limited the degree of popular participation. The protests might demonstrate that the students were capable of something resembling "mass action," but they tended to stay within academic precincts and did not spill out into the streets.

A case in point was the riot at the Nanking Academy in 1567. When the *sheng-yuan* candidates for the provincial examination learned of the drastic reduction in the number of successful candidates, they directed their anger against the two presiding examination officials, whom they verbally abused and insulted. Despite the participation of several hundred students, the demonstration hardly spread outside of the gates of the Nanking Academy.[16] There was little street action. Similar protests against corruption, bribery, or preferential treatment during the examinations also tended to be limited in popular participation, unless such grievances could be combined with other issues.[17]

The Retention of Prefect Li at Sung-chiang in 1593

Whereas the Nanking Academy case involved only students, the retention of a popular prefect in 1593 had a very broad following among the townsmen of Sung-chiang. Several students became leaders of this movement. The popularity of the Sung-chiang prefect, Li To-chien (*chin-shih* 1574), a native of P'u-t'ien, Fukien, rested on his kindness toward the common people as well as on his simple and frugal conduct of office.[18] According to the local accounts, the prefect not only protected the ordinary Sung-chiang townsmen against the unjust encroachments of the powerful and wealthy local families, but also insisted that all the artisans be paid equitably for the work they performed. Thus, when the news arrived on March 17, 1593, that the prefect's superiors had just transferred him, the populace of Sung-chiang immediately began a campaign to retain him. Among the leaders of the movement were Ts'ai Ju-chung, a *sheng-yuan* degree holder, and P'eng Ju-jang, a student at the Imperial Academy.

The popular demonstrations in support of Prefect Li took several

forms. The crowd used placards, which called for the retention of
the prefect, and hung these from government office buildings and the
city walls.[19] They dispatched representatives to the imperial capital
to file a petition, pleading for a review of the transfer decision. Many
demonstrators blocked off the western gate of the city to prevent Li
from leaving. After the rumors spread that a powerful and wealthy
local resident, Lin Ching-yang, a former supervising secretary at the
Office of Scrutiny for Rites, was responsible for Li's transfer, the
crowd descended upon his house and forced him to flee.[20] The disturbance lasted for three weeks before the arrival of troops restored
order. With the arrest of the two riot leaders, Ts'ai and P'eng, the
Sung-chiang townsmen had little choice but to permit the prefect's
departure.

Although the demonstration in Sung-chiang proved to be abortive,
it did enjoy considerable popular participation. At the height of the
movement, there were daily gatherings of over ten thousand protesters in front of the prefectural building. For three weeks, the
Sung-chiang townsmen did gain a taste of power. But by April 5,
with the departure of the prefect, the protest collapsed, and the two
student leaders, Ts'ai and P'eng, were put in jail.[21] The Sung-chiang
case, however, did demonstrate how public opinion in the traditional
urban setting could be easily mobilized on behalf of a popular cause.

The Silk Weavers' Strike of 1601

The silk weavers' strike of 1601 was a dramatic outburst aginst the
arbitrary power of the eunuch tax commissioner, Sun Lung. It had
tacit support from the local elite, judging from the subsequent local
sympathies to the strike's leader; but on the whole, the strike was a
notable example of the weavers' initiative. It was made up mostly of
weavers, and it was led by a weaver, Ko Ch'eng (1568–1630). I have
found no mention of student participation in the whole affair.

The strike of 1601 took place against the background of the increasing fiscal needs of the Wan-li emperor (1573–1620). During the
1590s his troops had been involved in three major campaigns:
against the Mongol rebels in the north, the aboriginal tribesmen in
the southwest, and the Japanese invaders in Korea. As a result of
these expeditions, the annual military expenditures increased from
about 2,800,000 taels in 1570 to 10,000,000 taels in the 1590s.[22]

Moreover, the personal extravagance of the Wan-li court was stagger-
ing. For example, after the burning of some palaces, the wood for
the reconstruction in 1598 of three buildings alone cost 9,300,000
taels.[23] To meet these financial needs, the emperor dispatched
eunuchs as tax commissioners throughout the empire to collect new
impositions and surcharges. To enforce these collections, the various
eunuch commissioners used their agents, the Embroidered Uniform
Guardsmen, to spy upon, arrest, and torture those who resisted.
The silk weavers' strike was a remarkable demonstration of the
weavers' cohesion in defiance of authority and force. The movement was all the more extraordinary for its apparent lack of gentry
leadership.

The Soochow weavers began their opposition to the eunuch tax
commissioner Sun Lung in the belief that they were about to fall
victim to a crushing tax burden. Since 1599, Sun had set up an
elaborate ring of toll barriers and customhouses on land and water
around the Soochow area.[24] But until 1601, the taxes had fallen
only on transit goods, not on the resident weavers. However, early in
June 1601, when the slackening of trade and recent flooding caused
the government revenue to plummet, Sun, in his capacity as tax
commissioner as well as director of the Weaving and Dyeing Bureau,
decided to take remedial measures. On the advice of a local member
of his staff, Huang Chien-chieh, who happened to be on intimate
terms with some twelve local gangster families, Sun reportedly
decided to impose a tax of 0.3 tael of silver on every loom in the
city. Many of the silk-weaving establishments by this time had as
many as thirty to forty looms and required sixty to eighty weavers
for their operation.[25] Since the most skilled weaver earned only
0.8 tael per month, the reported tax appeared as a horrendous
imposition.[26] At about the same time, wild rumors circulated
through Soochow that the eunuch was planning to impose further
levies on special products such as satin and gauze. Driven by these
rumors to desperation, the weavers' establishments and loom households began to close their doors. By early July 1601, the social and
psychological ingredients of an urban riot were at hand.

There are several versions of what happened shortly thereafter.[27]
According to the *Ming Veritable Records,* the aroused weavers, acting without direction but with great spontaneity, killed their local

betrayer, Huang Chien-chieh, with rocks and then proceeded to
burn down the houses of two local gangsters, T'ang Hsin and Hsü
Ch'eng.[28] In this official version, the subsequent hero of the strike,
Ko Ch'eng, a weaver from K'un-shan, made his appearance only
after the officials had restored civil order and public trust by im-
prisoning the two local gangsters, T'ang and Hsü, and sentencing
them to wear the cangue. Only then did the relatively unknown Ko
come forward to offer himself for imprisonment as a substitute for
the crowd. After all, lives had been lost and properties destroyed.
Ko offered to take upon himself any punishment so that the officials would relent toward the rioters for their transgression of the
law.

In another version of the incident, however, Ko Ch'eng appears as
a ringleader who bore considerable responsibility for the direction
of the strike. The 1642 edition of the *Wu-hsien chih* notes that the
silk weavers staged their riot on July 2, when two thousand strikers
chose Ko as their leader. Ko then divided his followers into six
columns, which were then to be coordinated by signals from his
palm-leaf fan.[29] According to the more detailed local gazetteer,
having killed Huang and burned the two houses of T'ang and Hsü,
the crowd was still not pacified by the officials' token imprisonment of the two local gangsters. The rioters, in fact, continued their
rampage for three more days, during which they destroyed the house
of the other ten local gangsters. Furthermore, on July 6 the crowd
proceeded to lynch T'ang and Hsü, even while they were held under
official confinement and protection. Indeed, in this version, Ko
Ch'eng as the strike's leader did not volunteer to be imprisoned
but having been arrested, he merely "entered prison contentedly
and bore the ropes and beatings without regret."[30]

The denouement of the weavers' disturbance of 1601 was more a
vindication of social justice than of law and order. Frightened by the
display of popular anger, the eunuch Sun Lung had fled to Hangchow.[31] Other officials, however, were sympathetic to the weavers'
plight. In his report to the emperor, the assistant censor-in-chief
of Ying-t'ien, Ts'ao Shih-p'in (1548–1609, *chin-shih* 1571), noted
that the strikers were "worthy people who supported themselves by
their own efforts."[32] The commander of the troops, Chu Hsieh-
yüan (1566–1638, *chin-shih* 1592), was so moved by Ko Ch'eng's

sincerity that he conferred on him the personal name of Hsien or
Worthy, so that he was thereafter known as Ko Hsien until his death
in 1630.

The Soochow weavers' strike of 1601 had considerable significance
in strengthening the sense of urban identity. Although the silk
weavers bore the brunt of the confrontation with the authorities,
they also had the support of merchants, shopkeepers, and members
of the gentry in their elimination of the local gangsters. When Ko
made his way to the local prison, over ten thousand Soochow townsmen expressed their gratitude to him by lining his route with offer-
ings of food and wine.[33] After Ko's release from prison in 1613, he
was lionized as a local hero; in the 1620s, Ko made a trip to Peking,
in a role that might be described as local public opinion personified,
to plead the cause of a Soochow official who had been unjustly
accused of wrongdoing. On the strength of his plea, the accused,
Ch'en Wen-jui, was exonerated and reinstated as district magistrate
of Wu-hsien; he was still magistrate when the popular demonstration against the henchmen of Wei Chung-hsien in 1626 occurred.
As for Ko, when he died in 1630, the city of Soochow honored his
memory by having him buried in a particularly sacrosanct area next
to the Five Martyrs' Tombs on Shan-t'ang Street, near the Tiger
Hill.

There was little evidence that members of the local elite were out
in the streets with the weavers during the strike of 1601. The elite-
popular interaction apparently did not take this form. There is, however, little doubt that the gentry deeply resented the eunuchs' power
and could have easily formed a common front with the weavers. This
common antipathy helped to explain the fact that Ch'en Chi-ju,
a prolific writer and representative of the Chiang-nan gentry, wrote
a eulogistic epitaph for Ko, the hero of the weavers.[34] Ch'en, in fact,
addressed the deceased as "General Ko," no mean compliment to a
former professional weaver.

The Potters' Disturbances of 1601 and 1604

The voluminous information available on the Chiang-nan area, Soochow in particular, should not obscure the fact that there were urban
riots elsewhere. The Ching-te-chen potters' strike of 1601 also represented an urban riot led by and composed of nonelite elements. In

this instance, the target was another eunuch, P'an Hsiang, who was responsible for the tax collection at Ching-te-chen. Ching-te-chen was the pottery capital of China; it was not known as a cultural center, as was Soochow. But because of its pottery manufacturing, the town attracted migrants from far and wide in search of work. One estimate placed its transient population as high as 80 percent of its total.[35] The existence of such a large number of transients tended to keep wages for the potters low, because there was a constant pool of unemployed. The highest wages went to the master craftsmen with years of experience who worked on the dragon bowls; they received an annual wage of 12.6 taels. The skilled potters and sketchers received an annual wage of 9 taels, while the unskilled laborers who mixed colors received only 0.3 tael per month.[36] Since many of the potters could not make ends meet, they would resort to pilfering the Mohammedan blue glaze material or even finished pieces, which they then sold to other private kilns.

The eunuch P'an Hsiang had been director of the Imperial Manufactory at Ching-te-chen as well as mine-tax commissioner since 1598. Greedy and cruel, P'an wanted to produce as many as possible of the intricate dragon bowls for the palace in order to advance his own standing. It is said that he did not shrink from using whips on the potters, one of whom, T'ung Pin, cast himself into the blazing kiln out of desperation, to register his protest.[37] Some time during the ninth month (September 26–October 25), P'an's orders to increase porcelain production and to construct ships for their transport led to the potters' outburst. Over ten thousand of them sought to kill him, but failing that, they burned down the newly constructed storage areas and destroyed countless pieces of porcelain. Only through the efforts of the assistant prefect of Jao-chou was the crowd of potters gradually appeased. But P'an was far from being grateful. Having fled to safety, he accused the assistant prefect of negligence. Two months after the riot, the assistant prefect was himself under arrest and eventually died in prison.[38]

The Ching-te-chen riot of 1604 centered on a different issue, that of natives of the town against outsiders. In this instance, the merchants and kiln operators of Tu-ch'ang, a town located to the west of Ching-te-chen in northern Kiangsi, were the targets of the riot, since they dominated much of the private pottery industry at Ching-te-chen. Scuffling and hand fighting took place between the non-Tu-ch'ang workers and the Tu-ch'ang employers. The workers marched upon the Tu-ch'ang *hui-kuan* or guild hall, seeking to burn it down. It took the mediation of the officials before order could be restored.[39]

Of the two Ching-te-chen riots, one was ostensibly against authority of the government, the other was not. But in both instances, the potters themselves apparently took the leading role. There was little if any gentry support in both of these incidents. Neither riot was long sustained; both were from the best available evidence one-day affairs. Ching-te-chen had the reputation of being an unruly manufacturing town; certainly the presence of a large number of unemployed helped to ignite mass discontent. But neither of the two riots seems to have had much effect; the riot of 1601 only temporarily checked the abuses of the eunuch tax commissioner; P'an was soon back as powerful as ever. Similarly, the riot of 1604 did not end the domination of the Tu-ch'ang merchants over the Ching-te-chen's private pottery industry.

The Soochow Riots of 1603 and 1626

In contrast to the single-industry town of Ching-te-chen, Soochow was, during the late Ming and early Ch'ing, an outstanding city of culture and commerce. Its riots therefore also had greater variation of theme and actors. The riot of 1603 was basically an examination riot that attracted some subelite participation; as such, it was of more significant scope than the examination riot of 1567. The Soochow riot of 1626, on the other hand, was an event of national significance; it not only drew the attention of the court and the powerful eunuch Wei Chung-hsien, but also gave a powerful display of gentry-commoner cooperation.

Although the details of the examination riot of 1603 differed from the student riot of 1567, there were remarkable similarities in the sources of the students' irritation and in the style of their protest. The official *Ming Veritable Records* contains only a succinct note that the Prefect of Soochow, Chou I-wu, was forced to resign his post during the seventh lunar month (August 7–September 4), 1603, on account of a disturbance of *sheng-yuan*.[40] From private sources, we learn that the prefect, a northerner from Shansi, who had an overbearing and covetous reputation, supervised a prefectural examination where the examination papers of well-qualified candidates reportedly were maliciously tampered with. As a result, the unlucky papers were placed at the bottom of the pile and the candidates did not pass.[41]

Whereas the student protesters at the Nanking Academy in 1567 had merely shouted abuse at the examination officials, those at Soochow in 1603 eventually resorted to physical force. During the next round of examinations that Prefect Chou supervised, some of the students taking the examination became deliberately unruly and obstreperous. When the prefect retaliated by having one student beaten with ten strokes, the others within the examination hall called upon the crowd that had already gathered outside to enter and help them. Having grown to several hundred townsmen and students, the crowd began to throw rocks and bricks. The rioters eventually seized the prefect and began to rain blows on him and to tear at his robe and belt.[42] Chou fortunately had his seal officer to shield him from serious injury; he dodged the attacks and was able to escape under cover of darkness during the ensuing confusion.

The incident at the examination hall in 1603 dramatized the intense emotionalism that surrounded the examination system. The *Ming Veritable Records* simply notes that the prefect resigned his post after the disturbance; it makes no mention of any punishments being meted out to the rioters, if indeed there was an official inquiry into the case. The Ming authorities quite likely regarded the riot as a reflection of the prefect's own bungling. Undoubtedly, as many of the examination candidates were from local elite families, their complaints against the prefect could not be lightly dismissed. As Chou's harsh actions had alienated the townspeople, the students' demonstration immediately attracted their support. Thus an examination protest became a popular disturbance.

In comparison with the examination riot of 1603, the Soochow disturbance of 1626 was of much greater scope and significance. The issue was also far more sharply drawn; in the popular imagination, it appeared as a just cause against arbitrary eunuch power. The riot was touched off by the arrest of the respected retired official, Chou Shun-ch'ang, who had been noted for his pleas on behalf of his fellow Soochow townsmen before the local officials, as well as for

his criticisms of the chief eunuch, Wei Chung-hsien.[43] Since Chou
was an associate of the Tung-lin movement, his arrest was not unexpected during the chief eunuch's crackdown on his opponents. On
April 14, 1626, when the news of Chou's arrest reached the Soochow
townsmen, a crowd quickly gathered to register its protest and to
seek his release. Ten thousand commoners, as well as five hundred
students dressed in formal attire, reportedly were on hand at the
demonstration; the figures may be somewhat exaggerated. In the
subsequent confrontation with the guardsmen, the commoners, led
by five activists, including a wholesaler, a clothing merchant, and a
sedan-chair bearer, killed at least one guardsman and, for a time,
threatened the lives of the chief eunuch's henchmen, including the
governor of Ying-t'ien, Mao I-lu.[44] The commoners, fortified by their
numbers, resorted to violence after the students had spoken in vain on
Chou's behalf. The confrontation between the sixty guardsmen protecting Mao and the crowd lasted at least four days, during which the
guardsmen were on the defensive. At the height of the crisis, Soochow appeared to be on the brink of revolt, with placards attacking
the eunuchs and the burning of incense to add solemnity to the
occasion. But government forces were on the side of Wei Chung-
hsien; with the arrival of fresh orders from Peking, the eunuch's
power finally prevailed. Chou was forcibly removed to prison in
Peking, where he was put to death in July. The five commoners who
had stirred the crowd to action were arrested and later that year also
put to death.[45]

The participation of such a large crowd of townspeople in support
of Chou Shun-ch'ang and his Tung-lin associates, as well as the duration and intensity of the struggle, suggest that here might have developed a growing sense of urban identity. The relationship with the
Tung-lin party, as well as its offshoots—the Ying-she and the Fu-she
on the one hand, and the urban commercial interests on the other—
is a subject that deserves further scrutiny. Although the Tung-lin
partisans opposed the more extreme versions of Wang Yang-ming's
doctrines that had found such a wide following in the cities in the
late sixteenth century, their few economic pronouncements showed
much ground for common action with mercantile interests, calling
for relaxed government restraints, the curbing of official exactions,
and the elimination of the eunuchs as tax commissioners.[46] Li

San-ts'ai, generally regarded as the "generalissimo" of the Tung-lin party by his political enemies, for example, was blunt in his memorial to the Wan-li emperor while serving as the governor of the Huai river area:

> Ever since the staggering growth of the mine taxes, ten thousand people have lost their jobs. Your Majesty should regard the people as of the essence. You not only do not clothe them, you in fact take away their clothes from them. You not only do not feed them, you in fact take away their food from them.[47]

Indeed, Li's anti-eunuch position, if not his Mencian concern for the common people, was shared by the urban craftsmen and merchants, who resented the eunuchs' exactions. It might be risky to push the Tung-lin's connection with the mercantile interests too far, but one of the opponents of the Tung-lin party described it as composed of "ambitious politicians, unscrupulous scoundrels, retired officials, as well as rich merchants."[48]

The anti-eunuch demonstration in Soochow was not an isolated instance; it was supported by a similar popular outburst in neighboring Chiang-yin. The two events took place within the same month of April 1626. At Chiang-yin, it was the arrest of another Tung-lin partisan, Li Ying-sheng, a censor and a sharp critic of Wei Chung-hsien, that touched off the riot.[49] Several thousand townspeople gathered and demonstrated on behalf of the arrested Li. As the arrest order was being read, ten young men, each carrying a short stick, headed for the magistrate's office and set upon the military guards with blows. One teenager, a former sugar-cane peddler, was able to get close enough to a fat guardsman to cut off a piece of his flesh. According to a contemporary narrative, the teenager threw the meat to a dog to feed upon, while shouting, "This is how much I hate you!" a striking example of the intensity of emotion that was aroused and expressed in public action in these riots. Still, Wei Chung-hsien had his way in Chiang-yin as in Soochow, and Li Ying-sheng was put to death shortly thereafter.[50]

The events of 1626 had a dramatic impact on a new generation of urban leaders, the founders of the Ying-she and Fu-she, who carried on the tradition of the Tung-lin. Such members of both societies as Chang P'u, Yang T'ing-shu, and Wen Chen-meng all received their initiations into political action at the Soochow demonstration. Chang P'u wrote an essay in 1627 eulogizing the five martyrs who had given their lives in defense of Chou Shun-ch'ang.[51] As a friend of Chou, Yang, the founder of the Ying-she, was an eyewitness of, if not an active participant in, the Soochow riot; he too wrote an account of the demonstration of April 1626.[52] Wen Chen-meng, a leader of the Fu-she who subsequently took a high office at Peking after the death of Wei Chung-hsien in 1627, had one of his sons married to Chou's daughter; his brother Wen Chen-heng (1585–1645), also a witness of the demonstration, was probably the author of still another account of the affair.[53] In other words, there were intimate links throughout these anti-eunuch urban riots that cast light on the politics of the late Ming empire. These riots seem to have been crucial events in the emergence of a sense of urban identity in some of China's cities and in the shaping of some of a new generation of activist scholar-officials. Both were to be severely tested in the first years of the Ch'ing.

TOWARD A DEFINITION OF URBAN STRIFE

In the various late Ming urban riots, the extent of popular participation, the degree of organization, as well as the objects of protest might differ from one to the next. Yet all these Ming riots took place against rulers and officials who were also Chinese, like the rioters themselves. With the conquest of China by the Ch'ing, the tenor and style of protest were to undergo a somewhat abrupt change, dictated by the harsher reality of alien rule. In their opposition to the Ming authorities, the urban populace used placards to carry their petitions, resorted to wailings and lamentations to demonstrate their righteousness, and ultimately, when peaceful tactics failed, relied on physical force. None of these tactics was to prove to be effective with the Manchu rulers and their Chinese allies. Before we examine the reasons as well as the circumstances of these early Ch'ing protests, a definition of certain key terms might clarify our conceptual understanding of civil strife.

According to the political scientist Ted Gurr in his comparative study of civil strife, there are generically three general kinds of such strife: turmoil, conspiracy, and internal war. According to Gurr, turmoil involves "relatively spontaneous, unorganized strife with substantial popular participation" in the form of demonstrations, strikes, and riots. In contrast to turmoil, conspiracies are a highly organized form of strife, with limited participation which take such forms as antigovernment plots, mutinies, and coups d'état. Finally, internal war is "a highly organized strife with widespread popular participation, accompanied by extensive violence and including large-scale terrorism and guerrilla wars."[54]

To be sure, there are other ways of classifying urban riots. They can be classified on the basis of political, economic, or social objectives or by the characteristics of the persons arrested for participation.[55] Still another way is to arrange the various disturbances on a descending scale based on their duration, geographic spread, number of participants, as well as the amount of violence.[56] Unfortunately, much of the needed data prove to be lacking for the late Ming and early Ch'ing riots.

Gurr's definition of the three types of civil strife might be more applicable to the Chinese examples. Many of the late Ming urban disturbances, such as the examination riots, the anti-eunuch demonstrations, and the movement to retain a popular prefect, involved relatively spontaneous, unorganized strife; as such, they may be considered in the category of "turmoil." During the early Ch'ing, there were also examination riots and demonstrations with lamentations, such as the famous k'u-miao case of 1661 (discussed below), but the responses of the Ch'ing authorities were much more thorough, sweeping, and generally retaliatory. In any case, the greater frequency of conspiracies during the Ch'ing, especially by Soochow calenderers, was a remarkable testament to the temper of the times. In the light of the increasing commercial growth of the early Ch'ing during a period of prolonged internal peace, these instances of conspiracy were definitely evidence of internal discontent, whether racially or economically inspired.

Finally, Gurr's definition of "internal war" might be applied to the events of 1645–46, when the Ch'ing forces crushed the Ming loyalist resistance in a number of cities, such as Sung-chiang, Wu-chiang, Chia-ting, Chiang-yin, and K'un-shan. In the case of the urban riots, the conflict between the rioters and the authorities took place within the city, but in the case of "internal war," the leaders sought to incite the cities themselves to act as single entities against an external enemy. Whether the experience of past elite-popular interaction in the late Ming riots helped to cement the loyalists' resistance in the 1640s has yet to be proven. It may be noted for the present that a number of Fu-she members, who had been influenced by the Chou Shun-ch'ang case of 1626, played an active role in the loyalist resistance—for example, Ch'en Tzu-lung (1608–47) and Hsia Yün-i (1596–1645) at Sung-chiang, as well as Hou T'ung-tseng (1591–1645) and Huang Ch'un-yao (1605–45) at Chia-ting.[57]

THE EARLY CH'ING URBAN DISTURBANCES

After the fall of the key fortress of Yangchow on May 20, 1645, the Chiang-nan region lay nearly defenseless before the Ch'ing armies. The ensuing ten-day massacre of the conquered Yangchow population was meant to be a severe reminder to those who would resist of the consequences of such action. Once Nanking, the restoration capital, surrendered without resistance on June 7, the Ch'ing pacification of Chiang-nan was merely a matter of time.[58] Slowly, new Ch'ing officials began to arrive at various Chiang-nan cities to receive the local registers and maps. By the middle of July, when the newly appointed Ch'ing magistrates arrived at Chiang-yin and Chia-ting to do their duty, relative calm prevailed.

But the new Ch'ing order for the Chinese to cut their hair and wear the queue soon became the key issue that cemented local elite-popular resistance. There was an immediate outcry from the local gentry and populace alike. By the third week in July at Chiang-yin and by the first week in August at Chia-ting, the urban populations of these two cities had chosen the path of resistance. The battle cry in these two cities, as well as several others, was, "My head might be cut off, my blood may flow, but I shall never let my hair be cut."[59] The queue issue thus became a catalyst for urban unity of sentiment, but the military odds were overwhelming, and intraelite and elite-popular tensions within the cities made effective resistance very difficult. At Chia-ting the end came swiftly; by August 24 the city had fallen. But at Chiang-yin the siege was to last eighty-one days; it fell to the Manchu forces only on October 8.[60] As in Yangchow genocidal massacres and pillage were visited upon the conquered population. The new rulers would not brook further resistance.

The difference in style and frequency between late Ming and early Ch'ing urban riots was partially the outcome of the differences in imperial leadership. During the late Ming, the emperors were remote and distant. In contrast, the early Ch'ing rulers, being able and intelligent men, were highly interventionist in their actions; to them it was imperative to extend the emperor's primacy in matters of administration.[61] The K'ang-hsi emperor (1661–1722) was noted for his six Southern Tours, during which he checked into the conditions of his empire; both he and his successor, the Yung-cheng emperor (1723–36), made extensive use of the secret palace-memorial system, through which they received confidential reports from provincial officials as well as imperial bondservants scattered throughout the land. One may appreciate the vigor of the early C'hing controls not only in the literary inquisition cases, which are well known, but also in the official steps taken to check urban dissent. In the following cases, we shall examine the response of early Ch'ing rulers to tax grievances, examination abuses, and workers' conspiracies.

The "Laments in the Temple" (k'u-miao) Incident of 1661

The expression of lament at a Confucian temple was a traditional device often used by the local elite to register dissatisfaction or irritation with officialdom. The sanctity of a Confucian temple lent an air of moral righteousness and scholarly purity to the protest. In 1661, the Soochow lamenters demanded the removal of the hated magistrate of Wu-hsien (Soochow), Jen Wei-ch'u (d. 1662), who had been using ruthless methods, including flogging, to collect tax arrears from the local population.[62] On March 4, over one hundred scholars appeared before the Kiangsu governor, Chu Kuo-chih, and with loud cries they urged the magistrate's dismissal. However, the occasion was hardly appropriate for such a protest; for the governor with other dignitaries was then at the temple conducting the mourning ceremonies for the recently deceased Shun-chih emperor (1643–61). Chu lost no time in having the leaders of the students seized and imprisoned.

The Ch'ing authorities' handling of the *k'u-miao* incident represented a harsh approach toward the Chiang-nan elite, for the case eventually led to a severe crackdown on tax evasion in the area. As the new emperor was then still a child of seven, the four Manchu regents in Peking gave the orders to mete out heavy punishments.[63]

During the summer trial, the Ch'ing investigators and the Kiangsu
governor linked the student rioters with the loyalists under Cheng
Ch'eng-kung, who had entered the Yangtze and besieged Nanking
in 1659. During the interrogation, the eighteen scholars accused,
among whom was the eminent writer Chin Jen-jui, (1610?–61) were
repeatedly beaten. On August 7, the trial came to an end with their
mass execution. But for the Chiang-nan elite, the tax case was only
the beginning of their troubles, as the governor proceeded with his
investigation of tax arrears throughout the Chiang-nan area. The
lucky members of the gentry who rushed to pay their taxes escaped
punishment. But numerous officials and scholars lost their government posts and ranks; before its conclusion, the Chiang-nan tax case
led to the removal of 11,346 individuals from the *sheng-yuan* rolls in
the area around Soochow and Sung-chiang.[64]

In the *k'u-miao* incident, there was little popular support for elite
protest; commoners probably felt little sympathy for the sufferings
of elite tax-evaders. Whereas during the late Ming there was considerable popular support for the local elite's resistance to abuses
by the eunuchs which affected all classes, such support seems rare
during the early Ch'ing. The *k'u-miao* case further supports the
impression that when an elite protest challenged the ruling power, it
was much more thoroughly suppressed by the Ch'ing authorities than
similar riots had been by their Ming counterparts.

However, by the middle K'ang-hsi years, if not earlier, it probably
was easier for Chinese scholar-officials to get along with Manchus
than it had been to get along with eunuchs, who had poisoned much
of Ming political life. On the one hand, the sagacious K'ang-hsi
emperor helped to direct the Chinese elite's energies into safer and
more orthodox channels through such means as the *po-hsüeh hung-
ju* examination of 1679. On the other hand, Chinese bannermen and
bondservants helped to break down the institutional barriers between
the bureaucracy and the inner palace.

The Student Riot at Yangchow in 1711

By 1711, the Ch'ing state was enjoying an unprecedented prosperity
under the K'ang-hsi emperor, who was a great patron of Chinese
scholarship and institutions. But as an increasing number of Chinese
scholars participated in the examination system, the severe competi-

tion led to scandals. As early as 1657, an investigation into the Chihli provincial examination found widespread bribery among the examining officials, as well as tampering with the examination papers.[65] The upshot of the affair was that seven officials received the execution sentence, and twenty-five others were exiled with their families. In the Shun-t'ien (Peking) provincial examination of 1699, there were reports of irregularities, as a result of which the chief examiner was banished and the assistant examiner sent to prison; later they were found to be innocent.[66] Again in 1705, the candidates at the Shun-t'ien provincial examination brought psychological pressure to bear on the examining officials by parading through the streets and by beheading symbolically two straw images of the chief and assistant examiners.[67] But none of these examination scandals matched the Yangchow case in terms of political significance. For during the subsequent riot and its investigation, the conflict between the Manchu governor-general of Liang-chiang, Gali, and the Chinese governor of Kiangsu, Chang Po-hsing, and ultimately between their respective factions, broke out into the open.

The Yangchow student riot itself followed the general pattern of late Ming examination riots. When the examination results revealed on October 20, 1711, that among the new chü-jen holders were many sons of wealthy salt merchants, the unsuccessful candidates accused Gali and the deputy examiner of selling the coveted degrees.[68] By November 4, over a thousand students took to the streets in Yangchow; they pasted derogatory statements at conspicuous locations, ridiculed the accused officials with degrading puns, and some even broke into the prefectural school, where they kept the director of studies their prisoner. The authorities arrested two of the new chü-jen, one of whom reportedly had given bribes to various officials.[69] The investigation itself, however, came to a halt when two members of the investigative commission, Gali and Chang Po-hsing, impeached each other in their respective memorials to the K'ang-hsi emperor. In order not to favor either high official, the emperor dismissed both of them on March 10, 1712. The political casualties stemming from the examination riot thus mounted.

With the examination scandal still waiting to be settled, the K'ang-hsi emperor's dismissal of Gali touched off another urban phenomenon, the pa-shih, or market strike. As in the Soochow weavers'

strike of 1601, the people of Yangchow closed their shops on March
24 and March 25, and halted all business transactions.[70] If the tactics were similar to the late Ming Soochow case, the ostensible motive
of the market strike was to secure the retention of the Manchu
governor-general Gali, a replay of the theme of trying to retain the
popular Sung-chiang prefect in 1593. The precise causes for Gali's
popularity with the Yangchow populace are, however, not clear.
It may be of some significance that soldiers joined in the popular
demonstration.[71] The impact of military pressure or compulsion
on the populace cannot be fully ascertained. Gali, an ally of the disgraced former heir-apparent Yin-jeng, may have fomented the
demonstration in a desperate effort to save his own position. In this
regard, the secret palace memorial of Ts'ao Yin, one of the emperor's
trusted bondservants, was revealing. Written at the beginning of May
1712, the confidential report noted that the popular agitation at
Yangchow had died down and that the populace despised both Gali
and Chang Po-hsing for their pettiness and selfishness.[72]

The K'ang-hsi emperor was, however, made of tougher and wiser
stuff than his late Ming predecessor, the Wan-li emperor, who gave
his eunuchs a free rein. Through a series of bold, personal interven-
tions, the Manchu monarch made it abundantly clear that he was
both an upholder of Confucian tradition as well as an impartial arbiter
between the Manchus and the Chinese. Informed at every step of the
investigation, the emperor appointed three successive investigative
commissions; but in the end, after nine months, he meted out what
he considered to be proper punishment. Both Gali and Chang received
their dismissals, though the emperor later transferred Chang to
another post. The punishments for those found guilty of bribery and
cheating were severe; the chief examiner and his associate examiners,
as well as the licentiate candidates found guilty, all were condemned
to death.[73] If the K'ang-hsi emperor appeared a despot, he was at
least a highly responsible and level-headed one.

The Calenderers' Riots and Conspiracies, 1670–1729

Neither the k'u-miao riot nor the Yangchow examination-hall riot
had the participation of the urban lower classes, except for the
ambiguous case of the demonstrations in support of Gali. The early
Ch'ing unrest among the Soochow calenderers, therefore, serves as

a useful balance to these instances of elite protest. Although the
calenderers' riots and plots were quite frequent, their participation
involved relatively insignificant numbers. Many of the late Ming
urban disturbances involved large numbers, such as 2,000 in Soochow
in 1601, but there were few such large riots in the early Ch'ing. Moreover, we have an exceptionally interesting body of source material
for the calenderers' disturbances. The contractors and merchants
who were menaced by them and who had to work out means of controlling them made a permanent and public record of the events and
the control measures in a series of stone inscriptions. These have
been published by researchers in the People's Republic, who have
found them exceptionally interesting as evidence of incipient
bourgeois-proletarian conflict in early modern China.[74]

There were several reasons why the calenderers became such important disturbers of the urban peace. First of all, they had to be
tough and physically robust to be able to work with the large foot-
rollers, which weighed as much as 1,000 catties (1,100 pounds).[75]
On certain occasions they would use their physical strength to take
the law into their own hands. Second, being for the most part
recent migrants from outlying areas of Soochow prefecture, the
calenderers were without families and rootless in the large city, with
which they felt little identification. Third, their wages were among
the lowest of urban workers: in 1670 they were paid 0.011 tael of
silver for every bolt (each bolt was 68 feet) of cloth calendered; in
1720 they were still paid 0.0113 tael per bolt.[76] For their accommodation and equipment, most of the calenderers had to pay the
contractors (pao-t'ou) 0.36 tael per month. It has been estimated
that a calenderer had to finish at least one bolt of cloth per day or
30 bolts per month just to break even; his normal capacity was 33
bolts per month.[77] It is not surprising, therefore, that these calenderers would repeatedly demand higher wages for their labors.
On such occasions, the Ch'ing authorities invariably came to the
support of the contractors against the calenderers.

There was a series of labor disputes between the calenderers and
their contractors from 1670 onward. In 1670, some twenty-one
calenderers under the leadership of Wang Nan-kuan were accused by
local cloth merchants in Soochow of destroying property.[78] The case
arose because of rising grain prices; the calenderers had demanded

higher wages and threatened to strike if their demands were not met during the sixth month (July 17–August 14). When the workshop owner, Li Sheng-mao, refused to make any concessions, the calenderers gathered outside his house and proceeded to destroy his property. The local cloth merchants naturally supported Li's recalcitrant stand; in their inscription, dated the tenth month (November 13–December 11), they reaffirmed the standard wage of the calenderers at 0.011 tael per bolt and averred that all trouble-makers such as Wang and his men should be dismissed from their jobs.[79]

By 1692, the contractors and cloth merchants were concerned not just with trouble-makers but with the infiltration of the city's racketeers among the calenderers. In that year, a number of cloth merchants in Soochow, led by Chu Jih-mao, accused some sixteen calenderers of being ex-racketeers who had assumed the calenderers' calling to generate discontent among their ranks.[80] The cloth merchants charged that the calenderers had gathered in unruly bands that committed violent acts and robberies, and even destroyed governmental proclamations. Eventually, on October 9, 1692, the Soochow prefectural government sentenced the accused ringleaders to wear the cangue for thirty days and to receive thirty bamboo strokes afterward.[81] The inscription, to which some seventy-six cloth merchants affixed their names, affirmed that such punishments would be a clear warning to future trouble-makers.

A few years later, another incident led the contractors to impose a special private adaptation of the government's collective responsibility institutions on their rowdy employees. In 1700, several hundred calenderers began a brawl in the midst of a theatrical performance during the fourth month (May 19–June 16). After the racketeers joined in the scuffling, so the accusing cloth merchants contended, the fight got out of control. The disorder forced many of the calendering establishments to close while the ruffians broke into a number of commercial shops.[82] To prevent any such future outbreaks of lawlessness, the contractors instituted a system of collective surveillance and responsibility. The contractors would keep strict registration of groups of ten households; should any contractor harbor any trouble-maker, both he and his neighbors would be punished.[83] The regulations further forbade the calenderers to drink alcohol, to gamble, or to venture out at night.

On their part, the calenderers, whose occasional misbehavior had
led to the increasing restraints on their life style, sought ways to
improve their lot through organization. In 1715, under the leadership of Wang Te, the calenderers not only demanded a raise in wages
by threatening to strike, but also asked for the right to build a hospital, orphanage, and a *hui-kuan* or guildhall for themselves.[84] The
response of the cloth merchants and the contractors was outrage.
They pointed out that the calenderers had only recently received a
wage increase from 0.011 tael to 0.0113 tael for every bolt of cloth
finished. The idea of having a *hui-kuan* for the calenderers was particularly objectionable: "Once a *hui-kuan* is completed, all those
vagabonds without any proper registration will be quartering there
with their factions and crowds, and the harm will be incalculable."[85]
A group of seventy-two cloth merchants accused Wang Te and his
five associates of inciting unrest and argued that, since the calenderers
were ignorant and illiterate, their desire to build a hospital and
nursery was simply to squeeze the merchants' profits.[86] The Soochow prefectural government concurred with the cloth merchants'
position and, on October 7, 1715, sentenced Wang Te and five of
his associates to heavy blows with the bamboo.[87] This persistent
government favoritism toward the cloth merchants and contractors,
while scarcely surprising,[88] does help to explain the subsequent plots
of the calenderers against the government.

Although the Soochow calenderers' conspiracy of 1729 was more
serious because of its much greater support from other classes of
Ch'ing society, the conspiracy of 1723 was the forerunner and a
necessary catalyst. Much of the evidence, coming as it does from
official sources, tends to be prejudicial to the plotters, viewing them
as underworld figures intent on sedition and destruction. In the
secret palace memorials of Li Wei, governor of Chekiang in 1725,
promoted to governor-general of the same province in 1727 and
given the additional task of governing southeastern Kiangsu in
1728, one sees a conscientious official doing his duty to catch
all evil-doers.[89] Two other officials assisted Li Wei in the investigation into the calenderers' conspiracy of 1729: Yin-chi-shan, who
became acting governor of Kiangsu in 1728 and the full governor of
the province the following year; and Shih I-chih, who was both
the senior vice-president of the Board of Civil Office and acting

governor-general of Liang-chiang during 1730.[90] In summarizing the calenderers' plot of 1723 in their investigative report on the antigovernment conspiracies in 1729, all these officials sought to prove their efficiency and thoroughness so as to win the favor of the Yung-cheng emperor, who had succeeded his father, the K'ang-hsi emperor, in 1722.

After a general account of the nature and working conditions of the calenderers in the Soochow area, the three officials' report of 1730 dealt with the unruliness of these workers and pointed to the conspiracy in 1723, whose two ringleaders were still at large in 1730.[91] According to the official report, the two calenderers Luan Chin-kung and Hsü Lo-yeh originally planned to seize ships and put out to sea. But their contractor got wind of the plot and immediately reported the conspiracy to the government. Thirty-five of the conspirators were caught, but both Luan and Hsü were able to make good their escape. The government sentenced thirteen of those arrested to death and awarded the contractor-informer with twenty taels of silver. The three officials concluded their report by noting the recent arrest of the infamous robber Hsi Kuei-ch'ing, many of whose followers apparently had assumed the calenderers' calling to evade the law.[92] Li Wei and his two associates were much concerned with the trouble-making potential of this gang, for in 1730 they had discovered a wide ring of conspirators, of whom the calenderers were only a part. The ring, in fact, included not only the Soochow calenderers, but also *sheng-yuan,* fortune-tellers, roving swordsmen, and salt merchants—some, if not most of whom, had designs to overturn the dynasty.[93]

According to the Li Wei report, the calenderers had aroused official suspicions by taking taking the oath of brotherhood and by their ties with the conspirators of 1723. On October 18, 1729, twenty-two calenderers, under the leadership of Luan Erh-chi, the nephew of Luan Chin-kung, made sacrifices to the gods and drank wine as a part of the ceremony of initiation.[94] As soon as the calenderers' brotherhood came to light, the government lost no time in having its members arrested. The fact that Luan Erh-chi was the nephew of the escaped Luan Chin-kung made any defense for the brotherhood difficult. Early in 1730, while holding the arrested calenderers in prison for sentencing, Li Wei worriedly reported to the emperor that

the number of Soochow calenderers that had at one time been
estimated at seven to eight thousand had grown recently by two
thousand, among whom could be found a large number of former
outlaws.[95] Above all, the discovery that the calenderers had been
joined by other conspiratorial groups was a matter of grave concern.

According to Li Wei, the large conspiracy included men from many
walks of life besides calendering. One of the most crucial figures
was the swordsman, Kan Feng-ch'ih, a man of immense physical
strength, who reportedly could squeeze lead and tin into their
liquid form.[96] Li Wei believed that Kan practiced breathing exer-
cises and possessed magical powers, and the wily governor-general
resorted to devious means to trick Kan into confession, first hiring
Kan to teach his own son in the martial arts, then enticing Kan's son
to reveal the whereabouts of his father's associates, and finally confronting Kan with his arrested accomplices.[97] In the end, Kan had
little choice but to give a full confession and to beg forgiveness. The
questions remain, though, whether Kan might have embroidered the
extent of his conspiracy to gain credence with Li Wei, and whether
the governor-general might not have exaggerated the participation
of some neophytes in order to claim credit with the emperor.

Although the conspiracy was abortive, thanks to Li Wei's alert-
ness, its avowed aims and supposed ringleaders encompassed a
variety of subversive tendencies. There was the theme of Ming restoration, as one of the leaders, Chou K'un-lai of Nanking, claimed to be
a descendant of the prince of Chou of the imperial line.[98] Another
ringleader, Lu T'ung-an of P'ing-hu, a *sheng-yuan,* reputedly had
maintained contacts ever since 1714 with another descendant of the
Ming house, who had been residing in Luzon in the Philippines. To
plan his uprising against the government, Lu made extensive surveys
of the topography of the area of Soochow and Sung-chiang, bought
a villa at K'un-shan, and had his followers trained there in the ways of
insurrection.[99] In addition, Li Wei accused Lu of worshipping the
writings of Lü Liu-liang (1629–83), whose anti-Manchu views were
just coming to light during the recent investigation into the case of
Tseng Ching (1679–1736). Tseng was arrested in December 1729,
for trying to foment a military rebellion in Shensi against the Yung-
cheng emperor.[100] In his secret memorial, Li Wei lumped Lu T'ung-
an with Tseng Ching as men of the same class in their worship of

Lü Liu-liang, though he did not identify Tseng as a member of Lu's conspiracy.

Among the conspirators, Li Wei included not only the calenderers of Soochow, the swordsman Kan Feng-ch'ih, the *sheng-yuan* Lu T'ung-an, and the Ming claimant Chou K'un-lai, but also fortune-tellers, salt merchants, and petty tradesmen. One of the accused was the fortune-teller, Ts'ai "the Beard" of An-ch'ing, who had made a prediction that the following fall would be an appropriate time for an uprising. At the home of another fortune-teller, Chang Yün-ju, under whom Kan Feng-ch'ih had reportedly studied the martial arts, the government found some fifty different calling cards belonging to salt merchants, gentry members, and even bannermen.[101] Li Wei lost no time in having the fifty people, including the head of the Yangchow salt merchants, investigated. He even placed the movements of a flower tradesman under observation. Basing additional information on the testimony of a *sheng-yuan* informer, the governor-general claimed that the conspirators had been active in a wide area that included Kiangsu, Chekiang, Anhwei, Kiangsi, and Fukien; though he did not have their precise numbers or plans, he was sure their aims were anti-Ch'ing.

The veracity of the informers might not be above suspicion. In the case of the Soochow calenderers, the economic grievances of poor wages and working conditions no doubt reinforced the racial antipathies toward the Manchu rulers. But when the conspirators resorted to secret society rituals, practiced Taoist modes of physical training, collaborated with Ming claimants, and read subversive works, an official of Li Wei's caliber could not but conclude that a large conspiracy was at hand. Quite possibly, in view of Tseng Ching's attempted uprising of 1729, the governor-general saw imaginary enemies of the state lurking everywhere. But prior to the unraveling of the conspiratorial ring, aside from the few rowdy acts of the calenderers there had been neither demonstrations nor petitions to forewarn the government. There was indeed a sharp distinction between these attempts at subversion and the late Ming urban popular disturbances.

CONCLUSION

The urban riots and disturbances of the late Ming and early Ch'ing should be properly placed in the perspective of other developments in the urban scene of the time: the growth of commerce and the handicrafts, the proliferation of the *hui-kuan,* the increasing use of silver, and the popularity of vernacular literature. It was a period of stirring change and unfulfilled expectations. Some historians in the People's Republic have contended that sixteenth-to-seventeenth-century China contained the "sprouts of capitalism," some of which continued to grow during the Ch'ing while others were nipped in the bud by the Manchus.[102] Although the term *capitalism* may not accurately describe the economic and social development of the time, by the late Ming there was definitely increasing concentration among the urban inhabitants, especially in the Chiang-nan area, on the monetary, commercial, and material aspects of their existence. Novels such as the *Chin P'ing Mei* and short stories like those found in the *San-yen* described the mundane and often unedifying side of urban life with singular realism. The growing dimension and sophistication of the silk and cotton industries, the expansion of inter-regional trade, the increasing outflow of Chinese silk and porcelain and inflow of silver—all gave eloquent testimony to the vibrant tempo and style of the time.

But these developments did not ultimately lead to the rise of an independent urban order. The Chinese merchants and artisans never obtained the charters of autonomy and immunities that their European counterparts received in the early modern West. The classic explanation offered to account for this discrepancy centered on the overwhelming administrative and military power of the Chinese bureaucracy. In other words, bureaucratic control of the traditional Chinese city prevented the urban classes from exercising any initiative. It has been further argued that the urban population remained consistently passive and docile. The study of urban unrest during the late Ming and early Ch'ing, however, proved that the Chinese townsmen did on occasion take the law into their own hands. The traditional urban populace, in fact, posed a serious and recurrent challenge to the Ming and Ch'ing governments.

The late Ming and early Ch'ing urban riots shared certain continuities and recurring themes. Few of the riots were politically motivated. The examination candidates rioted because they wanted to belong to the existing political system, not to overturn it. The silk weavers' strike of 1601, the potters' strike of the same year, and the *k'u-miao* incident of 1661, were the outcome largely of economic grievances based on tax impositions. With the exception of the conspiracies of 1723 and 1729, most of the calenderers' disturbances were also basically prompted by demands for higher wages, better living arrangements, the building of a hospital, nursery, or *hui-kuan*. In contrast to modern mass movements, these rioters resorted to force without the support of an ideology. E. J. Hobsbawm has called such urban rioters the "pre-industrial mob" and the "primitive rebels."[103]

The late Ming and early Ch'ing urban riots also shared a low level of discipline and organization. Highly dependent on mass spontaneity of the moment, these urban rioters found outlets in assaulting unpopular local figures and burning houses and property. Upper-class agitations also had few goals beyond the elimination of immediate abuses. One of the nonviolent acts of urban disturbance was the use of the *pa-shih* or "market strike," when the artisans would stop their looms and the merchants close their shops.[104] The use of "lamentations" constituted yet another tactic aimed primarily at soliciting the sympathies of the authorities. Tried during both the late Ming and early Ch'ing, the effectiveness of this tactic depended totally on the official's good will and moral conscience. During the demonstrations of 1626 as well as 1661, when the local officials had to carry out certain orders from above, such a display of outward emotions by the protestors proved to be completely futile.

What were some of the differences between the late Ming and early Ch'ing riots? First, during the late Ming, there was apparently a greater cohesion between the elite and the populace in the urban disturbances; presumably the existence of a common target, the eunuchs and their agents, sustained this alliance. In the weavers' riot of 1601 and the pro-Chou Shun-ch'ang riot of 1626, artisans, merchants, and laborers made common cause with the urban gentry in resisting the eunuchs' exactions and arbitrary power. But after the anti-queue resistance of 1645, such elite-popular interaction became increasingly rare during the early Ch'ing.

A contributing factor to this development was, perhaps, the lowered status of the urban working class during the early Ch'ing. Whereas during the late Ming, a professional weaver such as Ko Ch'eng could achieve honor and prestige among the gentry, such an occurrence appeared remote during the early Ch'ing. There was probably also greater functional specialization in the Ch'ing handicrafts, so that the bottom-level workers such as the calenderers became even more isolated from the decision maker; in fact, they became social rejects and a security problem. During the early Ch'ing, the relative absence of literati allies in the later disturbances might also have been the result of the loss of leaders during the conquest period and the systematic wooing of the elite by the K'ang-hsi emperor. Indeed, it became increasingly unlikely that the Ch'ing literati would ally themselves with the populace on an urban issue.

Second, the Ch'ing authorities tended to be more repressive and forceful in their handling of urban unrest. Despite the arbitrary power of the eunuchs, the Ming townsmen could and did express their views with arguments based on justice and fair play. Not only did the silk weavers of 1601 go unpunished except for the token imprisonment of Ko Ch'eng, but most of the student rioters during the late Ming also tended to get off lightly for their defiance of the law. In reacting to urban unrest, the Ch'ing government took countermeasures with greater dispatch and more thoroughness. There was an unyielding single-mindedness in the performances of such Ch'ing bureaucrats as Chu Kuo-chih, the Kiangsu governor in 1661, and the governor-general Li Wei in 1730. Because of the more autocratic nature of the Ch'ing government, these officials probably also had less flexibility and initiative with which to deal with local problems than their Ming counterparts and could give little if any cooptation to the dissenters:[105] their all-embracing concern was the preservation of order in the cities. Just as the Ch'ing officials in their memorials to the emperor emphasized their abject servility, so they expected an attitude of cringing submissiveness from the people they governed. The smothering of urban riots and conspiracies in their infancy represented, as much as the famous literary inquisition cases, the overpowering hand of the Ch'ing state.

APPENDIX

A Summary List of Urban Riots 1560–1730

Year	Location	Background and Causes
1567	Nanking	Southern Academy students vs. examiners

Year	Location	Background and Causes
1571	Sung-chiang	Students' protest
1578	Hui-chou	Opposition to the silk tax
1582	Hangchow	Troop mutiny supported by the populace
1592	Sung-chiang	Populace vs. the Fan clan
1593	Sung-chiang	Populace for the retention of prefect Li
1596	Wu-han	Populace vs. eunuchs and mine taxes
1597	Kua-chou	Market strike by merchants and populace
1599	I-chen	Populace vs. eunuchs and taxes
1600	T'ung-chou, Wu-han, Lin-ch'ing Canton, Hsin-hui	Populace vs. the eunuchs and taxes
1601	Soochow	Silk weavers' expulsion of eunuch Sun Lung
	Hsiang-t'an, Pao-ching	Populace vs. eunuch
	Ching-te-chen	Potters' disturbance vs. eunuch P'an Hsiang
1602	Soochow	Silk weavers vs. eunuch
1603	Soochow	Students vs. the prefect Chou I-wu
	Ch'ang-shu	Students vs. local official
	Shang-jao	Students vs. eunuch
1604	Ching-te-chen	Potters disturbance vs. T'u-ch'ang merchants
1607	Foochow	Populace vs. eunuchs and taxes
	Hsü-chou	Students' agitation
1626	Soochow	Populace vs. the eunuchs: the Chou Shun-ch'ang case
	Chiang-yin	Populace vs. the eunuchs
1641	Sung-chiang	Populace's rice riot
1660	Lu-an	Market strike due to reduced imperial silk orders
1661	Soochow	K'u-miao case
1670	Soochow	Calenderers' disturbance vs. workshop owner
1680	Wu-hu	Market strike vs. surtaxes
1682	Hang-chou	Market strike vs. usurers
1698	P'u-ch'eng	Market strike vs. magistrate
1700	Soochow	Calenderers' disturbance
1711	Yangchow	Examination candidates' riot

Year	Location	Background and Causes
1712	Yangchow	Populace for retention of Gali
	Nanking	Market strike for tax reduction
	Chen-chiang	Market strike for tax reduction
1723	Soochow	Calenderers' conspiracy foiled
1726	Canton	Market strike vs. rice prices
	Ting-chou	Populace's robbing of grain ships and market strike
1729	Soochow and other Chiang-nan cities	Calenderers, fortune-tellers, swordsmen sought to commit conspiracy

NOTES TO CHAPTER 8

Abbreviations

MSL — *Ming shih-lu* [Ming veritable records]. Taipei: Chung-yang yen-chiu yüan li-shih yü-yen yen-chiu so, 1962.

PKTL — *Chiang-su sheng Ming-Ch'ing i-lai pei-k'o tzǔ-liao hsüan-chi* [Selected stone-inscription source materials in Kiangsu since Ming and Ch'ing times]. Edited by Kiangsu Provincial Museum. Peking, 1959.

YCCP — *Yung-cheng chu-p'i yü-chih* [The vermillion endorsements of the Yung-cheng emperor]. Taipei: Wen-hai ch'u-pan shê, 1965.

1. Rhoads Murphey, "The City as a Center of Change: Western Europe and China," *Annals of the Association of American Geographers* 44, no. 4 (1954): 353, 358-59; for a recent restatement of the same theme, see Gilbert Rozman, *Urban Networks in Ch'ing China and Tokugawa Japan* (Princeton, 1973), pp. 90, 95. On Western urban disturbances, one may profitably consult George Rudé, *Paris and London in the 18th Century: Studies in Popular Protest* (London, 1970), and Lauro Martines, ed., *Violence and Civil Disorder in Italian Cities 1200-1500* (Berkeley, 1972).

2. Among the Chinese works were *Chung-kuo tzǔ-pen-chu-i meng-ya wen-t'i t'ao-lun chi* [Symposium on the question of the germination of Chinese capitalism]. (Peking, 1957), and *Ming-Ch'ing shê-hui ching-chi hsing-t'ai ti yen-chiu* [A study of the social and economic posture of the Ming and Ch'ing periods] (Shanghai, 1957). For a critical review of these works, see Albert Feuerwerker, "From 'Feudalism' to 'Capitalism' in Recent Historical Writing from Mainland China," *Journal of Asian Studies* 18, no. 1 (1958):107-15. On Japanese writings, see Tanaka Masatoshi, 'Chūgoku rekishi gakkai ni okeru 'shihon shugi no hōga' kenkyū" [The study of the "germination of capitalism" in the Chinese historical circles], in *Chūgoku shi no jidai kubun* [Periodization of Chinese history], ed. Suzuki Shun and Nishijima Sadao (Tokyo, 1957), pp. 219-52.

3. For the use of certain indices in the study of disturbances, see Pitirim A. Sorokin, *Social and Cultural Dynamics,* revised and abridged version (Boston,

1957), pp. 574–78; see also Charles Tilly, "How Protest Modernized in France, 1845–1855," in William O. Aydelotte, Allan G. Bogue, and Robert W. Fogel, eds., *The Dimensions of Quantitative Research in History* (Princeton, 1972), p. 243.

4. See Map 3, p. 282.

5. E. J. Hobsbawm, "City and Insurrections," in Hobsbawm, *Revolutionaries: Contemporary Essays* (London, 1973), pp. 221–22.

6. The conservative figure is given by Frederick W. Mote, "A Millennium of Chinese Urban History: Form, Time, and Space Concepts in Soochow," in *Rice University Studies* 59 (Fall 1973):39; the much higher figure probably applies to the entire Soochow prefecture, though this fact is not clear; see Huang P'ei-chin, "Kuan-yü Ming-tai kuo-nei shih-ch'ang wen-t'i ti k'ao-ch'a" [An investigation concerning the problem of the domestic market during the Ming period], in *Ming-Ch'ing she-hui ching-chi hsing-t'ai ti yen-chiu*, pp. 210–13.

7. *Wu-hsien chih* [Gazetteer of Wu district], 1933 ed., 44/7a.

8. *Ching-te-chen t'ao-tz'u shih-kao* [Draft history of Ching-te-chen ceramics] (Peking, 1959), p. 109.

9. E. Stuzhina, "The Economic Meaning of Some Terms in Chinese Feudal Handicrafts," *Archiv Orientalni* 35, no. 2 (1967):236–38; the question whether the hired labor was truly "free" has been much debated among Mainland historians; see Lo Yao-chin,"Tsai-lun Ming-ch'ao Wan-li nien-chien ku-yung lao-tung ti hsing-chih" [Further discussion on the character of hired labor during the Wan-li years of the Ming period], *Li-shih yen chiu*, no. 4 (1962), pp. 78–103. See also Fu I-ling, "Wo tui-yü Ming-tai chung-yeh i-hou ku-yung lao-tung ti tsai jen-shih" (My further consideration of the hired labor after the middle of the Ming period), *Li-shih yen-chiu*, no. 3 (1961), pp. 59–78, where Fu maintained that workers during the late Ming were becoming "freer."

10. Ramon H. Myers, "Some Issues on Economic Organization during the Ming and Ch'ing Periods: A Review Article," *Ch'ing-shih wen-t'i* 3, no. 2 (1974): 81–82; Ping-ti Ho, *The Ladder of Success in Imperial China* (New York, 1962), pp. 57–58.

11. *MSL* (Shen-tsung), *chüan* 361, vol. 112, p. 6742; the translation is done by Mark Elvin in his *The Pattern of the Chinese Past* (Stanford, 1973), p. 278.

12. *YCCP*, 8:4515.

13. Gustave LeBon, *The Crowd: A Study of the Popular Mind*, introduction by Robert K. Merton (New York, 1960), pp. 35–36.

14. Gustave LeBon, *The Psychology of Revolution*, trans. Bernard Miall (Wells, Vt., 1968), p. 70.

15. The crucial importance of the provincial examination is discussed in Ho, *Ladder of Success*, p. 193.

16. *MSL* (Mu-tsung), *chüan* 12, vol. 92, p. 0341; see also Fu-I-ling, *Ming-tai Chiang-nan shih-min ching-chi shih-t'an* [A preliminary inquiry into the economy of the townsmen of Kiangnan during the Ming period] (Shanghai, 1957), p. 111.

17. See, for example, Chang Chung-li, *The Chinese Gentry* (Seattle, 1955), pp. 188–97, on later corruption of the system.

18. Fan Lien, "Yün-chien chü-mu ch'ao," in *Pi-chi hsiao-shuo ta-kuan* (Taipei, 1962), 1:1278.

19. *Sung-chiang fu-chih* [Prefectural gazetteer of Sung-chiang], 1819 ed., 42/22b–23b; Fu, *Ming-tai Chiang-nan*, pp. 115–16.

20. Fan, "Yün-chien chü-mu ch'ao," 1:1279; Lin is mentioned in *Ming-shih* [Ming history] (Taipei, 1963), 4:2573.

21. Fan, ibid.

2. Li Wen-chih, *Wan-Ming min-pien* [Popular revolts in the late Ming period] (Hong Kong, 1966), p. 1.

23. Ibid. p. 2.

24. *MSL* (Shen-tsung), *chüan* 331, vol. 110, p. 6125.

25. Shih Hung-ta, "Ming-tai ssǔ-chih sheng-ch'an-li ch'u-t'an" [A preliminary inquiry on the productivity of silk-weaving in the Ming period], *Wen-shih-chê* [Literature-history-philosophy] 60 (1957–58):3431.

26. Saeki Yūichi, "Mindai shōckisei no hōkai to toshi kinuori-monogyō ryūtsū shijo no tenkai" [The decline of the Ming artisans system and the development of urban textile flows to markets], *Tōyō bunka kenkyūjo kiyō* 10 (1956): 368–69.

27. For extracts of these versions, see Saeki Yūichi, "Mimmatsu shokkō bōdō shiryō ruishu" [Collection of selected historical materials on the weavers' disturbance at the end of the Ming], in *Shimizu Hakase tsuito kinen mindaishi ronsō* [Studies on the Ming period in memory of the late Dr. Shimizu] (Tokyo, 1962), pp. 611–35.

28. *MSL* (Shen-tsung), *chüan* 361, vol. 112, p. 6742; Saeki, "Mimmatsu shokkō," p. 613.

29. *Wu-hsien chih* [Gazetteer of Wu district], 1642 ed., 11/39b–40b, 30. A detailed description of the riot is also found in Yokoyoma Suguru, "Chūgoku ni okeru shōkōgyō rōdōsha no hatten to yakuwari-Mimmatsu ni okeru Sōshū o chūshin to shite" [The development of commercial and industrial workers and their role in China, with special reference to Soochow at the end of the Ming], *Rekishigaku kenkyū* 160 (November 1952):9.

30. *Wu-hsien chih*, 1642 ed., 11/40b; the differences between the two accounts may be explained by the officials' desires (as we can trace them in *MSL*) to minimize the seriousness of the disturbance and to show the lawbreakers' contribution in the face of government power.

31. Chu Kuo-chen, *Huang Ming shih-kai* [Historical resumé of the Ming], 1632 ed., 44/32a.

32. *MSL* (Shen-tsung), *chüan* 361, vol. 112, p. 6742.

33. Ch'en Chi-ju, "Obituary inscription," in *PKTL*, p. 416; Chu Hsieh-yuan's biography appears in *Ming-shih*, *chüan* 249, vol. 4, pp. 2825–28.

34. *PKTL*, p. 417,

35. Takanaka Toshie, "Minshin jidai Keitokuchin no tōgyō" [The ceramic industry of Ching-te-chen during the Ming and Ch'ing period], *Shakai keizai shigaku* [Studies in socioeconomic history] 32, nos. 5–6 (1967):583.

36. *Ching-te-chen t'ao-tz'u shih-kao,* p. 105.

37. Wen Ping, *Ting-ling chu-lüeh,* Library of Congress microfilm ed., 5/32a; Sakuma Shigeo, "Mimmatsu Keitokuchin no minyō no hatten to minhen" [The development of private kilns and the popular disturbances at Ching-te-chen during the late Ming], in *Suzuki kyōju kanreki kinen Tōyōshi ronsō* [Oriental Studies presented to Professor Suzuki on the occasion of his sixtieth birthday] (Tokyo, 1964), p. 277.

38. *Fu-liang hsien-chih* [District gazetteer of Fu-liang], 1682 ed., 4/39b–40a; Sakuma, p. 278. *MSL* (Shen-tsung), *chüan,* 379, vol. 113, pp. 7137, 7140–41.

39. *Ching-te-chen t'ao-tz'u shih-kao,* p. 240; Sakuma, p. 275.

40. *Wu-hsien chih* [Gazetteer of Wu district], 1642 ed., 11/43a–b; *MSL* (Shen-tsung), *chüan* 386, vol. 113, p. 7254.

41. Hsü Fu-tso, *Hua-tang-ko ts'ung-t'an,* Chieh-yüeh shan-fang hui-ch'ao ed., 5/38b–39a.

42. Ibid., 5/39b–40a; cf. Fu I-ling, *Ming-tai Chiang-nan,* p. 112.

43. The most detailed account of this incident is found in Charles O. Hucker, "Su-chou and the Agents of Wei Chung-hsien, 1626," reprinted in Hucker's *Two Studies on Ming History* (Ann Arbor, 1971), pp. 41–83; recent Chinese accounts can be found in Liu Yen, "Ming-mo ch'eng-shih ching-chi fa-chan hsia ti ch'u-ch'i shih min yün-tung" [Early townsmen's movement during the late Ming urban economic development], *Li-shih yen-chiu* [Historical studies] 6 (1955):422–24; and Fu I-ling, *Ming-tai Chiang-nan,* pp. 116–18.

44. Hucker, "Su-chou," pp. 60–62; cf. Wen Ping, *Hsien-po chih-shih,* in *Chung-kuo nei-luan wai-huo li-shih ts'ung-shu* (Shanghai, 1947), pp. 187–89; Chi Liu-ch'i, *Ming-chi pei-lüeh,* in *Chung-kuo fang-lüeh ts'ung-shu* (Taipei, 1968), pp. 164–67.

45. The five men's obituary as it appears in a stone inscription can be found in *PKTL,* pp. 411–14; see also *Wu-hsien chih,* 1642 ed., 11/47a–48b.

46. Tso Yun-p'êng and Liu Chung-jih, "Ming-tai tung-lin tang-cheng ti shê-hui pei-ching chi ch'i yü shih-min yün-tung ti kuan-hsi" [The social background of the Tung-lin party struggle and its relationship with the townsmen's movement during the Ming period], *Hsin chien-shê* [New construction], 10 (1957): pp. 37–38; on the Tung-lin's relationship to the Ch'eng-Chu and Wang Yang-ming school, see Ian McMorran, "Wang Fu-chih and Neo-Confucian Tradition," in Wm. Theodore DeBary, ed., *The Unfolding of Neo-Confucianism* (New York, 1975), pp. 423–24.

47. The statement is included in Li's biography, *Ming-shih,* 4:2660. See *Ming-shih chi-shih pen-mo* (Taipei: Commercial Press, 1965), 9:79.

48. *MSL* (Shen-tsung), *chüan* 513, vol. 119, p. 9692.

49. A brief biography of Li appears in Chi Liu-ch'i, *Ming-chi pei-lüeh,* pp. 187–89.

50. Wen Ping, *Hsien-po chih-shih,* p. 190; cf. Hsia Hsieh, *Ming T'ung-chien* [Ming universal mirror] (Peking, 1959), 4:3089.

51. *PKTL,* pp. 411–13; for an account of the Fu-she that Chang founded, see William S. Atwell, "From Education to Politics: The Fu She," in DeBary, *Unfolding,* pp. 333–65.

52. The account, "Ch'üan Wu chi-lüeh," can be found in *Ch'ung-chen ch'ang-pien* (Taipei, 1964).

53. Wen's official career is treated in Chi Liu-ch'i, *Ming-chi pei-lüeh,* 419–21; see also Hucker, "Su-chou," p. 70; cf. Ōkubo Eiko, "Mimmatsu dokushojin kessha to kyōiku katsudō" [Associations of scholars and their educational activities during the late Ming], in *Kinsei Chūgoku kyōikushi kenkyū* [Studies on the history of Chinese education during the early modern period[(Tokyo, 1958), pp. 203–04.

54. Ted Robert Gurr, "A Comparative Study of Civil Strife," in Hugh D. Graham and Ted. R. Gurr, eds., *Violence in America: Historical and Comparative Perspectives* (New York, 1970), p. 574.

55. See, for example, Tilly's approach in "How Protest Modernized in France," pp. 245–47.

56. See Gurr, "A Comparative Study," pp. 627–28; the application of quantification of domestic violence can be seen in Raymond Tanter, "International War and Domestic Turmoil: Some Contemporary Evidence," in Graham and Gurr, *Violence in America,* pp. 557–65; Barbara A. Wilson, *Topology of Internal Conflict: An Essay* (Washington, D.C., 1968), p. 8; Ted Gurr with Charles Ruttenberg, *Cross-national Studies of Civil Violence* (Washington, D.C., 1969), pp. 31–33.

57. Hsiao I-shan, *Ch'ing-tai t'ung-shih* (Taipei, 1963), 1:316–18; Atwell, "Fu She," pp. 356–57; see also "Yen-t'ang chien-wen tsa-chi," in *T'ung-shih* [A history of suffering] (Taipei, 1968), pp. 15b, 27a.

58. Hsü Tzu, *Hsiao-t'ien chi-nien fu-k'ao* (Peking, 1957), pp. 359–61; the classic account of the fall of Yang-chou is found in Wang Hsiu-ch'u, *Yang-chou shih-jih chi* [An account of the ten days of Yang-chou], in *Chung-kuo chin-tai nei-luan wai-huo li-shih ts'ung-shu* (Shanghai, 1946).

59. Han T'an, *Chiang-yin ch'eng-shou chi* [An account of the defense of Chiang-yin], in *Chung-kuo chin-tai nei-luan wai-huo li-shih ts'ung-shu* (Shanghai, 1946), pp. 45–46; Chu Tzǔ-su, *Chia-ting hsien i-yu chi-shih* [An account of events in Chia-ting in 1645], in *T'ung-shih* [A history of suffering] (Taipei, 1968), p. 3a; Hsü Tzu, *Hsiao-t'ien chi-nien fu-k'ao,* pp. 403–04, 422–23; on the significance of the hair-cutting issue as a symbol of Han racial authenticity, see Yang K'uan, "I-liu-ssǔ-wu nien Chia-ting jen-min ti k'ang-Ch'ing tou-cheng" [The popular anti-Ch'ing struggle at Chia-ting in 1645], in *Ming-Ch'ing shih lun-ts'ung* [Collected essays on Ming and Ch'ing history] (Wuhan, 1957), pp. 215–16. See also Frederic Wakeman, Jr., "Localism and Loyalism," pp. 58–60; on Chia-ting, see Jerry P. Dennerline, "The Mandarins and the Massacre of Chia-ting: An Analysis of the Local Heritage and the Resistance to the Manchu Invasion in 1645" (Ph.D. diss., Yale University, 1973).

60. Hsü Tzu, *Hsiao-t'ien chi-nien fu-k'ao* pp. 422–23; Lai Chia-tu, "I-liu ssǔ-

wu nien Chiang-yin jen-min ti k'ang-Ch'ing tou-cheng" [The popular anti-Ch'ing
struggle at Chiang-yin in 1645], in *Ming-Ch'ing shih lun-ts'ung,* p. 195; cf. Wakeman, "Localism and Loyalism," passim.

61. Harold L. Kahn, "Some Mid-Ch'ing Views of the Monarchy," *Journal of
Asian Studies* 24, no. 2 (1965):229–31; a theoretical treatment of the "authority's viewpoint" can be found in Nathan Leites and Charles Wolf, Jr., *Rebellion
and Authority: An Analytic Essay on Insurgent Conflicts* (Chicago, 1970), pp.
71–83.

62. The two main contemporary sources on this incident are almost identical:
see *K'u-miao chi-lüeh* [An account of the K'u-miao affair], in *T'ung-shih* [A
history of suffering] (Taipei, 1968), pp. 1a–b; and *Hsin-ch'ou chi-wen* [An account of (the year) 1661], in *Ming-Ch'ing shih-liao hui-pien* (Taipei, 1967), 2d
ser., 16:1235–36; there is also a brief account in "Yen-t'ang chien-wen tsa-chi"
in *T'ung-shih,* p. 35a; see also Lawrence D. Kessler, "Chinese Scholars and the
Early Manchu State," *Harvard Journal of Asiatic Studies* 31 (1971):184–86.

63. Robert B. Oxnam, *Ruling from Horseback: Manchu Politics in the Oboi
Regency 1661–1669* (Chicago, 1975), pp. 106–07.

64. Yeh Meng-chu, *Yüeh shih pien* [A survey of the age], in *Ming-Ch'ing
shih-liao hui-pien* (Taipei, 1969), 6th ser., vol. 56, pp. 158, 355.

65. Shang Yen-liu, *Ch'ing-tai k'o-chü k'ao-shih shu-lu* [A study of the examination system in the Ch'ing dynasty] (Peking, 1958), pp. 299–301.

66. Ibid., p. 306; on this case, see Arthur Hummel, ed., *Eminent Chinese of
the Ch'ing Period* (Washington, D.C., 1943), 1:135–36.

67. Shang, *Ch'ing-tai,* p. 309; see Jonathan D. Spence, *Ts'ao Yin and the
K'ang-hsi Emperor: Bondservant and Master* (New Haven and London, 1966),
p. 241.

68. Li Hsü, "Su-chou chih-tsao Li Hsü tsou-che" [The palace memorials of
the Soochow textile commissioner Li Hsü], in *Wen-hsien ts'ung-pien* (Taipei,
1964), 2:867, dated February 22, 1712; a detailed study of the examination-hall
case of 1711 is found in Spence, *Ts'ao Yin,* pp. 240–54; see also Silas H. L. Wu,
Communication and Imperial Control in China, Evolution of the Palace Memorial System 1693–1735 (Cambridge, Mass., 1970), pp. 143–44.

69. Li Hsü, "Su-chou," p. 869; *Shih-lu* (K'ang-hsi) (Taipei, 1964), 6:3308–
09; cf. Shang Yen-lin, *Ch'ing-tai,* pp. 309–10.

70. Li Hsü, p. 868; *Shih-lu* (K'ang-hsi), pp. 3324–25, 3342–43; cf. Silas Wu,
Communication and Imperial Control, p. 145; Spence, *Ts'ao Yin,* pp. 245–46.

71. Li Hsü, p. 867.

72. Spence, *Ts'ao Yin,* p. 291; Hsiao Shih, *Yung-hsien-lu* [Historical records
of the Yung-cheng reign] (Shanghai, 1959), p. 306; Silas Wu, pp. 53, 146–48.

73. *Shih-lu* (K'ang-hsi), pp. 3377–78; cf. Spence, pp. 252–53.

74. *PKTL,* passim.

75. Terada Takanobu, *Sansei shōnin no kenkyū* [A study of Shansi merchants] (Kyoto, 1972), p. 394; cf. Yokoyama Suguru, "Shindai ni okeru tambugyō no keiei keitai" [Structure of the cotton calendering industry in the
Ch'ing period], *Tōyōshi kenkyū* [Studies in Oriental history] 19, nos. 3–4
(1960):337–49 and 451–67.

76. The wages for 1670 were given in *PKTL*, p. 34; those for 1720, in *PKTL*, p. 44.

77. Terada, *Sansei*, pp. 357–58.

78. The inscription on this incident, 141 cm. high and 68 cm. wide, was located at 34 Hsiang-fu Monastery Lane in Soochow; see *PKTL*, pp. 13–14.

79. *PKTL*, p. 14; Terada, pp. 343–44.

80. This inscription, 174 cm. high and 88.5 cm wide, was located near the Kuang-chi Bridge; see *PKTL*, p. 34

81. *PKTL*, p. 35; Terada, p. 344.

82. *PKTL*, p. 38. Such brawls during theatrical performances were apparently common and prompted the government to exercise closer supervision over such amusements; see Colin P. Mackerras, *The Rise of the Peking Opera 1770–1870: Social Aspects of the Theatre in Manchu China* (Oxford, 1972), pp. 36–37.

83. *PKTL*, pp. 38–39; Terada, pp. 345, 366–67.

84. The inscription, 185 cm. high and 90 cm. wide, was also located near the Kuang-chi Bridge; see *PKTL*, pp. 40–41.

85. *PKTL*, p. 41; for a study of *hui-kuan*, see Ho Ping-ti, *Chung-kuo hui-kuan shih-lun* [A historical survey of *Landsmannschaften* in China] (Taipei, 1966); see also Gideon Sjoberg, *The Preindustrial City: Past and Present* (Glencoe, Ill., 1960), pp. 187–96.

86. *PKTL*, pp. 41–43;

87. Ibid., p. 42.

88. On the government's functions in policing deviant behavior, see S. N. Eisenstadt, *The Political Systems of Empires* (New York, 1969), pp. 146–47.

89. For a detailed biography of Li Wei, see *Ch'ing-shih lieh-chuan* [Ch'ing dynasty biographies] (Taipei, 1964), 2:13/37–43; cf. Hummel, *Eminent Chinese*, 2:720–21. See also Silas Wu, *Communication and Imperial Control*, pp. 74–76; and Pei Huang, *Autocracy at Work: A Study of the Yung-cheng Period, 1723–1735* (Bloomington and London, 1974), pp. 234–35.

90. For a biography of Yin-chi-shan, see *Ch'ing-shih lieh-chuan*, 3:18/26–34, and Hummel, *Eminent Chinese*, 2:920–21; for that of Shih I-chih, see *Ch'ing-shih lieh-chuan*, 3:15/39–45, and *Eminent Chinese*, 2:650–51.

91. *YCCP*, 8:4514–15; the report, while undated, is between two reports dated September 7, 1730, and October 1, 1730.

92. Ibid., p. 4515; for other details on this incident, see Li Hua, "Shih lun Ch'ing-tai ch'ien-ch'i ti shih-min tou-cheng" [Preliminary study of townsmen's struggle during the early Ch'ing period], *Wen-shih-chê* [Literature-history-philosophy] 10 (1957):58–59.

93. For the entire secret memorial, see *YCCP*, 7:4455–61.

94. Ibid., pp. 4457–58; see also Sasaki Masaya, *Shin matsu no himitsu kessha* [Secret societies of the late Ch'ing] (Tokyo, 1970), pp. 78–79.

95. *YCCP*, 7:4458; on the structure of the urban lower class, see Sjoberg, *The Preindustrial City*, pp. 121–23.

96. A brief biography of Kan Feng-tz'u appears in *Ch'ing-shih kao* [Draft history of the Ch'ing period], ed. Chao Erh-hsün et al. (Peking, 1928), 504/2b; a useful reconstruction of Kan's career is in Sasaki, *Shin matsu* pp. 65, 73–74.

97. *YCCP*, 7:4456; see also Li Wei's biography in *Ch'ing-shih lieh-chuan* 2:13/40.

98. Sasaki, pp. 74–75.

99. *YCCP*, 7:4457; see also Hsiao I-shan, *Ch'ing-tai t'ung-shih*, 1:932.

100. On the Tseng Ching Case, see Hummel, *Eminent Chinese*, 2:747–49; L. Carrington Goodrich, *The Literary Inquisition of Ch'ien-lung* (Baltimore, 1935), pp. 84–87; Pei Huang, *Autocracy at Work*, pp. 215–20.

101. *YCCP*, 7:4459; Sasaki, p. 79.

102. Li Hua, "Shih lun Ch'ing-tai," pp. 61–62; Li Hsün, *Ming Ch'ing shih* [History of Ming and Ch'ing] (Peking, 1956), pp. 201–02.

103. E. J. Hobsbawm, *Primitive Rebels* (New York, 1959), p. 110; for a critique of Hobsbawm's ideas, see Henry Bienen, *Violence and Social Change* (Chicago, 1968), pp. 41, 84–85.

104. A discussion of four instances of *pa-shih* during the early Ch'ing can be found in Yang Lien-sheng, "Government Control of Urban Merchants in Traditional China," *Tsing Hua Journal of Chinese Studies* 8, nos. 1–2 (1970):199–203.

105. Silas Wu, *Communication and Imperial Control*, pp. 12–22; Pei Huang, *Autocracy at Work*, pp. 306–07; on the use of cooptation as a control mechanism, see William A. Gamson, *Power and Discontent* (Homewood, Ill., 1968), pp. 134–35.

9

Ambivalence and Action
Some Frustrated Scholars of the K'ang-hsi Period

by Lynn A. Struve

Scholars and Heroes

Since the late nineteenth century, our general views of early Ch'ing thought have tended to be dominated by such figures as Ku Yen-wu, Wang Fu-chih, and Huang Tsung-hsi; this dominance was partly because of their very real intellectual distinction, but also in part because the effects of the Manchu conquest on their careers, and their frank responses to that conquest, met the needs of an emergent Chinese nationalism. This concentration led to much fruitful scholarly analysis but also to a narrowing of focus, since a rather special kind of political attitude and approach to political thought was taken as being representative. Our knowledge of the background to the philosophical stances of the seventeenth century has recently been immeasurably expanded by two volumes edited by William Theodre de Bary, Self and Society in Ming Thought *and* The Unfolding of Neo-Confucianism, *and in this essay Lynn Struve seeks to move the discussion on into a new realm of discourse. Her aim, in examining such post-conquest Ch'ing writers as Wang Yüan, Wen Jui-lin, and Liu Hsien-t'ing, is to show us what we can learn from studying, not the theories of historiography, but living historians at work. By so doing, she leads us to a more organic sense of how thought functions in society; she is interested not only in the ways in which certain intellectual giants may have influenced their less eminent contemporary thinkers but also in the degree to which such giants may have been expressing in a particularly cogent way thoughts and feelings that were widely current in their milieu.*

Study of these less well-known figures of the early Ch'ing period is difficult: many works were lost, either in response to the efficient Ch'ing censorship or because there was inadequate incentive, in either the late nineteenth or in the twentieth century, to reprint them. Biographies are sparse, and many are found only in yeh-shih, *thus requiring patient verification. And the Ch'ing state, historiographically sensitive, made a systematic effort to suppress certain frank contemporary sources on the Southern Ming.*

Nevertheless, Struve manages to describe a group of writers, and their patrons, in a way that illuminates the social and intellectual world of the early Ch'ing and introduces certain definite continuities with later Ming trends, both in ching-shih *(statecraft studies), and in k'ao-cheng (textual research). We begin to see how empirical research in such a field as geography, for instance, could be a panacea for a deep inner restlessness, and how the cult of the hsia (the wanderer or "knight errant") could be lived out in one's own life or studied historically. A friend could lament of Chiang Jih-sheng that "everything he did was untimely"; this essay helps us to see how such a perception could be lived with.*

The chaotic disintegration of the Ming order and its rapid replacement by a regime controlled by an alien, "barbarian" people came as a profound shock to the intelligentsia of mid-seventeenth-century China. The debate over reasons behind this overwhelming calamity began almost immediately after the fall of Nanking in 1645 and was intensely personal to surviving men of prominence who had been caught in their maturity by a cataclysmic change of Heaven's Mandate. Writings of the 1650s and 1660s were filled with partisan recriminations, sectarian fault-finding, and expiatory confessions of wayward behavior, as men painfully sought to apportion the guilt in a generation that would always be held collectively responsible for the ruin of a great dynasty.

But what about the next generation? How did the conquest affect their thoughts and feelings as they weighed aspirations, career prospects, and social responsibilities—public, filial, and familial? Though responses were as varied as human personality itself, in general men who grew to maturity after 1644 did not inherit their fathers' anguish. But they were tugged and pulled by a number of factors that instilled an uncomfortable ambivalence toward conventions of public service, scholarship, and personal conduct, factors which in some ways were peculiar to the middle decades of the K'ang-hsi reign (1662–1722) but which must be understood in relation to late Ming trends in politics philosophy, and scholarship. Theirs was a variegated ambivalence, with at least four shades of difficulty:

> 1. Mixed feelings about the recent pathos-filled fall of the once great Ming dynasty, and about the concomitant establishment and consolidation, by armed force, of a new, attractive, but "barbarian" dynastic order.

2. Dissatisfaction with the accepted modes, language, and pre-occupations of scholarly writing and the typical sedate scholars' life style (especially after the Ming collapse, which seriously indicted late Ming literati culture), on the part of men who still desired status and reputation as members of the educated elite.

3. Alternate relish and disdain for public service careers at a time when prestigeful, regular bureaucratic positions were especially hard to come by for Han Chinese, but when the emperor was active in creating challenges and opportunities for specially selected men of talent and ability.

4. Vaunted scorn for power, prominence, and influence in the political or academic hierarchies appearing in men who depended on patrons of wealth and high position, greatly admired the K'ang-hsi emperor, and sought access to scholarly resources collected under imperial auspices and by major cultural arbiters of the day.

In each of these spheres I shall discuss how feelings of ambivalence could give rise to the sort of martial, heroic, active, and practical values which especially marked intellectuals of this generation. And in each case I shall point out how such ambivalences and values resulted in part from conquest-induced intensification of late Ming trends. It is to be hoped that an examination of conditions underlying the peculiarly robust ethos of K'ang-hsi times will better prepare us to explain the somewhat puzzling disappearance of that ethos in the eighteenth century.

It is not surprising to find the sorts of ambivalence outlined above etched most sharply in middle-level figures, men who were socially acceptable to the scholar-official elite but not completely part of it, affected by (more than affecting) major developments of their time, but who constituted an important substratum of the intellectual and political terrain in early Ch'ing times. Examples are drawn in this essay primarily from men who in some way were connected with official historical work, especially on the recently fallen Ming dynasty, for this is the point at which emotional responses to the recent past, attitudes toward government service, and values in scholarship come to a head.

Particular attention will be devoted to three figures who have not received due notice in Western research of this period. Wang Yüan

(1648–1710), Liu Hsien-t'ing (1648–95), and Wen Jui-lin (fl. 1690–1710) were three friends who sought relief from the discomfort of ambivalence through bold declarations of independent values. These men became aware of shared aspirations and frustrations in the 1680s and 1690s when they functioned as assistants to leading scholars at work on two projects of great importance in legitimating Ch'ing rule: compilation of the official *Ming History* and of the monumental geography, *Treatise on the Great Ch'ing Empire* (*Ta-Ch'ing i-t'ung chih*).[1] Like others among their contemporaries, they responded to uncertainties—both in their milieu and in their own minds—by cultivating esteem for vigorous physical activity and pragmatic scholarship (especially geography and military history), admiration for heroes of the recent past, and devil-may-care aloofness toward contemporary standards of success and renown. Frustrated in their desire to seize great but elusive opportunities, these men reacted both by asserting their individuality and by recalling times when meaningful, direct, physical action had been possible in righting human affairs.

In past studies, particularly from the Republican period, such values among men of the mid-K'ang-hsi reign have been cited both as evidence of continuing "Ming loyalism" and as support for the argument that the "practical learning" advocated so rigorously by Yen Yüan and Li Kung (discussed below) would have flourished from the outset had it not been for the Manchus' imposition of a repressive, ultraorthodox brand of Neo-Confucianism on China's intelligentsia. But the attitudes and behavior of these men and their contemporaries were shaped by factors—some peculiar to K'ang-hsi and others of longer standing—more subtle and complex than the presence of one or two maverick philosophers or lingering hopes, on the part of some, for a viable Ming restoration.

"LOYALISM" AND AMBIVALENCE TOWARD THE CH'ING

When a dynasty fell, traditional morality called for a mortal sacrifice on the part of men (and their womenfolk) who had placed themselves in direct relation to the ruling house by earning formal degrees, accepting imperially bestowed honors, or by holding official military or bureaucratic positions. Ideally, such men were ex-

pected to find significant opportunities literally to lay down their
lives; but symbolic death, usually in the form of a radical change in
life style and adoption of a new set of personal names, was also
acceptable, especially if the man had not held an important post in
the defunct government.[2] And preserving oneself—though in relative
seclusion—as the last surviving male who could maintain the welfare
of family and clan was also an honored alternative. The term "Ming
loyalist" could apply meaningfully to anyone who pointedly altered
his or her life patterns and goals to demonstrate unalterable personal
identification with the fallen order. The term need not be restricted
to men who worked actively for a Ming revival or who clearly harbored seditious intentions. On the other hand, it should not be used
indiscriminately in reference to men who wrote or spoke with
enthusiasm or admiration for heroes and martyrs of the Ming demise.

Nor should we assume that scholars who reached adulthood under
the Ming and eschewed serving in the Ch'ing government did so
largely or wholly out of loyalty to "their" dynasty. The ambivalence
felt by many K'ang-hsi scholars regarding employment under the
foreign conquest dynasty should be viewed integrally with long-
standing misgivings toward the civil service examinations (whether
under Ming or Ch'ing auspices), and toward public service itself,
as careers in literature, the fine arts, and private scholarship gained
recognition as full-fledged alternatives—rather than as "poor sisters"
or supplements—to official careers.[3] Much of the anguished introspection characteristic of Ming philosophical discourse was rooted in
the spiritual starvation and perversion of Confucianism's finer
potentialities by the stultifying "eight-legged" essay form of the
increasingly competitive state examinations, success in which was
viewed as almost mandatory for making a mark in the world.[4]

And difficult questions as to the real value of various official and
nonofficial life styles, wrestled with by early Ming intellectuals,
developed another dimension—questions as to the real value of
various official and nonofficial scholarly orientations—as Ming
thought gradually "unfolded" from its early preoccupation with
self-cultivation into wider realms of literary consciousness and
positive scholastic endeavor from the latter half of the sixteenth
century onward.[5] Late Ming factional strife had encouraged total
commitment to partisan political positions and had given more

and more scholars a taste of an ethically sanctioned total disengagement from official life when their faction lost out. For some, the conquest simply provided an objective ethical justification for their subjective disinclination to enter the sometimes distressing social and political competition of government service.[6]

"Loyalist" refusal to serve was one end of a spectrum of attitudes toward government service; other shades can be seen in the responses of Chinese intellectuals to Ch'ing summonses to participate in the compilation of the official *Ming History*. The *Ming History* project was part of a conscious attempt on the part of the K'ang-hsi emperor to unify the country and mollify the Han Chinese intelligentsia after suppression of the San-fan Rebellion. As such, it was launched with considerable fanfare in 1679 by conducting a special *po-hsüeh hung-ju* ("broad learning and vast erudition") examination among a select body of recommendees who were regarded as the most talented and respected of Han Chinese intellectuals remaining outside government service. Although several prominent figures refused to compromise their scruples against serving two dynasties, most of those who were recommended felt honored to participate; and the prospect of being among the fifty successful candidates who would be assigned to work on various parts of the *Ming History* was a definite attraction for some who theretofore had stayed aloof.[7] Despite grandiose beginnings, however, it was not long before most of the original fifty "requested scholars" were retired, dismissed, or transferred to other duties—not because their political allegiance was questioned, but because few of them proved to be especially skilled or avid Ming historians and because some were temperamentally ill suited to bureaucratic scholarship.[8]

The *Ming History* project, begun thirty-five years after the fall of Peking to the Ch'ing, involved primarily men who were born in the last years of the Ming or the early Ch'ing. Most educated members of this generation saw themselves as Ch'ing subjects, associated freely with Ch'ing officials, and in general responded positively to opportunities for public service under the new order. But the *degree* of involvement desired by various men often was influenced by the directness and intensity of their fathers' identification with the old order and mode of response to the conquest.

The "patriot historian" Wan Ssu-t'ung (1638–1702) was the most respected historian of the K'ang-hsi period, and reportedly could recite the entire *Ming Shih-lu*. He was a pupil of the famous loyalist Huang Tsung-hsi (1610–95), and the dying wish of his father, Wan T'ai (1598–1657), was that his son in some way make up for his own failure to gird the southern Ming cause. Wan labored long years, to the day of his death, as backbone of the *Ming History* project, but he steadfastly refused to take any Ch'ing examinations, accept any official designation, or receive any bureaucratic stipend for his services.[9] Wang Yüan, whose father had been an officer in the Ming Imperial Bodyguard and scarcely managed to save himself and his family from destruction during the conquest, at first worked in the History Office on terms similar to those of Wan Ssu-t'ung. Eventually Wang was piqued into proving his literary ability by obtaining a *chü-jen* degree, but he eschewed striving for any higher honors. And Wen Jui-lin, though proud of his uncle's celebrated martyrdom in the Ch'ing subjugation of Anhwei, joined his father in hobnobbing with Peking luminaries, was ready to do his best for the Manchu court, and expressed the view that Heaven bestowed success on sons and grandsons in public service under Ch'ing rule to compensate for the sacrifices of elders who had fought for or maintained personal identity with the Ming.[10]

Moreover, the emotions and imaginations of men who matured in the conquest's wake constantly were stirred by vivid reconstructions of the Ming resistance saga—through privately circulated firsthand accounts, the reminiscences of clan elders, and tales told by aging veterans who congregated in urban or monastic centers. Politically speaking, the younger generation's loyalties lay with the Ch'ing. Nevertheless, the admiration, sympathy, and sorrow they felt for older men so close at hand or so fresh in the collective memory naturally limited the emotional component of their loyalty, and to that extent qualified their commitment to the new order.

But these emotions did not always lead to a nostalgia for the Ming. Many of Huang Tsung-hsi's associates in the Restoration Society (Fushe) were martyrs of the Ch'ing conquest, but Huang's father and other principled men of his time had been martyrs of the Tung-lin opposition to Wei Chung-hsien. No well-read scholar could forget the terrible bureaucratic strife of the late Ming, and how conscientious generals were defeated more by pervasive incompetence and

venality in Ming officialdom than by military enemies, be they bandits or "barbarians." Even during the minor "restoration" of the last
Ming reign in Peking, there came to be a lamentable dearth of talent
and integrity at court, as the suspicious and impatient Ch'ung-chen
emperor (r. 1628–44) went through fifty grand secretaries in seven-
teen years and average official tenure—if not morale—dropped to its
lowest level since the founding of the dynasty.[11]

For some scholars, these attitudes toward serving the Ch'ing were
further complicated by their views on government-sponsored
history-writing. Concomitant with steady growth in the number,
detail, quality, and availability of government documents, records,
and publications since mid-Ming times, there was a deepening ambivalence among conscientious scholars toward large-scale, state-
sponsored research and compilation.[12] It is well known that the great
philosopher-historian Wang Fu-chih (1619–92) stayed close to home
in Hunan after the conquest (with the unhappy exception described
in Ian McMorran's essay in this volume) and that, as a result, his
work remained in relative obscurity until the nineteenth century.[13]
Wang and his disciple Hu Ch'eng-no chose to sacrifice the metropolitan scholar's access to officially compiled or collected materials
in favor of redressing from the provinces what they felt to be a growing imbalance. Hu explicitly objected to the centuries-long trend
toward regarding "history" as "official state history"; and he complained that the concentration of historical materials in imperial
capitals, increasing steadily since Han times, had resulted in: (a) emphasis on a few major (perhaps unworthy) figures to the neglect of
truly salutary achievements on the local level, (b) the study of powerful men rather than the more appropriate analysis of policies and
institutions, and (c) making writers of history vulnerable to pressures from rulers and influential personages at court.[14]

Wan Ssu-t'ung shared his contemporaries' high regard for most
government records and publications; and he favored the History
Office practice of using the "Veritable Records" as a firm outline to
be supplemented at appropriate points with information from other
kinds of material. But Wan took history-writing as a delicate, highly
personal charge and saw conglomerate, bureaucratic historical production as comparable to gathering a crowd off the street to come
in and deliberate the affairs of a household. No sound, informed

judgments could ever arise from the ensuing chaos.[15] Laboring as a private citizen outside the History Office proper, Wan hoped to ameliorate through his own constant endeavor the error, inconsistency, irrational avoidance, and meaningless homogenization of committee-style compilation. Thus his conscientiousness as a historian and his personal scruples about serving the Ch'ing reinforced each other.

In sum, misgivings about government service, in political or scholarly capacities, and about officially sponsored historiography, were not new during those first decades of Ch'ing rule. But widespread feelings of at least emotional loyalty to the fallen dynasty, or sympathy for those fraught with such feelings, intensified ambivalence about service among those who had experienced the conquest, and their offspring. The pain of nostalgia and empathy, combined with career uncertainties, often produced heightened admiration for nonscholarly, nonbureaucratic, heroic, down-to-earth, and unconventional life styles. Scholarly scruples about official historiography went hand in hand with mistrust of conventional bureaucratic categories and factional labels. These themes are discussed in the next section.

SKEPTICISM, EMPIRICISM, AND RESISTANCE ACTIVITY

Naturally, many lives had been lost, fortunes destroyed, and careers ruined in the so-called peasant rebellions that wracked north and west China prior to the Ch'ing invasion, which in turn was resisted most actively in the south and east. Subsequent admiring accounts of persons who made great sacrifices in this chaotic period generally stress such timeless qualities as courage, steadfastness, and loyalty, without emphasizing—sometimes without even mentioning—the agent that necessitated their sacrifice. A great many biographies describe in rather similar terms various perspicacious magistrates who foresaw calamity but, when "the state changed," stuck to their posts, exhorted the inhabitants of their districts to self-defense, and eventually managed to dash off some poetic sentiments as they committed ritual suicide or were captured and ceremoniously executed as a matter of course after firmly refusing all inducements to switch allegiances.

A remarkable feature of certain mid-K'ang-hsi writings, however, is that in choosing timeless qualities for emphasis, a marked
preference is shown for a more martial brand of heroism similar to
that of the traditional Chinese "knight-errant" (*yu-hsia*), and for
subjects who, though they may not have *died* in the changeover,
took vigorous, necessary, practical, and physically demanding action
to save their dynasty and their people. The following biographical
sketch by Wang Yüan shows several characteristics—an obscure
subject, martial audacity, attention to strategy, loyalty among
peers, and plenty of action:

> Wang the Righteous Fighter—his real name is not known—was
> a native of Shantung and as a youth engaged in farming. One
> night he accompanied his older brother to do the plowing. At
> that time there were many robbers, and his brother cautioned
> him saying, "Be very quiet. If the robbers hear us, they'll make
> off with our ox." The Righteous Fighter, who had just turned
> eight *sui,* shook his whip and shouted, "I'll kill any bandit who
> comes around!" His brother was so frightened that he went
> home, but the Righteous Fighter drove the ox and plowed until
> dawn. People in the locality were quite astonished. He grew up to
> be very strong, was skilled with both swords and firearms, and
> had extraordinary courage and strategic talent. . . . He was eight
> feet tall, very ugly, and though slow of speech, was loyal and
> sincere in his very nature. . . . A certain Chu T'ien-yu was a great
> adventurer in Honan—swift, agile, and adept in combat. He had
> become angered at the rampaging of the pernicious bandits and
> wanted to join with some duty-conscious soldiers to aid his
> monarch, so he formed a bond of brotherhood with the Righ-
> teous Fighter and they planned a great undertaking. . . . They
> began as forty-two men at Feng-hsiang, where the bandits at-
> tacked them furiously with two thousand footsoldiers and
> cavalrymen. Drums rolling, they moved forward, T'ien-yu split-
> ting his men into two wings of twenty each for a counterat-
> tack. They beheaded one subordinate [bandit] general and
> killed over a hundred others. Startled into disorder, the ban-
> dits had to retreat several *li,* regroup, and advance again in a
> circular formation. With arrows falling like rain, the forty-two

men chatted and joked as they joined in battle, again slaying several hundred; but after three days and nights of hard fighting, the bandits were more numerous than before. As his strength gave out, T'ien-yu became surrounded by a thick ring of bandits. The Righteous Fighter gave a mighty hoot, leaped onto his horse, and galloped in, bringing a spear with his left hand and using his right to remove his armor for T'ien-yu. When T'ien-yu refused to accept, the Righteous Fighter said, "The world can do without me, but not without you, Sir." Forcing him to put on the armor, [the Righteous Fighter] broke the encirclement and helped T'ien-yu get free. [Then] the forty other men contended in cheering, "Master Wang truly is a Righteous Fighter!"[16]

As for men in the educated elite, Wen Jui-lin's favorite figure was Ying T'ing-chi, who served as righthand man to the Southern Ming's greatest martyr, Shih K'o-fa. Variously employed as a troop supervisor, logistics director, personnel manager, and trusted policy advisor, Ying derived special virtue from combining practical experience and common sense with book-learning in astrology and prognostication for immediate application to pressing problems. He halted the mounting of cannon on a sandy riverbank, opposed a military colonization plan in spite of its longstanding precedent, accurately read the (usually dire) significance of abnormal biological and celestial phenomena, and supervised Shih's "hall for honoring worthy men" (li-hsien kuan). Almost to a man, those chosen from this cadre pool in a "special selection" (p'o-ko chih hsüan) stayed with Shih to the death at Yangchow; but the fact that Ying T'ing-chi escaped that awful massacre by being on a logistical assignment at the time did not reduce Wen Jui-lin's admiration.[17]

Among those who reacted more passively to the conquest, special attention is drawn to men who found consolation and physical release in mundane toil and backbending agronomy, and to others whose psychological nonacceptance of the postconquest status quo found expression in mysterious, chimerical, outlandish, and even crazed behavior. What reasons can be suggested for this attention to martial heroism, pragmatic activity, and unconventional behavior, especially when displayed by obscure men in the recent past? Again, various kinds of ambivalence exhibited by seventeenth-century

intellectuals, and men of the K'ang-hsi period in particular, seem
relevant in answering this question.

First, emphasis on men's activities, no matter how strange, rather
than on their words or philosophical stances, and on the actual per-
petration of events by a wide range of men, rather than on a few
morally exemplary but perhaps ineffectual figures, was in keeping
with trends in Chinese thought that had been developing throughout the Ming. William Theodore de Bary, in discussing broad continuities in Chinese thought from late Sung into Ch'ing times, points
to the secularization of both Neo-Confucian and Buddhist strains,
that is, gradual loss of interest in the individual's quest for spiritu-
ality (or sagehood) compensated by growing interest in critical,
broadly informed, yet humane intellectuality and scholarship.
Manifestations of the dominant Ming reaction against "empty"
speculative metaphysics generally took as objects of criticism the
quiescence of the Ch'eng-Chu school (or "Sung Learning" as a
whole), the existentialist element in Wang Yang-ming thought, or
the irresponsibility and irrelevance of Buddhism. But de Bary argues
persuasively that this reaction owed much to the respect for doubt
and questioning, the open (hsü) state of mind, receptivity to manifest principles, and objectivity through self-transcendence which
always had been fundamental in Neo-Confucianism—and characteristic, as well, of the pluralistic standpoint and critical detachment
fostered by Buddhism.[18]

> . . . there was a constant interplay in the development of Neo-
> Confucianism, with its intense moral concern complemented
> by spiritual transcendence and intellectual detachment, and the
> latter at times providing a lofty perspective on the narrowness
> and rigidities of the moralistic approach. From this point of
> view the new learning or "enlightenment" of the seventeenth and
> eighteenth centuries, with its great stress on practicality and its
> distinctive "humanistic pragmatism" can be seen in part as the
> offspring of underlying tendencies in Neo-Confucianism, while
> at the same time it rebelled against its parent, using the very
> weapons of intellectual objectivity and practical concern which
> the latter had put into its hands.[19]

De Bary adds that the critical and iconoclastic writings of men such as Li Chih (1527–1602) and Chiao Hung (1540?–1620)[20] "shook the intellectual world of late Ming Confucians as nothing had before. Later, with the added shock of dynastic collapse and the damage to Chinese self-confidence of subjection to alien rule, the intellectual despair of the Confucian at midcentury was such that it generated both a deeper questioning of tradition and an effort to establish it on more solid foundations."[21]

Perhaps the most thoroughgoing critic of both Sung and Ming approaches to Confucian cultivation was the Chihli fundamentalist Yen Yüan (1635–1704), whose personal crisis in seeking sagehood was directly affected by family dislocations of the conquest years. Suddenly repudiating the Neo-Confucian tradition that almost literally had consumed him in his early adulthood, Yen charged that the Sung legacy of the Ch'eng brothers and Chu Hsi (condemned together with Wang Yang-ming) had perverted the entire sense of "learning"—a very physical, immediate, practical pursuit inseparable from moral cultivation in all-around men of classical times—into dabbling, pen-and-ink mimicry and rarefied, abstract speculation. This view, he said, had stultified bodies and minds and rendered national leadership ineffectual for the ensuing six hundred years. At times both a farmer and a medical doctor, Yen rigorously maintained a rustic regimen in comparative isolation, when he taught, stressing actual performance of the classical six arts (ceremony, music, archery, charioteering, writing, and mathematics), and supplementing institutional historical studies with applied science and military training.[22] Although Yen's thought was not influential again until the late nineteenth century, it found fertile ground in the K'ang-hsi period among men who held fresh admiration for the many heroes who had taken action to save the Ming dynasty and had struggled in vain against pervasive ineptitude in the official class.

The cultural attraction to concrete fact and personal action, and the high drama and historical importance of the events of the conquest, reinforced an already powerful interest in the gathering and examination of evidence on the recent past. Interest in recent history had been growing throughout the Ming period, during which more men wrote histories of their own dynasty—with heightened critical awareness and attention to historical growth and change—than ever before.[23] Late Ming scholars like Wang Shih-chen, Chiao Hung, and

Ch'en Jen-hsi[24] had begun to develop critical methods for the study
of recent history, emphasizing the distinction between *chang-ku*
(historical documents) and *yeh-shih* (miscellaneous private accounts).
Among the many K'ang-hsi scholars who carried on this endeavor
was Hsü Ping-i (1633–1711), who built an unrivaled collection of
private histories from the Ming-end and conquest decades, less out of
fascination than out of suspicion. Through comparison and interviewing, Hsü doggedly sought to establish the actual circumstances
of men's deaths in order to offset the tendency of family histories
and hack *yeh-shih* to dramatize and embellish the passing of almost
any man who happened to die in times of turmoil.[25] Increasingly,
thinkers wanted to know in very concrete terms what had actually
existed and transpired in the world, especially in the recent past.

This "evidential" orientation fed and was fed by a growing ambivalence toward the authority of the written word—its capacity to distort through abstraction, but its immense importance as the key to
continuity with the past and projection into the future. David Nivison has attributed this "suspicion of words," this denial of value in
abstraction and general statement, to the gradual erosion of Sung
Neo-Confucianism's dominance by intuitionist Wang Yang-ming
thought, in its various ramifications.[26] This philosophical development was paralleled by changes in the media of communication
available to intellectuals. As the scale and techniques of printing
improved throughout the Ming, and documentation—both official
and otherwise—increased in volume and variety, intellectuals gradually came to discriminate more and more carefully among different kinds of source material. As a consequence, literary societies
were able to center their meetings frequently on discussions of
divergencies in various copies and editions of key classical texts.[27]

By the latter part of the seventeenth century, scholars had become acutely aware of semantic pitfalls and the insidious capacity
of arbitrary or biased verbal constructs to distort reality and delude
or mislead posterity. Scholars of all philosophical backgrounds
enthusiastically welcomed two particularly great exegetical studies
that were completed (building on Ming skills) in the last decade of
the seventeenth century, and which proved conclusively the spurious-
ness of whole portions of long-venerated works: Yen Jo-chü's *Inquiry
into the Authenticity of the Ancient-text 'Classic of History' (Ku-*

wen Shang-shu shu-cheng) and Hu Wei's *Clarification of Diagrams to the 'Classic of Changes' (I-t'u ming-pien).* And sensitivity to the undesirable political and philosophical consequences of employing ill-chosen biographical rubrics is especially evident in Huang Tsung-hsi's successful argument against perpetuating in the *Ming History* the previous official distinction between (more exalted) adherents of orthodox Sung Neo-Confucianism and all other (slightly disparaged) philosophers, including the Wang Yang-ming school.[28]

Nor was Wang Yüan one to be fettered or duped by hand-me-down forms in writing. In one essay he urged the flexible adoption of whatever mode might best suit the historian's intent and purpose.

> A common saying [in praise of historical prose] is "it's just like *The Mean.*" But actually, there is nothing that deludes the posterity of everyone in the world more than the written word. [Writing styles] invariably follow the views of different periods and change with the atmosphere of the times. Really, though, what agent is it that causes this change? Men, of course. Though men write under [the influence of] such change, should they be considered incapable of getting atop change [and mastering it]? Mencius said that any man can be another Yao or Shun; and I humbly submit that any man can be another Tso [-ch'iu Ming] or [Ssu-] ma Ch'ien.[29]

Perhaps Wen Jui-lin was the friend to whom Wang Yüan's exhortation was directed. In any case, considering seventeenth-century skepticism toward facilely assigned labels and rubrics, it is not so surprising that Wen pointedly—and quite unconventionally—rejected the idea of categorizing the most important biographies in his general history of the Southern Ming. His intention was to focus on men's active responses to the most crucial of all moral tests, namely, the destruction of a great dynasty, and to record the bearing of men's actions on the outcome of events. In Wen's view, the capacity to take significant, effective steps in times of crisis leveled all social distinctions and rendered irrelevant such traditional biographical designations as "great ministers," "Confucian scholars," and "litterateurs."[30] Wen's work is an example of the way in which self-expression could take historiographical form, and in which attention to observable activity could enable an author to avoid the imposition of unsatisfactory concepts that might hamper the independent judgment of subsequent generations.

Wen Jui-lin's history also shows another kind of avoidance which illustrates postconquest intensification of Ming skepticism and resulting emphasis on action in historical portrayals. Because physical (preferably pragmatic) manifestations of personal cultivation and men's actual impact on events were prime criteria for Wen, he tends to point out, wherever possible, his subjects' affinity for high-spirited adventurers or noble fighters and their willingness to gather comrades and practice martial skills when chaotic times seemed imminent. Left in studied neglect are scholarly pedigrees and politicoliterary associations, allegations of partisan motivations behind certain policies, and men known chiefly for their fiery memorials and other high-minded writings—matters that occupy page after page in earlier private histories more concerned with court and partisan affairs—though Wen never fails to mention interest in "learning of practical applicability in ordering affairs" (*ching-shih chih-yung*).[31] Complementing Wen's indifference to the specific content of factional wrangling is his praise for aloofness from partisanship and his favorable treatment of any nonpartisan or moderating role. In treating the most crucial purge of the Southern Ming Hung-kuang period (1644–45), for instance, Wen is unconcerned about the actual guilt of parties on either side of the case and finds fitting and predictable the demise of any who venture into the deadly games of court chicanery and partisan trickery.[32]

Early in the seventeenth century, as factional struggles undermined coherent administration, ruined promising careers, and even produced some martyrs, more scholar-officials had come to doubt the value of partisan crusades and countercrusades; and disillusionment overtook fear in the Ch'ung-chen period, as the Restoration Society and its affiliate politicoliterary associations, founded in strong moral-ethical conviction, became bandwagons for men of unclear commitment who aspired to fame, influence, and high office.[33] To outsiders on the local level, membership in such societies increasingly appeared to license petty elitists in throwing their weight around the community. Conscientious partisans condemned machine politics on all sides. For example, Hsia Yün-i (1596–1645), despite the strident objections of Huang Tsung-hsi, saw some "pernicious clique" actions as understandable responses to "righteous" excess. Just prior to the conquest, Hsia, reflecting on the Tung-lin experience, wrote that, although cliques could be mechanisms for facilitating governance, nevertheless they tended to degenerate, bring out the worst in men, and cause disaster for the state.[34] A prime example of disaffection with polemical confrontation after the Ming demise is the contrast between combative Huang Tsung-hsi and his own best student, the quiet, self-effacing, uncontentious Wan Ssu-t'ung, who confessed that he had turned away from debate to solitary, concentrated reading of the classics and histories after incurring the wrath of his master and fellow students for keeping an open mind toward a heterodox thinker inimical to Huang.[35]

Wen Jui-lin was one among many in mid-K'ang-hsi times who preferred to avoid voicing opinions on prominent figures of the preceding several decades, during which factional struggles had produced vast quantities of deceitful, biased writing, blatant propaganda, and even surreptitious destruction and alteration of the most closely guarded official records. This tawdry literary legacy alone might have been sufficient to cause thorough skepticism toward partisan dogma and pat sectarian judgments. But men of Wen's generation also could survey events of the Ming collapse and easily conclude that no faction or element, despite past rhetoric, had held any monopoly on either righteousness or perfidy.[36] Granted, the Manchus took definite steps to eradicate factional contention among the Han educated elite; and factional concerns naturally subsided as ultimate control of governmental affairs passed to the Manchus, out of the hands of Chinese ministers who had not served the Ch'ing court before 1644.[37] But it should be noted that Wen Jui-lin was not unique in his ability to trace immediate ancestors on both the "pure" and the "pernicious" sides of late Ming struggles. Also, it was widely felt that debilitating factional and sectarian squabbling had led directly to China's humiliating subjugation by barbarians and that such quarrelsome behavior should be left behind, both for the good of Chinese culture and to dispel painful memories.

Whatever a K'ang-hsi writer's reasons might have been for wishing to avoid political issues in recent history, a stress on martial exploits and practical activity, especially when engaged in by unsung heroes

of low rank or commoner status, allowed a shift of focus away from
major court figures and military commanders, who invariably wore—
or were assigned—party tags. It should be clear to anyone familiar
with the eighteenth-century flowering of *k'ao-cheng* (text-critical)
research that a healthy spirit of doubt toward written records continued to gain strength after the K'ang-hsi period. Less immediately
apparent is the fact that interest in actions by a wide variety of individuals, skepticism about partisan labels, and the search for reliable
evidence in all kinds of sources—all "enlightened" developments in
de Bary's broad sense—were compatible with neglect of larger concerns, such as political organization for morality and effectiveness in
governance, for which eighteenth-century *k'ao-cheng* scholarship is
notorious.

Thus we have seen in seventeenth-century culture a peculiar connection between distrust of the concept-sealing power of the written,
transmitted word—rhetoric, classification, interpretation—in both
politics and scholarship, which was serving both destructive and con-
structive purposes in late Ming, and the ambivalence of K'ang-hsi-
period scholars toward conventional frames of record and discourse,
which was heightened by the ineffectuality of the educated elite
during the Ming collapse. Though more ambivalent than rebellious,
many K'ang-hsi scholars shifted significantly away from traditional
elite preoccupations (with "important" men, factional and sectarian maneuverings, philosophical niceties, etc.) toward such con-
ventionally disvalued concerns as little-known eccentrics, hero
figures, inglorious historical periods, and the physically active,
full-spirited, martial way of life—all especially easy to pursue in
those decades of newfound peace and stability.

WANDERLUST, DISRUPTION, AND NONLITERARY VALUES

Of course, heightened interest in the recent past was natural just
following a period of dramatic change. Moreover, enthusiasm for
ching-shih chih-yung studies, which had been growing since the mid-
sixteenth century, enhanced interest in the recent past as an especially accessible source of raw information for men who sought
economic, institutional, and geographical answers to practical problems of governance and warfare. But the study of history—whether
recent or remote, *ching-shih* or otherwise—was, after all, a scholarly

pursuit, and many men who grew to maturity just following the conquest had not fallen neatly into the conventional scholar's mold. The misgivings they felt about the desirability or feasibility of striving to attain the traditional literatus life style tended to accentuate admiration for nonliterary qualities.

The Ch'ing success had skewed men's academic orientations in several ways. It almost goes without saying that decades of bandit depredations and conquest by an alien element had caused a great deal of economic and social disruption. Of course, conflicts developed between Manchus and Chinese; but also, where enmity smoldered within Han Chinese society itself, the conquest situation often fired it anew.[38] Conditions remained unstable through much of the K'ang-hsi reign; in some cases, well-to-do families were ruined, and their educated male members were forced into farming, trade, or such fairly erudite but pragmatic professions as medicine. Since merchants and drug-peddlers often were itinerant, these roles proved especially suitable for men who had to move about avoiding the authorities or local enemies—the most outstanding figures in such circumstances being Ku Yen-wu (1613–82) and Fang I-chih (d. 1671?).[39] And traditional association of druggists and healers with Taoist heterodoxy may even have made such guises seem ruefully appropriate to cultivated and self-conscious victims of human affairs.

In other instances, men of military background who joined the Ch'ing side were able to assume civil positions and perform quasi-literary functions. A case in point is Chiang Jih-sheng, who completed his admiring chronicle of the Cheng clan's resistance on Taiwan and elsewhere and planned to submit it to the History Office at a time (1704) when most writers shunned the topic. Chiang's father had been a Ming commander in Fukien but was made magistrate of a subprefecture after changing his allegiance to the Ch'ing. Because Chiang, then still a child, accompanied his father continually, he was able to learn all about current affairs from an early age; and as an adult he hung around the yamen working as a litigation specialist while writing his account of exploits across the waves. A friend, prefacing Chiang's work, had this lament:

> Ah! With talent like his, hitting on a time of unusual opportunities, everyone said he surely would find something suitable. But

what can be done when fate goes against the times? Repeatedly [Chiang] fell into grief, everything he did was untimely, and he encountered numerous pitfalls. He was fated to make plans with friends and then have them come to naught. Like the oriole, he wanted to whistle up [companions and be a] righteous adventurer; but in the end there was [only] the slanderous, suspicious chatter of little sparrows.[40]

For those who retained the capacity to enter the civil service, success in the onerous, intellectually stifling examinations—already terribly competitive owing to increases in population and literacy through the Ming period—became even more difficult under K'ang-hsi conditions, as the Ch'ing, for reasons of security and partly out of sinophobia, made severe cuts in the examination quotas for Han Chinese and consistently awarded the most important provincial posts to Chinese bannermen, then considered more reliable than Chinese who had not fought on the Manchu side.[41] And prestigious positions that were opened to Han Chinese initially tended to be sinecures offered to established leaders of the literati elite in an effort to win tacit endorsements and general acquiescence in Ch'ing rule. Throughout the K'ang-hsi period, young scholars in general found it particularly difficult to advance via the regular examination route and obtain even minor bureaucratic posts—if, indeed, they deemed it worth their time and effort to try.

Despite Ch'ing parsimony in awarding actual civil and military positions to Han Chinese through the regular examination system, during the K'ang-hsi reign various consolidation tasks of the new dynasty (controlling the Yellow River, rehabilitating the Grand Canal, defeating Wu San-kuei, the Taiwan regime, and the Central Asian Eleuths, mapping and assessing the land, and so on) provided ample employment for educated men skilled in transport, drafting, engineering, surveying, accounting, and general management. This labor demand was filled, outside the purely military sphere, through ad hoc recommendation, patronage, and utilization of private aides (*mu-yu*) attached to responsible officials, without altering the low civil-service examination quotas. Wen Jui-lin, for one, found both interesting and invigorating his trip through Manchuria as an illustrator for the surveying expedition of 1693, launched ostensibly in conjunction with work on the *I-t'ung chih,* but also in the wake of a Manchu diplomatic and military campaign to halt Russian penetration in the northeast and delineate the northern boundary of the empire. In his account of that trip, as in his history of the Southern Ming, Wen repeatedly expresses his admiration for the Manchus' integration of social and military organization, their fighting skill, and for men who could adjust to hard riding life on the steppe.[42] Indeed, the pervasiveness of energetic, purposeful movement during this period—often though not always under official auspices—suggests that, in his robust vitality, the K'ang-hsi emperor was exemplifying more than leading the temporary rise of a virile ethos.

Of course, not all men turned to seeking fulfillment in less prestigious careers involving physical skill and activity. When the usual avenues to full scholarly recognition and prominence in public affairs appeared blocked, some naturally became embittered. The K'ang-hsi scholar Tai Ming-shih (1653–1713), who eventually was executed for his imprudence, is an example of the way in which frustrated aspirations could result in deliberately offensive behavior and caustic ridicule of ordinary practices in literati society.[43] But several of Tai's associates, though they may have enjoyed his flaunting nonconformity, did not share his negative attitude. Tai's close friend and literary mentor, Fang Pao (1668–1749), later a very prominent patron himself, expressed great admiration for men he had come to know in the capital (to his regret, all slightly older than himself) who devoted their attention and energies to recent and contemporary affairs and enhanced both their reputations and self-respect by refusing to bend under pressures from powerful patrons and examiners.[44] One of Fang's favorites was Wang Yüan, who, having been reared by his father among swordsman-adventurers, championed robust values and a full-spirited approach to life, as opposed to the effete, degenerate values of typical mincing, ineffectual scholar-officials. Despite his almost studied audacity and arrogance, Wang drew a large following among young men who were inspired by his insistence on the superiority of an active life and the importance of combining book-learning and moral cultivation with actual behavior and practical experience.

Among Wang Yüan's associates, Wen Jui-lin, in particular, drew on recent history to show how numberless gallant men who shared his values had been prevented from executing their plans or rising to positions of authority by pedantic, jealous, purblind, but high-ranking scholar-officials. Echoing the thought of Yen Yüan, Wen saw this domination of competence by incompetence as the result of abstract notions of cultivation and learning that had been inculcated (especially since Southern Sung times) by self-styled authorities who presumed on refined cerebration alone to maintain claims to superiority, with disastrous consequences for the state.

> After the Chin period when men esteemed "pure discussion" and Sung when the philosophy of rationalism became respected, military preparedness became regarded as an incidental matter and commanders as boorish fellows. Men adopted the rationales of armistice and demobilization to explain away their own incompetence, and the world faddishly followed along. Consequently, generals seldom were chosen for their moral character, and no mutual respect was shown in military families. Our best armor became rusty and dull, the ranks thin and weak until, when bandits ravaged and barbarous tribes encroached, coarse, violent desperadoes—at first treated with contempt but later feared—were respectfully awarded commands. Overbearing troops and ruthless generals took in bandits to strengthen themselves alone, as cowardly civil officials feared attempting to save the situation. Thus, China's decline in these later ages is entirely the fermented by-product of rotting scholars.[45]

In Wen's view, even bandits sometimes were worthy of respect for their unqualified sense of loyalty and willingness to take action for a cause. After all, they too often had been victims of the same elitist suppression that befell men who did not become outlaws but felt similar outrage against bureaucratic authority and all those elegantly useless "flowers of the examination roster." In recounting the never-say-die career of Li Ting-kuo, renegade defender of the last Southern Ming court, Wen Jui-lin exclaims, "Robbers and bandits are more worthy than the most successful examinees!"[46]

For men of the K'ang-hsi period who had no secure academic or bureaucratic standing, stories of energetic and effective heroes of the Ming demise could provide an outlet for feelings of sympathy and admiration toward men of their father's generation, and could affirm for them the potential worth of conscientious, capable men—perhaps like themselves—who were kept out of leadership positions by distorted cultural values. Such stories allowed indirect venting of frustration with self-satisfied arbiters in control of affairs who precluded challenges to their own status by ignoring true talent. Looking beyond the K'ang-hsi period, moreover, it is interesting to observe that the Southern Ming resistance was studied most avidly for personal pleasure by abrasive and overly candid Chinese scholars whose career expectations were thwarted or who failed to achieve their capacity in the "world of affairs." (The best examples are Ch'üan Tsu-wang [1705–55], Yang Feng-pao [1754–1816], and Tai Wang [1837–73]. Tai was also one of the first to begin reasserting Yen-Li pragmatism in the nineteenth century.)

Liu Hsien-t'ing, too, was inclined to deride his less pragmatic and less adventurous peers; but, unlike Wen Jui-lin, he did not blame a specific philosophy or a class of men for this divergence in values. He was closer to Wang Yüan in feeling that contemporary scholars exaggerated the weight of past accomplishments and sold short the capacities of their own generation. In 1692, when climbing Heng Mountain in east-central Hunan, Liu had this thought:

> In former times men travelled to the five sacred mountains
> in order to broaden their aspirations and vision and to augment
> their insight. It truly was complementary to reading, moral
> cultivation, social exchange, and experience in affairs. The only
> differences [among these activities] lay in degrees of visibility.
> [Such travel] increased their ability to think and express them-
> selves, so the benefit was enormous. . . . [Now if a man of] my
> generation climbs a famous mountain and scans a marvellous
> scene, he thinks to himself, "My ambitions and mental range are
> still those of an ignorant bumpkin. Why should I strain to waste
> several days' time, expending my energies, belaboring the muscles
> and bones of my servants, and using up the incense and food of
> the monasteries just to go climbing up and down? Really, drink-
> ing and snoozing under the eaves of a thatch hut would be so
> much more peaceful and comfortable." I must strictly guard
> against this in my own mind.[47]

Of course, Liu Hsien-t'ing was not unique. The turbulence of the Ming-Ch'ing changeover forced many people, from Ch'ing officials to refugees, to travel widely and to pay close attention to recent history.

The ardent Ming loyalist Ch'ü Ta-chün (1630–96) spent almost
twenty years avoiding probable arrest in his home district of P'an-yü,
Kwangtung. Shen Hsün-wei, author of a basic work on the bandit
scourge in Szechwan, suffered severe dislocation throughout his
younger years after his father's martyrdom as a Ming official in
Chengtu left him an orphan, far from his home in Kiangsu. And
among Ch'ing officials, Feng Su (1628–92) proved to be a singularly
empathetic and resourceful inquirer as his duties carried him all over
Kwangtung and the southwest in the wake of the conquest and
during the San-fan Rebellion.[48]

It should be pointed out, however, that men with remarkable zest
for travel and quasi-scientific observation had emerged among well-
educated Chinese prior to 1644. The most notable among these is the
indefatigable geographer Hsü Hung-tsu (1586–1641), who, though
comfortably well-to-do and certainly of the educated elite, chose
not to take the examination route to officialdom, and instead
pursued thirty-four years of wide-ranging geographical explorations,
the most ambitious of which was completed in 1640.[49] And specific
events of the conquest cannot account completely for the wanderlust of men like Liu Hsien-t'ing and Ku Yen-wu, or for the robust life
enjoyed by Ku's friend Li Yin-tu (1631–92). Having succeeded in the
po-hsüeh hung-ju examination, Li could have settled down to a comfortable and prestigious career in Peking, but he left the History
Office after only a few months and returned to his native Shensi,
where he delighted in mapmaking expeditions southward to the
Yangtze and northward beyond the Great Wall, perhaps recalling the
trips he had made as a youth to gather fighting men at the time of
the Ming collapse.[50]

Thus, complementing intellectual trends, we find the life situations
and career prospects of many K'ang-hsi men contributing to ambivalence toward staid, circumscribed, bureaucratic desk jobs—still
attractive, but when out of reach, scorned. The conquest accentuated sharply for a time the normal rate of change in men's careers
and social positions, stirring up an especially rich mixture of civil and
military, literary and nonliterary elements. The effect on scholarship,
however, was less abrupt and more sustained, as it reinforced late
Ming tendencies to get closer to the ground—and the lakes, rivers,
and canals—for "studies of practical use in governance."

HOPE AND HESITATION UNDER K'ANG-HSI PATRONAGE

As mentioned above, the difficulty of advancement through formal channels and deep misgivings as to the intellectual and practical value of studying for the state examinations both contributed to K'ang-hsi scholars' ambivalence toward entering the Manchu-dominated government. But minor functionaries and degree-holders who otherwise might have despaired of finding fulfillment in Ch'ing service were kept from complete alienation and pessimism and were encouraged to continue putting forth their best efforts by two factors that were especially operative in K'ang-hsi times: (1) the emperor's predilection for lifting men from relative obscurity into high positions, with scant regard for normal examination and promotion procedures, when he happened to take note of some special accomplishment; and (2) large-scale patronage engaged in by certain prominent and wealthy Ch'ing officials, who took in and supported scholars who impressed them in some way.

Among those who served the K'ang-hsi emperor with unusual dedication after being raised by fiat to the pinnacle of imperial confidence were the great hydraulic engineer Chin Fu, the bibliophile Chu I-tsun, and the trusted counselor Li Kuang-ti; and such special treatment provoked considerable resentment against the fast riser Wang Hao, who was allowed to sit for the palace examination and was placed in the Imperial Study without going through the usual preliminary testing stages. Though jealousies and procedural objections often resulted, the K'ang-hsi emperor made the most of both Manchu authoritarianism and Chinese esteem for a ruler who could recognize and utilize talent in providing a kind of firm and sagacious leadership that was welcome to those who remembered the paralysis of late Ming times. And in his personal style the emperor displayed a combination of martial vigor, insatiable curiosity, sensible tolerance, and down-to-earth concern for plain effectiveness that attracted capable men to his service.[51]

One minister who encouraged the emperor to conduct special selections was Wu Han.[52] In 1689 Wu became a tutor in the Imperial Academy, and in subsequent years he continued to assist the students of that institution. These *kung-sheng,* literally "tribute students," were recommended by authorities in their home districts to study in Peking, where they could take special examinations to obtain minor official positions, and where their chances of passing the *chü-jen* examinations were enhanced. Being in the capital, they also had more opportunity than licentiates in the provinces to become acquainted with, and receive recommendations from, influential officials and courtiers. Wu also was a major scholars' patron in the capital, his guests including Wang Yüan, Li Kung, and other men who became deeply impressed by the radically stringent approach to Confucian cultivation advocated by Yen Yüan.

Because Yen did not frequent metropolitan centers, his philosophy developed currency among K'ang-hsi intellectuals largely through the efforts of Li Kung, whose role in softening his mentor's thorough disparagement of textual pursuits was essential to its appeal to a generation attracted by physical activity, yet unwilling to forego the satisfactions of high culture. It was Wu Han who gave Li domicile in Peking and subsidized the printing of his *Clarification of Matters in the 'Great Learning'* (*Ta-hsüeh pien-yeh*), a work which excited such readers as Wen Jui-lin by rejecting study and contemplation as adequate ways to "investigate things."[53]

The patronage offered by Wu Han was small-scale compared to that of the famous "Three Hsü Brothers" (Ch'ien-hsüeh, Ping-i, and Yüan-wen), who all took top examination honors, served in a number of ministerial capacities, built huge book collections, and served in succession as directors of the *Ming History* compilation.[54] Their uncle, Ku Yen-wu, was among those independent scholars who did not look with favor on the type of aggregate literary activity sponsored by his nephews; and when his pupil P'an Lei was invited to join the Hsü entourage, Ku attempted to dissuade him, saying:

> The more lofty [Hsü Ch'ien-hsüeh's] position becomes, the more numerous are his guests; the sycophantic remain and the unbending leave. Now he intends to invite one or two scholarly gentlemen so as to cover up the hordes, but he does not understand that the fragrant and the offensive cannot be stored in the same spot. . . . Seeing the activities of those who hasten to him like flies and ants frightens me. . . . If you go, you will associate day and night with bullies and slaves; more than being unable to read or study, you will certainly suffer by associating with those villains.[55]

But those less eminent seldom could afford Ku's detachment.

Scores were grateful for the haven Hsü Ch'ien-hsüeh offered in hard times, for intangibles such as sympathy, encouragement, and the opportunity to make stimulating acquaintances, for access to his extensive library resources, and especially for his unfailing attention to such mundane matters as debts, travel and funeral expenses, and recommendations for income-sustaining employment. When Hsü was forced to leave Peking in 1690 (as a result of involvement in Manchu clique politics), the minor functionaries of all the imperial documentation offices are said to have sent him off wailing, "After you leave, Sir, who will keep us alive?"[56]

Since the selection and promotion of promising men by the emperor or by influential patrons occurred in no regular, predictable pattern, attainment of fame and success appeared tantalizingly unpredictable to the sort of man—often receptive to Li Kung's ideas—who relied more on demonstrating his practical abilities than on writing perfect eight-legged essays. And this factor seems to have had a distinct psychological effect on some lesser-known scholars in the mid-K'ang-hsi period. Hopeful but unrecognized men had to be ready for any sudden opportunity to display and utilize their talents (and perhaps to exhaust themselves at impossible tasks). At the same time, they had to be prepared to accept nonrecognition and live in obscurity, if that were their fate. To hope or not to hope? That was a subtly discomfiting question that could be dealt with by adopting (consciously or unconsciously) a nose-thumbing, devil-may-care attitude toward conventional standards of success and recognized authority.

Liu Hsien-t'ing, for instance, is said to have deliberately slept on a bench and snored through two days of lectures by a prominent Buddhist master before boldly taking the speaker's place and overwhelming everyone present with his own views.[57] And part of Liu's appeal to contemporaries was his utter disregard for the tattered, disheveled state of his clothing, his physical handicaps (one blind eye and a broken left arm), and the reaction that his odd appearance and frank opinions might provoke in other men. Small wonder that one of Liu's warmest admirers was Wang Yüan, who is described in the following terms by Li Kung:

> Wang regarded himself as a heroic figure. When night fell he
> would always set out some liquor and drink his fill. Then he

would lift his face and sit up straight—eyes like lightning, beard
like a two-pronged spear—and discourse on all kinds of topics
ranging through history. After becoming drunk he would casti-
gate high and mighty celebrities of the day, here and there
adding words of ridicule.[58]

Another friend recalled Wang's sentiments from a more somber
moment:

It really is not easy to gain release from melancholy,
But pouring wine with you, Sir, does cheer me somewhat.
Appreciation of talent has been rare since the heroes of old,
And finding fulfillment is difficult for my generation.
Aspirations dissipate as we amuse ourselves over precious swords.
Hope-filled dreams waste away as we travel aimlessly about.
After returning, we [can only] get drunk together in golden
    pavilions,
And look out on the desolation that surrounds us.[59]

And the poignant situation of high-spirited scholars in K'ang-hsi
times is further illustrated in this comment by Wang Yüan upon
viewing a portrait of Wen Jui-lin:

He sat, legs apart, on a deerskin spread over a large rock, holding
a book in his left hand and stroking his beard with the right,
surveying all before him with a look of sublime detachment in
his clear eyes. . . . Ah, Wen truly is a man of depth! I have observed his lofty vision and heroic vigor, his manner of discussion often distinguishing him from the common run of men.
Hmph. What sorts of mediocre fellows are in the capital these
days! And yet Wen retains his dignity moving among them. One
cannot tell whether such a man will ever meet his big chance in
life. Nevertheless, . . . that Wen, from inner stillness, has taken his
stand in purity and can observe all the affairs of the world, is this
not what we term "emerging from life's grime unsoiled"? What
does it matter to such a man if great opportunity never arises?[60]

Such descriptions suggest that the flamboyant, almost swaggering
indifference so notable in K'ang-hsi men who professed martial
values, grew out of the necessity to be constantly poised, if not for
the call to arms of bygone days, then for those less romantic big
chances that still might—or might never—come.

Of course, frustrated adventurers probably dotted the intelligentsia throughout Chinese history. But certain conditions peculiar to the K'ang-hsi period allowed several such figures to participate significantly in the greatest scholarly achievements of their time. Especially during this period, scholars who had a penchant for travel, personal inquiry, and firsthand observation (including many who shrank from serving the Ch'ing government) were able to interact on an informal basis, over long and short periods of time, with less mobile scholars who husbanded large quantities of documentation compiled or collected under official auspices, principally in Peking.

A prime example of such interaction is the close relationship between Wan Ssu-t'ung, a sedate bibliophile who suffered from poor health and failing eyesight while working on the *Ming History* as a houseguest of Hsü Yüan-wen, and the inquisitive, footloose, gregarious Liu Hsien-t'ing, who became intimately involved in the *Ming History* and *I-t'ung chih* projects as a private employee of Hsü Ch'ien-hsüeh. According to both men's biographer, Ch'üan Tsu-wang,

> Mr. Wan [always] spent the whole morning sitting in a dignified manner looking over his books, or else sitting quietly with his eyes closed. But [Liu] Chi-chuang liked to travel around and had to venture out each day, sometimes not turning back for the better part of a month. When he did return, [Liu] would tell Mr. Wan all about his experiences, and Mr. Wan, for his part, would use his books to verify [what Liu said]. When they finished talking, [Liu] would be off again.[61]

In this role, Liu Hsien-t'ing can be regarded as representative of the many peripatetic information-gatherers who were relied on by more sedentary documentation experts at a time of heightened interest in recent history and such empirical fields as geography and phonetics, which called for extensive travel, interviewing of subjects and witnesses, and the recording of personal observations. In 1690, Liu Hsien-t'ing took a day's time to jot down the names of new acquaintances he had made during the three years he had been in Peking—over three hundred of them! And he still regretted that "for each one recorded, I have never met ten others." This type of contact, so important in the late seventeenth-century flowering of *ching-shih* studies, was greatly facilitated by certain generous and tolerant project directors whose semiofficial patronage provided

inroads to the center of cultural production for scholars whose nonliterary values otherwise might have excluded them from participation.

Putting aside the purely personal gratifications that must have
accrued to such prominent ministers as the Hsü brothers, Wu Han,
and the *Draft Ming History* compiler Wang Hung-hsü, in befriending,
helping, and sometimes utilizing unfairly the brightest men in the
country, it is interesting to speculate whether the practice of gathering under the roofs of various hosts may have compensated somewhat for the reduction in politico-literary society activity following
the conquest. Though patrons could not hope to achieve the political
goals of Ming partisan leaders who had sought to place their supporters in key positions throughout the bureaucracy, still, Ch'ing
ministers could satisfy individual power drives and gain certain con-
veniences (particularly in less ideologically charged factional maneu-
vers) by staffing certain organs with functionaries and minor officials
who were personally indebted to them. And the men they helped
seemed to relish the new, apolitical camaraderie that developed
as they shared lodgings and books and pooled their enthusiasm for
various kinds of empirical study.

This special spirit among recipients of patronage in the K'ang-hsi
period was supplementary to traditional feelings of gratitude and
obligation toward sponsors, whose influence could augment the
success of certain competitors in the higher civil service examinations, and to feelings of lifelong mutual friendship and dependence
among men who struggled together through those ordeals. From the
Manchu viewpoint, such patronage did not threaten their dominance
(indeed, it could be manipulated in their favor) and had the advantage of bridging political differences within the Han Chinese
elite—between men who still felt late Ming partisan resentments, and
between those who were and those who were not willing to serve
outright in the Ch'ing government.

Moreover, by providing conditions for free and informal, direct and
indirect exchange among scholars who complemented one another in
their knowledge, values, and life styles, major director-patrons helped
to create an atmosphere that was academically productive and intellectually stimulating, as well. It was fruitful patronage partly because
it allowed for, and made the best of, two kinds of ambivalence men-

tioned above: (1) toward large-scale, bureau-type scholarly work carried on in major governmental centers, and (2) toward sedentary, book-bound research.

Hsü Ch'ien-hsüeh's patronage was particularly important for the *I-t'ung chih* compilation, of which he was director-general. When Hsü was forced to leave Peking, the quasi-personal nature of the project staff made it easy for him to transfer the whole undertaking, with the emperor's permission, to his villa on Tung-t'ing-shan, a peninsula stretching into Lake T'ai southwest of Soochow. There it flourished in the hands of such brilliant geographers (and thorough-going text-verifiers) as Yen Jo-chü (1636–1704) and Hu Wei (1633–1714), and the adamantly independent Ming loyalist Ku Tsu-yü (1631-92),[62] not to mention the eccentric Liu Hsien-t'ing. Many southern scholars, who might never have been willing or able to participate if the project had remained in Peking, labored for varying lengths of time on Tung-t'ing-shan.

One older man of the South who deeply influenced several members of the Tung-t'ing-shan group was Wang Yüan's mentor Wei Hsi (1624–81), patriarch of the famous "Nine Scholars of I-t'ang," an eremitic group which gathered on a nearly inaccessible pinnacle near Ning-tu in southern Kiangsi during the Ming disintegration. More conventional scholars admired Wei Hsi for his courageous refusal to sit for the *po-hsüeh hung-ju* examination, thereby maintaining his identity as a surviving man of the Ming. But Wang Yüan was more inspired by Wei Hsi's martial response to late Ming bandit depredations around Ning-tu, his strategic intelligence in recognizing the perfect defensibility of Ts'ui-wei Peak, his philosophical emphasis on absolute sincerity and candor in all matters, which transcended sectarian differences, his boundless energy and willingness to travel great distances to meet other high-spirited men, and the self-sufficiency of the I-t'ang scholars, who supported themselves by tilling fields, selling tea and medicine, and performing divinations.[63]

Wei Hsi's disciple, Liang Fen (1641–1728), whose consuming interest in the history, geography, and techniques of warfare sent him traveling thousands of miles (on foot, it is said), naturally became a close friend of Wang Yüan. And Liang's major work on the geography of North China proved of great interest to Liu Hsien-t'ing as he was gathering and copying material for the *I-t'ung chih*. [64] The feelings of these men as they passed their prime together are reflected in Wang Yüan's preface to Liang Fen's collected prose:

> When I was young and pupil of Mr. Wei [Hsi], he prefaced one of *my* writings with the expectation that I would become another Teng Chung-hua or Chou Kung-chin [both young and brilliant generals]. That was over forty years ago. Now Liang Fen and I are together here in the capital, lonely and despondent, old and spent, dependent on others. Our old acquaintances are senile and completely decrepit; and scarcely two or three others remain of our own generation. Unhappy and disappointed, we face each other with hoary heads, looking up and down, unable to do anything at all. The climate of public affairs changes with increasing absurdity, beyond the power of anyone to predict. Often we join hands and sob out our sorrow. [65]

In 1694 Liu Hsien-t'ing, then in his late forties, returned to the Soochow area from another of his long journeys and planned to settle down in quiet surroundings with a few friends to do some writing. He was dead within a year. Wang Yüan continued to serve as a tutor and secretary for several hosts in Chihli, Shensi, Kiangsi, and Kiangsu until his death in Huai-an in 1710, just as charges were being formulated that resulted in the imprisonment of many of his friends and the execution in 1713 of Tai Ming-shih, ostensibly because of the "wild, irrational, irresponsible" content of Tai's *Nan-shan chi*. [66] With implications of sedition being used as weapons in Peking's increasingly treacherous political environment, Wen Jui-lin prudently chose this time to pack up his nearly complete history of the Southern Ming and return to his patron's home district in Kiangsu, where he served as a tutor until his own death several years later.

The Tai Ming-shih case seems to mark the end of an era in two ways. First, occurring in the twilight of the sixty-year K'ang-hsi reign, when vicious struggles were developing over succession to the throne, this case signaled an end to the ameliorative atmosphere that had prevailed since the emperor's majority in 1669. [67] As clique-building took on deadly seriousness from this time into the first years of Yung-cheng (1723–35), the particularly expansive and accommodating semiofficial patronage that had formed such an important part of the K'ang-hsi tolerance policy also faded from the scene. Semiofficial patronage continued, but its spirit and function changed. Without question, the most powerful patron of Yung-cheng and early Ch'ien-lung times was Grand Councilor Chang T'ing-yü (1672–1755), whose numerous important duties included completion of the languishing *Ming History* project. But Chang, a thoroughly subservient minister to the throne whose scholarship was unexceptional, failed to retain capable scholars for this task and even repelled one outstanding contemporary intellectual, Ch'üan Tsu-wang, even though (modern portrayals notwithstanding) Ch'üan was hardly a Ming loyalist. Ch'üan relied instead on the munificent private patronage then flourishing in urban centers of the South, such as Hangchow and Yangchow.[68]

In a second sense, the *Nan-shan chi* case also shows an end to the need for tolerance. Tai Ming-shih himself was in his sixties when executed, and of the scholars who had enlivened the capital with efforts to preserve the action-filled history and heroic spirit of the recent past, only the nonagenarian Mao Ch'i-ling remained alive, having long since retired to Hangchow. Among prominent scholars in their prime, only the maverick Ch'üan Tsu-wang (who, qua historian, saw himself as the successor to Huang Tsung-hsi and Wan Ssu-t'ung) continued to be fascinated with heroes and martyrs of the conquest period, now with the zeal of a stone-turning eighteenth-century local historian.[69] Indeed, some of the energy and adventurousness that characterized hero-scholars of K'ang-hsi times seems to have lived on in many bookish *k'ao-cheng* scholars of the eighteenth century, if one considers the near fanaticism with which men like Ch'üan sought out scraps of evidence, including overgrown gravesites, wherever they might be found. Nevertheless, with Tai Ming-shih died what could be called the "ambivalent generation," whose fresh memories and frustrated dreams led them to combine color and romance with empiricism and pragmatism in a way that never recurred in the Ch'ing period.

I have written not so much of ambivalences as of overlapping spheres of ambivalence, first because the contradictory urgings that we find in and among K'ang-hsi scholars seldom appear in full complement in any individual, and second because such feelings and attitudes derive significance as integral parts of larger trends and institutional systems, which themselves were overlapping. One man strongly opposed to bureau-style scholarship or bureaucratic service might show little interest in heroic deeds, while another might devote himself entirely to peripatetic, physically demanding research but be wholly conventional in his use of literary forms or his attitudes toward wealth and power. But constellations of the ambivalences I have described were significant factors in the production of the K'ang-hsi reign's most important officially sponsored works, the *Ming History* and the *Ta-Ch'ing i-t'ung chih,* and in the patronage system, which linked talent not only with such scholarly activity but also with the variety of tasks generated by consolidation projects and the energy of the K'ang-hsi emperor himself. Systems of thought, too, drew impetus for change from the ambivalences of this period, various strands which eventually wove themselves into eighteenth-century "evidential research," being strengthened by K'ang-hsi scholars' penchant for active inquiry and impatience with con-ventional descriptive and explanatory formulas. Less easy to gauge, but perhaps of greatest long-term benefit to the stability of the new dynasty, was the expiatory effect which much of their dash and flare seems to have had in helping the postconquest generation to cope with the Ming, as it slipped out of memory into hallowed history.

NOTES TO CHAPTER 9

1. Wang Yüan (lit. name K'un-sheng; of Ta-hsing, Chihli): Arthur Hummel, ed., *Eminent Chinese of the Ch'ing Period* (hereafter cited as ECCP), pp. 842–44; Li Kung, *Shu-ku hou-chi* (*Chi-fu ts'ung-shu,* vols. 392–95), 6/14a–17b; Fang Pao, *Fang Wang-hsi hsien-sheng wen-chi* (*Ssu-pu ts'ung-k'an,* 1st ser. [1920], vol. 93), ch. 8, "Ssu chün-tzu chuan"; Preface, Family Biography, and Postscript attached to Wang Yüan's *Chü-yeh-t'ang wen-chi* (hereafter cited as CYT) (*Chi-fu ts'ung-shu,* vols. 414–19; *Ts'ung-shu chi-ch'eng,* 1st ser. [1936], vols. 2478–82).

Liu Hsien-t'ing (lit. name Chün-hsien, style name Chi-chuang; also of Ta-hsing, Chihli): ECCP, pp. 521–22; Ch'üan Tsu-wang, *Chi-ch'i-t'ing chi* (1805, 1872), 8/11a–16b; epitaph by Wang Yüan from CYT, ch. 18 (1936 ed., 4:285–87) prefaces the 1962 edition of Liu's *Kuang-yang tsa-chi* (see n. 47 below); Wang Ch'in-yü, "Liu Chi-chuang hsien-sheng nien-p'u ch'u-kao," *Che-chiang t'u-shu-kuan kuan-k'an* 4, nos. 4, 5 (August 1935):1–25, 1–31; Yin Keng, "Liu Chi-chuang chih sheng-p'ing chi ch'i hsüeh-shu kai-yao," *Ch'i-Ta chi-k'an* 1 (June 1933): 49–64.

Wen Jui-lin (lit. name Lin-i, style name Shen-yüan; of Wu-ch'eng, Chekiang):

fragments on Wen and his family from such sources as *Wu-ch'eng hsien-chih* (1880), *Nan-hsün chen-chih* (1858), Hsü Shih-ch'ang's *Yen—Li shih-ch'eng chi* [Yen—Li Study Society edition], 3/4a–b, Tai Ming-shih's *Nan-shan chi* (see n. 43 below), 7/21b–23a, and Wen's major extant work, *Nan-chiang i-shih,* 56 ch. (Shanghai, 1960; Tokyo, 1967; Hongkong, 1971); all have been utilized in writing a biographical sketch of Wen Jui-lin which constitutes chapter 1 of my Ph.D. dissertation, "Uses of History in Traditional Chinese Society: The Southern Ming in Ch'ing Historiography" (University of Michigan, 1974).

2. Frederick W. Mote discusses conventions of withdrawal from another period of conquest in "Confucian Eremitism in the Yüan Period," in *The Confucian Persuasion,* ed. Arthur Wright (Stanford, 1960), pp. 202–40.

3. Nelson Wu, in discussing the famous painter Tung Ch'i-ch'ang, points out that late Ming intellectuals often sought public office only in order to serve short perfunctory terms and then return as quickly as possible to private lives of aesthetic endeavor ("Apathy in Government and Fervor in Art," in *Confucian Personalities,* ed. Arthur Wright [Stanford, 1962], pp. 260–93). Chang Tai is another example of a totally immersed scholar and aesthete who cared nothing for government service and was caught utterly unprepared for exigencies of the dynastic changeover (see ECCP, pp. 53–54; my own unpublished paper, "Chang Tai: A Daydreaming Historian," draws on Chang's *Lang-hsüan wen chi* and *T'ao-an meng-i*). And Yoshikawa Kōjirō tells us that prominent late Ming litterateurs such as Ch'ien Ch'ien-i and Wu Wei-yeh who did, unhappily, become embroiled in politics still were primarily concerned with sensuousness and euphony in their poetry, exemplifying a gradual "disengagement" of literature from politics that became even more marked after the conquest ("Political Disengagement in Seventeenth-century Chinese Literature," paper presented at the Conference on Seventeenth-century Chinese Thought, Villa Serbelloni, Italy, 1970). That a highly developed aesthetic sense need not be associated with decadence is pointed out by Wm. Theodore de Bary (appropriately, in reference to the Tung-lin patriarch Kao P'an-lung) in "Neo-Confucian Cultivation and the Seventeenth-Century 'Enlightenment,'" in *The Unfolding of Neo-Confucianism,* ed. de Bary (New York, 1975), pp. 178–84.

4. W. T. de Bary, introduction to *Self and Society in Ming Thought* (New York, 1970), pp. 5–8; and David S. Nivison, "Protest Against Convention and Conventions of Protest," in *The Confucian Persuasion,* esp. pp. 181–99. Cf. Ho Ping-ti, note 41 below.

5. W. T. de Bary, introduction and "Neo-Confucian Cultivation," in *The Unfolding,* esp. pp. 29–32 and 184–204.

6. Willard J. Peterson points out that Ku Yen-wu was motivated to join Fu-she more out of literary than political motivations and was among all those "southern gentlemen" like Tung Ch'i-ch'ang who pursued scholarly and social interests in disregard of bandit uprisings and threats of Manchu invasion. Peterson also suggests that Ku found it convenient to assume a "loyalist" stance after the conquest, since he did not relish taking state examinations or competing in the political realm ("The Life of Ku Yen-wu, 1613–1682," *Harvard Journal of Asiatic Studies* 28 [1968]:129, 144–45).

7. Hellmut Wilhelm, "The Po-hsüeh Hung-ju Examination of 1679," *Journal of the American Oriental Society* 71 (1951): 60–66. On earlier attempts to start this compilation, see Huang Yün-mei, "Ming-shih pien-tsuan k'ao-lüeh," in *Ming-shih pien-tsuan k'ao,* ed. Pao Tsun-p'eng (Taipei, 1968), pp. 9–12.

8. Huang Yün-mei, "Ming-shih pien-tsuan k'ao-lüeh," pp. 16–17.

9. Wan Ssu-t'ung (lit. name Chi-yeh, scholarly appellation Shih-yüan hsien-sheng); youngest of the eight exceptional sons of Wan T'ai; of Yin District, Chekiang. Among numerous secondary writings on Wan, the most accessible and useful for a general overview of his life are: the biography by Tu Lien-che in ECCP, pp. 801–03; Chang Hsü, "Wan Chi-yeh yü Ming-shih," in *Ming-shih pien-tsuan k'ao,* pp. 211–26; Ma T'ai-hsüan, "Wan Ssu-t'ung chih sheng-p'ing chi ch'i chu-shu," *Kuo-li Chung-shan Ta-hsüeh yü-yen li-shih-hsüeh yen-chiu-so chou-k'an* 3, no. 18 (May 1928): 942–48; and Wang Huan-piao, "Wan Chi-yeh hsien-sheng hsi-nien yao-lu," *Shih-ti tsa-chih* 1, no. 2 (July 1937): 11–22.

10. Postscript to Wen Jui-lin's biography of his brother-in-law Ku Chu, *Nan-chiang i-shih,* ch. 40 (modern editions, p. 300).

11. Charles O. Hucker, "The Tung-lin Movement of the Late Ming Period," in *Chinese Thought and Institutions,* ed. John K. Fairbank (Chicago, 1957); and idem, *The Censorial System of Ming China* (Stanford, 1966), chap. 5. On factional struggles, as well as the Ch'ung-chen Grand Secretariat, see Hsieh Kuo-chen, *Ming-Ch'ing chih chi tang-she yün-tung k'ao,* 2d ed. (Taipei, 1968), esp. chap. 4. Charles O. Hucker, ed., *Chinese Government in Ming Times: Seven Studies* (New York, 1969) contains three articles that treat Ch'ung-chen bureaucratic conditions: Lo Jung-pang, "Policy Formulation and Decision-making on Issues Respecting Peace and War," pp. 46–49; Ray Huang, "Fiscal Administration during the Ming Dynasty," pp. 73–128; and especially James B. Parsons, "Ming Dynasty Bureaucracy: Aspects of Background Forces," pp. 177–81, 224–25 (also *Monumenta Serica* 22 [1963]: 343–406). Major primary sources on the tragic bureaucratic and military breakdown of this period are listed in Wolfgang Franke, *An Introduction to the Sources of Ming History* (Kuala Lumpur, 1968), sections 2.8 and 2.9. (The number of ministers who finally went to their deaths with the Ch'ung-chen emperor was considered woefully small by contemporary historians, as shown in Frederic Wakeman's contribution on the Shun Interregnum in this volume.)

12. Wolfgang Franke, introduction to *An Introduction to the Sources of Ming History,* pp. 4–8. (A portion of this introduction is substantially the same as Franke's article, "The Veritable Records of the Ming Dynasty, 1368–1644," in *Historians of China and Japan,* ed. W. G. Beasley and E. G. Pulleyblank (London, 1961), pp. 60–77. Franke cites the historian Wang Shih-chen (1526–90), whose critical standards starred the late sixteenth century, as one who, though well aware of numerous pitfalls in compiling official records, still recognized their great value (p. 19; "Veritable Records" article, pp. 67–68). Cf. note 27 below.

13. Cf. also Ian McMorran's intellectual biography of Wang Fu-chih, "Wang Fu-chih and the Neo-Confucian Tradition," in de Bary, ed., *The Unfolding,* pp. 413–67.

14. Synopsis of Hu Ch'eng-no's "Shih-hsüeh p'ien," *I-chih*, ch. 54, as presented in Naitō Torajirō, *Shina shigaku shi* (Tokyo, 1967 [1950]), pp. 398–99.

15. Fang Pao's epitaph for Wan Ssu-t'ung is in *Fang Wang-hsi hsien-sheng wen-chi*, ch. 12 (*Ssu-pu ts'ung-k'an* ed., p. 168); see also Wan Ssu-t'ung, *Shih-yüan wen-chi* (*Ssu-ming ts'ung-shu*, pt. 4, vol. 54), 7/1a–2b, also cited in Tu Wei-yün, "Wan Chi-yeh chih shih-hsüeh," in *Chung-kuo hsüeh-shu shih lun-chi*, ed. Ch'ien Mu, 4 vols. (Taipei, 1956), 2:4–5.

16. CYT, ch. 3 (*Ts'ung-shu chi-ch'eng* ed., pp. 42–43). The "adventurers" admired by writers like Wen Jui-lin and Wang Yüan do not conform precisely to the typologies presented by James J. Y. Liu in *The Chinese Knight-errant* (Chicago, 1967), pp. 1–13, or by Robert Ruhlmann in· "Traditional Heroes in Chinese Popular Fiction," in *The Confucian Persuasion*, ed. Arthur Wright (Stanford, 1960), pp. 166–72. While Wen and Wang generally reserve obtuseness, belligerence, and egocentrism for banditlike leaders of armed forces, their martially inclined activists do share the typical *hsia*'s straightforwardness and strong sense of justice. Liu points out that knights-errant of Ming-Ch'ing times tended to be on the side of the law (pp. 53, 194); and Ruhlmann agrees that their virtues were seen as appropriate for times of disorder, and aberrant in times of peace and good government (p. 176).

17. Biography of Ying T'ing-chi, in Wen Jui-lin's *Nan-chiang i-shih*, ch. 5, appended to biography of Shih K'o-fa.

18. W. T. De Bary, "Neo-Confucian Cultivation," esp. pp. 184–96. Also, regarding the development of empirical thought and the transitional nature of the late seventeenth century, see three articles by Yamanoi Yū on *ching-shih chih-yung* studies, Huang Tsung-hsi, and Ku Yen-wu, in *Tōhōgaku ronsyū* 1 (February 1954): 136–50, *Tōkyō Shinagaku hō* 3 (1957): 31–40, and *Chuō Daigaku Bungakubu kiyō* 35 (1964): 67–93, respectively.

19. W. T. de Bary, "Neo-Confucian Cultivation," p. 188.

20. Idem, "Individualism and Humanitarianism in Late Ming Thought," in *Self and Society*, pp. 188–225 (on Li Chih); and Edward T. Ch'ien, "Chiao Hung and the Revolt Against Ch'eng-Chu Orthodoxy," in *The Unfolding*, pp. 271–303.

21. W. T. de Bary, "Neo-Confucian Cultivation," p. 190.

22. Tu Wei-ming "Yen Yüan: From Inner Experience to Lived Concreteness," in *The Unfolding*, pp. 513–39. Standard secondary writings in Chinese on the thought of Yen Yüan and Li Kung include: Ch'ien Mu, *Chung-kuo chin san-pai-nien hsüeh-shu shih*, 2 vols. (Taipei, 1964 [1937]), vol. 1, chap. 5; Liang Ch'i-ch'ao's work of the same title (Taipei, 1966 [Chungking, 1944]), chap. 10; and Hou Wai-lu, *Chung-kuo tsao-ch'i ch'i-meng ssu-hsiang shih* (Peking, 1956), chap. 9. Also see biographies of Yen Yüan and Li Kung in ECCP, pp. 912–15 and 475–79, respectively. For primary materials, consult Hsü Shih-ch'ang, comp., *Yen-Li hsüeh san-chung* (Yen-Li Study Society, Republican Period).

23. W. T. de Bary, "Neo-Confucian Cultivation," pp. 196–99; and Wolfgang Franke, *An Introduction*, pp. 1, 4–5.

24. Franke, *An Introduction*, pp. 6–7; and Naitō, *Shina shigaku shi*, pp. 343–47.

25. For biographical information on Hsü Ping-i, see note 54 below. On Hsü's attitude toward Ming-end *yeh-shih,* see Ch'ien Ch'eng-chih's preface and Hsü's own explanatory introduction (*fan-li*) to *Ming-mo chung-lieh chi-shih* (microfilm of MS provided to the Library of Congress by the National Library of Peking), both of which are paraphrased in HsiehKuo-chen, *Wan-Ming shih-chi k'ao* (Peiping, 1932), 2/22a–26a, and in Chu Hsi-tsu, *Ming-chi shih-liao t'i-pa* (Taipei, 1968 [Peking, 1961]), pp. 81–85.

26. David S. Nivison, "'Knowledge' and 'Action' in Chinese Thought since Wang Yang-ming," in *Studies in Chinese Thought,* ed. Arthur Wright (Chicago, 1953), p. 121.

27. Regarding the increase of published materials, both private and official, see K. T. Wu, "Ming Printing and Printers," *Harvard Journal of Asiatic Studies* 7, no. 3 (February 1943): 203–60. On literary society discussions of classical texts, see Ono Kazuko, "Shinsho no kōkeikai ni tsuite," *Tōhō gakuhō* 36 (1964): 633–61.

28. On the *Ku-wen Shang-shu shu-cheng* and the *I-t'u ming-pien,* see Ch'ien Mu, *Chung-kuo chin san-pai-nien,* vol. 1, chap. 6, esp. pp. 236–42, and *Ssu-k'u ch'üan-shu tsung-mu t'i-yao,* 4 vols. (Shanghai, 1934), ch. 12 (1: 248–49). For Huang Tsung-hsi's arguments in the controversy over classifying scholars in the *Ming History,* see *Nan-lei wen-ting, ch'ien-chi* 1/9b–10a and 4/11a, *san-chi fu-lu* 7a–b.

29. CYT, ch. 6, "Yü yu-jen lun-shih shu" (p. 88). Yao and Shun, of course, are legendary sage rulers of Chinese antiquity. Tso-ch'iu Ming is the putative author of the fourth-century B.C. (?) Tso commentary to the *Spring and Autumn Annals,* and Ssu-ma Ch'ien wrote the second-century B.C. *Records of the Historian*—China's two most revered works on (what was to the authors) recent history.

30. Wen Jui-lin, *Nan-chiang i-shih, fan-li,* entries 10, 12.

31. Note, for instance, the *Nan-chiang i-shih* biographies of Kuo Fu-shen (ch. 15), Ho Kang (ch. 11), and Ch'en Tzu-lung (ch. 14), and Wen Jui-lin's complete omission of Wu Kua, a Tung-lin Fu-she mouthpiece in the censorial ranks whose pronouncements stretch through other works.

32. The persecution of Chou Piao, Chou Chung, and Lei Yen-tso: Wen Jui-lin, *Nan-chiang i-shih, fan-li,* 8th item; and ch. 12, author's postscript to biography of Lei Yen-tso.

33. Aspects of attrition in politicoliterary society ideals are discussed by S. K. Lao in "The Split within the Tung-lin Movement and Its Consequences," a paper presented to the Conference on Seventeenth-century Chinese Thought, Villa Serbelloni, Italy, 1970, esp. pp. 42–45. Also, see William S. Atwell, "From Education to Politics: The Fu She," in *The Unfolding,* pp. 349–54.

34. Frederic Wakeman, Jr., "The Price of Autonomy: Intellectuals in Ming and Ch'ing Politics," *Daedalus* 101 (Spring 1972): 42–43. Hsia Yün-i's general condemnation of all shortsighted factional bickering was reinforced by his son Wan-shun, who wrote a "Continuation" of the *Fortunately Surviving Record* (*Hsing-ts'un lu*) before he, too, sacrificed his life in anti-Manchu resistance ac-

tivities. Despite the Hsias' stature, both works elicited an acerbic reaction in Huang's *Clean-up of the Surviving Record* (*T'ai-ts'un lu*). For detail on these men and works, see my doctoral dissertation (cited in n. 1 above), pp. 63–64, nn. 20–30.

35. For Li Kung's biographical sketch of Wan Ssu-t'ung, see Hsü Shih-ch'ang, *Yen-Li shih-ch'eng chi*, 3/1b. On the thinker in question, P'an Yung-wei, see Ch'ien Mu, *Chung-kuo chin san-pai-nien*, 4:51–69.

36. Wen Jui-lin's clan uncle was Chief Grand Secretary Wen T'i-jen, who was widely regarded as ringleader of the "pernicious" or "eunuch" party in the Ch'ung-chen period; but his direct uncle, the paragon Wen Huang, had identified with the "pure" or "righteous" element by joining the Restoration Society.

Even before the conquest, partisan reversals also had a centering effect on the prominent Li Ch'ing (1602–83). In early life Li had been a student of Ni Yüan-lu, champion of Tung-lin partisans during the Ch'ung-chen period; but his grandfather, once listed on Tung-lin rolls, was condemned for cooperating with the eunuch Wei Chung-hsien during the T'ien-ch'i period (1621–27). Li's most controversially even-handed views are expressed in his *Notes from Three Offices of Scrutiny* (*San-yüan pi-chi*), completed after the fall of Nanking (*Ch'ing-shih kao*, chüan 505; and Franke, *An Introduction*, no. 4.2.9.).

37. Ono Kazuko, "Shinsho no shisō tōsei o megutte," *Tōyōshi kenkyū* 18, no. 3 (1959): 99–123. Though a few figures sought to utilize what remained of Tung-lin and anti-Tung-lin factional identifications, after the conquest cliques among Han Chinese officials tended to center on power factors within the Manchu elite (see Hsieh Kuo-chen, *Ming-Ch'ing chih chi tang-she*, chap. 6).

38. Feng-ch'en Ma, "Manchu-Chinese Social and Economic Conflicts in Early Ch'ing," in *Chinese Social History*, ed. and trans. E-tu Zen Sun and John de Francis (Washington, D.C., 1956), pp. 333–51. Hsieh Kuo-chen's work on the "removal of the coastal population" from southern Chekiang to western Kwangtung (translated in *Chinese Social and Political Science Review* 15 [1930–31]: 559–96) is appended to *Ming-Ch'ing chih chi tang-she yün-tung k'ao* along with his basic work on the late Ming "slave revolts." And Fu I-ling has written on unrest in the rural, urban, and mining sectors in his ground-breaking *Ming-tai Chiang-nan shih-min ching-chi shih-t'an* (Shanghai, 1957), esp. pp. 78–126, and in his *Ming-Ch'ing nung-ts'un she-hui ching-chi* (Peking, 1961), esp. pp. 68ff. Cf. Tsing Yüan's article on urban insurrection in Ming and Ch'ing times. One need not read many biographies from this period to see how the advent of Ch'ing power provided opportunities for grabbing long-coveted lands, settling old scores, and blackmailing former members of the Ming elite.

39. On Ku Yen-wu's mercantile activity, see Peterson's biography of Ku, *Harvard Journal of Asiatic Studies* 28 (1968): 151, and 29 (1969): 205. On Fang I-chih: ECCP, pp. 232–33; Hou Wai-lu, "Fang I-chih—Chung-kuo te pai-k'e-ch'üan-shu p'ai ta che-hsüeh-chia," *Li-shih yen-chiu* 57, no. 6 (June 1957): 1–21, and 57, no. 7 (July 1957): 1–25; Yü Ying-shih, *Fang I-chih wan chieh k'ao* (Hong Kong, 1972); and Willard J. Peterson, "Fang I-chih: Western Learning and the 'Investigation of Things,'" in *The Unfolding*, esp. pp. 369–76.

40. Preface by Cheng Ying-fa to Chiang Jih-sheng's *T'ai-wan wai-chi, Taiwan wen-hsien ts'ung-k'an*, no. 60, in 3 vols. (Taipei, 1960), p. 9.

41. Ho Ping-ti, *The Ladder of Success in Imperial China: Aspects of Social Mobility, 1368–1911* (New York, 1962), pp. 111–17, 172–83, and 219; Jonathan Spence, *Ts'ao Yin and the K'ang-hsi Emperor: Bondservant and Master* (New Haven, 1966), pp. 70–75. The findings of Lawrence Kessler, "Ethnic Composition of Provincial Leadership During the Ch'ing Dynasty," *Journal of Asian Studies* 28, no. 3 (May 1969): 489–511, are very similar to those of Narakino Shimezu, "Shindai jūyō shokkan Man-Kan hiritsu no hendō," *Gunma Daigaku kiyō—jimbun shakai kagaku hen* 17, no. 5 (1967): 47–70, and of Ishibashi Hideo, "Shindai Kanjin kanryō ni kansuru ikkōsatsu—toku ni Kanjin shinshi to tokubu to no kankei ni tsuite," *Shien* 26, nos. 2–3 (1966): 24–35.

42. Wen Jui-lin, *Ch'u-sai t'u-hua shan-ch'uan chi*, in *Shih-yüan ts'ung-shu* (1913–17), pt. 7, vol. 14. The following two works, though they do not mention the surveying expedition of 1639, are informative regarding Manchu objectives in the northeast during this period: Lawrence Kessler, "K'ang-hsi's Military Leadership and the Consolidation of Manchu Rule," paper presented at the Association for Asian Studies 23d Annual Conference, Washington, D.C., March 1971, esp. pp. 11–13; and Robert Lee, *The Manchurian Frontier in Ch'ing History* (Cambridge, Mass., 1970), esp. pp. 1–2, 9.

43. On Tai Ming-shih's life, see Hsiao Mu, "Tai Yu-an hsien-sheng shih-lüeh," in *Pei-chuan chi pu* 8/6b–17b, and in *Kuo-ts'ui hsüeh-pao* 6, no. 10 (October 1910); and T'ang Ch'uan-chi, "Tai Nan-shan yü T'ung-ch'eng p'ai," *Shih-Ta hsüeh-pao* 2 (June 1957): 227–36. Some selections from Tai's *Nan-shan chi* (*ou-ch'ao*), 14 ch., suppl. 3 ch. (1701, 1900) are translated by Lucien Mao in *T'ien Hsia Monthly* 5, no. 4 (November 1937): 382–99.

44. Fang Pao, *Fang Wang-hsi hsien-sheng wen-chi*, ch. 8, "Ssu-chün-tzu chuan."

45. Wen Jui-lin, *Nan-chiang i-shih*, ch. 8, author's postscript.

46. Ibid., ch. 52, author's postscript.

47. Liu Hsien-t'ing, *Kuang-yang tsa-chi*, 5 ch., printed in *Kung-shun-t'ang ts'ung-shu* (Kuang-hsü period, vols. 24–28) and in *Chi-fu ts'ung-shu* (but not in the 1966 Taipei edition); punctuated edition of Peking, 1959, reprinted by World Book Company of Taipei, 1962. This quotation is from chüan 2 (pp. 88–89).

48. Ch'ü Ta-chün: ECCP, pp. 201–03; Ch'en Po-t'ao, *Sheng-ch'ao Yüeh-tung i-min lu* (1916) 1/25b–29a; Liu Tso-mei, "Ch'ü Ta-chün 'Kuang-tung hsin-yü' te li-shih pei-ching," *Shu-mu chi-k'an* 2, no. 1 (September 1967): 61–66.

Shen Hsün-wei is the author of *Shu-nan hsü-lüeh*, the preface to which gives biographical information. Contained in *Chao-tai ts'ung-shu* (pt. F, vol. 71), *Chih-pu-tsu-chai ts'ung-shu* (pt. 18, vol. 6), *Pi-chi hsiao-shuo ta-kuan* (pt. 4), and *Ts'ung-shu chi-ch'eng* (vol. 3971).

Feng Su: *T'ai-chou fu-chih* (1895), *jen-wu* 11/7b–9b; *Ch'ing-ch'ao ch'i-hsien lei-cheng ch'u-pien* 5/18a–22b; Yu T'ung, *Liang-chai-chüan kao* 11/16a–19b; and Chu Hsi-tsu, *Ming-chi shih-liao t'i-pa* (Peking, 1961), pp. 64–68.

49. A biography of Hsü by Chang Ch'un-shu and a translation of one of

Hsü's travel diaries, plus a second biography by Li Chi, constitute the greater part of *Two Studies in Chinese Literature,* Michigan Papers in Chinese Studies No. 3 (University of Michigan Center for Chinese Studies, 1968). (See also ECCP, pp. 314–16.) Better known by his style name, Hsia-k'o, Hsü shared his scientific bent with several near contemporaries, such as the medical doctor Li Shih-chen (1518–93), author of *Pen-ts'ao kang-mu (The Great Pharmacopeia);* the natural scientist and statesman Hsü Kuang-ch'i (1562–1633), who wrote *Nung-cheng ch'üan-shu (Complete Treatise on Agriculture),* and Sung Ying-hsing (born ca. 1600), an official whose interest in production technology resulted in the remarkable treatise *T'ien-kung k'ai-wu (Exploitation of the Works of Nature).* Li Chi, in her biography of Hsü Hung-tsu, places him among figures like Hsü Kuang-ch'i and Fang I-chih in emphasizing the influence of Jesuit missionaries in spreading scientific thought in China during their time, an influence which became even stronger in the K'ang-hsi period *(The Love of Nature: Hsü Hsia-k'o and His Early Travels,* Occasional Paper No. 3 of the Program in East Asian Studies, Western Washington State College, 1971, pp. 37–40). Now superseded by the University of Hawaii Press publication of Li Chi's larger work on Hsü.

50. Li Yin-tu: Wu Huai-ch'ing, comp., *Li T'ien-sheng hsien-sheng nien-p'u,* in *Kuan-chung ts'ung-shu,* pt. 5, vol. 12; Teng Chih-ch'eng, *Ch'ing-shih chi-shih ch'u-pien,* 2 vols. (Shanghai, 1965; Taipei, 1970), 2:869–71.

51. An excellent portrayal of the K'ang-hsi emperor's style and concerns is Jonathan Spence's *Emperor of China: Self-portrait of K'ang-hsi* (New York, 1974).

52. Wu Han: *Ch'ing-ch'ao ch'i-hsien lei-cheng ch'u-pien* 60/24a–25a.

53. Li Kung, *Ta-hsüeh pien-yeh,* first printed in 1701; now in *Chi-fu ts'ung-shu* (1966 ed., vol. 208) and in *Yen-Li ts'ung-shu* (Peking, 1922), vol. 19.

54. Hsü Ch'ien-hsüeh and Hsü Yüan-wen: ECCP, pp. 310–12 and 327, respectively; biographies of all three brothers in *K'un-Hsin liang-hsien hsü-hsiu ho-chih* (1880) 24/26a–30a, 32a–37a.

55. Ku Yen-wu, *T'ing-lin yü-chi* 27a–b, in *T'ing-lin hsien-sheng i-shu* (1898), vol. 23 (as translated in Peterson, "The Life of Ku Yen-wu," [1969], pp. 225–26).

56. Han T'an, *Yu-huai-t'ang wen-kao* (1703) 18/10a–b.

57. Wang Yüan's epitaph for Liu Hsien-t'ing (see n. 1 above).

58. Li Kung, *Shu-ku hou-chi* 6/14b.

59. Ibid. 17a.

60. "Wen Lin-i hsiao-hsiang chi," CYT, ch. 19 (pp. 313–14); also in Hsü Shih-ch'ang, *Yen-Li shih-ch'eng chi* 3/4a.

61. Ch'üan Tsu-wang, postscript to "Liu Chi-chuang chuan," *Chi-ch'i-t'ing chi* 8/16a. Liu Hsien-t'ing, *Kuang-yang tsa-chi,* ch. 4 (1962 ed., p. 189). It is interesting to note that modern scholars see Liu as the connection through whom the work of Wang Fu-chih, secluded in Hunan, was known to Wan Ssu-t'ung in Peking (Liang Ch'i-ch'ao, *Chung-kuo chin san-pai nien,* p. 168, and Ch'ien Mu, *Chung-kuo chin san-pai nien,* p. 195). Liu's orientation was empirical

in the extreme. Though his writings on agriculture, irrigation, and phonetics were well known and respected during his lifetime, his only surviving work, cited here, is an unorganized collection of jottings about things he heard, saw, and thought about on his incessant travels—from tiger fetuses and strange insects to aboriginal dialects and tales of Ming-end heroes.

62. Ku Tsu-yü: ECCP, pp. 419–20; Wang Te-i, "Ku Tsu-yü nien-p'u," *Ku-kung wen-hsien* 1, no. 2 (March 1970): 21–34, and 1, no. 3 (June 1970): 45–59.

63. Wei Hsi: Wen Chü-min, comp., *Wei Shu-tzu nien-p'u* (Shanghai, 1936); Teng Chih-ch'eng, 2:199–201. The Nine Scholars of I-t'ang were: the three Wei brothers, Wei Chi-jui, Wei Hsi, and Wei Li (in descending order of age), Li T'eng-chiao, P'eng Jen, Tseng Ts'an, and the Weis' brother-in-law, the accomplished mathematician Ch'iu Wei-p'ing, all of Ning-tu, and from Nanchang, P'eng Shih-wang, and Ming imperial kinsman Chu I-p'ang, alias Lin Shih-i, who became well known in tea horticulture. They are said to have given shelter, aid, and solace to many displaced Ming "survivors," including Fang I-chih, and had frequent intercourse with the "Seven Anchorites of Chi-shan" (in Nan-k'ang Prefecture, Kiangsi), whose leader was Sung Chih-sheng, another man active in helping and recording the exploits of Ming-end heroes (*Ch'ing-shih lieh-chuan* 70/1a–3a, 66/20b–21a).

64. Liang Fen: T'ang Chung, comp., *Liang Chih-jen nien-p'u* (Shanghai, 1933), with some entries from scattered points in Liu Hsien-t'ing's *Kuang-yang tsa-chi.*

65. CYT, ch. 13 (pp. 209–10). References are to Teng Yü and Chou Yü. Teng helped Liu Hsin establish the Latter Han (*Hou-Han shu,* ch. 46), and Chou inflicted a crushing defeat on Ts'ao Ts'ao in the last years of that dynasty (*San-kuo chih,* Wu ch. 9, and *Ch'en shu,* ch. 10).

66. Most primary materials pertaining to this case have been reprinted in *Ko-ming yüan-yüan,* 2 vols., *Chung-hua min-kuo k'ai-kuo wu-shih-nien wen-hsien* (Taipei, 1963), vol. 2, including "Chi T'ung-ch'eng Fang-Tai liang-chia shu-an" from *Ku-hsüeh hui-k'an,* 6 vols. (Taipei, 1964), vol. 2. Also, see Meng Sen, *Ming-Ch'ing shih lun-chu chi-k'an* (Peking, 1959), p. 42.

67. Silas H. L. Wu, *Communication and Imperial Control in China* (Cambridge Mass., 1970), pp. 52–69.

68. On Chang T'ing-yü and Ch'üan Tsu-wang, see ECCP, pp. 54–56 and 203–05, respectively. Regarding Chang's directorship in the concluding stages of the *Ming History* project, consult articles by Huang Yün-mei and Li Chin-hua in Pao Tsun-p'eng ed., *Ming-shih pien-tsuan k'ao,* pp. 43–46 and 85–89, respectively. Numerous adulatory biographies have been written of Ch'üan by patriotic Chinese scholars of this century, the best known of which is by Liu Shih-p'ei (*Tso-an wai-chi,* ch. 18, and *Kuo-ts'ui hsüeh-pao* 1.11 [1905]); but more definitive is Chiang T'ien-shu, *Ch'üan Hsieh-shan nien-p'u* (Shanghai, 1932). For background on the patronage of which Ch'üan partook in the South, see Ho Ping-ti, "The Salt Merchants of Yangchow: A Study of Commercial Capitalism in Eighteenth-century China," *Harvard Journal of Asiatic Studies* 17 (1954): 130–68, esp. pp. 156–57.

69. Tu Wei-yün, *Ch'ing Ch'ien-Chia shih-tai chih shih-hsüeh yü shih-chia* (Taipei, 1963), pp. 49–58. Most of Ch'üan Tsu-wang's writings on conquest period figures, including many indications of how Ch'üan garnered his information, have been excerpted in *Chi-ch'i-t'ing chi hsüan-chi*, 2 vols., *T'ai-wan wen-hsien ts'ung-k'an* series, no. 217 (Taipei: Bank of Taiwan Economic Research Group, 1965).

Bibliography

Abe Takeo 安部健夫. *Shindai shi no kenkyū* 清代史の研究. Tokyo, 1971.

Aga-Oglu, Kamer. "Blue-and-White Porcelain Plates Made for Moslem Patrons." *Far Eastern Ceramic Bulletin* 3, no. 3 (September 1951): 12–16.

Akiyama Kenzō 秋山謙藏. *Nisshi kōshō shi kenkyū* 日支交渉史研究. Tokyo, 1939.

Algemeen Rijksarchief, The Hague. Archives of the Dutch East India Company.

An-hui t'ung chih 安徽通志. 1830.

Atwell, William S. "From Education to Politics: The Fu She." In W. T. de Bary, ed., The *Unfolding of Neo-Confucianism*, pp. 333–367.

Barthold, W. "Kāshgar." In *The Encyclopedia of Islam*, 2: 788. 4 vols. Leiden: E. J. Brill, 1913–1934.

Bawden, C. R. *The Modern History of Mongolia.* New York: Frederick Praeger, 1968.

Beasley, W. G., and Pulleyblank, E. G., eds. *Historians of China and Japan.* London and New York: Oxford University Press, 1961.

Beattie, Hilary J. "Land and Lineage in China: A Study of T'ung-ch'eng County, Anhwei, in the Ming and Ch'ing Dynasties." Ph. D. dissertation, Cambridge University, 1973. To be published by Cambridge University Press.

Bellew, H. W. "History of Kashghar." In T. D. Forsyth, ed. *Report of a Mission to Yarkund in 1873*, pp. 106–213. Calcutta: Foreign Department Press, 1875.

Bienen, Henry. *Violence and Social Change.* Chicago: University of Chicago Press, 1968.

Boxer, C. R. *The Christian Century in Japan, 1549–1650.* Berkeley and Los Angeles: University of California Press, 1951.

———. *The Great Ship from Amacon: Annals of Macao and the Old Japan Trade.* Lisbon: Centro de Estudos Históricos Ultramarinos, 1959.

———. "The Rise and Fall of Nicholas Iquan." *T'ien-hsia Monthly* 11 (1941): 401–39.

Boxer, C. R., ed. and trans. *South China in the Sixteenth Century.* Hakluyt Society, ser. 2, vol. 106. London, 1953.

Busch, H. "The Tung-lin Shu-yuan and its Political and Philosophical Significance." *Monumenta Serica* 14 (1949–55): 1–163.

Cartier, Michel. "Note sur l'histoire des prix en Chine." *Annales* 24, no. 4 (Aug.–Sept. 1969): 876–79.

Cha Chi-tso 查繼佐. *Lu Ch'un-ch'iu* 魯春秋. TW, no. 118.

————. *Tsui wei lu* 罪惟錄. *Ssu-pu Ts'ung-k'an* edition.

————. *Tsui wei lu hsüan-chi* 罪惟錄選輯. TW, no. 136.

Chan, Albert. "The Decline and Fall of the Ming Dynasty: A Study of the Internal Factors." Ph. D. dissertation, Harvard University, 1954.

Chan Wing-tsit. "The Ch'eng-Chu School of Early Ming." In de Bary, ed., *Self and Society in Ming Thought*, pp. 29–51. New York, 1970.

Chang Ch'un-shu, "Hsü Hsia-k'o." In *Two Studies in Chinese Literature*, pp. 24–46. Michigan Papers in Chinese Studies, 3 (1968).

Chang, Chung-li. *The Chinese Gentry, Studies in Their Role in Nineteenth Century Chinese Society*. Seattle: University of Washington Press, 1955.

Chang, Hajji Yusuf. "A Bibliographical Study of the History of Islam in China." M. A. thesis, Montreal: McGill University, 1960.

Chang Han 張瀚. *Sung-ch'uang meng-yü* 松窗夢語. In *Wu-lin hsien-che i-shu* 武林先哲遺書. N.d.

Chang Hsü 張須. "Wan Chi-yeh yü Ming-shih" 萬季野與明史. In Pao Tsun-p'eng 包遵彭, ed., *Ming-shih pien-tsuan k'ao* 明史編纂考 pp. 211–226. Taipei, 1968.

Chang Huang-yen 張煌言. "Pei-cheng lu" 北征錄. In *Chang Ts'ang-shui chi* 張蒼水集. Shanghai, 1964.

Chang Hung-hsiang 張鴻翔. "Ming hsi-pei kuei-hua-jen shih-hsi-piao" 明西北歸化人世系表. *Fu-jen hsueh-chih* 輔仁學誌 8, no. 2 (1939): 89–122.

Chang-shih tsung-p'u 張氏宗譜. 1890, T. 656.

Chang Ssu-shan 張斯善. "Kung te chi" 功德記. In Shih K'o-fa 史可法. *Shih Chung-cheng kung chi* 史忠正公集. Shanghai, 1937.

Chang Tai 張岱. *Lang-hsüan wen-chi* 瑯嬛文集. 1877.

————. *Shih kuei shu hou-chi* 石匱書後集. Taipei, 1960.

————. *Shih-kuei ts'ang-shu* 石匱藏書. Shanghai, 1959.

————. *T'ao-an meng-i* 陶庵夢憶. In *Yueh-ya t'ang ts'ung-shu* 粵雅堂叢書. 1852.

Chang Te-ch'ang. "The Economic Role of the Imperial Household (*Nei-wu-fu*) in the Ch'ing Dynasty." *Journal of Asian Studies* 31, no. 2 (February 1972): 243–72.

Chang T'ien-tse. *Sino-Portuguese Trade from 1514 to 1644*. Reprint, Leiden: Brill, 1969.

Chang Ts'ai 張采. "Chün-ch'u shuo" 軍儲說. In *Chih-wei t'ang wen ts'un* 知畏堂文存. 1675.

Chang Wei-hua 張維華. *Ming-shih Fo-lang-chi, Lü-sung, Ho-lan, I-ta-li-ya ssu-chuan chu-shih* 明史佛郎機呂宋和蘭意大里亞四傳注釋. Yenching Journal of Chinese Studies Monograph Series, no. 7. Peiping, 1934.

Chang Ying 張英. *Heng-ch'an so-yen* 恆產瑣言. In *Ts'ung-shu chi-ch'eng*, ch'u-pien, no. 977.

Chao Ch'i-na 趙綺娜. "Ch'ing-ch'u pa-ch'i Han-chün yen-chiu" 清初八旗漢軍研究. *Ku-kung wen-hsien* 故宮文獻 4, no. 2 (March 1973): 55–65.

Chao I 趙翼. *Nien-erh shih cha-chi* 廿二史劄記. *Ssu Pu Pei Yao* ed.

Chao-lien 昭槤. *Hsiao-t'ing tsa-lu* 嘯亭雜錄. 1680.

Chao Shih-chin 趙士錦. *Chia-shen chi-shih* 甲申紀事. In *Chia-shen chi-shih teng ssu-chung* 甲申紀事等四種, pp. 3–28. Shanghai, 1959.

Chao Tsung-fu 趙宗復. "Li Tzu-ch'eng p'an-luan shih-lüeh" 李自成叛亂史略. *Shih-hsüeh nien-pao* 史學年報 2, no. 4, pp. 127–57.

Chaunu, Pierre. *Les Philippines et le Pacifique des Ibériques (XVIe, XVIIe, XVIIIe siècles): introduction methodologique et indices d'activite*. Ports, Routes, Trafics, 11. Paris: S. E. V. P. E. N., 1960.

Chen-yang hsien chih 鎮陽縣志, n.d. (Ch'ien-lung edition).

Ch'en Chan-jo 陳湛若. "Lueh lun 'Hung-lou-meng' she-hui pei-ching" 略論 "紅樓夢" 社會背景. *Meng-ya*, 703–33.

Ch'en Chi-sheng 陳濟生. *Tsai-sheng chi-lüeh* 再生紀略. In *Hsüan-lan t'ang ts'ung-shu* 玄覽堂叢書, ed. Cheng Chen-to 鄭振鐸, *ts'e* 110–11. 2 *chüan*, Nanking, Nanking Central Library, 1947.

Ch'en Ch'ing-lung 陳慶隆. "Lun pai-shan tang yü hei-shan tang" 論白山黨與黑山黨. *Bulletin of the Institute of China Border Area Studies, National Chengchi University*, no. 2 (July 1971): 209–31.

Ch'en Jen-hsi 陳仁錫. *Huang Ming shih-fa lu* 皇明世法錄. Taipei, 1965 reprint.

Ch'en Mao-heng 陳懋恒. *Ming-tai wo-k'ou k'ao-lueh* 明代倭寇考略. Yenching Journal of Chinese Studies Monograph Series, no. 6, Peiping, 1934. Reprinted Peking, 1957.

Ch'en Po-t'ao 陳伯陶. *Sheng-ch'ao yüeh-tung i-min lu* 勝朝粵東遺民錄. Kowloon, 1916.

Ch'en Shih-ch'i 陳詩啓. *Ming-tai kuan shou-kung-yeh ti yen-chiu* 明代官手工業的研究. Wuhan, 1958.

Ch'en, Ta-tuan. "Investiture of Liu-ch'iu Kings in the Ch'ing Period." In John K. Fairbank, ed., *The Chinese World Order*, pp. 135–64, 315–20. Cambridge, Mass., 1968.

Ch'en Tzu-lung 陳子龍. "Nien-p'u" 年譜. In *Ch'en Chung-yü kung ch'üan-chi* 陳忠裕公全集. 1803.

Ch'en Tzu-lung 陳子龍 et al., eds., *Huang Ming ching-shih wen-pien* 皇明經世文編. 30 vols. Taipei, 1964.

Ch'en Wen-shih 陳文石. "Ch'ing-jen ju-kuan ch'ien ti nung-yeh sheng-huo" 清人入關前的農業生活, 2 pts. *Ta-lu tsa-chih* 大陸雜誌 (May 1961), 22, no. 9, pp. 8–13 and 22, no. 10, pp. 18–25.

———. *Ming Hung-wu Chia-ching chien ti hai-chin cheng-ts'e* 明洪武嘉靖間的海

禁政策. Taipei, 1966.

Cheng Jo-tseng 鄭若曾. *Chiang-nan ching-lüeh* 江南經略. In *Ssu-k'u ch'üan-shu chen-pen* 四庫全書珍本, 2d collection, vols. 179–81. Taipei, 1971.

Cheng-shih kuan-hsi wen-shu 鄭氏關係文書. TW, no. 69.

Cheng-shih shih-liao ch'u-pien 鄭氏史料初編. TW, no. 157.

Cheng-shih shih-liao hsu-pien 鄭氏史料續編. TW, no. 168.

Chi Liu-ch'i 計六奇. *Ming-chi nan-lüeh* 明季南略. Shanghai, 1958, and TW, no. 148.

——. *Ming-chi pei-lüeh* 明季北略 in *Chung-kuo fang-lüeh ts'ung-shu* 中國方略 叢書. Taipei, 1968, and also TW, no. 275.

Ssu-k'u ch'üan-shu tsung-mu t'i-yao 四庫全書總目提要 comp. Chi Yün 紀昀, 1782. 4 vols. Shanghai, 1934 ed.

Ch'i Kung-min 齊功民. "Ming-mo shih-min fan feng-chien tou-cheng" 明末市 民反封建鬥爭. *Wen-shih-che* 文史哲, no. 2 (1957): 3019–46.

Ch'i Piao-chia 祁彪佳. *Ch'i Piao-chia chi* 祁彪佳集. Shanghai, 1960.

——. *Chia-i jih-li* 甲乙日曆. Taipei, 1969.

Chia-ting hsien chih 嘉定縣志. 1673 edition.

Chiang Jih-sheng 江日昇. *T'ai-wan wai-chi* 臺灣外記. TW, no. 60.

Chiang-nan t'ung chih 江南通志. Editions of 1684 and 1737.

Chiang-su sheng Ming-Ch'ing i-lai pei-k'o tzu-liao hsüan-chi 江蘇省明清以來碑刻 資料選集, edited by Kiangsu Provincial Museum, Peking, 1959.

Chiang T'ien-shu 蔣天樞. *Ch'üan Hsieh-shan nien-p'u* 全謝山年譜. Shanghai, 1933.

Chiao Hung 焦竑 comp., *Kuo-ch'ao hsien-cheng lu* 國朝獻徵錄, 8 vols. Taipei reprint, 1965.

Chien Po-tsan 翦伯贊. *Chung-kuo shih-lun chi* 中國史論集 Shanghai, 1948.

Ch'ien Ch'eng-chih 錢澄之. *So-chih lu* 所知錄. TW, no. 86.

Ch'ien Ch'ien-i 錢謙益. *Mu-chai ch'üan-chi: ch'u-hsüeh chi* 牧齋全集：初學集. 1910.

Ch'ien, Edward T. "Chiao Hung and the Revolt Against Ch'eng-Chu Orthodoxy." In W. T. DeBary, ed., *The Unfolding of Neo-Confucianism*, pp. 271–303.

Ch'ien Hsing 錢駅. *Chia-shen ch'uan-hsin lu* 甲申傳信錄 in *Chung-kuo nei-luan wai-huo li-shih ts'ung-shu, ts'e* 12. Shanghai, 1940.

Ch'ien Hung 錢宏. "Ya-p'ien chan-cheng i-ch'ien Chung-kuo jo-kan shou-kung-yeh pu-men chung ti tzu-pen-chu-i meng-ya" 鴉片戰爭以前中國若干手工 業部門中的資本主義萌芽, *Meng-ya*, 238–71.

Ch'ien Mu 錢穆. *Chung-kuo chin san-pai-nien hsüeh-shu shih* 中國近三百年學術史. 1937; Taipei reprint 1964.

Ch'ien Pang-ch'i 錢邦芑. *Chia-shen chi-pien lu* 甲申紀變錄 in Lung-tao-jen 聾道 人. *Yü-pien chi-lueh* 遇變紀略, TW, no. 249, pp. 13–16.

Chin Pao 金保. *Ling-hai fen-yü* 嶺海焚餘. In *Shih-yuan ts'ung-shu* (適園叢書). 1916.

Chin Sheng 金聲. *Chin Chung-chieh kung wen-chi* 金忠節公文集. 1888.

Chin Wu-lan. See *K'un-Hsin liang-hsien hsü-hsiu ho-chih*. 1880 edition.

Ching-te-chen t'ao-tz'u shih-kao 景德鎮陶瓷史稿. Compiled by *Chiang-hsi ch'ing-kung-yeh-t'ing t'ao-tz'u yen-chiu so* 江西輕工業廳陶瓷研究所. Peking, 1959.

Ch'ing-ch'ao ch'i-hsien lei-cheng ch'u-pien 清朝耆獻類徵初編. Li Huan 李桓, comp., 1884. Taipei reprint, 1966.

Ch'ing-ch'ao hsü-wen-hsien t'ung-k'ao 清朝續文獻通考 ed., Liu Chin-tsao 劉錦藻. 1936; Taipei reprint, 1955.

Ch'ing-shih 清史. 8 vols. Taipei, 1961.

Ch'ing-shih kao 清史稿. Chao Erh-hsün 趙爾巽 et al., eds. Peking, 1928.

Ch'ing-shih-kao T'ai-wan tzu-liao chi-chi 清史稿臺灣資料集輯. TW, no. 243.

Ch'ing-shih lieh-chuan 清史列傳. Shanghai, 1928. Taipei reprint, 1964.

Ch'ing-tai pi-chi ts'ung-k'an 清代筆記叢刊. Shanghai, 1936.

Chiu Man-chou tang. T'ien-ts'ung chiu nien 舊滿洲檔. 天聰九年, translated by Kanda Nobuo 神田信夫, Matsumura Jun 松村潤, Okada Hidehiro 岡田英弘. Tokyo, 1972.

Choson wangjo sillok 朝鮮王朝實錄 [The Korean Veritable Records]. Sonjo 宣祖, Kwanghaegun ilgi 光海君日記, Injo 仁祖. N.d.

Ch'ien-chou chih-kao 乾州志稿. Chou Ming-ch'i 周銘旗, comp., 1884, Taipei reprint, 1969.

[*T'ung-ch'eng Yao-shih*] *Chou-shih Shang-i-t'ang chih-p'u* 桐城鷚石周氏尙義堂支譜. 1894, C.291.

Chu Hsi 朱熹. *Chin-ssu lu chi-chu* 近思錄集注, (Ssu-pu pei-yao edition). Shanghai, 1934.

Chu Hsi-tsu 朱希祖. *Ming-chi shih-liao t'i-pa* 明季史料題跋. Peking, 1961. Taipei reprint, 1968.

Chu Kuo-chen 朱國禎. *Huang Ming shih-kai* 皇明史概. 1632.

Chu Tzu-su 朱子素. *Chia-ting hsien i-yu chi-shih* 嘉定縣乙酉紀事 in *T'ung-shih* 痛史. Taipei reprint, 1968.

Chu Wen-chang 朱文長. *Shih K'o-fa chuan* 史可法傳. Chungking, 1943.

Chu Yü 朱裕. *Chia-ting chih chan* 嘉定之戰. Peking, 1956.

Ch'ü T'ung-tsu. *Local Government in China under the Ch'ing*. Cambridge, Mass.: Harvard University Press, 1962.

Chuan, Han-sheng, and Kraus, Richard A. *Mid-Ch'ing Rice Markets and Trade: an Essay in Price History*. Cambridge: Harvard University Press, 1975.

Ch'üan Tsu-wang 全祖望. *Chi-ch'i-t'ing chi* 鮚埼亭集 and *Chi-ch'i t'ing wai-pien* 外編 (1805, 1872); also *Ssu-pu ts'ung-k'an*; also *Ming-Ch'ing shih-*

liao hui-pien 明清史料彙編 (Taipei), pt. 5, vol. 3–9; also excerpted in *Chi-ch'i t'ing chi hsuan-chi* 選輯. TW, no. 217.

Chung-kuo nei-luan wai-huo li-shih ts'ung-shu 中國內亂外禍歷史叢書 ed. Wang Ling-kao 王靈皐. Shanghai, 1940, 1947–48.

Chung-kuo tzu-pen chu-i meng-ya wen-t'i t'ao-lun chi 中國資本主義萌芽問題討論集. Peking, 1957.

Ch'ung-chen ch'ang-pien. See Wan Yen.

Ch'ung-chen shih lu 崇禎實錄, compiler unknown, ed. Liang Hung-chih 梁鴻志. 1940, reprinted in *Ming Shih-lu*, Nan-kang, Taiwan, 1962–68.

Cocks, Richard. *The Diary of Richard Cocks, Cape-Merchant in the English Factory in Japan, 1615–1622*, 2 vols. Hakluyt Society, series 1, vol. 67, London, 1888.

Courant, Maurice. *L'Asie centrale aux xviie et xviiie siècles, empire kalmouk ou empire mantchou?* Paris: A. Rey, 1912.

Crawford, Robert B. "The Biography of Juan Ta-ch'eng." *Chinese Culture* 6, no. 2 (March 1965): 28–105.

Crawford, Robert. "Chang Chü-cheng's Confucian Legalism." In W. T. deBary, ed., *Self and Society in Ming Thought*, pp. 367–413.

CTPCTK. See *Ch'ing-tai pi-chi ts'ung-k'an*.

CT. See *Man-chou chiu-tang*.

CYT. See Wang Yüan.

da Cunha, Euclides. *Rebellion in the Backlands*. Translated by Samuel Putnam. Chicago: University of Chicago Press, 1944.

Dagh-register Gehouden in 't Casteel Batavia, 1628–1682. Batavia, 1887–1931.

Dardess, John W. *Conquerors and Confucians: Aspects of Political Change in Late Yüan China*. New York: Columbia University Press, 1973.

———. "The Late Ming Rebellions: Peasants and Problems of Interpretation." *Journal of Interdisciplinary History* 3 (1972): 103–17.

DeBary, Wm. Theodore. "Neo-Confucian Cultivation and the Seventeenth-Century 'Enlightenment.'" In DeBary, ed., *The Unfolding of Neo-Confucianism*, pp. 141–216.

DeBary, Wm. Theodore, ed. *Self and Society in Ming Thought*. New York: Columbia University Press, 1970.

———, ed. *The Unfolding of Neo-Confucianism*. New York: Columbia University Press, 1975.

DeBary, W. T. "Individualism and Humanitarianism in Late Ming Thought." In DeBary, ed., *Self and Society in Ming Thought*, pp. 145–245.

Dennerline, Jerry. "The Ch'ing Conquest and the Role of the Bureaucratic Elite." Paper, American Historical Association, 1974.

————. "Fiscal Reform and Local Control: The Gentry-Bureaucratic
Alliance Survives the Conquest." In Frederic Wakeman, Jr., and
Carolyn Grant, eds., *Conflict and Control in Late Imperial China*.

————. "The Mandarins and the Massacre of Chia-ting: An Analysis of
the Local Heritage and the Resistance to the Manchu Invasion in 1645."
Ph.D. dissertation, Yale University, 1973.

Dermigny, Louis. *La Chine et l'Occident: Le Commerce à Canton au
XVIIIe Siècle*. 3 vols. and album. Paris, 1964.

Dreyer, Edward L. "The Poyang Campaign, 1363: Inland Naval Warfare
in the Founding of the Ming Dynasty." In Frank Kierman, and
Fairbank, John K., eds. *Chinese Ways in Warfare*. Cambridge, Mass.,
1974.

ECCP. See Hummel, Arthur.

Eisenstadt, S. N. *The Political Systems of Empires*. New York: The Free
Press, 1969

Elias, Ney, ed. *A History of the Moghuls of Central Asia being the Tarikh-i-
Rashidi of Mirza Muhammad Haidar, Dughlat*. Translated by E. Denison
Ross. London: S. Low, Marston & Co., 1895.

Elvin, Mark. *The Pattern of the Chinese Past*. Stanford: Stanford
University Press, 1973.

Erh-ch'en chuan 貳臣傳. 12 *chüan*, Peking, exact publication date unknown,
ordered compiled in 1776.

Fairbank, John K., ed. *Chinese Thought and Institutions*. Chicago: Chicago
University Press, 1957.

————. *The Chinese World Order*. Cambridge, Mass.: Harvard University
Press, 1968.

Fan Lien 范濂. "Yün-chien chü-mu ch'ao" 雲間據目抄. In *Pi-chi hsiao-shuo
ta-kuan* 筆記小說大觀, pp. 1259–89. Taipei, 1962.

Fang Chao-ying. "A Technique for Estimating the Numerical Strength of
the Early Manchu Military Forces." *Harvard Journal of Asiatic Studies*
13 (1950): 192–215.

Fang Hao 方豪. "Ch'ung-chen ch'u Cheng Chih-lung i-min ju-T'ai shih"
崇禎初鄭芝龍移民入臺事. *T'ai-wan wen-hsien* 臺灣文獻 12, no. 1 (March 1961):
37–38.

Fang Hsüeh-chien 方學漸. *Erh-hsün* 邇訓. Reprinted 1883.

————. *T'ung-i chi hsü* 桐彝及續. Reprinted 1883.

Fang Hung-hsiao 方宏孝. *Ming mo liu k'ou chi-shih* 明末流寇紀事. Taipei, 1960.

Fang Pao 方苞. *Fang Wang-hsi hsien-sheng wen-chi* 方望溪先生文集. *Ssu-pu
ts'ung-k'an*.

Fei Hai-chi 費海璣. "Ch'üan Tsu-wang hsing-i k'ao" 全祖望行誼考. *Chung-hua
wen-hua fu-hsing yüeh-k'an* 中華文化復興月刊 2, no. 12 (December 1969):

38–43.

Fei Hsiao-t'ung. *Peasant Life in China*. London: G. Routledge and Sons, 1939.

Feng Meng-lung 馮夢龍. *Chia-shen chi-wen* 甲申紀聞. In *Hsüan-lan t'ang ts'ung-shu* 玄覽堂叢書, ed. Cheng Chen-to 鄭振鐸, *ts'e* 107. Nanking, 1947.

Feuerwerker, Albert. "From 'Feudalism' to 'Capitalism' in Recent Historical Writing from Mainland China." *Journal of Asian Studies* 18, no. 1 (1958): 107–15.

Fletcher, Joseph. "Central Asian Sufism and Ma Ming-hsin's New Teaching." Unpublished manuscript.

Fletcher, Joseph R. "China and Central Asia, 1368–1884." In John K. Fairbank, ed., *The Chinese World Order*, pp. 206–24.

Ford, J. F. "Some Chinese Muslims in the Seventeenth and Eighteenth Centuries." *Asian Affairs: Journal of the Royal Central Asian Society* 61, pt. 2 (June 1974): 144–56.

Franke, Wolfgang. *An Introduction to the Sources of Ming History*. Kuala Lumpur: University of Malaya Press, 1968.

Franke, Wolfgang. "The Veritable Records of the Ming Dynasty, 1368–1644." In W. G. Beasley and E. G. Pulleyblank, eds. *Historians of China and Japan*, pp. 60–77.

FSHSCL. See Wu Shan-chia.

Fu I-ling 傅衣凌. *Ming-Ch'ing nung-ts'un she-hui ching-chi* 明清農村社會經濟. Peking, 1961.

————. *Ming-tai Chiang-nan shih-min ching-chi shih-t'an* 明代江南市民經濟試探. Shanghai, 1957.

Fu-liang hsien-chih 浮梁縣志. 1682.

Fu-she hsing-shih 復社姓氏. K'ang hsi ed., Rare Books of the National Library of Peking. Microfilm, no. 562.

Fujii Hiroshi 藤井宏. "Shin-an shōnin no kenkyū" 新安商人の研究. *Tōyō gakuhō* 東洋学報 36, nos. 1–4 (1953–54): 1–44, 32–60, 65–118, 115–45.

Gallagher, Louis, trans. *China in the Sixteenth Century: The Journals of Matthew Ricci, 1583–1610*. New York: Random House, 1953.

Gamson, William A. *Power and Discontent*. Homewood, Ill.: Dorsey, 1968.

Goodrich, Luther Carrington. *The Literary Inquisition of Ch'ien-lung*. Baltimore: Waverly Press, 1935.

Gotō Shukudō 後藤粛堂. "Wakō-ō Ō Choku." 倭寇王王直. *Rekishi chiri* 歴史地理, vol. 50, nos. 1, 2, 4, pp. 32–40, 106–26, 289–309.

Graham, Hugh Davis, and Gurr, Ted Robert, *Violence in America: Historical and Comparative Perspectives*. New York: Bantam Books, 1970.

Groeneveldt, W. P. *De Nederlanders in China, Eerste Deel: De eerste bemoeiingen om den handel in China en de vestiging in de Pescadores (1601–1624)*. The Hague, 1898.

Gurr, Ted R. "A Comparative Study of Civil Strife." In Graham and Gurr, *Violence in America*, pp. 572–632.

Gurr, Ted, with Charles Ruttenberg. *Cross-national Studies of Civil Violence*. Washington: American University Center for Research in Social Systems, 1969.

Ha-mi chih 哈密志. Compiled by Chung Fang 鐘方. Taipei reprint, 1967.

Hambly, Gavin, ed. *Central Asia*. New York: Delacorte, 1969.

Han T'an 韓炎. "Chiang-yin ch'eng-shou chi" 江陰城守紀. In *Chung-kuo nei-luan wai-huo li-shih ts'ung-shu*. Shanghai, 1946.

———. *Yu-huai t'ang wen-kao* 有懷堂文稿. In his *Yu-huai t'ang wen-chi* 有懷堂文集. 1703.

Haneda Akira 羽田明. "Minmatsu Shinsho no higashi Torukistan" 明末清初の東トルキスタン. *Tōyōshi kenkyū* 東洋史研究 7, no. 5 (September–October 1942): 285–321.

Hatano Yoshihiro 波多野善大. *Chūgoku kindai kōgyō shi no kenkyū* 中国近代工業史の研究. Tokyo, 1961.

Hauer, E. "Li Tze-ch'eng [*sic*] und Chang Hsien-chung" Ein Beitrag zum Ende der Ming Dynastie," *Asia Major*, o.s. 2 (1925): 436–98, and 3 (1926): 268–87.

Hinton, William. *Fanshen*. New York: Monthly Review, 1966.

Ho Ch'ang-ling 賀長齡 ed. *Huang-ch'ao ching-shih wen-pien* 皇朝經世文編. 1826; Taipei reprint, 1963.

Ho Peng-yoke. "The Astronomical Bureau in Ming China." *Journal of Asian History* 3, no. 2 (1969): 137–57.

Ho Ping-ti 何炳棣. *Chung-kuo hui-kuan shih-lun* 中國會館史論. Taipei, 1966.

———. *The Ladder of Success in Imperial China: Aspects of Social Mobility, 1368–1911*. New York: Columbia University Press, 1962.

———. "The Salt Merchants of Yangchow: A Study of Commercial Capitalism in Eighteenth-century China." *Harvard Journal of Asiatic Studies* 17 (1954): 130–68.

———. *Studies of the Population of China, 1368–1953*. Cambridge, Mass.: Harvard University Press, 1959.

Hobsbawm, E. J. *Primitive Rebels*. New York: Norton, 1959.

———. *Social Bandits and Primitive Rebels*. Glencoe, Ill.: Free Press, 1959.

Hobsbawn, E. J., ed. *Revolutionaries: Contemporary Essays*. London: Weidenfeld and Nicolson, 1973.

Hou T'ung-tseng 侯峒曾. *Hou Chung-chieh kung ch'üan-chi* 侯忠節公全集. 1933.

Hou Wai-lu 侯外廬. *Chung-kuo tsao-ch'i ch'i-meng ssu-hsiang shih* 中國早期啓蒙

思想史. Peking, 1956. Also constitutes vol. 5 of his *Chung-kuo ssu-hsiang t'ung-shih* 中國思想通史. Peking, 1958.

———. "Fang I-chih—Chung-kuo ti pai-k'e ch'uan-shu p'ai ta che-hsueh-chia" 方以智—中國的百科全書派大哲學家 *Li-shih yen-chiu* 歷史研究, 1957, June, pp. 1–21, July, pp. 1–25.

Hou Yüan-ching 侯元瀞. "Nien-p'u" 年譜. In Hou T'ung-tseng, *Hou chung-chieh kung ch'üan-chi* 侯忠節公全集.

Hsi, Angela. "Wu San-kuei in 1644: A Reappraisal." *Journal of Asian Studies* 34, no. 2 (February 1975): 443–53.

Hsia, Hsieh 夏燮. *Ming T'ung-chien* 明通鑑. Peking, 1959.

Hsia-men chih 廈門志. Chou K'ai 周凱 ed. TW, no. 95.

Hsiao I-shan 蕭一山. *Ch'ing-tai t'ung-shih* 清代通史. Shanghai, 1927–32; Taipei reprint, 1962–67.

Hsiao Kung-ch'üan. *Rural China: Imperial Control in the Nineteenth Century*. Seattle: University of Washington Press, 1960.

Hsiao Mu 蕭穆. "Tai Yu-an hsien-sheng shih-lüeh" 戴憂庵先生事略. *Kuo-ts'ui hsueh-pao* 國粹學報 6, no. 10 (October 1910).

Hsiao Shih 蕭奭 comp. *Yung-hsien lu* 永憲錄. Shanghai, 1959.

Hsieh Ai-chih 謝愛之. "Ch'üan Tsu-wang hsien-sheng hsing-i k'ao" 全祖望先生行誼考, *Yu-shih yueh-k'an* 幼獅月刊 31, no. 1 (January 1970): 27–30.

Hsieh Kuo-chen 謝國楨. *Ch'ing-ch'u nung-min ch'i-i tzu-liao chi-lu* 清初農民起義資料輯錄. Shanghai, 1956.

———. "Ch'ing-ch'u tung-nan yen-hai ch'ien-chieh k'ao" 清初東南沿海遷界考. *Kuo-hsueh chi-k'an* 國學季刊 2, no. 4 (December 1930): 797–826; English translation, *Chinese Social and Political Science Review* 15 (1931): 559–96.

———. *Ming-Ch'ing chih chi tang-she yün-tung k'ao* 明清之際黨社運動考. Shanghai, 1934; Taipei reprint, 1967.

———. *Nan-Ming shih-lüeh* 南明史略. Shanghai, 1957.

———. *Wan-Ming shih-chi k'ao* 晚明史籍考. Peiping, 1932; Taipei reprint, 1968.

Hsin-ch'ou chi-wen 辛丑紀聞. In *Ming-Ch'ing shih-liao hui-pien* 明清史料彙編. 2d ser., vol. 16. Taipei, 1967.

Hsin-hua hsien-chih 新化縣志. 1549.

Hsiu-ning hsien-chih 休寧縣志. 1693.

Hsiu-shui hsien-chih 秀水縣志. Wan-li ed. and also 1684 ed.

Hsü Fu-tso 徐復祚. *Hua-tang-ko ts'ung-t'an* 花當閣叢談. In *Chieh-yüeh shan-fang hui-ch'ao* 借月山房彙鈔. N.d.

Hsü Fu-yüan 徐孚遠. *Tiao-heng t'ang ts'un-kao* 釣璜堂存藁. Chin-shan, 1926.

Hsü, Immanuel C. Y. "The Great Policy Debate in China, 1874: Maritime

Defense vs. Frontier Defense." *Harvard Journal of Asiatic Studies* 25 (1964–65): 212–28.

Hsü Kuang-ch'i 徐光啓. *Hsü Kuang-ch'i chi* 徐光啓集. Shanghai, 1961.

Hsü Ping-i 徐秉義. *Ming-mo chung-lieh chi-shih* 明末忠烈紀實. Manuscript, microfilm provided to Library of Congress by National Library of Peking.

Hsü Shih-ch'ang 徐世昌, comp. *Yen-Li shih-ch'eng chi* 顏李師承記. In *Yen-Li hsueh san-chung* 顏李學三種. Republican period.

Hsü Tzu 徐鼒 *Hsiao-t'ien chi-chuan* 小腆紀傳. Reprint TW, no. 168; also Peking, 1958.

———. *Hsiao-t'ien chi-nien* 小腆紀年. Reprint TW, no. 134.

———. *Hsiao-t'ien chi-nien fu-k'ao* 小腆紀年附考. Annotated by Wang Ch'ung-wu 王崇武. Shanghai, 1957.

Hsü wen-hsien t'ung-k'ao 續文獻通考. Shanghai, 1936; Taipei reprint, 1965.

Hsü Ying-fen 徐應芬. *Yü-pıen chi-lueh* 遇變紀略. In *Ching-t'o i-shih* 荊駝逸史 (Tao-kuang ed.), *ts'e* 19.

Hu Shan-yuan 胡山源. *Chia-ting i-min pieh-chuan* 嘉定義民別傳. Shanghai, 1938.

Hua Fu-li 華復蠡. *Liang-Kuang chi-lueh* 兩廣紀略. In *Ming-chi pai-shih hui-pien* （明季稗史彙編）. Shanghai, 1912.

Huai-ning hsien-chih 懷寧縣志. 1915.

Huang Ch'un-yueh 黃淳耀. *Huang T'ao-an chi* 黃陶菴集. 1924.

Huang, Pei. *Autocracy at Work: A Study of the Yung-cheng Period, 1723–1735.* Bloomington: Indiana University Press, 1974.

Huang P'ei-chin 黃佩瑾. "Kuan-yü Ming-tai kuo-nei shih-ch'ang wen't'i ti k'ao-ch'a" 關於明代國內市場問題的考察. *Ming Ch'ing she-hui ching-chi hsing-t'ai ti yen-chiu* 明清社會經濟形態的研究, pp. 198–262. Shanghai, 1957.

Huang, Ray. "Fiscal Administration during the Ming Dynasty." In Charles Hucker, ed., *Chinese Government in Ming Times*, pp. 73–128.

———. "Military Expenditures in Sixteenth Century Ming China." *Oriens Extremus* 17, nos. 1–2 (December 1970): 39–62.

———. "Merchants of the Late Ming as Presented in the *San-yen Stories*," *The Journal of the Institute of Chinese Studies of the Chinese University of Hong Kong* 7, no. (December 1974): 133–54.

———. "Ni Yuan-lu: 'Realism' in a Neo-Confucian Scholar Statesman." In W. T. de Bary, ed., *Self and Society in Ming Thought*, pp. 415–49.

———. *Taxation and Governmental Finance in Sixteenth Century Ming China.* Cambridge: Cambridge University Press, 1974.

Huang Tsung-hsi 黃宗羲. *Hai-wai t'ung-k'u chi* 海外慟哭記. TW, no. 135.

———. *Ming-i tai-fang lu* 明夷待訪錄. 1937; Peking, 1955.

———. *Ming-ju hsüeh-an* 明儒學案, 1882.

————. *Nan-lei wen-ting* 南雷文定. In *Huang Li-chou i-shu* 黃梨洲遺書. Hangchow, 1905; Taipei reprint, 1966.

Huang Yün-mei 黃雲眉. "Ming-shih pien-tsuan k'ao lueh" 明史編纂考略. In Pao Tsun-p'eng 包遵彭, ed., *Ming-shih pien-tsuan k'ao* 明史編纂考, pp. 9–52. Taipei, 1968.

Hucker, Charles O. *The Censorial System of Ming China*. Stanford: Stanford University Press, 1966.

Hucker, Charles O., "Hu Tsung-hsien's Campaign Against Hsü Hai, 1556." In Frank A. Kierman, Jr., and John K. Fairbank, eds., *Chinese Ways in Warfare*. Cambridge, Mass.: Harvard University Press, 1974, pp. 273–307.

————. "Su-chou and the Agents of Wei Chung-hsien, 1626." In *Silver Jubilee Volume of the Zinbun-Kagaku-Kenkyusyo, Kyoto University*, pp. 224–56. Kyoto, 1954. Also in Hucker, *Two Studies on Ming History*, Ann Arbor: University of Michigan Center for Chinese Studies, 1971.

————. "The Tung-lin Movement of the Late Ming Period." In John K. Fairbank, ed., *Chinese Thought and Institutions*, pp. 132–62. Chicago: University of Chicago Press, 1957.

Hucker, Charles O., ed. *Chinese Government in Ming Times: Seven Studies*. New York: Columbia University Press, 1969.

Hullu, J. de. "Over den Chinaschen Handel der Oost-Indische Compagnie in de Eerste Dertig Jaar van de 18ᵉ Eeuw." *Bijdragen tot de Taal-, Land- en Volkenkunde van Nederlandsch Indie* 78 (1917): 32–151.

Hummel, Arthur W., ed. *Eminent Chinese of the Ch'ing Period*. Washington: U.S. Government Printing Office, 1943–1944; Taipei reprints, 1964, 1972.

Hung Liang-chi 洪亮吉, comp. *Ch'ien-lung fu-t'ing-chou-hsien t'u-chih* 乾隆府廳州縣圖志. 1803.

Hung-kuei ch'un-meng 紅閨春夢. Taipei reprint, 1969.

I Man-hui 易曼暉. "Lun Wang Ch'uan-shan ti ts'ai-cheng ssu-hsiang" 論王船山的財政思想, *Wang Ch'uan-shan hsueh-shu t'ao-lun chi*, pp. 370–86.

Imbault-Huart, Camille. "Deux insurrections des mahometans du Kansou (1648–1783)." *Journal Asiatique*, ser. 14 (November-December, 1889): 494–525.

Inaba Iwakichi 稻葉岩吉. *Man-chou fa-ta shih* 滿州發達史. Tokyo, 1935. Translated by Yang Ch'eng-lung 楊成龍, *Ch'ing-shih tzu-liao* 清史資料, pt. 2, vol. 10. Taipei, 1968.

Ishibashi Hideo 石橋秀雄. "Shindai Kanjin kanryō ni kansuru ikkōsatsu— toku no kanjin shinshi to toku-bu to no kankei ni tsuite" 清代漢人官僚に関する一考察—特に漢人進士と督・撫との関係について, *Shien* 史苑 26, nos. 2–3 (1966): 24–35.

Ishihara Michihiro 石原道博. *Bunroku-keichō no eki* 文祿;慶長の役. Tokyo, 1963.

———. *Wakō* 倭寇. Tokyo, 1964.

Israeli, Raphael. "Chinese Versus Muslims: A Study of Cultural Confrontation." Ph.D. dissertation, University of California, Berkeley, 1974.

Iwao Seiichi. "Li Tan, Chief of the Chinese Residents at Hirado, Japan, in the Last Days of the Ming Dynasty." *Memoirs of the Research Department of the Toyo Bunko* 17 (1958): 27–83.

Iwao Seiichi. 岩生成一 "Shih-ch'i shih-chi Jih-pen-jen chih T'ai-wan chin-lüeh hsing-t'ung" 十七世紀日本人之臺灣侵畧行動. *T'ai-wan ching-chi shih pa-chi* 臺灣経済史八集. *T'ai-wan yen-chiu ts'ung-k'an*. 研究叢刊 no. 71 (1959), pp. 1–23.

Kahn, Harold L. "Some Mid-Ch'ing Views of the Monarchy." *Journal of Asian Studies* 24, no. 2 (1965): 229–43.

[*Huang Ch'ing*] *k'ai-kuo fang-lüeh* 皇清開國方略. Compiled by A-kuei 阿桂. 1774–86; reprint, Shanghai, 1889.

[*Huang Ch'ing*] *k'ai-kuo fang-lüeh*. Die Gründung des Mandschurischen Kaiserreiches. Translated by Erich Hauer. Berlin: Walter de Gruyter & Co., 1926.

Kessler, Lawrence D. "Chinese Scholars and the Early Manchu State." *Harvard Journal of Asiatic Studies* 31 (1971): 179–200.

———. "Ethnic Composition of Provincial Leadership During the Ch'ing Dynasty." *Journal of Asian Studies* 28, no. 3 (May 1969): 489–511.

———. *K'ang-hsi and the Consolidation of Ch'ing Rule, 1661–1684.* Chicago: Chicago University Press, 1976.

———. "K'ang-hsi's Military Leadership and the Consolidation of Manchu Rule." Paper. Association for Asian Studies, 1971.

Kierman, Frank, and Fairbank, John, eds. *Chinese Ways in Warfare.* Cambridge, Mass: Harvard University Press, 1974.

Ko Lin 葛麟, *Ko Chung-han i-chi* 葛中翰遺集. 1890.

Ko-ming yuan-yuan 革命遠源. In *Chung-hua min-kuo k'ai-kuo wu-shih-nien wen-hsien* 中華民國開國五十年文獻, 1st series. Taipei, 1963.

Kracke, E. A., Jr. *Civil Service in Early Sung China.* Cambridge, Mass.: Harvard University Press, 1954.

Ku-chin t'u-shu chi-ch'eng 古今圖書集成. 1886–89.

Ku Yen-wu 顧炎武. *Jih-chih lu chi-shih* 日知錄集釋, (Ssu-pu pei-yao ed.).

———. *Ming-chi san-ch'ao yeh-shih* 明季三朝野史 (Taipei reprint, 1961).

———. *Sheng-an pen-chi* 聖安本紀. Reprinted from *T'ing-lin i-shu hui-chi* 亭林遺書彙輯. In TW., no. 183, pp. 1–30.

———. *T'ien-hsia chün-kuo li-ping shu* 天下郡國利病書. Shanghai, 1936.

————. *T'ing-lin wen-chi* 亭林文集 and *Yü-chi* 餘集 in *T'ing-lin hsien-cheng i-shu* 亭林先生遺書 (1898), vols. 19, 23.

————. *T'ing-lin shih-wen chi* 亭林詩文集. Peking, 1959.

Ku Ying-t'ai 谷應泰. *Ming-shih chi-shih pen-mo* 明史紀事本末. *Chi-fu ts'ung-shu* 畿輔叢書 *ts'e* 285–302. 1879; also Shanghai, 1934, and Taipei reprint, 1965.

K'u-miao chi-lüeh 哭廟紀略. In *T'ung-shih* 痛史. Taipei, 1968, vol. 6.

Kuhn, Philip A. *Rebellion and Its Enemies in Late Imperial China.* Cambridge, Mass.: Harvard University Press, 1970.

K'un-Hsin liang-hsien hsü-hsiu ho-chih 崑新兩縣續修合志. 1880 edition.

Kung P'eng-chiu 龔鵬九. "Kuan-yü Wang Ch'uan-shan ti chieh-chi li-ch'ang wen-t'i" 關於王船山的階級立場問題. *Wang Ch'uan-shan hsueh-shu t'ao-lun chi*, pp. 430–56.

Kuo I-sheng 郭毅生. "T'ai-p'ing t'ien-kuo ch'ien-hsi shang-p'in huo-pi ching-chi ti fa-chan" 太平天國前夕商品貨幣經濟的發展. *Li-shih chiao-hsueh* 歷史教學 7 (1955): 47–52.

Kuo Mo-jo 郭沫若. *Chia-shen san-pai-nien chi* 甲申三百年祭. Peking, 1972.

Kuo-pien nan-ch'en ch'ao 國變難臣鈔 (anon.). In *San-ch'ao yeh-chi* 三朝野紀, in *Chung-kuo nei-luan wai-huo li-shih ts'ung-shu*, ser. 10 pp. 183–188. Shanghai, 1947.

Kuropatkin, A. N. *Kashgaria: Eastern or Chinese Turkestan.* Translated by Walter Gowan. Calcutta: Thacker, Spink and Co., 1882.

Lai Chia-tu 賴家度. "I-liu ssu-wu nien Chiang-yin jen-min ti k'ang-Ch'ing tou-cheng" 一六四五年江陰人民的抗清鬥爭. In Li Kuang-pi, ed., *Ming-Ch'ing shih lun-ts'ung* 明清史論叢.

Langlois, Ch. V. and Ch. Seignobos. *Introduction to the Study of History.* Translated by G. G. Berry. New York, 1913.

Lao, S. I. (Lao Yung-wei). "The Split within the Tung-lin Movement and its Consequences." Paper. Conference on Seventeenth-Century Chinese Thought. Bellagio, Italy, 1970.

Lattimore, Owen. *Inner Asian Frontiers of China.* Boston: Beacon Press, 1962 paperback.

Laufer, B. "Chinese Muhammedan Bronzes." *Ars Islamica* 1, no. 2 (1934): 133–46.

LeBon, Gustave. *The Crowd: A Study of the Popular Mind.* New York: Viking, 1960.

————. *The Psychology of Revolution.* Translated by Bernard Miall. Wells, Vt.: Fraser, 1968.

Lee, Robert H. G. *The Manchurian Frontier in Ch'ing History.* Cambridge, Mass.: Harvard University Press, 1970.

Leites, Nathan, and Wolf, Charles, Jr. *Rebellion and Authority: An*

Analytic Essay on Insurgent Conflicts. Chicago: Markham, 1970.

Li Chi. *The Love of Nature: Hsu Hsia-k'o and His Early Travels*. Western Washington State College, Program in East Asian Studies, Occasional Paper No. 3 (1971).

——. "Hsü Hsia-k'o's Huang Shan Travel Diaries." In *Two Studies in Chinese Literature*, pp. 1–23. Michigan Papers in Chinese Studies 3 (1968).

Li Chih-ch'in 李之勤. "Kuan-yü Chung-kuo Ch'ing-ch'u tzu-pen chu-i sheng-ch'an meng-ya ti fa-chan shui-p'ing wen-t'i" 關於中國清初資本主義生產萌芽的發展水平問題. *Meng-ya*, pp. 565–608.

Li Ch'ing 李清. *San-yüan pi-chi* 三垣筆紀. In *Ku-hsueh hui-k'an* 古學彙刊, ser. 1, ts'e 2–4. Shanghai, 1913; also Wu-hsing, 1927.

Li Hsü 李煦. "Su-chou chih-tsao Li Hsu tsou-che" 蘇州織造李煦奏摺. *Wen-hsien ts'ung-pien* 文獻叢編. Taipei, 1964.

Li Hsüeh-chih 李學智 and Kuang Lu 廣祿. "Lao-Man-wen yuan-tang yü Man-wen lao-tang chih pi-chiao yen-chiu" 老滿文原檔與滿文老檔之比較研究. *The China Council for East Asian Studies, Annual Bulletin*, vol. 4. Taipei, 1965.

Li Hsün 李洵. *Ming Ch'ing shih* 明清史. Peking, 1956.

Li Hsün-chih 李遜之. *Ch'ung-chen ch'ao yeh-chi* 崇禎朝野紀. TW, no. 250.

Li Hua 李華. "Shih-lun Ch'ing-tai ch'ien-ch'i ti shih-min tou-cheng" 試論清代前期的市民鬥爭, *Wen-Shih-Che* 文史哲 10 (1957): 54–62.

Li Kuang-ming 黎光明. *Chia-ching yü-Wo Chiang-Che chu-k'o-chün k'ao* 嘉靖禦倭江浙主客軍考. Yenching Journal of Chinese Studies Monograph Series 4. Peiping, 1933.

Li Kuang-pi 李光璧. *Ming-ch'ao shih lüeh* 明朝史略. Wuhan, 1957.

——, ed. *Ming Ch'ing shih lun-ts'ung* 明清史論叢. Wuhan, 1957.

——. *Ming-tai yü-Wo chan-cheng* 明代御倭戰爭. Shanghai, 1956.

Li Kuang-t'ao 李光濤, ed. *Ch'ao-hsien jen-ch'en Wo-huo shih-liao* 朝鮮壬辰倭禍史料. 5 vols. Taipei, 1970.

Li Kuang-t'ao 李光濤. *Ming-chi liu-k'ou shih-mo* 明季流寇始末. Taipei, 1965.

Li Kuang-t'ao 李光濤 and Li Hsueh-chih 李學智, eds. *Ming-Ch'ing tang-an ts'un-chen hsuan-chi* 明清檔案存眞選輯, 2 vols. Taipei, 1959, 1973.

Li Kung 李塨. *Shu-ku hou-chi* 恕谷後集. In *Chi-fu ts'ung-shu* 畿輔叢書, vols. 392–95. 1879.

——. *Ta-hsüeh pien-yeh* 大學辨業 (1701). Also in *Chi-fu ts'ung-shu*. Taipei reprint, 1966, vol. 208, and in *Yen-Li ts'ung-shu*, Peking, 1922.

Li Shih-chen 李士楨. *Fu-Chiang fu-Yüeh cheng-lüeh* 撫江撫粵政略. N.d. copy in Toyo Bunko, Tokyo.

Li Ti 李迪 et al., comp. *Kan-su t'ung-chih* 甘肅通志. 1737.

Li T'ien-yu 李天祐. *Ming-mo Chiang-yin Chia-ting jen-min ti k'ang-Ch'ing tou-cheng* 明末江陰嘉定人民的抗清鬥爭. Shanghai, 1955.

Li Tung-fang 黎東方. *Hsi-shuo Ch'ing-ch'ao* 細說清朝. Taipei, 1970.

———. *Hsi-shuo Ming-ch'ao* 細說明朝. Taipei, 1964.

Li Wen-chih 李文治. "Lun Ch'ing-tai ch'ien-ch'i ti t'u-ti chan-yu kuan-hsi" 論清代前期的土地佔有關係. *Li-shih yen-chiu*, 1963, no. 5, pp. 75–108.

———. *Wan-Ming min-pien* 晚明民變. Shanghai, 1948, and Hong Kong, 1948 and 1966).

Li Yen 李楘. *Tung-lin tang-chi k'ao* 東林黨籍考. Peking, 1957.

Li Yuan-tu 李元度, comp., *Kuo-ch'ao hsien-cheng shih-lueh* 國朝先正事略. 1866.

Liang Ch'i-ch'ao 梁啓超. *Chung-kuo chin san-pai-nien hsueh-shu shih* 中國近三百年學術史. Chungking, 1944; Taipei reprint, 1966.

Lin Shih-tui 林時對. *Ho-cha ts'ung-t'an* 荷牐叢談. TW, No. 153.

Ling Shun-sheng 凌純聲. "Chung-kuo ku-tai she chih yuan-liu" 中國古代社之源流. *Chung-yang yen-chiu-yuan: Min-tsu-hsueh yen-chiu-so chi-k'an* 中央研究院：民族學研究所集刊 17 (Spring 1964): 1–44.

Liu Chien-shao 劉建韶. *Fu-chien t'ung-chih cheng-shih lüeh* 福建通志政事略. Manuscript, n.d., Harvard-Yenching Library.

Liu Hsien-t'ing 劉献廷. *Kuang-yang tsa-chi* 廣陽雜記. CTPCTK; also *Kung-shun t'ang ts'ung-shu* 功順堂叢書. Kuang-hsu period, vol. 24–28; also *Chi-fu ts'ung-shu ch'u pien* 畿輔叢書初編 (not in 1966 Taipei reprint); also separate Taipei reprint, 1962.

Liu, Hui-chen Wang, *The Traditional Chinese Clan Rules*. Locust Valley, New York: J. J. Augustin, 1959.

Liu James J. Y., *The Chinese Knight-Errant*. Chicago: University of Chicago Press, 1966.

Liu, James T. C., *Ou-yang Hsiu: An Eleventh-Century Neo-Confucianist*. Stanford: Stanford University Press, 1967.

Liu Shang-yu 劉向友. *Ting-ssu hsiao-chi* 定思小紀. In Chao I-ch'en 趙詒琛 and Wang Ta-lung 王大隆, eds. *Ting-ch'ou ts'ung-pien* 丁丑叢編. Wu-hsi, 1937.

Liu Shih-p'ei 劉師培. [Liu Kuang-han 劉光漢]. "Ch'üan Tsu-wang chuan" 全祖望傳. *Kuo-ts'ui hsueh-pao* 國粹學報 1, no. 11 (1905): 6a–b.

Liu Tso-mei 柳作梅. "Ch'ü Ta-chün 'Kuang-tung hsin-yü' ti li-shih pei-ching" 屈大均「廣東新語」的歷史背景. *Shu-mu chi-k'an* 書目季刊 2, no. 1 (September 1967): 61–66.

Liu Yen 劉炎. "Ming-mo ch'eng-shih ching-chi fa-chan hsia ti ch'u-ch'i shih-min yun-tung" 明末城市經濟發展下的初期市民運動. In *Meng-ya*, pp. 401–435. Also in *Li-shih yen-chiu*, 1955, no. 6, pp. 29–60.

Lo Jung-pang. "Policy Formulation and Decision-Making on Issues Respecting Peace and War." In Charles O. Hucker, ed. *Chinese Government in Ming Times: Seven Studies*, pp. 41–72.

Lo Yao-chiu 羅耀九. "Tsai lun Ming-ch'ao Wan-li nien-chien ku-yung lao-tung ti hsing-chih" 再論明朝萬歷年間僱傭勞動的性質. *Li-shih yen-chiu*, 1962, no. 4, pp. 78–103.

Loewenthal, Rudolf. "Russian Contributions to the History of Islam in China." *Central Asiatic Journal* 3, no. 4 (1962): 312–15.

Loewenthal, Rudolf. "Russian Materials on Islam in China: A Preliminary Bibliography." *Monumenta Serica* 16 (1957): 449–79.

Lu K'o-tsao 魯可藻 (probable author). *Ling-piao chi-nien* 嶺表紀年. Manuscript. National Central Library, Taipei.

Lu Shih-i 陸世儀. *Fu-she chi-lüeh* 復社紀略. Taipei reprint, 1964.

Lü Wei-ch'i 呂維祺. *Ssu-i-kuan tse* 四譯館則. Kyoto, 1928.

Ma Ch'i-ch'ang 馬其昶. *T'ung-ch'eng ch'i-chiu chuan* 桐城耆舊傳. 1911; Taipei reprint, 1969.

Ma Feng-ch'en. "Manchu-Chinese Social and Economic Conflicts in Early Ch'ing." In *Chinese Social History*, edited and translated by E-tu Zen Sun and John de Francis, pp. 333–56. Washington: American Council of Learned Societies, 1956.

Ma T'ai-hsuan 馬太玄. "Wan Ssu-t'ung chih sheng-p'ing chi ch'i chu-tso" 萬斯同之生平及其著作. *Chung-shan ta-hsueh yü-yen li-shih yen-chiu-so chou-k'an* 中山大學語言歷史研究所週刊 3, no. 18 (May 1928): 942–48.

Mackerras, Colin. *The Rise of the Peking Opera 1770–1870: Social Aspects of the Theatre in Manchu China*. Oxford University Press, 1972.

MacSherry, Charles W. "Impairment of the Ming Tribute System as Exhibited in Trade through Fukien." Ph. D. dissertation, University of California, Berkeley, 1956.

Mambun rōtō 滿文老檔. Translated by Kanda Nobuo 神田信夫 et al. Tokyo, 1955–63.

Mammitzsch, Ulrich. "Wei Chung-hsien (1568–1628): A Reappraisal of the Eunuch and the Factional Strife at the Late Ming Court." Ph. D. dissertation, University of Hawaii, 1968.

Man-chou chiu-tang 滿洲舊檔. 10 vols. Taipei, 1969.

Man-chou lao-tang pi-lu 滿洲老檔秘錄, ed. Chin-liang 金梁. Taipei, 1929.

Mao Jui-cheng 茅瑞徵. *Huang Ming hsiang-hsü lu* 皇明象胥錄. Shanghai, 1937.

Mao, Lucien. "Tai Ming-shih," *T'ien-shia Monthly* 5, no. 4 (1937): 382–99.

Mao, Lucien, trans., "A Memoir of Ten Days' Massacre in Yangchow." *T'ien-hsia Monthly* (1937), pp. 515–37.

Mao Yuan-i 茅元儀. *Wu-pei chih* 武備志. T'u-shu chi-ch'eng ed.

Martin, B. G. "A Short History of the Khalwati Order of Dervishes." In Nikki R. Keddie, ed., *Scholars, Saints, and Sufis*, pp. 275–305. Berkeley: University of California Press, 1972.

Martines, Lauro, ed. *Violence and Civil Disorder in Italian Cities, 1200–1500*. Berkeley: University of California Press, 1972.

McMorran, Ian. "Wang Fu-chih and the Neo-Confucian Tradition." In
    W. T. de Bary, ed., *The Unfolding of Neo-Confucianism*, pp. 413–67.
Meilink-Roelofsz, M. A. P. *Asian Trade and European Influence in the
    Indonesian Archipelago between 1500 and about 1630*. The Hague, 1962.
Meng Cheng-fa 蒙正發. *San-hsiang ts'ung-shih lu* 三湘從事錄. Shanghai, 1947.
Meng Sen 孟森. *Ch'ing-shih ch'ien-chi* 清史前紀. 1930. Reprinted in *Ch'ing-
    shih tzu-liao* 清史資料, pt. 2, vol. 2. Taipei, 1968.
————. *Ming Ch'ing shih lun-chu chi-k'an* 明清史論著集刊. Peking, 1959;
    Taipei, 1959.
————. "Pa-ch'i chih-tu k'ao shih" 八旗制度考實. *Chung-yang yen-chiu yuan:
    Li-shih yü-yen yen-chiu-so chi-k'an* 6 (1936): 343–412. Reprinted in
    Meng Sen, *Ch'ing-tai shih* 清代史. Taipei, 1960.
Meng-ya. See *Chung-kuo tzu-pen chu-i meng-ya wen-t'i t'ao-lun chi*.
Michael, Franz. *The Origin of Manchu Rule in China*. Baltimore: Johns
    Hopkins Press, 1942.
Min Erh-ch'ang 閔爾昌, comp. *Pei-chuan chi pu* 碑傳集補. Peiping, 1932.
"Mindai no Kaikyō ni tsuite." 明代の回教に就て. *Kaikyō jijō* 回教事情 2, no. 3
    (1939): 3–14.
Mindai seiiki shiryō 明代西域資料. Kyoto, 1973.
Ming-chi Ho-lan-jen chin chü P'eng-hu ts'an tang 明季荷蘭人侵據彭湖殘檔. TW,
    no. 154.
Ming ching-shih wen-pien hsüan-lu 明經世文編選錄. TW, no. 289.
Ming Ch'ing she-hui ching-chi hsing-t'ai ti yen-chiu 明清社會經濟形態的研究.
    Shanghai, 1957.
Ming Ch'ing shih-liao 明清史料. Shanghai and Peiping, 1930 et seq.; Taipei
    reprint, 1973.
Ming Shih 明史, ed. Chang T'ing-yü 張廷玉 et al. Ssu-pu pei-yao; punctuated
    edition, Taipei, 1963.
Ming Shih-lu 明實錄. Taipei, 1962–1968.
Mote, Frederick W. "Confucian Eremitism in the Yuan Period." In
    Arthur F. Wright, ed., *The Confucian Persuasion*, pp. 202–40. Stanford:
    Stanford University Press, 1960.
————. "A Millennium of Chinese Urban History: Form, Time, and
    Space Concepts in Soochow." *Rice University Studies* 59 (Fall 1973):
    35–65.
MR. See *Mambun Rōtō*.
MS. See *Ming-shih*.
MSL. See *Ming Shih-lu*.
Murphey, Rhoads. "The City as a Center of Change: Western Europe and
    China." *Annals of the Association of American Geographers* 44, no. 4
    (1954): 349–62.

Myers, Ramon H. "Some Issues on Economic Organization during the Ming and Ch'ing Periods: A Review Article." *Ch'ing-shih wen-t'i* 3, no. 2 (1974): 77–93.

Naitō Torajirō 內藤虎次郎. *Shina Shigaku shi* 支那史学史. Tokyo, 1950, 1967.

Nan-hsün chen-chih 南潯鎮志. 1858 edition.

Nan-Ming yeh-shih 南明野史. "Nan-sha san-yü shih" 南沙三餘氏. Shanghai, 1930.

Naquin, Susan. *Millenarian Rebellion in China: The Eight Trigrams Uprising of 1813.* New Haven: Yale University Press, 1976.

Narakino Shimezu 楢木野宣. "Shindai juyō shokkan Man-Kan hiritsu no hendō" 清代重要職官満漢比率の変動. *Gunma Daigaku kiyō—jimbun shakai kagaku hen* 群馬大学紀要—人文社会科学篇 17, no. 5 (1967): 47–70.

Needham, Joseph. *Science and Civilization in China.* Cambridge: Cambridge University Press, 1954 et seq.

Ni Tsai-t'ien 倪在田. *Hsü Ming chi-shih pen-mo* 續明紀事本末. TW, no. 133.

Nivison, David S. " 'Knowledge' and 'Action' in Chinese Thought since Wang Yang-ming." In Arthur F. Wright, ed., *Studies in Chinese Thought*, pp. 112–145. Chicago: University of Chicago Press, 1953.

Nivison, David S. "Protest Against Convention and Conventions of Protest." In Arthur F. Wright, ed., *The Confucian Persuasion*, pp. 170–201. Stanford: Stanford University Press, 1960.

Okada Hidehiro 岡田英弘. "Ch'ing T'ai-tsung chi-wei k'ao-shih" 清太宗繼位考實. *Ku-kung wen-hsien* 故宮文獻 3, no. 2 (1972): 31–37.

Ōkubo Eiko 大久保英子. "Minmatsu dokushojin kessha to kyōiku katsudō" 明末読書人結社と教育活動. In Hayashi Tomoharu 林友春 ed., *Kinsei Chūgoku kyōikushi kenkyū* 近世中国教育史研究, pp. 155–206. Tokyo, 1958.

Ono Kazuko 小野和子. "Shinsho no kōkeikai ni tsuite" 清初の講経会について. *Tōhō gakuhō* 東方学報 36 (1964): 633–661.

———. "Shinsho no shisō tōsei o megutte" 清初の思想統制をめぐっ て. *Tōyōshi kenkyū* 東洋史研究 18, no. 3 (1959): 99–123.

Oxnam, Robert B. "Policies and Institutions of the Oboi Regency, 1661– 1669." *Journal of Asian Studies* 32, no. 2 (February 1973): 265–86.

Oxnam, Robert B. *Ruling from Horseback: Manchu Politics in the Oboi Regency, 1661–1669.* Chicago: University of Chicago Press, 1975.

Pa-ch'i t'ung-chih 八旗通志 ed. O-erh-t'ai 鄂爾泰. 1739; Taipei reprint, 1968.

[*Ch'in-ting*] *Pa-ch'i t'ung-chih* 欽定八旗通志 ed. Fu-lung-an 福隆安. 1796; Taipei reprint, 1968.

Pai Shou-i 白壽彝, ed. *Hui-min ch'i-i* 回民起義. Shanghai, 1952.

[*T'ung-ch'eng Mu-shan*] *P'an-shih tsung-p'u* 桐城木山潘氏宗譜. 1928, C. 818.

Pao-shan hsien-chih 寶山縣志. 1882.

Pao Tsun-p'eng 包遵彭, ed. *Ming-shih pien-tsuan k'ao* 明史編纂考. *Ming-shih lun-ts'ung* 明史論叢, vol. 1. Taipei, 1968.

Pao Yang-sheng 抱陽生. *Chia-shen ch'ao-shih hsiao-chi* 甲申朝事小紀. In *T'ung-shih* 痛史. Shanghai, 1912, no. 21.

Parsons, James B. "Ming Dynasty Bureaucracy: Aspects of Background Forces." In Charles O. Hucker, ed., *Chinese Government in Ming Times: Seven Studies*, pp. 175–231; also in *Monumenta Serica*, 22 (1963): 343–406.

Parsons, James B. *The Peasant Rebellions of the Late Ming Dynasty*. Tucson: University of Arizona Press, 1970.

Paske-Smith, M. *Western Barbarians in Japan and Formosa in Tokugawa Days, 1603–1868*. 2d ed. Reprint, New York, 1968.

Pearson, J. D., et al. *Index Islamicus, 1906–1955*. Cambridge: Heffer, 1958.

Pei-chuan chi 碑傳集, ed. Ch'ien I-chi 錢儀吉. 1893.

Pei-shih pu-i 北事補遺, anon. In *Hsuan-lan t'ang ts'ung-shu* 玄覽堂叢書 ed. Cheng Cheng-to 鄭振鐸, *ts'e* 112. Nanking, 1947.

Pelliot, Paul. "Le Hōja et le Sayyid Husain de l'Histoire des Ming." *T'oung Pao* 38, nos. 2–5 (1948): 81–292.

P'eng Sun-i 彭孫貽. *Ching-hai chih* 靖海志. TW, no. 35.

——. *P'ing-k'ou chih* 平寇志. Peiping, 1931.

P'eng Tse-i 彭澤益. "Ch'ing-tai Kuang-tung yang-hang chih-tu ti ch'i-yuan," 清代廣東洋行制度的起源. *Li-shih yen-chiu* 歷史研究, 1957, no. 1, pp. 1–25.

P'eng Yü-hsin 彭爾新. "Wang Ch'uan-shan ti fu-i-lun chi ch'i ssu-hsiang t'i-hsi" 王船山的賦役論及其思想體系. *Wang Ch'uan-shan hsueh-shu t'ao-lun chi*, pp. 348–69.

Peterson, Willard J. "Fang I-chih: Western Learning and the 'Investigation of Things.'" In W. T. de Bary, ed., *The Unfolding of Neo-Confucianism*, pp. 369–411.

Peterson, Willard J. "The Life of Ku Yen-wu (1613–1682)." *Harvard Journal of Asiatic Studies* 28 (1968): 114–56, 29 (1969): 201–47.

Pickens, Claude, Jr. *Annotated Bibliography of Literature on Islam in China*. Hankow: Society of Friends of the Moslems in China, 1950.

P'ing-wu shih-lüeh 平吳史略, anon. Taipei, 1968.

PKTL. See *Chiang-su sheng Ming Ch'ing i-lai pei-k'o tzu-liao hsuan-chi*.

Pokora, Timoteus. "A Pioneer of New Trends of Thought in the End of the Ming Period." *Archiv Orientalni* 29 (1961): 469–75.

Polanyi, Karl. *Dahomey and the Slave Trade*. Seattle: University of Washington Press, 1966.

Pratt, Mark S. "Japanese Materials on Islam in China." M.A. thesis, Georgetown University, Washington, D.C., 1962.

Rawski, Evelyn S. *Agricultural Change and the Peasant Economy of South China*. Cambridge, Mass.: Harvard University Press, 1972.

Rossabi, Morris. "Cheng Ho and Timur: Any Relation?" *Oriens Extremus* 20, no. 2 (December 1973): 129–36.

———. "The Jews in China." In Herbert Franke, ed., *Handbuch der Orientalistik*. Leiden: Brill, forthcoming.

———. "The Jurchen in the Yuan and the Ming." Manuscript for the Chin Dynastic History Project, directed by Herbert Franke.

———. "Khubilai Khan and Islam." Paper for the "Yuan Conference," 1976.

———. "Ming China and Turfan, 1406–1517." *Central Asiatic Journal* 16, no. 3 (1972): 206–25.

———. "The Tea and Horse Trade with Inner Asia during the Ming." *Journal of Asian History* 4, no. 2 (1970): 136–68.

———. "Trade Routes with Inner Asia." In Denis Sinor, ed., *Cambridge History of Inner Asia*. London: Cambridge University Press, forthcoming.

Rozman, Gilbert. *Urban Networks in Ch'ing China and Tokugawa Japan.* Princeton: Princeton University Press, 1973.

Rudé, George. *Paris and London in the 18th Century: Studies in Popular Protest.* London: Collins, 1970.

Ruhlmann, Robert. "Traditional Heroes in Chinese Popular Fiction." In Arthur F. Wright, ed., *The Confucian Persuasion*, pp. 141–76. Stanford: Stanford University Press, 1960.

Saeki Tomi 佐伯富. *Shindai ensei no kenkyū* 清代塩政の研究. Kyoto 1956.

Saeki Yūichi 佐伯有一. "Mindai shōekisei no hōkai to toshi kinuorimonogyō ryūtsū shijō no tenkai" 明代匠役制の崩壊と都市絹織物業流通市場の展開. *Tōyō bunka kenkyūjo kiyō* 10 (1956): 359–426.

———. "Minmatsu shokkō bōdō shiryō ruishu" 明末職工暴動史料類輯. In *Shimizu Hakushi tsuitō kinen Mindaishi ronsō* 清水博士追悼記念明代史論叢. Tokyo, 1962.

Sakuma Shigeo 佐久間重男. "Minmatsu keitokuchin no minyō no hatten to minhen" 明末景徳鎮の民窯の発展と民変. In *Suzuki kyōju kanreki kinen Tōyōshi ronsō* 鈴木教授還歴記念東洋史論叢, pp. 165–81. Tokyo, 1964.

Sansom, George. *A History of Japan, 1334–1615.* Stanford: Stanford University Press, 1961.

Sasaki Masaya 佐マ木正. *Shinmatsu no himitsu kessha* 清末の秘密結社. Tokyo, 1970.

Schurz, William L. *The Manila Galleon.* New York, 1939; paper, 1959.

Selden, Mark. *The Yenan Way in Revolutionary China.* Cambridge, Mass.: Harvard University Press, 1971.

Serruys, Henry. "The Mongols in China, 1400–1450." *Monumenta Serica* 27 (1968): 233–305.

Shang-hai hsien-chih 上海縣志 (Chia-ch'ing ed.).

Shang Yen-liu 商衍鎏. *Ch'ing-tai k'o-chü k'ao-shih shu-lu* 清代科學考試述錄.
    Peking, 1958.

Shen Hsün-wei 沈荀蔚. *Shu-nan hsu-lueh* 蜀難叙略. In *Chao-tai ts'ung-shu* 昭代
    叢書, ts'e 68; *Chih-pu-tsu chai ts'ung-shu* 知不足齋叢書, ts'e 142; *Pi-chi
    hsiao-shuo ta-kuan* 筆記小說大觀, pt. 4; *Ts'ung-shu chi-ch'eng* 叢書集成, vol.
    3971.

Shen Yu-jung 沈有容. *Min-hai tseng-yen* 閩海贈言. TW, no. 56.

[*Ta-Ch'ing shih-ch'ao*] *Sheng-hsun* 大清十朝聖訓. 1880; Taiwan reprint, 1965.

Shigeta Atsushi 重田德. "Shinsho ni okeru Konan kome shijō no ichi
    kōsatsu" 清初におけろ湖南米市場の一考察. *Tōyō bunka kenkyūjo kiyō* 東洋文化研究
    所紀要 (November 1956): 427–98.

Shih Hung-ta 史宏達. "Ming-tai ssu-chih sheng-ch'an-li ch'u-t'an" 明代絲織生
    產力初探. *Wen-shih-che* 文史哲 60 (1957–58): 3423–33.

Shih K'o-fa 史可法. *Shih Chung-cheng kung chi* 史忠正公集. Editions of 1897
    and Shanghai, 1937.

Shih Lang 施琅. *Ching-hai chi-shih* 靖海紀事. TW, no. 13.

[*Ta-Ch'ing li-ch'ao*] *Shih-lu* 大清歷朝實錄. Tokyo, 1937–38; Taipei reprints,
    1964, 1973, cited by reign period.

Shih-lu (T'ai-tsu). *Ta-Ch'ing T'ai-tsu Wu-huang-ti Nu-erh-ho-ch'i shih-lu* 大清
    太祖武皇帝弩兒哈奇實錄. 1636. In *Ch'ing-shih tzu-liao* 清史資料, pt. 2, vol. 5.
    Taipei, 1968.

Shih Tun 石惇. *Tung-yü tsa-chi* 憧餘雜記. In Chao Shih-chin 趙士錦, *Chia-shen
    chi-shih* 甲申紀事, pp. 61–94.

Shimizu Taiji 清水泰次. "Mindai no ryūmin to ryūzoku" 明代の流民と流賊.
    Shigaku zasshi 史学雑誌 46, no. 2 (February 1935): 200–06.

"Shinsho no tai Kaikyō seisaku" 清初の對回教政策. *Kaikyō jijō* 回教事情 2, no. 4
    (1939): 33–53.

Simonovskaia, Larisa V. *Antifeodal'naia bor'ba kitaiskikh krest'ian vXVII
    veke.* Moscow: Moskovski gosudarstvennyi universitet imeni M. V.
    Lomonosova, 1966.

Sinor, Denis. "Horse and Pasture in Inner Asian History." *Oriens
    Extremus* 19, nos. 1–2 (December 1972): 171–83.

Sjoberg, Gideon. *The Preindustrial City: Past and Present.* Glencoe, Ill.:
    Free Press, 1960.

Skachkov, Petr Emel'ianovich. *Bibliografia kitaia.* Moscow: Akademiia
    Nauk SSSR, Institut Narodov Azii, 1960.

So, Kwan-wai. *Japanese Piracy in Ming China during the 16th Century.*
    East Lansing, Mich.: Michigan State University Press, 1975.

Sorokin, Pitirim A. *Social and Cultural Dynamics.* Revised and abridged
    edition. Boston: Porter Sargent, 1957.

Spence, Jonathan D. *Emperor of China: Self-Portrait of K'ang-hsi*. New
    York: Knopf, 1974.
————. *Ts'ao Yin and the K'ang-hsi Emperor: Bondservant and Master*.
    New Haven: Yale University Press, 1966.
Spuler, B. "Central Asia from the Sixteenth Century to the Russian
    Conquests." In P. M. Holt, Ann K. S. Lambton, and B. Lewis, eds., *The
    Cambridge History of Islam*, vol. 1, pp. 468–94. London: Cambridge
    University Press, 1970.
Spuler, B., ed. *Geschichte Mittelasiens*. In *Handbuch der Orientalistik* 5,
    no. 5. Leiden: Brill, 1966.
Ssu-ma Kuang 司馬光. *Hsin-chiao Tzu-chih t'ung-chien chu* 新校資治通鑑注.
    Edited by Yang Chia-lo 楊家駱. Taipei, 1962.
Steensgaard, Niels. *Carracks, Caravans, and Companies*. Copenhagen:
    Scandinavian Institute of Asian Studies, 1973.
Struve, Lynn A. "Chang Tai: A Daydreaming Historian." Unpublished
    manuscript.
————. "Uses of History in Traditional Chinese Society: The Southern
    Ming in Ch'ing Historiography." Ph.D. dissertation, University of
    Michigan, 1974.
Stuzhina, E. "The Economic Meaning of Some Terms in Chinese Feudal
    Handicrafts." *Archiv Orientalni* 35, no. 2 (1967): 232–43.
Sun Chen-t'ao 孫甄陶. *Ch'ing-shih shu-lun* 清史述論. Taipei, 1957.
Sun, E-tu Zen. "Sericulture and Silk Textile Production in Ch'ing China."
    In W. E. Willmott, ed., *Economic Organization in Chinese Society*,
    pp. 79–108. Stanford: Stanford University Press, 1972.
Sung-chiang fu-chih 松江府志. 1819.
Sung Chih-cheng 宋之正. "Liu-an-sheng tz'u-chi" 六安生祠記. In Shih K'o-fa,
    Shih Chung-cheng kung chi.
Sung Po-lu 宋伯魯 et al. *Hsin-chiang chien-chih chih* 新疆建置志. Taipei
    reprint, 1963.
Ta-Ch'ing hui-tien 大清會典. 1732.
Ta-Ming hui-tien 大明會典. 1587.
Taga Akigoro 多賀秋五郎. *Sōfu no kenkyū* 宗譜の研究. Tokyo, 1960.
Tai Li 戴笠 and Wu Shu 吳殳. *Huai-ling liu-k'ou shih-chung lu* 懷陵流寇始終錄.
    See under Li Kuang-t'ao, *Ming-chi liu-k'o shih-mo*.
Tai Ming-shih 戴名世. *Chieh-i lu* 孑遺錄. Taipei, 1969; this work is also in his
    Nan-shan chi.
————. *Nan-shan chi* 南山集. 1701; 1900; Taipei reprint, 1970.
[*Wan-T'ung Hsiang-shan*] *Tai-shih tsung-p'u* 皖桐香山戴氏宗譜. 1868; T. 1136.
T'ai-chou fu-chih 台州府志. 1895.
T'ai-wan wen-hsien ts'ung-k'an (*TW*) 臺灣文獻叢刊. Taipei, 1958 et seq.

Takanaka Toshie 高中利恵. "Minshin jidai no keitokuchin no tōgyō" 明清時代の景德鎮の陶業. *Shakai keizai shigaku* 社会経済史学 32, nos. 5–6 (1967): 562–97.

T'an Ch'ien 談遷. *Kuo-ch'üeh* 國榷. Peking reprint, 1958.

———. *Pei-yu lu* 北游錄. Hong Kong, 1969.

———. *Tsao-lin tsa-tsu* 棗林雜俎. Taipei, 1960.

T'an Ssu-t'ung 譚嗣同. *T'an Ssu-t'ung ch'üan-chi* 譚嗣同全集. Peking, 1954.

T'ang Ch'uan-chi 唐傳基. "Tai Nan-shan yü T'ung-ch'cng p'ai" 戴南山與桐城派. *Shih-Ta hsüeh pao* 師大學報 2 (June 1957): 227–36.

T'ang Chün-i. "Liu Tsung-chou's Doctrine of Moral Mind and Practice and His Critique of Wang Yang-ming." In W. T. de Bary, ed., *The Unfolding of Neo-Confucianism*, pp. 305–31.

T'ang Chung 湯中, comp. *Liang Chih-jen nien-p'u* 梁質人年譜. Shanghai, 1933.

Tanaka Masatoshi 田中正俊. "Chūgoku rekishi gakkai ni okeru 'Shihon shugi no hōga' kenkyū" 中国歷史学界における「資本主義の萌芽」研究. In *Chūgoku shi no jidai kubun* 中国史の時代区分 ed. Suzuki Shun 鈴木俊 and Nishijima Sadao 西山島定生, pp. 219–59. Tokyo, 1957.

Tani Mitsutaka 谷光隆. *Mindai basei no kenkyū* 明代馬政の研究. Kyoto, 1972.

Tani Mitsutaka. "A Study on Horse Administration in the Ming Dynasty." *Acta Asiatica* 21 (1971): 73–97.

Tanter, Raymond. "International War and Domestic Turmoil: Some Contemporary Evidence." In Hugh Davis Graham and Ted Robert Gurr, eds., *Violence in America*, pp. 550–69.

T'ao Hsi-sheng 陶希聖. "Man-tsu wei ju-kuan ch'ien ti fu-lu yu hsiang-jen" 滿族未入關前的俘虜與降人. *Shih-huo* 食貨 2, no. 12 (November 1935): 31–37.

Tazaka Kōdō 田坂興道. *Chūgoku ni okeru kaikyō no denrai to sono gutsū* 中国における回教の傳来とその弘通. *Tōyō bunko ronsō* 東洋文庫論叢, 43. 2 vols. Tokyo, 1964.

———. "Mindai koki no kaikyōto ryūzoku" 明代後期の回教流賊. *Tōyō gakuhō* 東洋學報 37, no. 1 (June 1954): 46–68.

———. "Mindai ni okeru gairaikei isuramu kyōto no kaisei ni tsuite" 明代における外来系イスラム教徒の改姓について. *Shigaku zasshi* 史學雜誌 65, no. 4 (1956): 49–66.

TCHC. See *T'ung-ch'eng hsien-chih*.

Teng Chih-ch'eng 鄧之誠. *Ch'ing-shih chi-shih ch'u-pien* 清詩紀事初編. In *Li-tai shih-shih ch'ang-pien* 歷代詩事長編, vol. 36–37. Taipei reprint, 1971; also separate reprints, Shanghai, 1965, and Taipei, 1970.

Terada Takanobu 寺田隆信. *Sansei shōnin no kenkyū* 山西商人の研究. Kyoto, 1972.

Thiersant, Claude P. Dabry de. *Le Mahométisme en Chine et dans le Turkestan Oriental*. 2 vols. Paris: Ernest Leroux, 1878.

Thompson, Laurence G. "The Junk Passage Across the Taiwan Strait: Two Early Chinese Accounts." *Harvard Journal of Asiatic Studies* 28 (1968): 170–94.

T'ien-ts'ung ch'ao ch'en kung tsou-i 天聰朝臣工奏議. In Lo Chen-yü 羅振玉, ed., *Shih-liao ts'ung-k'an ch'u-pien* 史料叢刊初編, *ts'e* 2–3. 1924; Taipei reprint, 1964.

Tilly, Charles. "How Protest Modernized in France, 1845–1855." In William O. Aydelotte, Allan G. Bogue, and Robert W. Fogel, eds., *The Dimensions of Quantitative Research in History*, 192–255. Princeton: Princeton University Press, 1972.

Torbert, Preston. "The Ch'ing Imperial Household Department: A Study of Its Organization and Principal Functions, 1662–1796." Ph.D. dissertation, University of Chicago, 1973.

Trimingham, J. Spencer. *The Sufi Orders in Islam*. London: Oxford University Press, 1971.

Tsao Kai-fu. "The Rebellion of the Three Feudatories against the Manchu Throne in China: Its Setting and Significance." Ph.D. dissertation, Columbia University, 1965.

Ts'ao Lü-t'ai 曹履泰. *Ching-hai chi-lueh* 靖海紀略. TW, no. 33.

Tseng Wen-wu 曾問吾. *Chung-kuo ching-ying Hsi-yü shih* 中國經營西域史. Shanghai, 1936.

Tso-shih tsung-p'u 左氏宗譜. 1849; T. 126.

Tso Yun-p'eng 左雲鵬 and Liu Chung-jih 劉重日. "Ming-tai Tung-lin tang-cheng ti she-hui pei-ching chi ch'i yü shih-min yun-tung ti kuan-hsi" 明代東林黨爭的社會背景及其與市民運動的關係. *Hsin chien-she* 新建設 10 (1957): 33–38.

Tsou I 鄒漪. *Ch'i Chen yeh-ch'eng* 啓禎野乘. Peiping, 1936; Taipei reprint, n.d.

———. *Ming-chi i-wen* 明季遺聞. TW, no. 112.

Tu Chen 杜臻. *Yüeh-Min hsün-shih chi-lüeh* 粵閩巡視紀略. N.d.: Copies in Kuwabara Collection, Library of the History Department, Kyoto University, and in Ssu-k'u ch'üan-shu, Palace Museum, Taiwan.

Tu Wei-ming. "Yen Yuan: From Inner Experience to Lived Concreteness." In W. T. de Bary, ed., *The Unfolding of Neo-Confucianism*, pp. 511–41.

Tu Wei-yün 杜維運. *Ch'ing Ch'ien-Chia shih-tai chih shih-hsueh yü shih-chia* 清乾嘉時代之史學與史家. Taipei, 1964.

———. "Wan Chi-yeh chih shih-hsüeh" 萬季野之史學. In Ch'ien Mu 錢穆, ed., *Chung-kuo hsüeh-shu shih lun-chi* 中國學術史論集, vol. 2. Taipei, 1956.

[*Shih-i-ch'ao*] *Tung-hua lu* 十一朝東華錄. Wang Hsien-ch'ien 王先謙, ed. 1899; Taipei reprint, 1968.

Tung-yang hsien-chih 東陽縣志. Tao-kuang ed.

Tung-yang ping-pien 東陽兵變, anon. In *Ching-t'o i-shih* 荊駝逸史. 1812.

T'ung-ch'eng hsien-chih, TCHC 桐城縣志 Editions of 1673 and 1696 and 1827.

TW. See *T'ai-wan wen-hsien ts'ung-k'an.*

Übelhör, Monika. "Hsu Kuang-ch'i (1562–1633) und seine Einstellung zum Christentum." *Oriens Extremus* 15, no. 2 (December 1968): 191–257; 16, no. 1 (June 1969): 41–74.

Vierheller, E. *Nation und Elite im Denken von Wang Fu-chih (1619–1692).* Hamburg: Gesellschaft für Natur- und Völkerkunde Ostasiens, 1968.

Vissière, A. *Études Sino-Mahométanes.* Paris: Ernest Leroux, 1911.

Wakeman, Frederic, Jr. "High Ch'ing 1683–1839." In James B. Crowley, ed., *Modern East Asia: Essays in Interpretation*, pp. 1–28. New York: Harcourt, Brace, and World, 1970.

Wakeman, Frederic, Jr., with Carolyn Grant, eds. *Conflict and Control in Late Imperial China.* Berkeley and Los Angeles: University of California Press, 1975.

Wakeman, Frederic, Jr. "Localism and Loyalism during the Ch'ing Conquest of Chiang-nan: The Siege of Chiang-yin." In Wakeman and Grant, *Conflict and Control*, pp. 43–85.

————. "The Price of Autonomy: Intellectuals in Ming and Ch'ing Politics." *Daedalus*, no. 101 (Spring 1972): 35–70.

Waley, Arthur, trans. *The Analects of Confucius.* London, 1938; paperback, New York, n.d.

Wallerstein, Immanuel. *The Modern World-System: Capitalist Agriculture and the Origins of the European World-Economy in the Sixteenth Century.* New York: Academic Press, 1974.

Wan Ssu-t'ung 萬斯同. *Shih-yüan wen-chi* 石園文集. In *Ssu-ming ts'ung-shu* 四明叢書, pt. 4, vol. 54. (1936).

Wan Yen 萬言. *Ch'ung-chen ch'ang-pien* 崇禎長編. In *Chung-kuo nei-luan wai-huo li-shih ts'ung-shu*, ser. 10, pp. 11–114; also Taipei reprint, 1964, and TW, no. 270.

Wang Ch'in-yü 王勤堉. "Liu Chi-chuang hsien-sheng nien-p'u ch'u-kao" 劉繼庄先生年譜初蒿. *Che-chiang t'u-shu-kuan kuan-k'an* 浙江圖書館館刊 4, no. 4: 1–25, 4, no. 5 (August 1935): 1–31.

Wang Ch'uan-shan hsueh-shu t'ao-lun chi 王船山學術討論集. Peking, 1965.

Wang Fu-chih 王夫之. *Ch'uan-shan i-shu* 船山遺書. T'ai-ping-yang edition, Shanghai, 1933. Titles cited: *Chang-ling fu* 章靈賦; *Chia-shih chieh-lu* 家世節錄; *Chiang-chai kung hsing-shu* 薑齋公行述; *Chiang-chai shih fen-t'i kao* 薑齋詩分體稿; *Chiang-chai wen-chi* 薑齋文集; *Chiang-chai wen-chi pu-i* 薑齋文集補遺; *Chiu chao* 九昭; *Chou-i wai-chuan* 周易外傳; *Ch'u-tz'u t'ung-shih*

楚辭通釋 ; *Ch'u-tz'u t'ung-shih hsu-li* 楚辭通釋序例 ; *Ch'u-tz'u t'ung-shih chüan-mo* 楚辭通釋卷末 ; *Ch'uan-shan hsien-sheng chuan* 船山先生傳 ; *Ch'un-ch'iu chia-shuo* 春秋家說 ; *E-meng* 噩夢 ; *Ho Mei-hua pai-yun shih* 和梅花百韻詩 ; *Huang-shu* 黃書 ; *I-te* 意得 ; *Li-chi chang-chü* 禮記章句 ; *Lien-feng chih* 蓮峰志 ; *Lung-yuan yeh-hua* 龍源夜話 ; *Nan-ch'uang man-chi* 南窗漫記 ; *Ssu-wen-lu wai-p'ien* 思問錄外篇 ; *Sung lun* 宋論 ; *Tu Ssu-shu ta-ch'üan shuo* 讀四書大全說 ; *Tu T'ung-chien lun* 讀通鑑論 ; *Wu-shih tzu-ting kao* 五十自定稿 ; *Yung-li shih-lu* 永曆實錄.

Wang Fu-chih 王夫之 . *Huang-shu, O-meng* 黃書噩夢. Peking, 1956.

———. *Shang-shu yin-i* 尚書引義. Peking, 1962.

Wang Gung-wu. "Feng Tao: An Essay on Confucian Loyalty." In Arthur F. Wright and Denis Twitchett, eds., *Confucian Personalities*, 123–45. Stanford: Stanford University Press, 1962.

Wang Hsiu-ch'u 王修楚 . *Yang-chou shih-jih chi* 揚州十日記 . In *Chung-kuo nei-luan wai-huo li-shih ts'ung-shu*. Shanghai, 1946.

Wang Huai-ling 汪槐齡 . "Ming Wan-li nien-chien ti shih-min yun-tung" 明萬曆年間的市民運動 . *Li-shih chiao-hsueh* 歷史教學, 1959, no. 6, pp. 23–30.

Wang Huan-piao 王煥鑣 . "Wan Chi-yeh hsien-sheng hsi-nien yao-lu" 萬季野先生繫年要錄 . *Shih-ti tsa-chih* 史地雜誌 1, no. 2 (July 1937): 11–22.

Wang Ming-lun 王明倫 . "Ya-p'ien chan-cheng ch'ien Yun-nan t'ung-k'uang-yeh chung ti tzu-pen chu-i meng-ya" 鴉片戰爭前雲南銅礦業中的資本主義萌芽 . *Meng-ya*, pp. 673–84.

Wang Ssu-jen 王思任 . *Ch'i Chung-min kung nien-p'u* 祁忠敏公年譜 . In Ch'i Piao-chia, *Chia-i jih-li*.

Wang Te-i 王德毅 . "Ku Tsu-yü nien-p'u" 顧祖禹年譜 . *Ku-kung wen-hsien* 故宮文獻 1, no. 2 (March 1970): 21–34 and 1, no. 3 (June 1970): 45–59.

Wang Yeh-chien. *Land Taxation in Imperial China, 1750–1911*. Cambridge, Mass.: Harvard University Press, 1973.

Wang Yüan 王源 . *Chü-yeh-t'ang wen-chi* 居業堂文集 (CYT) 1831. In *Chi-fu ts'ung-shu* 畿輔叢書 , vols. 331–36.

Wang Yueh-chen 王曰槙 , comp. *Nan-hsun chen-chih* 南潯鎮志 . 1858.

Watt, John R. *The District Magistrate in Late Imperial China*. New York: Columbia University Press, 1972.

Wei Yuan 魏源 . *Sheng-wu-chi* 聖武記 . Taipei reprint, 1967.

Wen Chü-min 溫聚民 , comp. *Wei Shu-tzu nien-p'u* 魏叔子年譜 . Shanghai, 1936.

Wen-hsien ts'ung-pien 文獻叢編 . Taipei reprint, 1964.

Wen Jui-lin 溫睿臨 . *Ch'u-sai t'u-hua shan-ch'uan chi* 出塞圖劃山川記 . In *Shih-yuan ts'ung-shu* 適園叢書 (1913–17), pt. 7, vol. 14.

Wen Jui-lin 溫睿臨 . *Nan-chiang i-shih* 南疆繹史 . 1915; reprints, TW, no. 132; Shanghai, 1960 and 1971; Tokyo, 1967, in *Wan-Ming shih-liao ts'ung-shu (ch'i-chung)*; Hong Kong, 1971.

Wen Ping 文秉. *Hsien-po chih-shih* 先撥志始. In *Chung-kuo nei-luan wai-huo li-shih ts'ung-shu*. Shanghai, 1947.

———. *Lieh-huang hsiao-chih* 烈皇小志. In *Chung-kuo nei-luan wai-huo li-shih ts'ung-shu* Shanghai, 1947.

———. *Ting-ling chu-lüeh* 定陵註略. N.d. Microfilm, Library of Congress.

Wessels, C. *Early Jesuit Travellers in Central Asia, 1603–1721*. The Hague: Nijhoff, 1924.

Whitbeck, B. H. "The Tea System of the Ch'ing Dynasty." B.A. thesis, Harvard College, 1965.

White, William C. *Chinese Jews*. 3 vols. Toronto: University of Toronto Press, 1912.

Wiethoff, Bodo. *Chinas dritte Grenze: Der traditionelle chinesische Staat und der Küstennahe Seeraum*. Wiesbaden: Harrassowitz, 1969.

———. *Die chinesische Seeverbotspolitik und der private Überseehandel von 1368 bis 1567*. Mitteilungen der Gesellschaft für Natur- und Volkerkunde Ostasiens, vol. 45. Hamburg, 1963.

Wilhelm, Hellmut. "From Myth to Myth: The Case of Yueh Fei's Biography." In Arthur F. Wright and Denis Twitchett, eds., *Confucian Personalities*, pp. 146–61. Stanford, 1962.

———. "The Po-hsueh Hung-ju Examination of 1679." *Journal of the American Oriental Society* 71 (1951): 60–66.

Wills, John E., Jr. "Ch'ing Relations with the Dutch, 1662–1690." Ph.D. dissertation, Harvard University, 1967.

———. *Pepper, Guns, and Parleys: The Dutch East India Company and China, 1662–1681*. Cambridge, Mass.: Harvard University Press, 1974.

———. "Early Sino-European Relations: Problems, Opportunities, and Archives." *Ch'ing-shih wen-t'i* 3, no. 2 (December 1974): 50–76.

Wilson, Barbara Anne. *Topology of Internal Conflict: An Essay*. Washington: American University, Center for Research in Social Systems, 1968.

Wu-ch'eng hsien-chih 烏程縣志. 1880 edition.

Wu Ch'ien 吳騫. *Tung-chiang i-shih* 東江遺史, ed. Lo Chen-yü 羅振玉. 1935.

Wu Chin 吳津. *Hsiu-ning hsien-shih Wu-shih pen-tsung p'u* 休寧縣市吳氏本宗譜. Chia-ch'ing ed.

Wu Ching-tzu. *The Scholars*. Translated by Yang Hsien-yi and Gladys Yang. Peking, 1957.

Wu-hsien chih 吳縣志, 1642 and 1933 editions.

Wu Huai-ch'ing 吳懷清, comp. *Li T'ien-sheng hsien-sheng nien-p'u* 李天生先生年譜. In *Kuan-chung ts'ung-shu* 關中叢書, pt. 5, vol. 12.

Wu, K. T. "Ming Printing and Printers." *Harvard Journal of Asiatic Studies* 7, no. 3 (February 1943): 203–60.

Wu, Nelson. "Tung Ch'i-ch'ang (1555–1636): Apathy in Government and Fervor in Art." In Arthur F. Wright and Denis Twitchett, eds., *Confucian Personalities*, pp. 260–93. Stanford: Stanford University Press, 1962.

Wu Shan-chia 吳山嘉. *Fu-she hsing-shih chuan-lueh* 復社姓氏傳略. 1831; reprinted, Hangchow, 1961.

Wu Shu 吳甡 et al. *Huai-ling liu-k'ou shih-chung lu* 懷陵流寇始終錄. Taipei reprint, 1969.

Wu, Silas H. L. *Communication and Imperial Control in China: Evolution of the Palace Memorial System, 1693–1735*. Cambridge, Mass.: Harvard University Press, 1970.

Wu T'ing-hsieh 吳廷燮. *Ming tu-fu nien-piao* 明督撫年表. N.d.; Harvard-Yenching Library.

Wu Wei-yeh 吳偉業. *Wu-shih chi-lan* 吳詩集覽. Annotated by Chin Jung-fan 靳榮藩, and including Chin's *Wu-shih pu-chu* 吳詩補注 Ssu-pu pei-yao. Taipei, 1966.

Yamanoi Yū 山井湧. "Hō Sō-gi no gakumon—Mingaku kara Shingaku e no itsuyu no ichi yōsō" 黃宗羲の学問―明学カラ清学への移行の一様相. *Tōkyō Shinagaku hō* 東京支那学報 3 (1957): 31–40.

———. "Ko En-bu no gakumon kan—Mingaku kara Shingaku e no tenkan no kanten kara" 顧炎武の学問觀―明学から清学への轉換の觀点カラ. *Chūō Daigaku Bungakubu kiyō* 中央大学文学部紀要 35 (1964): 67–93.

———. "Minmatsu Shinsho ni okeru keisei chiyō no gaku" 明末清初に於ける経世致用の学. *Tōhōgaku ronsyū* 東方学論集 1 (February 1954): 136–50.

———. "Minmatsu Shinsho shisō ni tsuite no ikkosatsu" 明末清初思想についての一考察. *Tōkyō Shinagaku hō* 東京支那学報 11 (1965): 37–54.

Yang K'uan 楊寬. "I-liu-ssu-wu-nien Chia-ting jen-min ti k'ang-Ch'ing tou-cheng" 一六四五年嘉定人民的抗清鬥爭. In Li Kuang-pi, ed., *Ming-Ching shih lun-ts'ung* 明清史論叢.

Yang Lien-sheng. "Government Control of Urban Merchants in Traditional China." *Tsing Hua Journal of Chinese Studies* 8, nos. 1–2 (1970): 186–209.

Yang Te-en 楊德恩. *Shih K'o-fa nien-p'u* 史可法年譜. Changsha, 1940.

Yang T'ing-shu 楊廷樞. "Ch'üan-Wu chi-lueh" 全吳紀略. In Wan Yen, *Ch'ung-chen ch'ang-pien*. Taipei, 1964 ed.

Yang Ying 楊英. *Ts'ung-cheng shih-lu* 從征實錄. TW, no. 32.

Yao Ming-ta 姚名達. *Liu Tsung-chou nien-p'u* 劉宗周年譜. Shanghai, 1934.

[*Ma-hsi*] *Yao-shih tsung-p'u* 麻溪姚氏宗譜. 1921, T. 428.

Yao Ying 姚瑩. *Chung-fu t'ang ch'üan-chi* 中復堂全集. 1867.

YCCP. See *Yung-cheng chu-p'i yü-chih*.

Yeh Meng-chu 葉夢珠. *Yüeh-shih pien* 閱世編. In *Shang-hai chang-ku ts'ung-shu* 上海掌故叢書 (1936), First Collection, *ts'e* 3–5; also in *Ming-Ch'ing shih-liao hui-pien* 明清史料彙編, vol. 56, pp. 111–542. Taipei, 1969.

Yen Jù-yü 嚴如煜. *San-sheng shan-nei pien-fang lun* 三省山內邊防論. Ch'ing ed.

"Yen-t'ang chien-wen tsa-chi" 研堂見聞雜記. Shanghai, 1911. Also in *T'ung-shih* 痛史, vol. 6. Taipei, 1968.

Yin Keng 尹耕. "Liu Chi-chuang chih sheng-p'ing chi ch'i hsueh-shu kai-yao" 劉繼庄之生平及其學術概要. *Ch'i-Ta chi-k'an* 齊大季刊 1 (June 1933): 49–64.

Yoboko Jōtarō 呼子丈太郎. *Wakō shikō* 倭寇史考. Tokyo, 1971.

Yokoyama Suguru 横山英. "Chūgoku ni okeru shōkōgyō rōdōsha no hatten to yakuwari—Minmatsu ni okeru Sōshū o chūshin to shite" 中国における商工業勞働者の發展と役割—明末における蘇州を中心として. *Rekishigaku kenkyū* 歴史学研究 160 (November 1952): 1–13.

——. "Shindai ni okeru tambugyō no keiei keitai" 清代における踹布業の経営形態. *Tōyōshi kenkyū* 東洋史研究 19.3: 337–49, 19.4: 451–67 (1960).

Yoshikawa Kōjirō. "Political Disengagement in Seventeenth-Century Chinese Literature." Paper for the Conference on Seventeenth-Century Chinese Thought, 1970.

Yu T'ung 尤侗. *Ken-chai chüan-kao wen-chi* 艮齋倦藁文集. In his *Hsi-t'ang yü-chi* 西堂餘集. 1691.

Yü Ying-shih 余英時. *Fang I-chih wan-chieh k'ao* 方以智晚節考. Hong Kong, 1972.

Yüan T'ung-li and Watanabe Hiroshi. *Shinkyō kenkyū bunken mokuroku, Classified Bibliography of Japanese Books and Articles Concerning Sinkiang, 1866–1962*. Tokyo: Sinkiang Research Library, 1962.

Yung-cheng chu-p'i yü-chih 雍正硃批諭旨. Taipei, 1965.

Yung-li shih-lu. See under Wang Fu-chih.

Glossary

This list does not include authors and titles for which characters can be found in the Bibliography.

A-pu-tu-la 阿布都喇
Aita 愛塔
An-ch'ing 安慶
Anhwei (An-hui) 安徽
An Lu-shan 安祿山
An-lung 安隆
ch'a-ma ssu 茶馬司
Chang Ch'ao-chen 張朝珍
Chang Ch'i 張琦
Chang Chia-yü 張家玉
Chang Chin-yen 張縉嚴
Chang Chü-cheng 張居正
Chang Feng-i 張鳳翼
Chang Hsiao-ch'i 張孝起
Chang Hsien-chung 張獻忠
Chang Huang-yen 張煌言
Chang-i (gate) 彰義
Chang Ju 張儒
chang-ku 掌故
Chang K'uang 章曠
Chang Kuo-wei 張國維
Chang Liang 張亮
Chang Lin-jan 張璘然
Chang Lu 張巇
Chang Ping-chen 張秉貞
Chang Ping-ch'ien 張秉謙
Chang Ping-i 張秉彝
Chang Ping-wen 張秉文
Chang P'u 張溥
Chang Shen-yen 張慎言
Chang T'ing-yü 張廷玉
Chang Tsai 張載
Chang Ts'un-jen 張存仁
Chang Tsung-hsiang 張宗祥
Chang Ying 張英
Chang Yun-ju 張雲如
Ch'ang-an 長安

ch'ang-pan 長班
Ch'ang-sha 長沙
Ch'ang-shu 常熟
Ch'ang-te 常德
Ch'ang Yü-ch'un 常遇春
Chao-ch'ing 肇慶
Chao I 趙翼
Chao Shih-chin 趙士錦
Chao Wen-hua 趙文華
Chao Yü-sen 趙玉森
Chekiang (Che-chiang) 浙江
Ch'e-chia-shan 車架山
chen 鎮
Chen-chiang 鎮江
Ch'en Chi-ju 陳繼儒
Ch'en-ch'i 辰溪
Ch'en Jen-hsi 陳仁錫
Ch'en Pa 陳霸
Ch'en Pang-fu 陳邦傅
Ch'en Tzu-lung 陳子龍
Ch'en Wen-jui 陳文瑞
Ch'en Yen 陳演
cheng 征 / cheng 正
Cheng Ch'eng-kung 鄭成功
Cheng Chih-lung 鄭芝龍
Cheng Ching 鄭經
Cheng Ho 鄭和
Cheng Hsi 鄭襲
Cheng Hung-k'uei 鄭鴻逵
Cheng San-chün 鄭三俊
Cheng T'ai 鄭泰
Cheng-te 正德
Cheng Ts'ai 鄭彩
cheng-t'ung 正統
Cheng-yang (gate) 正陽
Ch'eng-Chu 程朱
Ch'eng Hao 程顥

397

Ch'eng-kuo (Duke) 成國
Ch'eng-t'ien (gate) 承天
Ch'eng-tu 成都
Ch'eng Yuan 程源
chi 稷
chi-hu 機戶
Chi Liu-ch'i 計六奇
Chi-nan 濟南
Chi-shan 髻山
Chi Shao 嵇紹
Chi-she 幾社
Ch'i Chi-kuang 戚繼光
Ch'i Piao-chia 祁彪佳
Chia-ch'ing 嘉慶
chia-hsun 家訓
chia-kuei 家規
chia-shen 甲申
Chia-ting 嘉定
chiang (artisan) 匠
Chiang Ch'en 蔣臣
Chiang Jih-sheng 江日昇
Chiang Kuo-t'ai 江國泰
Chiang-nan 江南
Chiang-ning 江寧
Chiang-yin 江陰
Chiao Hung 焦竑
chieh-chi 接濟
Chieh Sung-nien 介松年
chien-li 奸吏
Ch'ien-an 遷安
Ch'ien-chou (Shensi) 乾州
Ch'ien-lung 乾隆
Ch'ien-men 前門
Ch'ien Ping-teng (Ch'eng-chih) 錢秉鐙(澄之)
Chin 金
Chin-chou (1) 錦州
Chin-chou (2) 金州
Chin-hua 金華
chin-i-wei 錦衣衛
Chin Jen-jui 金人瑞
Chin Pao 金保
Chin P'ing Mei 金瓶梅
Chin Sheng 金聲
Chin Sheng-huan 金聲桓
chin-shih 進士
Ch'in Hsien 秦汧
Ch'in Shih Huang-ti 秦始皇帝
Ch'in-t'ien-chien 欽天監
Ching-k'ou 京口
ching-shih chih-yung 經世致用
Ching-shih wen-pien 經世文編
Ching-te-chen 景德鎮
ch'ing 頃
ch'ing-liu 清流
Chiu-chiang 九江
Ch'iu Shan 邱山
Ch'iu Wei-p'ing 邱維屏
Ch'iu Yü 丘瑜
Chou (Empress) 周
Chou of Yao-shih 周，鷂石
Chou Ch'i 周岐
Chou Chung 周鍾
Chou I-wu 周一梧
Chou K'uei 周奎
Chou K'un-lai 周昆來
Chou Kung-chin (Yü) 周公瑾（瑜）
Chou-shui chih huo 咒水之禍
Chou Shun-ch'ang 周順昌
Chou Wu-wang 周武王
chu-ching 主靜
Chu Hsi 朱熹
Chu Hsieh-yuan 朱爕元
Chu I-kuei 朱一貴
Chu I-p'ang (Lin Shih-i) 朱議雱（林時益）
Chu I-tsun 朱彝尊
Chu Kuo-chih 朱國治
Chu Jih-mao 朱日茂
Chusan Island (Chou-shan) 舟山
Chu Shun-ch'en 朱純臣
Chu T'ien-lin 朱天麟
Chu T'ien-yu 朱天祐
Chu Wan 朱紈
Ch'u 楚
Ch'u-tz'u 楚辭
chü-jen 舉人
Chü-yung (pass) 居庸
ch'ü 區
ch'ü-hsiang 取餉

Ch'ü Shih-ssu　瞿式耜
Ch'ü Ta-chün　屈大均
Ch'ü Yuan　屈原
ch'üan　權
ch'üan-kuei　權貴
Ch'üan Tsu-wang　全祖望
chuang-ting　壯丁
ch'uang-wang　闖王
Ch'un-ch'iu (period)　春秋
chung　忠
chung-ch'en　忠臣
chung-hsing　中興
Ch'ung-chen　崇禎
Ch'ung-te　崇德
Dorgon　多爾袞
Fan Ching-wen　范景文
Fan-ho　范河
fan-jen　凡人
Fan Wen-ch'eng　范文程
Fang Chung-t'ung　方中通
Fang Hsueh-chien　方學漸
Fang I-chih　方以智
Fang K'ung-chao　方孔炤
Fang K'ung-shih　方孔時
Fang Kuo-an　方國安
Fang Pao　方苞
Fang Ta-jen　方大任
Fang Wen　方文
Feng-hsiang　鳳翔
Feng Su　馮甦
Feng Tao　馮道
Feng-yang　鳳陽
Fu, Prince of　福王
Fukien (Fu-chien)　福建
Fu-she　復社
Fu-shun　撫順
Gali　噶禮
Giyešu (Chieh-shu)　傑書
Goto Islands　五島
Hai-ch'eng　海澄
Hai-chou　海州
Han-chung　漢中
Han Kao-tsu　漢高祖
Han Lin　韓霖
hang　行

Hang Ch'i-su　杭齊蘇
Hangchow (Hang-chou)　杭州
Heng-chou　衡州
Heng-shan　衡山
Heng-yang　衡陽
Hirado　平戶
Ho Ju-ch'ung　何如寵
Ho Jui-cheng　何瑞徵
Ho Kang　何剛
Ho Kuang　何廣
Ho-nan-fu　河南府
Ho Shu-heng　何叔衡
Ho T'eng-chiao　何騰蛟
Hou T'ung-tseng　侯峒曾
Hsi-hua (gate)　西華
Hsi Kuei-ch'ing　奚貴卿
Hsi-yü　西域
Hsia　夏
Hsia　俠
Hsia Ju-pi　夏汝弼
Hsia Kuo-hsiang　夏國祥
Hsia Wan-ch'un　夏完淳
Hsia Yun-i　夏允彝
Hsiang (river)　湘
hsiang　餉
Hsiang-hsiang　湘鄉
hsiang-ping　鄉兵
Hsiang-yang　襄陽
Hsiang-yin　湘陰
hsiang-yueh　鄉約
hsien-kung　閑工
Hsing-hua　興化
hsing-jen　行人
hsing-tsai　行在
Hsing-ts'un lu　幸存錄
hsiu-ts'ai　秀才
Hsu[a]　許
Hsu[b]　須
hsu　虛
Hsu A-chi　徐阿寄
Hsu Ch'eng　徐成
Hsu Ch'ien-hsueh　徐乾學
Hsu Fu-yuan　徐孚遠
Hsu Hsin-su　許心素
Hsu Hung-kang　許宏綱

Hsu Hung-tsu　徐宏祖
Hsu Kuang-ch'i　徐光啓
Hsu Lo-yeh　徐樂也
Hsu Ping-i　徐秉義
Hsu Ta-tao　許達道
Hsu Tu　許都
Hsu Tung　許棟
Hsu Yuan-wen　徐元文
Hsu Ying-fen　徐應芬
Hsuan-tsung　玄宗
hsun-an　巡按
Hu　胡
Hu Ch'eng-no　胡承諾
Hu San-sheng　胡三省
Hu Tsung-hsien　胡宗憲
hu-t'ung　胡同
Hu Wei　胡渭
Hua-t'ing　華亭
Huai-an　淮安
Huai-ning　懷寧
Huang Chien-chieh　黃建節
Huang Ch'un-yao　黃淳耀
Huang Pin-ch'ing　黃斌卿
Huang Taiji　皇太極
Huang Te-kung　黃得功
Huang Wen-ting　黃文鼎
Huang Wu　黃梧
Hui-chou　徽州
hui-kuan　會館
hui-t'ung-kuan　會同館
Hung Ch'eng-ch'ou　洪承疇
Hung-kuang　弘光
Hung T'a-shih　弘他時
Hung Taiji　洪台吉
Hung T'ai-shih　洪太氏
Hung-wen-kuan　宏文館
Hung-wu　洪武
hung-yeh　弘業
i　義
i-cheng　議政
I-lu　懿路
I-t'ang　易堂
i-ti　夷狄
I-t'u ming-pien　易圖明辨
[*Ta-Ch'ing*] *I-t'ung-chih*　大清一統志

Jen Wei-ch'u　任維初
Juan Ta-ch'eng　阮大鋮
K'ai-yuan　開原
Kan-chou　甘州
Kan Feng-ch'ih　甘鳳池
K'ang-hsi　康熙
Kao P'an-lung　高攀龍
Kao Pi-cheng　高必正
Kao Shih-t'ai　高世泰
k'ao-cheng　考證
Keng Ching-chung　耿精忠
Keng Chung-ming　耿仲明
Ko Ch'eng　葛成
Ko Hsien　葛賢
Ko Lin　葛麟
ku　賈
Ku Chün-en　顧君恩
Ku Hsien-ch'eng　顧憲成
Ku Tsu-yü　顧祖禹
Ku-wen shang-shu shu-cheng
　古文尚書疏證
Ku Yen-wu　顧炎武
k'u-miao　哭廟
Kua-chou　瓜州
kuan-k'u　管庫
kuan-shao　管哨
Kuan Ssu-ch'iu　管嗣裘
Kuang-ning　廣寧
Kuang Shih-heng　光時亨
k'uang-chüan　狂狷
K'uang-she　匡社
kuei　貴
Kuei　桂
Kuei-lin　桂林
kuei-mei　歸妹
k'uei　癸
k'un　坤
K'un-i (Princess)　坤一
K'un-shan　崑山
kung-sheng　貢生
Kung Yü　鞏煜
K'ung-ch'eng　孔城
K'ung Yu-te　孔有德
kuo　國
Kuo Chieh　郭節

Kuo Chih-ch'i 郭之奇
Kuo Chih-wei 郭之緯
Kwangtung (Kuang-tung) 廣東
Lan-chou 蘭州
Lao Hui-hui 老回回
Lao-tzu 老子
Lei Te-fu 雷德復
li 里
Li Chen-sheng 李振聲
Li Ch'eng-liang 李成梁
Li Ch'eng-tung 李成棟
Li Chien-t'ai 李建泰
Li Chih 李贄
Li Chih-sheng 黎志陞
Li Ching-po 李精白
li-hsien kuan 禮賢館
Li Hsu 李煦
li-hsueh 理學
Li Kuang-ti 李光地
Li Kuang-t'ou 李光頭
Li Kung 李塨
Li Kuo 李過
Li Kuo-chen 李國楨
Li Ming-jui 李明睿
Li Pang-hua 李邦華
Li San-ts'ai 李三才
Li Sheng-mao 李升茂
Li Shih-chen 李時珍
[Li] Ta-liang 李大梁
Li Ta-lu 李大祿
Li Tan 李旦
Li T'eng-chiao 李騰蛟
Li Ting-kuo 李定國
Li To-chien 李多見
Li Tzu-ch'eng 李自成
Li Wei 李衞
Li Yen 李巖
Li Yin-tu 李因篤
Li Ying-sheng 李應昇
Li Yuan-yin 李元胤
Li Yung-chi 李用楫
Li Yung-fang 李永芳
liang-chang 糧長
Liang Chao-yang 梁兆陽
Liang-chiang 兩江

Liang-chou 涼州
Liang Fen 梁份
Liao-hsi 遼西
liao-li chün-shih 料理軍事
Liaotung 遼東
Liao-yang 遼陽
lien 連
Lin Ching-yang 林景暘
Lin-ch'ing 臨清
Ling-wu 靈武
Liu Hsiang-k'o 劉湘客
Liu Hsien-t'ing (Chi-chuang)
    劉獻廷（繼莊）
Liu Hsiu 劉秀
Liu Jen-hsi 劉人熙
Liu K'un 劉琨
liu-pu 六部
Liu-shih tzu-ting kao 六十自定稿
Liu T'ien-lu 劉天祿
Liu Tsung-chou 劉宗周
Liu Tsung-min 劉宗敏
Liu Yin-tung 柳寅東
Liu Yü-sung 劉毓崧
Liu Yueh-shih 劉越石
Lo Chiu-wu 羅九武
Lu 陸
Lu, Prince of ("administrator of
    realm" in Chekiang) 魯王，監國
Lu, Honan Prince of 潞王
Lu T'ung-an 陸同菴
Lu-Wang 陸王
Lu-chou 廬州
Lü Liu-liang 呂留良
Lü Pi-chou 呂弼周
Luan Chin-kung 欒晉公
Luan-chou 灤州
Luan Erh-chi 欒爾集
Lung-wu 隆武
Ma Chi-hsiang 馬吉祥
Ma Ch'i-ch'ang 馬其昶
Ma Chin-chung 馬進忠
Ma Kuang-yuan 馬光遠
Ma Lao-hu 馬老虎
Ma Shih-ying 馬士英
Ma Shou-ying 馬守應

Ma Wen-sheng　馬文升
mang-kung　忙工
Mao Ch'i-ling　毛奇齡
Mao I-lu　毛一鷺
Mao Wen-lung　毛文龍
Matsuura　松浦
Mei-shan　煤山
Meng Cheng-fa　蒙正發
Meng Ch'iao-fang　孟喬芳
Mi La-yin　米喇印
Min-chou　岷州
mu (mou)　畝
mu-yu　幕友
Nan-chihli　南直隸
Nan-k'ang　南康
Nei-ko　內閣
Nanking (Nan-ching)　南京
nei-chu　內主
ni tang　逆黨
Ni Yuan-lu　倪元璐
Ninghsia　寧夏
Ningpo　寧波
Ning-tu　寧都
Ning Wan-wo　甯完我
Ningyuan　寧原
Niu Chin-hsing　牛金星
nu-p'u　奴僕
Nung-cheng ch'üan-shu　農政全書
Ōuchi　大內
Ou-yang Hsiu　歐陽修
Pa-pai　巴拜
pa-shih　罷市
pan-chiang　班匠
P'an Hsiang　潘相
P'an Lei　潘耒
P'an-yü　番禺
P'ang T'ien-shou　龐天壽
Pao-chi　寶雞
pao-chia　保甲
pao-i　包衣
pao-shui　報水
Pao-ting　保定
pao-t'ou　包頭
Pen-ts'ao kang-mu　本草綱目
P'eng Jen　彭任

P'eng Ju-jang　彭汝讓
P'eng Shih-wang　彭士望
P'i-tao　皮島
pien　便
ping-shang　病商
P'ing-hu　平湖
P'ing-yang　平陽
po　撥
Po Ching-hsing　博景星
po-hsueh hung-ju　博學鴻儒
po-hsueh hung-tz'u　博學鴻詞
p'o-ko chih hsuan　破格之選
Pu-ho　蒲河
P'u-ch'eng　浦城
San-fan Rebellion　三藩之亂
San-yen　三言
San-yuan pi-chi　三垣筆記
Sarhu　撒爾滸
Shan-hai-kuan　山海關
Shan-t'ang　山塘
Shantung　山東
Shan-yin　山陰
shang　賞
shang (merchants)　商
Shang Chih-hsin　尚之信
Shang-ch'iu　商邱
Shang Chiung　尚絅
Shanghai　上海
shang-huang t'ien-ti　上皇天帝
Shang K'o-hsi　尚可喜
shang-ku　商賈
Shang-lo [shan]　商雒山
Shao-hsing　紹興
she　社
she-chi　社稷
Shen Chih-hsiang　沈志祥
shen-chin　紳衿
Shen Hsun-wei　沈荀蔚
Shen I-kuan　沈一貫
Shen Shang-ta　沈上達
Shen T'ing-yang　沈廷揚
Shen-yang　瀋陽
Sheng Chih-ch'i　陞之祺
sheng-yuan　生員
shih　時

shih 石
shih 士
Shih I-chih 史眙直
Shih K'o-fa 史可法
Shih Lang 施琅
Shih-lu 實錄
shih-pa-tzu 十八子
Shih Pang-yueh 施邦曜
Shih Shih-ying 石世英
Shih T'ing-chu 石廷柱
shou-hsing 受刑
Shu (Szechwan) 蜀
Shu-fang 書房
Shuang-hsu 雙嶼
Shui-hu chuan 水湖傳
shui-shih 水師
Shun (dynasty) 順
Shun (legendary emperor) 舜
Shun-min 順民
Shun-t'ien 順天
Soochow (Su-chou) 蘇州
ssu ("selfish") 私
ssu-i kuan 四夷館
Ssu-ling 思陵
Ssu-ma Ch'ien 司馬遷
Su-chou (Kansu) 肅州
Su-Sung 蘇松
Su-tsung 肅宗
sui 歲
Sun Chin 孫晉
Sun I 孫頤
Sun K'o-wang 孫可望
Sun Lin 孫臨
Sun Lung 孫隆
Sun Te-sheng 孫得勝
Sun T'ing 孫鋌
Sung Ch'i-chiao 宋企郊
Sung-chiang 松江
Sung Chih-sheng 宋之盛
Sung Chin 宋金
Sung Hsien-ts'e 宋獻策
Sung-shan 松山
Szechwan (Ssu-ch'uan) 四川
Ta-hsueh pien-yeh 大學辨業
Ta-ling-ho 大凌河

Ta-Shun 大順
Ta-t'ung 大同
Tai Chün-ts'ai 戴君采
Tai Ming-shih 戴名世
tai-pao chün-fu chih ch'ou hui-kuan
　　　代報君父之仇會館
Tai Wang 戴望
T'ai-chou 泰州
T'ai-hu (Lake T'ai) 太湖
T'ai-ts'ang 太倉
[Ming] T'ai-tsu [明]太祖
T'ai-ts'un lu 汰存錄
T'an Ssu-t'ung 譚嗣同
tang 黨
T'ang, Prince of 唐王
T'ang Hsin 湯莘
[T'ang] T'ai-tsung [唐]太宗
tao 道
t'ao-wu 淘物
Teng Chung-hua (Yü) 鄧仲華(禹)
T'ieh-ling 鉄嶺
tien-shih 典史
Tientsin (T'ien-chin) 天津
T'ien-ch'i 天啓
T'ien-kung k'ai-wu 工工開物
t'ien-ming 天命
T'ien-ts'ung 天聰
t'ien-tzu 天子
ting 丁
Ting Kuo-tung 丁國棟
Ting Shih-k'uei 丁時魁
Ts'ai the Beard 蔡鬍子
Ts'ai Ju-chung 蔡汝中
Ts'ai Shan-chi 蔡善繼
Ts'ao Shih-p'in 曹時聘
Ts'ao Ts'ao 曹操
Ts'ao Yin 曹寅
ts'e 册
Tseng Ching 曾靜
Tseng Ts'an 曾燦
Tseng Ying-lin 曾應遴
Tso-ch'iu Ming 左丘明
Tso Kuang-hsien 左光先
Tso Kuang-tou 左光斗
Tso Kuo-lin 左國林

Tso Kuo-ts'ai　左國材
Tso Liang-yü　左良玉
Tso Meng-keng　左夢庚
Tsou I　鄒漪
Tsu K'o-fa　祖可法
Tsu Ta-shou　祖大壽
Tsu Tse-hung　祖澤洪
Ts'ui-wei Peak　翠微峯
Tsun-hua　尊化
tsung-ping-kuan　總兵官
Tu-ch'a-yuan　督察院
Tu-ch'ang　都昌
Tu Hsun　杜勳
tu-t'ang　都堂
Tu Yin-hsi　堵胤錫
T'u-lun-t'ai　土倫泰
tuan-kung　短工
t'un-t'ien　屯田
Tung-hua (gate)　東華
Tung-kuan　東莞
Tung-lin　東林
Tung-t'ing-shan　洞庭山
Tung-yang　東陽
Tung Yün-hsiang　董雲驤
T'ung (Liaotung family)　佟
t'ung　統
T'ung-ch'eng　桐城
T'ung-chou　通州
t'ung-hsiang　同鄉
T'ung-kuan　桐關
t'ung-nien　同年
T'ung-pien jih-lu　桐變日錄
T'ung Pin　童賓
T'ung Yang-hsing　佟養性
T'ung Yen　佟延
Tzu-mo　子莫
Tzu-t'ung　梓潼
tz'u　賜
Wan Ao　萬翺
Wan-li　萬歷
Wan-shou (hill)　萬壽
Wan Ssu-t'ung　萬嗣同
Wang　王
Wang Ch'eng-en　王承恩
Wang Chih　王直

Wang Hao　王灝
Wang Hsi-lieh　王希烈
Wang Hua-ch'eng　王化澄
Wang Hung-hsu　王鴻緒
Wang Kuo-hua　汪國華
Wang Nan-kuan　王南觀
Wang Shih-chen　王世貞
Wang Sun-hui　王孫蕙
Wang Te　王德
Wang Te-jen　王得仁
Wang Te-hua　王德化
Wang Wei-kung　王維恭
Wang Wen-yao　王雯燿
Wang Yang-ming (Shou-jen)　王陽明(守仁)
Wang Ying-hsiung　王應熊
Wang Yuan　王源
Wei Chi-jui　魏際瑞
Wei Chung-hsien　魏忠賢
Wei Hsi　魏禧
Wei Hsueh-lien　魏學濂
Wei Li　魏禮
Wei Tsao-te　魏藻德
Wen　溫
Wen Chen-heng　文震亨
Wen Chen-meng　文震孟
wen-hsien-yuan　文閑員
Wen-hua (palace)　文華
Wen Huang　溫璜
Wen Jui-lin　溫睿臨
Wen-kuan　文館
Wen T'i-jen　溫體仁
Wen T'ien-hsiang　文天祥
Wu　吳
Wu Ch'ang-shih　吳昌時
Wu Chen-yü　吳貞毓
Wu-chiang　吳江
Wu Ch'ien　吳騫
Wu Chin-chao　吳晉昭
Wu Ching-tzu　吳敬梓
Wu-chou　梧州
Wu Han　吳涵
Wu-hsi　無錫
Wu-hsien　吳縣
Wu Hsing-tso　吳興祚

Wu-hu 蕪湖
Wu-kang 武岡
Wu-kung 武功
Wu San-kuei 吳三桂
Wu Te-ts'ao 吳德操
Wu Tse-t'ien 武則天
Wu Tzu-ch'ang 吳孳昌
Wu Wei-yeh 吳偉業
Wu-ying (palace) 武英
Wu Yung-hsien 吳用先
Yalu 鴨綠
Yang Chen-tsung 楊鎮宗
Yang Chi-sheng 楊繼盛
Yang Chien-lieh 楊建烈
Yangchow (Yang-chou) 楊州
Yang Feng-pao 楊鳳苞
yang-hang 洋行
Yang Hu-li 楊虎力
Yang Kuan-kuang 楊觀光
Yang Kuei-fei 楊貴妃
Yang Lien 楊漣
Yang Ssu-ch'ang 楊嗣昌
Yang T'ing-shu 楊廷樞
Yang Wen-ts'ung 楊文驄
Yang Yü-lin 楊玉林
Yao 堯
Yao Ch'i-sheng 姚啓聖
Yao Ch'i-ying 姚七英
Yao-chou 耀州
Yao Nai 姚鼐
Yao Sun-chü 姚孫榘

Yao Sun-fei 姚孫棐
Yao Sun-lin 姚孫林
Yao Wen-jan 姚文然
yeh-shih 野史
Yeh Ts'an 葉燦
Yen Ch'i-heng 嚴起恆
Yen Jo-chü 閻若璩
Yen Sung 嚴嵩
Yen Yuan 顏元
Yin-chi-shan 尹繼善
Yin-jeng 胤礽
ying 營
Ying-t'ien 應天
Ying T'ing-chi 應廷吉
Ying-tsung 英宗
yu-hsia 遊俠
Yü Chung-hua 于重華
Yü-fu (mountains) 魚腹
Yü Ta-yu 俞大猷
Yü Tzu-kao 俞咨皋
Yuan Ch'ung-huan 袁崇煥
Yuan-ma ssu 苑馬寺
Yuan P'eng-nien 袁彭年
yueh 約
Yueh Ch'i-luan 岳起鸞
Yung-ch'ang 永昌
Yung-cheng 雍正
Yung-li 永曆
Yung-lo 永樂
Yung-p'ing 永平

Index

951
Fro   From Ming to Ch'ing.